Corporate Financial Reporting

A Global Perspective

Hervé Stolowy & Michel J. Lebas

THOMSON

Austria • Canada • Mexico • Singapore • Spain • United Kingdom • United States

THOMSON

Corporate Financial Reporting – A Global Perspective

Copyright © Hervé Stolowy and Michel J. Lebas, 2002

The Thomson logo is a registered trademark used herein under licence.

For more information, contact Thomson, High Holborn House, 50–51 Bedford Row, London WC1R 4LR or visit us on the World Wide Web at: http://www.thomsonlearning.co.uk

All rights reserved by Thomson 2002. The text of this publication, or any part thereof, may not be reproduced or transmitted in any form or by any means, electronic or mechanical, including photocopying, recording, storage in an information retrieval system, or otherwise, without prior permission of the publisher.

While the publisher has taken all reasonable care in the preparation of this book the publisher makes no representation, express or implied, with regard to the accuracy of the information contained in this book and cannot accept any legal responsibility or liability for any errors or omissions from the book or the consequences thereof.

Products and services that are referred to in this book may be either trademarks and/or registered trademarks of their respective owners. The publisher and authors make no claim to these trademarks.

British Library Cataloguing-in-Publication data
A catalogue record for this book is available from the British Library

ISBN 1-86152-753-5

First edition 2002

Typeset by Saxon Graphics Ltd, Derby, UK

Printed in Italy by G. Canale & C.

Corporate Financial Reporting

Dedication

To Nicole, Natacha, and Audrey

To Michael

For their indefatigable support and immense patience

Dedication

To Nicole, Natasha, and Audrey

And also

Together in darkness, sorrow, and in dense nature

contents

I Introduction to financial accounting 1

1 Accounting: The language of business 3

2 Introduction to financial statements 43

Tangible fixed assets 247

 Intangible assets 287

list of figures

list of tables

about the authors

Hervé Stolowy is Professor of Accounting at the HEC School of Management (Jouy-en-Josas, France). He holds a degree in business administration (ESCP–Paris Graduate School of Management), a masters' degree in private law (Université Paris-Val de Marne), a BA in Russian and American studies (Université Paris-Sorbonne), a PhD in financial accounting (Université Paris-Panthéon-Sorbonne) and an *"habilitation à diriger des recherches"* (which certifies him as a qualified doctoral dissertation adviser). He is a certified and practising *"expert comptable"* (French equivalent of a chartered accountant or certified public accountant).

He has authored and co-authored 9 books, chapters in 8 collective works and published over 60 articles in academic and applied journals, such as *Advances in International Accounting, Comptabilité – Contrôle – Audit, The European Accounting Review, The International Journal of Accounting, Les Echos*, the *Revue de Droit Comptable* and the *Revue Française de Comptabilité*.

His research and teaching interests span financial and international accounting, and focus more specifically on intangibles, accounts manipulation, and design and use of cash flow statements. Professor Stolowy is a member of the Association Française de Comptabilité (AFC), European Accounting Association (EAA), American Accounting Association (AAA), and Canadian Academic Accounting Association (CAAA). He is a past treasurer of AFC and past secretary-treasurer of IAAER.

Hervé Stolowy teaches financial accounting in the different graduate programs of the HEC School of Management: introduction to financial accounting (HEC-MBA Program (isa) and HEC *Grande Ecole* (first year)); intermediate accounting (HEC *Grande Ecole* (second year)), and both advanced accounting and international accounting (HEC *Grande Ecole* (third year)).

Michel J. Lebas is Professor of Management Accounting and Management Control. He currently holds a joint appointment at the HEC School of Management in Paris and at the University of Washington Business School in Seattle. He was educated both in France (HEC) and in the United States (Tuck School at Dartmouth College and Stanford University Graduate School of Business). After a brief career as an economic analyst for an American multinational and later as a staff consultant in the New York office of then Price Waterhouse, he joined the academic profession while maintaining a freelance consulting practice.

His field of research and consulting concentrates on advanced practices in management accounting and performance management systems. He is an academic research associate in the Beyond Budgeting Round Table Program of the Consortium for Advanced Manufacturing-International (CAM-I); from July 1992 until July 2000 he represented the *French Ordre des Experts Comptables* and the *Compagnie des Commissaires aux Comptes* on the Financial and Management Accounting Committee (FMAC) of the International Federation of Accountants (IFAC). He is the founder, and was from 1992 until 1996 co-editor of the management accounting section of the *Revue Française de Comptabilité*.

His recent publications include chapters in 3 major international collective works, co-authorship of a *Glossary of Accounting English*, co-authorship of a *Management Accounting Glossary*, as well as a management accounting textbook. He co-authored a CAM-I monograph on *Best Practices in World Class Organizations* with Ken Euske and C.J. McNair. His articles have been published in many academic and professional journals including *Administracion de Empresas* (Argentina), *Cahiers Français* (France), *De Accountant* (NL), *European Accounting Review* (UK), *European Management Journal* (UK), *International Journal of Production Economics* (NL), *Journal of Management Studies* (UK), *Management Accounting Research* (UK), *Performances Humaines et Techniques* (F), *Problemi di Gestione* (I), *Revue Française de Comptabilité* (F), *Revue Française de Gestion Industrielle* (F), *Sviluppo & Organizzazione* (I), *Travail* (F).

Beside his research and teaching at the HEC School of Management, he has been teaching for the past 10 years in the executive MBA of the Helsinki School of Economics International Center. He has been Associate Dean for Academic Affairs of the HEC *Grande Ecole* (1986–1989), and has held visiting appointments at SDA Bocconi in Milan, the University of Washington School of Business, and at the Darden Graduate School of Business at the University of Virginia where he held the P&H Rust Chaired Professorship. During 1999–2001 he held the K. Hanson Endowment Visiting Professorship Chair at the University of Washington.

The author team is a reflection of the spirit and the tone of the text. Hervé Stolowy brings an accounting and reporting practitioner/researcher and external financial analysis viewpoint, while Michel Lebas brings the internal and managerial preoccupations in the design of information systems and the interpretation of accounting information.

preface

A book to meet changing student and faculty expectations

In the past, most students of Financial Accounting in Continental European universities or schools, even in the best programs, studied local practice in their local language. Exceptionally UK or US textbooks were used, often creating conflict between the approach of the 'foreign authors' and local accounting standards and practices.

The fact that each country has its own accounting standards is becoming a thing of the past and Financial Accounting and Reporting courses today need to recognize both the diversity of national traditions and the trend towards accounting harmonization.

The profile of students in Financial Accounting courses in (mainly) European graduate and undergraduate business programs is changing.

- Student bodies are now real melting pots fed from a variety of countries. Students do not just come from Western and now Eastern Europe, but also from Africa, Asia, the Middle East, Latin and Central America as well as from North America and from the Southern Pacific, Australia and New Zealand.

- To these students, English has become the *lingua franca* of business and more and more business programs are taught in part or completely in International English.

- Most of these mobile and 'delocalized' students have only rarely been exposed to the Financial Accounting practices of their home country.

- Most of these students will, upon graduation, work in an international context (i.e. not where they grew up and often not even where they were educated).

- They need therefore to be trained to appreciate, understand and analyze a variety of Accounting and Reporting problems from a theoretical and generic point of view, rather than just memorize the local regulatory solution prescribed in any given country or context. They will have to adapt and apply their understanding of generic Accounting and Reporting principles and practices to the local circumstances they will face.

- They need to familiarize themselves with financial information as it is presented in a variety of countries and be able to decode, without error, messages about the economic performance of a business that come in an assortment of formats.

A book with multiple perspectives on financial accounting

Today, business courses (graduate and undergraduate, BA, Masters of Accounting or MBA) have a really *international* audience. This book recognizes the needs created by this situation and was conceived to teach Financial Accounting and Reporting with the following three perspectives in mind:

- First it provides an *a-national* approach in that the issues are explained as natural business and common sense problems with multiple possible solutions and positions. In as much as possible, all possible solutions are examined with their logic and pros and cons.

- Second it takes on an *international point of view* because national practices are rapidly evolving in response to complex external (foreign in many cases) pressures coming from International Accounting Standards (IASC, now IASB), US GAAP, and regulations promulgated by Financial Market regulators such as IOSCO and SEC.

- Lastly it continuously offers the possibility to *compare and contrast the rules and practices of different countries*, especially from a user viewpoint. The students need to familiarize themselves with comparative accounting and be able to interpret signals or information coming from a diversity of international or national rules and standards.

Purpose of this text

This text offers an introduction to Financial Accounting and Reporting. It is designed for business students following their course of studies in institutions where knowledge of a single accounting system is recognized as being insufficient preparation for the world where the graduates will work.

This is a book on recording and measurement of value created (and aggregate value creation from the point of view of outside decision-makers) and not a book on the process through which accounting information contributes to the detailed value creation process inside the firm (decision-making support or managerial accounting).

Our approach derives from the characteristics of our targeted audience

The approach is based on the following ideas:

- We adopted a *user*, rather than a *producer* perspective. Our choice results from our deeply held belief that business students (graduate or undergraduate), regardless of the major they will select or the career they will embrace will be users of financial statements. Financial Accounting and Reporting is a universal knowledge base required from all students intending to become economic actors. Whether they will use accounting and financial information as internal managers or executives, or as external users (investors, credit analysts, etc.) they will need to interpret accounting data. Their knowledge of the preparation of accounting and reporting numbers needs to encompass only enough comprehension of key principles to allow the user to not be at the mercy of the information preparer. The book incorporates numerous unedited examples taken from annual reports of companies and many excerpts from the financial press. Some of these short excerpts from annual reports are commented, in order to prepare the students with reading and interpreting annual reports and articles in the financial press.

- Rather than providing a regulatory (technical) solution to a (simple or complex) reporting or measurement issue, we have chosen to first examine the economic logic of the problem and identify generic possible solutions and what impact each might have on a company's or decision maker's decisions. This requires an *a-national* or *non-national* approach. The authors find it more pedagogically useful and intellectually exciting to take time explaining the various possible solutions and their implications than studying the way a particular country handles the issue. In the first part of the book, all developments are based on a *generic* country, not on any specific country. Throughout the book, we examine the various possible ways of recording transactions and measuring and reporting value creation (such as unearned revenues and prepaid expenses, inventories, sale of fixed assets). We use a lot of examples, graphs and case studies in order to show the different potential solutions.

- Throughout the book and whenever appropriate, we cite the IASC (today IASB) standards. We strongly believe that, in many situations, the IASB recommendations, with the leeway and flexibility they contain, offer a good *a-national* approach but we do not hesitate highlighting the areas where there is still an open debate or where we feel in disagreement, always taking the point of view of the user, with aspects of a 'recommended' solution.

- In each chapter, we are providing a clear difference between what we feel is essential and what, in our opinion, might be considered more advanced or specialized knowledge. Each chapter is divided into 7 parts giving the instructor great flexibility in defining her or his customized approach: (1) Core Issues, (2) Advanced Issues, (3) Key Points, (4) Review Exercises, (5) Assignments, (6) References and (7) Further Readings. The term *Advanced issues* does not mean that the topics are not important or are outside the scope of a basic course. It only means that these topics could be covered after the core issues, at a later date, or not at all, depending on the instructor's preference.

- The comparative parts of the text follow a topical (issue oriented) approach, rather than a country-by-country approach. They include however many comparative tables that are structured by countries.

- The authors have written this text with the intention of showing that accounting and reporting are far from being a sterile over-regulated domain but on the contrary offer opportunities to think and search for what is the most suitable solution. Preparing accounting records, statements or reports is as creative as journalism. Good journalism follows rules and is only limited by professionalism, language and tradition. However the talent of the journalist rests in her or his ability to give a true and fair view of events while staying within these limits. An accountant faces a similar challenge to describe the economic reality of enterprises by using a specialized language, which we hope to have demystified in this book.

As practitioners and consultants the authors know how hard and complex, and intellectually stimulating the valuation, recording and reporting decisions can be. We are aware that these decisions have a great impact on value recognition and timing and thus on the behavior of myriads of economic actors. Accounting is serious business with great societal implications and it is an exciting profession. We have made the utmost effort to reflect our practical experience and wrote this book to communicate our passion and practice to the students who use the output of Accounting and Reporting processes.

A few practical considerations

- As the choice of currency unit has no bearing on the logic of our arguments or presentation, we use, throughout the book, a generic Currency Unit (or CU) except when we refer to real-life examples in which case the original currency is always used.
- All assignments based on actual business organizations are identified in the name of the assignment with a star next to the name of the company.
- In journal entries, we use the following conventions:

  BS(A+) = balance sheet, increase in assets
  BS(A–) = balance sheet, decrease in assets
  BS(L+) = balance sheet, increase in shareholders' equity and liabilities
  BS(L–) = balance sheet, decrease in shareholders' equity and liabilities
  IS(E+) = income statement, increase in expenses
  IS(E–) = income statement, decrease in expenses
  IS(R+) = income statement, increase in revenues
  IS(R–) = income statement, decrease in revenues.

- In some tables, based on real-life examples, the use of parentheses is equivalent to a negative sign, as it is a common practice in some countries.
- Tables and figures are numbered by chapter. Those in appendices are referred to with a letter A after the number.

Level of the text

The text is pitched at an introductory level for both graduate students with business experience (MBA, essentially) and undergraduate students with minimal business experience. Because of the dual level of complexity in each chapter, the book can also be used in intermediate courses on Financial Statement Analysis, Financial Reporting or International Accounting.

Supplementary support materials for students and teachers

Supplementary support material is available for both students and instructors and teachers on the book's website.

For students
- Excel™ files with the text of a certain number of assignments
- Appendices (Text and Journal entries)
- Multilingual glossary of accounting terms.

For instructors and teachers

- PowerPoint™ slides of the figures and tables included in the text.
- Additional PowerPoint™ presentation slides.
- Solutions to the end-of-chapter assignments. We sometimes wrote special notes to the instructor indicating the frequently made mistakes and alternative solutions.
- Additional assignments and solutions.
- Excel file solutions.

The supplementary material may be found of the Internet at the following address: http://www.thomsonlearning.co.uk/accountingandfinance/stolowylebas

Access will be given to academics through several levels of password protection. The appendices and glossary are also provided on the enclosed CD Rom.

Acknowledgments

Jennifer Pegg, our commissioning editor at Thomson Learning, provided us with constant and caring support and occasional prodding when needed. Without her continuous attention, the birthing of this book might never have taken place or would probably have been much slower. Ever since our initial contact with her when we first casually shared, with no specific intention of ever writing a textbook, the frustrations we felt with existing material inadequately meeting the needs of our students, Jennifer has had the great wisdom of putting us in the driver seat to create the material we were calling for. Her challenges, encouragements, wise and, at times, comforting comments as well as her quick decisions have helped us shape our project in the form of this book. We want to recognize Jennifer Pegg as the first person we wish to acknowledge for this book. Without her, we would not be writing these lines.

Our appreciation also goes to all the staff at Thomson who have contributed to the creation of this book and especially to Jenny Clapham, Paula McMahon, Jackie Wrout and Coralie Hudson.

We also wish to acknowledge the contribution of Stéphanie Chauveau, our secretary at HEC, who supported our many drafts.

Anonymous reviewers paid a significant role in shaping the finished product. From the first outline to the test chapters, their constructive comments helped us narrow down or focus our views and improve the pedagogical approach. They 'kept us honest' by telling us not to blow our pet-topics out of proportion and also by suggesting topics a balanced text would require and which we might have underplayed without their wise observations. Some of these evaluators have accepted to lose their anonymity and we gladly acknowledge in person these friends and kindred souls:

- Ignace de Beelde, University of Gent
- Axel Haller, University of Linz
- Begoña Giner Inchausti, University of Valencia

- Ann Jorissen, University of Antwerp
- Josephine Maltby, University of Sheffield
- Pat Sucher, Royal Holloway College, University of London
- Anne Ullathorne, University of Central England
- Stefano Zambon, University of Ferrara
- Peter Walton, ESSEC
- Charles P. van Wymeersch, University of Namur

The idea of this book and the ideas in this book have germinated and grown over the years, and notably in our teaching the introductory courses in both the bilingual H.E.C. MBA Program (*isa* Program) and the English speaking sections of the H.E.C. *Grande Ecole* program (both introductory and advanced courses). The students of these programs, the users from all over the world we have in mind as our audience, have been our first and often toughest evaluators. They have tested, criticized and commented-on earlier drafts of this book. Our greatest appreciation goes to these truly international students (they, together, represent over 45 nationalities) for their patience and tolerance with our occasional lack of clarity and weaknesses and for their generally constructive comments.

Some of these students' contributions were particularly detailed and useful. We want to recognize Mireia Ideaquiez, Hallgeir Varsi, Armando Capobianco and Ragnvald Mällberg. Special thanks and recognition go to Nils Clotteau, our student assistant on this project. They became dedicated advocates for the future readers. Their work has allowed us to considerably improve our successive drafts by incorporating the observations of enlightened users.

The multi-lingual glossary is a collective work and we are pleased to acknowledge our co-authors: Eva Eberhartinger (Professor, Chair of Accounting and Tax Management, University of Münster, Germany), José Antonio Gonzalo (Professor of Accounting and Financial Economics, Department of Managerial Science, University of Alcalá, Spain), and Stefano Zambon (Professor of Business Economics, Faculty of Economics, University of Ferrara, Italy).

We thank all these contributors for the generosity of their time and intelligence. The authors, nonetheless, assume full responsibility for the ideas expressed and for any errors or omissions.

We will appreciate any and all comments from readers and users.

Hervé Stolowy, Jouy-en-Josas
Michel J. Lebas, Seattle
March 2002

Contact:
stolowy@hec.fr
lebas@u.washington.edu

Introduction to financial accounting

Accounting: The language of business

Accounting is inseparable from business and management. In this book on accounting and reporting we will be discussing business issues and decisions by management and investors. "Accounting is the language of business" is a frequently heard expression. Let us see what is behind what has by now become a banal expression.

A model of business activity

Business is about action (transformation of resources) and involves several people (Robinson Crusoe, alone on his island may have had undertakings but could not have had a business).

Business involves both suppliers and customers but also a variety of people, each bringing to the business a specialized skill set that will be used in the enterprise's transformation process.

Business is about transforming resources into something else (product or service, tangible or intangible) that will meet a customer's expectation and create "profit" in doing so. Each skill set provided by individuals or groups of individuals (marketing, R&D, purchasing, manufacturing, selling, hiring, coordinating, managing, measuring, etc.) contributes to the transformation process of resources into making available a product offering to a (solvent) customer base.

Business decisions involve how resources will be acquired, allocated to each skill set and utilized to serve customers. All decisions in an enterprise are therefore built on a *representation* of the transformation process that includes a description of the role of each skill set. Each firm has its own vision of its transformation process (and therefore about its allocation of resources): it is its specific strategy. The strategy of Scania Trucks is, for example, different from that of Volvo Trucks. Both firms try to provide customers with the ability to find the truck that serves their needs as perfectly as possible. They have, however, opted for very different business processes. Scania opted, more than 20 years ago, for a modular design of its products that allows great possibilities for customization while limiting complexity at the manufacturing level at the expense of a large investment in upfront research for flexibility and compatibility. Meanwhile, Volvo Trucks, having grown largely through external acquisitions, has a rich product offering coming from a much more complex transformation process to create a great diversity of discrete truck models thus creating a market offering which is about as rich as Scania's. Both enterprises are leaders in their market and accounting must be able to compare them. Accounting must, therefore, be generic enough to be applicable to a variety of situations and business models.

A generic representation of the activity of any business is shown in Figure 1.1 as a "figure eight" cycle. In this cycle, resources are transformed into a value proposition, physically "packaged" in goods or services delivered to customers. These, in turn, exchange cash for said goods and that cash is, in due course, used for the acquisition of additional resources. The "figure eight" cycle is essentially endless as long as the enterprise can acquire resources and continues giving satisfaction to customers (at least better than competitors) and receive more cash from customers than it must give to all suppliers (including labor) that allow the transformation cycle to take place.

This cycle needs to be monitored by the managers of the firm. Every transaction (between suppliers and the enterprise or between the enterprise and its customers, but also inside the transformation process) needs to be recorded in order to serve as a basis for analysis over time (for example: does the enterprise need more or fewer resources than during the previous period in order to find a customer?) and comparatively to competitors (does the enterprise require more resources than its competitor to find a reliable supplier of resources?).

The only way for the various managers and actors in the firm (actors in the "figure eight") to be able to analyze transactions and take any action required to maintain the competitiveness of the firm is to agree on shared descriptions of transactions so they can communicate with one another. In other words, they need to share a language with its vocabulary, grammar and syntax to describe events and transactions that need to be examined in order to manage the "figure eight". That language is called accounting.

Accounting: a language for business

Accounting is a specialized language that has the specificity of being able to:

● Describe a state or a result (such as: "the sales revenue obtained from customers in the month of October amounted to 12 million CU").

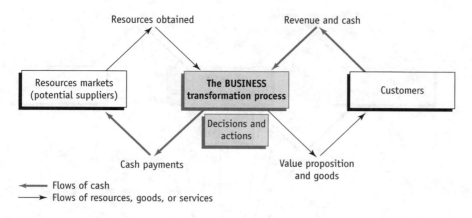

Resources obtained

Revenue and cash

Resources markets
(potential suppliers)

The BUSINESS
transformation process

Customers

Decisions and
actions

Cash payments

Value proposition
and goods

← Flows of cash
→ Flows of resources, goods, or services

Figure 1.1 The generic business model is a "figure eight" cycle

- Describe the events that led to that result (such as: "An advertising campaign worth 750,000 CU was run on TV in the first week of October; market share increased by 10% between October 1 and October 31; prices were reduced by 5% on October 1 from what they had been since last year; additional customers were acquired, etc.").
- Provide a rank ordering of results allowing evaluators of accounting signals to be able to say "This result – be it for a time period or for a market or a responsibility center – is better (or worse) than that result."

Figure 1.1 must therefore be amended to show that accounting is needed to support decision making. Figure 1.2 illustrates such amendment.

Accounting records all flows through the "figure eight" of the business cycle. Accounting records principally economic variables using monetary units. It can, however, also describe non-financial parameters. Accounting is an integral part of the life of business. It is as inseparable from business activity as the shadow is to the illuminated object. Accounting helps managers know what was done so they can modify their future actions in order for the future to yield results that are more coherent with their intent.

However the reader will remember that the title of this book is *Corporate Financial **Reporting***. Why reporting?

Business creates an agency relationship that calls for reporting

Business is about delegation. Delegation from the capital providers to the enterprise in charge of creating wealth with the capital they were awarded; and delegation within the organization to specialized managers to work in a coordinated and coherent way to create wealth (among other things for capital providers, but also for other participants in the business process). Delegation means control that the devolution and autonomy granted was used appropriately. Control means that information be provided about what the "delegatee" did and what results were achieved. This flow of information allowing control by the "delegator" is called reporting. Reporting is accounting for what the subordinate or delegatee has done with the resources she or he has received from her or his superior. A report may document effort or results or both. If effort is reported, accounting will be detailed and will be providing values of

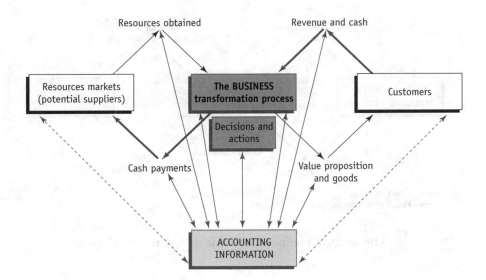

Figure 1.2 Accounting describes all parts of the activity of the firm

parameters throughout the business process transforming resources. Reporting on effort will be business specific (we will later call it "managerial accounting"). If, on the contrary, only results are reported, the report may be generic since the questions are essentially the same regardless of the nature of the business (this type of report will be the focus of this text and is part of what we will call "financial accounting"). The questions are about (a) whether the business has created value (i.e., a positive return) – and will continue to do so – for capital providers (current or potential), and (b) whether the business is viable for the future (that question being of prime importance for employees, customers, and suppliers among many).

Reporting to capital providers

The "figure eight" cycle described in Figure 1.1 is not completely operational. Like any pump, the "figure eight" cycle must be primed. How can the business acquire resources to feed its transformation process unless there is already some cash in the enterprise before it starts to operate? Suppliers might extend credit to prime the pump, but the operating (transformation) cycle might be much longer than the duration of the credit the suppliers are willing to extend.

There must be capital providers who provide initial financial resources that will be used to prime the transformation cycle. The business manager is therefore the agent of the capital provider: she or he has received the mandate to use the capital to earn a positive return within acceptable risk-taking practices. In some cases the entrepreneur/manager and the capital provider might be one and the same person but, as we will see later, it is essential to distinguish the business's activities from those engaged in *privately* by the individuals who are either providing capital or are the operators of the transformation process.

Since the providers of capital are not doing so without the motive of earning a return on their investment, it is normal for a business to report on what they used the funds for and what outcome was obtained from their application to the transformation process.

There are two kinds of capital providers:

- Those (known as shareholders in the case of an incorporated business) who are willing to assume (vicariously or directly) the risks of the business (in exchange for a variable but hopefully large return) and who are investing capital for an unspecified long term.

- Those (known as lenders) who are not willing to assume much of the risks of the business and want a guaranteed return on their provision of funds within a specified short, medium or long term.

Each category has specific needs in terms of reporting which the accounting information system will need to satisfy. Lenders are mainly interested in being kept informed about the ability of the business to reimburse the money it has borrowed. The emphasis is therefore on the cash generation potential of the firm.

Shareholders, by way of contrast, are interested in two types of information: on the one hand, from a fiduciary point of view, shareholders want to know periodically what the firm they have invested in owns (and what their share is), and be sure that appropriate controls are in place to avoid inappropriate disbursement of resources (we call this accounting report the **statement of financial position** or **balance sheet**); on the other hand, they are interested in knowing how much residual wealth was created in the transformation process that they can claim as theirs (we call this accounting report the **income statement**).

In addition, both lenders and capital providers are interested in knowing more about the plans of the business and the dynamics of the evolution of the relevant and specifically defined "figure eight".

Figure 1.2 can now be enriched yet again to recognize the complexity of all processes behind the life of an enterprise. Figure 1.3 illustrates not only a representation of the business cycle (the "figure eight" of the transformation process), but also positions accounting as the medium of communication inside the firm as well as with its partners, be they capital providers, lenders, suppliers of material or of labor force and intelligence, or providers of the license to operate granted to the business.

In addition Figure 1.3 illustrates the fact that an initial flow of capital is essential to start the value creation cycle (transformation process) and that capital providers need to be rewarded by either dividends or interest payment but also by a provision of information (reporting) about how well the business is functioning.

Reporting to business partners

Although technically the firm is not an agent of employees, customers or suppliers (the firm has not received a mandate from them), it is normal, if the relationship is to be durable, that they be kept informed. Others who need to evaluate the risks of a business and the likelihood of its survival will use accounting reports that were originally prepared mainly for capital providers. These other users will do so by surmising the business model and looking at telltale ratios or metrics describing the "health" of the "figure eight" process both in terms of efficiency and relevance, but also in terms of security of provision of funds by capital providers (we call this "financial statement analysis" and Chapter 15 is devoted entirely to that activity).

Reporting to superiors and peers

Accounting describes transactions and results of actions and decisions. It is normal (and convenient, since the information already has been captured to

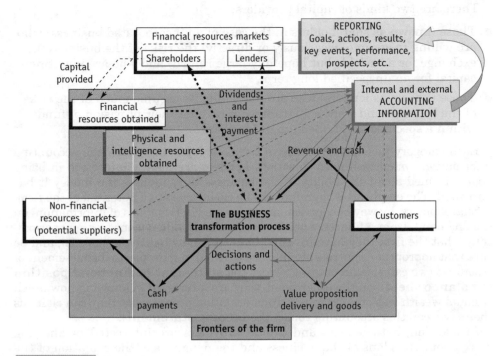

Figure 1.3 A generic representation of the operations of a business and the role of accounting

satisfy capital providers) that a superior uses accounting information to verify the subordinate discharged her or his responsibility appropriately. If the superior is only interested in results, information in a format similar to the one used to report to capital providers might prove to be sufficient (financial accounting is results oriented), while, if the superior is interested in evaluating the effort of the subordinate, she or he might be interested in the detailed steps undertaken by the subordinate in fulfilling her or his mission. In this case the accounting report will be more process oriented and will be called as already mentioned "managerial accounting".

Accounting is a living language

As we have seen accounting describes what actors in the transformation process of the firm do. The process of the "figure eight" is one of value creation. Business makes sense only if more resources (in the broad sense of the term resources, i.e., financial and non-financial) are created as the outcome of the transformation process than were consumed in its course.

The process of doing business changes over time (the application of the generic "figure eight" changes continuously). Business relationships are affected by technology. For example, the introduction of the web had greatly modified the way the transformation process is organized. Web-based market-places and speed of communication change the relationships between enterprises, suppliers and customers. Similarly, new issues appear with the evolution of society. For example, 75 years ago, few businesses paid significant attention to the possible creation of a retirement income for their former employees. New business issues are born every day that accounting must be able to describe. The new description must be an enrichment that is added to previously established modes of description of economic reality. The reality that accounting describes is alive and evolving continuously. The accounting language must therefore be very strong and flexible and rest on solid principles that will allow that flexibility.

Accounting is a language and its "words" are symbols that reflect a certain view of the world. Just like our everyday language evolves continuously, accounting must be able to adapt to the needs of the time.

Accounting is a very special language in that the way it describes the world of business affects the timing and measurement of wealth creation. Just to give a brief example, when one buys a machine, one could offset the purchase against the revenue generated by the use of the machine during the first year (cash accounting), or one could consider that the machine will be useful to generate sales over several years and therefore one would offset in the first year only a part of the cost of the machine (depreciation or accrual accounting). Clearly, the choice between these two approaches will affect greatly the perceived timing of the wealth created by the use of the machine to serve customers. Accounting is so important for the smooth operation of a society that few countries have allowed its evolution to go unchecked.

Language is essential to the operation of any organized society. Cardinal de Richelieu, Prime Minister to the French King Louis XIII, founded the Académie Française to create, standardize, and regulate the French language. His decision was totally political. It was part of a process to unify the kingdom and facilitate both government and inter-regional trade. In a process similar to the unique case of the French attempt at standardizing their language, accounting standards-setting bodies have been created in many countries to define (regulate) the terms of this special language to facilitate measurement of wealth creation and therefore open exchanges and facilitate the support financial markets provide to the development of businesses.

Today, regulation of the accounting language is carried out on a global level because businesses trade globally and also because financial markets span the globe (see later, in "Core Issues").

Accounting is a language with some maneuvering room

Accounting, because of the variety of requirements placed on its applicability and evolution, remains, by necessity, built on very generic principles and leaves some room for customizing the representations it creates to the specific needs of businesses or classes of users of accounting information. The accounting language must be able to describe any business activity. It must allow any user (also defined in "Core Issues") to shape their opinion about an economic entity by looking at the entity's financial statements. These statements are like the "final product" of the accounting business process.

The users' opinion is built on several aspects of a business entity's potential: financial situation (through the balance sheet), sales performance and efficiency in its consumption of resources for the generation of sales (through the income statement), and cash generation (through the cash flow statement).

Financial statements allow users to take very concrete decisions such as whether to invest or not in the business entity, acquiring additional resources for the entity, giving (or receiving) credit terms for settling accounts between customers (or suppliers) and the business entity, the granting of a loan by a financial institution to a business entity, providing the basis for calculation of taxation of business entities by tax authorities, etc.

Since there are different (yet perfectly legitimate[1] ways of describing the same reality (and especially the timing of recognition of profit), the choice of an accounting "solution" (embodiment of principles into practice) will impact on the perception financial markets hold about a business.

The stakes are high in communicating fairly and effectively the potential represented by the business they manage. Practitioners, managers, and the media have even coined the expression "accounting strategy" to reflect the fact that there is "wiggle room" in describing a given reality. An accounting strategy means that, sometimes, when needed (in theory, to better serve the users), one can alter the accounting representation to better serve the purpose of communicating at that time. Clearly that maneuvering space has to be regulated (see "Core Issues"). Although room exists for variations in measurement, timing, and classification of a given reality, over the long run the results are always the same (but the decisions of the users of accounting information may have been affected in the meantime). Some quotes illustrate this point:

> Acatos & Hutcheson, the UK edible oils and manufacturing fats group revealed it had only just managed to stay in the black in its first half of 1999. However, analysts said that were it not for complex changes in accounting policy on the valuation of inventory of oil stocks, Acatos would have reported losses of about £3m. (adapted from: *Financial Times*, 8 December 1999)

Here the change in accounting methods helped reduce the loss of a given period by distributing it over several periods – but it must be noted that the analysts, and thus the decision makers, were not fooled by this "cosmetic" modification.

> Air France announced in 1998 that it had changed certain accounting methods to bring them in line with best international practice. The changes had no significant impact on the results [i.e., no effect on the wealth created this period], but had reduced shareholders' funds [equivalent of net worth i.e., wealth created in the past] by about FF1billion. (*Financial Times*, 27 May 1998)

Such a modification (which acknowledged that profits had effectively been overstated in the past) certainly was very important for a business that was about to be privatized. The view it gave of the business was truer than before.

> When Nissan Motors, the Japanese carmaker, was having financial difficulties, analysts cautioned that a change in accounting practices disguised the actual decline. Nissan adjusted its accounting methods to include royalties in pre-tax profits. Excluding Y19bn in royalties, pre-tax profits fell 97 per cent. (adapted from: *Financial Times*, 11 November 1998)

> Mr. Godsell, chief executive of Anglogold, the world's largest gold mining company based in South Africa, introduced international accounting methods, so that he could compare the performance of his mines with those of his foreign rivals, namely in Australia and North America. (adapted from: *Financial Times*, 12 July 1998)

Here, the reference to international accounting standards allows comparability of performance metrics, which is useful for shareholders and potential investors, and the management of Anglogold itself.

These examples also illustrate the fact that accounting is never deterministic. This is why the field has drawn so much interest for so long: within a limited set of rules and principles, the language of accounting is there to serve the users by giving the most useful, true, and fair description of a sometimes ambiguous reality (especially when it comes to timing).

This chapter's Core Issues define financial accounting, introduce the various users of financial information, and describe the international accounting standard setting process as well as some elements of the accounting process.

The Advanced Issues section revisits the distinction between reporting issues to management and to third parties (financial accounting), and issues of efficiency in the use of resources (managerial accounting) we briefly touched on in the introduction. This section also emphasizes that accounting is almost as old as human economic activity. We therefore provide a short overview of the history and evolution of accounting over the years. Accounting, being the language of business, is an open language just as there are many ways an artist can use to create a portrait of the model.

CORE ISSUES

Definition of financial accounting

Accounting

Accounting is about information. To account for something is to acknowledge its existence and describe it. To count is to measure and quantify. Accounting does both: it is a method of counting and a method of accounting for economic parameters describing the life of an enterprise (be it "for" or "not-for" profit). Accounting is about providing users with information (i.e., more than just data) about the economic and financial aspects of the life of an enterprise.

Broadly speaking, accounting information is an essential decision-support tool for the users of accounting information. Most decisions in a business are about resource planning, resource acquisition, and resource allocation in order to fulfill the firm's strategic intent (see, for example, Lebas 1999: 54). These decisions are based on financial and non-financial (i.e., operational) information.

Such information is the output of an ongoing process of identifying, capturing, managing, analyzing, interpreting, and distributing data and information describing the economic activity of the firm.

Accounting has two key missions:

- To facilitate value creation by supporting resource acquisition and allocation decision making. Value can be reduced to economic wealth if one refers only to shareholders who are looking for a financial return on their investment. However, we will keep using the term "value" because it refers to the broader concept of being better off for a variety of stakeholders[2] whose utility functions may not be expressed solely in economic or monetary terms.

- To measure and report to stakeholders the amount of value created during a given period.

Although accounting is a complete discipline, this duality of missions has traditionally led to separating it in two (although closely interactive) subclasses on the basis of the different users who have access to its output:

- The first is called managerial accounting. It deals with a rather detailed account of how resources (which may include non-financial resources such as employee or customer loyalty or ability to create a network of resources) are acquired, managed, and used in the various business processes constituting the firm and is thus of particular interest to managers inside the firm.

- The second one is called regulated or financial accounting. It is the focus of this text. It is aimed at reporting, in a somewhat aggregated way, the (economic) performance of the firm to essential external users such as shareholders, bankers, creditors, customers, unions, tax authorities, etc. Financial accounting focusses on the financial or monetary aspects of performance. Since its output will be used by outside investors and stakeholders to allocate their own resources, accounting information is a social good and therefore is generally regulated so that all classes of users receive signals of equivalent significance.

As we will see later, such a distinction between the accounting subclasses is somewhat artificial and often causes debates as to where the frontier should be placed between them.

Financial accounting

Financial accounting is a **process** of description of the various events that take place in the life of a firm. These events are essentially **transactions** between the firm and outside partners (suppliers of resources and customers of the firm's output). The description of each elemental transaction is **materialized** by source documents that contain both financial and non-financial elements to allow a **valuation** of that transaction. These are **recorded**, classified, and **analyzed** so as to allow for the **periodic** creation of synthetic reports called **financial statements**. These generally comprise an income statement, a balance sheet, and a cash flow statement (all three with footnotes which explain choices made by the firm and give more details about some transactions). Financial statements are established periodically and it is traditional to create these synthetic documents at least once every year, generally around a date when sales activity is the slowest.

The origin of the annual nature of financial statements can probably be traced back to the agricultural cycle. After the harvest was completed, the farmer calculated the amount of wealth created before it could be distributed between the various stakeholders according to the contract binding the partners (owner of the land and provider of the labor force that created the harvest) in such formats as sharecropping (shared risks), farming (the landowner takes no risk), or salaried labor force (the landowner takes all the risks). It was traditional to close the "books" on the harvest at the end of the production cycle, i.e., at the end of the year. Therefore many countries have retained a preference for a civil "year-end" closing. However, in businesses such as retail sales, home electronics, toys, or gifts sales, a civil year-end closing would not make much sense as that is a period of boom and it would be more logical to close (i.e., prepare the synthetic financial statements), for example, in February when business is slack and the wealth or value created by the business cycle will be pretty well definitively acquired (few returns two months after the year-end boom sales). The topic of the choice of a closing date is developed further in Appendix 1.1.

From the definition of financial accounting several keywords merit attention:

Process: The method of describing events and transactions and collecting the descriptors is organized by what is called the accounting process. It is a set of rules and practices, supported by dedicated hardware and software, and coordinated by the activities of a variety of people, extending well beyond the staff of the accounting department.

Transactions include such events as the acquisition of resources, selling the firm's output, securing work space through the signing of a lease, payment of the monthly rent, obtaining a loan from a financial institution, etc. Financial accounting only recognizes transactions that have or will have monetary implications, i.e., which will result in an exchange of cash at some point. However, rules that govern financial accounting create certain exceptions such as depreciation in which the cash transaction (acquisition of the fixed asset) takes place before the recognition of the value creation event (recognition of the consumption of the value creation potential of a piece of equipment or an asset) (see Chapters 2 and 7).

Materialization of transactions: Each transaction is materialized by a concrete document (invoice, bank statement, voucher, receipt, etc.). If a transaction is not documented, the accountant cannot recognize and record it. For example, if a business were to acquire a resource without a corresponding invoice, it would be impossible to record it.

Analysis of transactions consists of defining the category or class they belong to so they may be aggregated into homogeneous classes. This step in the accounting process (described in Chapter 4) is often manual (with the possibility of human error and inconsistencies). This classification and aggregation tends, however, to be replaced by automated procedures, for example by the definition of bar codes placed on types of documents corresponding to certain transactions or by linking software such as the accounting recording and invoicing software so that transactions are automatically recorded in the appropriate category.

Recording is generally carried out on a regular periodic basis (most frequently, daily), and in chronological order. This may explain why the record of these transactions is called the **journal** (see Chapter 4).

Valuation consists in giving a monetary value to the transaction so it can be recorded. It is often easy to place a monetary value when there is an invoice, but often it is more subjective as in the case of the recording in the acquirer's books of the purchase price of an acquired business that is comprised of both physical assets and a loyal clientele.

Financial statements also called "accounts" or "annual accounts": They provide a synthesis of the performance of the firm in terms of value creation. The balance sheet describes the "stock" of resources of the firm and the claims on that stock. The income statement describes how and how much value was created between two "balance sheets" dates and the cash flow statement describes the cash situation, and how it changed during the period.

Periodicity of financial statements has been generally agreed to be at least one calendar year, but these can be established for any period duration, if it is useful for decision makers. Closing the books (i.e., establishing the financial statements), however, consumes both time and resources and managers tend to limit the number of periods within a year so as to not waste the resources of the firm.

Users of financial accounting

Financial accounting reflects the economic activity of the firm. Its purpose is to allow users to understand its situation in global and synthetic ways. It produces information for managers as well as for third-party stakeholders. Financial accounting is also often used to document tax obligations, and is therefore subject to regulation and control by tax authorities. Creditors expect from financial accounting that it will help them better understand the profitability of the firm as well as its ability to generate cash in the future to repay its lenders. Customers, suppliers, and employees alike look to financial accounting for information about the ongoing nature of the business.

There are many users of financial accounting and they have, by definition, different needs and expectations. The first user of financial accounting information is the firm itself. Managers need to have a synthetic view of their collective performance. It is impossible to create a hierarchy of users. Such rank ordering would be context and culture specific. Figure 1.4 illustrates a generic structure of potential financial accounting users and is not meant to carry any idea of rank ordering.

The diversity of needs of the different users is analyzed in further detail in Table 1.1[3] that illustrates how each class of users may employ financial statements for their own purposes.

While all the information needs of these users cannot conceivably be met by only one set of financial statements, there are needs that are common to all users. As investors are providers of risk capital to the enterprise, the provision of financial statements that meet their needs and expectations will also likely meet many or most of the needs of other users who are interested in estimating risks and potential rewards attached to the operations of a given enterprise.

Limited liability companies must periodically file financial statements with a regulatory organization such as the Registrar in the UK, the Commercial Register in Spain or the Commercial Courts in France (see Appendix 15.7 on the website). Such filings are required in each European Union member country for the protection of third parties. The European Union reinforced such an obligation by the 1st (9 March 1968) and 4th Directives (25 July 1978). The EU Directive no. 90–605 (8 November 1990) essentially extends to all incorporated businesses, the requirement to file financial statements.

Table 1.1   Users and their different needs

Users	Needs	Source documents	Accessible information	Delay to obtain information
Management	Information to plan, make strategic and resource allocation decisions and control	Financial statements	Total access, from source documents to financial statements	Information is accessible on an ongoing basis. It depends on the organization itself
Shareholders/ investors	Are concerned with the risk inherent in, and return provided by, their investments: • Information to help them determine whether they should buy, hold or sell • Information to assess the ability of the enterprise to pay dividends	Financial statements	Financial statements plus additional publicly available information about the successes of the firm in its markets and in its operations	The date on which the financial statements must be made available before the general assembly is regulated in each and every country. The trend is towards earlier publication
Bankers, lenders	Information to determine whether their loans, and the interest attached to them, will be paid when due	Financial statements, both historical and pro forma (forecasts)	Financial statements	A business will produce the ad hoc documents whenever it needs to raise funds from banks or on the market
Suppliers and other trade creditors	Information to determine whether amounts owed to them will be paid when due. Trade creditors are likely to be interested in an enterprise over a shorter period than lenders unless they are dependent on the continuation of the enterprise as a major customer	Financial statements	In theory these users have no particular claim on financial information beyond the financial statements but by benchmarking and comparative analysis plus an organized intelligence watch, they can interpret financial information in a detailed manner	Case by case
Customers	Information about the going concern nature of an enterprise, especially when they have a long-term involvement with, or are dependent on, the enterprise Customers are especially interested in evaluating the viability of the firm as an ongoing supplier	Financial statements	Just like suppliers, customers will ask information directly and cross-reference it to be able to have leading signals indicating possible opportunities or problems	Case by case

continued overleaf

Table 1.1 continued

Competitors	To compare relative performance	Financial statements	Competitive analysis will be the output of large databases of financial statements, cross-referenced with business intelligence and a good understanding of the economic sector	Case by case, as a function of the amount of resources dedicated to information gathering
Employees	Information about the stability and profitability of their employer Information to assess the ability of the enterprise to provide remuneration, retirement benefits, and employment opportunities	Financial statements	Access is regulated through legislation in every country	Case by case moderated by local legislation
Government, regulatory agencies, tax authorities	Are interested in resource allocation and, therefore, want to know about the activities of enterprises. Also use information to stimulate the economy, to determine taxation policies and assessments. Also use some or all the information in the calculation of national economic statistics	Financial statements, often recast in a pre-defined tax-based format possibly following different rules	On a recurring basis the tax-formatted financial statements plus, in the case of a tax audit, access to all source documents	Each country has specific rules. For example, in France tax-formatted statements must be ready within three to four months after the closing
General public	Enterprises affect members of the public individually and collectively. For example, enterprises may make a substantial contribution to the local economy in many ways, including the number of people they employ and their patronage of local suppliers Financial statements may assist the public by providing information about the trends and recent developments in the prosperity of the enterprise and the range of its activities	Financial statements	Regulated access	Case by case

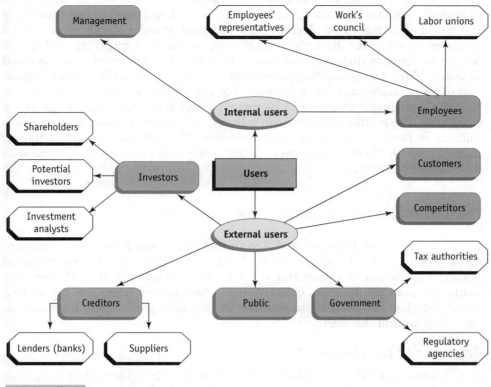

Figure 1.4 A set of financial accounting users

Financial reporting standards

Necessity of financial reporting standards

The various (and numerous) users of financial statements mentioned in the previous section need to understand financial information in the same way. For that reason, within each country, local regulators issue generally accepted accounting principles[4] (GAAP) that are called **accounting standards** or **financial reporting standards**. Accounting standards are authoritative statements of how particular types of transaction and other events should be reflected in financial statements. These standards include specific principles, bases, conventions, rules, and practices necessary to prepare the financial statements.

In each country, regulatory bodies (such as the Accounting Standards Board in the UK or the German Accounting Standards Committee in Germany) and/or the professional accountancy bodies promulgate financial reporting standards. Each national official source of regulation issues pronouncements, which include standards, laws, doctrines, etc.

Because of differences in culture and traditions, taxation policy, sources of financing, importance and recognition of the accounting profession, nature of accounting regulation, etc., there are differences of form and content between the published financial reporting standards of most countries. However, comparability of financial information is a key issue in an international environment. The various users act more and more globally and should be able to understand, and also trust, the financial statements issued in any country of the world. Further, lack of commonly accepted standards can increase the preparation costs for financial reports: for instance a multinational group having to prepare financial statements in a certain number of countries and following different accounting standards in each would incur a much higher cost of preparation (and a possible loss of quality of the aggregate description of the whole business) than would be incurred had there been one single set of standards. The relationship between internal and external reporting would also militate in favor of accounting harmonization. More precisely, a group having harmonized its internal measure of performance could also want to harmonize its external reporting.

The International Accounting Standards Board

In this context, the International Accounting Standards Board is an independent, private sector body, formed in 1973, under the name of International Accounting Standards Committee (IASC), and restructured in 2001 when the name was changed. Its main objective is to promote convergence of accounting principles that are used by businesses and other organizations for financial reporting around the world.

Objectives of the IASB

The objectives of IASB, as stated in its new constitution (IASC 2001: § 2), are:

a   "To develop, in the public interest, a single set of high quality, understandable and enforceable global accounting standards that require high quality, transparent and comparable information in financial statements and other financial reporting to help participants in the world's capital markets and other users make economic decisions;

b   To promote the use and rigorous application of those standards; and

c   To bring about convergence of national accounting standards and International Accounting Standards to high quality solutions."

History of the IASB

The confidence crisis which began in 1998 in certain Asian countries and spread to other regions of the world showed the need for reliable and transparent accounting to support sound decision making by investors, lenders, and regulatory authorities. This led to a restructuring process that culminated on 1 April 2001, when the IASB assumed accounting standard setting responsibilities from its predecessor body, the IASC. The IASB met in technical session for the first time on 18–20 April 2001.

Structure

In March 2001, the IASC Foundation, a not-for-profit corporation incorporated in the state of Delaware, USA, was formed and is the parent entity of the IASB, which is based in London, UK. The new structure has the following main features: the IASC Foundation is an independent organization having two main bodies, the trustees, coming from the accounting and financial community, and the IASB, as well as a Standards Advisory Council and the Standing Interpretations Committee. The IASC Foundation trustees appoint the IASB members, exercise oversight, and raise the funds needed, whereas IASB has sole responsibility for setting accounting standards. The Standards Advisory Council provides a formal vehicle for groups and individuals having diverse geographic and functional backgrounds to give advice to the IASB. Figure 1.5 summarizes this structure.

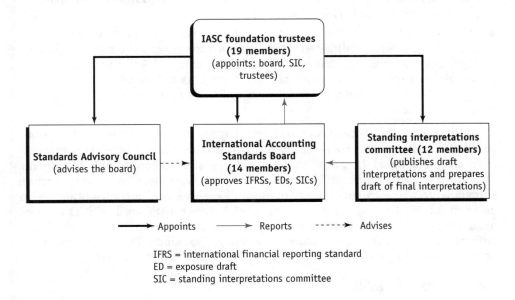

IFRS = international financial reporting standard
ED = exposure draft
SIC = standing interpretations committee

Figure 1.5 The IASB structure
Source: Adapted from IASB overview: www.iasb.org.uk

Past international accounting standards

In April 2001, the IASB approved that "all standards and interpretations issued under previous constitutions continue to be applicable unless and until they are amended or withdrawn".

New terminology

The IASB announced in April 2001 that the IASC Foundation trustees have agreed that accounting standards issued by IASB shall be designated "International Financial Reporting Standards" (IFRS for one standard – or IFRSs in the plural).

List of standards

Appendix 1.2 provides a list of the International Accounting Standards issued as of 1 April 2001.

Implementation of International Accounting (Financial Reporting) Standards (IASs or IFRSs)

The IASB has no authority to require compliance with its accounting standards. However, many countries already endorse, require, or recommend IASs and

IFRSs as their own either without amendment, or with minor additions or deletions (as was the case for Armenia, Barbados, Botswana, Croatia, Cyprus, Czech Republic, Egypt, Georgia, Hungary, Kenya, Latvia, Lesotho, Macedonia, Malta, Nepal, Philippines).

Furthermore, important developments have taken place in Europe:

- Austria, Belgium, France, Germany, Italy, and Spain have passed laws allowing certain companies to use IASB standards for domestic reporting purposes, subject to certain conditions.
- On 13 June 2000, the European Commission issued a communication proposing to require all listed EU companies to prepare their consolidated financial statements in accordance with International Accounting Standards from 2005 onwards, at the latest. This communication was followed by a proposal for a regulation in February 2001, including the same requirement.

Additionally, the International Organization of Securities Commissions (IOSCO), which is the representative body of the world's securities markets regulators[5], decided in May 2000 to endorse the International Accounting Standards (IASs), while still allowing national regulators to require certain supplementary treatments (reconciliation, disclosure, and interpretation). This decision followed an agreement dating 1995 between IASC and IOSCO to work on a program of "core standards", which could be used by publicly listed enterprises when offering securities in foreign jurisdictions. The "core standards" project resulted in 15 new or revised IASs and was completed in 1999.

Future impact of IASB

The next few years will be crucial for IASB, as its success will depend on two factors:

- Agreement by European governments to implement IASs (and IFRSs) in their listed companies by 2005.
- Attitude of stock markets regulators, and in particular of the United States' Security and Exchange Commission (SEC), towards the IASs. Our expectation is that the SEC will decide to recognize these standards as they are, or with a certain amount of additional disclosure (which could lead to effectively transforming IASs into US accounting standards).

Introduction to the accounting process

An illustration will show how the need for accounting arises from a simple set of transactions between persons or corporations and how the accounting process is created to monitor and record these transactions.

Let us assume we are at the end of the 15th century in Venice. Mantzaros, a young merchant of Greek origin, wants to become rich and powerful. A quick survey of his environment leads him to the conclusion that the most effective way for him to achieve his objective is to trade with the Orient. His family had endowed him with some 100 gold ducats. In order to not mix his own "estate" with the risky venture he is considering, Mantzaros, as an individual, creates a separate entity he calls "Venture Mantzaros" or VM for short. This entity (VM) is endowed by Mantzaros with his 100 ducats. Mantzaros, as the sole investor in this business venture, holds claim to all the profit the venture might create in the future. He is a 100% shareholder.

However, if profit is to be created, this endowment of 100 ducats is not enough to buy and commission a ship to start trading with the Orient. Such an activity would require about 1,000 ducats. Thus Mantzaros, now as the *manager* of the venture, visits a Florentine banker who agrees to lend the venture the 900 additional ducats it needs for the acquisition and outfitting of a ship. The loan will be for not more than 5 years and will carry an annual interest rate of 10% (to be paid in a lump sum on the date when the principal will be reimbursed).

The venture must record that it has entered into obligations: it has agreed to refund the money it received from the banker not later than 5 years from now, and it has agreed to pay an interest charge of 10% a year for as many years as the money will be borrowed. In a blank note book, let us call it a "journal", Mantzaros, as manager of VM, records the commitment the venture has made. If VM were to "take stock" of its wealth at that moment, it would show on one side the cash it holds (the original 100 ducats provided by Mantzaros, the individual, plus the cash received from the banker), and it also would record the debt commitment that, if – and when – it were called, would diminish the wealth of the venture.

Essentially, VM's "net situation" has evolved this way:

- Situation before the agreement of the banker: Wealth = 100 ducats.
- Situation after the agreement with the banker: Wealth = 100 ducats plus 900 ducats received minus a debt of 900 ducats = 100 ducats.

Borrowing, in itself, does not create wealth. It is what the money will be used for that, eventually, creates wealth.

The "wealth account" of the venture at this stage is presented in Table 1.2.

Table 1.2   VM's "wealth account" at step 1

Venture Mantzaros owns		Venture Mantzaros owes	
Cash in hand (100 + 900)	1,000 ducats	Owed to banker	900 ducats
Total	1,000 ducats	Total	900 ducats
		Net "worth" of Venture Mantzaros	100 ducats

Accounting alone (i.e., recording) does not create wealth[6]. It only keeps track of what the economic entity (here it is the Venture Mantzaros) does and is worth at any point in time. The owner's or capitalist's claim is equal to what the enterprise is worth at any moment. Since the venture has done nothing so far to create wealth (no transformation activity and no trading of output with third parties), the claim of Mantzaros, the individual, is still equal to the 100 gold ducats he invested in the business.

Mantzaros (as the manager of VM) then uses the 1,000 ducats to buy a good ship, outfit it, staff it, and load the hold with cargo and merchandise the captain of the ship will trade for the venture in the Orient (actually the Near Orient or Middle East at the eastern end of the Mediterranean). Venture Mantzaros' wealth has not changed. Cash has simply been changed into tangible goods. If VM were in a perfect market, whether it holds cash or merchandise should not make any difference. Both are resources that VM, as an economic entity, can and will use to try to create future wealth.

The VM "wealth account" after the expedition is about ready to depart reads like Table 1.3.

Table 1.3 "Wealth account" after step 2

Venture Mantzaros owns		Venture Mantzaros owes	
Cash in hand (petty cash)	10 ducats	Owed to banker	900 ducats
Cash in the hands of the captain for sailors' future wages, maintenance of the ship and trading	150 ducats		
Inventory of food and supplies on board	330 ducats		
Inventory of merchandise to be traded	350 ducats		
Ship and equipment	160 ducats		
Total	1,000 ducats	Total	900 ducats
		Net "worth" of Venture Mantzaros	100 ducats

Since VM owns goods, a ship and cash worth 1,000 ducats but owes 900, its net wealth (or net worth) is still 100 ducats. Not only does Table 1.3 show VM's net worth, it also lists all that the venture owns, structured in different classes or categories. Such a document is of great importance for "controlling" the efforts of the captain (Venture Mantzaros' agent) in his efforts to create more wealth. It can also be used to verify that no pilferage takes place (internal control). At any time, Mantzaros, or someone else, can verify the physical existence of what the venture owns.

The fact that Mantzaros was able to select a good captain, a good crew, and a solid ship is very important: the likelihood of success rests on the quality of the captain and his or her crew. Mantzaros (as an individual) now not only represents the reality of what he owns (he is the sole proprietor of VM), but that ownership now represents a potential profit to come if and when the ship returns and is sold along with its cargo for more than VM owes the banker. His hope and intention is that the captain of his venture will bring back more than just one ship. He has encouraged him or her to behave as a privateer and capture as many "enemy" ships and place them under his (her) control. Mantzaros is looking forward to the success of the VM expedition.

Mantzaros is expecting it will take 4 years before the ship can be expected to return, hopefully loaded with more valuable merchandise than it sailed out with. Mantzaros needs resources to live on while the venture runs its course. He realizes that not only has he handed over all his cash to the venture but also he is not even entirely confident in its success. He wants to hedge his bet (i.e., diversify his risks). He therefore seeks partners who are willing to share the risks and the returns of his planned "expedition". He finds a wealthy friend who agrees Mantzaros has bought a solid ship and hired an excellent and entrepreneurial captain who will be likely to return with his hold loaded with valuable goods. This friend buys, in exchange for 500 ducats in cash, a half "share" of the rights and claims Mantzaros (as an individual) holds over the venture: i.e., half of the net worth today, which includes the right to receive 50% of the possible profit realized if and when the ship returns. Essentially, Mantzaros (individual) sold privately a state conditional claim (50% of future profits) for 500 ducats, thus reducing his own claim on future profits from 100% to 50%.

The wealth of the venture remains at 100 ducats, although the wealth of Mantzaros, the individual, has been modified by his receiving 500 ducats in cash. The fundamental advantage of having created Venture Mantzaros is that the "shares" (i.e., unit claims on future profits) can be sold by "shareholders" privately and completely independently of the venture itself. Mantzaros' claim on the future profit of the venture has been reduced to 50% while it used to be 100% before his private transaction with his friend. Mantzaros' personal wealth before the sale of a half of his share was "zero ducats in hand – he had handed over all of his cash wealth to the venture – plus a 100% claim on the profits of the venture".

His wealth after the private sale of a 50% interest in the venture is now "500 ducats in hand plus an only 50% interest in the future profits of the Venture". Mantzaros traded his rights to 100% of an uncertain reward (future profits) for 500 ducats in hand plus only 50% of the uncertain future reward. He has diversified his risk but reduced the possible high return he would eventually claim from the venture when it is concluded.

The wealth account of VM integrating the fact Mantzaros sold half his personal contingent claim on future profit is summarized in Table 1.4. As the reader can see the sale of Mantzaros' half-interest in the venture is completely external to the venture itself. It is a private matter between the two partners, both now shareholders. The only element recorded is that if the venture were to be liquidated or make money, there are now two equal claimants on the net worth or profit, where there was only one before.

It can be noticed that the claim held by the "share" holders is not recorded in the same way as the amount payable to the banker. Although the shareholders (Mantzaros and his friend) certainly hope to recover their capital, it will not be by reimbursement but by sharing in the profit of the venture. Each "share" holder has a right over the future profits. The 500 ducats the friend paid were part of the net worth of Mantzaros the individual, not part of the venture's net worth. The change in the ownership structure of the venture does not create wealth for the Venture[7]. If we were to look at the immediate net worth of each shareholder, it would be half of the net worth of the venture or 50 ducats each. The friend essentially bought from Mantzaros for 500 ducats what is immediately worth only 50 but has attached to it a claim on future returns to be obtained in the next few years. The friend paid 450 gold ducats more than the "book value" of what he holds because he thinks future returns will be greater than the "premium" he paid.

Mantzaros' personal wealth is now 500 ducats plus a claim of only 50% on the future profit of the venture. The venture is a separate entity from Mantzaros as a person. It is essential in accounting to know exactly the perimeter of the economic entity of which one speaks. From now on, we will speak only of the "venture" as the relevant economic entity. We can record the situation for the "sailing/trading expedition" by saying it "owns" physical goods (or "assets") in the amount of 1,000 ducats, and owes 900 ducats. The net worth of the venture to date (and at any point in the future until the contract between Mantzaros and his partner is ended) is to be distributed half to his partner and half to him. When the ship returns, hopefully within the time frame originally intended, the merchandise the ship (ships) carries (carry) is sold. The profit will be calculated after the banker has been reimbursed (with interest), and any bonuses have been paid to the captain and the crew, etc.

Let us assume that, after only 4 years, the captain of Mantzaros' expedition brings back 3 ships, and that the merchandise is sold and brings in 10,008 ducats in cash. Since Mantzaros wants, at that time, to end the contract that

Table 1.4 'Wealth account' of VM after step 3

Venture Mantzaros owns		Venture Mantzaros owes	
Cash in hand	10 ducats	Owed to banker	900 ducats
Cash given to the captain for wages	150 ducats		
Inventory of food and supplies	330 ducats		
Inventory of merchandise to be traded	350 ducats		
Ship and equipment	160 ducats		
Total	1,000 ducats	Total	900 ducats
		Net "worth" of the venture	100 ducats
		Share of net worth held by Mantzaros	50%
		Share held by friend	50%

binds him and his friend to the venture, he will also sell the vessels to get a situation that is totally liquid. Let us assume the 3 vessels are sold for an aggregate of 300 ducats in total. The first ship's original value of 160 ducats has been reduced to, say, 100 ducats due to wear and tear. If we were not dissolving the venture (i.e., liquidating all assets) we would need to recognize the loss of value of that ship (i.e., its loss of sailing potential) as "depreciation" (amounting, here, to 60 ducats) and charge it against revenue in the calculation of profit.

Given the great success of the expedition[8], Mantzaros decides to grant a bonus of 1,000 ducats to the captain and his or her crew over and above the agreed salary of 150 ducats. The venture must also repay the banker the 900 ducats of principal plus the 417.69 ducats of interest for 4 years ($900 \times 1.10^4 - 900$) (rounded to 418). Only the interest is an expense.

In order to summarize the elements related to the expedition and its 'final outcome', we prepare Table 1.5, called "income statement" or report of the business activity.

Table 1.5 Report on the activity of the Venture Mantzaros for the 4 years of its activity

Revenues	
Sales of merchandise	10,008
Sale of the ships*	300
Expenses	
Wages and expenses (covered by the original cash)	– 150
Bonus paid to the captain and crew	– 1,000
Consumption of inventory of food and supplies	– 330
Consumption of inventory of merchandise to be traded	– 350
Interest expense paid to banker	– 418
Value of the original ship*	– 160
Income	7,900

*The reader will notice that by counting the original ship at its original cost of 160 ducats in the expenses and for the 100 ducats its sale brings in the revenues, we are in fact charging the venture with a depreciation expense equal to 160 – 100 = 60 ducats

The positive elements creating wealth are called "revenues" and the negative ones consuming (destroying) wealth are called "expenses". The difference between the revenues and the expenses represent the income (or the wealth) generated by the business.

The ending cash balance is computed in Table 1.6.

Table 1.6	Cash balance

Initial balance	100
Receipts	
Sales of merchandise	10,008
Amount received from the banker	900
Sale of ships	300
Payments	
Different payments (cash for wages, inventory, food, ship)	– 990
Payment of bonus to captain and crew	– 1,000
Interest expense	– 418
Debt principal repayment	– 900
Ending balance	8,000
Cash flow generated during the period	7,900

We can also see the evolution of the "wealth account" in Table 1.7.

Table 1.7	"Wealth account" after step 4 (return of the expedition)

Venture Mantzaros owns		Venture Mantzaros owes	
Cash in hand (see Table 1.6)	8,000 ducats	Owed to banker	0 ducats
Total	8,000 ducats	Total	0 ducats
		Net "worth" of the venture	8,000 – 0 = 8,000 ducats
		Percentage of the net worth owned by the shareholder friend	50%
		Percentage of the net worth owned by Mantzaros himself	50%

Compared to the original net worth of 100 ducats, the net worth of VM has increased by 7,900 ducats (8,000 – 100). This difference represents the profit of the venture. Since we are looking at the accounts of the Venture Mantzaros over its complete lifecycle, net worth and ending cash balance show the same amount. It will be extremely unusual, in the real world, to be able to look at the complete lifecycle of any business venture. Most businesses are created in the belief of their ongoing nature, without any specified predetermined liquidation date (a business venture with a specified date of "birth" and date of "end" is generally called a campaign or project, not an enterprise). Thus, in general, cash on hand and net worth will never be the same (more on this in Chapters 2 and 3).

The venture is liquidated according to the terms of the original agreements. The outcome of the liquidation is shown in Table 1.8.

Table 1.8 Liquidation of the venture

Original net worth	100
Profit of the venture	7,900
Total net worth upon liquidation	8,000
Amount received by Mantzaros:	
• His 50% share of the original net worth	50
• Share of the profit of the venture (50%)	3,950
Total	4,000
Amount for his shareholder friend	
• His 50% share of the original net worth	50
• Share of the profit of the venture (50%)	3,950
Total	4,000

Mantzaros (the individual, since the venture has been dissolved and no longer exists) can now use his 4,000 ducats (plus whatever he has left of the 500 ducats that were given to him 4 years ago when he sold a half-share in VM) to start another expedition (perhaps even a bigger one) and have enough money left to build a modest but comfortably equipped house. He has achieved his original objective.

Notice that Mantzaros, who was the initiator of the whole business process called VM, earned a greater return on his investment than did his friend (although the latter fared pretty well too – but is not "high risk–high return" the name of the game in business?). Mantzaros invested 100 ducats and received 500 ducats from his friend "early in the game" (for surrendering a half-share in the Venture's possible profits) plus 4,000 ducats at the end. If we ignore the time value of money (an acknowledgedly unrealistic hypothesis which will be relaxed in Chapter 12), his original 100 ducats became 4,500 ducats, i.e., an individual profit of 4,400 ducats. His friend invested 500 ducats in buying a 50% share of a state conditional claim owned by Mantzaros and got a return of 4,000. His individual profit is 3,500 ducats. The difference in return between Mantzaros and his friend is the reward for the entrepreneurial initiative of Mantzaros. Notice in passing, that profit to the individual shareholders and to the business are not the same at all, thus reinforcing the need for the separation of entities that had led Mantzaros to create "Venture Mantzaros" in the first place.

In this short story, we have shown the need to:

● Record the financial position or the condition of an economic entity called the "venture" (we will call this a balance sheet and we established one at the beginning, one at the end and two in between).

● Acknowledge the business entity as being separate from its shareholders.

● Record the composition of the resources of the business entity at any time.

● Record the sharing of future profit.

- Establish the base line against which wealth creation will be calculated.

- Establish rules about how wealth created will be calculated before it can be shared.

- Establish a synthetic document recording how much value was created by the economic activity of the venture (the income statement).

- Understand how the captain (a manager or an agent acting on behalf of the two co-owners of the venture) came about to have three fully loaded ships on her or his return so as to allow Mantzaros (the initiator of this venture and potentially future ventures) to learn about patterns of how the expedition could have been run more efficiently or where additional resources would have facilitated the process of value creation. Looking at a "journal" in which the captain would have recorded every transaction that took place during the 4 years of the "campaign" would be very helpful.

- Provide proof of the success of the first venture to secure more funds from the banker or from other potential partners for a second venture.

We can also notice that:

- The income of the period and the cash flow of the period happen to be the same. This situation is exceptional and happens only because of the complete liquidation of all assets and claims. Such a situation is clearly not a common practice of business (most businesses are conceived as going concerns that, theoretically and if well managed, should never cease their activity). The normal relationship between profit and cash in an ongoing business will be studied in more detail in Chapters 3 and 14.

- The profit computed directly from the activity is equal to the change in net wealth arising from the business. This situation is no coincidence, as we will show in Chapter 2.

Accounting is the whole process of recording and analyzing and reporting relevant information, whether with the intention of helping settle the claims at the end of the business venture, or for a better understanding (and thus better management of) the business processes leading to value creation.

ADVANCED ISSUES

Financial accounting and managerial accounting

As mentioned earlier, accounting is separated between financial (external reporting) and managerial components to reflect the distinction between the users, either mainly external or mainly internal.

Managerial accounting deals with the informational needs of decision makers inside the organization. It therefore deals with complex issues such as the diffusion of information inside the firm to create a mobilization of the energies of all members of the personnel and staff. It spans a wide range of fields from cost issues to management of performance including anticipatory management, motivation and commitment building, and the analysis of deviations.

Financial accounting and managerial accounting use the same basic information for different purposes. They cannot describe events in different ways. Simply put, financial accounting tends to be "recording" historical events while managerial accounting uses the same information to forecast future situations through a fine modeling of business processes. In the end, both types of information processing should lead to the very same *ex post* measure of value created.

Apart from being linked at the beginning (one single basic record of the same event for both) and at the end (one single income statement), financial and managerial accounting are also linked during the data analysis processes itself in that the costing aspect of managerial accounting, although used primarily for product and customer portfolio management is also used, by financial accounting, for the valuation of inventories of finished or semi-finished goods and of work in progress. Table 1.9 presents some key differences between financial accounting and managerial accounting.

It is very important to remember that there is only one discipline called accounting. Although each approach deals with a specific angle of analysis, in the end they must be reconciled to give the same figure for the increase in the net worth, i.e., the amount of value created.

Figure 1.6 illustrates how the same data are processed according to two parallel but different approaches. They give, however, the same figure in the end. The types of decision that are taken on the basis of either approach differs, of course, because of the degree of fineness of both the data and the analysis which is vastly different between the two approaches

Qualitative characteristics of useful financial statements

According to the IASC (1989: § 24), the qualitative characteristics of useful financial statements are the attributes that make the information provided in financial statements relevant to users. Figure 1.7 highlights the characteristics of useful financial information and the constraints it must satisfy.

The four principal qualitative characteristics are understandability, relevance, reliability, and comparability.

Understandability

The information provided in financial statements should be readily understandable by users. For this purpose, users are assumed to have a reasonable knowledge of generic business processes (as, for example, those shown in Figures 1.1 to 1.3) and economic activities and accounting. They should also have a willingness to study the information with reasonable diligence.

Relevance

Definition

To be useful, information must be relevant to the decision-making process of users. Information has the quality of relevance when it has the potential to

Table 1.9 Differences between managerial and financial accounting

	Managerial accounting	Financial accounting
Purpose	Understand how value is created in detail so as to assist internal decisions	Measure the performance of the firm as a whole and report it to external decision makers
Principal users of the output	Managers and decision makers at all levels inside the firm and in a responsibility orientation	Essentially external users who look at the firm as a whole: investors, banks, customers, personnel, etc.
Regulatory context	None, but focus on continuous progress in a philosophy of balancing costs and benefits	Financial accounting information is a social good and is therefore regulated at least by the bodies regulating financial markets, by tax authorities and by the profession itself in a spirit of true and fair view
Behavioral implications	Aimed at mobilizing energies inside the firm by the distribution of the appropriate information after ad hoc analyses	Does not attempt to influence behavior and, on the contrary, tries to be as fair as possible to all parties involved
Time frame	Oriented toward anticipation (based on fine modeling of internal and market-linked business processes), and analysis of deviations between anticipated and observed results	An objective record of what was actually realized, thus mainly oriented towards the past but the comparison of periods allows for extrapolation
Time horizon	Flexible and continuous. Information is collected on any time period deemed interesting to the decision maker	Less flexible in that financial statements must be made available at fixed intervals
Orientation	Detailed units of analysis such as: business processes, activities, functions, knowledge sets, markets, customers, products, resources, etc.	A process of systematic aggregation of records of discrete simple and elemental events to create categories of like transactions and create in the end financial statements that give a synthetic view of the situation of the firm on a given date
Fineness	Accent is placed on interactions and on the operation of business models	Aggregate and *ex post facto* vision
Frontiers	Defined by the usefulness of the data: importance of commercial, strategic, behavioral, economic aspects in decision-making aspects. It is totally normal in managerial accounting to extend the analysis beyond the legal borders of the entity	Often defined and constrained by the regulatory and legal context, Financial accounting is limited to be within the definition of the legal (or otherwise specified) perimeter of the entity

influence the economic decisions of users by helping them evaluate past, present, or future events and either confirming, or correcting past evaluations.

Link with materiality

The relevance of information is affected by its nature and materiality. Information is material if its omission or misstatement could influence the economic decisions of users taken on the basis of the financial statements. Materiality depends on the size of the item or of a possible error, judged in the particular circumstances of its omission or misstatement. Materiality is often related to a "materiality level" or "materiality threshold". Concretely, financial statements may contain approximations and minor errors not worth fixing in the spirit of a cost/benefit balance. It is of no consequence as long as their "materiality" places them under a threshold of significance. With the speed of

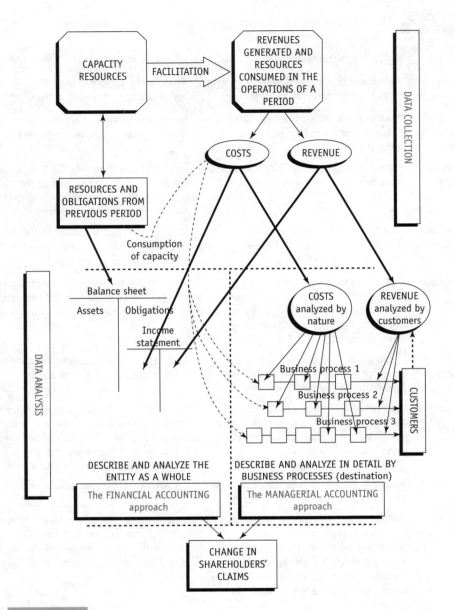

Figure 1.6 The unity of accounting: different but coherent approaches

decision making and the size of the stakes of these decisions in the "new economy", issues of materiality have become extremely relevant and are often discussed in the press and more and more often in court cases (weak signals can be leading indicators – or forerunners – of significant shifts in opportunities or problems).

Reliability

To be useful, information should also be reliable, in that financial statements:

1   represent faithfully the results and financial position of the enterprise

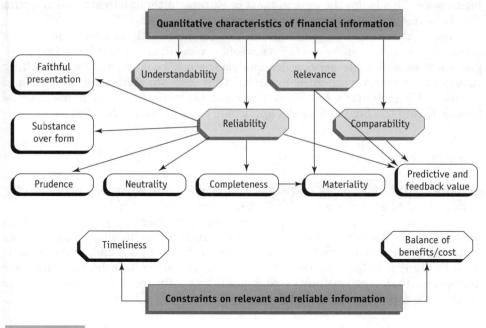

Figure 1.7 Useful information

2   reflect the economic substance of events and transactions and not merely their legal form
3   are neutral, that is free from bias
4   are prudent
5   are complete in all material respects (IAS 1) (IASC 1997: §20).

These aspects will be developed later in Chapter 5.

Comparability

Users must be able to compare the financial statements of an enterprise through time in order to identify trends in its financial position and perform- ance. Hence, the measurement and display of the financial effect of like transactions and other events must be carried out in a consistent way throughout an enterprise and over time.

Users also would like to be able to compare the financial statements of different enterprises in order to evaluate their relative financial position, performance, and changes in financial position. However, this is often in contra- diction with the requirement of relevance as the definition of a common coding process between firms because like events may lead to the choice of a "lowest common denominator" through which, in the end, very little is learned. In fact, if left to their own devices, each firm would probably be inclined to code events in a way that corresponds in the best way to the very strategic view it holds of its business process. The debate about the pros and cons of common coding of events and common presentation of accounts between firms is never closed. France, for one, immediately after World War II, opted for a common presenta- tion and imposes a constraining chart of accounts (see Chapter 4) to all businesses. This is not the case in most of Europe (although Spain and Belgium also have a standardized chart of accounts).

Given that enterprises generally do not follow exactly the same format as other firms in the same sector, there is an arbitraging business provided, generally as a sellable service, by analysts, stock brokers, banks, consulting firms, or semi-governmental agencies that use sophisticated models and additional information to recast financial statements in an homogeneous format fitting the business model applicable to any given industrial sector.

Predictive and feedback value

Accounting information is useful both to account for what was done and for anticipating what decisions will be taken or modified if any.

It is, therefore, important to remember that the rules and principles such as understandability, relevance, comparability, prudence, neutrality, completeness, materiality, etc. need to be subjected to the filter that in the end information is useful only if it helps understand the past (and particularly how agents have discharged their responsibility), and predict the future (by extrapolation or other more sophisticated models).

Constraints on useful information

Timeliness

If there is undue delay in the reporting of information, it may lose its relevance. Management may need to balance the relative merits of timely reporting and the provision of reliable information. Balancing timeliness and relevance is a day-to-day issue for all businesses. Timely information is expensive, but missing an opportunity may be even more expensive. The issue is therefore: What is best? A piece of information that may be timely but not reliable, or reliable information that may not be timely?

Benefits/cost relation

The benefits derived from information should exceed the cost of providing it.

Balance between qualitative characteristics

In practice, a balancing, or trade-off, between qualitative characteristics is often necessary. Generally, the aim is to achieve an appropriate balance among the characteristics in order to meet the objective of financial statements. The relative importance of the characteristics in different cases is a matter of professional judgment.

History of accounting: from Sumer to Luca Pacioli

Accounting is not the new kid on the block. Some historians (Colasse 2000: 12) assert that marks found on bones dating as far back as 20 or 30,000 years ago were a form of accounting, recording claims of various tribe members on the result of hunting expeditions. Let us see how modern accounting originated from before the time of the Hammurabi Code in the times of ancient Sumer to the founding work of Fra Luca Pacioli that recorded the accounting practices of Venetian merchants and allowed for the development of modern accounting[9].

Sumerian times

The origins of accounting are often traced to the times of Sumer, in Mesopotamia, in the 4th millennium BC. The Sumerian civilization pre-dates that of ancient Egypt by a few centuries. Archeological explorations in the region between Tigris and Euphrates rivers have unearthed innumerable vestiges of accounting documents recorded on stone or clay tablets. The very fragility of the material was the guarantee of the security of the record because any attempt at falsification would have caused its destruction. The efforts to protect these tablets were commensurate with the likely desire to uphold the contracted commitment and the corresponding counting.

As far back as the 3rd millennium BC, during the Ur Dynasty, accounting entries became both more complex and precise. All features of a modern account were recorded on clay tablets: nature of objects being transacted, names of the parties to the contract, quantities of goods, and their equivalent value in other goods or currency. Some tablets even carry over the balance of the previous period, separate increases from decreases, and also show the end of period balance.

In some cases, rules were discovered that required use of materials such as stone, more sturdy than clay, to record official or sacred accounts or statements. One such example is the Hammurabi Code, which dates back to the 18th century BC. This "document" reflects societal rules in Babylon. This text, essentially about contracts and family law, contains notions of accounting and management that refer to an agency contract. This implies that the agent keep clear accounts or, more likely, that some specified transactions be recorded in the form of accounts. Accounting, then and since, has always been placed in an agency context: the issue is to define the profit resulting from transactions carried by the agent in the name of the principal and provide the basis for sharing it between the principal and the agent.

Surprisingly, this first "accounting civilization" seems to have rapidly disappeared when the cuneiform language[10] it used was supplanted by the "more efficient" Aramaic and Phoenician languages and writing techniques.

Accounting in Egypt

Accounting was well developed in ancient Egypt. Scribes had a simplified script (less complex than hieroglyphics) dedicated to home and business economics. They were required to know both arithmetic and bookkeeping. They kept their records on papyrus, a lighter and more flexible medium but more vulnerable than stone or clay tablets. Transactions were registered first in draft form before being recopied carefully in "definitive" chronological records. From time to time, and at least once a year, chronological records were summarized in synthetic documents. Accounts had all the characteristics of "universal accounts": name of the account, date, and amount. Receipts were distinguished from disbursements. From 300 BC, Egyptians, who were then part of the Greek cultural universe, adopted the Greek language and practices in banking. These include account-to-account transfers, which are an essential step in the development of modern accounting as it provides a way to add to or subtract from any account without actually going through a cash transaction.

Accounting in Greece

Greek accounting was, as already mentioned, very advanced. Some historians believe that temples were the first organizations to need accounting (and incidentally to play the role of bankers). Exactly as was the case in ancient Babylon or in Egypt, offerings to the gods were recorded on marble or limestone tablets. Greek bankers kept thorough accounts. The complexity of the banking network led to the development of accounting control systems, the predecessors of auditing. As far back as 300 BC, Athens had an audit court comprised of 10 "logists" who had the responsibility of controlling accounts. The set of practices, including completeness of records, thorough controls and existence of public records, and accountability, obvious signs of democracy, vanished with its demise.

Accounting in Rome

In Rome, each family (a much broader concept than the nuclear family of the 21st century AD – a family included all parents from all generations plus uncles and aunts and a multitude of servants and slaves) was in fact an economic entity with its own production and trading systems. Keeping books was the responsibility of the head of the household (*pater familias*) as it is the responsibility today of a person heading an enterprise. According to Cicero (143–106 BC), who described the set of books kept in his time, the main document was the *Codex Accepti et Expansi* or journal of receipts and payments. Entries were first recorded in a draft before being organized in the Codex. The *Codex Rationum* was the permanent document with value of proof. It was the predecessor of what we now call the general ledger (see Chapter 4). The demise of the Roman civilization caused the disappearance of this body of accounting knowledge.

Accounting in the Middle Ages

Although the Barbarians overran the western part of the Roman Empire early on, the eastern part of the empire, including Greece, Constantinople, and the Middle East remained untouched for a while. The Greek accounting expertise was preserved in the Byzantine empire. The development of the Arab civilization and its intense trading activity capitalized on the accounting knowledge of the territories it conquered and developed it even further by incorporating refinements derived from mathematics and astronomy.

It is not clear whether the western European merchants learned from their Byzantine and Arab partners or whether they actually rediscovered administrative and accounting practices. The fact is accounting underwent a rebirth in western Europe, mainly in Northern Italy and in the Netherlands and Flanders as early as the 13th century.

Whether merchants formed large, multi-establishment "companies" (the predecessors of our multinational corporations), or dealt through mercantile or commission agents, they needed rigorous accounting. Accounting recorded the transactions and the wealth created and transferred between establishments. This allowed the agents to be accountable for their activity. The development of international trade, of companies, and of agency contracts is the major cause of the re-emergence of accounting in the Middle Ages. This extended period has known three sequential phases: memorial, single entry and double entry bookkeeping.

Memorial

The memorial is essentially a journal recording the transactions on a daily basis without any attempt at regrouping transactions of similar nature. It is essentially the rudimentary practice that was predominant in early antiquity.

Single entry bookkeeping

Single entry bookkeeping is a significant improvement to the simplistic memorial method. The growing complexity of the operations of medieval merchants led to the partitioning of the memorial into separate accounts of similar nature. Each type of transaction or establishment is recorded in its own coherent table keeping track of all relevant specific events, thus forming an account.

Double entry bookkeeping

Double entry bookkeeping marks the birth of modern accounting. Each transaction is recorded by entries in two accounts: one entry "credits" one account and the other one "debits" another one. The earliest record of double entry bookkeeping is found in the books of the *Massari* (treasurers of the city state of Genoa) around 1340 AD. However, it is the Franciscan monk, Luca Pacioli, who formalized and extensively described these procedures in his 1494 mathematics text entitled *Summa de arithmetica, geometria, proportioni et proportionalita*. Incidentally, his purpose in inserting a chapter on accounting in his book was not to write a business text, but to illustrate one way of handling the concept of "zero" which had been lost to western European mathematicians (although not to Arabic ones, but the western European merchants and the Arabic ones were not exactly on "friendly terms" at the time). In effect, the fundamental equation of accounting "debits = credits" or "assets = obligations to outside parties" shows that, if this is true, the balance has to be zero, i.e., "nothing", a very difficult concept to apprehend at the time. It was especially important for accountants to be able to show, for example, a debt had been paid back or extinguished and that the borrower in fact owed "nothing". This was done easily by crediting (reducing) cash and debiting the debt account where the borrower's debt was recorded (i.e., eliminating the debt – since debt and cash are on opposite sides of the financial situation account, the terms debit and credit work in opposite ways. (More on this in Chapter 4.) Modern accounting was born with Luca Pacioli, and this text will deal only with double entry bookkeeping, and with the accounting that derives from such practice.

- Accounting is a language that allows any person interested in the economic life of a business to communicate with others with the same interest about the past, present, and future of the business as an economic entity.

- Broadly speaking, accounting information is an essential decision-support tool. Most decisions in a business are about resource planning, acquisition, and resource allocation in order to fulfill the firm's strategic intent.

- Accounting information is the output of an ongoing process of identifying, capturing, managing, analyzing, interpreting, and distributing data and information describing the economic transactions of the firm.

- Accounting is inseparable from and necessary to any business activity. It allows any user to shape their opinion about the economic aspects of an economic entity by looking at its financial statements.

- Financial statements are the synthetic "final product" of the accounting business process. These generally include an income statement, a balance sheet, and a cash flow statement (all three with footnotes which explain choices made by the firm and provide more detail regarding some complex or critical transactions).

- Financial statements are established periodically and it is traditional to create these synthetic documents at least once every year, generally around a date when the sales activity is the least active in the year.

- The various (and numerous) users of financial statements need to understand the financial information in the same way. For that reason, within each country, local regulations issue generally accepted accounting principles (GAAP) that are called accounting standards, or financial reporting standards, which include specific principles, bases, conventions, rules, and practices necessary to prepare the financial statements.

- The International Accounting Standards Board's main objective is to promote convergence of accounting principles that are used by businesses and other organizations for financial reporting around the world.

- Accounting is separated between financial (external reporting) and managerial components to reflect the distinction between the decision needs of users, either mainly external or mainly internal.

- Financial statements relevant to users meet four criteria: understandability, relevance, reliability, and comparability.

REVIEW

Review 1.1

Multiple-choice questions
Type: Individual exercise
Related part of the chapter: Core Issues

1   **In general, financial statements are comprised of the following documents (several possible answers)**
    (a) Balance sheet
    (b) Cash flow statement
    (c) Notes to financial statements

    (d) Income statement
    (e) Value added statement
    (f) Value created statement

2   Only an event with a monetary implication (potential impact on the cash situation) must be recorded in financial accounting
    (a) True
    (b) False

3   Financial accounting offers the great advantage of being completely objective and thus leaves no room for being subjective
    (a) True
    (b) False

4   Bookkeeping is a subset of … (choose one answer)
    (a) Managerial accounting
    (b) Financial accounting
    (c) Auditing

Answers

1 (a), (c), (d), and, in certain countries, (b).
The statement of changes in shareholders' equity, which presents the changes in the "net worth" (as described in the introduction to the chapter) has not been included in this list. It is, however, a compulsory financial statement in some countries. This statement will be explored further in Chapter 11.

2 False.
Many transactions have no impact on cash, either because the impact is postponed to a later date (as in the case of a sale on account) or because there never will be a direct cash impact as we will see later (see Chapters 2 and 7) in the case of the recognition of the loss of value of physical assets (depreciation).

3 False.
Financial accounting does not always have clear or complete documents supporting the exact value placed on a transaction. The value is often subjective. For example, the risk of uncollectibility on a credit sale may be estimated statistically but cannot be known exactly for each transaction before settlement or an incident actually occurs.

4 (b).
Bookkeeping means recording transactions. It is therefore part of financial accounting since recording of transactions is compulsory. Managerial accounting can also use the recorded data for its own analyses.

ASSIGNMENTS

Assignment 1.1

Discussion questions
Type: Group exercise
Related part of the chapter: Core Issues

    1 Should managers of a company (i.e. decision makers who are inside the business entity) be considered to be part of the population of "users" of financial accounting?

2 Are there possible conflicts of interests between the various users of financial information?

3 How can a decision maker obtain a copy of a firm's financial statements if the latter does not make them public (for example, an unlisted business or of a closely held competitor)? Identify concrete examples in a given country.

4 Why are suppliers and customers interested in studying the financial statements of a company?

5 What sources of information on a business's economic situation, other than financial statements, are available to the general public?

Assignment 1.2 Xenakis

Topic: Financial situation
Type: Individual exercise
Related part of the chapter: Core Issues

Xenakis, a young Greek person, arrives on the first day of summer in Byblos, a Phoenician harbor city. His parents, respectable rich merchants in Athens have sent him on a "world" journey to discover himself and learn about business. They have given him some material goods and a little money.

When he arrives in Byblos for a planned 10-day stay, Xenakis' personal wealth is as follows:

● 6 gold flatware pieces, worth 50 drachmas each

● 10 crystal glassware pieces, worth 15 drachmas each

● 102 drachmas in cash (down from the 150 drachmas he left home with – his sea passage had cost him 48 drachmas).

As soon as he sets foot on land, he rents a room at the Cedar Inn. The innkeeper offers full room and board for 10 days for one drachma a day. Once settled in, he goes out looking for the Phoenician merchants his parents have recommended to him. As he ambles along the narrow streets and through sunny piazzas, he reminisces about the basic rule his tutor had taught him: "Keep a detailed account of all operations and transactions you engage in."

Xenakis met a glass merchant who agreed to buy all of Xenakis' 6 pieces of gold flatware for 70 drachmas each. Next, Xenakis sold his crystal pieces for 25 drachmas each. He bought a dozen amphorae of assorted spices and he paid 45 drachmas for each. He also bought two pieces of silk fabric for 90 drachmas each. Very happy with his transactions, he bought his return fare to Athens for which he paid 50 drachmas in cash. Feeling a little short of cash to be able to live in the style he was accustomed to until his departure, he asked a Greek friend he had met on the wharf to lend him ten drachmas. As soon as he was back in Athens he sold all the merchandise he had brought back at the locally accepted prices:

● 60 drachmas per amphora of assorted spices,

● 120 drachmas per silk piece.

Required

1 Describe Xenakis' "net worth" on the day of his departure from Athens for Byblos.

2 How much cash does Xenakis have after he sold all his merchandise after his return to Athens?

3 Compute the income generated by Xenakis on his round trip.

4 Describe Xenakis' "net worth" after his return to Athens.

INTRODUCTION TO FINANCIAL ACCOUNTING

Assignment 1.3 Theodorakis

Topic: Users of financial information
Type: Individual exercise
Related part of the chapter: Core Issues

Required

Identify at least 5 classes of users (including at least one non-profit organization) of financial information about a given business (specify clearly the characteristics of the business you choose) and list on what specific aspects of the life of the business (including short and long term if necessary) each class of users might like to be informed. Show whether accounting, as described in the chapter, is likely to satisfy these classes of users. If you feel accounting statements do not provide all the relevant information needed, elaborate on at least three legitimate reasons why accounting information falls short of expectation of this or these classes.

Assignment 1.4 Horn of Abundance

Topic: Users of financial information and investors
Type: Group exercise
Related part of the chapter: Core Issues

The following list contains data or information that might be provided about a business:

1 List of managers and directors.
2 Compensation package of directors and managers.
3 List of major competitors by markets and by product groups.
4 Allocation of responsibility in the business.
5 Age distribution pyramid of employees and managers.
6 Result of labor union elections in the establishments of the business.
7 Social climate in each department of the business.
8 Financial statements (balance sheet, income statement, cash flow statement).
9 Map of the layout of the plant and the warehouse.
10 Location, size and staffing of all points of sale.
11 Evolution of sales of each key product group over the past 3 years.
12 Age distribution of products (products still sold launched 1, 2 or 3 years ago or more).
13 Number of employees.
14 Distribution of shares ownership (with major shareholders and percentage they own as well as percentage of total shares traded in a normal month).
15 Details of the loans received (amounts and reimbursement schedule).
16 Cost of capital (weighted current average cost of capital).
17 Opportunities for investments in the business and their expected rate of return.
18 Major capital investment projects approved over the last 3 years.
19 Partition of assets between owned and leased.
20 Percent of completion of investment projects started in the last 3 years.
21 Outside expert report on the technological and physical obsolescence of assets owned by the business.
22 Details on the incentive plans implemented in this business (including stock options).

23 Evolution of the share price of the business on the Euronext Stock Markets over the past 3 years (including a comparison with other firms in the same economic sector).

24 Description of the sales technology and techniques used in each of the markets in which the products are sold.

25 Amount spent on acquiring new customers and creating demand (marketing, advertising, promotion and sales expenses).

26 Tax filings for the past 3 years and amount of taxes still owed.

27 Cash or liquid assets position.

28 Description of key customers with length of relationship and evolution of percentage each represents in the business's total sales.

29 Opinion of the senior management team about how they see the future of the firm and its markets.

30 Amounts spent on R&D, structured by types of research.

31 Evolution of the duration of R&D projects until success or abandonment and percentage of successful projects in the last 10 years.

32 Percentage of sales (per product group) carried out in currencies other than that of the home country of the business. Percent of physical volume of sales exported.

33 Existence, details, and status of any court litigation against the business or which the business has originated against others.

34 A summary of the history of the business.

35 By-laws or articles of incorporation.

36 Existence, value, and relevance of proprietary technology owned by the business (own research or purchased?).

37 Percent of total expenses spent on humanitarian or not-for-profit activities (and the list of these activities).

38 Environmental report by an external independent agency evaluating the effect of the business on noise, air and water quality as well as the health environment of both workers and citizens in a 10-kilometer radius around the plant.

39 Statistics of the work-related injuries and deaths over the past 10 years.

40 Partnership agreements with suppliers and customers.

41 List of subsidiaries and affiliates.

42 Percentage of employees (structured by homogeneous classes) connected effectively via a broadband intranet/internet system.

Required

From the list select the 10 most important items you feel an investor might want to find, for her or his analysis and review, in a business's annual report. Explain why you selected these and rejected the others. Examine whether the items you wish to provide investors originate in the accounting or in other information systems. If they do not originate in the accounting systems, explain which aspect of accounting regulation or practice may explain why these items have been excluded from the traditional reach of accounting.

References

Chatfield, M., and Vangermersch, R. (eds) (1996) *The History of Accounting: An International Encyclopedia*, Garland Publishing, New York & London.

Colasse, B. (2000) *Comptabilité générale*, 6th edn, Economica, Paris.

Degos, J.G. (1998) *Histoire de la comptabilité*, Que-sais-je? no. 3398, PUF, Paris.

IASC (1989) Framework for the Preparation and Presentation of Financial Statements, London.

IASC (1997) International Accounting Standard No. 1, Presentation of Financial Statements, London.

IASC (2001) Constitution in *International Accounting Standards*, bound volume, London.

Lebas, M.J. (ed.) (1999) *Management Accounting Glossary*, ECM, Paris and CIMA, London.

PricewaterhouseCoopers (PwC) (1999) *Student's Manual of Accounting*, ITBP, London.

Further readings

Aiken, M., and Lu, W. (1998) The evolution of bookkeeping in China: Integrating historical trends with western influences. *Abacus*, 34(2), September, 220–42.

Murphy, A.B. (2000) The impact of adopting international accounting standards on the harmonization of accounting practices. *International Journal of Accounting*, 35(4), 417–93.

Murphy, A.B. (2000) Firm characteristics of Swiss companies that utilize international accounting standards. *International Journal of Accounting*, 34(1), 121–31.

Street, D.L., Gray, S.J., and Bryant, S.M. (1999) Acceptance and observance of international accounting standards: An empirical study of companies claiming to comply with IASs. *International Journal of Accounting*, 34(1), 11–48.

Additional material on the website

Go to http://www.thomsonlearning.co.uk/accountingandfinance/stolowylebas for further information, journal entries and extra assignments for each chapter.

The following appendices to this chapter are available on the dedicated website:

Appendix 1.1: The reporting period
Appendix 1.2: List of International Accounting Standards

Notes

1 A German and a North American user may not require that the same reality, for example income, be couched in the same format and terms. The German user of accounting information, coming from a culture where business, banks and labor unions are quite intermingled, may tend to have a long-term view of business and probably would support wholeheartedly an accounting language that would smooth over peaks and valleys in the reporting and timing of value creation. Her or his North American counterpart, coming from a culture of rapid movement and short-term investment decisions where 'a dollar today is always better than a dollar tomorrow,' might, however, be more short-term minded and might support an accounting language that would be as reactive as possible and would not allow smoothing of good or bad events or news.

2 Stakeholders are any party that has a "stake" in the outcome and output resulting from the activity of an enterprise. They include a variety of parties. A far from exhaustive list may include the following stakeholders in addition to the obvious capital providers which, in the western economies, tend to be seen as the major stakeholders (see also Figure 1.4):

● Employees whose interest is in the long-term stability of their employment and/or in the ability for the firm to maintain the employability of its personnel (i.e., stability of employment outside the firm as well as inside the firm).

- Customers who want to be certain their supplier will be able to serve them in the future. This is both a question of security and of efficiency because finding a good supplier is expensive.

- Suppliers whose interest is to have a long-lasting buyer for their output. (It is costly to find a good customer.)

- Health authorities, as the economic activity of the enterprise can impact on the health of employees, of the community surrounding the plants, of the community of users of the output, etc.

- Government authorities who are looking at the effect of the economic activity of the firm on the country's balance of payment (net importer or net exporter) or employment level.

- Social watchdog organizations looking for the enforcement of evolving societal values such as "no child labor" or "no prisoner labor", "no discrimination in employment", or sourcing or selling, etc.

3 For *investors, employees, lenders, suppliers, customers, government,* and the *general public* the needs listed in Table 1.1 are adapted from IASC (1989).

4 The AICPA (American Institute of Certified Public Accountants) in its APB Statement No. 4 Basic Concepts and Accounting Principles Underlying Financial Statements of Business Enterprises (New York, 1970) defines a GAAP as encompassing "conventions, rules and procedures necessary to define accepted accounting practice at a particular time. It includes not only broad guidelines of general application but also detailed practices and procedures. Those conventions, rules, and procedures provide a standard by which to measure financial presentations." Every country, every culture or society creates its own GAAP, adapted to its tradition, principles, values, and practices.

5 Members include the Australian Securities and Investments Commission, the members of the Canadian Securities Administrators (CSA), the French *Commission des Opérations de Bourse* (COB), the Italian *Commissione Nazionale per le Società e la Borsa* (CONSOB), the UK's Financial Services Authority (FSA), and the United States Securities and Exchange Commission (SEC).

6 But wealth and wealth creation cannot be measured unless assets, obligations, and transactions are recorded and "accounts" drawn.

7 Here the capital or endowment of the venture was not modified by the private sale of shares. We will see in Chapter 11 how a business can issue shares and increase its capital.

8 And also because of the honesty of the captain that is attested by an examination of the log or journal he/she kept of his/her periodic authorization of payments, trades and transactions.

9 This section draws heavily, by permission of the author, on Degos (1998). This short abstract is, however, our entire responsibility. The reader can also refer to Chatfield and Vangermersch (1996).

10 Cuneiform refers to a scripture based on a combination of wedge-shaped marks resembling "little nails", thus its name from the Latin *cuneus* or nail.

Introduction to financial statements

We have seen in the previous chapter that **financial statements** are one of the key "outputs" of the financial accounting process. They form the reporting package and comprised several documents:

- The balance sheet, the income statement, and notes to these documents (common to all countries' accounting standards).

- One or more of the following: a cash flow statement (or funds flow statement – developed in Chapters 3 and 14), a statement of retained earnings (developed in Chapter 11), and a statement of changes in equity (required in some, but not all countries – developed in Chapter 11).

This chapter introduces the minimum set of documents: balance sheet, income statement, and notes. In doing so we develop the "basic business equation" also known as the "balance sheet equation" or "accounting equation". In the "Advanced Issues" section, we introduce important concepts which are developed in later chapters, such as depreciation, profit appropriation, and inventory.

Major topics

Balance sheet

Business equation

Income statement

Depreciation

Profit appropriation

Inventory

Financial statement analysis

The "basic" financial statements are the balance sheet, the income statement, and the notes to financial statements.

Balance sheet or statement of financial position

In the course of the life of a business, any business manager needs to know its position at any given time in order to decide how to allocate resources and create value for its owners. She or he therefore needs to know what its resources and what its obligations to third parties are.

The very term **balance sheet** contains a message about its format. It is a set of two lists: resources on one side (also called assets) and obligations to external parties on the other side (liabilities to creditors and the residual due to shareholders or owners). The totals of the two lists, expressed as we have stated in Chapter 1 in monetary terms, must be equal or balanced.

In languages other than English, the term used for balance sheet emphasizes more the *status* of the firm's position at a particular point in time than the *balancing* aspect of the statement. (For example, *Bilanz* in German or *bilan* in French imply drawing a statement of up-to-date information – rather like a photo – but the idea of equilibrium between resources and obligations is not explicitly present.)

The balance sheet, also called "**statement of financial position**", shows the value or net worth of a business at a given point in time. It is the document that allows a netting of what the firm possesses, i.e., its resources to engage in the fulfillment of its strategic intent to create value, and what it owes, i.e., what obligations it has contracted in order to obtain these resources.

The obligation side is generally separated in two parts: the *liabilities* and the *shareholders' equity*. **Liabilities** are what is owed (with certainty) to third parties that are not participants in the ownership or management of the business (and therefore are not sharing the risks taken by the business venture). The **equity** is what remains when resources (assets) are offset against the external obligations (liabilities). Shareholders' equity represents the obligation the firm has towards its shareholders or, conversely, it is the claim the owners of the business have collectively over the firm's current net worth and potential future wealth. Each shareholder's claim is proportional to their contribution to the capital.

The balance sheet can therefore be represented by an equation:

Resources (or assets) = Obligations to third parties (liabilities)
plus Equity (shareholders' claims)
or
Assets *minus* Liabilities = Net assets = Shareholders' equity

We choose to qualify this equation as the "business equation" rather than calling it "balance sheet equation" because it anchors accounting in the domain of business modeling, i.e., the identification and reporting of a dynamic set of relationships, flows, and stocks which, when appropriately coordinated, create value for the owners.

The balance sheet is a table that records in detail all resources and all obligations that have definite monetary implications and for which an amount can be determined without ambiguity. Obligations or resources which are probable but not certain (such as the one that could result from a litigation in a court of law), or which are conditional on external events (such as guarantees given) are often listed, for the sake of exhaustiveness, with a range of possible monetary values, in the footnotes to the financial statements and are considered "off balance sheet".

A balance sheet is a snapshot[1] of the status of the financial position of a business entity at a given point in time. It focusses on the composition of the financial position (see Figure 2.1 and Table 2.1).

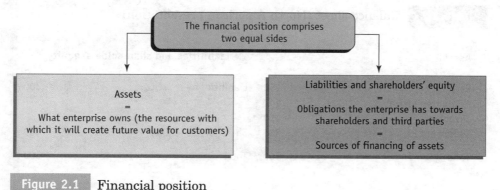

The financial position comprises two equal sides

Assets
=
What enterprise owns (the resources with which it will create future value for customers)

Liabilities and shareholders' equity
=
Obligations the enterprise has towards shareholders and third parties
=
Sources of financing of assets

Figure 2.1 Financial position

The list of obligations and resources can be structured in either increasing or decreasing order of liquidity. Although the rank ordering of resources and obligations in terms of relative liquidity does not change anything of substance in the situation of the firm, the behavioral implications may be meaningful in the sense that what appears on the top of a list is often considered, at least in the western world, to be the most important item(s). If the firm wishes to focus the attention of the reader on their potential for future value creation, management may prefer to show buildings, machinery, and inventories on the top of the asset list. If, on the contrary, a business wishes to communicate its ability to pay its short-term obligations, it might choose to present its cash balance and marketable securities at the top of the list of assets.

Continental European tradition tends to favor reporting the "stock" of assets first, thus emphasizing the long-term potential; the North American tradition, by way of contrast, tends to favor reporting first the data that help understand the short-term survival potential of the firm.

In Table 2.1, assets are presented in order from least to most liquid ("increasing liquidity") and liabilities are presented with longer term liabilities first and shorter term last (increasing degree of maturity). Some countries, such as the United States and Canada, use the reverse order (see Table 2.2).

Chapter 3, devoted to financial statements, will explore further the pros and cons of each presentation. At this point, the way the balance sheet is presented is not important. Whatever the order of the various elements, what matters is that both sides be balanced and that the basic business equation be respected.

Table 2.1 Balance sheet (continental European Presentation)

Assets	000CU		
		Shareholders' equity and liabilities	
Equipment	200	Shareholders' equity	300
Inventory	150		
Accounts receivable	100		
Cash	50	Liabilities	200
Total	500	Total	500

Table 2.2 Balance sheet (North American presentation)

Assets		Liabilities and shareholders' equity	
Cash	50	Liabilities	200
Accounts receivable	100		
Inventory	150		
Equipment	200	Shareholders' equity	300
Total	500	Total	500

Any imbalance between the two sides would mean that the shareholders' equity would need to be adjusted (up or down, reflecting a gain or a loss) until balance is regained.

Basic business equation or balance sheet equation

Basic principle

Any transaction in a business affects some element of the balance sheet. Even though the total of each side of the balance sheet may be modified, the net effect of the transaction is that there will always be a perfect balance between the two sides. This principle is part of the very foundation of modern accounting.

Transactions can take place between assets (reduce cash and increase inventory of goods for sale, for example), between liabilities (a portion of a long-term debt becomes current or payable), or can involve both sides (reduce cash and reduce accounts payable when one settles a debt to a supplier or reduce inventory due to a sale, increase in cash for more than the inventory value (hopefully!), and, therefore, increase the shareholders' equity, by the creation of value through the sale).

Terminology

Assets

An **asset** is a "resource controlled by an enterprise as a result of past events and from which future economic benefits are expected to flow to the enterprise" (IASC 2001).

Liabilities

A **liability** is a "present obligation of the enterprise arising from past events, the settlement of which is expected to result in an outflow from the enterprise of resources embodying economic benefits" (IASC 2001).

Shareholders' equity *or* equity capital

Equity is a claim, a right or an interest one has over some net worth. Equity, taken globally, represents the claim of all shareholders. Equity is generally represented by some form of "shares" indicating how much of the total claim accrues to each of the parties comprising the group of shareholders.

Equity is defined (IASC 2001) as "the residual interest in the assets of the enterprise after deducting all its liabilities":

$$\text{Assets} - \text{Liabilities} = \text{Shareholders' equity}$$

Shareholders' equity is itself composed of two components, identical in nature (they represent claims shareholders have over the firm's net worth), but not in their origin. They are "share capital" and "retained earnings".

Share capital is the historical value of the contributions to the firm all shareholders have made in the beginning and during the life of the firm by making external resources available to the firm and giving up control over these resources (cash, effort or ideas, physical assets, etc.).

Retained earnings represent that part of the value created through the firm's operations that shareholders have chosen not to take out of the firm. It is a de facto increase in their contribution to the ongoing activity of the firm.

Earnings

Earnings are the result of the difference between the resources created by the economic activity of the business (revenue), and the resources consumed in operating the firm (expenses). In essence, earnings are the net increase (profit) or decrease (loss) of the shareholders' equity due to the operations of the business.

Revenue is "the gross inflow of economic benefits during the period arising in the course of the ordinary activities of an enterprise when those inflows result in increases in equity, other than increases relating to contributions from equity participants" (IASC 2001). In other words, revenues are increases in shareholders' equity that originate from the business of the company such as a sale of goods or services or interest received from short-term investments.

Expenses represent "decreases in economic benefits during the accounting period in the form of outflows or consumption (destruction or reduction of future potential) of assets or incurrence of liabilities that result in decreases in equity, other than those relating to distributions to equity participants" (IASC 2001). Expenses originate from activities of the firm such as purchase of services, payment of salaries or remuneration to employees, payment of rent for the use of certain physical facilities, wear and tear on equipment, royalties for the right to use someone else's idea, etc. In other words, expenses are decreases in shareholders' equity that originate from carrying out the business of the company.

Net income (or period **earnings**) is thus the difference between total revenue and total expenses recorded during a period. It represents the profit or loss of a period. Net income is an increase (profit) or a decrease (loss) of the equity shareholders collectively have in the business. It describes the value created through the activity of the business. The following equation applies:

Net income (period t)
=
Shareholders' equity (at the end of period t)
minus
Shareholders' equity (at the beginning of period t)
(all things otherwise being equal)

The net income is generally calculated in a separate and subsidiary account called "income statement" (in US accounting terms) or "profit and loss account" (P&L) (in British accounting terms). This special account or statement will be further developed later in this chapter. The income statement allows managers to follow revenue and expenses separately without measuring changes in shareholders' equity at each transaction. The balance of the income statement (or P&L) is the net income, i.e., the amount that describes the net effect of one period's activity on the shareholders' equity.

Transactions

The operation of the basic business equation is best demonstrated by looking at several illustrative transactions. As a convention, we have chosen to follow the rank ordering of items on the balance sheet where the most liquid items are listed first, and the least liquid are listed last. It is important to remind the reader at this point that the rank ordering preferences have no impact on the output of accounting. One important element to keep in mind is that the rank ordering preference must apply homogeneously to both assets and liabilities and equity.

Transaction 1 – Initial investment by shareholders

Stefania, a professional photographer, and her life partner Stefano, a graphic design artist, decide to create an advertising agency on 1 January 20X1. The financial resources they wish to invest in their business venture amount to 90 CU. They create their business with a capital contribution of 90. It is agreed between them that Stefania receives 60 shares with a nominal value of 1 currency unit (implying she contributed two-thirds of the initial capital) while Stefano receives 30 shares. They choose to name their business venture "Verdi" and open a bank **account**[3] in that name. Each shareholder deposits the agreed upon amount of cash on the bank account. Once in the Verdi bank account, the funds now belong to neither Stefania nor Stefano. They are now part of the net worth of Verdi. Stefania has a claim of two-thirds over that net worth, while

Stefano has a claim of one-third. The personal net worth of the "shareholders" is always (at least conceptually) distinct from that of the business in which they have invested. Various legal structures exist that reinforce the separation of net worth of the entity from that of the individual shareholders – limited liability companies for example – or weaken the separation – individual entrepreneur for example. These will be covered in Chapter 11.

Figure 2.2 illustrates the effect of the company's creation as a separate economic entity on the basic equation.

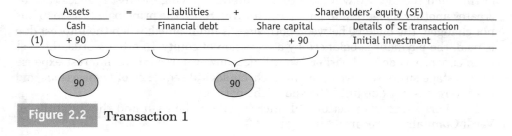

	Assets	=	Liabilities	+	Shareholders' equity (SE)	
	Cash		Financial debt		Share capital	Details of SE transaction
(1)	+ 90				+ 90	Initial investment

Figure 2.2 Transaction 1

The transaction results in an increase by the same amount (from zero to 90) in both assets and shareholders' equity. Investments by shareholders do not represent revenues and are excluded from the determination of net income. "Cash" and "share capital" will eventually have to be set up as individual "accounts" so as to allow the tracing of the many transactions that will impact on their balance in the normal course of the life of the agency.

The equation is balanced because "assets" equals "liabilities plus equity". Equity will, in time, become more complex and income will be added to the capital brought initially by shareholders. The shareholders' equity will eventually be equal to share capital plus income from previous years reinvested by shareholders (retained earnings) plus income of the most recently concluded period.

The net income for the period is zero since in this transaction no value was created (value is only created through transactions with customers), and no value was destroyed (value is destroyed by transactions with suppliers or consumption of assets).

Income corresponds to a period of time, while the balance sheet corresponds to an instant in time. Net income is calculated at the end of a period of any duration. Conceptually, income (change in shareholders' equity) could be calculated for each transaction but it would be very cumbersome. It is generally required to report the net income once a year for the previous year to shareholders, but management and, increasingly, the financial markets require more frequent reporting of net income so as to help managers and investors alike evaluate the performance trend on which the firm operates. Managers will be interested in adjusting the course of action they have selected, on the basis of the confrontation between expected and observed and also on the basis of the evolution of the external competitive conditions under which the firm operates. Shareholders, meanwhile, will essentially use the information to review their investment decision.

Transaction 2 – Verdi obtains a loan

Early in January 20X1, Verdi obtains a 60 currency unit loan from its bank (or from another financial institution – the nature of the lender has no bearing on our accounting for it). The principal of the loan is deposited in Verdi's bank account.

When the business contracts for the loan, it is actually "acquiring" an obligation to repay 60 CU in the future and also the obligation to pay interest on the principal outstanding. Since the external obligations of Verdi are increased by their obtaining a loan, the liabilities record will be increased by 60 CU (interest is not due yet, thus only the principal will be recorded). Of course, the counterbalancing event is that the cash balance increased by the same amount. Since we have increased both sides of the equation, the impact on equity is zero. Borrowing in itself does not create or destroy wealth; at least not until we consider the passage of time and the fact we will have to pay interest (paying interest reduces cash or creates another obligation to pay in the future). Since the principal of the loan has not changed, the balance between both sides is maintained: when the interest due is paid, the payment is balanced by a reduction of equity. In other words, interest is an expense as defined earlier. We will not, however, record the interest expense at this stage since we have opted for a chronological sequence of transactions and the interest is not due until the end of the period.

This borrowing transaction will increase both the cash and the liabilities of Verdi Company as recorded in Figure 2.3.

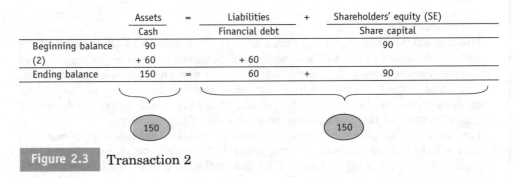

| | Assets | = | Liabilities | + | Shareholders' equity (SE) |
	Cash		Financial debt		Share capital
Beginning balance	90				90
(2)	+ 60		+ 60		
Ending balance	150	=	60	+	90

Figure 2.3 Transaction 2

Figure 2.3 shows the cumulative effect of the previous transactions, the specific effect of the current transaction and the cumulative effect of all transactions. After this transaction, net income is still zero. No value was created by the simple acquisition of additional funding.

Transaction 3 – Purchase of equipment in exchange for liquidity

On 1 January 20X1 Verdi acquires some equipment (a computer, a color printer, and an art/drawing software program). They cost 125 CU in total. The supplier is paid for this purchase with a check drawn on Verdi's bank account.

This equipment will be used in the future to create (or contribute to the creation of) services that will be sold to customers in keeping with the chosen strategy. Such equipment has the potential of creating future streams of revenue (economic benefits). It is now a resource of the business and is considered to be a part of its net worth (as defined in Chapter 1).

An interesting question bears on the definition of the value at which the resource will be recognized in Verdi's net worth. The "basic equation" gives us the answer: since the equipment costs originally 125 CU (consumption of a resource, i.e., cash), the asset or resource will be valued at this invoiced price (also known as its historical cost). The substitution of a resource for another does not, in itself, create value: value creation happens only when there is increase in the equity the shareholders have in the business and clearly a resource substitution does not, in itself, create value. Even if the asset substitution modifies the potential of value creation, the prudence rules call for ignoring the modification until the use of the new resource actually generates additional resources.

The acquired equipment increases Verdi's total assets by 125 CU and *simultaneously*, because of the payment to the supplier, the bank account is decreased by 125 CU and thus the event "acquisition of a piece of equipment" has the following net effect: $(+125) + (-125) = 0$.

The business has neither gained nor lost wealth due to this investment in physical equipment. However, this will not be the case in the future, as two sequences of events will normally take place: (a) a stream of revenue will derive (directly or indirectly) from the sales generated by the use of the equipment, i.e., additional resources will be created, and (b) the equipment will be consumed, i.e., its future ability to create resources will be diminished and thus its value in the list of resources composing the net worth of the firm will have to be decreased. Thus, in the future, the net effect of the use of the equipment will be to create resources – that is create profit (or to destroy resources – which is called a loss).

In summary, the asset acquisition transaction results in an equal increase and decrease in total assets and does not change the total assets, liabilities or the shareholders' equity of Verdi Company. Figure 2.4 shows that this transaction only changed the composition of company's assets by increasing equipment and decreasing cash.

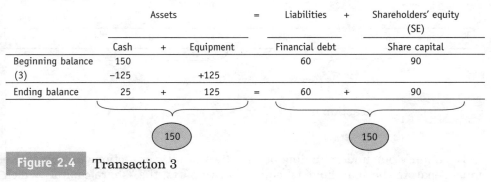

	Assets			=	Liabilities	+	Shareholders' equity (SE)
	Cash	+	Equipment		Financial debt		Share capital
Beginning balance	150				60		90
(3)	−125		+125				
Ending balance	25	+	125	=	60	+	90
		150				150	

Figure 2.4 Transaction 3

Transaction 4 – Services rendered

Sam Suffit, a retailer, approaches Verdi on 14 January and contracts for an advertising campaign to be carried out in February for his spring season products. After discussion about the content and format of the campaign, Sam agrees to pay 250 CU for the service Verdi will render. He also agrees to pay the full amount 30 days after he receives the invoice, which will be sent after the advertising campaign has been implemented. Therefore, he agrees to pay the full amount on 31 March. Verdi has, therefore, engaged in a transaction that will generate a sales revenue of 250 CU which will be recognizable on 1 March when Verdi invoices Sam (to recognize a revenue – or an expense – is to record it formally and officially in the accounts that will serve in preparing the financial statements). The likelihood that Sam will actually give the promised cash is extremely high and we can anticipate the future cash inflow. Simply, we will recognize the 250 currency unit sales as "potential cash" under the name of **accounts receivable**. It is not really cash but represents a claim on Sam that Verdi will exercise on 31 March. In fact, such claim could be sold for cash now (at a discount, of course, because of the time value of money – see this concept in Chapter 12) just like any other resource.

Since there is an increase in the resources side of the basic equation, there must be a counterbalancing entry which can either be an increase in the equity component of the net worth (which will be called income) or a reduction in other resources. It could even be a combination of both (as we will see after transaction 6).

At this stage, in this simplistic example, let us assume, for the time being, there are no costs attached to the actual execution of the advertising campaign. The net effect on the balance sheet is that, on the left-hand side, the claim on the customer (accounts receivable) has increased by 250 (increase in assets: the receivable is a resource that could be exchanged or transformed to create more resources) while on the right-hand side, equity has increased by the same amount (debt was unaffected).

Revenues increase shareholders' equity. Because the "sale of services" is not for cash, assets other than cash will increase: this is done through the recognition of the accounts receivable. Revenue is included in the determination of net income (see Figure 2.5).

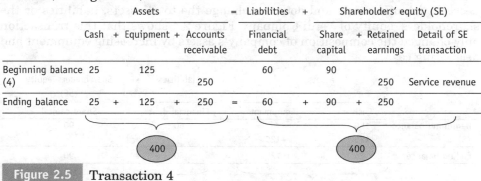

	Assets			=	Liabilities	+	Shareholders' equity (SE)		
	Cash	+ Equipment +	Accounts receivable		Financial debt		Share capital	+ Retained earnings	Detail of SE transaction
Beginning balance	25	125			60		90		
(4)			250					250	Service revenue
Ending balance	25 +	125 +	250	=	60	+	90 +	250	

Figure 2.5 Transaction 4

To simplify our understanding of the effect of all transactions on equity, we must separate the shareholders' equity in two parts: the "share capital" which recognizes the initial amount brought in by the investors (two investors in Verdi's case) and the "earnings" which record the net cumulative effect on equity of any and all transactions. Earnings are in fact the property of the owners of the firm (shareholders). If they choose to not withdraw the earnings over which they have a claim, these earnings become "retained earnings" (i.e., retained in the business to allow it to conserve its resources pool – especially cash – and allow the shareholders to increase their stake in the firm while supporting its ability to grow).

Remark 1: Retained earnings are no longer zero. Because we have (for the time being) assumed there were no costs attached to the creation of the revenue, the latter is plainly an increase in the shareholders' equity. This is so because the accounts receivable have increased the left-hand side of the balance sheet but there is no counterpart other than "sales revenue" which is in fact a subsidiary account of shareholders' equity (revenue minus costs equals income or increase – or decrease – in shareholders' equity). When net additional resources enter the financial position of the firm without resources being decreased or new obligations created to third parties, value is created.

Remark 2: The balance sheet remains balanced (by recognizing the net income – retained earnings – the equilibrium is maintained).

Remark 3: The cash position has not been modified because the customer has not paid yet. This sale was on credit and this fact is reflected in the "accounts receivable" account. Such an account is clearly an asset (or a resource) since Verdi has a legal claim on Sam to request payment and can even go to court to collect if Sam were to fail to pay on the due date.

Transaction 5 – Receipt of cash in settlement of the account receivable

When Sam Suffit sends a check to pay 180 of the 250 CU debt to Verdi, this check is immediately deposited in Verdi's bank account on 31 March. The claim is only partially settled.

As was the case in transaction 3, this transaction results in an equal increase and decrease in total assets and does not change the total assets, liabilities, and shareholders' equity of Verdi Company. It changes the composition of the company's assets by increasing cash and decreasing accounts receivable. However, the accounts receivable transaction related to the transaction between Sam Suffit and Verdi is not entirely completed. The new balances are as shown in Figure 2.6.

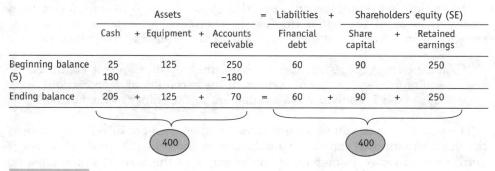

	Assets			=	Liabilities	+	Shareholders' equity (SE)		
	Cash	+ Equipment	+ Accounts receivable		Financial debt		Share capital	+	Retained earnings
Beginning balance	25	125	250		60		90		250
(5)	180		−180						
Ending balance	205 +	125	+ 70	=	60	+	90	+	250

400 = 400

Figure 2.6   Transaction 5

As the 180 CU actual payment of the revenue has already been "earned" (included in transaction 4), it cannot increase shareholders' equity a second time. The balance of accounts receivable (here it is 70, since the original balance was 250 and the customer paid 180) represents the amount which still remains to be collected.

Transaction 6 – Expenses either in cash or on account

In order to carry out the advertising campaign mentioned in transaction 4, Verdi had to pay wages to one employee in the amount of 101 CU, including social contributions, and fringe benefits. For the sake of simplicity, we will assume here that the wage cost plus social contributions and fringe benefits are paid in a single operation. This payment will be carried out by writing a check. In addition, the lending institution withdraws at the end of the period the interest accrued which amounts to 4 CU. Lastly, Verdi has received an invoice from a supplier (a subcontracted special effects artist) who worked on specific aspects of the Sam Suffit campaign. The invoice is in the amount of 85 CU and is due within 60 days of receipt.

Services purchased from suppliers, or work realized by employees, are not free of charge. They are the foundation of claims by these parties on the resources of the enterprise. The recognition of these claims creates what we call expenses (i.e., consumption of resources). When the claims will eventually be settled (extinguished), it will be by paying cash; and the conclusion of these transactions will reduce Verdi's cash account balance (i.e., reduce resources). Note that when the claim by a supplier is not settled immediately for cash, it is first recognized under the name of "**accounts payable**" (a debt owed by Verdi) before finally being settled through a transfer of cash in the hands of the creditors – supplier and employee in this case.

For example, Verdi Company has consumed 85 CU worth of resources to acquire and consume external services from a supplier (this consumption is called external expenses). That amount has a direct impact on equity. Even if the invoice were to be paid in two installments, for example of 80 and 5, the way the claim is settled would have no impact on equity (see transaction 7 for details).

When the financial institution lent money to Verdi, they were expecting repayment of the principal (the nominal amount lent) and the payment of interest on any remaining balance on the loan at scheduled intervals. The **interest** represents the fee for having the right to use the money that belongs to the bank. That rental fee will be settled by giving up (consuming) resources (cash) in favor of the bank. Interest is, therefore, an expense and will be recognized on the agreed anniversary dates. This is called a "financial expense".

> An expense is the recognition of a consumption of resources creating a claim on current or future cash (with the exception of depreciation).
> An expense is equivalent to a reduction in the equity of the business.

The way the claim will be settled (now or later) does not affect the equity of the firm. The interest expense is a reduction in the equity of Verdi. However, if Verdi were to repay all or part of the principal of the loan, it would have no impact on the equity because there is a simultaneous reduction of cash on the asset side and of the debt payable on the liability side (see transaction 8).

To sum up, any expense (with the exception of depreciation) will eventually be settled in cash. The recognition of an expense causes a reduction in the equity in a way similar to the recognition of a revenue (see, for example, transaction 4) causes an increase in the equity of the firm. The way the expense will actually be settled does not affect equity.

The effect of these transactions on the basic equation is shown in Figure 2.7.

	Assets			=	Liabilities		+	Shareholders' equity (SE)		
	Cash	+ Equipment	+ Accounts receivable		Accounts payable	+ Financial debt		Share capital	+ Retained earnings	Detail of SE transaction
Beginning balance	205	125	70			60		90	250	
(6)	− 101								−101	Salaries expense
	− 4								−4	Interest expense
					85				−85	External expense
Ending balance	100 +	125 +	70	=	85 +	60	+	90 +	60	
		295					295			

Figure 2.7   Transaction 6

Equity is decreased when an expense is incurred. Transaction 7 shows how the settlement of a delayed claim affects the books. The three types of expense listed here are completely consumed in the course of Verdi's activity. It confirms that it is generally critical to consume resources in order to create revenue. (In old Dutch: *De cost gaet for de baet* or "the cost is what 'gets' – i.e., drives – the [sales] revenue".)

Expenses and revenues affect retained earnings. It might be interesting to regroup expenses by homogeneous type so as to gain a better understanding of how the business model of the firm actually creates wealth or value. Here, we distinguished expenses by their nature (external, operational, financial) but we will see in Chapter 3 that they could also usefully be regrouped by function or destination. The expense classification is secondary to understanding the impact of the expenses on retained earnings and shareholders' equity.

Transaction 7 – Settlement of accounts payable

Verdi only settles 80 out of the 85 currency unit supplier's claim (accounts payable) on the due date. The remaining 5 units will be settled later. The supplier's invoice has been previously recorded (see transaction 6) as an account payable. This payment will decrease both assets (cash) and liabil-ities (accounts payable). The effect of this transaction on the equation is illustrated in Figure 2.8.

	Assets			=	Liabilities			+	Shareholders' equity (SE)		
	Cash +	Equipment +	Accounts receivable		Accounts payable	+	Financial debt		Share capital	+	Retained earnings
Beginning balance	100	125	70		85		60		90		60
(7)	– 80				– 80						
Ending balance	20 +	125 +	70	=	5	+	60	+	90	+	60

215   215

Figure 2.8　Transaction 7

When 80 CU worth are paid in cash, there is simultaneously a reduction of the asset side of the basic equation, and a reduction of the claim amount recognized in the accounts payable on the right-hand (liability) side. Thus, since both sides are incremented in exactly the same amount, there is no impact on equity. The fact that 5 CU remain unsettled simply means we are recognizing it as a residual claim to be settled in the future.

No value was created or destroyed by this operation. The impact on equity was recorded in transaction 6 and cannot be recorded a second time.

Transaction 8 – Repayment of a debt

- Verdi reimburses the lender 15 CU out of the loan principal of 60.
- The asset side will be reduced by 15 (reduction of cash).
- Debt is also simultaneously reduced by 15 CU.

By reimbursing part of its debt, Verdi did not create value. It neither gained nor lost wealth! Since the reimbursement affects simultaneously both sides of the fundamental business equation, there is no impact on equity.

Here we see an important limitation of accounting. Although the statement that Verdi neither gained nor lost wealth is arithmetically (and accounting-wise) perfectly correct, the leverage effect would lead us to think otherwise. Hopefully, the business could use the cash represented by the reimbursement to generate a sale activity that would yield a return that would exceed the interest expense avoided. Thus, if the firm had opportunities that could yield more income or earnings than the avoided interest rate on the same amount of resources, it should not have reimbursed the principal early. Reimbursing early when more profitable alternative uses of cash exist deprives the shareholders of future earnings, therefore making them lose wealth. If, on the contrary, no such opportunity existed, it would be best for the shareholders to have Verdi reimburse the principal on the loan because the interest expense avoided is greater than the earnings that would have been generated through the use of these resources. When no profitable alternative use of cash exists, early reimbursement of the loan actually avoids future expenses and is therefore equivalent to a creation of wealth. Accounting, however, will not recognize these possible opportunities because they are not known with certainty.

Accounting is essentially prudent and only recognizes or considers elements that are certain and perfectly known, i.e., that are historical or not set in an uncertain future. This transaction is very close in nature to the previous one: decrease in assets (cash) and decrease in liabilities (financial debt). Figure 2.9 illustrates the effect of this transaction on the business equation.

	Assets			=	Liabilities		+	Shareholders' equity (SE)	
	Cash +	Equipment +	Accounts receivable		Accounts payable	+ Financial debt		Share capital	+ Retained earnings
Beginning balance (8)	20 − 15	125	70		5	60 − 15		90	60
Ending balance	5 +	125 +	70	=	5	+ 45	+	90	+ 60

200

200

Figure 2.9   Transaction 8

Summary

A summary of the eight transactions affecting Verdi Company is presented in Figure 2.10.

After all these transactions have been recorded, the synthetic financial position account (the balance sheet) appears as shown in Table 2.3.

Table 2.3   Balance sheet on 30 April 20X1

Assets		Equity and liabilities		
Fixed assets		Shareholders' equity		150
Equipment	125	Capital	90	
		Retained earnings (net income)	60	
Current assets		Liabilities		
Accounts receivable	70	Financial debt		45
Cash at bank	5	Accounts payable		5
Total assets	200	Total equity and liabilities		200

	Assets			=	Liabilities		+	Shareholders' equity (SE)		
	Cash	+ Equipment	+ Accounts receivable	=	Accounts payable	+ Financial debt	+	Share capital	+ Retained earnings	Detail of SE transaction
(1)	+ 90							+ 90		Initial investment
(2)	+ 60					+ 60				
(3)	− 125	+ 125								
(4)			+ 250						+ 250	Service revenue
(5)	+ 180		− 180							
(6)	− 101								− 101	Salaries expense
(6)	−4								− 4	Interest expense
(6)					85				− 85	External expense
(7)	− 80				− 80					
(8)	− 15					− 15				
End balance	5	+ 125	+ 70	=	5	+ 45	+	90	+ 60	

200 (Assets) = 200 (Liabilities + Shareholders' equity)

Figure 2.10 Summary table

Conclusion – Some key points

The previous illustrative transactions illustrate the following points:

1 *Both sides of the business equation must always be balanced with one another.*

2 *Each transaction must be analyzed specifically to identify its possible impact on shareholders' equity.*

3 *The result of a transaction that creates or consumes value is summarized in the "retained earnings" account.*

The change in the amount of the retained earnings at the end of a period represents the net income of that period (in our example, it was + 60). However, since income belongs to the shareholders, part or all of it can be distributed in the form of dividends. Income for the period is only reflective of what happened during that period. If the shareholders decide to withdraw some of the wealth created, it is their right and therefore the retained earnings (RE) in any balance sheet will be the result of the following equation:

(Beginning RE balance) + (Income from the period) – (Dividends) = (Ending RE balance)

The retained earnings account reflects the cumulated effect of the earnings the shareholders have chosen not to withdraw from the business.

4 *What creates income?*

There was no income (impact on retained earnings) until transaction 4 (sale of services). This transaction was the first operation in our illustrative sequence that affected the shareholders' equity and therefore the retained earnings. Any transaction that affects either the assets or liabilities and the retained earnings affects income. Any transaction that only affects the structure of the balance sheet is not a source of value creation. Only transactions with outside customers are susceptible to create revenue. Transactions with outside customers always require the consumption of resources, i.e., destroy "value".

Income is the difference between the value created in the customer-based transaction and the value destroyed by consuming resources to serve the customer.

5 *Net income is different from cash.*

Since our example only looked at the first period and no dividends have been paid out, the net income of the period and the retained earnings show identical amounts, namely + 60 CU. However, the ending cash balance (in the bank) is + 5. Such a difference is not happenstance. The cases where cash balance and profit are the same are extremely rare and unusual and offer no opportunity for generalization. How can we explain this difference? Two main explanations can be proposed:

● Some transactions only have an impact on the bank's cash balance and not on retained earnings. For example, transaction 1 (constitution of the business' capital), transaction 2 (obtaining a loan), and transaction 3 (acquisition of an asset or equipment).

● The fact that some sales lead to extending credit to customers (and, conversely, some acquisitions of resources lead to credit being extended by the supplier) creates a situation in which the retained earnings account is modified when the transaction takes place and not when it is finally settled through payment from the customer or to the supplier. This was the case in transaction 4 (sale of services) in which retained earnings were increased but not the cash account. Similarly, transaction 6 (purchasing resources or services from an outside supplier) generated a reduction in retained earnings without modifying the bank balance at the same moment.

The effect on retained earnings (and the counterbalancing claim) is recognized when the triggering event (transaction) takes place. There is no need to take into account this transaction when the claim is actually settled by the exchange of cash or other commodity.

The different timing between cash and profit is crucial, especially in a fast growing business. Let us build a simple example to illustrate the situation. Assume there is a business whose sales double each period. Expenses are 80% of revenue. Customers pay two periods after the sales take place and suppliers require payment within one period after the delivery. The resources are acquired in the same period when the sales take place (see Table 2.4).

Table 2.4 Cash versus profit

Period	1	2	3	4	5	6	7
Sales	10	20	40	80	160	320	640
Expenses	8	16	32	64	128	256	512
Profit	**2**	**4**	**8**	**16**	**32**	**64**	**128**
Opening cash	0	0	-8	-14	-26	-50	-98
Cash inflow	0	0	10	20	40	80	160
Cash outflow	0	8	16	32	64	128	256
Ending cash	**0**	**-8**	**-14**	**-26**	**-50**	**-98**	**-194**

We have here a business which is clearly extremely profitable but for which the cash situation is dramatically dangerous and probably will lead to bankruptcy unless something is done such as obtaining more starting cash (upfront capital), changing the credit terms given to customers (not always possible for a start-up business), or obtaining better credit terms from the suppliers (here again, not an easy task for a small enterprise). Many fast growing businesses actually go bankrupt because they cannot generate enough long-term capital to provide stable resources to keep the firm alive through this fast growth phase.

The cash flow statement (see Chapters 3 and 14) describes in detail the relationship between the income and cash situation.

6 *The order in which items are listed on the balance sheet is not random.*

Each national or enterprise culture lists items in a sequential order that matches their value system. Chapter 3 shows that several countries go as far as defining a standard order. One of the reputed advantages of a normalized order is that it facilitates comparability of financial statements between comparable enterprises (the opposite is, of course, that comparability is useless if it is obtained at the detriment of the quality and descriptive flexibility of accounting). Most multinational companies have imposed on their subsidiaries all over the globe the obligation to report (to the parent) in similar formats (regardless of the locally required format) and also to use the same definition of terms so as to facilitate the comparative evaluation of the value creation potential of each subsidiary by senior management in the headquarters. Similarly, financial analysts and investment advisors are interested in homogeneous reporting so as to facilitate their task of identifying superior performers in an industrial sector.

Typical transactions

Table 2.5 lists some typical transactions and their impact on assets, liabilities, and shareholders' equity. This table is in no way exhaustive and we have deliberately focussed on the most common transactions.

Table 2.5 Impact of most common transactions

Example	Assets	=	Liabilities	+	Shareholders' equity
Creation of the company by capital contribution	+				+ C
Reduction of capital (repayment of the capital)	–				– C
Purchase of equipment for cash	+ and –				
Purchase of equipment on credit	+		+		
Collection of accounts receivable	+ and –				
Obtaining a loan	+		+		
Payment of a liability (e.g., accounts payable)	–		–		
Conversion of a debt into share capital			–		+ C
Sales revenue for cash or on account	+				+ RE
Expense for cash	–				–RE
Expense on account			+		–RE

The shareholders' equity account is separated between C = capital and RE = retained earnings

In the previous section, revenues and expenses were recorded through their impact on the "retained earnings" account. This choice was made to show the fundamental mechanism of the business equation. The number of transactions in the life of a business is, however, so large that it would be extremely cumbersome to record each change individually in the retained earnings or to handle the revenue and expense accounts as a subsidiary account of shareholders' equity in the balance sheet. It would also be difficult to carry out analyses of transactions to understand the business model of value creation during the period (remember that the balance of retained earnings reflects the cumulated impact of all transactions – including distribution of income to shareholders – since the firm was created). In practice, transactions will be recorded in specific accounts opened only for a given period of time. These accounts will form the "income statement". These allow us to analyze the processes through which income of the period was created and thus how retained earnings will be modified. In the end, only the income statement's net balance at the end of the period will be transferred to the balance sheet account (as part of the shareholders' equity). The income statement will be the record of what happened during the period that caused the observed income (profit or loss). This separate record of actions can be subjected to analysis so as to identify which decisions can be modified to create even more profit for the next period.

The balance sheet will remain a "still photograph" of the financial position of the firm while the income statement will record the dynamics of how such position changed during a period of time. In a way, if the balance sheet were a still photograph, the income statement is like the "film" of the "activity" of the business during a given period that explains how the appearance of the two still photos (beginning and closing balances) was modified during the period.

Some key terms have been introduced here:

Activity: This term refers to both the industrial or commercial sector a business operates in and the level of intensity of its transactions (level of activity). The term activity refers to what the firm does. The income statement reflects the activity of the firm; it gives a view of how one went from one balance sheet to the next. It, therefore, does not give the financial position (or record of the "net worth" of the firm); it is providing a dynamic view of what the firm did during the period. It will record the consumption of resources and the creation of revenue. Resources can be short lived as would be the case for salaries, supplies, energy, etc., or can be long lived such as physical assets (machinery, fixtures, office equipment, etc.). In the case of the latter we will only record the reduction in value due to usage (wear and tear, obsolescence, etc.).

During a given period: The income statement is a recapitulation of all transactions linked to serving customers during a given period of time (the concept of "accounting period" was defined in Chapter 1).

The income statement will allow us to track revenues (conventionally placed on the right-hand side to mirror the fact that revenues are equivalent to an increase in shareholders' equity) and the expenses or costs (conventionally placed on the left-hand side). The positioning of the revenues and expenses is not fortuitous. The income statement is a temporary account that will be "closed" at the end of the period by the transfer of its balance to the "retained earnings" account on the balance sheet. If expenses are less than revenues, there is profit, which appears as the amount required to balance both sides of the income statement. The "profit", on the left-hand side, is therefore the counterbalancing entry to the recognition of the increase in the shareholders' equity, on the right-hand side of the balance sheet.

This co-temporal recognition of related revenue and expenses, which is made possible by the **accrual principle**, is essential for the usefulness of financial statements. This principle means that a revenue (expense) is recorded in the income statement at the time of the transaction that causes it and not at the time of the cash inflow (or outflow, as the case may be). Both managers and outside information users can read directly from the income statement (established on an accrual basis) how much of the business's resources must be mobilized to create revenue and by comparing several successive periods, these users can also see whether the "productivity" of the business' resources is improving or deteriorating (due to any combination of quality of management, changes in competitive conditions, relevance of value offering to customers, etc.).

Business equation and income statement

Figure 2.11 illustrates the link between the basic business or accounting equation (the balance sheet) and the income statement.

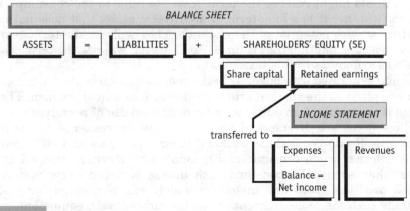

Figure 2.11 Links between balance sheet and income statement

Elements of the income statement

Revenue

A revenue is an influx of economic resources for the firm, coming from third parties and whose origin is generally a commercial transaction. A revenue is always an increase in shareholders' equity.

The ultimate purpose of an enterprise is to create a profit so as to give a positive return to (or increase the wealth of) its shareholders. The way an enterprise creates profit is by satisfying its customers. The **sales** revenue (or sales turnover) is the metric that reflects how successful is the firm at creating and delivering a customer value proposition at any given point. Note that the concept of value offering or value proposition includes provision of goods or services as well as rental of facilities, technologies, or goods. The concept of rental revenue recognition is of increasing interest in the "new economy" and will be further explored in Chapter 6. The growth of the sales revenue is an even better indicator of the appreciation by the customer of the firm's value proposition or value offering than the absolute value of the sales revenue, as is shown in Chapter 15. Sales are measured in accounting by the recording of some form of invoice, which is the material proof of the existence of the transaction.

Accounting records the sale based on the assumption that the customer will pay the invoice on the agreed date. It is therefore critical to understand that "revenue" and "receipt of funds" are very different. The actual receipt of funds may happen (1) earlier than when the revenue is recognized (as in the case of a down payment), (2) simultaneously with the revenue recognition (as in the case of a cash sale), or (3) later than the revenue recognition (as in the case of a credit sale or sale on account).

Revenue may also come from a financial investment made by the firm (interest or return on investment). For example if a retailer receives cash from a customer 30 days before the supplier must be paid, the retailer can invest the cash received for 30 days and earn additional revenue on the sale in the form of interest revenue.

Expenses

An expense is a consumption of resources, i.e., a reduction in shareholders' equity. Purists might reserve the term "cost" to refer to the consumption of a resource (whether it is a long-term or short-term asset) that does not destroy the future service potential of the resource. They will use the term "expense" to refer to a consumption that is final. We, however, will use the terms cost and expense as synonyms in this text.

Revenue generated by a business is the representation of the exchange value customers place on the value offering or value proposition of the firm. The value offering is the result of an efficient and coordinated use of resources (consumption). Resources are diverse and they all can be expressed in terms of cash equivalents. Resources include workers' labor, employees and staff (materialized by salaries which consume cash), supplies or services provided by third parties (they eventually consume cash unless bartered), raw materials or finished products (consume inventory which was purchased for cash and eventually cash for replenishment of the inventory level), equipment, such as machinery, computers, telephone systems, commercial facilities (the value of an asset is equal to the net present value of the future cash flows it will generate; the "consumption" of a fixed asset recognizes the fact that usage and obsolescence reduce future cash flows), etc.

One critical issue in revenue and expense recognition is their "**matching**". Resource consumption for research and development, acquiring customers, or for promoting a new product may not take place in the same period as the revenue that will result from these cash outlays and/or resource consumption. Accounting will pay great attention to the "matching" of revenue and expenses. An income statement will attempt to show side by side the revenue and the expenses corresponding to the same business activity for a given period. Matching will be further addressed in Chapter 5.

Income or "bottom line"

Every year (or at the end of any "accounting period" or "accounting year"), the balance between all revenues and expenses is drawn. This is done by balancing all of the increases and decreases in shareholders' equity that result from the normal business operations. If the revenues are greater than the expenses, the shareholders' equity has a net increase and we have what is called a profit (often called net income). If, however, the revenues of the period are not enough to cover the expenses, it means the shareholders' equity has been reduced during the period, and this is called a loss. The profit or loss appears as the last line (bottom) of the two lists of revenues and expenses, and thus it has become colloquially acceptable to refer to the profit or loss as the "bottom line".

In summary, during any given period we have the following equation:

$$\text{Revenues} - \text{Expenses} = \text{Income (profit or loss)}$$

Application to Verdi

During the year 20X1, Verdi Company has recognized net sales or net revenue of 250. This means it has produced invoices in the amount of 250 CU. It has concurrently consumed resources (services and supplies) that outside suppliers invoiced to Verdi for a total amount of 85. In addition Verdi consumed the labor force of its employees and incurred for such consumption an expense of 101 CU (salaries, and fringe and social benefits). Lastly, Verdi was able to generate the 250 CU of revenue because it had been able to use its resources, including some which have been financed through the loan. The interest expense of 4 CU is thus a relevant cost that must be matched against the revenue of 250.

The operations of Verdi Company are summarized in Table 2.6.

Table 2.6	Income statement of Verdi Company

Total revenues		250
incl. sales	250	
Total expenses		190
incl. services and supplies	85	
incl. personnel expenses	101	
incl. interest expenses	4	
Income (revenues – expenses)	=	+ 60

During 20X1, Verdi's business activities have created a profit of 60 (before income tax). In the statement, revenues and expenses were presented in a vertical list (vertical format). It can also be shown as a subset of the shareholders' equity account, i.e., using the convention of showing increases in shareholders' equity on the right-hand side and decreases on the left-hand side. Such a format is known as the horizontal format and is illustrated in Table 2.7.

In the Verdi example, expenses are listed by nature, simply summarizing transactions of a similar nature, without any other calculations besides simple additions. Some countries, such as the United States and Canada, have chosen

Table 2.7   Income statement

Expenses		Revenues	
Purchases and external expenses	85	Sales	250
Personnel expenses	101		
Interest expenses	4		
Profit	*60*		
Total	250	Total	250

to present expenses by regrouping them further by destination (or function). In their model, expenses are shown in "blocks" grouping expenses having the same purpose (and the details of these expenses is not considered useful for the decider) such as cost of sales, cost of acquiring a customer, administrative expenses, etc. The functional approach distinguishes between "cost of goods sold", "cost of selling", "cost of administering", and "cost of financing". This aspect will be further developed in Chapter 3, which is devoted to financial statements. At this point, the format of presentation of the income statement is not important for our purpose.

In the previous formats of the income statement, "profit" appears to be in the same column as expenses or costs. It is simply the result of the fact the net income is the balance of revenues minus expenses and would be written as a way to update the shareholders' equity account (see Figure 2.12).

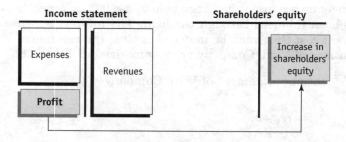

Figure 2.12   Link between profit and shareholders' equity

Of course, had there been a loss (i.e., expenses exceed revenue), the net income would have been shown on the right-hand side of the income statement because the counterpart would have been a decrease in shareholders' equity.

Impact of transactions on financial statements

So far, we have recorded transactions, one by one, by applying the basic business equation model (Assets = Liabilities + Shareholders' equity). We will now focus on the transactions that impact the financial statements as a stand-alone document. The income statement will no longer be considered being a subpart of shareholders' equity at each step, but will be connected to the balance sheet only at the end of the period (see Figure 2.13). This will thus create the income statement as a document that records all transactions and only the balance in the end will be carried over to the balance sheet as a modification of shareholders' equity.

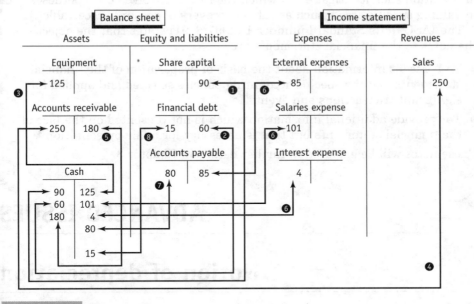

Figure 2.13 Impact on financial statements

From now on, we will use this T-account-based format to illustrate the handling of transactions. The double arrows linking elements of a record imply that the two or more elements connected cannot be separated. The set of transactions records will always be balanced by definition.

Balance sheet and value creation

Appendix 2.1 shows how the change between two balance sheets can be related to the value creation.

Notes to financial statements

The accounting system must provide relevant information with as much precision and reliability as possible so that users of the financial statements trust their informational content. Such understandability requires that no ambiguity remains about how they were developed. The rules, procedures, and principles that were followed in the establishment of the financial statements must be made clear so that the users can interpret their implications and, if needed, re-code the information to suit their specific needs. In some countries, as we will see later, accounting rules and regulations governing the establishment of financial statements are very precisely defined. Other countries leave more room for interpretation of these descriptors of the financial position of the firm.

Notes to financial statements constitute a clarification and a supplement to the balance sheet and the income statement. They list "off balance sheet" information such as litigation in which the firm is involved or hypotheses used in valuing specific assets such as rate of recovery of accounts receivable.

The IASC in its Standard number 1 (1997: § 91) states that the objectives of the notes to the financial statements are:

- To "present information about the basis of preparation of the financial statements and the specific accounting policies selected and applied for significant transactions and events".

- To "provide additional information which is not presented on the face of the financial statements but that is necessary for a fair presentation".

These notes will be explored in further details in Chapter 3.

ADVANCED ISSUES

Notion of depreciation

Principle

In order to fulfill its mission of creating value for shareholders by providing value to customers (in the form of goods or services) a business needs to invest in permanent "means of production". These can be in the form of plant, machinery, warehouses, retail facilities, fixtures, computers, vehicles, distribution systems, etc. Most of these assets have a useful life that exceeds the duration of the accounting period. They are called "fixed assets" to distinguish them from the "current assets" which are acquired and consumed within the duration of the operating cycle or the accounting period (whichever is the shorter).

Fixed assets gradually lose value (i.e., potential of creating future economic benefits, or sellable goods or services in the future) due to usage, aging, or obsolescence. They must be replaced periodically to maintain the value creation ability of the business. The loss of value of such a "fixed" asset due to any of the previously mentioned causes is considered a cost since it is an actual "consumption" of an asset. The consumption of a fixed asset is called "**depreciation expense**" since it reflects the gradual loss of value of these assets.

Depreciation is the process of adjusting (downwards) the value of an asset by recognizing it is consumed in a way that does not completely eliminate the resource. It would have been a violation of the matching principle to recognize the full value of the equipment as being consumed in the very period when it was acquired since benefits will continue to derive in the future years from owning the asset. (Verdi knew their equipment would create a flow of revenues for several years.) Depreciation is the procedure that allows a business to match revenue and fixed asset resource consumption, when the asset will benefit several periods.

The **accumulated depreciation** expense of any fixed asset will eventually be equal to the amount initially paid to acquire it. The fixed asset will then be recorded as "fully depreciated" and have a zero book value.

A **depreciation expense** is recognized every year in the income statement just as supplies or salary expenses are. Depreciation, however, will be recognized at the end of the period and not each time the asset is used.

Application to Verdi

Verdi had acquired fixed assets (a computer, a color printer, and an art/drawing software) at the beginning of the period for 125 CU. Let us assume these assets have an expected useful life of 5 years (i.e., they will be able to contribute to the generation of economic benefits for 5 years). This means that, in 5 years, they will be worthless and will no longer be productive assets. Verdi will have consumed the asset completely over 5 years. If we choose a simple approach, we may recognize that these fixed assets lose 20% of their value every year. We will see in Chapter 7 that methods other than this **"straight-line"** approach (proportional to the passage of time) are possible but the choice of method, although it modifies the timing of recognition of the depreciation expense, does not modify the principle of depreciation: all outputs created by using a fixed asset must bear a part of the cost of the depreciation of the asset. In Verdi's case, the depreciation expense for the year is thus 25 CU (for each year since we selected a method – straight-line depreciation – which creates an equal amount of depreciation each year). At the end of the first period, the book value of these fixed assets would now be 125 minus 25 or 100. The yearly depreciation expense of 25 units is another expense in the income statement. It will be offset against the revenues to help determine the income for the period. Thus, for the next 5 years, an expense of 25 will be recognized in the annual income statement to acknowledge the consumption of the productive capacity. At the end of the 5 years, the net (book) value of the equipment will be zero. In theory, the equipment will have to be replaced at the end of the 5-year period if the exhaustion of the value creation potential of the asset is also physical in addition to being financial.

An "improved", i.e., more complete, representation of the situation of Verdi Company appears as Figure 2.14.

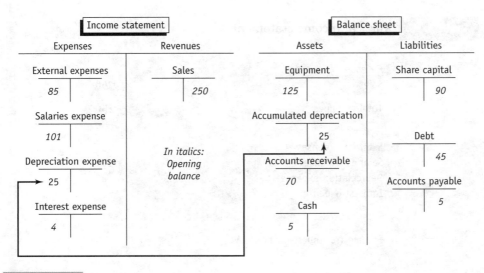

Figure 2.14 Recording the depreciation

The balance sheet is adjusted as shown in Table 2.8.

Table 2.8 Balance sheet after depreciation

Assets	Balance sheet on 31 December 20X1		Equity and liabilities	
Equipment	Gross value 125	100	Shareholders' equity	
	– Depreciation 25		Capital	90
Accounts receivable		70	Retained earnings	35
Cash		5	Liabilities	
			Debt	45
			Accounts payable	5
	Total assets	175	Total liabilities	175

The income statement is also modified (see Table 2.9).

Table 2.9 Income statement after depreciation

Income statement			
Expenses		**Revenues**	
External expenses	85	Sales	250
Salaries expense	101		
Depreciation expense	25		
Interest expense	4		
Profit	35		
	250		250

Remark: Had we chosen the *vertical* presentation of the income statement, the latter would look as described in Table 2.10.

Table 2.10 Vertical income statement

Revenues	
Sales	250
Total revenues	250
Expenses	
External expenses	85
Salaries expenses	101
Depreciation expense	25
Interest expense	4
Total expenses	215
Income (revenues – expenses)	35

Profit appropriation

Principle

The income (profit or loss) calculated in the balance sheet is an increase or a reduction of shareholders' equity and reflects whether the business created any net additional wealth. When shareholders contribute their own personal resources to create a business (cash, intellectual property, effort, or transfer control of a physical asset, for example), these contributions form the capital from the point of view of the business. They are considered an investment from the point of view of the shareholders. The latter expect a return on their investment.

As we said earlier, profit represents the increase in wealth created by the operation of the firm and literally belongs to the shareholders. The shareholders can choose to take all or part of that increase in their equity out of the business in the form of dividends. Whatever part of the profit is not distributed is considered to be "retained" earnings.

In a limited liability company (public or private limited company in the UK, *société anonyme* or *société à responsabilité limitée*, in France, *Aktiengesellschaft* or *GmbH* in Germany, *SpA* in Italy, etc.), there are generally many shareholders and it would be difficult to allow each individual shareholder to decide whether or not they wish to withdraw their share of the added wealth to which they are personally entitled (based on the percentage of their contribution to the share capital and opening balance of earnings retained from previous periods). The decision is, therefore, made by a vote of the general meeting of the shareholders and their decision applies uniformly to all shareholders.

Practically, the decision regarding what to do with profit of the period consists in choosing among any of three possibilities:

1 Distribute the profit entirely to the shareholders as dividends.
2 Distribute the profit partially to the shareholders as dividends, and the balance is considered to be an increase of the investment of the shareholders in the proportion of their previous contributions.
3 Not distribute profit at all, and the investors (shareholders) reinvest their claim in its entirety in the business.

The debate about whether or not to distribute the profit implies an arbitration between the individual needs of shareholders for cash income and the medium to long-term interest of the firm. When dividends are paid out, there is a reduction of shareholders' equity, and a simultaneous reduction in cash. This drain on the cash situation of the firm may create a serious limitation of the ability of the firm to pursue its operations (remember that profit and cash flow are often disconnected – see Table 2.4). The problem is generally to try to partition the profit of the firm between owners and the firm itself in such a way that the shareholders receive enough cash for their needs and the firm is not drained out of cash, which is the fuel for its smooth operation and growth.

The part of the profit that is paid out to the shareholders is first recognized as a short-term debt to shareholders (dividend payable) after the distribution has been approved by shareholders. When the dividend is actually paid out, the debt is canceled and cash is reduced appropriately.

The profit retained in the business is aggregated to the shareholders' equity but remains, often for legal or regulatory reasons, distinct from the strictly defined "capital". Profit retained in the business is called either "retained earnings" (for example, in the United States or in Canada) or "reserves" (for example, in the Nordic countries, Germany, France, or the UK).

It should be clear that retained earnings (or reserves) are in no way equivalent to available cash. Since income and cash are disconnected through credit terms and different timing of financial flows on the revenue and the expense sides of the income statement, we can have a situation where there is a lot of profit (and potentially a large addition to the retained earnings) but a negative cash position (see Table 2.4).

The topic of **profit appropriation** will be further developed in Chapter 11, and reporting for retained earnings and reserves is presented in Appendix 2.2.

Application to Verdi

The shareholders of Verdi Company observe their business results during the recently closed accounting period and determine that they made a profit of 35 (after depreciation). They decide to award themselves a dividend of 3 CU or, in other words, they decide to keep in the business 32 of the profit of 35 as a reserve or retained earnings. In fact, this is equivalent to their reinvesting that same amount into the business (with the significant tax advantage that since the amount reinvested was never distributed, the shareholders have not been individually taxed on the investment income they now choose to reinvest). The shareholders' decision to pay a dividend will be recorded immediately by recognizing the immediate liability to the shareholders under the name of "dividends payable". The impact on cash, however, will not take place until the actual payout takes place (here we can assume it will not take place before 20X2).

The transaction of "declaring dividends" results in a decrease in retained earnings and creation of a liability for the same amount. On the date of payment, this liability account is canceled and cash is decreased. The impact on the basic financial statements (only the necessary accounts are presented) is shown in Figure 2.15. For the sake of simplification, we have ignored the tax implications in this illustration. In the "real world", before recording it on the balance sheet, income would first have been subject to taxation according to the rules of the country where Verdi is operating. Let's add that depending on the country or the company, retained earnings and reserves can be reported in two different ways (see Appendix 2.2).

Cash, profit, and reserves

The term "reserves" or "retained earnings" proves to be misleading at times to students (and executives alike) who do not fully grasp the distinction between profit and cash balance. As was shown earlier (and in Table 2.4 especially), a business can be very profitable but extremely cash poor, or the converse can be true as illustrated in Table 2.11 for a business whose unprofitable sales double each period. For each currency unit of revenue the cost is 1.1. However, the customers pay immediately but the business does not have to pay the supplier(s) until two periods after the cash sale was realized.

We can see from this illustration that this business is a cash-generating machine although it is actually "losing money" on every sale. In Table 2.11, if we ignore that the cash generated could be invested profitably, the business is

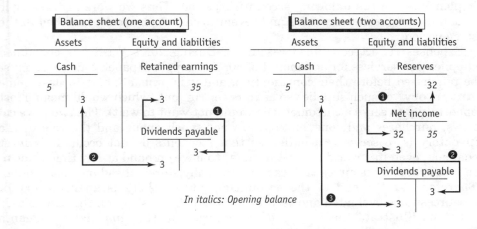

Balance sheet (one account)

Assets | Equity and liabilities

Cash | Retained earnings

In italics: Opening balance

❶ Transfer to dividends payable
❷ Payment of dividends

Balance sheet (two accounts)

Assets | Equity and liabilities

Cash | Reserves

Net income

Dividends payable

❶ Transfer of net income to reserves
❷ Transfer of net income to dividends payable. The net income account is de facto emptied to zero by these two entries
❸ Payment of dividends

Figure 2.15 Recording profit appropriation

Table 2.11 Cash versus profit

Period	1	2	3	4	5	6	7
Sales	10	20	40	80	160	320	640
Expenses	11	22	44	88	176	352	704
Income (here a loss)	**(1)**	**(2)**	**(4)**	**(8)**	**(16)**	**(32)**	**(64)**
Opening cash	0	10	30	59	117	233	465
Cash inflow	10	20	40	80	160	320	640
Cash outflow	0	0	11	22	44	88	176
Ending cash	**10**	**30**	**59**	**117**	**233**	**465**	**929**

literally destroying the capital (losses are equivalent to negative reserves, reducing equity). Negative reserves are no more equivalent to cash shortage than retained earnings or reserves are equivalent to available cash.

Consumption of resources and inventory

We will introduce the subject only briefly as it is further developed in Chapter 9. In the Verdi example, the concept of inventory was not needed since Verdi sold a service that could not be stored for sale at a later date. Further, we assumed that no preparation work had been incurred during the accounting period for advertising campaigns ordered by customers that would be implemented in the following accounting period. Thus we were in the simple situation in which all expenses and revenues can be physically matched in the same period.

Expenses reflect consumed resources. During 20X1 Verdi has consumed supplies and services for an amount of 80. The supplies (paper, toner, etc.) must be purchased before their consumption, and it is probably best to have some "**inventory**" of such supplies so as to never run out (which would mean a lost opportunity to serve a customer who would not want to wait). The two physical flows, purchases and consumption, are not synchronous and the role of the inventory is to serve as a buffer, so that stockouts do not occur. It is most common, even in a world of "just in time" to have on hand at any time some of the consumable resources that can be physically stored ahead of consumption. Therefore, at the end of the accounting period, there is an inventory of resources to be evaluated and recorded in the balance sheet on the asset side.

Let us illustrate the impact of inventories on the financial statements through the case illustration of Puccini, an umbrella manufacturer.

Goods purchased for resale or for use in a transformation process

Assume that Puccini acquires, with cash for 100 CU, the raw materials and parts necessary for the manufacturing of umbrellas (ribs, handles, mechanisms, fabric, thread, boxes, etc.). During the accounting period, Puccini consumed only 80 CU worth and therefore it still holds 20 CU worth of parts and materials at the end of the period.

Two different approaches exist for recording this situation. The first records each consumption of goods (materials and parts) incurred to satisfy customers. The second calculates the total consumption at the end of the period by measuring what remains on hand.

Method 1: Purchases recorded as inventory in the balance sheet

In this method, withdrawals from inventory or consumption to satisfy customers are recorded as they occur. The parts and materials purchased are considered to enter first in the inventory of Puccini. Therefore the counterpart of the purchase is an increase in the "inventory" account on the asset side of the balance sheet. When parts and materials are required for the manufacturing of umbrellas (probably on several occasions during the period), a requisition is issued by the plant (or from the retail store if we are not in a manufacturing context) and the goods are withdrawn from inventory. The parts and materials are, therefore, withdrawn for immediate consumption. Their value will be recognized, each time a withdrawal takes place, as both an expense (consumption of a resource) and a reduction of the asset amount listed under the heading "inventory". The total of all withdrawals will be recognized under the name of "cost of merchandise sold" if there is only a resale without transformation, otherwise the withdrawals will be a component of the "cost of goods manufactured" (or "cost of goods sold").

We can summarize this process very simply:

	Beginning inventory
Plus	Purchases (sum of all invoices of the period)
Minus	*Consumption (sum of all recorded material or merchandise requisitions)*
Equals	Ending inventory (which can be validated by a physical stocktaking)

In 20X1 in which there was no beginning inventory, the impact of inventories, carried under this first method, on the basic business equation is as shown in Table 2.12.

Table 2.12   Impact on the basic equation – Year 20X1

	Assets		Shareholders' equity (SE)	
	Cash +	Inventory =	Retained earnings	Detail of SE transaction
Purchases	−100	+100		
Withdrawals for consumption		−80	−80	Cost of goods sold
Ending balance	−100 +	20 =	−80	

The impact of inventories on the financial statements is as follows in Table 2.13.

Table 2.13   Impact on financial statements

Balance sheet at 31.12.20X1		Income statement year 20X1	
Assets	Equity and liabilities	Expenses	Revenues
Inventory 20		Cost of goods sold 80	

Suppose that during 20X2, Puccini purchases supplies for an amount of 200 CU. The value of the "supplies available" for consumption in the normal operations of the firm is 200 *plus* the existing beginning inventory of 20, which means a total available for use worth 220 CU. Consumption (i.e., sum of the withdrawals) during the year equals 211 CU. As a consequence, the ending inventory is computed by difference: 9 or (20 + 200 − 211). The impact on the accounting business equation is shown in Table 2.14.

Table 2.14   Impact on the basic business equation – Year 20X2

	Assets		Shareholders' equity (SE)		
	Cash +	Inventory =	Capital +	Retained earnings	Detail of SE transaction
Beginning balance	−100	20		−80	
Purchases	−200	+200			
Consumption		−211		−211	Cost of goods sold
Ending balance	−300 +	9 =		− 291	

Method 2: Purchases recorded as expense in the income statement

In this approach, instead of assuming all materials or parts acquired for future production are first going through an inventory account, we make the hypothesis that all that is purchased (100 CU worth in Puccini's case) is supposed to be consumed (either through resale or consumed in the manufacturing process) and is therefore considered to be expensed for the full amount at the time of purchase.

At the end of the period, when Puccini orders a physical stocktaking (i.e., counting what really exists in the inventory), it will observe that the hypothesis of exhaustive consumption of materials and parts may not have been quite correct. In our example, there are still 20 CU worth of goods left in inventory. Expenses have, therefore, been overestimated in our simplifying hypothesis and they must be adjusted *ex post* to recognize (the matching principle strikes again) only that part of the "materials and parts" that have been consumed so as to match them against revenue from sales. This second method is very simple and relatively less expensive than the first inventory approach (no record keeping of withdrawals from inventory during the period) but does not give the same control over consumption or the same fineness of information (which managers and external users of information may want to have in their resource allocation decision). Computerization tends to make the second inventory approach obsolete since it has become rather economical today to record every movement of materials or parts. However, the physical inventory taking is still a necessity in order to validate the quality of the computerized recording process of withdrawals and prevent pilferage and human errors in counting.

The equation defining the relation between inventories is modified. Instead of having the unknown be the ending inventory, the unknown is now the consumption of materials:

	Beginning inventory
Plus	Purchases (sum of all invoices of the period)
Equals	Available for consumption to satisfy customers
Minus	*Ending inventory (which results from a physical stocktaking)*
Equals	Consumption

At the end of the period the physical stocktaking carried out shows the final inventory to be worth 20 CU. The amount recorded as an expense must therefore be adjusted so as to reflect the correct value for the consumption of materials and parts. We create an "ending inventory account" which takes on the value of 20 CU. If we want to use a crude physical illustration of what happens, the inventory is taken out of the "plant" (the income statement), where is was "temporarily" stored (under the name of expense) and stored in a "warehouse" (the inventory account in the balance sheet).

Table 2.15 illustrates how accounting records the transaction under this approach. The impact of inventories on the accounting business equation is as follows (since there is no impact on liabilities, they can be ignored).

Table 2.15 Impact on the basic equation

	Assets		=	Shareholders' equity (SE)	
	Cash	+ Inventory	=	Retained earnings	Detail of SE transaction
Purchases	– 100			– 100	Purchase of supplies (during the year)
Ending inventory		+ 20		+ 20	Ending inventory
Ending balance	– 100 +	20	=	– 80	

Note: In this example, we have made the hypothesis that purchases have an immediate impact on income and that the consumption is adjusted *ex post* via a physical inventory taking. We have already seen, and will also see in greater details in Chapter 9, that another approach exists.

The impact of inventories on the financial statements is as follows (see Table 2.16).

Table 2.16 Impact on financial statements

Balance sheet at 31.12.20X1		Income statement year 20X1	
Assets	Equity and liabilities	Expenses	Revenues
		Purchases 100	
Inventory 20		– Ending inventory – 20	
		Consumed purchases 80	

In this method, since purchases were assumed to have been immediately consumed (i.e., turned into costs to be deducted from revenue), the ending inventory must be deducted from the expenses recognized so far in order to create a cost of consumption of parts and materials equal to what was actually consumed.

To further understand the entries recorded in the income statement, let us see what happens the following year. During the following year, purchases are 200 CU and the final inventory measured by stocktaking at the end of the year is estimated to be worth 9 CU.

The beginning inventory (ending inventory of the previous period) was worth 20 CU. The ending inventory is valued at 9 CU. The accounting change in inventory is therefore +11 (i.e., BI – EI, or 20 – 9), and the cost of materials consumed to satisfy customers is the full 200 purchased plus the reduction of inventory or 200 + 11 = 211 CU.

	Purchases	200
Plus	Beginning inventory	20
Minus	Ending inventory	– 9
Equals	Total consumed supplies	211

The impact of inventory on the accounting equation for 20X2 appears in Table 2.17.

Table 2.17 Impact of inventory on the basic equation

	Assets			Shareholders' equity (SE)		
	Cash	+ Inventory	=	Capital +	Retained earnings	Detail of SE transaction
Beginning balance	– 100	+ 20			– 80	
Beginning inventory		– 20			– 20	Consumption of beginning inventory
Purchases	– 200				– 200	Purchase of supplies (during the year)
Ending inventory		+ 9			+ 9	Ending inventory
Ending balance	– 300	+ 9	=		– 291	

The reader will note that the example is simplified in that purchases are assumed to have been paid for in cash (they could have been purchased on account) (see Table 2.18).

Table 2.18 Impact on the financial statements – Year 20X2

Balance sheet 20X2			Income statement		
Assets		**Liabilities**	**Expenses**		**Revenues**
			Purchases	200	
Inventory	9		Beginning inventory	20 ⎫	
			– Ending inventory	–9 ⎬ 11	
			Consumed supplies	211	

Note: Accountants call "variations in inventory level" or "changes in inventory" of raw materials, supplies, and merchandise the difference of "beginning inventory (BI) minus ending inventory (EI)". Traditionally, and by convention, the change in inventory level is generally shown on the expenses side of the income statement.

If the ending inventory has a larger value than that of the beginning inventory, the change in inventory is negative by our convention. This means that some of the resources incurred during the period have been devoted not to the creation and delivery of the value proposition but to the creation of an increased inventory. Incidentally an increased inventory can be a good thing in that it prepares the firm better to meet demand with short response time. Since in this (continental European) approach the expenses recognized on the left-hand side of the income statement are the ones that were incurred during the period, creating a "change in inventory" account reduces (or increases) the expenses of the period so that the balance is equal to the cost that needs to be matched with the revenue. The way of calculating the "change in inventory" as "BI – EI" adjusts the accounts automatically to recognize the amount of materials (or components or parts) expenses that matches the revenue, regardless of when these were acquired.

Intuitively (more logically, maybe?), we could have written:

> Consumption = Purchases *minus* Increase (or *plus* decrease) in inventories

(with increase and decrease defined as the difference (ending minus beginning inventories) which would lead us to define consumption as being equal to "purchases" minus ("ending inventory" – "beginning inventory").

The choice between the first and the second inventory methods depends on the tradition of each country and enterprise. Moreover, the 2 methods give exactly the same results in a non-inflationary world. Additionally, their impact on the financial statements is almost identical, if we take the case of goods purchased for resale or transformation. The only difference is the reporting of one account ("cost of goods sold") or two accounts ("purchases" and "change in inventory") in the income statement.

Goods manufactured

The main objective of Puccini is to manufacture and sell umbrellas. It could also offer a service of maintenance and repairs on its umbrellas. Service cannot, by definition, be stored. At the end of any period Puccini may, however, happen to have the following types of inventories:

- Inventory of finished umbrellas, ready for sale.
- Inventory of semi-finished umbrellas. For example, the mechanical parts of the umbrella and the fabric may be manufactured in two different workshops before final assembly in a third workshop. Each workshop may create an inventory of semi-finished umbrellas or umbrella subsystems.
- Work in progress (umbrellas or subsystems that are still being worked on when the period ends). They are neither finished nor semi-finished but somewhere in between. In industries where the transformation process is very long, this inventory may be very significant and its correct evaluation may be essential to the estimation of the income of the period.
- "Inventory" of development projects (R&D, engineering, development of new machinery by the manufacturing personnel themselves, etc.).

For all these "inventories", the logic of valuation is absolutely similar to the one followed earlier for raw materials, goods, merchandise, or parts and components for consumption or resale. Instead of being consumed to satisfy customer requests directly, raw materials and parts are first consumed in a production process, and then the finished products are made available to customers and are hopefully sold. This presents us with the following schematics (see Figure 2.16).

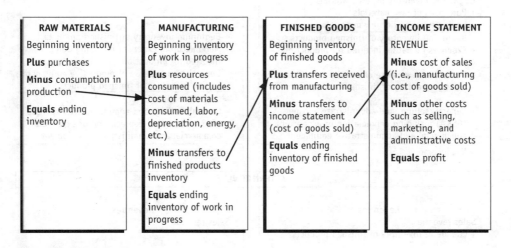

RAW MATERIALS	MANUFACTURING	FINISHED GOODS	INCOME STATEMENT
Beginning inventory	Beginning inventory of work in progress	Beginning inventory of finished goods	REVENUE
Plus purchases	**Plus** resources consumed (includes cost of materials consumed, labor, depreciation, energy, etc.)	**Plus** transfers received from manufacturing	**Minus** cost of sales (i.e., manufacturing cost of goods sold)
Minus consumption in production		**Minus** transfers to income statement (cost of goods sold)	**Minus** other costs such as selling, marketing, and administrative costs
Equals ending inventory	**Minus** transfers to finished products inventory	**Equals** ending inventory of finished goods	**Equals** profit
	Equals ending inventory of work in progress		

Figure 2.16 The logic of inventories

In each box the same equation applies: Beginning inventory plus New "entries" minus "Withdrawals" equals "Ending inventory".

Logically, there are two compatible income statement presentations as illustrated in Figure 2.17.

If the income statement is prepared according to Method 1 for inventory recording, only cost of goods sold and general, selling, and administrative expenses will be recognized with little details (inventory levels will only be found by looking at the balance sheet).

If, on the contrary, method 2 of recording inventories is followed, the income statement will, in this case, record more details of both purchases and inventories. Any variation of inventory level will automatically be provided, either by a one-line item (balance) or by providing the three components that define the balance.

Where to place the balance of the change in inventory is a question of choice and of meaningfulness of the financial statement. It may appear interesting to some to be able to find a measure of the evolution of inventories over the period (i.e., a measure of the preparedness of the firm for subsequent periods) next to information pertaining to the profitability of current sales. What matters is that either method 1 or method 2 provides a good matching of expenses with revenue. The income for the period is, of course, the same, regardless of the method used.

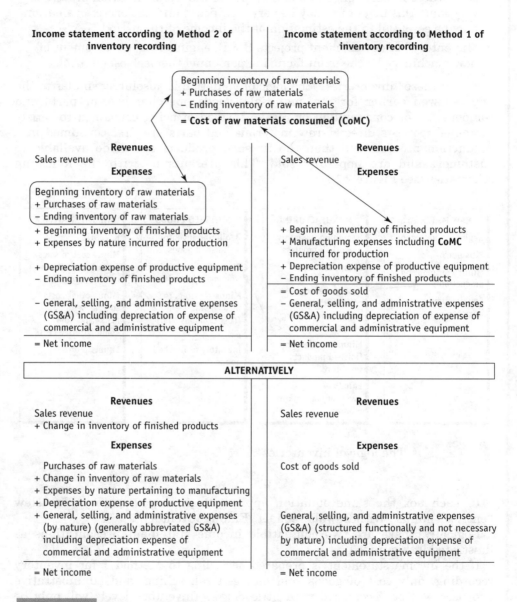

Figure 2.17 Income statement and inventory

Financial statement analysis

Financial statements are prepared by businesses and used by different stakeholders in their decision making. Investors are looking for both understanding of how profit was created (analysis of the income statement) and being able to build an evaluation of the prognosis for survival of the firm. In this context, ratios (i.e., a metric that describes the relation between two variables that are key to the success of the firm) may prove to be useful in providing a quick idea about the soundness of the financial structure and the quality of the financial performance of the company. Although financial statement analysis will be revisited in almost all the following chapters and specifically in Chapter 15, we wanted to introduce some basic ratios right now to reinforce the message of usefulness of financial statements.

Balance sheet ratios

Short-term liquidity ratios

The following ratios assess the firm's ability to finance its day-to-day operations and to pay its liabilities as they fall due.

> **Current ratio =**
> Current assets/Current liabilities (amounts falling due within one year)

The current ratio shows the firm's ability to pay its current liabilities from its current assets, i.e., the probability that a slowdown in the economy or in the operating cycle will place the firm in a difficult liquidity position.

> **Cash ratio =**
> (Cash + Marketable securities)/Current liabilities

The objective of the cash ratio is to evidence the firm's ability to pay its current liabilities from its cash and cash equivalents (i.e., the ability of the firm to cover its short-term obligations even without having to wait until the end of the operating cycle).

> **Average collection period =**
> [(Accounts receivable Year 2 + Accounts receivable Year 1)/2 × 365]/Sales

The average length of time to collect accounts receivable is an important indicator relating to the management of receivables but also a metric describing part of the operating cycle. The longer the collection period, the longer the cycle is that transforms cash into cash again. The longer the operating cash to cash cycle is, the more long-term financing the firm needs.

Long-term solvency ratios

The objective is now to determine the firm's ability to pay its long-term liabilities.

> **Long-term debt to equity ratio =**
> Long-term debt/Equity

This ratio is often known as the degree of financial leverage. If two, well nigh equivalent firms differ only on this ratio, the one with the highest leverage will provide the better return to their shareholders (interest expense is not proportional to sales but to the level of indebtedness, all things being equal). But, of course, that firm is also the one that takes a higher risk because it has more external debt than the lesser leveraged firm. If a firm is too leveraged, the interest expense that arises from the long-term debt may place that firm in a difficult position in terms of profitability.

Income statement ratios

The main ratios are known as "profitability ratios" as they measure the firm's performance.

> **Return on sales (net profit margin) =**
> Net income/Sales

This ratio computes the percentage of each sales currency unit that contributes to net income. It can be used internally to compare markets or customers and externally to compare the firm with others in the same sector (same risk and opportunities environment).

> **Return on shareholders' equity (ROE) =**
> Net income/Average equity[4] (or Income before interest and tax/Average equity)

This ratio emphasizes the return to shareholders, i.e., the profit generated during a period on the capital invested by the shareholders.

> **Return on investment (ROI) (return on capital employed or ROCE) =**
> Net income/(Average long-term liabilities + Average equity) = Net income/Capital employed or Earnings before interest and tax (EBIT)/Capital employed

This ratio measures the income earned on invested capital.

> **Return on assets (ROA) =**
> Net income/[(Assets Year 2 + Assets Year 1)/2]

This ratio measures the firm's ability to use its assets to create profits.

- Financial statements include a minimum set of documents: balance sheet, income statement, and notes. Additionally, they may comprise a cash flow statement and a statement of changes in equity.
- A balance sheet is a set of two lists of resources on one side (also called assets) and of obligations to external parties on the other side (liabilities to creditors and residual interest due to the shareholders or owners). The two lists must be equal in value or balanced.
- Shareholders' equity represents the obligation the firm has towards its shareholders or the claim the owners of the business have collectively over the firm's current net worth and potential future wealth.
- The balance sheet can be represented by an equation: Assets (resources) = Liabilities (obligations to third parties) plus Equity (claims of shareholders).
- An asset is a resource controlled by an enterprise as a result of past events and from which future economic benefits are expected to flow to the enterprise.
- A liability is a present obligation of the enterprise arising from past events. Its settlement is expected to result in an outflow from the enterprise of resources generating economic benefits.
- An income statement describes the processes through which income of the period was created and thus how retained earnings have been modified.
- Revenues are increases in shareholders' equity that originate from the business of the company such as a sale of goods or services or interest received from short-term investment.
- Expenses are decreases in shareholders' equity that originate from the business of the company such as services purchased, salaries paid to the employees, rent paid for the use of certain physical facilities, wear and tear on equipment, etc.
- Net income is thus the difference between total revenue and total expenses recorded during a period.
- Retained earnings represent that part of the value created through the firm's operations that shareholders have chosen not to take out of the firm.
- Net income is different from cash.
- Notes to financial statements constitute a clarification and a supplement to the balance sheet and the income statement.
- Depreciation is the recognition of the consumption of a fixed asset.
- Profit appropriation is the decision taken by the shareholders to distribute entirely, partially, or not at all the profit of the year.

REVIEW

Review 2.1 Vivaldi Company (1)

Topic: Transactions and the business equation
Type: Individual exercise
Related part of the chapter: Core/Advanced Issues

Vivaldi Company is a retailer. During one accounting period it carried the following transactions.

A Creation of the business and provision by shareholders of assets in the amount of 40 and of cash for 60 CU.

B Purchase merchandise for resale: 40 (on account).

C Advertising expense: 7 (on account).

D Sale of merchandise to customers (on account): 120 CU. The merchandise that was sold had been purchased for 30 CU.

E Personnel expenses for the period: salaries 30, social charges and fringe benefits 15 (these will be paid out in cash during the next period).

F Miscellaneous business taxes: 20 (will be paid cash during the next period).

G Cash received from customers (who had bought on account): 60 CU.

H Payment to the merchandise suppliers: 35.

I Payment of salaries: 30.

J The assets brought as a capital contribution when the business was created are expected to have a useful life of 10 years. The loss of value of the asset is expected to be the same each year for 10 years.

K The value of the merchandise on hand at the end of the year (ending inventory) is 10.

Required

1 Show the impact of each event on the basic business equation (recording the purchases of merchandise in expenses).

2 Prepare the year-end balance sheet reflecting the events listed in A to K.

3 Prepare the income statement for the period reflecting the events listed in A to K.

Solution

1 Basic business equation (see opposite)

2 Preparation of the year-end balance sheet

Assets		Liabilities	
Fixed assets (equipment)	40	Capital	100
Equipment depreciation	–4	Net income	14
Fixed assets (net value)	36	Accounts payable (40 + 7 – 35)	12
Merchandise inventory	10	Salaries and social expenses payable	
Accounts receivable (120 – 60)	60	(30 + 15 – 30)	15
Cash at bank (60 + 60 – 35 – 30)	55	Taxes payable	20
Total	161	Total	161

	Cash	+ Accounts receivable	+ Merchandise inventory	+ Equipment	− Accumulated depreciation	= Taxes payable	+ Salaries payable	+ Accounts payable	+ Retained earnings	+ Share capital	Details of SE transactions
(A)	+60			+40						+100	Initial investment
(B)								+40	−40		Purchases of merchandise
(C)								+7	−7		External expense
(D)		+120							+120		Sales of merchandise
(E)							+45		−45		Personnel expenses
(F)						+20			−20		Tax expenses
(G)	+60	−60									
(H)	−35										
(I)	−30						−30	−35			
(J)					4				−4		Depreciation expenses
(K)			+10						+10		Change in inventory
End balance	55	+ 60	+ 10	40	− 4	= 20	+ 15	+ 12	+ 14	+ 100	

Assets = **161**

Liabilities + Shareholders' equity (SE) = **161**

3 Preparation of the income statement

Expenses		Revenues	
Purchases of merchandise	40	Sales of merchandise	120
Change in inventory of merchandise	−10		
Other purchases and external expenses	7		
Taxes	20		
Personnel expenses (30 + 15)	45		
Depreciation expenses	4		
Net income	14		
Total	120	Total	120

Remarks

- The balance sheet is itself an account which is documented by the balances of all balance sheet subsidiary accounts. The profit or the loss is itself the balance of the balance sheet account.

- The income statement is the account that records the balances of all the expense and revenue accounts. Income (profit or loss) is the balance of the income statement.

- The income is the same, by construction, in the balance sheet and the income statement.

Review 2.2 Vivaldi Company (2)

Topic: Transactions and impact on the financial statements
Type: Individual exercise
Related part of the chapter: Core/Advanced Issues

Refer to the Vivaldi (1) exercise.

Required

Record the transactions in the appropriate accounts.

Solution

Equipment	Accumulated depreciation of equipment	Capital
(A) 40	(J) 4	(A) 100
Balance = 40	Balance = 4	Balance = 100

Inventory	Accounts receivable	Accounts payable	Salaries and social security payable

(K) 10	(D) 120 (G) 60	(H) 35 (B) 40
		       (C) 7
		 35 47
			(I) 30 30 (E)
			       15 (E)
			 30 45

Balance = 10	Balance = 60	Balance = 12	Balance = 15

Cash at bank	Taxes payable
(A) 60 (H) 35 (G) 60 (I) 30 120 65	(F) 20
Balance = 55	Balance = 20

Expenses   **Income statement**   Revenues

Purchases of merchandise	Sales of merchandise
(B) 40	(D) 120
Change in inventory of merchandise	
(K) 10	
Other purchases and external expenses	
(C) 7	
Taxes	
(F) 20	
Personnel expenses	
(E) 30	
(E) 15	
Depreciation expense	
(J) 4	

Assignments

Assignment 2.1

Multiple-choice questions
Type: Individual exercise
Related part of the chapter: Core/Advanced Issues

Select the right answer (only one possible answer unless otherwise stated).

1 **Raw materials and merchandise purchased can be included in (two solutions)**

  (a) Cash
  (b) Expenses
  (c) Fixed assets
  (d) Current assets
  (e) None of these

2 **Obtaining a long-term loan affects which of the following accounts**

  (a) Operating liabilities
  (b) Financial liabilities
  (c) Shareholders' equity
  (d) Retained earnings
  (e) None of these

3 **Land, buildings, furniture, and computers are included in**

  (a) Current assets
  (b) Fixed assets
  (c) Cash
  (d) Inventory
  (e) None of these

4 **The document reporting all the expenses and revenues for a given period is the**

  (a) Balance sheet
  (b) Cash flow statement
  (c) Income statement
  (d) Notes to financial statement
  (e) Statement of changes in equity
  (f) None of these

5 **A balance sheet is presented**

  (a) Only after profit appropriation
  (b) Only before profit appropriation
  (c) Before or after profit appropriation
  (d) None of these

6 **An income statement is presented**

  (a) Only after profit appropriation
  (b) Only before profit appropriation
  (c) Before or after profit appropriation
  (d) None of these

7 **Advance payments received from customers are included in**

  (a) Revenues
  (b) Assets
  (c) Liabilities
  (d) Shareholders' equity
  (e) Expenses
  (f) None of these

8 **Advance payments to suppliers are included in**

  (a) Revenues
  (b) Assets
  (c) Liabilities
  (d) Shareholders' equity
  (e) Expenses
  (f) None of these

9 The depreciation recorded in the balance sheet includes

    (a) Accumulated depreciation for past years

    (b) Depreciation for the current year

    (c) Both

    (d) None of these

10 An example of an item that is not a current asset is

    (a) Accounts receivable

    (b) Inventory

    (c) Equipment

    (d) Cash

    (f) None of these

Assignment 2.2 Vivaldi Company (3)

Topic: Transactions and the business equation
Type: Individual exercise
Related part of the chapter: Core/Advanced Issues

Refer to Vivaldi (1) exercise.

Required

1 Show the impact of each event on the accounting equation (recording the purchases of merchandise in inventory in the balance sheet).

2 Prepare the year-end balance sheet reflecting the events listed in A to K.

3 Prepare the income statement for the period reflecting the events listed in A to K.

Assignment 2.3 Corelli Company

Topic: Classification of accounts
Type: Individual exercise
Related part of the chapter: Core/Advanced Issues

Corelli Company provides the following listing (in alphabetical order) of all the accounts it uses (far left column). For each line you are provided five choices of families of accounts to which the account listed on the left can be related.

Required

Indicate by a checkmark to which account family or families each account is related.

	Assets	Shareholders' equity	Liabilities	Revenues	Expenses
Accounts payable					
Accounts receivable					
Accumulated depreciation					
Administrative expense					
Advance payments received from customers					
Advance payments to suppliers					
Buildings					
Cash at bank					
Cash on hand					
Computing equipment					

continued overleaf

	Assets	Shareholders' equity	Liabilities	Revenues	Expenses
Cost of goods sold					
Financial debts					
Finished products					
Income tax expense					
Income tax payable					
Industrial equipment					
Insurance expense					
Interest expense					
Interest revenue					
Loans					
Marketable securities					
Merchandise					
Net income					
Purchases of merchandise					
Purchases of supplies					
Raw materials					
Repair and maintenance expense					
Reserves					
Retained earnings					
Salaries payable					
Salary expense					
Sales of merchandise					
Selling expense					
Share capital					
Social security payable					

Assignment 2.4 Stora Enso*

Topic: Financial statement analysis
Type: Group exercise
Related part of the chapter: Advanced Issues

Stora Enso is a Finnish company involved in paper production. From its 1999 and 1998 annual reports we extracted the following balance sheets and income statements, which have been prepared in accordance with International Accounting Standards. (The figures for 1997 have been converted from Finnish marks to euros – 1 euro = 5.94573 markka.)

Consolidated balance sheet (€ millions)			
Assets	31 Dec. 1999	31 Dec. 1998	31 Dec. 1997
Fixed assets and other long-term investments			
Intangible assets	60.3	42.0	42.2
Goodwill on consolidation	466.4	540.5	509.4
Property, plant, and equipment	10,717.6	10,424.6	10,731.5
Shares, associated companies	165.5	334.1	317.9
Shares, other companies	280.4	128.8	57.0
Capital investment shares	49.3	48.0	37.9
Non-current loan receivables	66.8	90.1	77.8
Deferred tax assets	5.9	7.8	11.6
Other non-current assets	88.6	79.2	78.6
	11,900.8	11,695.1	11,863.9

Current assets

	31 Dec. 1999	31 Dec. 1998	31 Dec. 1997
Inventories	1,265.6	1,332.3	1,289.1
Tax assets	71.9	3.4	0.3
Short-term receivables	2,090.4	1,783.4	2,040.5
Short-term investments and receivables	265.9	250.4	110.0
Cash and cash equivalents	439.4	348.5	249.7
	4,133.2	3,718.0	3,689.6
Total assets	16,034.0	15,413.1	15,553.5

Shareholders' equity and liabilities	31 Dec. 1999	31 Dec. 1998	31 Dec. 1997
Shareholders' equity			
Share capital	1,277.6	1,277.5	1,277.5
Restricted equity	698.2	704.6	736.1
Retained earnings	3,224.9	3,093.2	3,090.5
Profit for the period	752.5	191.0	409.0
	5,953.2	5,266.3	5,513.1
Minority interests	202.0	278.8	271.7
Long-term liabilities			
Pension provision	575.5	569.6	564.0
Deferred tax liability	1,488.9	1,326.6	1,373.8
Other provisions	186.5	256.0	121.5
Long-term debt	3,846.2	4,294.1	4,209.1
Other long-term liabilities	87.0	90.7	84.4
	6,184.1	6,537.0	6,352.8
Current liabilities			
Current portion of long-term debt	446.7	1,218.4	1,202.1
Short-term borrowings	1,476.6	475.4	590.1
Other current liabilities	1,507.8	1,451.7	1,485.6
Tax liability	263.6	185.5	138.1
	3,694.7	3,331.0	3,415.9
Total shareholders' equity and liabilities	16,034.0	15,413.1	15,553.5

Consolidated income statement

€ millions	1999	1998
Sales	10,635.7	10,489.6
Finished and semi-finished goods, decrease (–)	–119.4	41.8
Share of profits of associated companies	9.7	9.9
Other operating income	126.1	44.9
Materials and services	–4,843.3	–5,033.5
Freights and sales commissions	–993.5	–1,016.0
Personnel expenses	–1,754.3	–1,805.2
Depreciation and value adjustments	–885.4	–1,151.4
Other operating expenses	–757.5	–861.5
Operating profit	1,418.1	718.6
Financing	–266.6	–379.2
Profit before tax and minority items	1,151.5	339.4
Tax	–394.5	–148.2
Profit after taxes	757.0	191.2
Minority interests	–4.5	–0.2
Profit for the period	752.5	191.0

Required

1 Compute the ratios you feel are important for the evaluation of the business for the years 1999 and 1998.

2 Evaluate the evolution of the context (either use your common sense or visit the Stora Enso website at www.storaenso.com) and of the performance of the firm on the basis of these ratios. What risks seem to be increasing?

Notice that minority interests[5] are often included in equity in the computation of ratios based on this concept.

References

IASC (1997) International Accounting Standard No. 1, Presentation of Financial Statements, London.

IASC (2001) Glossary of terms in *International Accounting Standards*, bound volume, London.

Further readings

Additional material on the website

Go to http://www.thomsonlearning.co.uk/accountingandfinance/stolowylebas for further information, journal entries and extra assignments for each chapter.

The following appendices to this chapter are available on the dedicated website:

Appendix 2.1: Balance sheet and value creation

Appendix 2.2: Reporting for retained earnings and reserves

Notes

1 The snapshot, however, represents the picture only at its "historical" value. For example, a piece of land will be shown at its purchase price, even if events subsequent to the purchase may have modified the potential resale value of the land. If, for example, the development of a shopping area next to the plot has increased its value, such a change in value will not be recorded in the accounts. Accounting must be credible without ambiguity or debate. Since the value of a resource (exchange or resale value or potential to create sellable objects or services in the future) changes continuously, accounting practitioners have chosen long ago to prefer reliability over accuracy.

2 As indicated in the preface, the choice of the currency unit has no bearing on the logic of our presentation. We will specify the currency only when presenting real cases.

3 Each amount is recorded in an "account", i.e., a table with several columns that classifies entries between increase or decrease. There is an account for every type of resource or obligation, and therefore for revenue and expenses (cash, capital, accounts payable, etc.). By convention, accounts are often presented in the form of a T (thus the term T-account), separating movement in homogeneous categories on either side of the vertical bar of the T (see an illustration in Chapter 4).

4 Average equity = (Beginning shareholders' equity + Ending shareholders' equity)/2.

5 They represent the part of the net results of operations of a subsidiary attributable to interests which are not owned, directly or indirectly through subsidiaries, by the parent company (minority shareholders). This item will be presented in a more detailed manner in Chapter 13.

Financial statements presentation

In the first two chapters we briefly introduced three of the main documents that are part of the managerial information set called financial statements. These documents report the financial situation of the firm and are essential for the needs of decision makers and users of accounting information. They are the balance sheet, the income statement, and the notes to financial statements.

The 4th European directive (EU 1978) specifies in its article 2 that: "The annual accounts shall comprise the balance sheet, the profit and loss account and the notes on the accounts". A large majority of countries, whether part of the European Union or not, require at least these three documents. Many countries add the cash flow statement (see later and Chapter 14) and/or a statement of changes in shareholders' equity (see Chapter 11) to the required reporting package to be sure investors, accounting information users, and shareholders are well informed about the situation of a business.

In its Accounting Standard no. 1 (IASC 1997: § 7), the International Accounting Standards Committee (IASC) offers a definition of **financial statements** by stating that "a complete set of financial statements includes the following components:

(a)   balance sheet;

(b)   income statement;

(c)   a statement showing either:

   –   all changes in equity; or

   –   changes in equity other than those arising from capital transactions with owners and distributions to owners;

Major topics

Balance sheet

Income statement

Notes to financial statements

Cash flow statement

Annual report

Terminology

(d)   cash flow statement; and

(e)   accounting policies and explanatory notes."

The purpose of this chapter is to develop further the three core components of financial statements (balance sheet, income statement, and notes), and to briefly introduce the cash flow statement, which will be fully developed in Chapter 14.

As mentioned earlier, the issue of comparability of financial situation of firms is essential for accounting information users. However, this objective of ease of comparability is far from being achieved today. Many countries have either encouraged, required, or accepted a diversity of formats of presentation of the key documents. Each presentation emanates from a certain vision of the business model financial statements are supposed to describe. Chapter 2 already mentioned that the order in which assets and liabilities are listed in a balance sheet depends on the choice of the image the firm wants to give to information users (or the regulatory authorities want businesses to give). For example, a firm is secure because it has solid productive capacity or solid because it is very liquid. Neither choice is intrinsically better. Each is coherent with a certain philosophy and communication approach.

This chapter will be an opportunity to explore the different presentations of a content that is essentially the same. We will focus on the format of the statements and not on specific accounts which will only be introduced in later chapters.

CORE ISSUES

As mentioned in the IASC Conceptual Framework (IASC 1989: § 47): "Financial statements portray the financial effects of transactions and other events by grouping them into broad classes according to their economic characteristics. These broad classes are termed the elements of financial statements".

Balance sheet

Definition

The **balance sheet** shows the financial position of a business on a given date. The IASC specifies that "the elements directly related to the measurement of financial position are assets, liabilities and equity" (IASC 1989: § 49).

Possible presentations

The key choices are essentially pertaining to format of the list and to the degree of fineness (single or multiple step) and the type of classification (by term or by nature; see Figure 3.1)

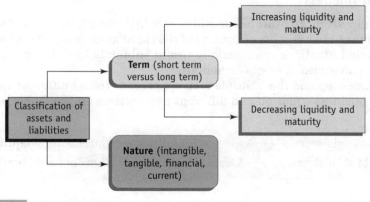

Figure 3.1 Presentations of the balance sheet

Formats

The balance sheet is a list of account balances. The list can be continuous (vertical format; see Figure 3.2), or presented as two lists side by side (horizontal format; see Figure 3.3).

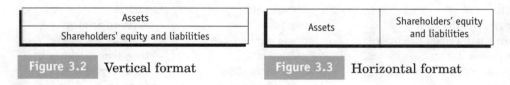

Figure 3.2 Vertical format   **Figure 3.3** Horizontal format

The "horizontal" format is often represented as two blocks as in Figure 3.4.

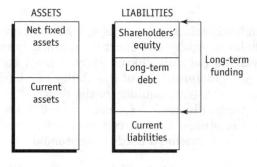

Figure 3.4 Balance sheet format

Degree of fineness

The **"single-step" format** list provides very little detail, while the **"multiple-step" format** creates a list of subsets of the three main categories of assets and liabilities and identifies managerially useful subtotals by subtracting relevant other sub-categories of assets or liabilities.

The single-step and the multiple-step approaches reflect different readings of the basic business equation and different perspectives on the firm's position:

Single-step	→	Assets = Liabilities + Shareholders' equity
Multiple-step	→	Assets − Liabilities = Shareholders' equity

The examples of multiple-step format provided in Table 3.1 illustrate the fact that any balance sheet presentation is essentially a specific expansion of the business equation.

Table 3.1   Balance sheet examples using the "multiple-step" vertical format

Example 1	Example 2	Example 3
Assets	Current assets	Capital
− Current liabilities	− Current liabilities	+ Retained earnings
= Assets minus current liabilities	= Working capital	= Shareholders' equity
− Non-current liabilities	+ Fixed assets	+ Long-term liabilities
= Total net assets	− Long-term liabilities	= Long-term sources
= Equity	= Shareholders' equity	− Fixed assets
Control: Net asset = Equity	− Retained earnings	= Working capital
	= Capital	− Current assets
		= Current liabilities

Example 1 highlights shareholders' equity while example 2 focusses attention on both shareholders' equity and short-term liquidity of the firm. Meanwhile, example 3 highlights not only shareholders' equity, but also the structure of long-term financing (determinant of the ability of a business to be an ongoing venture), and the short-term liquidity of the firm.

None of the three illustrated formats provides an intrinsically superior presentation to the others. Each is coherent with a certain vision of the firm and the perceived informational needs of shareholders.

Classifications of assets and liabilities

Assets and liabilities can be classified on the basis of either the cycle time of their transformation into cash (short term versus long term, or fixed versus current), or by nature of asset (tangible versus intangible, or financial versus operating).

Short-term versus long-term or current versus fixed

For example, liabilities can be classified in the following subsets:

- Long-term (non-current) liabilities (amounts falling due after more than one year):
  - financial debts (long-term portion)
  - accounts payable (for payables due in more than one year).
- Short-term (current) liabilities (amounts falling due within one year):
  - financial debts (short-term portion)
  - bank overdrafts
  - accounts payable (for which the due date is typically less than 1 year from the date of reference for the balance sheet).

A parallel classification must also be applied to assets: long-term assets will be recognized as fixed assets (the stream of economic benefits they create for the firm extends beyond one year) and will be distinguished from short-term or current assets which are part of the normal **operating cycle** illustrated in Figure 3.5.

IAS 1 (IASC 1997: § 54) specifies that, and many countries' regulation concur: "An enterprise should disclose, for each asset and liability item that combines amounts expected to be recovered or settled both before and after twelve months from the balance sheet date, the amount expected to be recovered or settled after more than twelve months."

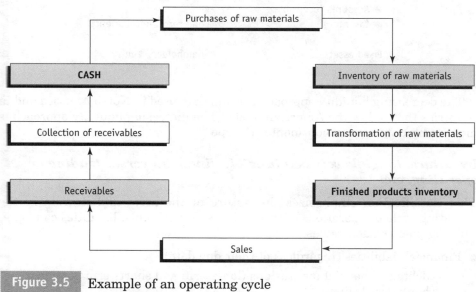

Figure 3.5 Example of an operating cycle

The four current assets in Figure 3.5 are chronologically: cash, inventory of raw materials, finished goods inventory, and accounts receivable. They are "used" more than once during the operating cycle of the firm.

When the balance sheet is presented according to the length of the transformation cycle into cash, two approaches exist: increasing (Table 3.2) or decreasing (Table 3.3) order of liquidity. Each approach emphasizes a different point: long-term strength or short-term liquidity. Neither one is, however, intrinsically superior to the other one.

Table 3.2 Increasing liquidity and maturity

Assets	Shareholders' equity and liabilities
Fixed assets	Shareholders' equity
Current assets: ● Inventory ● Accounts receivable ● Cash	Liabilities: ● Long term (non-current) ● Short term (current)

Table 3.3 Decreasing liquidity and maturity

Assets	Liabilities and shareholders' equity
Current assets: ● Cash ● Accounts receivable ● Inventory	Liabilities: ● Short term (current) ● Long term (non-current)
Fixed assets	Shareholders' equity

The decreasing liquidity approach is commonly used in North America and in countries that follow the American model. The increasing liquidity approach is more commonly used in continental Europe.

By nature: tangible versus intangible, financial versus trading or operating, etc.

This classification emphasizes the nature of the asset and its role in the operating cycle or operations of the business. For example, liabilities can be, in this approach, structured as:

● Financial liabilities (regardless of their due date):
  – debts to financial institutions (long-term and short-term portions)
  – bank overdrafts.
● Trading (or operating) liabilities (debt linked to trading and relations with other partners):
  – advance payments received from customers on contracts to be delivered in the future
  – accounts payable (debt contracted from suppliers in the course of running the business)
  – debt to tax authorities.

On the asset side a parallel distinction will apply. Financial assets are financial investments or a loan to an associate, while trading assets are connected to the cycle of operations. Inventories and accounts receivable are considered to be trading assets.

Trading and operating liabilities and trading and operating assets are generally referred to as "current liabilities" or "current assets". In this context, the term "current" is not synonymous with "short term" but means "related to the operating cycle of the business".

Income statement

Definition

The **income statement** reports the revenues and expenses incurred during a period and serves to establish the net income. Net income is the remainder after all expenses have been deducted from revenues. It is a measure of the wealth created by an economic entity (increased shareholders' equity) during an accounting period. The income statement reports how the company's financial performance was achieved.

Possible presentations

As was the case for the balance sheet, there are several ways of presenting an income statement (horizontal or vertical format) and a choice of degree of fineness as well as of types of account classifications (see Figure 3.6).

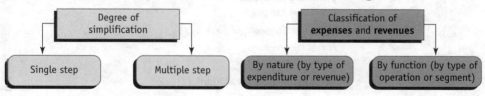

Figure 3.6 Choices in the presentation of income statements

Formats

An income statement is a list of account balances. The list can be presented as a continuous list (vertical format), or as two lists side by side (horizontal format; see Figure 3.7).

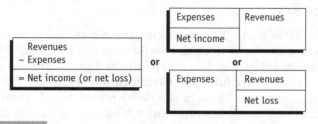

Figure 3.7 Vertical versus horizontal presentations

Although not commonly used in business reporting, the horizontal format is very practical in a pedagogical context. We will often present the income statement in the form of a T-account.

Degree of fineness

Expenses are first grouped in homogeneous meaningful categories, and then deducted step by step from revenues. The choice is between single and multiple steps.

Single step

It is the most simplified version of the income statement. Expenses and revenues are each considered as one category (see for example the left panel of Figure 3.7).

Multiple step

Revenue and expense categories are paired so as to highlight the components of total net income (see Table 3.4). For example, trading revenue and trading expenses will be grouped to create the trading income. Financial revenues and expenses will be offset against one another to inform the users about the role of the financial activity in total net income. This format is also used in reporting income by segments such as types of business, product, market, region, etc. (see Chapter 15).

Table 3.4 Example of multiple-step income statement (vertical)

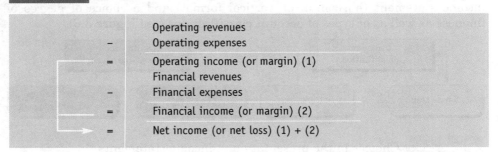

		Operating revenues
–		Operating expenses
	=	Operating income (or margin) (1)
		Financial revenues
–		Financial expenses
	=	Financial income (or margin) (2)
	=	Net income (or net loss) (1) + (2)

This rich format of reporting income is the most commonly used in business reports because it is more informative than the single-step approach. Its usefulness rests on the ability for the firm to separate revenue and expenses on sound and meaningful bases, without using rules of allocation that would create doubt about the usefulness for decision making of the sub-categories of the net income.

Classification of expenses

IASC (1997: §§ 77–85) states that: "Expense items are sub-classified in order to highlight a range of components of financial performance, which may differ in terms of stability, potential for gain or loss and predictability." This information is provided either by nature or by function. Classification issues are especially important for operating expenses. Thus, in the development in this chapter we do not explore classification schemes beyond those of operating income as most other sources of income are self-explanatory.

Classification by nature (or "nature of expenditure method")

Expenses are aggregated in the income statement directly according to their nature (for example, purchases of materials, transportation costs, taxes other than income tax, salaries and social expenses, depreciation, etc.) (see Table 3.5). This method is simple to apply, even in small enterprises, because no allocation or partition of expenses or costs is required.

Classification by function (or "cost of sales method")

This method classifies expenses according to their role in the determination of income (cost of goods sold, commercial, distribution or administrative expenses are common distinctions in this case) (see Table 3.6).

Table 3.5	Table 3.6
Income statement by nature (vertical)	Income statement by function (vertical)

Net sales + Other operating revenues − Purchases of merchandise − Change in inventories of merchandise − Labor and personnel expenses − Other operating expenses − Depreciation expense = Operating income	Net sales revenue − Cost of goods sold (cost of sales) = Gross margin − Commercial and distribution expenses − Administrative expenses − Other operating expenses = Operating income

Choice of a classification approach

The criteria "degree of fineness" and "classification of expenses" are not exclusionary and can form a 2 × 2 matrix. For example, an income statement by nature can be presented according to the single- or the multiple-step method. An income statement prepared according to the functional approach can be either single or multiple step. The "horizontal × functional" approach is, however, rather rare and thus is ignored here.

No single format of the multiple-step approach appears to be dominating in practice. Each firm chooses the representation that best communicates its intended emphasis on specific points and messages:

● Preference for a classification by nature often reflects pressure exercised by some governmental statistics agencies to ease their own work of consolidation of income and expenses in their preparation of the national accounts (this is often the case in continental and East European countries[1]). Such a presentation is often difficult to decipher by users, especially if they want, as is the purpose of financial reporting, to make forecasts.

● Preference for a functional presentation often reflects an emphasis on the income creation process. It is the preferred method in North America and is also used by most firms quoted on the New York Stock Exchange. The informational content of such annual statements is easily understandable and usable by ordinary users.

The IASC chooses sides by stating that the presentation by function "provides more relevant information to users than the classification of expenses by nature" (IASC 1997: § 82). It draws the attention of the report preparer, in the very same paragraph, to the fact that "the allocation of costs to functions can be arbitrary and involves considerable judgment". However paragraph 84 recognizes that "the choice of analysis between the cost of sales method and the nature of expenditure method depends on both historical and industry factors and the nature of the organization". Both methods provide an indication of those costs, which might be expected to vary, directly or indirectly, with the level of sales or production of the enterprise.

Proponents of the classification by nature highlight the fact that this method may allow for a user-specific analysis of the performance of the firm. They point out that, in theory, the cost of goods sold (or the cost of sales) can be reconstructed to suit the analysis of the user. However, most reports presented by nature fail to offer any partition of key natures of expenses between manufacturing and selling. Proponents of the classification by function highlight the fact that gross profit and the commercial and distribution expenses are two key figures in monitoring the performance of a business and are easily understandable by any user.

In conclusion, we will not choose sides and will agree with IASC that "each method of presentation has merit for different types of enterprise" (IASC 1997: §84). We will go further and acknowledge the fact that the choice between classifications must be in favor of that which "most fairly presents the elements of the enterprise's performance".

However, since information on the nature of expenses can prove useful in predicting future cash flows, additional disclosure must be provided when the classification by function ("cost of sales") is used. Depreciation and amortization (a concept equivalent to depreciation and applied to intangible assets – see Chapter 8) must critically be disclosed in a footnote or in the cash flow statement. It can prove useful for forecasting purposes, especially in internal reporting, to break up the cost of goods sold through a local application of the "by nature" approach, distinguishing consumption of consumables, raw materials and parts from labor, and services purchased from third parties.

In the second part of this chapter we will sketch the landscape of practice in the domain of income statement presentation in several countries.

Notes to financial statements

Principles

Since the purpose of the financial statements is to give a true and fair view of a business's financial performance, the **notes to the financial statements** (often called "footnotes") are essential. They will allow for the provision of any additional information the format of presentation selected failed to communicate since no format of presentation is actually perfect or serves the interests of all parties.

The European Union emphasizes this point in stating in article 2 of the 4th European Directive that "these documents" (the financial statements, including the notes) "shall constitute a composite whole". The notes should not be forgotten or omitted by preparers, a practice that was quite common on the part of medium and small enterprises before the publication of the 4th Directive.

IAS 1 (IASC 1997: § 91) states that the purposes of the notes are the following:

● To "present information about the basis of preparation of the financial statements and the specific accounting policies selected and applied for significant transaction and events."

- To "disclose information required by International Accounting Standards that is not presented elsewhere in the financial statements."
- To "provide additional information which is not presented on the face of the financial statements but that is necessary for a fair presentation."

Notes to the statements are a set of qualitative and quantitative comments or specification of hypotheses required to provide a really "true and fair view" of both the financial position of the firm and of its financial performance over the previous period and periods. They state the valuation hypotheses used and principles followed by management in establishing the figures that are in the financial statements.

Notes should not, however, become so cumbersome that they defeat their purpose of clarification. They should be reserved for remarks that are significant and may have a material effect on the meaning of figures.

Table 3.7 offers a list of some commonly found remarks in notes to financial statements.

| Table 3.7 | Example of information found in the notes |

Qualitative information	Quantitative information
Accounting policies: ● Accounting principles ● Basis of consolidation Measurement bases Specific accounting policy	Fixed assets – movements for the year Depreciation – movements for the year Amortization and provision – movements for the year Analysis of debt by maturity

Real-life example

The structure of the notes to the 1999 financial statements of Munksjö, a Swedish company that operates in four business areas (paper, packaging, pulp, and hygiene) is presented below (*source*: annual report 1999).

Accounting principles (accounting and valuation principles)
- Consolidated accounts
  - Definition of group companies
  - Consolidation principles
  - Treatment of untaxed reserve
  - Translation of foreign subsidiaries accounts
  - Accounting for associated companies
- Other accounting and valuation principles
  - Receivables and liabilities in foreign currencies
  - Valuation of stock and receivables
  - Tangible assets and leasing agreements
  - Planned depreciation
  - Work performed by the company for its own use and capitalized as asset
  - Shareholders' and group contributions
  - Deferred tax
  - Pension commitments

Notes

Operating income	Shares in associated companies
Other external costs	Other financial assets
Personnel	Stock
Planned depreciation	Receivables from operations
Items affecting comparability	Cash and bank balances
Result from participation in subsidiaries	Shareholders' equity
Participation in associated companies	Share capital
Interest income and similar items	Untaxed reserves
Interest expenses and similar items	Non-interest-bearing provisions
Taxes	Convertible loans
Intangible assets	Other long-term liabilities
Tangible assets	Operating liabilities
Group and the parent company shares and participation	Pledged assets and contingent liabilities

Cash flow statement

Although the **cash flow statement** is a required component of financial statements only in some countries, our position is that it constitutes an essential document for understanding the financial life of a business. The vision given through both balance sheet and income statement may appear to be restrictive because:

- the balance sheet offers only a static vision of the financial position
- the income statement, based on accruals, fails to show the importance of cash in the operation of the firm.

Cash is the blood of any organization as shown, for example, in Figure 3.5. Neither the balance sheet nor the income statement emphasizes the dynamics of the cash flowing in and out of the business. Comparing two consecutive balance sheets certainly allows the user to calculate the net change in cash position. However, that is not sufficient to understand *how* this change happened to be. Operations bring in and take out cash, but plenty of other events affect the cash balance such as additional cash contributions by shareholders, payment of dividends, acquisition or disposal of fixed assets, acquisition or granting of rights to operate specific technologies, etc. All these events need to be understood before the full meaning of the ending cash balance itself can be understood. Where did cash come from and what was it used for are the two key questions the cash flow statement will address.

We will present here only a brief outline of this statement and Chapter 14 will give us the opportunity to explore the document further. We do emphasize here, however, the relations between the three documents: balance sheet, income statement, and cash flow statement.

Accrual basis of accounting

The need for the cash flow statement arises from the choice made of the **accrual** approach for the recognition of revenue and expenses. IAS 1 (IASC

1997: § 25) states that: "An enterprise should prepare its financial statements, except for cash flow information, under the accrual basis of accounting." Under this method, transactions and events are recognized when they occur (and not as cash or its equivalent is received or paid) and they are recorded in the accounting records and reported in the financial statements of the periods to which they relate. Such a principle distinguishes modern accounting from cash basis accounting in which transactions and events are recorded at the time of the flow of cash they trigger. Accrual accounting creates a timing difference between recognition of revenue or expenses and their cash implications. The cash flow statement explains this timing difference.

Evolution

After many years of diversity of orientation and presentation, the cash flow statement has become a relatively standardized document. The requirement to publish one has spread rapidly from the mid-1980s. Canada was first in requiring a cash flow statement in 1985, followed by the USA (1987), France (1988), and the UK (1991). Most importantly, the cash flow statement became part of the standard reporting package required under IASC rules in 1992 reflecting an international generally accepted model. It offers a template that allows each country and tradition the possibility of attaching some specific (but minor) modifications to serve their particular needs.

According to the IAS 7 (IASC 1992: § 10): "The cash flow statement should report cash flows during the period classified by operating, investing and financing activities." This creates a document structured to distinguish three fundamental phases of life in an enterprise: operations, investing, and financing. Table 3.8 offers an illustration of the IASC model cash flow statement.

Table 3.8 Illustrative cash flow statement

Cash flows from operating activities		
Cash received from customers		80
Cash paid to suppliers and employees		−30
Net cash from operating activities	(1)	*50*
Cash flows from investing activities		
Purchase of property, plant and equipment		−15
Proceeds from sale of equipment		5
Net cash used in investing activities	(2)	*−10*
Cash flows from financing activities		
Proceeds from issuance of share capital		35
Proceeds from long-term borrowings		10
Dividends paid		−20
Net cash from financing activities	(3)	*25*
Net increase in cash and cash equivalents	**(4)=(1)+(2)+(3)**	**65**
Cash and cash equivalents at beginning of year	(5)	5
Cash and cash equivalents at end of year	(6)	70
Change in cash	(7)=(6)−(5)	65
Control	(4)=(7)	

Practically speaking, and without changing the logic of the approach, the cash flow statement can start with the opening cash balance and conclude with the closing balance. Then, using the same figures as previously, we can present the cash flow statement for the period as illustrated in Table 3.9.

Table 3.9 Cash flow statement – alternative presentation

Cash and cash equivalents at beginning of year	(1)	5
Net cash from operating activities	(2)	50
Net cash used in investing activities	(3)	–10
Net cash from financing activities	(4)	25
Cash and cash equivalents at end of year	(5)= (1)+(2)+(3)+(4)	70

Link between balance sheet, income statement and cash flow statement

The balance sheet, the income statement and the cash flow statement are totally linked as is shown in Figure 3.8. They form a closed system in which everything that happens in the life of the business is recorded so that the user of accounting information can understand very well how value was created (income statement) and how the liquidity of the firm (availability of cash) has been affected by operations and decisions during the period (cash flow statement). The balance sheet records the situation that is the outcome of the previously mentioned transactions recorded in the other two documents of the financial statements.

Each key relation is now explored in further detail. (Each number refers to Figure 3.8.)

❶ The cash balance in the opening balance sheet is the opening cash balance in the cash flow statement. This transfer from the balance sheet is not a flow of cash per se but only an accounting entry that is used to start the cash flow statement. The same line of reasoning will be used to transfer back the closing cash balance in the cash flow statement to the closing balance sheet.

❷ The income statement impact on the cash flow statement is through revenues and expenses collected or paid during the year.

❸ Revenues and expenses of the previous year that were not collected or paid during that year will, in principle, be collected or paid during the current year. They will impact the cash flow statement.

❹ Conversely, if revenues and expenses of the current period are not collected or paid during this period they will be in the following period. They are recognized as part of the receivables and payables balances in the closing balance sheet.

❺ Items in the opening balance sheet that are connected to investment or financing may also have an impact on the cash flow statement. For example, repaying all or part of the principal of a debt will generate a cash outflow, whereas proceeds from the sale of a fixed asset will create a cash inflow.

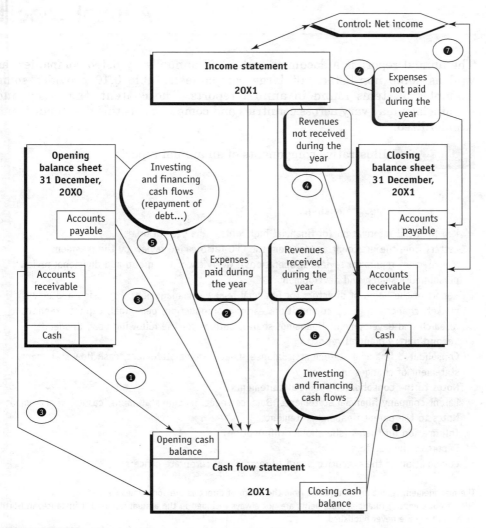

Figure 3.8 Link between balance sheet, income statement and cash flow statement

❻ Some investing or financing cash flows will also impact on the closing balance sheet. They can, for example, be the floatation of a new bond issue or the issuance of new share capital.

❼ When the income statement and closing balance sheet have been prepared, it is critical to double-check that the net income is the same in both documents. This is the closing relation to make sure the system is truly comprehensive and "balanced".

Figure 3.8 is illustrated through quantified examples in Review 3.3 "Beethoven Company".

The set of relations illustrated in Figure 3.8 can be used either from a historical (*ex post*) perspective in reports to shareholders and external users, but, most importantly, it can be and is used by managers and analysts alike in an anticipatory way (*ex ante*) to prepare a pro forma, budgeted or forecasted cash flow statement which will be used for decision making.

The annual report is a document published annually by listed companies (as well as some non-listed but large companies). Table 3.10 provides some examples of items found in annual reports. The content, the order, and terminology may vary across countries and companies, as this document is not standardized.

Table 3.10 Illustrative components of an annual report

First part: Business reporting

Key financial information (or financial highlights – the year in brief)
Letters from the president and/or from the CEO (also called review by the president)
Management report (or review of operations): Overview of the group and divisional reviews, personnel, research and development
Report of the board of directors (or financial review – management discussion and analysis): market, changes in group composition, earnings, production, personnel, capital expenditure, research and development, financing, shares, outlook for the following year, dividend
Second part: Financial reporting
Consolidated financial statements: Balance sheet, income statement, cash flow statement, statement of changes in equity
Notes to the consolidated financial statements
Parent company financial statements: Balance sheet, income statement, cash flow statement
Notes to the parent financial statements
Information on shares (shareholder information)
Report of the auditors
Composition of the executive board (directors and corporate officers)

The management report and the report from the board of directors are sometimes merged
The parent company financial statements are not always included in the annual report. For instance, in North America, they are never published
The consolidated and parent company financial statements are often mixed. This is particularly obvious in the notes (see for instance Irish, Nordic countries or UK annual reports)
The statement of movements of fixed assets (see Chapters 7 and 8) is often reported as a separate document after the balance sheet and income statement in Austria and Germany. Similarly, segment reports (see Chapter 15) are sometimes presented as a separate document in Austria

ADVANCED ISSUES

Balance sheet

This section provides illustrations of the various presentations of the balance sheets we introduced earlier.

European "models"

Practice in European countries is shaped by the 4th European Directive, which was issued in July 1978 (EU 1978). In the United Kingdom, for example, limited companies must use one of the two formats prescribed in the Companies Act. The two formats are illustrated in Tables 3.11 and 3.12 and are variations on the same "vertical balance sheet".

Table 3.11 UK format 1 – Multiple-step vertical balance sheet

Fixed assets	(1)	100
Current assets	(2)	70
Creditors (amounts falling due within one year)	(3)	–60
Net current assets/(liabilities)	(4)=(2+3)	10
Total assets minus current liabilities	(5)=(1+4)	110
Creditors (amounts falling due after more than one year)	(6)	–20
Provisions for liabilities and charges	(7)	–10
Total net assets	(8)=(5+6+7)	80
Capital and reserves	(9)	80
Total equity	(10)=(9)	80
The balance sheet balances with (10)=(8)		

Table 3.12 UK format 2 – Single-step vertical balance sheet

Fixed assets	(1)	100
Current assets	(2)	70
Total assets	(3)=(1+2)	170
Capital and reserves	(4)	80
Provisions for liabilities and charges	(5)	10
Creditors	(6)	80
Total equity and liabilities	(7)=(4+5+6)	170
The balance sheet balances with (7)=(3)		

In practice, most UK companies have adopted format 1 while most continental European firms tend to report under format 2.

US "model"

As opposed to a continental European balance sheet that reflects a patrimonial approach and thus lists fixed assets at the top, a North American approach tends to emphasize the short-term liquidity of the firm, and thus lists assets in the order of decreasing liquidity with fixed assets at the bottom of the list. Table 3.13 illustrates a "typical" North American balance sheet structure.

Table 3.13 A typical US balance sheet

ASSETS	
Current assets	
Cash and cash equivalents	
Accounts receivable	
Inventories	
Prepaid expenses and other current assets	
Total current assets	*(1)*
Fixed assets	
Investments	
Property, plant and equipment	
Intangible assets	
Total fixed assets	*(2)*
Total assets	**(3)=(1)+(2)**
LIABILITIES AND STOCKHOLDERS' EQUITY	
Current liabilities	
Accounts payable	
Income taxes payable	
Accrued expenses	
Dividends payable	
Current portion of long-term debt	
Total current liabilities	*(4)*
Long-term debt	
Borrowings	
Other long-term liabilities	
Total long-term debt	*(5)*
Stockholders' equity	
Capital stock	
Capital in excess of par value of stock	
Retained earnings	
Total stockholders' equity	*(6)*
Total liabilities and stockholders' equity	**(7) = (4)+(5)+(6)**
Balance	**(3)=(7)**

Synthesis

Appendix 3.1 summarizes the rules and most frequent practices regarding presentation of the balance sheet in a variety of countries.

Income statement

European "models"

The 4th European Directive (EU 1978) allows 4 formats by crossing in a 2 by 2 matrix the horizontal/vertical option with the nature/function option. Table 3.14 summarizes the principles underlying these formats.

Table 3.14 Income statement formats

Article of the 4th EU Directive	Vertical or horizontal format	Presentation by nature or by function
Art. 23	Vertical	Nature
Art. 24	Horizontal	Nature
Art. 25	Vertical	Function
Art. 26	Horizontal	Function

In the UK, for example, where the income statement is called profit and loss account (P&L), businesses are allowed to use any one of the four formats prescribed in the Companies Act which are the 4 EU-sanctioned formats. Tables 3.15 and 3.16 illustrate some of the most commonly found formats in the UK and in Europe in general.

Table 3.15 Article 25 format (vertical and by function)

Turnover (sales revenue)	(1)	100
Cost of sales (cost of goods sold)	(2)	−65
Gross profit (loss)	(3)=(1+2)	35
Commercial and Distribution costs	(4)	−5
Administrative expense	(5)	−21
Other operating income	(6)	9
Profit before interest and taxation (operating profit)	(7)=(3+4+5+6)	18
(EBIT = earnings before interest and taxation)		
Net interest income (charge)	(8)	−5
Profit on ordinary activities before taxation	(9)=(7+8)	13
Taxation on profit on ordinary activities	(10)	−8
Profit on ordinary activities after taxation	(11)=(9+10)	5
Extraordinary profit (loss)	(12)	3
Taxation on profit on extraordinary activities	(13)	−1
Profit (loss) for the financial year	(14)=(11+12+13)	7

Table 3.16 Article 23 format (vertical and by nature)

Turnover (sales revenue)	100
Change in stocks of finished goods and in work in progress	5
Own work capitalized	3
Other operating income	9
Raw materials and consumables consumed	−20
Other external charges	−25
Staff (labor) costs	−30
Depreciation and other amounts written off tangible and intangible fixed assets	−10
Exceptional amounts written off current assets	−4
Other operating charges	−10
Profit (earnings) before interest and taxation (operating profit) (EBIT)	18

In Table 3.16 we did not go beyond the level of operating profit as the remaining lines of the income statement are identical to those shown in Table 3.15.

US "model"

Table 3.17 illustrates a commonly found multiple-step income statement.

Table 3.17 US multi-step income statement

Net sales	(1)
Cost of goods sold	(2)
Gross profit	**(3)=(1)−(2)**
Selling and distribution expenses	(4)
Administrative expenses	(5)
Operating income	**(6)=(3)−(4)−(5)**
Interest expense	(7)
Gain or loss on sale of equipment	(8)
Pretax income from continuing operations	**(9)=(6)−(7)±(8)**
Income tax expense	(10)
Income from continuing operations	**(11)=(9)−(10)**
Discontinued operations (gain or loss on disposal)	(12)
Extraordinary items	(13)
Cumulative effect of change in accounting principle	(14)
Net income	**(15)= (11)±(12)±(13)±(14)**

Cost of goods sold

Expenses in the income statement by function are divided in three or four main categories:

- cost of sales (or **cost of goods sold**) (this concept is further developed in Appendix 3.2)
- selling and distribution expenses

- administrative expenses
- some companies add research & development (R&D) expenses to this list.

In order to compare presentations of an income statement by nature and by function, let us look at a quantified example. Brahms Company is a retailer. Its beginning inventory of merchandise is valued at 2,000 (all figures are in thousands of CU). During the period we are considering, Brahms Co. incurred total purchases of 8,000 and recorded invoicing customers for 17,000. The cost of the goods sold pertaining to these sales was 9,000. Thus the ending inventory of merchandise is 1,000 (i.e., 2,000 + 8,000 – 9,000). Labor and personnel expenses include the compensation of the sales force (4,000), and of the accounting and administration staff (2,000). The depreciation of administrative equipment for the period was estimated at 1,000.

Table 3.18 shows, side by side, the calculation of the operating income by nature and by function. As is clear from what we said earlier, the net operating income we will find under both approaches will, mechanically, be exactly the same. The possible interpretation and uses of the information contained in the income statement may, however, be different.

Table 3.18 Comparison between income statement by nature and by function

Income statement by nature		Income statement by function	
Sales of merchandise	17,000	Sales of merchandise	17,000
− Purchases of merchandise	−8,000	− Cost of goods sold	−9,000
− Merchandise inventory change (a)	−1,000	= Gross margin	8,000
− Personnel expenses (b)	−6,000	− Selling expenses (c)	−4,000
− Depreciation expenses	−1,000	− Administrative expenses (d)	−3,000
= Operating income	1,000	= Operating income	1,000
(a) beginning minus ending		(c) salesperson	
(b) 4,000 + 2,000		(d) 2,000 + 1,000	

Synthesis

Appendix 3.3 summarizes the rules and practices with regard to the presentation of the income statement in a variety of countries.

Terminology

As early as Chapter 2 we made it clear that differences existed between US and UK terminology. For example, we pointed out that the income statement in North America is generally called profit and loss account in the UK. However, since the vocabulary is not standardized within most countries, there exist plenty variations on a same theme as is the case in the United States. To make things somewhat more complex, the IASC tends to use its own terminology, which mixes both US and UK terminology, and leaves a lot of room for individual choices. However, comparability implies that any terminology covers definitions that are essentially coherent and we will therefore try to stay with one set of terms.

Table 3.19 recapitulates the differences and defines the terminology we will use in this text. Our choice has been to stay as close as possible to the IASC terminology but to make a clear choice when the official terminology leaves some leeway. We opted for simple options that reflect practice as reflected in the hundreds of annual reports we have consulted.

Table 3.19 Accounting terminology differences

USA	UK	IASC	Terminology used in this book
Financial statements	**Accounts**	**Financial statements**	**Financial statements**
Balance sheet			
Balance sheet (or statement of financial position)	Balance sheet	Balance sheet	Balance sheet
Long-term assets	Fixed assets	Non-current assets	Fixed assets
Real estate	Land and buildings	Land and buildings	Land and buildings
Property, plant and equipment	Tangible fixed assets	Property, plant and equipment	Tangible assets
Inventories	Stocks	Inventories	Inventories
Work in process	Work in progress	Work in progress	Work in progress
Receivables	Debtors	Receivables	Receivables
Accounts receivable	Trade debtors	Accounts receivable	Accounts receivable
Doubtful accounts	Bad debts, doubtful debts	Bad debts	Doubtful accounts
Allowance for doubtful accounts	Provision for doubtful debts	Allowance for bad debts	Provision for doubtful accounts
Treasury stock	Own shares	Treasury shares	Treasury shares
Stockholders' equity	Shareholders' equity, Shareholders' funds (or capital and reserves)	Shareholders' equity	Shareholders' equity
Common stock	Ordinary shares	Share capital	Share capital
Preferred stock	Preference shares	—	Preference shares
Additional paid-in capital	Share premium	—	Share premium
Retained earnings, retained income	Reserves, retained profit, profit and loss account	Reserves, accumulated profits (losses)	Retained earnings, retained income, reserves
Loans	Debts	Loans	Borrowings
Bonds, notes payable	Debenture loan	—	Bonds
Long-term liabilities	Creditors: Amounts falling due after more than one year	Non-current liabilities	Long-term liabilities
Payables	Creditors	Payables	Payables
Current liabilities	Creditors: Amounts falling due within one year	Current liabilities	Current liabilities
Accounts payable	Trade creditors	Accounts payable	Accounts payable
Income statement			
Income statement, statement of operations	Profit and loss account	Income statement	Income statement
Sales	Turnover	Revenue	Sales or sales revenue
Expense	Charge	Expense	Expense
Interest expense	Interest payable	Finance cost	Interest expense
Interest income	Interest received	—	Interest income
Income	Profit	Profit	Income
Others			
Statement of cash flows	Cash flow statement	Cash flow statement	Cash flow statement
Leverage	Gearing	—	Leverage
Stock	Share	Share	Share
Residual value, salvage value, terminal value	Scrap value	Residual value	Residual value
Declining balance method	Reducing balance method	—	Declining balance method
Pay check	Pay slip	—	Pay slip
Corporation	Company	—	Company
Conservatism	Prudence	Prudence	Prudence

KEY POINTS

- Financial statements include, as a minimum, a balance sheet, an income statement, and notes to financial statements. Additionally, they tend to also comprise a cash flow statement and a statement of changes in shareholders' equity.

- The several possibilities of presentation that exist for the balance sheet do not affect its generic content.

- There are several ways of presenting an income statement. They all provide the same bottom line.

- The choice between a presentation by nature or by function is debatable.

- The notes to the financial statements (often called "footnotes") are an essential component of the information provided through financial statements.

- The cash flow statement explains the timing difference existing between the recognition of revenues and expenses and their impact on cash.

- An annual report includes information on the activity of a company as well as financial information.

REVIEW

Review 3.1 Adidas*

Topic: Constructing an income statement
Type: Individual exercise
Related part of the chapter: Core Issues

Adidas is a German sporting good company. It acquired Salomon in 1998. The following lists in alphabetical order, items and amounts taken from the consolidated income statement for the accounting year ending on 31 December 1998, for Adidas alone, i.e., excluding the numbers resulting from the acquisition. All numbers are in millions of German marks (DM).

Cost of sales	−4,885	Minority interests	−18
Depreciation and amortization	−93	Net sales	8,441
Extraordinary income	24	Royalty and commission income	87
Financial result	−118	Selling, general, and administrative	
Income taxes	−208	expenses	−2,712

NB: Minority interests represent the part of the net results of operations of a subsidiary attributable to interests which are not owned, directly or indirectly through subsidiaries, by the parent company (minority shareholders). This item will be presented in a more detailed manner in the section in Chapter 13 devoted to consolidation.

Required

1 Reconstruct the income statement in a multiple-step format, showing separately gross profit, income from operations, income before taxes, net income before minority interests and net income. (Check figure: 518.)

2 Is the income statement organized by nature or by function?

Solution

1 Construct the income statement.

Income statement (millions of DM)	
	1998
Net sales	8,441
Cost of sales	−4,885
Gross profit	**3,556**
Selling, general, and administrative expenses	−2,712
Depreciation and amortization	−93
Income from operations	**751**
Royalty and commission income	87
Financial result	−118
Extraordinary income	24
Income before taxes	**744**
Income taxes	−208
Net income before minority interests	**536**
Minority interests	−18
Net income	**518**

2 Income statement format.

The income statement is organized by function, as we find the "cost of sales" and "selling, general, and administrative expenses".

Review 3.2 Statoil Group*

Topic: Constructing a balance sheet
Type: Individual exercise
Related part of the chapter: Core Issues

Statoil is a Norwegian company engaged in crude oil and oil derivatives, refined products, electricity, gas trade, and retailing. The following lists, in alphabetical order, items and amounts taken from the consolidated balance sheet as of 31 December 1999. All numbers are in millions of Norwegian kroner (NOK).

Accounts payable	24,544	Minority shareholders' interests	1,046
Accounts receivable	27,820	Other current liabilities	11,487
Current financial investments	9,525	Other receivables	11,543
Dividend payable	1,702	Provisions for liabilities and charges	32,540
Finished products	3,360	Raw materials	2,134
Intangible fixed assets	4,190	Retained earnings	35,624
Interest-bearing debt	3,858	Share capital	4,940
Investments	13,532	Tangible fixed assets	91,961
Liquid assets	4,072	Taxes payable	6,366
Long-term debt	46,030		

NB:
- Minority interests see note to Review 3.1.
- "Provisions for liabilities and charges" should be considered as a long-term liability.

Required

Prepare the balance sheet, showing separately fixed and current assets, shareholders' equity, long-term and current liabilities. (Check figure: total assets = 168,137.) The balance sheet should be drawn up in a horizontal increasing liquidity and maturity format.

Solution

Balance sheet as of 31 December, 1999 (in millions of NOK)			
ASSETS		**EQUITY AND LIABILITIES**	
FIXED ASSETS		**EQUITY**	
Intangible fixed assets	4,190	Share capital	4,940
Tangible fixed assets	91,961	Retained earnings	35,624
Investments	13,532	Minority shareholders' interests	1,046
Total fixed assets	**109,683**	**Total equity**	**41,610**
CURRENT ASSETS		**LIABILITIES**	
Inventories		*Provisions for liabilities and charges*	32,540
Raw materials	2,134		
Finished products	3,360	*Long-term debt*	46,030
Receivables		*Current liabilities*	
Accounts receivable	27,820	Interest-bearing debt	3,858
Other receivables	11,543	Accounts payable	24,544
		Taxes payable	6,366
Current financial investments	9,525	Dividend payable	1,702
Liquid assets	4,072	Other current liabilities	11,487
Total current assets	**58,454**	**Total current liabilities**	**47,957**
TOTAL ASSETS	**168,137**	**TOTAL EQUITY AND LIABILITIES**	**168,137**

This balance is presented by term, following an increasing liquidity and maturity approach.

Review 3.3 Beethoven Company

Topic: Link between balance sheet, income statement and cash flow statement
Type: Individual exercise
Related part of the chapter: Core Issues

Beethoven Company, a limited liability company that was incorporated in 20X1, has a commercial activity. It buys and sells books and CDs devoted to the learning of foreign languages. (The founder of the company speaks at least 10 languages fluently.)

The balance sheet at 31 December, 20X1 is presented as follows.

Balance sheet at 31 December, 20X1 (in 000 CU)			
ASSETS		**SHAREHOLDERS' EQUITY AND LIABILITIES**	
Fixed assets		*Shareholders' equity*	
Equipment (net value)	800	Capital	710
		Reserves	300
		Net income for 20X1 (a)	216
Current assets		*Liabilities*	
Merchandise inventory	150		
Accounts receivable (b)	400	Financial debt	110
		Accounts payable (c)	120
Cash at bank	250	Income tax payable (c)	144
Total	1,600	Total	1,600

a   to be appropriated in 20X2: one-third will be distributed
b   to be received in 20X2
c   to be paid in 20X2

The following budgeted figures are given for 20X2 (in 000 CU):

1   Sales budget: 1,600 (1,400 will be received from customers during the year).
2   Purchases budget (merchandise): 510 (400 will be paid to suppliers during the year).
3   Budgeted ending merchandise inventory:130.
4   Finance budget: repayment of financial debt for 80.
5   Salaries and social expenses budget: 430 (paid during the year).
6   Advertising expenses budget: 250 (paid during the year).
7   Miscellaneous taxes budget: 120 (paid during the year).
8   Depreciation budget: 40.
9   Fixed assets have been purchased: 300 (paid during the year).
The income tax rate is 40 %.

Required

Prepare the following documents: income statement, balance sheet and cash flow budget for the year 20X2.

Solution

Income statement (000 CU)			
Operating expenses		**Operating revenues**	
Purchases of raw materials	510	Sales	1,600
Merchandise inventory change (B – E)	20		
External expenses	250		
Miscellaneous taxes	120		
Personnel expenses	430		
Depreciation expense	40		
Financial expenses	0	**Financial income**	0
Exceptional expenses	0	**Exceptional income**	0
Subtotal	1,370	Subtotal	1,600
Income tax	92		
Net income	*138*	*Net loss*	*0*
Total	1,600	Total	1,600

Balance sheet (000 CU)

Fixed assets		Shareholders' equity	
Manufacturing equipment (net)	1,060	Capital	710
		Reserves	444
		Net income/loss	138
Current Assets		Subtotal	1,292
		Liabilities	
Merchandise inventory	130	Financial debts	30
		Bank overdraft	0
Accounts receivable	200	Accounts payable	110
Cash at bank	134	Income tax payable	92
Total	1,524	Total	1,524

Cash flow budget (000 CU)

Cash flows from operating activities	
Cash from sales	1,400
Cash from receivables (see preceding balance sheet)	400
Purchases for the year	−400
Accounts payable (see preceding balance sheet)	−120
Income tax payable	−144
Miscellaneous taxes	−120
Personnel expenses	−430
Advertising expenses	−250
Financial expenses	0
Net cash flows from operating activities (1)	*336*
Cash flows from investing activities	
Investments	−300
Other (sale of fixed assets)	0
Net cash flows used in investing activities (2)	*−300*
Cash flows from financing activities	
Other (capital)	0
Repayment of debts	−80
Dividends paid	−72
Net cash flows used in financing activities (3)	*−152*
Net increase (decrease) in cash and cash equivalents (4)=(1)+(2)+(3)	−116
Opening balance (5)	250
Ending balance (6)=(4)+(5)	134

Assignment 3.1

Industry identification
Type: Group exercise
Related part of the chapter: Core Issues[2]

Common-size statements and selected ratio values, related to the same financial year, are provided in Exhibit 1 for 6 well-known French companies. The name and some characteristics of these companies are given in Exhibit 2.

Required

Use your knowledge of general business practices to match the industries to the company data.

Exhibit 1 Common-size balance sheets						
	Company A %	Company B %	Company C %	Company D %	Company E %	Company F %
Balance sheet						
Assets						
Intangible fixed assets	0.1	0	0	0.1	0.1	1.0
Tangible fixed assets (net)	59.0	25.3	18.8	19.9	29.6	19.3
Financial fixed assets	20.8	15.9	17.5	21.9	25.6	3.6
Inventories	1.3	12.9	24.8	27.4	0	36.0
Accounts receivable	6.5	0.6	4.6	26.7	1.4	35.8
Other receivables	8.5	36.0	15.0	2.9	30.6	4.0
Cash	3.8	9.3	19.3	1.1	12.7	0.3
Total assets	100.0	100.0	100.0	100.0	100.0	100.0
Shareholders' equity and liabilities						
Capital and reserves	68.9	21.4	29.4	37.2	68.5	18.6
Net income	1.9	6.4	11.2	3.9	8.9	−4.9
Provisions for risks	11.9	1.1	0.1	0.4	6.0	0.5
Financial liabilities	4.3	12.8	13.4	21.2	12.3	21.2
Accounts payable	0.9	44.7	20.3	21.0	0.7	25.3
Other debts	12.1	13.6	25.6	16.3	3.6	39.3
Total equity and liabilities	100.0	100.0	100.0	100.0	100.0	100.0
Financial ratios						
Sales/total assets (%)	30	243	266	110	20	146
Salaries and social charges/total assets (%)	9	20	24	34	3	57
Inventory turnover	24.6	18.5	12.0	4.0	?	4.3
Average collection period (days)	78	1	6	12	20	72

Exhibit 2 Name and characteristics of the companies

Carrefour

This company, incorporated in 1959, operates, directly or indirectly through subsidiaries, an international chain of super- and hypermarkets. Its stores sell all consumer goods. It has enjoyed a dazzling growth with a high level of profitability. It is ranked first of all French commercial companies in the distribution sector.

Synthelabo

This holding company controls a specialized pharmaceutical group (brain and cardio-vascular therapeutics) which has 3% market share of the French pharmaceutical market. The company by itself has no industrial or commercial activity. Its role is mainly financial. It manages a large portfolio of financial investments and patents. It also manages lands and buildings.

Lyonnaise des eaux (now Suez-Lyonnaise)

Incorporated in 1880, this company and its subsidiaries deal with the following activities: water treatment and distribution, sewage treatment and disposal, garbage collection and disposal. In the water distribution sector, it is ranked as number 2 in France, immediately behind the "Generale des Eaux" (now Vivendi). It is the parent company of a diversified industrial group but still carries directly significant industrial and commercial activities. It is considered a "mixed" holding.

Dunlop

The main activity of this French subsidiary of a Japanese tire manufacturer is the production and sale of tires. It has to face very sharp competition and knows some difficulties. It also manufactures and sells sports articles, mattresses, and precision seals and gaskets for the air and space industry.

Rossignol

Well known to skiers, this company, whose main activity is the production and the sale of skis, has decided to manufacture and sell ski boots and, more recently, tennis rackets. Its growth is supported by important capital investment.

Darty

This company (subsidiary of the UK distributor Kingfisher) is a retail distributor of household equipments (brown and white goods). Its stores are located in the Paris area but it is the parent company of a group which operates stores in many other urban centers (about 50 stores in France). This company enjoys a very high turnover growth.

Assignment 3.2 Pernod-Ricard*

Topic: Constructing an income statement
Type: Individual exercise
Related part of the chapter: Core Issues

The Pernod-Ricard group is a French company operating in the wine, spirits and food flavoring industry. It manages brands like Pernod, Ricard, Jameson, Wild Turkey and Jacob's Creek. The following lists, in alphabetical order, items and amounts taken from the consolidated income statement for the accounting year ending on 31 December 1999. All numbers are in millions of €.

Amortization of goodwill	−21.1	Minority interests	−7.1
Cost of goods sold	−1,792.8	Net interest expense	−32.1
Exceptional items	−8.2	Net sales excluding taxes and duties	3,590.3
Income taxes	−92.8	Other income (exceptional)	2.3
Marketing and distribution expenses	−863.8	Production costs and overhead	−561.4

NB:
- Minority interests, see note to Review 3.1.
- Goodwill represents any excess of the cost of the acquisition over the acquirer's interest in the fair value of the identifiable assets and liabilities acquired as at the date of the exchange transaction.

These items will be presented in a more detailed manner in the section in Chapter 13 devoted to consolidation.

Required

1 Prepare the income statement in a multiple-step format, showing separately gross margin, operating profit, pre-tax profit before exceptional items, net income before amortization of goodwill, net income before minority interests and net income (check figure: 213.3).

2 Is the income statement organized by nature or by function?

Assignment 3.3 Adidas-Salomon*

Topic: Constructing a balance sheet
Type: Individual exercise
Related part of the chapter: Core Issues

In March 1998 Adidas completed its acquisition of Salomon. The newly created Adidas-Salomon group is a major international actor in the sporting goods market. The group manages brands like Adidas, Mavic, Salomon and Taylor Made.

The following lists, in alphabetical order, items and amounts taken from the consolidated balance sheet as of 31 December 1998. All numbers are in millions of German marks (DM). Some items have been grouped, in order to simplify the balance sheet.

Accounts payable	732	Other current assets	439
Accounts receivable	1,568	Other current liabilities	193
Accrued liabilities and provisions	688	Other intangible assets	107
Cash and cash equivalents	101	Other non-current assets	338
Goodwill	1,315	Other non-current liabilities	149
Income taxes payable	187	Property and equipment	496
Inventories	1,906	Shareholders' equity	906
Long-term borrowings	484	Short-term bank borrowings	2,856
Minority interests	75		

NB:
- Minority interests, see note to Review 3.1.
- Goodwill, see note to Assignment 3.2.

These items will be presented in a more detailed manner in the section in Chapter 13.

Required

Prepare a vertical balance sheet, knowing that the German group refers to the US accounting principles. (Check figure: total assets = 6,270.)

INTRODUCTION TO FINANCIAL ACCOUNTING

Assignment 3.4 Nokia* and others

Topic: Determination of financial statements format
Type: Group exercise
Related part of the chapter: Core Issues

Appendices 1 and 2 contain the balance sheets and income statements from seven different companies:

- Nokia (Finland) and Ericsson (Sweden) are among the leaders in the communication industry, with emphasis on cellular phones and other wireless solutions.
- Club Méditerranée (France) is an active service provider in the field of leisure with, in particular, its famous "villages".
- Norsk Hydro (Norway) is engaged in production of fertilizers, energy production and downstream distribution, as well as production of aluminum and magnesium.
- The Carlsberg Group (Denmark) is one of the world's major international brewing groups, with its Carlsberg and Tuborg brands being the two most widely sold beers on a global scale.
- Eircom is Ireland's largest communication company, and the principal provider of fixed-line and mobile telecommunication services in Ireland.
- Royal Vopak (Netherlands) is one of the largest service providers in the world in the field of logistics and distribution of chemicals and oil products.

Required

Analyze the financial statements and classify each balance sheet and income statement as described in the following table.

Company	Balance sheet			
	Format	**Classification**		**Presentation**
	Vertical Horizontal	Nature Term	Single step Multiple step	Increasing Decreasing
Nokia (Finland) Ericsson (Sweden) Club Méditerranée (France) Norsk Hydro (Norway) Carlsberg (Denmark) Eircom (Ireland) Royal Vopak (Netherlands)				

Company	Income statement		
	Format	**Classification of expenses**	**Degree of simplification**
	Vertical Horizontal	Nature Function	Single step Multiple step
Nokia (Finland) Ericsson (Sweden) Club Méditerranée (France) Norsk Hydro (Norway) Carlsberg (Denmark) Eircom (Ireland) Royal Vopak (Netherlands)			

Appendix 1: Balance sheets

The balance sheets listed hereafter are excerpted from the actual annual reports of the companies. Some of the data were simplified for pedagogical reasons. Whenever we did simplify, essentially by consolidating several lines that were distinct in the original statement, an asterisk next to the item indicates this.

Nokia – Consolidated balance sheet (International Accounting Standards) financial year ended 31 December 1999 (in millions of euros)

Assets	
Fixed assets and other non-current assets	
Intangible assets	838
Property, plant, and equipment	2,031
Investments in associated companies	76
Investments in other companies	68
Other assets*	474
Subtotal fixed assets	*3,487*
Current assets	
Inventories	1,772
Receivables	4,861
Short-term investments	3,136
Bank and cash	1,023
Subtotal current assets	*10,792*
Total assets	14,279
Shareholders' equity and liabilities	
Shareholders' equity	
Share capital	279
Share issue premium*	1,055
Translation differences	243
Retained earnings	5,801
Subtotal shareholders' equity	*7,378*
Minority interests	*122*
Long-term liabilities	
Long-term interest-bearing liabilities	269
Other long-term liabilities*	138
Subtotal long-term liabilities	*407*
Current liabilities	
Short-term borrowings	792
Current portion of long-term debt	1
Accounts payable	2,202
Accrued expenses	3,377
Subtotal current liabilities	*6,372*
Total shareholders' equity and liabilities	14,279

Source: Nokia, annual report 1999

Ericsson – Consolidated balance sheet
31 December 1999 (in millions of Swedish kroner – SEK)

ASSETS

Fixed assets
Intangible assets	10,548
Tangible assets	24,719
Financial assets	16,092
	51,359

Current assets
Inventories	25,701
Receivables	96,560
Short-term cash investments	13,415
Cash and bank	15,593
	151,269

Total assets	**202,628**

STOCKHOLDERS' EQUITY, PROVISIONS, AND LIABILITIES

Stockholders' equity
Capital stock	4,893
Reserves not available for distribution	32,618
Restricted equity	37,511
Retained earnings	19,535
Net income	12,130
Non-restricted equity	31,665
	69,176

Minority interest in equity of consolidated subsidiaries	2,182

Provisions	22,552

Long-term liabilities
Notes and bond loans	17,486
Convertible debentures	5,453
Liabilities to financial institutions	1,448
Other long-term liabilities	567
	24,954

Current liabilities
Current maturities of long-term debt	1,491
Current liabilities to financial institutions	10,519
Advances from customers	6,437
Accounts payable – trade	21,618
Income tax liabilities	2,397
Other current liabilities	41,302
	83,764

Total stockholders' equity, provisions, and liabilities	**202,628**

Source: Ericsson, annual report 1999

Club Méditerranée – Consolidated balance sheet
31 October 1999 (in millions of euros)

ASSETS

Intangible assets	**173**
Goodwill	100
Other	73
Tangible assets	**926**
Land	137
Property, plant, and equipment	646
Other	143
Financial assets	**95**
Investments, loans, and advances	48
Deposits and other	47
TOTAL FIXED ASSETS	**1,194**
Inventories	27
Trade receivables	52
Other receivables	104
Marketable securities	13
Bank and cash	90
TOTAL CURRENT ASSETS	**286**
Prepaid expenses and deferred charges	49
TOTAL ASSETS	**1,529**
LIABILITIES AND SHAREHOLDERS' EQUITY	
Capital stock	59
Additional paid-in capital	434
Reserves and cumulative translation adjustment	5
Group net (loss) income	38
SHAREHOLDERS' EQUITY	**536**
MINORITY INTEREST	**16**
PROVISIONS FOR CONTINGENCIES AND CHARGES	**143**
Bonds	288
Bank loans and debts	206
Trade payables	101
Amounts received for future vacations	128
Other	92
Total debt	**815**
Accrued expenses and deferred income	19
TOTAL LIABILITIES AND SHAREHOLDERS' EQUITY	**1,529**

Source: Club Méditerranée, annual report 1998–1999

Norsk Hydro – Consolidated balance sheet (Norwegian GAAP)
31 December 1998 (in millions of Norwegian kroner – NOK)

ASSETS

Current assets

Cash and cash equivalents	1,936
Other liquid assets	2,194
Accounts receivable, net*	19,219
Inventories	15,494
Prepaid expenses and other current assets	4,971
Total current assets	**43,814**

Non-current assets

Investments	7,153
Property, plant and equipment, net	55,633
Prepaid pensions	6,926
Other non-current assets*	175
Total non-current assets	**69,887**
Total assets	**113,701**

LIABILITIES AND SHAREHOLDERS' EQUITY

Current liabilities

Bank loans and other interest-bearing short-term debt	5,150
Current portion of long-term debt	1,587
Other current liabilities	19,735
Dividends payable	1,718
Total current liabilities	**28,190**

Long-term liabilities

Long-term debt	24,105
Accrued pension liabilities	1,812
Other long-term liabilities*	14,796
Total long-term liabilities	**40,713**
Minority shareholders' interest in consolidated subsidiaries	**1,266**

Shareholders' equity	
Share capital and restricted reserves	13,259
Distributable equity	30,273
Total shareholders' equity	**43,532**
Total liabilities and shareholders' equity	**113,701**

Source: Norsk Hydro, annual report 1998

Carlsberg Group – Balance sheet at 30 September 1999
(in millions of Danish kroner – DKK)

ASSETS		EQUITY AND LIABILITIES	
Fixed assets		**Equity**	
Tangible fixed assets		Share capital	1,278
Land and buildings	4,730	Reserves	9,113
Plant and machinery	5,737		**10,391**
Other fixtures and fittings, tools and equipment	3,082	Minority interests	1,462
Construction in progress	374	**Total equity**	**11,853**
	13,923		
Financial fixed assets		**Provisions**	
Shares and loans in associated companies*	773	Pensions and similar commitments	280
Other investments and shareholdings	624	Liability for deposits on returnable packaging	791
Other loans	1,516	Deferred tax	682
Deferred tax	1,077	Other	1,589
	3,990	**Total provisions**	**3,342**
Total fixed assets	**17,913**		
		Liabilities	
Current fixed assets		**Long-term liabilities**	
Stocks and debtors		Bond loans	2,997
Stocks	2,150	Credit institutions and other*	2,626
Trade debtors	4,665		**5,623**
Other debtors*	1,674	**Current liabilities**	
Pre-payments and accrued income	247	Bond loans	1,180
	8,736	Credit institutions	689
		Trade creditors	2,606
Marketable securities and liquid assets		Corporation tax, excise duties and VAT*	1,524
Shares, bonds and other securities*	1,447	Other creditors*	1,604
Cash at bank and in hand	1,793	Accrual and deferred income	1,212
	3,240	Proposed dividend	256
Total current assets	**11,976**		**9,071**
		Total liabilities	**14,694**
Total assets	**29,889**	**Total equity and liabilities**	**29,889**

Eircom – Group balance sheet as of 1 April 1999
(in millions of €)

Fixed assets	
Tangible assets	1,865
Financial assets	299
Investment in associated undertakings	5
Goodwill	6
	2,175
Current assets	
Stocks	41
Debtors: amounts falling due within one year	444
Debtors: amounts falling due after one year	0
Cash at bank and in hand	22
	507

continued opposite

Creditors: amounts falling due within one year	
Loans and other debt	280
Other creditors	550
Proposed dividend	54
	884
Net current liabilities	−377
Total assets less current liabilities	1,798
Creditors: amounts falling due after more than one year	
Loans and other debt	229
Provisions for liabilities and charges	203
Capital grants	8
	440
Net assets	1,358
Capital and reserves	
Called-up share capital	561
Share premium	144
Revenue reserves	467
Revaluation reserve	173
Equity shareholders' funds	1,345
Equity minority interests	13
	1,358

Source: Eircom, annual report 1998–1999

Royal Vopak – Consolidated balance sheet at 31 December 1999, after proposed distribution of net income (in millions of €)		
Property, plant and equipment	1,598	
Financial fixed assets	432	
Total fixed assets		2,030
Inventories	314	
Accounts receivable	767	
Prepaid expenses and accrued income	56	
Securities	16	
Cash and cash equivalents	99	
Total current assets		1,252
Amounts owed to banks	141	
Current portion of long-term debt	107	
Trade accounts and other accounts payable	860	
Dividends	69	
Total current liabilities		1,177
Current assets less current liabilities		75
Total assets less current liabilities		2,105
Long-term debt		788
Provision for deferred tax liabilities	97	
Provision for pensions	30	
Other provisions	214	
Total provisions		341
Third-party interests	42	
Stockholders' equity	934	
Group equity		976
Total		2,105

Source: Royal Vopak, annual report 1999

Appendix 2: Income statements

The income statements listed hereafter are excerpted from the actual annual reports of the companies. Some of the data were simplified for pedagogical reasons. Whenever we did simplify, essentially by consolidating several lines that were distinct in the original statement, an asterisk next to the item indicates this.

Nokia – Consolidated profit and loss account (International Accounting Standards)
Financial year ended 31 December 1999 (in millions of €)

Net sales	**19,772**
Cost of goods sold	–12,227
Research and development expenses	–1,755
Selling, general, and administrative expenses	–1,811
Amortization of goodwill	–71
Operating profit	**3,908**
Financial income and expenses	–63
Profit before tax and minority interests	**3,845**
Tax	–1,189
Minority interests	–79
Net profit	**2,577**

Source: Nokia, annual report 1999

Ericsson – Consolidated income statement
Year ended 31 December 1999 (in millions of Swedish kroner – SEK)

Net sales	215,403
Cost of goods sold	–125,881
Gross margin	**89,522**
Research and development expenses and other technical expenses	–33,123
Selling expenses	–31,205
Administrative expenses	–10,078
Other operating revenues	2,224
Share in earnings of associated companies	250
Operating margin	**17,590**
Financial income	2,273
Financial expenses	–2,971
Income after financial items	**16,892**
Minority interest in income before taxes	–506
Income before taxes	**16,386**
Income taxes for the year	–4,358
Minority interest in the taxes	102
Net income	**12,130**

Source: Ericsson, annual report 1999

Club Méditerranée – Consolidated income statement 1998–1999 (in millions of €)

Revenues	**1,478**
Other operating income	25
Total operating revenues	**1,503**
Purchases	−658
External services	−400
Payroll expenses	−298
Other operating expenses	−39
Depreciation and amortization expense	−67
Provision expense (net)	30
Operating expenses	**−1,432**
Operating (loss) income	**71**
Net financial income	**−17**
(Loss) income from continuing operations, before tax	**54**
Net income from equity companies	−2
Net (loss) income before exceptional items and amortization of goodwill	**52**
Net exceptional (expense) income	−2
Income tax	−5
Amortization of goodwill	−6
Net (loss) income before minority interests	**39**
Minority interests	0
Group net (loss) income	**39**

Source: Club Méditerranée, annual report 1998–1999

Norsk Hydro – Consolidated income statement (Norwegian GAAP) 1998 (in millions of Norwegian kroner – NOK)

Operating revenues	97,468
Operating costs and expenses	
Raw materials and energy costs	62,339
Payroll and related costs	13,081
Depreciation, depletion and amortization	6,779
Other	8,599
Total operating costs and expenses	90,798
Operating income	6,670
Equity in net income of non-consolidated investees	410
Financial income (expense), net	−788
Income before taxes and minority interest	6,292
Current income tax expense	−1,379
Deferred income tax expense	−807
Tax effect of changes in law	11
Minority interest	−98
Net income	4,019

Source: Norsk Hydro, annual report 1998

Carlsberg Group – Profit and loss account 1998/99 (in millions of Danish kroner – DKK)		
Turnover	31,285	+
Production cost	12,699	–
Excise duties on beer and soft drinks, etc.	7,131	–
Gross profit	**11,455**	
Sales and distribution expenses	8,194	–
Administrative expenses	1,743	–
Other operating income, net	91	+
Profit before tax of other associated companies	64	+
Operating profit	**1,673**	
Special items, net	79	+
Profit before financial items	**1,752**	
Financial income*	639	+
Financial expenses*	758	–
Profit before tax	**1,633**	
Corporation tax	477	–
Group profit	**1,156**	
Minority interests	–8	–
Profit for the year, Carlsberg A/S's share	**1,164**	

Source: Carlsberg, annual report 1998–1999

NB. The column with the "+" and "–" signs has been added by the authors, in order to facilitate the comprehension of the different steps in the calculation of the net income.

Eircom – Group profit and loss account for the year ended 1 April 1999 (in millions of €)		
Turnover	1,822	+
Cost of sales	286	–
Gross profit	1,536	
Operating costs	814	–
Contribution on ordinary activities	722	
Exceptional items	174	–
Depreciation and amortization	411	–
Operating profit	137	
Share on operating losses (profits) of associated undertakings	2	–
Interest payable and similar charges	16	–
Profit on ordinary activities before taxation	119	
Tax on profit on ordinary activities	36	–
Profit on ordinary activities after taxation	83	
Minority interests	–5	+
Profit attributable to group shareholders	78	

Source: Eircom, annual report 1998–1999

NB. The column with the "+" and "–" signs has been added by the authors, in order to facilitate the comprehension of the different steps in the calculation of the net income.

Royal Vopak – Consolidated income statement 1999
(in millions of €)

Net sales	3,582	+
Other operating income	6	+
Total operating income	3,588	
Cost of goods sold	2,279	–
Gross margin	1,309	
Wages, salaries, and social security charges	517	+
Depreciation	129	+
Other operating expenses	423	+
Total operating expenses	1,069	–
Operating income	240	
Income from equity participations	59	+
Group operating income	299	
Interest income	17	
Interest expense	–71	
Interest	–54	
Income from ordinary activities before income taxes	245	
Income taxes	–79	
Income from ordinary activities after income taxes	166	
Extraordinary expense	–127	
Extraordinary income	53	
Taxes on extraordinary income and expense	22	
Extraordinary expense/income after income taxes	–52	
Consolidated net income	114	
Third-party interests in consolidated income	–8	
Net income	106	

Source: Royal Vopak, annual report 1999

NB The column with the "+" and "–" signs has been added by the authors, in order to facilitate the comprehension of the different steps in the calculation of the net income.

Assignment 3.5 Schumann Company

Topic: Link between balance sheet, income statement and cash flow statement
Type: Individual exercise
Related part of the chapter: Core Issues

The small Schumann company makes and sells computers on a limited domestic market. The balance sheet at 31 December 20X1 is as follows.

Balance sheet at 31 December 20X1 (in 000 CU)			
ASSETS		**SHAREHOLDERS' EQUITY AND LIABILITIES**	
Fixed assets		*Shareholders' equity*	
Equipment (net value)	600	Capital	500
		Reserves	200
Current assets		Net income for 20X1 (a)	168
Inventories		*Liabilities*	
• Raw materials	80	Financial debt	100
• Finished products	120		
		Accounts payable (c)	120
Accounts receivable (b)	140		
Cash at bank	260	Income tax payable (c)	112
Total	1,200	Total	1,200

(a) to be appropriated in 20X2: one-half will be distributed
(b) to be received in 20X2
(c) to be paid in 20X2

The following budgets are given (in thousands of units):

1 Sales budget: 1,300 (1,140 will be received from customers during the year).
2 Purchases budget (raw materials): 520 (380 will be paid to suppliers during the year).
3 Renting expenses budget: 220 (paid during the year).
4 Other taxes budget: 100 (paid during the year).
5 Salaries and social charges budget: 400 (paid during the year).
6 Finance budget: repayment of financial debt for 60. Interest expense: 10 (paid during the year).
7 Investment budget: acquisition of fixed assets for 200 (paid during the year).
8 Depreciation budget: 20.
9 The capital has been increased, in cash, by 100.
10 Inventories budget:
   • finished products ending inventory: 140.
   • raw materials ending inventory: 120.

The income tax rate is 40 % (paid in the following year).

Required

Prepare the following proforma documents: cash flow budget, income statement, and balance sheet, for the year 20X2.

Assignment 3.6 Bach Company

Topic: Link between balance sheet, income statement, and cash flow statement – notion of management
Type: Group business game
Related part of the chapter: Core/Advanced Issues

1 Introduction

Bach is a business game created to give realistic training in the use of accounting and financial concepts, language, and documents. To this end, the participants in the game are expected to prepare their budgeted balance sheets, income statements, and cash flow statements, after making all the necessary calculations relating to them.

2 Your company and its market

The company, which you take the control of at 1 January 20X3, is small. It makes and sells hairdryers on a limited domestic market. At the beginning of the game, the market is shared equally, between 5 companies, all of similar size[3].

The overall market for the year 20X3 is about 500,000 units. It is reasonable to anticipate that the market will increase at a rate of about 10% per year, but this will depend on the decisions taken by the companies in such matters as sales prices and their evolution, publicity and marketing expenses and so on. Your market is excessively sensitive to the prices proposed.

3 Manufacturing equipment

At the opening date (1 January 20X3), the production capacity of each company consists of 9 assembly lines, each one of which can produce a maximum 10,000 units per year. An additional line represents an investment of 400,000 CU (CU), depreciated over 5 years on the straight-line method – that is 80,000 CU per year.

A more detailed analysis of the existing equipment shows that the 9 assembly lines are composed, for each company, of:

2	lines which	4 years	Their accounting	$(2 \times 400{,}000)$	–	$(2 \times 320{,}000)$	=	$(2 \times 80{,}000)$
3	have	3 years	book	$(3 \times 400{,}000)$	–	$(3 \times 240{,}000)$	=	$(3 \times 160{,}000)$
3	already	2 years	value is	$(3 \times 400{,}000)$	–	$(3 \times 160{,}000)$	=	$(3 \times 240{,}000)$
1	operated for	1 year	therefore	400,000	–	80,000	=	320,000

Each company may invest in new assembly lines, which start production in the period of purchase. Once an assembly line is fully depreciated, it is scrapped.

4 Inventories

The companies have to acquire various motors and parts, which enter into the assembly. These items consist of purchased motors (cost 30 CU per unit in 20X3) and various parts (cost 50 CU per unit in 20X3). The total material cost is therefore 80 CU for each hairdryer.

At 1 January 20X3, the inventory consists of motors and parts necessary for making 10,000 hairdryers. In addition, the company has 5,000 finished products in inventory, ready for delivery, whose unit direct cost (materials and labor) amounts to 170 CU made up as follows:

Motor, per unit	30
Parts, per unit	50
Direct labor	
• Annual salary cost of one worker	180,000 CU
• Number of dryers made in a year	2,000
→ Labor cost of one dryer	90
Total cost	**170**

5 Personnel

At 1 January 20X3, 50 employees are working on production. Each worker can normally assemble 2,000 hairdryers in a year. As far as production is concerned, each company can hire additional personnel or dismiss them. Every dismissal must be notified to the ministry of labor inspector, and will be subject to the payment of an indemnity of 4 months' salary.

In 20X3 the minimum annual salary will be 120,000 CU. The employees social charges are estimated at 50% of this amount. This makes a total salary cost of 180,000 CU per year for each employee.

Management and administrative personnel have a total payroll cost of 1 million CU per year in 20X3. This will be subject to increases in the same proportion as the increase of salaries granted to the assembly production personnel. Social security charges also amount to 50%. This personnel fulfils an essential function in the company and cannot be dismissed.

6 Financing

The opening balance sheet that follows indicates that the shareholders have paid in 1,600,000 CU and that the company has realized profits in the past, since the reserves amount to 680,000 CU.

A debt of 1,300,000 CU was contracted in 20X1 with interest payable at the rate of 10%. It is repayable at 31 December 20X4. The interest is due every 12 months at the end of the period. The amount of any new debt will be negotiated in the light of your needs.

Requests for additional debts or increases of capital must be examined by the bankers or the stockholders. The decision is taken after your financial situation has been studied.

Temporary financial needs can be covered by a short-term overdraft granted by the bank. Interest is charged at the rate of 10% on the overdraft needed at the end of the year.

Balance sheet at 31 December 20X2 (in CU)			
ASSETS		**LIABILITIES AND SHAREHOLDERS' EQUITY**	
Fixed assets		*Shareholders' equity*	
Manufacturing equipment (3,600,000 − 1,920,000)	1,680,000	Capital	1,600,000
		Reserves	680,000
		Net income for 20X2 (to be appropriated in 20X3)	400,000
Current assets		*Liabilities*	
Inventories		Debts 10% 20X1	1,300,000
● Raw materials (80 × 10,000)	800,000		
● Finished products (170 × 5,000)	850,000	Accounts payable	1,600,000
Accounts receivable	2,000,000	Income tax payable	200,000
Cash at bank	450,000		
Total	5,780,000	Total	5,780,000

7 Other purchases and external charges

- The rent expense for the buildings amounts to 600,000 CU.
- The various utility services (water, gas, and electricity) amount to 1,000,000 CU.
- Various taxes amount to 300,000 CU.

The amount of other expenses results from your decisions: publicity, marketing, and promotion expenses. Expenses of this nature are calculated as percentages of sales; for instance: 2 to 5%.

8 Credit conditions

Investments in manufacturing equipment, personnel expenditure, other purchases, and external charges are paid for during the period concerned:

- 85% of the purchases for motors and parts are paid in the period concerned.
- The remaining 15% (debts to suppliers) are paid in the immediately following period.

Customers pay the company 80% of the value of invoice during the period of delivery. The outstanding amount of 20% is included in accounts receivable and encashed in the following year.

9 Income tax and dividends

If the result is a profit, it is assessed for income tax at a rate of 40%. Income tax is due to the state at the end of the year and paid the following year. No fixed minimum tax is due when the company makes a loss.

The net income after tax may be distributed wholly or partially as a dividend to shareholders. The amount of the dividend (if any) distributed during a year is based on the income of the preceding year.

10 Decisions to be taken by the board

See Appendix 1.

11 Procedure for one year simulation

A Prepare the batch of budget documents (balance sheet, income statement, and cash flow forecast) to test the validity of the decisions.

B Hand-in your decision sheet to the instructor.

C Note the market's response: each company will be advised of the amount of its realized sales for the period. This amount is a maximum figure calculated in relation to the decision taken both by the company and its competitors.

D Prepare the resulting definitive accounting documents (which will be presented to the shareholders – balance sheet, income statement, cash flow statement). These documents have to be certified by the statutory auditor.

NAME OF THE COMPANY:		YEAR:

Appendix 1: Decision sheet

1 Sales

1.1 Unit sales price (in CU)

1.2 Quantities sold

2 Production

2.1 Investment (number of available assembly lines)

2.2 Production launched (quantity)

2.3 Outside purchases of raw materials and parts (quantity)

2.4 Consumption of motors and parts (quantity)

3 Personnel

3.1 New hires (number of persons)

3.2 Personnel dismissed (number of persons)

3.3 Annual total remuneration (excluding employers' social security charges) – in CU per employee

4 External charges (in 000s of CU)

4.1 Budget for publicity, marketing and promotion

5 Dividends and others

5.1 Dividends distributed (in 000s of CU)

5.2 Increase in capital (according to agreements made)

5.3 Incorporation of reserves

Appendix 2: Summary financial statements

COMPANY   YEAR

CASH FLOW BUDGET (in 000 of CU)

Cash flows from operating activities

Cash from sales (80%) ....
Cash from receivables (see preceding balance sheet) ....
Cash purchases: 85% of annual purchases ....
Accounts payable (see preceding balance sheet) ....
Income tax payable ....
Other taxes ....
Personnel expenses ....
Rent expense ....
Utility services ....
Advertising expenses ....
Auditing fees ....
Financial expenses ....

Net cash flows from operating activities (1) ....

Cash flows from investing activities

Investments (assembly lines) ....
Other (sale of fixed assets) ....

Net cash flows used in investing activities (2) ....

Cash flows from financing activities

Increase in capital ....
New debts ....
Repayment of debts ....
Dividends paid ....

Net cash flows used in financing activities (3) ....

Net increase (decrease) in cash (4)=(1)+(2)+(3) ....
Opening balance (5) ....
Ending balance (6)=(4)+(5) ....

INCOME STATEMENT (in 000 of CU)

Operating expenses		Operating revenues	
Purchases of motors and parts	....	Sales	....
Change in inv. of raw materials (B–E)	....	Change in inv. of finished products (E–B)	....
External expenses	....		
Other taxes	....		
Personnel expenses	....		
Depreciation	....		
Financial expenses		**Financial income**	....
Exceptional expenses		**Exceptional income**	....
Subtotal	....	Subtotal	....
Income tax	....		
Net income	....	Net loss	....
Total		Total	

BALANCE SHEET (in 000 of CU)

Fixed assets		*Shareholders' equity*	
Manufacturing equipment	....	Capital	....
		Reserves	....
Current assets		Net income/loss	....
Inventories		Subtotal	....
● Motors and parts			
● Finished products		*Liabilities*	
Accounts receivable (20%)	....	Debt 10% 20X1	....
		Bank overdraft	....
Cash at bank	....	Accounts payable (15%)	....
		Income tax payable	
Total		Total	

References

Colasse, B. (1993) *Gestion financière*, 3rd edn, PUF, Paris.

Drury, C. (2000) *Management and Cost Accounting*, Thomson Learning, London.

EU (European Union) (1978) 4th Directive on the annual accounts of certain types of companies no. 78/660/EEC. *Official Journal of the European Communities*, 14 August.

IASC (1989) Framework for the Preparation and Presentation of Financial Statements, London.

IASC (1992) International Accounting Standard No. 7, Cash Flow Statements, London.

IASC (1997) International Accounting Standard No. 1, Presentation of Financial Statements, London.

Further readings

Parker, R.H. (1996) Harmonizing the notes in the UK and France: A case study in *de jure* harmonization. *European Accounting Review*, 5(2), 317–37.

Additional material on the website

Go to http://www.thomsonlearning.co.uk/accountingandfinance/stolowylebas for further information, journal entries and extra assignments for each chapter.

The following appendices to this chapter are available on the dedicated website:

  Appendix 3.1: Balance sheet presentation
  Appendix 3.2: Cost of goods sold
  Appendix 3.3: Income statement presentation

Notes

1 This presentation allows the calculation of the so-called "value added" of the firm. This concept emanates essentially from a tax preoccupation (value added tax) and a national statistics viewpoint. It will be further explored in Chapters 10 and 15. Simply stated this value added concept (not to be confused with that of "economic value added" – developed in Chapter 15 – used in the rank ordering of firm performance, essentially operating profit minus cost of capital employed) measures the amount of value created by the firm beyond "what it acquired from outside the economic entity". The definition of the business perimeter, although provided by tax authorities, rarely reflects a decision-makers' preoccupation.

2 Freely adapted from Colasse (1993).

3 The number of companies in the game will, in fact, vary according to the number of participants. The average amount of units sold is always 100,000.

The accounting process

In order to establish financial statements a business needs to set up an organized accounting system. Such a system consists of a multi-stage process, illustrated in this chapter. The accounting process relies not only on the use of technical tools, but requires human intervention and interpretation. The importance of this factor must never be underestimated.

CORE ISSUES

Double entry bookkeeping and the recording of transactions

The accounts principle

Chapter 2 provided a direct illustration of the impact of economic transactions on the balance sheet, or on both balance sheet and income statement. Business organizations deal with very large numbers of transactions, and some degree of organization quickly becomes necessary to avoid chaos. Each balance sheet item or line of the income statement may undergo thousands of modifications during an accounting period. These successive modifications affect specialized accounts that result from subdivisions of balance sheet and income statement items according to the type of transaction. At year-end, only the summary position of the accounts, their balance, are used in establishing the balance sheet and income statement.

In the Verdi Co. example, discussed in Chapter 2 (Figures 2.2 to 2.10), the company's cash on 1 January, 20X1 was 90 CU. This initial amount (or opening balance) underwent several modifications (entries) following transactions either raising this amount (+240) or lowering it (–325), such that the year-end cash showed a positive balance of 5 (Table 2.3). This last figure is reported in the balance sheet assets on 30 April 20X1 (see Table 4.1): it is one of the components of the financial position of Verdi.

Table 4.1 Cash account of Verdi Co.

"Cash" account			
Cash inflows		**Cash outflows**	
Beginning balance	90	Cash payments to suppliers	80
Cash receipts from customers	180	Cash payment on equipment	125
Cash receipt on debt	60	Cash payments to employees	101
		Cash payment on debt	15
		Cash payment on interest	4
Total cash inflows	330	Total cash outflows	325
Ending balance[1]	5		

NB. We have not specified what sort of "Cash" this account covers. It could, in fact, be cash in hand, cash at bank, or in a post office current account (for countries where the post office operates as a bank).

The concepts of debit and credit

Basic principles

Since the concepts of increases and decreases to monetary amounts in the accounts can be confusing, the respective sides must be clearly defined. *By convention*, the left-hand side of a T-account is called the debit side, and the right-hand side the credit side. Thus, the "cash" account (an asset account) increases on the debit side and decreases on the credit side. The initial positive amount is a debit balance. Similarly, a "debt" account (part of shareholders' equity and liabilities) increases on the credit side (the right-hand side), and decreases on the debit side (the left-hand side). The balance of this account, when the borrowing is not totally repaid, is thus a credit balance.

In general, the asset side of the balance sheet is designed to summarize balance sheet accounts with debit balances, while the shareholders' equity and liabilities side contains the balance sheet accounts with credit balances. Since the balance sheet always balances, it means the total of debit balances (the assets) equals the total of credit balances (shareholders' equity and liabilities). Expense accounts function similarly to asset accounts, while revenue accounts function in the same way as shareholders' equity and liabilities.

A schematic presentation of these rules is shown in Figure 4.1, using the basic business equation.

It is important to note that the terms "**debit**" and "**credit**" correspond to the left and right-hand sides, and are not synonymous with "increase" and "decrease". To understand the meaning of debits and credits for accounts recording expenses and revenues, suffice it to remember that revenues increase shareholders' equity, but expenses reduce it. For this reason, revenue accounts

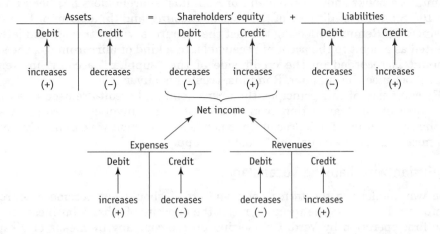

Figure 4.1 Basic business equation and concepts of debit and credit

"behave" in a way similar to that of shareholders' equity accounts (Credit = Increase, and Debit = Decrease), while for expense accounts the opposite applies.

Figure 4.1 also shows that net income is the difference between revenues and expenses, and becomes a component of shareholders' equity (retained earnings).

Origins of the concept

To understand the concepts of debit and credit, we must go back to the origin of the terms. According to Vlaemminck (1979: 63), they "are derived from the Latin words used in the Middle Ages 'debet' (verb *debere*: to owe) and 'credit' (verb *'credere'*: to lend or to trust)." The terms debit and credit refer to the other party's position in relation to the business. In other words, a debit means a claim *of the business* on something (equipment, inventory, or a promise to pay by a customer), while a credit reflects a claim of a third party *on the business*.

As an illustration, let us use the example of a sale of merchandise on credit by Romulus to Remus for 100 sesterces (S). This transaction will be recorded as shown in Figure 4.2.

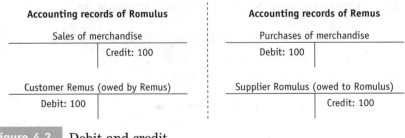

Figure 4.2 Debit and credit

In Romulus' books the sale, worth 100 S, is recorded on the credit side (Romulus is getting richer), and this is recorded by recognizing the counterbalancing entry which is a debit to an account receivable called "customer Remus" which shows that Romulus holds a claim of 100 S over Remus. This entry in

Romulus's books shows (a) a claim of Romulus' shareholders has been created for 100 S on the credit side of the "sales" account, and (b) a claim of Romulus' business on Remus (reflecting the fact the resources will be transferred later) is created as a debit to the account receivable. In a kind of mirror image, the same amount is recorded on the credit side of the "supplier" account in Remus' books, because the supplier, Romulus, trusts his buyer.

By extension of this principle, the terms debit and credit are used to position the effect of any transaction even those that do not involve a third party such as the recognition of a depreciation expense even though we can hardly say the old meanings of "owes us", or "trusts us" apply.

Confusion with banking vocabulary

The way banks use the terms debit and credit should not become a source of confusion. Banks use the terms to mean the opposite of what a business records. The first operation by Verdi Co. (setting up the company by means of a capital contribution of 90 CU) consisted in the business opening a bank account with an original deposit of 90 CU. In Verdi Co.'s books, the amount of 90 is recorded on the debit side of the cash account entitled Bank of Venice. However, the bank records the same amount as a credit to the Verdi's account, because from the bank's point of view, Verdi Co. is showing its trust by depositing its money, and thus for the bank the figure represents a credit (Figure 4.3).

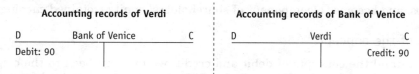

Accounting records of Verdi				**Accounting records of Bank of Venice**	
D	Bank of Venice	C	D	Verdi	C
Debit: 90					Credit: 90

Figure 4.3 Debit and credit from a bank's perspective

We have often observed that when students of accounting use the terms debit and credit, they first think of their own bank statements, and thus adopt the bank's point of view. In fact, these statements are extracted from the individual's account taken from the financial institution's accounts, and not the opposite. Another approach, based on the concepts of "use" and "source" is possible and presented in Appendix 4.1.

Figure 4.4 summarizes these basic rules in diagrammatic form.

Assets or expenses	
Debit	Credit
Left	Right
Increase	Decrease

Shareholders' equity, liabilities or revenues	
Debit	Credit
Left	Right
Decrease	Increase

Figure 4.4 Basic rules for debit and credit

In the end, the reader should use the vocabulary he or she finds most helpful. The most important thing is to translate the true impact of the transactions recorded on the position of the firm, whatever code is used.

The accounting process

Description of the process

Double entry bookkeeping is entirely based on a fundamental idea: each individual accounting transaction has two sides, which are always balanced. In accounting for cash, for example, double entry explains, on the one hand, the reasons why money has been received, and, on the other, what was done with it.

On the one hand, for practical reasons evoked earlier, it is impossible to report the full effect of every transaction on the shareholders' equity. On the other hand, in order to leave a clear audit trail (i.e., a possibility of *ex post* verification) all transactions must be recorded. The accounting process consists in a structured multi-step progressive aggregation of elemental data which is designed to be both exhaustive and efficient. It is illustrated in Figure 4.5.

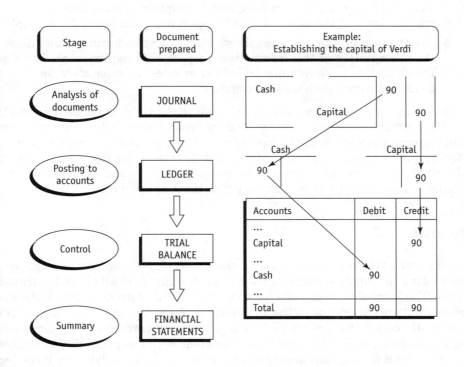

Figure 4.5 Accounting process/accounting system

Each accounting transaction originates in a **document**. Such a document serves as the basis for an entry in a **journal**. The journal provides a chronological list of all transactions. The next step is to distribute the effects of events between specialized **ledger** accounts where they can be accumulated in homogenous classes of nature and type of transaction. The ledger balances (net sum of a class of effect of transactions) will in turn be aggregated in the two main components of the **financial statements** (balance sheet, and income statement).

Documents

All recognized relevant transactions give rise to a "supporting document" or "source document". These are legal documents (invoices, checks, insurance premium receipts, contracts, tax and social security filings, etc.) that must be recorded in the accounts. In some cases (e.g., for depreciation and amortization, provisions, or adjusting entries), no specific document exists, and the operation is classified as "miscellaneous".

When a document pertaining to a transaction is received, the accounting department's first job is to verify that it is relevant. Relevance can be determined by the answers to the following five questions:

1 Is the document addressed specifically to the company, using its correct corporate name?

2 Does the document contain the necessary legal and personal references of the organization or individual who sent it (business registration number, name and address)?

3 Are the mathematical calculations correct?

4 Does the document give an adequate description of the nature of the transaction and the authority for it (reference to an order, for example)?

5 Are the unit and total values shown clearly on the document and does the presentation of this information respect legal requirements (such as the obligation to show value added tax or sales tax separately, for countries where such taxes are applied)?

Question 1 is essential because of the need to clearly distinguish between the business entity (or a legal entity) and individual shareholders or employees (sometimes problematic in the case of a sole proprietorship – see Chapter 11). Recording personal expenses, unrelated to the company's business and objectives, is a misappropriation of company assets and a fraud which is disallowed by tax authorities and may give rise to litigation.

Journal

As its name implies, the journal is the day-to-day chronological register of accounting information found in the source documents of all allowable transactions. The journal is often referred to as the record of prime entry or the book of original entry, since it is the first formal phase in the accounting process, frequently called "journalizing". The information recorded in the journal must be sufficiently detailed to provide management with the possibility of analyses required both for ongoing management needs and for complying with the legal obligations pertaining to the annual financial statements.

Bookkeeping entries for the eight transactions of Verdi Co. (see Chapter 2) are shown in Table 4.2 following the standardized form adopted when the journal is maintained as one centralized register.

Table 4.2   Verdi Co. journal

		(1)		
BS (A+)	Cash		90	
	BS (L+)	Capital		90
		(2)		
BS (A+)	Cash		60	
	BS (L+)	Financial debt		60
BS (A+)	Equipment	**(3)**	125	
	BS (A–)	Cash		125
		(4)		
BS (A+)	Accounts receivable		250	
	IS (R+)	Service revenue		250
		(5)		
BS (A+)	Cash		180	
	BS (A–)	Accounts receivable		180
		(6)		
IS (E+)	Payroll expenses		101	
	BS (A–)	Cash		101
IS (E+)	Interest expense		4	
	BS (A–)	Cash		4
IS (E+)	External expense		85	
	BS (L+)	Accounts payable		85
		(7)		
BS (L–)	Accounts payable		80	
	BS (A–)	Cash		80
		(8)		
BS (L–)	Financial debt		15	
	BS (A–)	Cash		15
			990	**990**

Since the journal's actual format depends on the computer software used, the following explanations concerning Table 4.2 may be useful:

● In practice, the first 2 columns (or computer fields or zones) are used to record the code numbers of the accounts debited and credited – each account has its own number. The principles of account numbers and charts of accounts will be discussed later in this chapter. This book does not use account numbers. We have, however, kept the two columns, to indicate the impact of each account on the financial statements. This decision was made because of its pedagogical value, and because it provides a constant reminder of the link between the accounts and the financial statements, even at the journal stage. The abbreviations used are as follows:

    – BS balance sheet

    – IS income statement

    – A+ increase in assets

    – A– decrease in assets

    – L+ increase in shareholders' equity and liabilities

    – L– decrease in shareholders' equity and liabilities

    – R+ increase in revenues

    – R– decrease in revenues

- E+ increase in expenses
- E– decrease in expenses.

- The two central columns are used for the names of the accounts debited or credited. By convention, the debited account(s) is (are) recorded first, to the left on the upper line, while the credited account(s) is (are) shown to the right on a line below (a single transaction may require that more than 2 accounts be used).

- The last two columns (one for debits and one for credits) show the amounts relevant to the entry.

- Another column in the middle is used for the number (or date, or reference) of the transaction.

- In practice, there is also often another column used to explain and describe the transaction, under the heading "Transaction".

The debit and credit columns must be totaled, and the absolute equality of the totals shows that the principles of double entry have been properly applied. At this stage, no error, not even a difference of one currency unit, can be tolerated.

The journal recording only recognizes the existence of the elements of the transaction. The subsequent steps will organize, classify, and aggregate the data in significant groupings (as on the balance sheet, for example) allowing comparison with prior information from the same company, or with industry benchmarks. This is done in ledgers.

Ledger

The general ledger is made up of specialized numbered ledgers, each regrouping one relevant aspect of transactions (as defined by management in their quest for effective and efficient running of the business – cash, purchases, sales…)[2]. The data recorded in the journal are integrally transcribed in the general ledger and in the specialized ledgers, still in chronological order in their category. The ledgers do not create data. They, however, reveal their informational content by creating meaningful aggregates.

The process of transferring entries from the journal to the ledger is called "posting". Each account debited or credited in the journal is thus transferred as a debit or credit of the relevant account in the general ledger and the specialized ledgers. Posting is a purely mechanical task, with no analysis required. Indeed, one of the first advantages of dedicated accounting software is that they automate this task, saving companies considerable time and eliminating errors (see the later section "Trial balance" for further discussion of errors).

Table 4.3 shows Verdi Co.'s ledger where accounts are listed according to their position in the financial statements.

1. We chose for pedagogical reasons to represent each account as a T-account. Real accounts do not follow this presentation, as each amount recorded must have an associated date and heading.

2. For transactions with customers and suppliers, one account alone (a "collective" or "general" account) is not enough. These accounts must be subdivided into one account per customer and per supplier, and all individual customer and supplier accounts taken together form the accounts receivable and accounts payable specialized ledgers (also called special or subsidiary ledgers).

Table 4.3   Verdi Co. ledger

Balance sheet

Assets			Shareholders' equity and liabilities		
D	Equipment	C	D	Capital	C
	125 (3)				90 (1)
D balance = 125					**C balance = 90**
D	Accounts receivable	C	D	Financial debt	C
	250 (4) 180 (5)			15 (8)	60 (2)
D balance = 70					**C balance = 45**
D	Cash	C	D	Accounts payable	C
	90 (1) 125 (3)			80 (7)	85 (6)
	60 (2) 101 (6)				
	180 (5) 4 (6)				**C balance = 5**
	330 80 (7)				
	15 (8)				
	325				
D balance = 5					

Numbers in parentheses next to the entry refer to the transaction number in the journal (see Table 4.2)

Income statement

Expenses				Revenues	
D	External expenses	C	D	Sales	C
	85 (6)				250 (4)
D balance = 85					**C balance = 250**
D	Payroll expenses	C			
	101 (6)				
D balance = 101					
D	Interest expense	C			
	4 (6)				
D balance = 4					

D: debit and C: credit

3 The totals of each column of an account are called "footings". The difference between the debit footing and the credit footing is called the balance of the account.

4 For learning purposes, we chose to record transactions directly in T-accounts, which has the advantage of providing a clear view of the impact of a transaction on each account.

5 In the summary of balance sheet accounts:
   –   The total of debit balances (D) is 125 + 70 + 5 = 200.
   –   The total of credit balances (C) is 90 + 45 + 5 = 140.

- Therefore, since the debit balances and credit balances are equal, the shortfall of 60 on the liabilities side corresponds to the net income of the period.

6 In the summary of the income statement accounts:
- The total of debit balances is 85 + 101 + 4 = 190.
- The total of credit balances is 250.
- There is thus a positive net income of 60.

As expected, the amount (net income/loss) to be added to the shareholders' equity is the same regardless of whether we use the balance sheet or the income statement approach. It was easy in our example to calculate the net income/loss both ways because so few accounts were involved. When a company's accounts comprise thousands of individual accounts, they must first be controlled by transcribing the balances in the trial balance.

Trial balance

Principle

Before establishing the financial statements, the accountant will prepare a "trial balance" which is simply a list of the debit and credit footings for each account in the general ledger. The object of this exercise is to check that the sum of all the debit balances is equal to the sum of all the credit balances. In other words it is the verification that Total debits = Total credits.

The format of the trial balance varies from one company (or software) to another. Table 4.4 illustrates a model of trial balance, using the Verdi Co. data.

Table 4.4   Verdi trial balance

Accounts	Debit entries	Credit entries	Debit balances	Credit balances
Equipment	125		125	
Accounts receivable	250	180	70	
Cash	330	325	5	
Capital		90		90
Financial debt	15	60		45
Accounts payable	80	85		5
External expenses	85		85	
Payroll expenses	101		101	
Interest expense	4		4	
Sales		250		250
Total	990	990	390	390

Accounts are listed nearly always in the order of the company's account codes. To simplify matters, our example follows the order used in the financial statements, i.e., asset accounts first, followed by liability accounts in the upper portion of Table 4.4, expense accounts and revenue accounts are listed sequentially in the lower part of the table.

The trial balance is used to verify two fundamental equations:

Sum of debit entries = Sum of credit entries
Sum of debit balances = Sum of credit balances

The initial purpose of the trial balance was a straightforward arithmetical verification. Above all, it was used to check that the amounts in the journal had been correctly copied into the ledger, and that the double entry principle had been respected. Today, thanks to the use of computer software, both of these equations are (fortunately) always verified. And yet – perhaps surprisingly – the trial balance is still established, essentially for the following three reasons:

1 It is a useful instrument in auditing accounts, since the trial balance reveals potential errors (e.g., accounts with an abnormal type of balance, for instance, a capital account with a debit balance or an equipment account with a credit balance – Table 4.5 lists "normal" balances) and anomalies (for instance, balances that are higher or lower than usual or than during a previous relevant period, accounts missing or wrongly included, etc.).

2 It is a necessary stage in the rational procedure for establishing both balance sheet and income statement, since there must be no errors or omissions.

3 It provides a simple determination of the net income/loss without having to establish a balance sheet or income statement. Whatever the system of codes attributed to the accounts, the trial balance generally comprises two distinct parts (as in Table 4.4): balance sheet accounts, followed by income statement accounts. The following equations permit a rapid calculation of the income of the period:

> Using only balance sheet accounts:
> Sum of debit balances minus Sum of credit balances = Net income
> Using only income statement accounts:
> Sum of credit balances minus Sum of debit balances = Net income

Table 4.4 was structured in such a way. The net income/loss is thus determined as follows:

> Using only balance sheet accounts:
> Debit balances – Credit balances = 200 – 140 = 60
> Using only income statement accounts:
> Credit balances – Debit balances = 250 – 190 = 60

Normal account balances

Table 4.5 lists common accounts and indicates the expected nature of their balance.

Table 4.5 Examples of "normal" account balances

Accounts	Debit	Credit
Assets	x	
Set-up expenses	x	
Land	x	
Office equipment	x	
Accumulated depreciation of office equipment		x
Investments	x	
Provision for depreciation of investments		x
Deposits and guarantees	x	
Merchandise inventories	x	
Provision for depreciation of merchandise		x
Accounts receivable	x	
Doubtful debt accounts	x	
Provision for doubtful debts		x
Income tax receivable	x	
Prepaid rent	x	
Cash at bank	x	
Cash in hand	x	
Shareholders' equity		x
Share capital		x
Reserves or retained earnings		x
Losses brought forward	x	
Profits brought forward		x
Liabilities		x
Long-term debts		x
Bonds payable		x
Bank overdrafts		x
Accounts payable		x
Salaries payable		x
Revenues		x
Sales of merchandise (goods purchased for resale)		x
Sales of finished products		x
Change in finished product inventory (2 possible normal balances)	x	x
Other trade revenues		x
Financial income		x
Expenses	x	
Purchases of merchandise (goods for resale)	x	
Change in merchandise inventory (2 possible normal balances)	x	x
Purchases of raw materials	x	
Change in raw materials inventory (2 possible normal balances)	x	x
Cost of goods sold	x	
Selling and marketing expenses	x	
General and administrative expenses	x	
R&D expenses	x	
External services – electricity, utilities	x	
Insurance and other services	x	
Miscellaneous payroll taxes	x	
Wages and salaries	x	
License fees	x	
Financial expenses and interest	x	
Exceptional items	x	
Extraordinary items	x	

Trial balance errors

Appendix 4.2 provides some explanations on errors which might be found in a trial balance.

Financial statements

This is the final stage of the accounting process. We have already discussed financial statements, principally in Chapter 3. Certain operations are undertaken specifically to establish the year-end financial statements. These are known as "end-of-period entries", and are discussed in the following chapter.

Going back to the example of Verdi Co., we have a balance sheet on 31 December 20X1 that summarizes the debit balances on the asset side (excess of debits over credits) and the credit balances on the liability side (excess of credits over debits) and an income statement (see Table 4.6).

Table 4.6	Financial statements of Verdi

Balance sheet on 31 December 20X1				
Assets			Shareholders' equity and liabilities	
Equipment	125		Shareholders' equity	
Accounts receivable	70		Capital	90
Cash	5		Net income (profit)	60
			Liabilities	
			Debt	45
			Accounts payable	5
Total assets	200		Total liabilities	200
Σ balances D	200		Σ balances C	200
Income statement for 20X1				
Expenses				Revenues
External expenses	85	Sales		250
Payroll expenses	101			
Interest expenses	4			
Total expenses	190			
Net income	60			
	250			250

Thanks to the double entry system, it is possible to establish both the balance sheet and the income statement at the same time. The balance sheet registers a profit of 60, and the income statement explains how it was obtained.

The accounts kept by a company serve three essential purposes:

1 They constitute legal evidence, and as such, must be easily accessible to controllers (e.g., tax inspectors or auditors) and comply with laws and regulations.

2 They are an instrument for business management. For example, the accounts payable should tell, with accuracy and timeliness, how much the company owes its suppliers; or the accounts receivable should reflect how much is owed by its customers, etc.

3 They are a source of management information. The accounting process, and the accounts that comprise it, allow reports on value creation (or subset thereof, such as sales by segment or costs by nature) at any desired interval, including the minimum legally required annual financial statements.

To be effective, the organization of the accounting system must, therefore, strike the best balance between these objectives or constraints, and the related costs.

Organization of the accounting system

Appendix 4.3 provides some developments on the organization of the accounting system, in terms of timing, specialized journals, and computer software. It also describes the accounting function within the company.

The chart of accounts

A chart of accounts is a logically organized list of all recognized accounts used in recording all transactions in a firm. A chart of accounts generally assigns a unique code to each account.

Principles

As indicated earlier in this chapter, each account must be identified by some code. The code is necessary for quick reference in processing transactions to the accounts, and absolutely vital for IT systems. Several coding methods are possible, mainly:

- alphabetical
- numerical
- alphanumerical.

Alphabetical coding appears to be the most simple: no numbers to remember, and only the names of the accounts to know. But in practice, it is not a good solution, because:

- It proved in the past to be complicated for programming IT systems.
- It may prove to be time consuming to enter the full name of an account, unless the name is given a code, which makes matters more complex again.
- Each account must have a specific name, and no variants (such as spelling errors or unspecified abbreviations) will be recognized: once again, this leads to practical difficulties.

For these reasons, account codes are almost always numerical or alphanumerical (for example, accounts receivable might be coded 31, and account "31soprano" records sales transactions to the Soprano family whereas "31tessitura" records sales transactions with Tessitura Inc.

In general, charts of accounts are based on hierarchical classification, in which classes or groups of accounts are identified and subdivided as the need requires. There can be as many subclasses or nested subdivisions as the company requires. Figure 4.6 illustrates one possible chart of accounts.

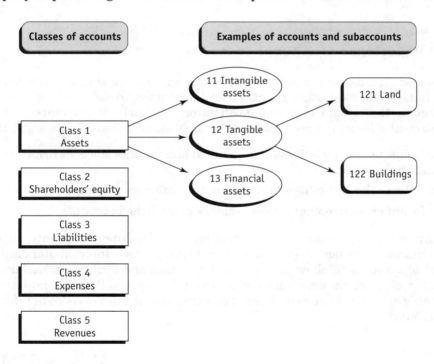

Figure 4.6 A possible chart of accounts

Standardized chart of accounts

In countries such as Belgium, France and Spain, the overall structure of the accounts code is laid down nationally while in several other European countries the choice of structure is left entirely up to company management (e.g., the Netherlands and the UK). For example Table 4.7 illustrates how the French national chart of account's overall structure corresponds to the order in which accounts appear in the financial statements.

Table 4.7   French chart of accounts

Account classes	Class headings
1	Shareholders' equity
2	Fixed assets
3	Inventories
4	Relations with third parties
5	Financial accounts
6	Expenses
7	Revenues

From this list it can be seen that the first five groups of numbered accounts relate to accounts included in the balance sheet and the other two to accounts included in the income statement.

The importance of account codes

As stated already, some countries (but not many) have a standardized chart of accounts, while most other countries let the company decide on its own chart. Although the debate over standardization of charts of accounts is not a fundamental issue, the proponents of national standardized charts argue that:

● It facilitates the mobility of the qualified accountants since all firms use the same basic structure.

● It reduces the cost of designing accounting software packages.

● It facilitate intercompany comparability of published accounts.

Any large organization with multiple establishments, plants, and/or subsidiaries is sooner or later forced to create its own internal standardized chart of accounts to allow managerial discussions and facilitate consolidation. The list of codes chosen either nationally or by any one firm has no intrinsic meaning and we deliberately chose to de-emphasize the use of codes in referring to accounts.

KEY POINTS

● In order to prepare its financial statements, a company needs to set up an organized accounting process supported by an accounting system.

● By convention, the left-hand side of any account is called the debit side, and the right-hand side the credit side.

● Each accounting transaction has its origin in a source document.

● This document serves as the basis for making a descriptive entry in a journal.

● The journal provides a chronological list of the transactions. After journalizing accounting entries, they are posted in the general ledger where the components of the description of the transaction are structured by nature and/or type of transaction.

- The general ledger is the preliminary step to the establishment the 2 main financial statements (balance sheet, and income statement).
- Detailed individual accounts entries are grouped together and replaced by the balance of the account, and recapitulated in the trial balance.
- All companies use a chart of accounts, i.e., a predetermined structured list of accepted account codes.

REVIEW

Review 4.1 Grieg Company (1)

Topic: The accounting process: From the journal to the financial statements
Type: Individual/group exercise
Related part of the chapter: Core Issues

The Grieg Company was incorporated on 1 January, 20X1. Grieg had five holders of share capital.

Part 1

The following events occurred during January 20X1:
1. The company was incorporated. Common shareholders invested 10,000 CU cash.
2. Equipment for a value of 1,200 CU was acquired for cash.
3. Merchandise inventory was purchased on credit, 9,000 CU.
4. Cash was borrowed from a bank, 500 CU.
5. Merchandise carried in inventory at a cost of 7,000 CU was sold for cash for 6,000 CU and on credit for 5,000 CU.
6. Collection of the accounts receivable, 4,000 CU.
7. Payment of accounts payable, 8,000 CU (see transaction 3).

Required

- Prepare an analysis of Grieg Company's transactions and record the entries in the general journal, assuming that the purchases of merchandise are first recorded in inventory (see "Advanced Issues" in Chapter 2).
- Post the entries to the ledger, entering your postings by transaction number.
- Prepare a trial balance, as of 31 January 20X1.
- Prepare a balance sheet as of 31 January 20X1, and an income statement for the month of January.

Part 2

The following event is now taken into account:
8. Depreciation expense of 120 CU was recognized.

Required

- Record the entry just mentioned in the general journal.
- Modify the general ledger.
- Modify the trial balance, as of 31 January 20X1.
- Modify the balance sheet as of 31 January 20X1 and the income statement for the month of January.

Solution

		Journal entries – Part 1		
1	BS (A+)	Cash at bank	10,000	
	BS (L+)	Shareholders' equity		10,000
2	BS (A+)	Equipment	1,200	
	BS (A–)	Cash at bank		1,200
3	BS (A+)	Merchandise inventory	9,000	
	BS (L+)	Accounts payable		9,000
4	BS (A+)	Cash at bank	500	
	BS (L+)	Debt		500
5	IS (E+)	Cost of goods sold	7,000	
	BS (A–)	Merchandise inventory		7,000
	BS (A+)	Cash at bank	6,000	
	BS (A+)	Accounts receivable	5,000	
	IS (R+)	Sales		11,000
6	BS (A+)	Cash at bank	4,000	
	BS (A–)	Accounts receivable		4,000
7	BS (L–)	Accounts payable	8,000	
	BS (A–)	Cash at bank		8,000
			50,700	50,700

Ledger – Part 1

Assets accounts

Equipment

2	1,200		
		1,200	Bal
	1,200	1,200	

Merchandise inventory

3	9,000	7,000	5
		2,000	Bal
	9,000	9,000	

Accounts receivable

5	5,000	4,000	6
		1,000	Bal
	5,000	5,000	

Cash at bank

1	10,000	1,200	2
4	500	8,000	7
5	6,000		
6	4,000		
		11,300	Bal
	20,500	20,500	

Equity and liabilities accounts

Capital

		10,000	1
Bal	10,000		
	10,000	10,000	

Debt

		500	4
Bal	500		
	500	500	

Accounts payable

7	8,000	9,000	3
Bal	1,000		
	9,000	9,000	

Expense accounts

Cost of goods sold

5	7,000		
		7,000	Bal
	7,000	7,000	

Revenue accounts

Sales

		11,000	5
Bal	11,000		
	11,000	11,000	

Comments

- Bal = balance.
- The balances are shown on the opposite side to their nature, in order to balance the account.
- The accounts have been divided into four main categories: assets, equity and liabilities, expenses, and revenues.

Trial balance – Part 1

| | Entries of the period | | Ending balance | |
	D	C	D	C
Equipment	1,200		1,200	
Merchandise inventory	9,000	7,000	2,000	
Accounts receivable	5,000	4,000	1,000	
Cash at bank	20,500	9,200	11,300	
Share capital		10,000		10,000
Accounts payable	8,000	9,000		1,000
Debt		500		500
Cost of goods sold	7,000		7,000	
Sales		11,000		11,000
Total	50,700	50,700	22,500	22,500

Balance sheet and income statement – Part 1

See Part 2.

Journal entry – Part 2

| 8 | IS (E+) | Depreciation expense | 120 | |
| | BS (A-) | Accumulated depreciation, equipment | | 120 |

Ledger – Part 2

	Accumulated depreciation				**Depreciation expense**	
		120 **8**	**8**	120		
Bal	*120*				*120*	Bal
	120	120		120	120	

Trial balance – Part 2

	Entries of the period D	Entries of the period C	Ending balance D	Ending balance C
Equipment	1,200		1,200	
Accumulated depreciation		120		120
Merchandise inventory	9,000	7,000	2,000	
Accounts receivable	5,000	4,000	1,000	
Cash at bank	20,500	9,200	11,300	
Share capital		10,000		10,000
Debt		500		500
Accounts payable	8,000	9,000		1,000
Cost of goods sold	7,000		7,000	
Depreciation expense	120		120	
Sales		11,000		11,000
Total	50,820	50,820	22,620	22,620

Balance sheet – Parts 1 and 2

The same table is used to show the balance sheet from Parts 1 and 2.

Balance sheet at 31 January 20X1					
ASSETS	Part 1	Part 2	LIABILITIES	Part 1	Part 2
Fixed assets			**Shareholders' equity**		
Equipment	1,200	1,200	Share capital	10,000	10,000
Accumulated depreciation	0	−120	Income for the month	4,000	3,880
Net amount	1,200	1,080			
Current assets			**Debts**		
Merchandise inventory	2,000	2,000	Debt	500	500
Accounts receivable	1,000	1,000	Accounts payable	1,000	1,000
Cash at bank	11,300	11,300			
Total assets	15,500	15,380	Total liabilities	15,500	15,380

Comment

● In Part 2, the new balance sheet total results from the depreciation expense (120).

Income statement – Parts 1 and 2

The same table shows the income statement from Parts 1 and 2.

Income statement for the month ended 31 January 20X1		
	Part 1	Part 2
REVENUES		
Sales	11,000	11,000
Total revenues (1)	11,000	11,000
EXPENSES		
Cost of goods sold	7,000	7,000
Depreciation expense	0	120
Total expenses (2)	7,000	7,120
Net income (1) – (2)	4,000	3,880

Comment

- The net income as calculated in the income statement is the same as that in the balance sheet.

Review 4.2 Grieg Company (2)

Topic: The accounting process: from the journal to the financial statements
Type: Individual/group exercise
Related part of the chapter: Core Issues

The Grieg Company was incorporated on 1 January 20X1. Grieg had five holders of share capital.

Part 1

Required

- Prepare an analysis of Grieg Company's transactions (see Review 4.1, 1–7) and record the entries in the general journal, assuming that the purchases of merchandise are first recorded in the income statement (see "Advanced Issues" in Chapter 2).
- Post the entries to the ledger, entering your postings by transaction number.
- Prepare a trial balance, as of 31 January 20X1.
- Prepare a balance sheet as of 31 January 20X1, and an income statement for the month of January.

Part 2

The following events are now taken into account:

8 Depreciation expense of 120 CU was recognized.

9 Ending inventory was valued at cost, i.e. 2,000 CU.

Required

- Record the entries mentioned in the general journal.
- Modify the general ledger.
- Modify the trial balance, as of 31 January 20X1.
- Modify the balance sheet as of 31 January 20X1 and the income statement for the month of January.

Solution

		Journal entries – Part 1		
1	BS (A+)	Cash at bank	10,000	
	BS (L+)	Shareholders' equity		10,000
2	BS (A+)	Equipment	1,200	
	BS (A–)	Cash at bank		1,200
3	IS (E+)	Purchase of merchandise for resale	9,000	
	BS (L+)	Accounts payable		9,000
4	BS (A+)	Cash at bank	500	
	BS (L+)	Debt		500
5	BS (A+)	Cash at bank	6,000	
	BS (A+)	Accounts receivable	5,000	
	IS (R+)	Sales		11,000
6	BS (A+)	Cash at bank	4,000	
	BS (A–)	Accounts receivable		4,000
7	BS (L–)	Accounts payable	8,000	
	BS (A–)	Cash at bank		8,000
			50,700	50,700

Ledger – Part 1

Assets accounts

Equipment

2	1,200			
		1,200	Bal	
	1,200	1,200		

Accounts receivable

5	5,000	4,000	6	
		1,000	Bal	
	5,000	5,000		

Cash at bank

1	10,000	1,200	2	
4	500	8,000	7	
5	6,000			
6	4,000			
		11,300	Bal	
	20,500	20,500		

Equity and liabilities accounts

Share capital

		10,000	1	
Bal	10,000			
	10,000	10,000		

Debt

		500	4	
Bal	500			
	500	500		

Accounts payable

7	8,000	9,000	3	
Bal	1,000			
	9,000	9,000		

Expense accounts

Purchase of merchandise

3	9,000			
		9,000	Bal	
	9,000	9,000		

Revenue accounts

Sales

		11,000	5	
Bal	11,000			
	11,000	11,000		

Comments

- Bal = balance.
- The balances are shown on the opposite side to their nature, in order to balance the account.
- The accounts have been divided into four main categories: assets, equity and liabilities, expenses and revenues.

Trial balance – Part 1

	Entries of the period		Ending balance	
	D	C	D	C
Equipment	1,200		1,200	
Accounts receivable	5,000	4,000	1,000	
Cash at bank	20,500	9,200	11,300	
Share capital		10,000		10,000
Debt		500		500
Accounts payable	8,000	9,000		1,000
Purchase of merchandise	9,000		9,000	
Sales		11,000		11,000
Total	43,700	43,700	22,500	22,500

Balance sheet and income statement – Part 1

See Part 2.

Journal entries – Part 2

8	IS (E+)	Depreciation expense		120	
	BS (A–)		Accumulated depreciation, equipment		120
9	BS (A+)	Merchandise inventory		2,000	
	IS (E–)		Change in inventories		2,000

Ledger – Part 2

	Merchandise inventory		
9	2,000		
		2,000	Bal
	2,000	2,000	

	Accumulated depreciation		
		120	8
Bal	120		
	120	120	

	Change in inventories		
		2,000	9
Bal	2,000		
	2,000	2,000	

	Depreciation expense		
8	120		
		120	Bal
	120	120	

Trial balance – Part 2

	Entries of the period D	Entries of the period C	Ending balance D	Ending balance C
Equipment	1,200		1,200	
Accumulated depreciation		120		120
Merchandise inventory	2,000		2,000	
Accounts receivable	5,000	4,000	1,000	
Cash at bank	20,500	9,200	11,300	
Share capital		10,000		10,000
Debt		500		500
Accounts payable	8,000	9,000		1,000
Purchase of merchandise	9,000		9,000	
Change in inventories		2,000		2,000
Depreciation expense	120		120	
Sales		11,000		11,000
Total	45,820	45,820	24,620	24,620

Balance sheet – Parts 1 and 2

The same table is used to show the balance sheet from Parts 1 and 2.

Balance sheet at 31 January 20X1					
ASSETS	Part 1	Part 2	LIABILITIES	Part 1	Part 2
Fixed assets			**Shareholders' equity**		
Equipment	1,200	1,200	Share capital	10,000	10,000
Accumulated depreciation	0	−120	*Income for the month*	*2,000*	*3,880*
Net amount	1,200	1,080			
Current assets			**Debts**		
Merchandise inventory	0	2,000	Debt	500	500
Accounts receivable	1,000	1,000	Accounts payable	1,000	1,000
Cash at bank	11,300	11,300			
Total assets	13,500	15,380	Total liabilities	13,500	15,380

Comment

● In Part 2, the new balance sheet total results from the depreciation expense (120) and the final inventory (2,000).

Income statement – Parts 1 and 2

The same table shows the income statement from Parts 1 and 2.

Income statement for the month ended 31 January 20X1		
	Part 1	Part 2
REVENUES		
Sales	11,000	11,000
Total revenues (1)	11,000	11,000
EXPENSES		
Purchase of merchandise	9,000	9,000
Change in inventories		−2,000
Depreciation expense	0	120
Total expenses (2)	9,000	7,120
Net income (1) – (2)	2,000	3,880

Comments

- The net income as calculated in the income statement is the same as that in the balance sheet.
- If we compare the review problems Grieg (1) and Grieg (2) we notice that the total "purchases + change in inventories" is equal to the "cost of goods sold". This is normal (see Chapters 2 and 9).

ASSIGNMENTS

Assignment 4.1 Sibelius Company

Topic: The beginning of the accounting process: The journal
Type: Individual/group exercise
Related part of the chapter: Core Issues

The Sibelius Company was incorporated in March 20X1. It has a commercial activity. The following transactions were undertaken during the first month:

1	March 1	Sibelius company incorporated with a share capital of 600 CU. A bank account was opened with Commercial Credit.
2	March 6	Purchased merchandise on credit: 350 CU.
3	March 12	Paid telephone expense for the month of March: 50 CU.
4	March 20	Sold merchandise for 500 CU (260 CU cash and 240 CU on credit). (The purchase price of the merchandise sold was 300 CU.)
5	March 29	Paid the supplier of merchandise (see transaction 2).
6	March 30	Organized a physical inventory and computed an ending inventory of 50 CU.

Required

Prepare the journal entries for the month of March 20X1.
   Note that:

- The company wants to compute income that reflects the economic situation at 30 March. Consequently, the ending inventory must appear in the records of the company.
- In order to record purchases, sales, and inventory, you can choose to record the purchases of merchandise either in the inventory (balance sheet) or in the purchases (income statement). You must indicate your choice clearly at the top of your journal.
- An extract from the chart of accounts of Sibelius company is as follows.

Accounts payable	Inventories
Accounts receivable	Purchases of merchandise (if purchases recorded in the income statement)
Capital	Sales of merchandise
Cash in bank	Telephone expenses
Cost of goods sold (if purchases recorded in the balance sheet)	Change in inventories (if purchases recorded in the income statement)

Model journal

Transaction number	Date	Accounts		Amounts	
		Debit	Credit	D	C

Assignment 4.2

Internet-based exercise
Type: Individual/group exercise
Related part of the chapter: Advanced Issues

- Search the web for job offers concerning vacancies for accounting and related personnel (auditor, financial director, management controller, treasurer, etc.).
- Using the offers located, draw up a list of the characteristics of each position.
- Compare and contrast the accounting and related professions.

Assignment 4.3

Accounting history
Type: Group presentation
Related part of the chapter: Advanced Issues

- Prepare a 15-minute oral presentation on the history of charts of accounts, with particular reference to the French chart of accounts (dating from 1942).
- Prepare a 15-minute oral presentation of how accounts have been kept and presented in the past up to the present day.

Reference

Vlaemminck, J.H. (1979) *Histoire et doctrines de la comptabilité*, Pragnos (quoted by Colasse, B. (2000) *Comptabilité générale*, 6th edn, Economica, Paris, p. 131).

Further readings

Chauveau, B. (1995) The Spanish *Plan General de Contabilidad*: Agent of development and innovation? *European Accounting Review*, 4(1), 125–38.
Inchausti, B.G. (1993) The Spanish accounting framework: Some comments. *European Accounting Review*, 2(2), 379–86.
Richard, J. (1995) The evolution of accounting chart models in Europe from 1900 to 1945: Some historical elements. *European Accounting Review*, 4(1), 87–124.

Additional material on the website

Go to http://www.thomsonlearning.co.uk/accountingandfinance/stolowylebas for further information, journal entries and extra assignments for each chapter.

The following appendices to this chapter are available on the dedicated website:

Appendix 4.1: Concepts of use and source
Appendix 4.2: Trial balance errors
Appendix 4.3: Organization of the accounting system

Notes

1   Which will be the beginning balance for the subsequent period. Also called "balance carried forward".
2   As a simplification, the "general ledger" is often called "ledger".

Accounting principles and end-of-period adjustments

The preceding chapter described how accounting records transactions during the year. We explained how data enter the accounting process and how they are recorded in the journal and ledger(s). The overall objectives of the accounting procedures during that recording phase are to ensure that:

- All data recorded are relevant to the description of the financial performance of the entity.
- The descriptors of every transaction can be verified from source documents.
- The structure of the data in the ledger is relevant to the business model held by management and to their decision-making needs.
- Accurate and significant data can be extracted rapidly from the ledgers on a periodical basis.

In order for the techniques introduced in Chapter 4 to deliver data that meet these objectives, transactions recording follows a certain number of guidelines or principles which are accepted by accountants around the world.

This chapter will present these key principles (conventions, broad guidelines, rules, and detailed procedures) around which accounting is organized. These principles apply to all accounting entries and provide a common foundation for greater understandability and comparability of financial statements.

One of these principles is the matching principle, introduced in Chapter 2, which is connected to the definition of the accounting period. The matching principle specifies that cost or expenses should be recorded at the same time as the revenue to which

Major topics

Accounting principles

End-of-period entries

Reporting of adjusting entries

Correction of errors

Closing entries

they correspond, i.e., cost and revenues that are linked during an accounting period should be reported in the same period. What we have recorded in Chapter 4 are the current operations of a business. However the cut-off between periods (specifying to which period a revenue or an expense "belongs") will require carrying out end-of-period adjustments. These allow one to close the books of one period and open those of the next. This chapter will, therefore, also introduce these entries that are essential to the completion of the periodic accounting cycle.

CORE ISSUES

Accounting principles

As indicated in Chapter 1, accounting produces a social good. The output of accounting is aimed at a variety of users who will use it in their decision making. It is therefore crucial that a large number of users can understand the meaning of the accounting reports, and that these describe fairly the situation of the economic entity. It is therefore necessary that "rules of the game" be established and followed. These rules, as mentioned previously are the accounting principles. These form a coherent set (see Figure 5.1) of behavioral rules and guidelines that range from pure concepts to the very operational guidelines about practice. Words used to refer to these principles vary between authors, between practitioners, and between countries. What we call principles is called elsewhere "concept", "convention", or "assumptions". In a given country, the set of principles is referred to in short as the local **GAAP** (for generally accepted accounting principles, a concept defined in Chapter 1). We will therefore specify the GAAP set when it is useful in understanding a specific real-world example. We will thus speak of US GAAP or Dutch GAAP or German GAAP. The trend is, however, to evolve towards two GAAPs: the US GAAP, largely influenced by the US financial market regulators, and the IAS GAAP which reflects the views of a broad international community of users. Some would even support the idea of an evolution towards one single set of GAAP (which would maximize comparability). Which of the leading two contenders will win is, however, pure speculation at this time.

It is useful to understand why these principles have been retained over time as they help producers and users as well understand the value and the limits of accounting information. It also provides an opportunity to explore how the usefulness and quality of accounting information can be improved (the qualitative characteristics of useful information have been presented in Chapter 1 – see Figure 1.7).

Figure 5.1 aims at classifying the accounting principles in four broad categories based on four critical requirements or constraints information users place on accounting.

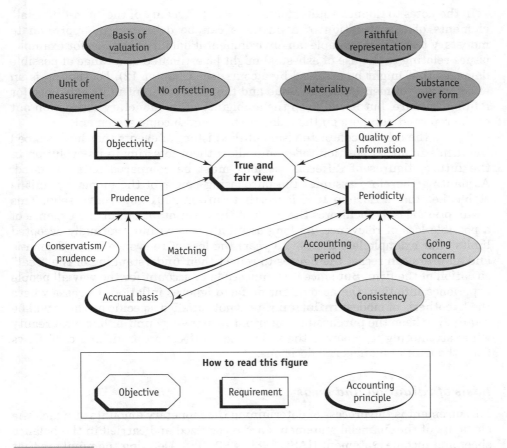

Figure 5.1 Accounting principles

Requirements

Objectivity

Unit of measurement

Financial accounting only records transactions expressed in financial units (euro, British pound, US dollar, ruble, etc.). No principle prevents accounting from keeping accounts of value creation and value consumption in terms other than financial. For example, it is conceivable to account for the environmental effect of a firm's behavior or its impact on the health of a population, and some specialized accounting approaches exist to handle such issues. However, all alternative valuation bases have a subjective component. The only objective common denominator between events and transactions is the financial measure of their economic impact which can be expressed only in monetary terms. Clearly, this limitation to financial elements is a loss of the richness of the description of the reality of a situation. However, the fact that everyone uses the same valuation bases creates coherence and allows all users to understand figures to mean the same thing.

In the notes to financial statements, some of the reality of the "non-financial" elements of the situation of a business can be described in approximate monetary terms. For example, an environmental liability (such as, for example, issues relating to the use of asbestos) might be estimated as a range of possible damages that might be assessed by a court (see Chapter 12). Footnoting is an effective way of mentioning an issue and the risks inherent in its existence for a full disclosure, but it will keep the ambiguity of its monetary estimation out of the reported numbers on the balance sheet and income statement.

To give the users a complete vision of the history of events that have shaped the firm's financial position today and allow them to estimate its evolution in the future, figures of different periods must be compared or aggregated. Accounting therefore assumes the purchasing power of the monetary unit is stable, i.e., that a Euro in 1999 is worth a Euro in 2001 (and conversely). This assumption clearly facilitates the work of the accountant but at the expense of a possible loss of relevance. As long as inflation is within "normally accepted limits" (for example less than 3% a year) the loss of relevance is not dramatic and all users can recast the figures to reflect their understanding of the "real" situation of the firm. But since it is impossible to account for the way all people experience inflation, the accountant de facto ignores inflation. In cases where the hypothesis of modest **inflation** rate is not satisfied, specific methods will be required to keep the purchasing power of the monetary unit in line with reality while attempting to separate the inflationary effects on profit and cash flows from the fruit of managerial decisions.

Basis of valuation and measurement

Measurement is the process of determining the monetary amounts at which the elements of the financial statements are recognized and carried in the balance sheet and income statement (IASC 1989: § 99–100). Defining the numbers that describe the effects of a transaction involves the selection of a particular basis of measurement. A number of different measurement bases can be employed and even mixed to different degrees in financial statements. They include the following:

- **Historical cost**: Assets are recorded at the amount of cash or cash equivalents paid or the fair value of the consideration given to acquire them at the time of their acquisition. Liabilities are recorded at the amount or proceeds received in exchange for the obligation, or in some circumstances (for example, income taxes), at the amounts of cash or cash equivalents expected to be paid to satisfy the liability in the normal course of business.

- **Current (or replacement) cost**: Assets are carried at the amount of cash or cash equivalents that would have to be paid if the same or an equivalent asset were acquired currently. Liabilities are carried at the undiscounted amount of cash or cash equivalents that would be required to settle the obligation right now.

- **Realizable (settlement or liquidation) value**: Assets are carried at the amount of cash or cash equivalents that could currently be obtained by selling the asset in an orderly disposal. Liabilities are carried at their settlement values; that is, the undiscounted amounts of cash or cash equivalents expected to be paid to satisfy the liabilities in the normal course of business.

- **Present value**: Assets are carried at the net present value of the future net cash inflows that the item is expected to generate in the normal course of business. Liabilities are carried at the net present value of the future net cash outflows that are expected to be required to settle the liabilities in the normal course of business.

The measurement basis most commonly adopted by enterprises in preparing the financial statements is historical cost since it is the one that requires the fewest hypotheses. This choice is coherent with the philosophy of "better approximate, unchallengeable and understandable than more descriptive but debatable and difficult to interpret". Historical costing is usually combined with other measurement bases. For example, inventories are usually carried at the lower of (historical) cost and net realizable value. Such a choice makes sense, especially in high-tech fields where the cost of components (i.e., their price on the market) falls very rapidly. It would not be fair to shareholders to describe an asset at its purchase price if the replacement value (or the resale value) is lower as is probably the case in the microelectronics field. We have to keep in mind that the objective of financial statements is to report to shareholders the financial situation of their investment.

Some countries choose to allow marketable securities (see Chapter 10) to be carried at market value (i.e., their resale value). Such practice may create some problems should a market downturn occur. Paper profits on marketable securities recognized in previous periods may have to be reduced, and possibly eliminated by what may appear to be paper losses. Pension liabilities (see Chapter 12) are carried at their net present value.

No offsetting

Offsetting of opposite net effects of different transactions could hide some of the richness of the situation accounting is supposed to report on. Such practice would obscure the reality of the risks faced by the firm in each transaction. Two transactions may have the same absolute value effect with opposite algebraic signs but their balance, which would arithmetically be zero, would not reflect the truth. For example, an overdrawn account at one bank and a positive bank balance with another bank may have equivalent amounts but the risks they carry are not equivalent.

Accountants have established the principle that assets and liabilities should not be offset except when offsetting is specifically required or permitted by an accounting standard. Similarly, items of income and expense should be offset when, and only when: (a) an accounting standard requires or permits it, or (b) gains, losses and related expenses arising from the same or similar transactions and events are not material (IASC 1997: § 33–34).

For this reason all ledgers and subsidiary ledgers provide the richest of records where all details of all transactions remain un-offset against one another even if the subsidiary ledger has been closed and the net balance transferred to the general ledger or to the balance sheet or income statement. Accounting is not only the way to report on the financial position of the firm, it is also the way to create and maintain a full archive of how such a position was achieved. Such an archive is essential for better understanding what went right and what went wrong so that more performance can be created in the future.

Example 1

If a business has 2 bank accounts, one in Acme Bank with a positive balance of 1,000 CU and a second one in Everyone Thrift Bank with a negative balance of 400 CU, offsetting would be to report a net balance of a positive 600. However, the no offsetting principle requires that the positive balance be reported on the asset side and the negative balance be reported on the liability side of the balance sheet.

Example 2

If a business owes a supplier 5,000 CU and simultaneously has a claim on that very supplier for the same amount (for example, as the result of a downpayment) it would not make sense to offset the two events as they reflect different parts of the business. The debt will be on the liability side and the claim on the supplier will be an asset.

Quality of financial statements

The usefulness of financial statements to decision makers rests on the reports being detailed enough but not too detailed to be overwhelming (materiality and aggregation principle), providing a faithful description of the economic situation of the business (faithful presentation principle), and being meaningful in the sense that they choose substance over form.

Materiality and aggregation

"Information is material if its non-disclosure could influence the economic decisions of users taken on the basis of the financial statements. Each material item should be presented separately in the financial statements. Immaterial amounts should be aggregated with amounts of a similar nature or function and need not to be presented separately" (IASC 1997: § 31 and § 29). However, all data must be reported.

Faithful presentation

"To be reliable, information must represent faithfully the transactions and other events it either purports to represent or could reasonably be expected to represent. Thus, for example, a balance sheet should represent faithfully the transactions and other events that result in assets, liabilities and equity of the enterprise at the reporting date (...). Most financial information is subject to some risk of being less than a faithful representation of that which it purports to portray. This is not due to bias, but rather to inherent difficulties either in identifying the transaction and other events to be measured or in devising and applying measurement and presentation techniques that can convey messages that communicate the full complexity of those transactions and events" (IASC 1989: § 33–34).

Substance over form

"If information is to represent faithfully the transactions and other events that it purports to represent, it is necessary that they are accounted for and presented in accordance with their substance and economic reality and not merely their legal form. The substance of transactions or other events is not always consistent with that which is apparent from their legal or contrived form. For example, an enterprise may dispose of an asset to another party in such a way that the documentation purports to pass legal ownership to that party; nevertheless, agreements to pay exist that ensure that the enterprise continues to enjoy the future economic benefits embodied in the asset. In such circumstances, the reporting of a sale would not represent faithfully the transaction entered into (if indeed there was a transaction)" (IASC 1989: § 35).

An operation such as the one described in the preceding paragraph is called a leaseback (see Chapter 12) and is commonly used by businesses to create cash. For example, a business may sell the building in which their headquarters is housed and lease it back immediately from the buyer. A proper way of recording such an operation would be to recognize, on one hand, the sale and the cash it generated and, on the other hand, recognize the fact the business now has a commitment to pay rent which can be measured through the net present value of the rental payments (liability) and an asset of equivalent amount that recognizes the building is actually at the disposal of the firm and will therefore permit future economic benefits. The retained earnings are not affected since we have the same amount on both sides of the balance sheet, but now the document fully reflects the reality of the situation.

Such a principle, although useful, is not universally accepted. To make an oversimplification, the substance over form principle is accepted and used mainly in the North American zone of influence. Many countries have adopted specific rules or principles for the recording of leases (see Chapter 12).

Prudence

The accountant is prudent by nature. She or he does not wish to recognize profit (or loss) before it has been earned with certainty. Three principles serve to achieve this objective: conservatism, accrual, and matching.

Conservatism

Preparers of financial statements have to contend with uncertainties that inevitably surround many events and circumstances, such as the collectability of doubtful receivables, the probable useful life of plant and equipment, and the number of warranty claims that may occur. Such uncertainties are recognized by the disclosure of their nature and extent and by the exercise of conservatism (or prudence) in the preparation of the financial statements. Prudence is the inclusion of a degree of caution in the exercise of the judgements needed in making the estimates required under conditions of uncertainty, such that assets or income are not overstated and liabilities or expenses are not understated (IASC 1989: § 37).

The exercise of prudence does not allow, for example, the creation of hidden reserves or excessive provisions, the deliberate understatement of assets or income, the deliberate overstatement of assets or income, or the deliberate overstatement of liabilities or expenses, because the financial statements would not be neutral, and, therefore, not have the quality of reliability.

The 4th EU Directive (1978: art. 31) states that "valuation must be made on a prudent basis, and in particular:

1 only profits concretely and definitively earned on the balance sheet date may be included;

2 account must be taken of all foreseeable liabilities and potential losses arising in the course of the financial year concerned or of a previous one, even if such liabilities or losses become apparent only between the date of the balance sheet and the date on which it is drawn up;

3 account must be taken of all depreciation whether the result of the financial year is a loss or a profit".

Practically, this principle means that profits should not be anticipated. They should only be taken into the accounts when they are realized. For example, sales should be recorded only when the goods have been shipped and invoiced and not when the order was received.

As far as losses are concerned they should be recognized as soon as the events giving rise to them take place. For example, when the resale value of an item in inventory decreases below its acquisition or manufacturing cost, the loss in value should be recognized immediately, even if the item is not sold. One example of a practice coherent with conservatism is that of always valuing inventories at the lower of cost or market. Provisions or valuation allowances used to recognize these losses will be further explored later in this chapter.

Conservatism is, like historical basis in the measurement unit, generally accepted but still controversial at times as there are many situations in which its usefulness is debatable, as is the case in the valuation of marketable securities in a volatile market.

Accrual basis

As we showed in Chapter 2, the accrual principle consists in recognizing or recording an event when it occurs and not when the cash transactions it induces have been completed. IAS 1 (IASC 1997: § 25) stipulates that an enterprise should prepare its financial statements, except for cash flow information, under the accrual basis of accounting. Financial statements must only reflect revenue, expenses, and income that relate to a given accounting period. The resulting difference between cash transactions and amounts recognized under the accrual basis must be shown as either an accrued expense (liability), a prepaid expense (asset), accrued revenue (asset), or prepaid revenue (liability) (see the next section in this chapter).

Matching

According to this principle, also introduced earlier, and coherently with the accrual basis, expenses are recognized in the income statement on the basis of their direct association with the revenue also recognized. Matching of costs with revenues is defined in IAS 1 (IASC 1997: § 26) and IASC Framework (IASC 1989: § 95) as the simultaneous or combined recognition of revenues and expenses that result directly and jointly from the same transactions or other events.

Periodicity

This objective or requirement consists of three principles: accounting period, going concern, and consistency of presentation and is also connected to the accrual and matching concepts introduced earlier.

Accounting period

As stated in Chapter 1, reporting to shareholders occurs at regular intervals, these defining the accounting period. The yearly accounting period is generally some arbitrary segmentation of the lifecycle of any business.

The outcome of the managers' decisions and actions (income) must be known for at least the following economical and legal reasons:

1 Need to know the performance potential of the firm and evaluate the quality of the management and of their decisions as agents of the shareholders.
2 Need to share the income between partners or shareholders.
3 Need to provide a basis for the state to levy taxes based on income.

The only definitive measure of the income or value created by a business is the one that would be established through an income statement that would span the entire life of the firm. However, no shareholder or regulatory agency wants to have to wait that long to know (a) how much wealth has been created, and (b) whether the managers, who are the shareholders' agents, are making the right decisions or at least decisions that the shareholders approve. Businesses are controlled by checking the outcome of decisions against the firm's strategic intent. Corrective actions are decided (both by investors and by managers) to bring the firm's financial position ever closer to fulfilling its strategic intent. The year-long accounting period is the longest periodicity that appears acceptable to all parties, many require more frequent information. In fact, most financial markets require reporting the financial position of listed firms on a quarterly basis.

The measurement of income is carried in contiguous yet clearly separated time slices. The accrual principle and the end-of-period entries (see later in this chapter) permit this partitioning of time and income in coherent sets useful for forecasting and decision making.

Going concern

The ability to allocate income between time periods rests on the assumption that a business entity has a long life expectancy. This assumption of continuity is called the "going concern principle". Unless the accountant has specific knowledge to the contrary, she or he will assume continuity when establishing the financial statements. It is management's responsibility to take decisions so the business goes on as long as possible for the benefit of the shareholders. Failure in exercising this responsibility leads to bankruptcy or to the business entity being bought out.

The going concern principle is a key reason for valuing assets and resources or liabilities at their historical costs rather than at their liquidation value. During the next periods the company will be able to gain economic benefits from the existence of these assets. The least debatable proxy for the net present value of these future benefits remains the purchase price of the asset, eventually adjusted over time through depreciation to recognize reduction of the potential since acquisition.

IAS 1 (IASC 1997: § 23) stipulates: "When preparing financial statements, management should make an assessment of an enterprise's ability to continue as a going concern. Financial statements should be prepared on a going concern basis unless management either intends to liquidate the enterprise or to cease trading, or has no realistic alternative but to do so. When management is aware, in making its assessment, of material uncertainties related to events or conditions which may cast significant doubt upon the enterprise's ability to continue as a going concern, those uncertainties should be disclosed. When the financial statements are not prepared on a going concern basis, that fact should be disclosed, together with the basis on which the financial statements are prepared and the reason why the enterprise is not considered to be a going concern".

Similarly the EU 4th Directive (1978: art. 31) prescribes that "the company must be presumed to be carrying on its business as a going concern". In other words, this principle means that there is no reason to suppose that the company will not be carrying on its business throughout the following financial year and years.

Consistency of presentation

Financial statements must be useful to decision makers. They must provide not only comparability with other firms involved in the same line of business (same risk factors) but also comparability from period to period to be able to detect trends and evolutions. It is therefore critical that the financial statements be presented in consistent fashion and over consistent parameters. If principles of presentation or parameter change following alterations of strategy or necessity, it will be essencial, in order to give a true and fair view of the firm's situation, to recast the new and the old data so that a minimum number of years are presented in homogeneous fashion for comparison purposes. This principle allows changes and regulates how these can be implemented (see Chapter 6 for more details).

IAS 1 (IASC 1997: § 27) indicates that "the presentation and classification of items in the financial statements should be retained from one period to the next unless:

(a) a significant change in the nature of the operations of the enterprise or a review of its financial statement presentation demonstrates that the change will result in a more appropriate presentation of events or transactions; or

(b) a change in presentation is required by an International Accounting Standard".

The standard adds that a change in presentation to comply with national requirements is permitted as long as the revised presentation is consistent with the requirements of IAS 1.

The 4th EU Directive (1978: art. 31) states that "the methods of valuation must be applied consistently from one financial year to another". In practice, this means that the valuation method used at the end of a financial year must be the same as that applied at the end of the preceding year. The effect of this is that the comparative figures for the preceding year appearing in a balance sheet (which are required by IAS 1, by the 4th EU Directive (EU 1978) and by many other national standards) are fully comparable with the figures for the current year. The importance of this principle will become apparent when we look later at the different methods of valuation used for various assets (concepts of depreciation and provision or valuation allowance).

Main objective of accounting principles: give a true and fair view

We have used the term **"true and fair view"** in Chapter 3. It does not really represent a principle per se but defines the intent of the adoption of the principles we listed earlier, as shown in Figure 5.1:

True means that the financial statements do not falsify or dissimulate the financial situation of the company at period-end or its profits (or losses) for the period then ended.

Fair applies to accounts that give accounting users complete and relevant information for decision making.

There is, in fact, no officially recognized and generally accepted definition of "true and fair" as it applies to financial statements. The term is used but never precisely defined. For instance, IAS 1 (IASC 1997: § 10) requires that financials statements "present fairly the financial position, financial performance and cash flows of an enterprise". The 4th EU Directive (1978: art. 2) prescribes that the annual accounts "give a true and fair view of the company's assets, liabilities, financial position and profit or loss". Neither, however, ever defines clearly the concepts they use.

The entity concept

Although not quite a principle, the entity concept which we introduced in Chapter 1 is a key foundation of accounting and of financial reports. It specifies that regardless of the legal form of the economic entity (sole proprietorship, partnership, limited company, etc. – see Chapter 11), economic transactions carried by the entity must be recorded separately from that of the personal transactions of actors involved in or with the entity.

End-of-period entries

Accounting principles, and especially the matching, accrual and periodicity principles, create the need to know exactly what pertains to a period (and provide the techniques to handle that requirement). Some events that took place during the period are linked to the passage of time or other causes such that they are not effectively documented through a transaction with a paper or electronic support. Other events straddle two periods and need to be partitioned between the two. Inventory and some asset values have to be adjusted if their market value has decreased, assets must be depreciated, etc.

End-of-period entries refer to any such entries that are necessary to give a true and fair view of both the financial position at the end of an accounting period and the income statement for the accounting period. These entries will be carried out every time one closes the books (yearly, half-yearly, quarterly, monthly, etc.).

Figure 5.2 outlines the main categories of end-of-period entries and identifies the principles that are at the source of the issue.

The accounting principles studied earlier in this chapter become particularly important when the year-end entries are recorded. In order to apply these principles, management has to exercise considerable judgement. This confirms that accounting cannot be considered to be an exact mathematical science.

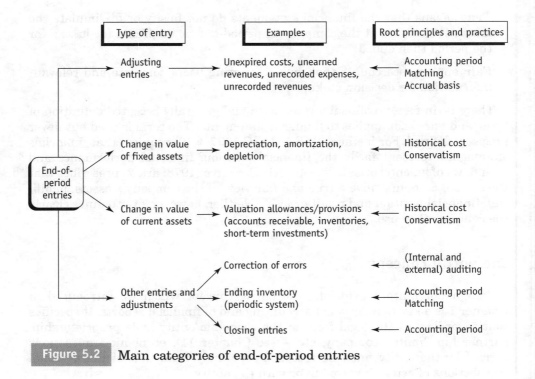

Figure 5.2 Main categories of end-of-period entries

Adjusting entries

The fundamental difficulty encountered with year-end financial statements is that the accounting period (generally the year, and even more so in the case of quarterly reporting) does not correspond to the duration of a normal operating cycle, whatever the company's activities. In manufacturing, distribution, services, utilities, etc., the economic cycle may be either longer or shorter than that of the reporting period.

However, in order to provide regular periodic information to shareholders, employees, financial institutions and markets, and, incidentally, to tax authorities, annual financial statements have to be prepared despite the economic entity continuing to carry on its operational activities on an ongoing basis. This means that a cut-off date has to be selected by company management in agreement with the shareholders. This date will be used as a watershed separating transactions pertaining to the closing period and those pertaining to the next one. As a result, many year-end adjustments are related to the influence of time: for example, an insurance premium invoice is probably not going to be received on the first day of a 12-month accounting period, and since it generally corresponds to an insurance coverage for a year, the amount of the premium must be partitioned between at least 2 accounting periods.

The 4th EU Directive (1978: art. 18) states: "Expenditure incurred during the financial year but relating to a subsequent financial year, together with any income which, though relating to the financial year in question, is not due until after its expiry must be shown under Prepayments and Accrued Income." Similarly article 21 mandates that: "Income receivable before the balance sheet date but relating to a subsequent financial year, together with any charges which, though relating to the financial year in question, will be paid only in the course of the subsequent financial year, must be shown under Accruals and Deferred Income."

The most common adjusting entries may be classified in four categories as shown in Figure 5.3.

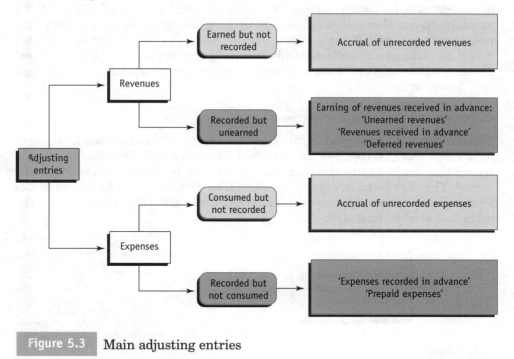

Figure 5.3 Main adjusting entries

Revenues

The principles of revenue recognition, which will be developed in Chapter 6, prescribe that revenues affect net income in the period during which they are earned, and not the period in which their cash equivalent is collected. In other words, net income must include all and only the revenues which have been earned during the accounting period. This principle has two major consequences:

1 Revenues which have been earned but not recorded, in particular because the triggering event has not occurred yet (for example, interest (on a loan) to be received after the closing date, sales delivered but not invoiced, etc.), must be recorded and "attached" to the current net income.

2 Conversely, revenues which have been recorded in advance and which cover a service to be rendered at a later date (for example, rent received in advance, subscription received from a customer for a newspaper service) must be adjusted to leave in the period only the relevant part.

Revenues earned but not recorded

It is necessary to recognize revenues that have been earned but have not yet been recorded. No entry has been recorded, mainly due to the fact that the event which would lead to the revenue will only happen in the future. For example, let us assume that interest revenue on a loan (for example, granted to a customer) becomes due only on the anniversary of the loan, let us say at the end of February. When the financial statements are drawn on the closing date of 31 December, the triggering event has not happened yet. However, during the period ending on that date, the firm has earned 10/12th of the annual interest on the loan. However the interest revenue is not due by the customer. No document will be issued saying the customer owes the firm 10/12th of the annual interest. However, it is essential to recognize, since interest is due to the passage of time, part of the annual interest revenue in this period even though it will be claimed and collected only during the next period. This unrecorded revenue will be accrued and recognized as revenue and capitalized as an asset (see details in Advanced Issues).

Revenues recorded but unearned

When a revenue is received in advance (for example, rent received in advance for several months, retainer fee, etc.) two alternative solutions can be used to record this event and to recognize the revenue in the appropriate accounting period. They are listed in Figure 5.4 and will be detailed in the Advanced Issues section. In each country, one of the alternatives is generally preferred but the other one is often tolerated.

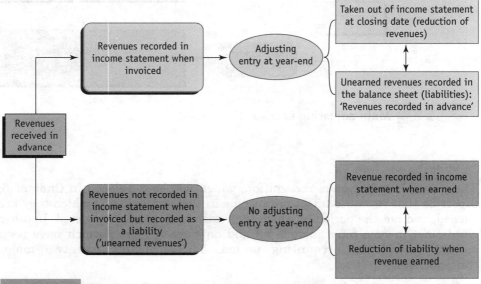

Figure 5.4 Revenues recorded but unearned

Expenses

Expenses should affect net income in the period during which the resources they represent are consumed, and not the period in which their acquisition transaction is settled in cash or cash equivalent. In other words, net income must include all and only the expenses which have been consumed during the accounting period. This principle has two major consequences:

1 Expenses which have been consumed but not recorded, in particular because the triggering event has not occurred (interest to be paid after closing date, purchases received but invoice not received from supplier, etc.) must be recorded and "attached" to the current net income calculation.

2 Conversely, expenses which have been recorded in advance (for example, rent paid in advance, retainer fee paid to lawyer) must be adjusted so as to recognize in the income statement only that part which is relevant for the accounting period.

Expenses consumed but not recorded

It is necessary to recognize expenses that have been consumed but not yet recorded (because the triggering event that will create the source document which will initiate the recording has not yet occurred). This would, for example, be the case of an interest expense on debt which would be due, say, on 30 June while the closing date is 31 December. Interest from 1 July to 31 December has actually built up and represents an expense of the closing period. However, it will not be due until 30 June of the next period. This accrued but unrecorded expense must be recognized as both an expense in the income statement and a liability as interest due in the balance sheet (see example later).

Expenses recorded but not consumed

When an expense is paid in advance it often straddles two accounting periods. For example, subscription fee to a software help line is generally paid in advance for the coming year but these 12 months rarely correspond to the accounting period. Two solutions can be used to record such an event and to recognize the expense in the proper period. Figure 5.5 illustrates the choice. Although each country's accounting regulators generally indicate a preferred approach, it is not unusual to see both approaches coexist.

A comparison of the two methods is presented later in Advanced Issues.

Value adjustments to fixed asset accounts

Principles

Fixed or tangible assets are defined in the IASC Glossary (IASC 2001) as assets:

- held by an enterprise for use in the production or supply of goods or services, for rental to others, or for administrative purposes
- expected to be used during more than one period.

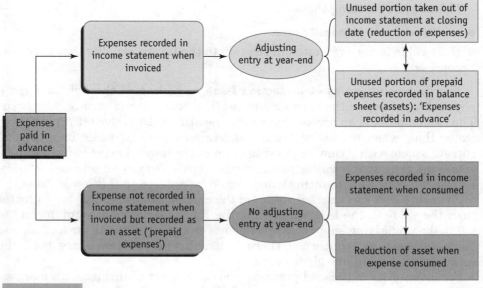

| Figure 5.5 | Expenses paid in advance

The value of fixed assets in the balance sheet is initially carried at their purchase price or acquisition cost (i.e., purchase price plus all costs incurred to make the asset useable in the context of the business strategy). This value needs to be adjusted periodically to recognize either or both of the wear and tear on the equipment (reduction of potential to create a stream of future economic benefits) and its technological obsolescence.

The 4th EU Directive which defines fixed assets (1978: art. 15) as comprising "those assets which are intended for use on a continuing basis for the purposes of the undertaking's activities" specifies that their accounting value ("the purchase price or production") "must be reduced by value adjustments" (which we call depreciation) "calculated to write off the value of such assets systematically over their useful economic lives" (article 35 b). This rule, it adds, should only be applied to assets with a limited economic life. For example, land is not considered subject to these downward value adjustments (although it satisfies all the criteria of definition of an asset) because the stream of future economic benefits is not affected by use. Incidentally, any increase in value of land is going to be unrecorded in accounting because of the prudence principle.

Depreciation is the process of allocating the cost of a tangible or fixed asset (with the exception of land) over the period during which economic benefits will be received by the firm. The justification for this process is found in the matching principle because each period benefits from the existence of the asset and is therefore deemed to consume a share of the original cost. Depreciation has already been mentioned in Chapter 2. Chapter 7 will give us the opportunity to explore further the depreciation mechanisms and their implication in the management of the business (see example opposite).

Value adjustments to current asset accounts

The application of the prudence/conservatism principle so that information given in the annual accounts satisfies the true and fair view objective, implies that the accounting values recorded during the year for current assets be validated against economic realities at year-end.

This implies checking that:

● assets really do physically exist
● their value is not overstated in relation to the future benefits that they represent.

The first point, an asset protection issue, is addressed through carrying a physical inventory of the existing current (and fixed) assets on a regular basis. The second point is an accounting issue. The 4th EU Directive (1978: art. 30 b) states that, when necessary, "value adjustments shall be made in respect of current assets with a view to showing them at the lower market value": that is, where the price that a willing purchaser is prepared to pay for an asset is below its original cost, its accounting value should be reduced to this lower value.

To ensure that the "market value" of the current assets is equal to or greater than the value in the ledger accounts, the Ravel Company accountant had to study the underlying supporting documents and other data. As far as cash and bank balances are concerned there is usually no problem since both the accounts are held in one given currency unit.

For inventories of finished products, the accountant confirmed with management that the current sales prices and the future sales forecasts gave every assurance that the future customers would pay an amount at least equal to the

The accountant has been informed by the local tax authorities that the normal useful life for Ravel Co.'s buildings was 50 years. This means that the acquisition cost of the building (5,000 CU) should be distributed over that period of time. The directors agreed with the accountant that a fixed annual depreciation charge of 100 CU should be attached to each accounting period.

Tax authorities and most accounting regulatory bodies endorse the no offsetting principle whose application forbids, netting the cost of acquisition, and the accumulated depreciation of any asset. As long as an asset is the property of the economic entity, it should be shown in its financial statements. The acquisition cost of a fixed asset will be shown separately from the accumulated depreciation. This separate depreciation account is called a "**contra asset**" account because it will be listed in the balance sheet on the asset side but with a negative (credit) balance.

As far as the calculation of income is concerned, depreciation is treated in the same way as any expense item, even though it is a "calculated charge", i.e., a charge that relates to a cash outflow that took place in possibly another period and will benefit several periods.

Figure 5.6 illustrates the entries required to account for depreciation.

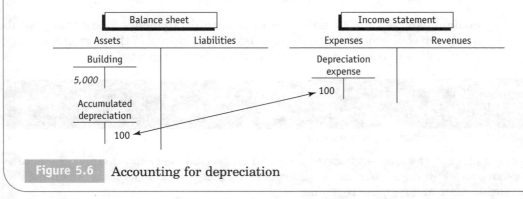

Figure 5.6 Accounting for depreciation

cost recorded in the accounts. For inventories of raw materials, the production program indicated clearly that all the items held in inventory would be used and the invested cost recovered through future saleable products. Therefore, for these categories of current assets no value adjustment is necessary.

The accountant also needs to evaluate the probability that Ravel Company will recover the full value of claims held by Ravel over its customers (accounts receivable). To do this, he studies the situation of each individual customer, looking for example at the following aspects:

- Has the customer challenged the validity of the receivable?
- Has the customer returned goods and/or complained about Ravel Co.'s service?
- Is the customer up to date with payments according to the agreed contractual terms governing the sales?
- Is there any correspondence (or other data) indicating that the customer had financial difficulties?
- Have any letters from Ravel Company been returned as undeliverable from the customer's address?

Although value adjustment to current assets will be developed more fully in Chapter 10, suffice it to say at this stage that a loss of value of a current asset will be recorded through contra asset accounts such as provisions or allowances for which the mechanism is very similar to that of depreciation. It is illustrated in Figure 5.7. Provision or allowance entries are in conformance with the no offsetting principle as well as the lower of cost or market value seen under the units of measurement principle.

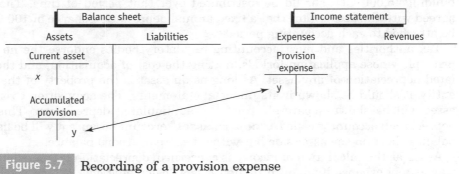

Figure 5.7   Recording of a provision expense

Reporting for adjusting entries

Some illustrations of actual notes to financial statements follow that provide details, in conformance with the no offsetting principle, of the elements affected by adjusting entries and which create the balances reported.

Pirelli
(Italy —Italian GAAP – Source: Annual report 1999 – Tires, cables, and systems)

Notes to the financial statements

Accrued income: the amount is determined on an accrual basis and mainly relates to the portion of [foreign] exchange differences on hedging transactions, insurance, interest income and hedging revenues.

Prepaid expenses (…) mainly refer to prepaid insurance, property rent, etc.
Accrued liabilities (…) include the portion of [foreign] exchange differences on hedging transactions, property leases payable, hedging costs; etc.

Deferred income (…) includes advance installment payments.

Philips
(Netherlands – Dutch/US GAAP – Source: Annual report 1999 – Consumer electronic products)

Accrued liabilities include "salaries and wages payable", "income tax payable", "accrued holiday rights", "accrued pension costs", "commissions, freight, interest and rent payable" and "other liabilities" (deferred payment in connection with the acquisition of a company).

Uno Restaurant Corporation

(USA – US GAAP – Source: Annual report 1999 – Pizzerias Uno, Chicago Bar & Grill restaurants, owned or franchised)

Excerpts from the balance sheet at year end

Year ended (amounts in thousands of dollars)	3 October 1999	27 September 1998
ASSETS		
(...)		
Prepaid expenses	1,757	815
(...)		
LIABILITIES AND SHAREHOLDERS' EQUITY		
(...)		
Accrued expenses	8,668	7,949
(...)		

Notes to financial statements

8 Prepaid expenses

Prepaid expenses consist of the following:

Year ended (amounts in thousands of dollars)	3 October 1999	27 September 1998
Prepaid rent	1,430	442
Prepaid operating costs	269	234
Prepaid insurance	58	139
	1,757	815

9 Accrued expenses

Accrued expenses consist of the following:

Year ended (amounts in thousands of dollars)	3 October 1999	27 September 1998
Accrued store closure	2,197	1,826
Accrued rent	1,483	1,372
Accrued insurance	1,627	793
Accrued utilities	653	785
Accrued vacation	737	680
Accrued advertising	482	557
Franchise fee deposits	273	486
Other	1,216	1,450
	8,668	7,949

The consolidated balance sheet of the company does not include any deferred income or accrued income.

ADVANCED ISSUES

At year-end, adjusting entries, correction of errors, entries relating to ending inventories, and closing entries will be recorded.

Recording of adjusting entries

After the introduction of the main types of adjusting entries, we will now explore the details of how each is being recorded in accounting.

Revenues earned but not recorded

Let us use the example of a royalty revenue not invoiced because the department in charge has been overworked and lags behind in invoicing. At the end of the year the accountant records for an amount of 20 CU an estimate of the royalty to be recovered. During the next accounting period, when the royalty department has time to calculate the correct amount to claim, an invoice is issued for 25 CU. Figures 5.8 and 5.9 describe the way to handle the situation.

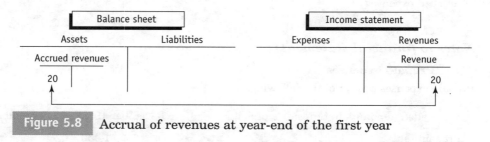

Figure 5.8 Accrual of revenues at year-end of the first year

Two solutions are possible for handling the completion of the transaction in the second period are illustrated in Figure 5.9.

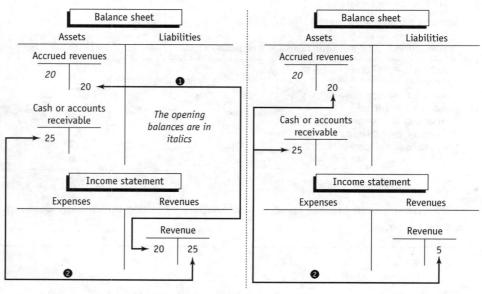

❶ Opening date (of the following accounting period)
❷ Reception of the document or date of the event

Figure 5.9 Accrual of revenues the following year

Appendix 5.1 analyzes the two solutions.

Revenues recorded but unearned

The general principles for handling such an entry have been introduced in the first part of the chapter. Two possible methods have been mentioned. We now present an example comparing the two methods.

Example

Rent for 200 CU is received from a tenant on 15 December, in advance for the second half of December of this current accounting period plus January and the first half of February of the next accounting period. The closing date for the books is 31 December. Figure 5.10 illustrates how accounting will record the situation.

Solution 1 – Revenue is recorded in advance and adjusted

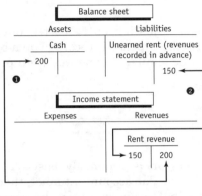

Solution 2 – Revenue is not recorded in advance

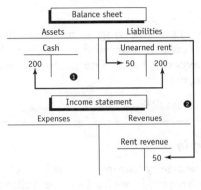

❶ 15 December: recording of the receipt of rent

❷ 31 December: adjusting entry in solution 1. In solution 2, the entry records the revenue. It is not an adjusting entry in the strict sense

Figure 5.10 Revenues recorded in advance – Year 1

Entries for the following year are presented in Figure 5.11.

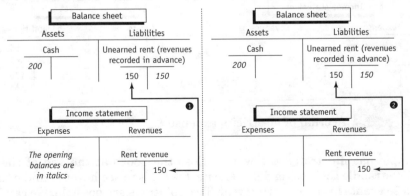

❶ 1 January: reversal of adjusting entry

❷ 15 February: recording of the revenue (solution 2)

Entries ❶ and ❷ are the same in both cases, except one is recorded on 1 January while the other one is recorded on 15 February. Comments on the 2 solutions are listed in Appendix 5.2

Figure 5.11 Accounting entries in Year 2

Expenses consumed but not recorded

Principle

The basic accounting entry is shown in Figure 5.12.

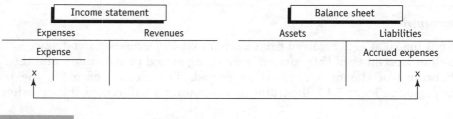

Figure 5.12 Expenses consumed but not recorded

The following is an illustration of adjusting entry corresponding to the accrual of unrecorded expenses. Here, the expense is recorded on a by nature of expense basis. The procedure would be similar if expenses were presented by function.

Example

The electricity company invoices customers on a bimonthly basis. The last invoice received was for October and November. The accountant must, therefore, calculate the cost of electricity consumed in December. From the company's electrical engineer he receives an estimate of the number of kWh (kilowatt hours) consumed in December. Thus using the rate known from previous invoices, the accountant calculates that the electricity expense for December Year 1 amounts to 175 CU (see Figure 5.13).

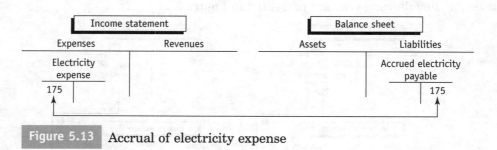

Figure 5.13 Accrual of electricity expense

This example has illustrated the way to close the books at the end of the year for events that straddle the closing date. The next issue is to see how to handle the second part of these events in the following year. Two solutions are possible. We can illustrate the procedure with this last transaction. Let us assume further that an analysis of the detailed invoice received in mid-February shows the real cost of electricity for December of Year 1 was 180 CU (instead of 175 anticipated). Figure 5.14 illustrates how accounting will handle the situation.

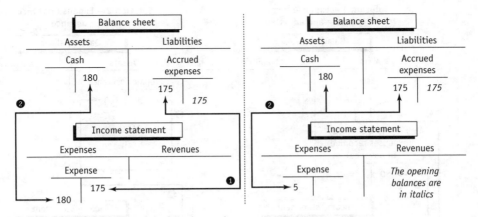

● Opening date (beginning of the following year)
❷ Reception of the document or date of the event

Figure 5.14 Recording in Year 2

Appendix 5.3 presents some comments on this type of entry.

Expenses recorded in advance

The two solutions that can be used to record expenses paid in advance have been mentioned in the first part of the chapter. Let us now look at some examples to illustrate these solutions.

Example

Insurance premium of 120 CU paid on 1 September for coverage during the next 12 months. The closing date for the accounts is 31 December.

Figure 5.15 illustrates Year 1 entries.

Year 2 entries are described in Figure 5.16.

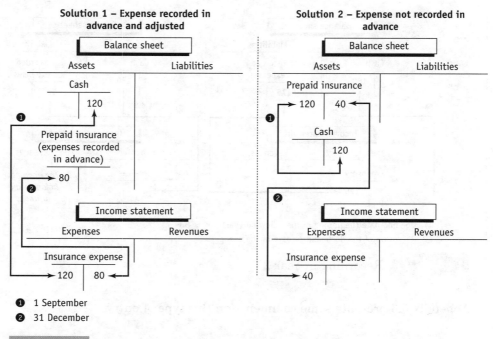

Solution 1 – Expense recorded in advance and adjusted

Solution 2 – Expense not recorded in advance

❶ 1 September
❷ 31 December

Figure 5.15 Expenses recorded in advance – Year 1

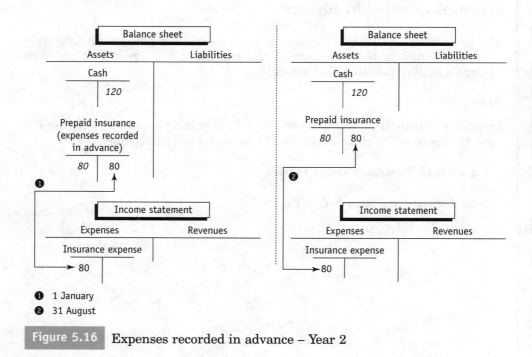

❶ 1 January
❷ 31 August

Figure 5.16 Expenses recorded in advance – Year 2

Entries are identical but they are not recorded on the same day. Appendix 5.4 compares and contrasts both methods.

Correction of errors

Accounting records may contain errors. We said in Chapter 4 that computerization of accounting could guarantee a quasi-perfect reliability of transfers between accounts but errors in the original recording may have been introduced without being immediately detected. It is part of normal procedures for all firms establishing financial statements to carry out an internal audit of their procedures and practices to create assurance that the figures are true and fair and devoid of mistakes. When carried out with rigor, this internal audit can detect the majority of errors and allow for their immediate correction. In addition, because financial statements are so important for a variety of users and especially the shareholders, these mandate an external accountant to carry an independent audit so as to make doubly sure that all figures are true and fair.

When an error is uncovered, the most common solution is the cancellation of the erroneous entry through a "reversing entry" and the correct reentry of the same event. Some accounting software packages allow a pure and simple cancellation or modification of an entry until it has been validated and rendered "definitive". Such a possibility is convenient but can be dangerous because it does not leave any trace of the original error, the identification of which, in many cases, can be source of improvement and learning.

Errors and omissions that are uncovered after the books are definitely closed and the financial statements drawn require a special procedure which will be dealt with in Chapter 6.

Ending inventory

Chapter 9 covers the end-of-period entries required for inventories when purchases are recorded as presumed consumption directly in the income statement (see Chapter 2).

Closing entries

Once the year-end accounting entries have been entered in the journal and the ledger accounts, the preparation of the financial statements can begin. This will be done by first closing all individual expenses and revenues accounts to the income statement and second by closing the income statement to the balance sheet to establish the income of the period.

Expenses and revenues accounts keep track of all the operating transactions that took place within the ending financial year. They provide a veritable archive of how the income figure that will be shown in the year's income statement and the year-end balance sheet was attained. The procedure of closing accounts consists in transferring the year-end balances from the individual accounts to a cascade of summary accounts until all the information has been transferred to the final summary account which is the balance sheet.

Balance sheet accounts are not "closed" at the end of the year: their closing balances for one accounting period are the opening balances for the following period. For instance, article 31 of the 4th EU directive states: "The opening balance sheet for each financial year must correspond to the closing balance sheet for the preceding financial year."

Limitations on the applicability of accounting principles

As indicated earlier in this chapter, some accounting principles have limits (see one example in Appendix 5.5).

KEY POINTS

- Accounting for transactions follows a certain number of guidelines or principles which are accepted by all accountants around the world.
- These principles apply to all accounting entries and provide a common foundation for improved understandability and comparability of financial statements.
- In order to reach the final objective of "true and fair view", accounting information must respect four major requirements: (1) objectivity (unit of measurement, basis of valuation, and no offsetting), (2) quality of information (materiality, faithful representation, and substance over form), (3) prudence (conservatism, accrual basis, and matching) and (4) periodicity (accounting, consistency, and going concern).
- End-of-period entry refers to any entry that is necessary to give a true and fair view of both the financial position and the income statement. These entries will be carried out every time one closes the books (yearly, half-yearly, quarterly, monthly, etc.).
- The main categories of end-of-period entries are: adjusting entries, entries relating to changes in value of fixed assets (depreciation and amortization), entries concerning changes in value of current assets (provision), corrections of errors, entries relating to ending inventory (if necessary), and closing entries.
- One fundamental difficulty encountered with year-end financial statements is that the accounting period (generally the year, and even more, as is the case of quarterly reporting) does not correspond to the duration of a normal operating cycle. Consequently, a cut-off date has to be selected and year-end adjustments must be recorded.
- The four categories of adjusting entries are: revenues earned but not recorded, revenues recorded but unearned, expenses consumed but not recorded, and expenses recorded but not consumed.

Review 5.1 Adam

Topic: Accounting principles and end-of-period entries
Type: Group exercise
Related part of the chapter: Core Issues

Eve Adam, a newly hired graduate at the accounting firm Dewey, Billem and How, is puzzled by the preliminary balance sheet of 4 of the clients she is in charge of.

Company 1 – Balance sheet on 31 December (in 000 of CU)			
Assets		**Shareholders' equity and liabilities**	
Fixed assets	300,000	*Shareholders' equity*	
Minus accumulated depreciation	–160,000	Share capital and reserves	330,000
Fixed assets (net)	140,000	Net income	20,000
Current assets		*Liabilities*	40,000
Inventories	120,000		
Accounts receivable	130,000		
Total assets	390,000	**Total shareholders' equity and liabilities**	390,000

Eve Adam has learned that a freeway is going to be built in the next year adjacent to one property the company had set aside to build housing for its employees. This piece of land is carried in the books at its historical acquisition cost of 100,000 CU. The market value of the land is expected to fall by 40% as soon as the construction of the freeway begins.

Company 2 – Balance sheet on 31 December (in 000 of CU)			
Assets		**Shareholders' equity and liabilities**	
Fixed assets	250,000	*Shareholders' equity*	
Minus accumulated depreciation	–130,000	Share capital and reserves	300,000
Fixed assets (net)	120,000	Net income	50,000
Current assets		*Liabilities*	20,000
Inventories	100,000		
Accounts receivable	150,000		
Total assets	370,000	**Total shareholders' equity and liabilities**	370,000

When analyzing the accounts receivable, Eve Adam finds out that the Lakme Corp. accounts receivable, has been in arrears for the past 3 years over an invoice of 60,000 CU. Company 2 has never handled the situation in accounting terms. Exploring a little further Eve Adam discovers that Lakme Corp. has actually filed for bankruptcy two years ago and that the probability of collecting on the receivable is probably nil.

Company 3 – Balance sheet on 31 December (in 000 of CU)				
Assets			**Shareholders' equity and liabilities**	
Fixed assets	500,000		*Shareholders' equity*	
Minus accumulated depreciation	–240,000		Share capital and reserves	520,000
Fixed assets (net)	260,000		Net income	20,000
Current assets			*Liabilities*	200,000
Inventories	330,000			
Accounts receivable	150,000			
Total assets	740,000		**Total shareholders' equity and liabilities**	740,000

Eve Adam is rather surprised by the valuation of the inventory of 300,000 gold pieces. On average, the gold pieces were acquired at a cost of 1,000 CU each. On 31 December the market value of the gold pieces is 1,100 CU each. The head accountant seems to have valued the inventory at its replacement cost.

Company 4 – Balance sheet on 31 December (in 000 of CU)				
Assets			**Shareholders' equity and liabilities**	
Fixed assets	210,000		*Shareholders' equity*	
Minus accumulated depreciation	–90,000		Share capital and reserves	150,000
Fixed assets (net)	120,000		Net income	10,000
Current assets			*Liabilities*	120,000
Inventories	40,000			
Accounts receivable	120,000			
Total assets	280,000		**Total shareholders' equity and liabilities**	280,000

Eve Adam observes that the income statement includes in the sales revenue one 100,000 CU sale to Godounov Inc. Despite being in an advanced stage of negotiation, the sale has, however, not yet been concluded but the chief salesperson feels very strongly the sale will actually be signed in the first days of the year. The goods that would be sold to Godounov Inc. have been acquired for 70,000 CU and would be sold with a margin on sales of 30%.

Required

Establish the definitive balance sheet for each of the four companies by incorporating the information provided. For each case, specify both the accounting principle concerned and the journal entry that should be recorded to correct the preliminary balance sheet. The impact of taxation will be omitted.

Solution

Company 1

Accounting principle involved: Prudence (conservatism).
Accounting entry: Provision for depreciation (in the balance sheet).

Company 1 – Modified balance sheet			
Assets		**Shareholders' equity and liabilities**	
Fixed assets	300,000	*Shareholders' equity*	
Minus accumulated depreciation (–40,000)	**–200,000**	Share capital and reserves	330,000
Fixed assets (net)	100,000	Net income (–40,000)	**–20,000**
Current assets		*Liabilities*	40,000
Inventories	120,000		
Accounts receivable	130,000		
Total assets	**350,000**	**Total shareholders' equity and liabilities**	**350,000**

In bold: Modified figures

Company 2

Accounting principle involved: Prudence (conservatism).
Accounting entry: Provision for depreciation (in the balance sheet).

Company 2 – Modified balance sheet			
Assets		**Shareholders' equity and liabilities**	
Fixed assets	250,000	*Shareholders' equity*	
Minus accumulated depreciation	–130,000	Share capital and reserves	300,000
Fixed assets (net)	120,000	Net income (–60,000)	**–10,000**
Current assets		*Liabilities*	20,000
Inventories	100,000		
Accounts receivable (–60,000)	**90,000**		
Total assets	**310,000**	**Total shareholders' equity and liabilities**	**310,000**

Company 3

Accounting principle involved: Historical cost.
Accounting entry: Cancellation of the profit recorded (300,000 × 10% = 30,000).

Company 3 – Modified balance sheet			
Assets		**Shareholders' equity and liabilities**	
Fixed assets	500,000	*Shareholders' equity*	
Minus accumulated depreciation	–240,000	Share capital and reserves	520,000
Fixed assets (net)	260,000	Net income (–30,000)	**–10,000**
Current assets		*Liabilities*	200,000
Inventories (–30,000)	**300,000**		
Accounts receivable	150,000		
Total assets	**710,000**	**Total shareholders' equity and liabilities**	**710,000**

Company 4
Accounting principle involved: Accounting period and prudence.
Accounting entry: Cancellation of the profit recorded (100,000 × 30% = 30,000).

Company 4 – Modified balance sheet				
Assets			**Shareholders' equity and liabilities**	
Fixed assets		210,000	*Shareholders' equity*	
Minus accumulated depreciation		–90,000	Share capital and reserves	150,000
Fixed assets (net)		120,000	Net income (–30,000)	**–20,000**
Current assets			*Liabilities*	120,000
Inventories (+70,000)		**110,000**		
Accounts receivable (–100,000)		**20,000**		
Total assets		**250,000**	**Total shareholders' equity and liabilities**	**250,000**

In all four cases the net income of the period goes from positive (profit) to negative (loss) after end-of-period adjustments.

ASSIGNMENTS

Assignment 5.1 Dukas Company

Type: Multiple-choice questions
Related part of the chapter: Advanced Issues

1   On June 1, the Dukas Company paid 3 months' rent in advance, for a total cost of 900 CU. At the time of payment, prepaid rent was increased by this amount. What adjusting entry is necessary as of 30 June (if financial statements are prepared on this date)?

   (a) Prepaid rent   300
        Rent expense   300
   (b) Rent expense   300
        Prepaid rent   300
   (c) Rent expense   600
        Prepaid rent   600
   (d) Prepaid rent   600
        Rent expense   600
   (e) No adjusting entry is necessary

2   The Dukas Company signed a 3,000 CU debit note to Bankix, their local bank on 1 September 20X3. At that time, the appropriate journal entry was made by the company. However, no other journal entry relating to the note has been made. Given that the bank is charging interest at a rate of 10%, what adjusting entry, if any, is necessary on Dukas Company's year-end date of 31 December 20X3?

   (a) Interest expense   300
        Interest payable   300
   (b) Interest expense   100
        Note payable   100
   (c) Interest expense   100
        Accrued interest payable   100

(d)	Interest expense	300	
	Note payable		300
(e)	Note payable	100	
	Interest expense		100
(f)	Note payable	300	
	Interest expense		300

3 **The Dukas Company owns offices which are rented to other companies. On 1 February Dukas rented some office space and received 6 months' rent in advance, totaling 6,000 CU. At that time, the entire amount was recorded to increase unearned rent. What adjusting entry is necessary on 28 February, if the company decides to prepare financial statements on that date?**

(a)	Unearned rent	1,000	
	Rent revenue		1,000
(b)	Rent revenue	1,000	
	Unearned rent		1,000
(c)	Unearned rent	5,000	
	Rent revenue		5,000
(d)	Rent revenue	5,000	
	Unearned rent		5,000
(e)	No adjusting entry is necessary		

4 **The Dukas Company owns an interest bearing note receivable with a nominal value of 1,000 currency units. Interest at 8% per annum on the note receivable has accrued for 3 months and is expected to be collected when the note is due in July. What adjusting entry is necessary on 31 March, if the Company decides to prepare financial statements at that date?**

(a)	Interest revenue	20	
	Accrued interest receivable		20
(b)	Note receivable	80	
	Interest revenue		80
(c)	Interest revenue	80	
	Note receivable		80
(d)	Accrued interest receivable	20	
	Interest revenue		20
(e)	Note receivable	20	
	Interest revenue		20
(f)	No adjusting entry is necessary		

Assignment 5.2 Gounod Company

Topic: Accounting principles
Type: Group case study
Related part of the chapter: Core Issues

Guillemette Gounod is CEO of the Gounod Corporation, a manufacturer of smartcards and electronic personal identification devices. As chair of the annual meeting of shareholders she is reporting on the performance of the previous period and commenting on some of the key points revealed by the financial statements. Her remarks follow.

1 Despite the figures you can observe in the comparative income statements, sales activity of 20X1 is significantly greater than that of period 20X0. Several major customers, essentially government and semi-government agencies with unused budget allowances in 20X0 had paid in advance in 20X0 for deliveries that did not take place until 20X1. This shifted sales that really took place in 20X1 towards 20X0, thus creating the erroneous perception that 20X1 sales were only 10% greater than those of 20X0. In reality the sales of your company have increased brilliantly by 40%.

2. Further to this understatement of the 20X1 sales, our 20X1 purchases have been inflated because we accepted early delivery of about 3 months' worth of card readers we purchase from MG-Electronics. MG-Electronics is a subsidiary of Silver Electric International and the CEO of MG-E asked us, and we accepted, to help him meet his 20X1 sales growth target by accepting early delivery and invoicing. He has extended us a 6-month credit term on the payable so this will have no impact on our cash situation.

   These two events, deflated sales and inflated purchases affect negatively the reported income of 20X1 as you can well understand.

3. You will observe that the balance sheet shows an asset called capitalized R&D which is lower this year, in comparison to last year. The R&D team is involved in a long-term project, a new-generation smartcard which we do not expect to see hitting the market for another year at least. The head count of our R&D team has been reduced this year by one person due to our seconding Dr. Thaddeusz Czapik to PT-Microelectronics to work on the development of the new generation of microchips we will use in our new smartcard.

4. As you know we capitalize the work (engineering and legal) that leads to our taking patents to protect our intellectual capital. In 20X1 we are valuing the new patents registered in our name for 160,000 CU, down from 340,000 in 20X0. I have been worried by this downward trend and have inquired to find that our patents department has been understaffed due to two sick leaves and is way behind in filing applications for new patents.

5. Our company's reputation and market share have been increasing significantly. I have been asking our external auditor repeatedly to allow us to recognize this increase in value of the firm due to both our name and the quality of our products and labor force in the larger sense. The auditor refused once again to recognize this value creation, fruit of the labor of my team and I will later propose a motion to change auditors.

6. Our tangible assets are essentially numerically controlled machines which still work magnificently well in the manufacturing of our products. These machines do not lose any of the potential they had when we bought them. However, I have had to reluctantly accept the demand by the CFO to depreciate them on the balance sheet. Fortunately the machines were purchased before a price increase and therefore that makes us comparatively more competitive.

7. The chief accountant has told me that each year he chooses the best methods for depreciating the building and fixtures in order to minimize taxable income. This year I understand we used the straight-line method but last year we had used the declining balance method, a form of accelerated depreciation.

8. My last remark, that also leads me to be critical of our auditor, is to say that I strongly feel our financial statements are overly prudent, bordering on pessimism. I still do not understand why we are not allowed to build a provision for the cost of laying-off all or most of our personnel. Such a provision would, of course, reduce taxes if it were allowed by the tax authority but mainly it would give us a true and fair view (accountants have been using this buzzword around me too much) of the situation of our company in case of a downturn in the economy.

Required

Ms. Guillemette Gounod seems to have an incomplete understanding of some key accounting principles. For each of the points of her speech to the shareholders, identify the accounting principle(s) that was (were) ignored or applied improperly.

Assignment 5.3 Lalo Company

Topic: End-of-period entries
Type: Group case study
Related part of the chapter: Core Issues

The company

Lalo Company, headquartered in Vaduz, is a listed company in Amsterdam, Paris and Zurich. It is the third largest small home appliance manufacturer in Europe. It was created in 1945 by the Patrimo family, which still holds 62% of the share capital. John Patrimo, the aging patriarch founder is the president of the company while his two sons Walter and Nicholas are executive directors. Walter is chief executive officer and chief financial officer while his brother Nicholas heads the international division.

Lalo has chosen 31 December as its year-end date, given its sales peaks are mainly in the late winter and early fall. Today is 10 January of year 20X2 and the books on year 20X1 are about to be closed. Current operations have been recorded and a preliminary income statement and balance sheet have been prepared (see Appendices 1 and 2).

A certain number of points remain to be debated about year-end adjustments and closing entries. Eric Faithfull, chief accountant, has organized a working meeting to which all parties holding divergent views about the year-end entries have been invited.

Attending the meeting are, among others, Eric Faithfull, Walter Patrimo (CEO and CFO) and Isabella Inkreese, head of financial communication.

Key actors

Eric Faithfull is a graduate of a French Graduate School of Business. After a brilliant audit career in one of the "Big 5" he joined Lalo two years ago as chief accountant. In his view, complete and faithful application of accounting principles is essential in the establishment of useful financial statements. He is absolutely opposed to any form of manipulation of accounts for whatever reason. He often declares: "Our mission is to give a true and fair view of the business of the company."

Walter Patrimo, a self-made man who rose through the ranks from salesperson to the position he currently holds, is the defender of the family's interest. He is firm believer in reinvesting profit and in generating cash flows to support growth without having to depend too much on financial institutions. His philosophy is that his accountant should "use tax law and all legal tax loopholes to minimize taxable income and avoid this useless drain on the cash flow of the company. A better future for all only comes from our ability to generate and reinvest as large a cash flow as possible."

After five years in the investor relations department of a large North American conglomerate, Isabella Inkreese assumed the responsibility of financial communication for Lalo some 12 months ago. She has been openly critical of what she calls the "closed mind and lack of ambitious vision of the family". She keeps saying that financial communication with the markets is key to the development of the firm. 'We must keep the loyalty of our shareholders and attract new ones. At the current rate of growth of the business we will soon need new share capital, especially in the context of mergers and acquisitions that leads to this worldwide consolidation of the industry."

Minutes of the meeting (irrelevant interventions have been deleted)

The meeting was convened at 10: 00 am and concluded at 12: 30 pm.
Attending were: WP, EF, II, DK, GS, and SB. Secretary: ICU.

1 Depreciation

Eric Faithfull: "On 1 July, 20X1, we purchased a machine tool for 1 million CU. The machine has been added to the equipment account and no decision has been made yet about its depreciation. Its technical useful life should be between 5 and 10 years according to Gunther (VP production – also present). We could choose either straight-line or accelerated."

Walter Patrimo: "This is a no-brainer; let's choose the accelerated method and let's do it over the shortest acceptable life, i.e., 5 years here. This will give us a large tax deduction and boost the cash flow. In addition, this machine may become obsolete in a few years, and I'd better have depreciated it a maximum before we have to scrap it, after all the production has benefited from that machine. Eric, the multiplier of straight line to get the accelerated is 2, right?"

EF: "Yes, it can be 2. This would give you a depreciation rate which would be twice as much as that of straight line, applied to the remaining balance, until you have to switch back to straight line when this rate is lower that the straight-line rate calculated on the remaining years. Moreover, to simplify the computations, I suggest that we start the depreciation on 1 July. Additionally, I remind you that, according to the accounting standards we follow, there is no rate limit for the accelerated depreciation."

Isabella Inkreese: "I do not agree with your tax-based decision. The products we are going to make on this machine have, in my mind, a remaining life expectancy of at least 10 years. I do not see the sales volume of these products changing much over the next 10 years or so. And, on top of that, I hear it is a good technology and the machine will not need to be replaced soon. Based on all this, I feel strongly the straight-line method is the one that is appropriate. Straight-line depreciation is also the method most commonly used in large international groups. Further, if we choose to depreciate over 10 years, we will show a more attractive income figure to the market. If the machine were to be made obsolete by some magic new technology, we would just expense the full residual value in the income statement at that time. It is very simple. Why penalize ourselves now in the eyes of shareholders?"

EF: "I do not agree with either of you. Our accounting records must reflect as faithfully as possible the actual position of Lalo. Gunther says that he thinks that given the new products in the pipeline, he does expect to use the machine fully for the next 8 years, beyond that he is not so sure we'll still use that technology. I would therefore suggest we take that 8-year time horizon in our depreciation calculations. As for the method of depreciation, the accelerated method seems to be the most appropriate to me because the market shows the resale value of the machine falling dramatically after the first year of operation. I would also suggest a multiplier of 2."

2   Provision on receivables

EF: "Our sale of microwaves of last 15 May to Worldapart for 200,000 CU is still outstanding and the receivables still unpaid. The salespeople estimate the probability of non-collectability from 60% to 90% with a highest probability at 70% chance of not collecting."

WP: "How about creating a provision for 90%? That is an easy decision to defend in front of the tax people if they start nitpicking."

II: "Why not 60%? The financial market is never happy if we show a mediocre income. Let us work on collecting these 40% instead of giving up so easily."

3   Provision for risk and expenses

EF: "We are involved in a law suit brought against us by Fairprice for patent infringement. They are asking for 200,000 of damages. I really see no merit to that suit but I really do not know which way the court is going to side. I see it as a 50–50 situation and would suggest provisioning half the amount they are seeking."

WP: "Absolutely not. Let us plan for the worst. What happens if our lawyers blow it? We should take a provision for the worst case, provision the full amount. It will always be possible to reverse it if our lawyers are good and we get off the hook."

II: "Oh come on! Another unneeded provision. The more you provision, the less income you report. This is, gentlemen, the era of the financial markets. You may not like their dictatorship, but they are the ones who make or break a company today. In any case the amount of damages Fairprice are seeking is ridiculously high. In a law suit you know very well that you always ask 5 if you want to get 1. I gave a call to Wim Winhall, our external lawyer, and he confirms what Eric said, namely that the suit is totally without merit. So please, gentlemen, let us not build this provision."

4 Receivables

EF: "We have a little problem with one element of the receivables. We shipped a truckload of mini-ovens to the warehouse of Price-Lead on 28 December. The invoice was not established until 2 January 20X2. We are talking about an invoice for 500,000 CU; that is not a small amount. The question is to decide between us whether to account for it in year 20X1 or keep it for year 20X2."

II: "Since the physical delivery took place in December of period 20X1, it seems logical to me to take the sales revenue into account for period 20X1."

WP: "But, wait a minute, the invoice was established and mailed in 20X2. The preliminary income figures I received from management accounting show that the operating income for 20X1 will be quite superb. Would it not be better to take the revenue for 20X2? Why make 20X1 even better and pay more taxes? In addition it would be good for the sales force to know they attack the year 20X2 with a little plus. Competition is getting harder every day and they know they have an uphill battle in front of them. Let us give them a push and record this sale as pertaining to 20X2, okay?"

5 Bonuses

EF: "Ramon Psikotic, in the HR department, has estimated the bonus earned by the employees for their contribution to our period 20X1 successes. These bonuses will, in any case, not be paid before the April 20X2 paycheck. The total bonus amounts is estimated at around 100,000 CU."

WP: "It is always the same thing, every year. Union representatives come and complain about the method of calculation of bonuses used by Ramon. I have already heard from them and they claim that the total bonus pool should be around 120,000 CU. We cannot afford a strike at this stage when we are building up inventories for the late winter rush. I feel that if they push hard, keep that under your hats, please, I will give them what they want. So I suggest we provision for 120,000 CU, we can always adjust the figure downwards later if we manage to have to give them less."

II: "Once again we see the disastrous effect of that bonus calculation formula which leaves a lot of room for interpretation. Personally, I have reviewed Ramon's calculations and I find the bonus pool should only be 80,000 CU. That is a number I truly prefer. If they go on strike we'll have to stand up to their ridiculous demands and, in case we have to cut them some rope, it will be a lot easier to limit the damage to below Ramon's 100,000 CU estimation if we can show them we have only provisioned 80,000 CU. A penny saved is a penny earned."

6 Deferred revenue

EF: "On 1 November of year 20X1, we received a 300,000 CU cash payment for the rent on the warehouse we have leased to Ready-Sol, our distributor in Palombaggia. This represents the rent for 3 months, i.e., through January 20X2. I know we have recorded the full payment as revenue for period 20X1."

II: "Since the cash is in, it must, of course, be recorded as a year 20X1 revenue."

WP: "Sorry Isabella, I do not agree! That is not correct, one month of that rent pertains to January and therefore one-third of the rent received should be recognized as revenue for January 20X2."

7 Deferred expenses

EF: "On 1 September 20X1 we paid our 90,000 CU annual liability insurance premium. We have expensed the full amount immediately. The period of coverage extends from 1 September 20X1, to 31 August 20X2."

WP: "What matters is when the payment took place. Keep it fully in the year 20X1 expenses."

II: "Wait a minute, here! The period during which we will receive the benefits derived from that premium is in 20X2. It would seem more logical to me to recognize that expense as belonging to period 20X2."

Required

The class has been divided into 3 subsections A, B and C. Each subsection prepares the version of the financial statements (balance sheet as of 31 December, 20X1 plus income statement for 20X1) fully reflecting the point of view of one of the three protagonists on each of the seven points evoked during the meeting:

- Subsection A: Position held by Walter Patrimo (profit minimization).
- Subsection B: Position held by Isabella Inkreese (profit maximization).
- Subsection C: Position held by Eric Faithfull (true and fair).

Exhibits 1 and 2 present the preliminary balance sheet and income statement before any year-end adjusting entry. All calculations should ignore the impact of both income tax and value added tax.

Appendix 1: Preliminary balance sheet before year-end adjustments, 31 December 20X1 (000 CU)

Assets		Shareholders' equity and liabilities	
Fixed assets (gross)	17,300	Capital	5,000
– Accumulated depreciation	–8,300	Reserves	3,000
Fixed assets (net)	9,000	Net income	200
Inventory	4,800		
Accounts receivable (gross)	2,400	Liabilities	8,700
– Accumulated provisions	–100		
Accounts receivable (net)	2,300		
Cash	800		
Total	16,900	Total	16,900

Appendix 2: Preliminary income statement for 20X1 before year-end adjustments (000 CU)

Sales	29,000
Rent revenue	300
Purchases	–20,000
External expenses	–230
Personnel expenses	–6,820
Depreciation expense	–1,100
Provision expense	–100
Operating income	1,050
Financial revenues	200
Financial expenses	–750
Financial income	–550
Current income	500
Exceptional income	–300
Preliminary income before income tax	200

Assignment 5.4 Poulenc Company

Topic: Adjusting entries
Type: Individual/group exercise
Related part of the chapter: Core/Advanced Issues

Poulenc & Associates, a consulting firm, was incorporated on 1 June. On 30 June the trial balance shows the following balances for selected accounts:

Notes payable (balance sheet)	20,000	Prepaid insurance (balance sheet)	3,600
Unearned fees (balance sheet)	1,200	Fees earned (income statement)	1,800

Analysis reveals the following additional data relating to these accounts (no adjusting entry has yet been recorded):

1. A customer paid 1,200 CU towards a yearly subscription to a service which started in June.
2. Prepaid insurance is the cost of a 9-month insurance policy, effective 1 June.
3. The note payable is dated 1 June. It is a 12-month, 10% note.
4. Services rendered to other customers but not billed at 30 June totaled 1,500 currency units.

Required

Show the impact on balance sheet and income statement for Poulenc Company as of 30 June, for each of these transactions.

Assignment 5.5 Debussy Company

Topic: End-of period entries and preparation of financial statements
Type: Individual/group exercise
Related part of the chapter: Advanced Issues

Debussy Company has prepared a set of financial statements in accordance with US GAAP: balance sheet, income statement and statement of retained earnings (see Appendix 1). The accounting period 20X1 ends on 30 September 20X1. Due to the illness of the company's accountant, the end-of-period entries have not been recorded.

Required

1. Show the impact on the financial statements of the end-of-period transactions or events that are described in Appendix 2.
2. Update the financial statements taking into account these transactions and events.

Appendix 1: Preliminary financial statements
(all amounts in 000 of CU)

Income statement
for the year ended 30 September 20X1

Sales	10,000
Cost of goods sold	−6,200
Gross profit	3,800
Operating expenses	
. Salaries	−1,300
. Advertising	−800
. Insurance	−30
. Telephone	−40
. Maintenance	−20
. Rent	−25
. Miscellaneous expense	−21
Total operating expenses	−2,236
Operating income	1,564
Deduct interest expense	−26
Income before income taxes	1,538

Balance sheet – 30 September 20X1

Assets			Liabilities and stockholders' equity	
Current assets			*Current liabilities*	
. Cash	1,000		. Accounts payable	600
. Accounts receivable	1,178		. Notes payable	300
. Note receivable	400		. Unearned rent revenue	60
. Merchandise inventory	2,000		Total current liabilities	960
. Unexpired insurance	20			
Total current assets	4,598			
Long-term assets			*Stockholders' equity*	
. Land	1,700		. Paid-in capital	5,000
. Building	3,000		. Retained income	3,038
. Accumulated depreciation	−300			
Total assets	8,998		Total liabilities and stockholders' equity	8,998

Statement of retained earnings

Retained income, 1 October 20X0	1,500
Net income for 20X1	1,538
Total	3,038
Cash dividends declared	
Retained income, 30 September 20X1	3,038

Appendix 2: End-of-period entries (all amounts in thousands CU)

1 Depreciation on the building for 20X1 is 80 CU.

2 Part of the building owned by the company has been rented to other companies with occupancy starting on 1 September, 20X1. The amount invoiced to the tenant (60) was paid in advance for 3 months and collected in cash. It has been recorded in the item "Unearned rent revenue".

3 Salaries are paid on a weekly basis. The amount corresponding to the last week of September (100 CU) will be paid at the beginning of October.

4 Interest on the note receivable has accrued for 1 month. It will be collected when the note is due in December. The rate is 6% per annum.

5 Income tax at the rate of 30% applies to 20X1. The tax owed will be paid in the following accounting period.

6 Cash dividends of 800 CU were declared in September 20X1. They will be paid out in October 20X1.

References

EU (European Union) (1978) 4th Directive on the annual accounts of certain types of companies no. 78/660/EEC. *Official Journal of the European Communities*, 14 August.

IASC (1989) Framework for the Preparation and Presentation of Financial Statements, London.

IASC (1997) International Accounting Standard No. 1, Presentation of Financial Statements, London.

IASC (2001) Glossary of terms in *International Accounting Standards*, bound volume, London.

Further readings

Alexander, D. (1993) A European true and fair view? *European Accounting Review*, 2(1), 59–80.

Brorstom, B. (1998) Accrual accounting, politics and politicians. *Financial Accountability & Management*, 14(4), November, 319–33.

Colasse, B. (1997) The French notion of the *image fidèle*: The power of words. *European Accounting Review*, 6(4), 681–91.

Dunk, A.S., and Kilgore, A. (2000) The reintroduction of the true and fair override and harmonization with IASC standards in Australia: Lessons from the EU and implications for financial reporting and international trade. *International Journal of Accounting*, 35(2), 213–26.

Evans, L., and Nobes, C. (1996) Some mysteries relating to the prudence principle in the Fourth Directive and in German and British Law. *European Accounting Review*, 5(2), 361–73.

Gangolly, J.S., and Hussein, M.E.A. (1996) Generally accepted accounting principles: Perspectives from philosophy of law. *Critical Perspectives on Accounting*, 7(4), August, 383–407.

Jonas, G.J., and Blanchet, J. (2000) Assessing quality of financial reporting. *Accounting Horizons*, 14(3), 353–63.

Jun Lin, Z., and Chen, F. (1999) Applicability of the conservatism accounting convention in China: Empirical evidence. *International Journal of Accounting*, 34(4), 517–37.

Ordelheide, D. (1993) True and fair view: A European and a German perspective. *European Accounting Review*, 2(1), 81–90.

Van Hulle, K. (1997) The true and fair view override in the European accounting Directives. *European Accounting Review*, 6(4), 711–20.

Zeff, S.A., Buijink, W., and Camfferman, K. (1999) 'True and fair' in the Netherlands: *inzicht* or *getrouw beeld*? *European Accounting Review*, 8(3), 523–48.

Additional material on the website

Go to http://www.thomsonlearning.co.uk/accountingandfinance/stolowylebas for further information, journal entries and extra assignments for each chapter.

The following appendices to this chapter are available on the dedicated website:

Appendix 5.1: Revenues earned but not recorded

Appendix 5.2: Revenues recorded but unearned

Appendix 5.3: Expenses consumed but not recorded

Appendix 5.4: Expenses recorded in advance

Appendix 5.5: Limitations on the applicability of accounting principles

International and comparative accounting: A topical approach

Revenue recognition issues

Before exploring in detail the various accounts composing the balance sheet (Chapters 7 through 12), it is essential to gain a better understanding of one of the most important balance sheet accounts, namely the income statement. As we saw in Chapter 2, the income statement is conceptually a subset of the balance sheet, summarizing those entries that affect shareholders' equity.

Beside the handling of costs and expenses which was covered in Chapters 4 and 5, three issues remain that need clarification:

- revenue recognition (when and how much)
- issues arising from the use of different purposes and accounting rules in tax and shareholders' reporting. (Both these topics raise some fundamental and universal issues which will be covered in the Core Issues section and some more complex or unusual issues that will be covered in the Advanced Issues section).
- handling of extraordinary events (i.e., not occurring in the normal course of business), which will also be dealt with in the Advanced Issues section.

Major topics

Principles of revenue recognition

Deferred taxation

Long-term contracts

Extraordinary items

Accounting changes

Comprehensive income

Government assistance

Issues of revenue recognition

Revenue is "the gross inflow of economic benefits during the period arising in the course of the ordinary activities of an enterprise when those inflows result in increases in equity, other than increases relating to contributions from equity participants" (IAS 18, IASC 1993c: § 7).

To recognize revenue is to record the impact of a transaction on the revenue component of the income statement. One major accounting issue, derived from the matching and periodicity principles (see "Core issues" in Chapter 5) is to determine when to recognize revenue. Some rules are specified in IAS 18 (IASC 1993c: § 1–5) guiding the revenue recognition process for the following 3 categories of transactions and events:

1 the sale of goods (goods purchased for resale or manufactured by the selling firm, or land and other property held for resale)
2 the rendering of services (performance by the enterprise of a contractually agreed task over an agreed period of time)
3 the use by others of enterprise assets yielding:
   – interest (charges for the use of cash or cash equivalents or amounts due to the enterprise)
   – royalties (charges for the use of long-term assets of the enterprise, for example, patents, trademarks, copyrights, and computer software)
   – dividends (distributions of profits to holders of equity investments in proportion to their holdings of a particular class of capital).

Criteria for recognition vary according to each type of transaction. Although some implementation differences may exist between countries, IAS 18 offers a set of generally accepted practices for revenue recognition. We will essentially adopt, in this chapter, the position presented in that standard.

Sale of goods

Revenue from the sale of goods should be recognized when all the following conditions have been satisfied (IAS 18, § 14):

(a) the enterprise has transferred to the buyer the significant risks and rewards of ownership of the goods
(b) the enterprise retains neither continuing managerial involvement to the degree usually associated with ownership nor effective control over the goods sold
(c) the amount of revenue can be measured reliably
(d) it is probable that the economic benefits associated with the transaction will flow to the enterprise
(e) the costs incurred or to be incurred in respect of the transaction can be measured reliably.

These five criteria call for several comments. The assessment of when an enterprise has transferred the significant risks and rewards of ownership to the buyer requires an examination of the circumstances of the transaction. In most cases, this transfer coincides with the transfer of the legal title or of possession to the buyer. This is the case for most retail sales. However, the seller, especially in business-to-business transactions, may retain a significant risk of ownership in a number of ways, such as:

- When the enterprise retains an obligation for unsatisfactory performance not covered by normal warranty provisions (for example, a sale conditional on a specific performance level clause).

- When the receipt of the revenue from a particular sale is contingent on the derivation of revenue by the buyer from its sale of the goods (for example, a consignment sales).

- When the goods are shipped subject to installation, and that installation is a significant part of the contract which has not yet been completed by the selling enterprise or on its behalf.

- When the buyer has the right to rescind the purchase for a reason specified in the sales contract and the enterprise is uncertain about the probability of return (for example, a sale on approval).

If an enterprise retains an insignificant risk of ownership, the transaction is considered to be a finalized sale and revenue should be recognized. An example would be a retail sale for which a refund is offered if the customer is not satisfied. Revenue in such a case would be recognized at the time of the sale, provided the seller can reliably estimate future returns, and recognizes a liability for returns based on previous experience and other relevant factors.

The rules that govern revenue recognition are all practical applications of the matching principle. They are conceived to facilitate the co-temporal recognition of revenue and expenses that are related to the same transaction or other event.

Some expenses or costs, including for example warranty work or recycling costs, are incurred after the shipment of the goods takes place and ownership changes hands. That is why co-temporality is an issue if we want to obey the matching principle. These expenses or costs can normally be estimated with statistical reliability and appropriately provisioned so as to be matched with the corresponding revenue.

A provision is an estimation of the future probable cost created by a risky situation (see Chapter 12). A provision allows the recognition of an expense at the time of the triggering event, therefore matching it to revenue. A provision is a cost or reduction in shareholders' equity. In order to keep the balance sheet balanced, the provision expense will lead to the creation of a liability for the very same amount. The provisioned liability will be used to compensate the actual expense when it is actually incurred. For example: assume a sale of 150 CU takes place that carries a 100% chance that the seller will need to provide additional costs of 40 two years from the date of the sale. The sale is recognized as 150 and a provision is taken for 40. In keeping with the no offsetting principle, the net effect of that sale in the income statement is 110 and a liability is created for 40 which acknowledges the anticipated recording of an expense. When the actual cost of 40 is incurred, it has all the characteristics of an expense but this cannot be the case since it has already been deducted from revenue. Therefore, that cost will be compensated by the cancellation of the provision taken as a liability two years before. With this procedure the matching principle has been fully respected, and the shareholders' equity has only been affected at the time of the triggering event, not when the actual cost is incurred.

If, however, it were difficult or impossible to estimate these post-sale expenses, the revenue should not be recognized at all at the time of shipment (and postponed until the uncertainties about these future costs is reduced sufficiently). Any cash or consideration received for the sale of the goods or service should be recognized as a debt towards the customer (if we increase cash and create a liability of the same amount, there is no impact on the shareholders' equity).

Rendering of services

Services rendered contracts such as long-term construction or consulting contracts, legal cases or research contracts tend to span several accounting periods. This creates specific problems of measurement of both periodic revenue and completion. We will cover these later in Advanced Issues.

IAS 18 (§ 20) states that, when the outcome of a transaction involving the rendering of services (such as in long-term contracts) can be estimated reliably, revenue associated with the transaction should be recognized as a function of the stage or percentage of completion of the transaction on the balance sheet date. The outcome of a transaction can be estimated reliably when all the following conditions are satisfied:

(a)   The amount of revenue that will be obtained upon completion can be measured reliably (i.e., the terms of the sales contract are clear).

(b)   It is probable that the economic benefits associated with the transaction will flow to the enterprise.

(c)   The stage or percentage of completion of the transaction on the balance sheet date can be measured reliably.

(d)   The costs incurred for the transaction and the costs to complete the transaction can be measured reliably.

The recognition of revenue by reference to the degree of completion of a transaction is often referred to as the percentage of completion method. Under this method, a portion of the final revenue is recognized in each of the accounting periods in which the services are rendered, in proportion to the increase in the degree of completion (total fulfillment of the contract) that took place during the period.

The percentage of completion of a transaction may be determined by a variety of methods. Each enterprise uses the method that, in their view, best measures reliably the services performed and gives what they feel is the fairest representation of the actual financial situation of the firm. Some methods are more suited for certain type of transactions. Methods include:

(a)   Actual measurement of work performed (feasible option when only one activity was performed).

(b)   Quantity of services performed to date as a percentage of total services to be performed (a feasible option when the completed, possibly complex service can be decomposed in small discrete and measurable sections or segments).

(c)   The proportion that costs incurred to date represented as a percentage of the re-estimated total costs of the transaction at completion, i.e., actual costs plus committed costs plus re-estimated costs remaining to be incurred until completion. (This is the preferred option when the service rendered is complex and requires the cooperation of several different types of expertise.)

Progress payments and advances received from customers often do not reflect the services performed. Even though agreed milestones of completion generally trigger invoicing for an agreed portion of the contractual revenue, it would be a rare case to find that the cumulative costs to date represent the same proportion of the total cost as the cumulative invoicing does. Given possible interpretations of the matching principle, three situations can occur at any point during the life of a long-term contract:

1 Cumulative actual costs exceed cumulative revenue: the seller finances the difference, it is equivalent to a hidden discount on the selling price.

2 Cumulative revenue exceeds cumulative actual costs: the customer finances the difference, it is equivalent to a hidden premium on the agreed upon sales price.

3 The two streams are pretty well balanced and the agreed sales price is relevant.

Clearly, the recognition of revenue leaves some room to choice. That is why long-term contracts are such an important subject in today's economy.

When the outcome of the transaction involving the rendering of services cannot be estimated reliably, revenue should be recognized only up to the amount of the recoverable recognized expenses (i.e., no profit should be recognized). When the outcome of a transaction cannot be estimated reliably and it is not probable that the costs incurred will be recovered, revenue should not be recognized and the costs incurred should be recognized immediately as an expense when incurred (principle of prudence and conservatism).

Interest, royalties, and dividends

When (a) it is probable that the economic benefits associated with the transaction will flow to the enterprise, and (b) the amount of the revenue can be measured reliably, revenue arising from the use by others of enterprise assets yielding interest, royalties and dividends should be recognized on the following bases:

- **Interest**: Proportionately to the length of the period during which the asset was actually made available and on the basis of the agreed interest rate.
- **Royalties**: On an accrual basis in accordance with the substance of the relevant agreement.
- **Dividends**: When the shareholder's right to receive payment is established (decision of the shareholders' general meeting).

Reporting for revenue recognition

Principles

The revenue recognition policy of a firm may have a significant impact on its income and on the image it will communicate of its future economic potential (going concern principle) to the variety of users of accounting information and especially to the financial markets. The rules can be applied with more or less flexibility, which can be used to anticipate or delay recognition of profit or losses. Such a deliberate action on the timing of recognition of revenue (and of expenses) creates what is called income smoothing (i.e., avoid reporting peaks and troughs in revenue and or income which might give an alarming message to financial markets – see Chapter 15).

Although financial markets can generally see through income smoothing practices, these may have a significant impact in terms of taxation, and, therefore, of impact on cash outflows. The consistency accounting principle is theoretically designed to prevent such abuses of flexibility but the recognition criteria have such a large built-in subjectivity component that flexibility always legitimately exists.

This is probably a reason why shareholders require that the notes to the financial statements reveal the methods of recognition retained and highlight any deviation therefrom (full disclosure). IAS 18, § 35 defines the minimum that an enterprise should disclose:

(a)   the accounting policies adopted for the recognition of revenue including the methods adopted to determine the stage or percentage of completion of transactions involving the rendering of services

(b)   the amount of each significant category of revenue recognized during the period including revenue arising from (i) the sale of goods, (ii) the rendering of services, (iii) interest, (iv) royalties, and (v) dividends

(c)   the amount of revenue arising from exchanges of goods or services (bartering) included in each significant category of revenue.

Real-life examples of notes to financial statements

Some illustrative notes excerpted from the financial statements of some large international corporations follow.

Bull

(France – French/US GAAP – Source: Annual report 1999 – International IT group)

Groupe Bull sells and leases computer equipment and data processing services under various contractual arrangements. Regular sales are recognized upon full execution, by Groupe Bull, of the terms of the contract, which generally coincides with delivery or acceptance. Sales contracts generally include a clause reserving title to the goods in countries where this is permitted by law.

Revenue from one-time charge licensed software is recognized upon execution of the license agreement and delivery of the software. Revenue from monthly software licenses is recognized as license fees accrue.

Services are either of a recurring nature invoiced periodically or contracts with progress deliveries. Recurring contracts generally cover maintenance and outsourcing services while progress delivery contracts mainly involve systems integration activities. Revenue is recorded at the end of each invoice period in the first instance and on each progress delivery in the second.

Ericsson

(Sweden – Swedish GAAP – Source: Annual report 1999 – Communications industry: cellular phones and other wireless solutions)

Sales revenue is recorded upon delivery of products, software and services according to contractual terms and represent amount realized, excluding value-added tax, and are net of goods returned, trade discounts and allowances.

Philips

(Netherlands – Dutch GAAP – Source: *Annual report 1999 – Lighting, consumer electronics and domestic appliances, components, semiconductors)*

Sales are generally recognized at the time the product is delivered to the customer, net of sales taxes, customer discounts, rebates and similar charges. Service revenue is recognized over the contractual period or as services are rendered. (…) Royalty income is recognized on an accrual basis. Government grants, other than those relating to assets, are recognized as income to the extent that it is more likely than not that these grants will be received.

Accounting for differences in net income calculations originating from diverging reporting and tax regulations

In most countries, an income tax is levied on taxable income (also referred to as "pre-tax income", "income before income taxes" or "book income"). Taxable income is generally defined as the difference between taxable revenues and deductible (or tax-deductible) expenses or costs. In principle, all sources of revenue are taxable and all ordinary and necessary expenses of doing business are deductible. But there are notable, large exceptions to this generalization.

However, the intent of the rules used for reporting to shareholders and for accounting for taxation are not at all coherent. Accounting rules and policies are designed to support a true and fair reporting of the financial situation of a firm (i.e., measuring and reporting fairly and usefully the wealth created in a period of time) to the shareholders and to other users.

Tax policies regarding calculation of the tax base (i.e., taxable income) are a practical compromise between stimulating the economy by encouraging certain behavior in a context of industrial policies, income redistribution, and the need for any state administration to obtain sufficient resources for its own policies. It is not within the scope of this book to explore exhaustively the tax regulations about costs deductibility and revenues taxability. Each country has its own rules established, for example, by the Internal Revenue Code in the USA, the *Code général des impôts* in France, or different sources of tax law in the UK (Income and Corporation Taxes Act, Value Added Tax Act, etc.).

This section deals with accounting for differences between reporting and taxation in unconsolidated financial statements. Accounting for income tax effects in consolidated financial statements will be covered in Chapter 13.

Pre-tax income and taxable income

Pre-tax income and taxable income do not derive from the same purposes and set of principles. Examples of differences in policies and practices include:

Depreciation is generally computed on a straight-line basis for financial reporting purposes, while an accelerated method is often used for tax purposes. This tax accepted acceleration of depreciation actually postpones the taxation of profits (larger deductions from taxable revenue in the early life of the asset, which create a larger cash flow from operations available early for reinvestment[1] and hopefully growth, thus encouraging the acquisition of assets and boosting the economy, which is often in the interest of the government).

Warranty costs are most often recognized for financial reporting purposes in the period in which the sale took place (matched with the sales revenue through the use of provisions for future warranty costs), while they are often deductible for tax purposes only when actually incurred. Here tax authorities do not want to leave open the door to possible easy abuses of provision expenses used to postpone paying taxes.

Expenses benefiting several years can be immediately deductible for tax purposes but can be amortized over several years for reporting purposes.

Differences between income tax rules and accounting rules lead to different versions of income and since only one serves as the actual tax basis (and thus affects the cash flow), it is important to reconcile the figures between the two versions of the same period so as to give a true and fair view of the financial position. Revenue and expense recognition rules for tax purposes can differ from accounting rules in two ways:

- *whether* or not an item is recognized (taxable or deductible)
- *when* an item is recognized (the current period when the triggering event takes place, or a subsequent period).

These differences in rules create two types of differences between tax basis income and pre-tax accounting income:

- permanent differences (linked to recognition or non-recognition)
- temporary differences (linked to the timing of recognition).

Figure 6.1 illustrates how these differences arise.

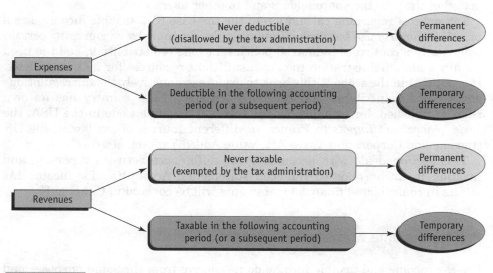

Figure 6.1 Differences between taxable and pre-tax income

Tables 6.1 and 6.2 illustrate the two routes for the calculation of taxable income: either a direct dedicated approach or by a reconciliation starting from the accounting income.

The direct dedicated route

Table 6.1   Method 1: Direct computation

	Taxable revenues
−	Deductible expenses
=	Taxable income

This approach is used in some countries where tax and financial accounting rules are the same (generally at the cost of a loss of relevance to the other users of financial information). It is also frequently used in unlisted small and medium enterprises. They do not wish to go through the reconciliation and keep only a set of tax books, applying tax rules for all recognition issues. Since the users are generally limited to the banker, the owners, or a limited group of close-knit shareholders, they often have an intimate knowledge of the reality of the situation of the firm and do not rely greatly on financial statements for interim information. Thus their loss of information is not significant. However larger businesses and especially listed companies must use the reporting format required by financial markets and thus may deviate from tax rules in their reporting.

Reconciliation and detailed description of steps

In this second approach, the steps describing the differences of rules and practices are detailed so that one can go step by step from the pre-tax income of the period to the taxable income. The interest of this method, when it is disclosed, is that it allows the reader of financial statements to better understand the choices made by the firm and to therefore anticipate better the future cash flows from operations.

Table 6.2   Method 2: Reconciliation in Year 20X1

	Pretax (i.e., reported accounting) income 20X1
	Positive tax adjustments
+	Expenses 20X1 never deductible
+	Expenses 20X1 deductible in 20X2 or after
+	Revenues 20X0 not taxable in 20X0 but taxable in 20X1
	Negative tax adjustments
−	Revenues 20X1 never taxable
−	Revenues 20X1 taxable in 20X2 or after
−	Expenses 20X0 not deductible in 20X0 but deductible in 20X1
=	**Taxable income 20X1**

Impact of permanent differences

Permanent differences are created by revenue and expense items that are recognized for accounting purposes but not for tax purposes or the converse, such as:

- interest revenue on state and municipal bonds are, in some countries, not taxable
- life insurance premiums (taken on the head of executives) paid by a company that is the designated beneficiary of the life insurance in case of death are not tax deductible
- penalties and fines for violation of laws are rarely tax deductible
- depreciation on certain assets may not be tax deductible (for instance, on cars in excess of certain tax specified limitation)
- interest expense on shareholders' current accounts in excess of certain tax specified limitation can be non-tax deductible in some countries
- provisions for doubtful accounts receivables are not always tax deductible
- non-deductibility of charitable contributions in excess of a tax-specified ceiling.

We will see how these permanent differences are affecting accounts through the example of non-tax-deductible parking violation fines for a firm whose main activity is the on-site maintenance of photocopying equipment in a small medieval town without public parking. From an accounting point of view, they are legitimate expenses because repair persons must continuously park illegally while visiting their customers. The tax authorities cannot condone the violation of the law and thus legitimately deny the deductibility of these parking violation fines. There is therefore a divergence between the two sets of rules. The pre-tax income before deducting the non deductible fines is 110 CU. The amount of parking fines is 20. The tax rate is 40%.

Table 6.3 illustrates the fact that, in the case of permanent differences, the accounting and tax approaches give the very same after-tax income.

Table 6.3 Permanent differences

Financial statements		Income tax return	
Pre-tax income before non-deductible penalty	110		
– Non-deductible penalty	–20		
= Pre-tax income	90 ⟶	Pre-tax income	90
		+ Permanent difference (expense added back)	20
		= Taxable income	110
– Income tax expense	44 ⟵	Income tax expense (taxable income	
= Net income (after tax) (pre-tax		× rate: 110 × 40%)	44
income – income tax: 90 – 44)	46		

Any other permanent difference would be handled in the same way. Thus we can state that "permanent differences" do not impair reporting:

- Permanent differences do not reverse themselves over time.
- They have no future tax consequences.

Temporary differences

As we saw in the example of warranty costs, the impact of the divergence between tax and accounting rules is on the timing of the recognition, not on the amount, to the contrary of what was the case for permanent differences. For example, some expenses are recognized immediately for reporting to shareholders and at a later date for tax purposes or the reverse. If the tax rules lead to a later recognition of the tax burden than under financial accounting rules, a tax liability is created which is called **deferred tax liability** (often shortened to "deferred taxes"). It is the most common case. If, on the contrary, the tax rules lead to recognizing taxes earlier than what would have been found according to financial accounting rules, a prepaid tax asset is created which is called **deferred tax asset**.

Figure 6.2 summarizes the process of creation of these deferred tax assets and liabilities (numbers refer to the examples that follow).

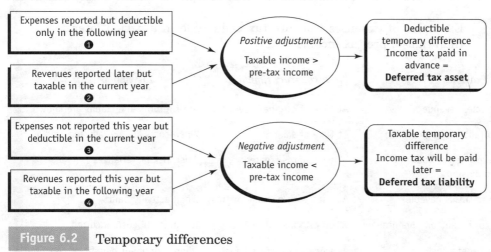

Figure 6.2 Temporary differences

The basic principle of deferred taxation is that the difference is expected to be reversed in future periods. These differences are said to originate in one period and be "capable of reversal" in one or more subsequent periods.

Temporary differences are often defined in a broader way. For example IAS 12 (IASC 1996, § 5) states that "temporary differences are differences between the carrying amount of an asset or liability in the balance sheet and its tax base". They "may be either:

(a) Taxable temporary differences, i.e. temporary differences that will result in taxable amounts in determining taxable profit (tax loss) of future periods when the carrying amount of the asset or liability is recovered or settled; or

(b) Deductible temporary differences; i.e. temporary differences that will result in amounts that are deductible in determining taxable profit (tax loss) of future periods when the carrying amount of the asset or liability is recovered or settled."

The tax base of an asset or liability is the value attributed to that asset or liability for tax purposes. For instance, if a provision for doubtful accounts receivables (see Chapter 10) is considered by tax authorities to have been overstated, the tax administration might disallow part of it. As a consequence, the tax value of the asset (accounts receivable net of accumulated provision) is greater than the carrying amount (net book value). This situation leads to the recording of a deferred tax asset as the provision expense will be reversed when the actual bad debt is recognized but will not be taxable at the time of reversal.

Temporary differences are essentially "timing differences". In practice many accountants use the terms "temporary" and "timing" interchangeably when discussing differences between tax accounting and accounting for reporting to shareholders.

Let us now illustrate some of the sources of temporary differences.

Examples of case ❶ – Expenses that are tax deductible in a later period than they are in the (financial accounting) pre-tax income

Table 6.4 provides for some examples that abound in the life of any business.

| Table 6.4 | Examples of expenses that are tax deductible in a period later than that of pre-tax income |

Examples	Accounting timing	Tax timing
Tax on net sales revenue	At time of original sale	After returns and claims are known
Product warranty costs provision	At time of sale	When costs are actually incurred
Bad debt expense (or doubtful accounts) provision	When claim is created	When risk materializes
Interest or royalties payable	Accrued with passage of time	When actually paid
Provisions for repairs and maintenance	When established	When actual costs incurred
Retirement benefit costs	As employee accrues benefits	When retirement benefit or contribution to pension fund is paid out
Research costs (incorporation or other start-up costs)	Year incurred	May be amortized over a few years

A quantified warranty provision example will illustrate the mechanism. Lorentz Co. sells products with a short lifecycle. Every year a new product replaces the previous year's product. In year 1, product A is still pretty experimental and Lorentz Co. feels it is appropriate to create a provision of 10 CU for future warranty costs on product A. Product B is introduced in year 2, completely replacing product A, which is no longer sold. B is a second-generation product and is considered to be extremely robust and, thus, in year 2, Lorentz Co. sees no need to create a provision for future warranty costs. In year 2 however, all the fears about the warranty service on product A materialize and the actual warranty service cost is 10 CU. The tax rate in this illustration is assumed to be 40%. The company has a pre-tax income before warranty expense and provision of 100 each year. The provision is tax deductible in the year of the actual expense (Year 20X2 in our example).

Two alternative accounting solutions exist: either the firm does report taxes as they are owed (no use of the deferred tax mechanism) as shown in Table 6.5 or they use the deferred tax mechanism as shown in Table 6.6.

First solution: the local GAAP does not allow the deferred tax mechanism

In year 2 the actual expense of 10 is compensated by the pre-existing provision. The recognition of the expense goes along with the cancellation of the provision, thus creating no impact on the income statement of year 2 as can be seen in Table 6.5.

Table 6.5 Effect of a provision when local GAAP does not allow deferred tax accounts

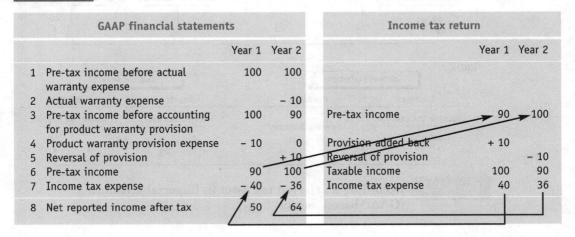

	GAAP financial statements			Income tax return		
		Year 1	Year 2		Year 1	Year 2
1	Pre-tax income before actual warranty expense	100	100			
2	Actual warranty expense		– 10			
3	Pre-tax income before accounting for product warranty provision	100	90	Pre-tax income	90	100
4	Product warranty provision expense	– 10	0	Provision added back	+ 10	
5	Reversal of provision		+ 10	Reversal of provision		– 10
6	Pre-tax income	90	100	Taxable income	100	90
7	Income tax expense	– 40	– 36	Income tax expense	40	36
8	Net reported income after tax	50	64			

Since no deferred taxes mechanism is used, the left panel of Table 6.5 shows what is recorded according to the local GAAP. The tax accrued in each year is the same in the fiscal calculation (right panel), and in the GAAP statements.

Second solution: the local GAAP accept or require the use of deferred tax accounting

Table 6.6 shows, in the left panel, that the tax recorded in financial accounting books is calculated on the basis of the pre-tax income (i.e., GAAP based). It is, in a way, a "theoretical" amount since the taxes that will really be owed to the tax authority are calculated as a function of the taxable income in the right panel of the table. There is a timing difference between the recorded tax expense, calculated on the basis of pre-tax income (36 in Year 1), and the tax due (40 in Year 1). The actual tax liability for year 1 is greater than the tax recorded in the books. Note that the taxes due accumulated over the two years of the illustration are the same (in nominal CU) regardless of whether one takes the GAAP or the tax basis.

Table 6.6 Accounting for deferred income taxes

Tax expense based on financial reporting			Tax expense based on tax return		
	Year 1	Year 2		Year 1	Year 2
Pre-tax income (from Table 6.5, line 6 on the left-hand side)	90	100	Pre-tax income (from Table 6.5, line 6)	90	100
Income tax expense (40 % of pre-tax income)	36	40	Income tax expense (40% of taxable income from Table 6.5 line 6 on the right-hand side)	40	36
Net income	54	60	Net income	50	64

The accounting tax expense is, like any expense, a reduction of the shareholders' equity. Thus, in order to keep the balance sheet balanced, we must recognize the creation of a "deferred tax asset" which is equivalent to saying we have "prepaid taxes" (see Figure 6.3).

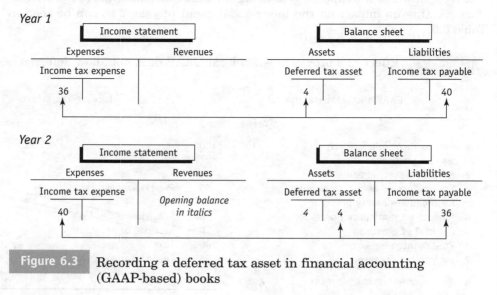

Figure 6.3 Recording a deferred tax asset in financial accounting (GAAP-based) books

The deferred tax asset records the temporary differences due to using differing rules and regulations accounting for taxes and accounting for reporting. This example shows that the deferred tax assets do indeed reverse in the second period. The deferred taxation mechanism's impact is only to modify the timing of the recognition of taxes on income.

Not all countries allow the deferred taxation mechanism. Some countries (see Table 6.9) require that the tax calculated according to tax rules be the one reported in financial accounting statements. In this case, the reported tax liability would be 40 for year 1 and 36 for year 2 in our example.

Examples of case ❷ – Revenues or gains that are taxable in an earlier period than they are recognized under financial accounting rules

Several such situations occur in the normal course of business:

- A latent gain on marketable securities (see Chapter 10) is in fact taxable, in some countries, in the period incurred but is reported under GAAP only at the time of the sale of these marketable securities. (Remember, the logic of taxation is sometimes just an expedient to get the cash into the coffers of the government sooner.)

- Cash received in advance for rent is sometimes taxable in the year received while it must be accrued under the local GAAP as prepaid rent (a liability) and recognized in the income statement of the period corresponding to the rent prepayment.

These temporary differences will generate a deferred tax asset because, as in the previous examples, there is a timing difference between the GAAP and the tax calculation.

Examples of case ❸ – Expenses or losses that are deductible in earlier periods for tax purposes than under the local GAAP for the calculation of the pre-tax income

This is for example the case for:

- Expenses spread over several years according to the local GAAP (matching principle) but tax deductible for the full amount in the year initially incurred. For example, development costs that have been capitalized and will be amortized in the income statement over several periods while the full amount is tax deductible in the period in which the development costs were incurred.

- Greater depreciation for tax purposes than for financial reporting purposes in the early periods of an asset's life, as is the case when accelerated depreciation is used for tax reporting while straight line is used for reporting to shareholders.

Such situations create a tax liability as is shown in the following very simple example of Gade Company. The pre-tax income before accounting for depreciation expense is 180 CU in both years and we will assume that depreciation expense for tax purposes will be fully incurred in year 1 while, under local GAAP, the asset depreciation is recognized over two years for reporting purposes.

Income before depreciation and taxes	180
Asset purchased	20
Depreciation for tax purposes (one year)	20
Depreciation for reporting purposes (two years)	10
Income taxes rate	40%

The impact of the different accounting and tax rules regarding depreciation expense is described in Tables 6.7 and 6.8. Two alternative treatments exist: either the financial accounting report shows the actual tax expense (calculated according to tax rules), or it reports taxes that would be owed if tax rules were the same as GAAP rules and shows a deferred tax liability account to reconcile the two different ways of calculating.

First alternative: GAAP indicates that financial statements report as tax expense the real tax owed (calculated according to tax rules)

Table 6.7 Case of an expense which is tax deductible earlier than under GAAP

Financial statements	Year 1	Year 2	Income tax return	Year 1	Year 2
Pre-tax income before accounting for depreciation expense	180	180	Pre-tax income	170	170
Depreciation expense	– 10	– 10	Reported depreciation expense added back	+ 10	+ 10
			Deductible expense	– 20	
Pre-tax income	170	170	Taxable income	160	180
Income tax expense	– 64	– 72	Income tax expense	64	72
Net income reported	106	98			

The left panel of Table 6.7 shows the reported statement while the right panel of Table 6.7 shows the calculation mechanism for the taxes on income that will actually be paid to the local fiscal administration.

Second alternative: local GAAP allows or states that reported tax expense should be calculated according to GAAP rules, and not according to tax rules (thus creating a deferred taxation issue)

Table 6.8 shows the calculations required for the establishment of the financial statements.

Table 6.8 Accounting for deferred income taxes

Tax expense based on financial reporting			Tax expense based on tax return		
	Year 1	Year 2		Year 1	Year 2
Pre-tax income based on local GAAP (see Table 6.7)	170	170	Pre-tax income based on local GAAP (see Table 6.7)	170	170
Income tax expense (40 % of pre-tax income)	68	68	Income tax expense (40% of taxable income) (Table 6.7)	64	72
Net income reported	102	102	Net income (tax rules)	106	98

There will exist a timing difference between the two flows: in the first year, for example, the tax expense actually owed to the fiscal administration is only 64 CU while under GAAP it will appear as 68. In the first year Gade Company pays 4 CU fewer in taxes than it reports. The situation is the reverse in year 2. Over the two years taken together, the taxes owed are the same (136) in nominal CU. Therefore it is essential for the financial statements to inform the shareholders that a debt to the tax authorities has been created by the GAAP rules in year 1. The accountant does so by recognizing a deferred tax liability of 4 CU at the end of year 1 (see Figure 6.4).

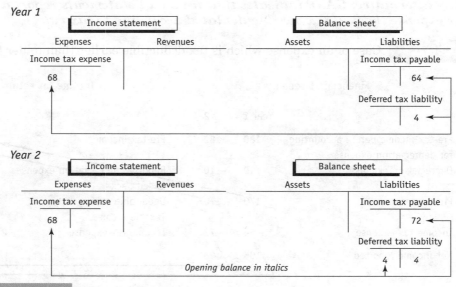

Figure 6.4 Recording a deferred tax liability

In this illustration, the deferred tax liability is indeed the result of a temporary difference since it clearly was reversed in the second year. Once again this illustrates the fact that the deferred tax mechanism only impacts the timing of recognition of the tax expense. The deferred tax liability may be classified as long-term or current liability (when the balance sheet distinguishes the time horizon of liabilities – see Chapter 3) as a function of the expected timing of the reversal.

Examples of case ❹ – Revenues or gains that are taxable in later periods than they are recognized under GAAP

This is the case or example in the following situations:

- In some countries, the revenue from credit sales (that give rise to an account receivable) may be fully recognized under GAAP when the sale takes place, but only be taxable for tax purposes on a cash basis, i.e., only when the customer settles their debt.

- Interest revenue is generally received in arrears and is included in GAAP accounting profit on a time-apportioned accrual basis (matching principle) but is included in taxable profit only on a cash basis.

These differences are only temporary as their effect will reverse over time. They generate a deferred tax liability.

Accounting for and reporting income taxes

Principles

The choice of reporting method for income taxes should answer the fundamental question: Should the expected tax consequences of the existing temporary differences be recognized in financial statements? In other words, should deferred taxation be reported?

Two basic alternatives can be identified:

1 **Taxes payable accounting** (or **flow-through method** or **integrated model**): This approach consists in ignoring the temporary difference, recognizing income tax expense (in the financial statements for shareholders) as identical to the income tax payable. This view is defended by experts and countries (see Table 6.9) which hold the view that taxation is, in fact, a sharing mechanism in which the tax is the share of income that should go to the state, government or fiscal administration (in return for granting the business the right to exist) rather than a cost of doing business that needs to be recorded in the income statement. This view is in opposition to the matching principle since there is no link between the tax recognized and the triggering event.

2 **Deferred taxation accounting** (or **full provision method** or **deferred tax model**): This approach consists in recognizing the tax consequences of the temporary difference by including its tax effect as **income tax expense** on the income statement and as an asset or a liability (called a **deferred tax asset** or a **deferred tax liability**) in the balance sheet. This method actually reports an economic tax expense based on the pretax income. This method is in full compliance with the matching principle.

While reporting for deferred taxation in the consolidated financial statements is an almost universal practice, many countries' GAAP do not include the use of deferred taxes in the unconsolidated financial statements, as shown in Table 6.9.

Table 6.9 Reporting for deferred income taxes in unconsolidated financial statements

Countries	Deferred taxes used in local GAAP for unconsolidated financial statements?		Countries	Deferred taxes used in local GAAP for unconsolidated financial statements?	
Australia	Yes		Japan		No
Austria		No	Luxembourg		No
Belgium		No	Netherlands	Yes	
Canada	Yes		Norway	Yes	
Denmark	Yes		Portugal	Yes	
Finland		No	Spain		No
France		No	Sweden		No
Germany	Yes		Switzerland		No
Greece		No	UK	Yes	
Ireland	Yes		USA	Yes	
Italy		No			

Real-life example

Procter & Gamble

Procter & Gamble, a diversified personal and home care US group involved among other activities in fabric and home care (Ariel, Mr. Clean), feminine protection (Always), healthcare, food and beverage, beauty care (Head & Shoulders) and baby care (Pampers), publishes in its annual report 1999 the following figures relating to income taxes:

Procter & Gamble
Consolidated statement of earnings (in millions of US $)
for the years ended 30 June 1997–1999 (source: annual report 1999)

In millions of $US	1999	1998	1997
Income taxes	2,075	1,928	1,834

In note 10 to the financial statements, the following information appears:

In millions of $US	1999	1998	1997
Current tax expense			
US federal	1,080	996	967
International	934	918	805
US state and local	121	115	88
	2,135	2,029	1,860
Deferred tax expense			
US federal	(74)	51	1
International	14	(152)	(27)
	(60)	(101)	(26)
Income taxes	2,075	1,928	1,834

ADVANCED ISSUES

Earlier sections of this chapter dealt with the general principles of revenue recognition. We will now examine the specific revenue recognition issues raised by some business practices.

Long-term contracts

As shown earlier in this chapter, long-term contracts represent a very common situation in which the revenue and cost recognition principles find all their usefulness.

Principles

Long-term contracts are referred to by IASC as "construction contracts" (IAS 11, IASC 1993b). We will however keep using the expression long-term contract since contracts that span several accounting periods include many other categories of contracts than construction contracts. For example, research contracts, contracts for the delivery of a series of locomotives or aircraft, facilities management contracts, computer service contracts, law suits, consulting contracts, etc., are all long-term contracts which span several accounting periods.

This section is largely inspired by IAS 11, which states the problems arising with the accounting for long-term contracts in a very clear way. The primary issue with long-term contracts is the allocation of contract revenue and contract costs to the accounting periods in which work is performed. The general rules of revenue recognition introduced in the "Core Issues" section of this chapter apply.

IAS 11 distinguished two types of long-term contracts based on the revenue determination formula:

- A fixed price contract is one in which the contractor agrees to a fixed contract price, or a fixed rate per unit of output, which in some cases is subject to cost escalation clauses to reflect inflation on the cost of resources consumed.

- A cost plus contract is one in which the contractor is reimbursed for allowable or otherwise defined costs, plus a percentage of these costs or a fixed fee.

When the outcome of a long-term contract can be estimated reliably, contract revenue and contract costs associated with this contract should be recognized as revenue and expenses respectively proportionately to the degree of completion of the contract activity at the balance sheet date. The IASC, and a majority of countries prefer the "percentage of completion method" over any other. It consists in recording costs and revenue associated with the contract as the increments in the degree of completion of the contract during the period.

The IASC states several conditions for their endorsement of this method. In the case, for example, of a fixed price contract, the outcome of the contract can be considered to have been reliably estimated when all the conditions mentioned earlier for recognition of services are satisfied. If any one of these conditions cannot be met, IAS 11 recommends a prudent approach for the recognition of revenue which is a variation on the percentage of completion method:

(a) Revenue should be recognized only up to the level of contract costs incurred that can unambiguously be considered recoverable.

(b) Contract costs should be recognized as an expense in the period in which they are incurred.

An alternative method exists that is not endorsed under IAS 11 but which is still used by many enterprises in countries that accept its use: the "completed contract method". Its mechanism consists in waiting until the contract is fully completed to recognize all its revenue and costs. Under this method the costs pertaining to the contract are capitalized as an asset and thus do not impact on the income of the firm until completion. This method is extremely simple to apply. It is built on the premise that the final outcome of a long-term contract cannot be known until the contract is fully completed because too many uncertainties taint any attempt at estimating the end result. While the percentage of completion method is a direct application of the matching principle, the completed contract method is a direct application of the prudence principle.

Regardless of the method used for the recognition of income pertaining to a long-term contract, both imply immediate recognition of potential losses on a contract as soon as they can be legitimately established. Appendix 6.1 provides a detailed illustration of both methods of recording long-term contracts.

Real-life examples

Some excerpts of long-term contract revenue recognition issues now follow as they appear in the financial statements of two large international businesses.

Ericsson
(Sweden – Swedish GAAP – Source: Annual report 1999)

Revenue from long-term customer contracts is recognized successively. If costs required to complete such contracts are estimated to exceed remaining revenues, provision is made for estimated losses.

Inventories (in millions of Swedish kronor)

	1999	1998
(...)		
Contract work in process	13,398	11,643
Less advances from customers	– 4,816	– 2,648
(...)		

Philips
(Netherlands – Dutch GAAP – Source: Annual report 1999)

Revenues from long-term contracts are recognized in accordance with the percentage of completion method. Provision for estimated contract losses, if any, is made in the period that such losses are determined.

Installment sales

Installment sales are quite common in some retail businesses such as mail order collector books, furniture, or automobiles. Under this practice the customer pays in several installments for a product or service over which she/he has acquired control before the full payment is completed. The issue of uncertainty about the full payment creates an interesting revenue recognition problem. Such a payment approach is generally referred to as an installment credit. The topic is quite complex and students who wish to explore it are invited to consult a more advanced text[2] than this one. In short the question is two-pronged: what date of recognition of revenue, and how much to recognize at what time. If revenue is fully recognized at the time of the signature of the sales contract, there is a major risk of payment default by some customers but that solution is coherent with the matching principle and a provision might be the right vector to recognize the risk. An issue here is to know whether the manager really wants the shareholders to be so well informed of the risks the business is taking.[3] Many installment sales are treated like long-term contracts and the gross profit margin (sales minus cost of acquisition or manufacturing by the seller of the goods sold) is recognized in proportion to the acquisition of the installment payments.

Deferred taxation

Recognition of a net deferred tax asset

The recognition of a net deferred tax asset (excess of deferred tax assets over deferred tax liabilities) raises an issue of both value and reality and is developed in Appendix 6.2.

Accounting for net operating losses

Some tax regulations allow the recording of carry-back and/or carry-forward of net operating losses. It means that the losses of one period can be carried back, i.e., used to offset profits made in previous periods (thus calling for a tax refund), or carried forward to be offset against future profits so as to avoid paying taxes in the future. The carry-back/carry-forward issue affects greatly the cash flow of businesses and is a major way of supporting start-up companies (the accumulated tax losses can be offset against future profits thus maintaining cash inside the firm when it needs it the most), and a significant element of financing in mergers and acquisitions (a profitable firm buys a business with large accumulated losses to shield its current and possibly future profits against taxation, thus affecting the net cash cost of the acquisition).

Table 6.10 indicates whether such practice is allowed in a given country (the list is not exhaustive and does not identify special cases).

Appendix 6.3 illustrates the mechanism of carry-back and carry-forward. A loss carry-back allows the business to carry the net operating loss back a certain number of years (generally between 1 and 3 years – see Table 6.10) and receive refunds for income taxes paid in those years.

Table 6.10 Net operating losses

Country	Loss carry-forward	Loss carry-back
Australia	Unlimited	No
Austria	7 years	No
Belgium	Unlimited	No
Canada	7 years	3 years
Denmark	5 years	No
Finland	5 years	No
France	5 years	3 years
Germany	Unlimited	2 years
Greece	5 years	No
Ireland	Unlimited	1 year
Italy	5 years	No
Japan	5 years	1 year
Luxembourg	Unlimited	No
Netherlands	8 years	3 years
Norway	10 years	2 years (if ceased activity)
Portugal	5 years	No
Spain	5 years	No
Sweden	2 years	No
Switzerland	3 years	No
United Kingdom	Unlimited	3 years
United States	15 years	3 years

BS (A+)	Income tax refund receivable	x
IS (R+) or	Benefit due to loss carry-back or	x
IS (E–)	income tax expense	

A **loss carry-back** is not a complex accounting issue as the claim on the tax authority is definite and real. Thus a journal entry on the model of the one just seen is perfectly legitimate. A **loss carry-forward** allows the enterprise to offset future taxable income against the accumulated losses for up to a certain number of years (15 in the USA, 5 in France, for example). The tax effect of a loss carry-forward represents future tax savings. To the contrary of a carry-back, the carry-forward encompasses a certain degree of uncertainty because the claim against future taxes can only be used if taxes payable result from future profits. In this context, the key accounting issue is whether the requirements for recognition of a deferred asset for operating loss carry-forwards should be different from those for deductible temporary differences.

The US answer is that there should not be different requirements. Different solutions have, however, been adopted in other countries. When local GAAP and regulation authorize the recognition of a deferred tax asset in the case of loss carry-forward, the following entry is recorded:

BS (A+)		Deferred tax asset	x
	IS (R+) or	Benefit due to loss carry-forward	x
	IS (E–)	or income tax expense	

Changes in tax rates

Appendix 6.4 develops the impact of changes in tax rates on deferred taxation.

Extraordinary and exceptional items

Most country-specific GAAP includes the principle that it is essential for an income statement to be useful in terms of evaluation of past performance and establishment of extrapolations of future performance. Consequently, an income statement presents separately and distinctly what pertains to "normal" and recurrent business activities and what pertains to actions, decisions, and events that are occasional and unusual.

There are, however, some divergent views (reflected in the choices of terms used to refer to this question) about what are "normal" (in the course of carrying out the business activity) and what are "abnormal" or unusual activities. The IASC, actually followed in their choice by many countries, distinguish extraordinary items from ordinary items. Others introduce a slightly different meaning by choosing other words: for example by distinguishing extraordinary from exceptional items and from current items (which means operating and financial). Rules adopted in the various country-specific GAAP lead to a fairly narrow definition of extraordinary but a much looser definition of exceptional items.

IAS 8 (IASC 1993a) states that "all items of income and expense recognized in a period should be included in the determination of the net profit or loss for the period unless an International Accounting Standard requires or permits otherwise" (§ 7). In this context, the net profit or loss for the period comprises the following components, both of which should be disclosed in the income statement:

● profit or loss from ordinary activities
● extraordinary items.

It goes further to define extraordinary items (§ 6): "Income and expenses that arise from events or transactions that are clearly distinct from the ordinary activities of the enterprise and therefore are not expected to occur frequently or regularly." The nature and the amount of each extraordinary item should be separately disclosed.

"Virtually all items of income and expense included in the determination of net profit or loss for the period arise in the course of the ordinary activities of the enterprise" (§ 12). These activities are undertaken by an enterprise as part of its normal business as defined by its strategic intent or mission. "Therefore, only on rare occasions does an event or transaction give rise to an extraordinary item" (§ 12).

IAS 8 (§ 13) adds: "Whether an event or transaction is clearly distinct from the ordinary activities of the enterprise is determined by the nature of the event or transaction in relation to the business ordinarily carried on by the enterprise rather than by the frequency with which such events are expected to occur. Therefore, an event or transaction may be extraordinary for one enterprise but not extraordinary for another enterprise because of the differences between their respective ordinary activities. For example, losses incurred as a result of an earthquake may qualify as an extraordinary item for many enterprises. However, claims by earthquake insurance policyholders arising from an earthquake do not qualify as an extraordinary item for an insurance company that insures against such risk."

Events or transactions that generally give rise to extraordinary items for most enterprises are generally events over which the management of the firm has no control such as an expropriation of assets or an act of God such as an earthquake or other natural disaster.

Appendix 6.5 provides further developments on the concepts of extraordinary and exceptional items.

Changes in accounting estimates

"As a result of the uncertainties inherent in business activities, many financial statement items cannot be measured with precision but can only be estimated. The estimation process involves judgements based on the latest information available at the time. Estimates may be required, for example, for bad debts, inventory obsolescence or the useful life or expected pattern of consumption of economic benefits of depreciable assets. The use of reasonable estimates is an essential part of the preparation of financial statements and does not undermine their reliability" (IAS 8, IASC 1993a: § 23).

An estimate may have to be revised if changes occur regarding the hypotheses and circumstances on which the estimate was based or as a result of new information, more experience or subsequent developments. By its nature, according to IAS 8 (§ 24), "a revision of an estimate does not bring the adjustment within the terms of the definition of either an extraordinary item or a fundamental error."

"Sometimes it is difficult to distinguish between a change in accounting policy [see later] and a change in an accounting estimate" (IAS 8: § 25). IAS 8 (§ 26) prescribes that the effect of a change in an accounting estimate should be included, when determining the net profit or loss, in the same income statement classification that was used for the estimate, and in the relevant period or periods. Appropriate disclosure in the footnotes of the reasons for the change in estimate is a logical next step not always satisfied.

Fundamental errors

"Errors in the preparation of the financial statements of one or more prior periods may be discovered in the current period. Errors may occur as a result of mathematical mistakes, mistakes in applying accounting policies, misinterpretation of facts, fraud or oversights. The correction of these errors is normally included in the determination of net profit or loss for the current period" (IAS 8, IASC 1993a: § 31).

"On rare occasions, an error has such a significant effect on the financial statements of one or more prior periods that those financial statements can no longer be considered to have been reliable at the date of their issue. These errors are referred to as fundamental errors. An example of a fundamental error would be the inclusion in the financial statements of a previous period of material amounts of work-in-progress and receivables in respect of fraudulent contracts which cannot be enforced" (IAS 8: § 32). Additionally, IAS 8 (§ 34) states: "The amount of the correction of a fundamental error that relates to prior results should be reported by adjusting the opening balance of retained earnings. Comparative information should be restated, unless it is impracticable to do so."

The restatement of comparative information does not necessarily give rise to the amendment of financial statements, which have been approved by shareholders or registered or filed with regulatory authorities. However, national laws may require the amendment of such financial statements.

IAS 8 adds that (§ 37) "an enterprise should disclose:

(a)   the nature of the fundamental error;
(b)   the amount of the correction for the current period and for each prior period presented;
(c)   the amount of the correction relating to periods prior to those included in the comparative information; and
(d)   the fact that comparative information has been restated or that it is impracticable to do so."

Changes in accounting policies

The consistency principle evoked in Chapter 5 states that identical accounting policies are normally adopted in each period in order to allow users to compare the financial statements of an enterprise over a period of time and to identify trends in its financial position, performance, and cash flows. Therefore, in this context, "a change in accounting policy should be made only if required by statute, or by an accounting standard-setting body, or if the change will result in a more appropriate [relevant or reliable] presentation of events or transactions in the financial statements of the enterprise" (IAS 8, § 42).

IAS 8 prescribes as benchmark treatment that "a change in accounting policy should be applied retrospectively unless the amount of any resulting adjustment that relates to prior periods is not reasonably determinable [or retrospectively material]. Any resulting adjustment should be reported as an adjustment to the opening balance of retained earnings. Comparative information should be restated unless it is impracticable to do so" (§ 49). The change in accounting policy should be applied prospectively when the amount of the adjustment to the opening balance of retained earnings cannot be reasonably determined. The International Accounting Standard also prescribes disclosure of:

- the reasons for the change
- the amount of the adjustment for the current period and for each period presented
- the amount of the adjustment relating to periods prior to those included in the comparative information
- the fact that comparative information has been restated or that it is impracticable to do so.

IAS 8 also accepts that the resulting adjustment be included in the determination of the net profit or loss for the current period, in a special caption "Cumulative effect of change in accounting policy."

Discontinuing operations

Any business must, in the normal course of its activity, discontinue or cede some segments of its activity so as to reallocate its resources towards potentially more profitable markets. Entire sections of a business will therefore be either sold or discontinued. Since users need to be able to interpret the current performance of the firm by comparing it against previous periods' performance, it is critical to be able to reconstitute an equivalent economic perimeter so that the basis of comparability be reestablished. The handling of discontinued operations is therefore a very important element of quality reporting.

Principles

As defined in IAS 35 (IASC 1998: § 2), "a discontinuing operation is a component of an enterprise:
  (a)   that the enterprise (...) is:
      – disposing of substantially in its entirety, such as by selling the component in a single transaction, by demerger or spin-off of ownership of the component to the enterprise's shareholders;
      – disposing of piecemeal, such as by selling off the component's assets and settling its liabilities individually; or
      – terminating through abandonment;
  (b)   that represents a separate major line of business or geographical area of operations; and
  (c)   that can be distinguished operationally and for financial reporting purposes."

The standard establishes principles for reporting information about discontinuing operations, thereby enhancing the ability of users of financial statements to make projections of an enterprise's cash flows, earnings-generating capacity, and financial position by segregating information about discontinuing operations from information about continuing operations.

An enterprise should include the following information relating to a discontinuing operation in its financial statements (IASC 1998: § 27):

- "a description of the discontinued operation;
- the business or geographical segment(s) in which it is reported (...);
- the date and nature of the initial disclosure event;
- the date or period in which the discontinuance is expected to be completed if known or determinable;
- the carrying amounts, as of the balance sheet date, of the total assets and the total liabilities to be disposed of;
- the amounts of revenue, expenses, and pre-tax profits or loss from ordinary activities attributable to the discontinuing operation during the current financial reporting period, and the income tax expense relating thereto (...);
- the amounts of net cash flows attributable to the operating, investing and financing activities of the discontinuing operation during the current financial reporting period."

These disclosures may be presented either in the notes to the financial statements or as a subsection of the financial statements themselves. The disclosure of the amount of the pre-tax gain, loss recognized on the disposal of assets, or settlement of liabilities attributable to the discontinuing operation should be shown clearly as an identified item in the income statement (IAS 35, IASC 1998: § 39).

Real-life example

Philips
(Netherlands – Dutch GAAP – *Source*: Annual report 1999)

Consolidated statements of income of the Philips Group

(in millions of €)	1999	1998	1997
(...)			
Discontinued operations			
Income from discontinued operations (less applicable income taxes of €75 million and €161 million for 1998 and 1997 respectively)	—	210	263
Gain on disposal of discontinued operations (no tax effect)	—	4,844	—
(...)			

Note 7 to the financial statements

In December 1998, Philips completed the sale of all of its 75% shareholding in PolyGram N.V. ("PolyGram"), to the Seagram Company Ltd. ("Seagram"). Philips received €5,233 million in cash and 47,831,952 Seagram shares, representing approximately 12% of the outstanding Seagram shares. The sale of PolyGram resulted in a gain of €4,844 million, or €13.45 per share, free of taxes. The results of PolyGram have been classified as discontinued operations in the accompanying financial statements.

PolyGram recorded sales of €4,818 million in 1998 through the date of its sale, and €5,035 million in 1997. Philips' share in net income of PolyGram in 1998 and 1997 amounted to €210 million and €263 million respectively, which is included under income from discontinued operations

Comprehensive income

Comprehensive income is defined as the sum of all "change[s] in equity of a business enterprise during a period [arising] from transactions and other events and circumstances," excluding those resulting from investments by owners and distributions to owners (FASB 1997: § 8).

Principles

Certain changes in assets and liabilities which, according to accounting principles, are considered neither ordinary nor exceptional or extraordinary and thus are not part of the net income, are sometimes not reported in the income statement for the period in which they are recognized but, instead, included directly in a separate component of equity in the balance sheet. For example, the potential gain resulting from a rise in the market value of "available-for-sale" marketable securities (see Chapter 10) is not recorded in the income statement but directly in the shareholders' equity.

Some users of financial statement information have expressed concerns about the increasing number of this type of items that bypass – or are not reported in – the income statement. In this context, in June 1997 the FASB issued the Statement of Financial Accounting Standard (SFAS) no. 130, Reporting Comprehensive Income, that discusses how to report and display these items within a "comprehensive income".

Those items "bypassing" the income statement are referred to as "other [elements of] comprehensive income". Figure 6.5 illustrates the three main sources of "other comprehensive income".

SFAS 130 encourages an enterprise to report "the components of other comprehensive income and total comprehensive income [separately and] below the total for net income in a statement that reports results of operations" ("one-statement approach"), "or in a separate statement of comprehensive income that begins with net income" ("two-statement approach") (FASB 1997: § 23). Comprehensive income and other comprehensive income may also be presented in a statement of changes in equity (see Chapter 11).

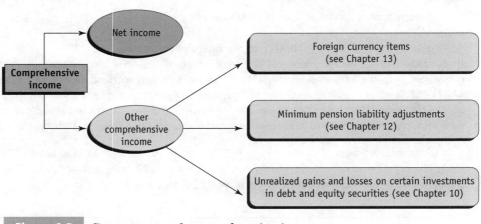

Figure 6.5 Components of comprehensive income

Examples

SFAS 130

SFAS 130 includes in its appendix an example of statement of income and comprehensive income. We are listing here the elements that are added to the net income to obtain the comprehensive income (see Table 6.11).

Table 6.11 Comprehensive income in SFAS 130

Net income		63,250
Other comprehensive income, net of tax:		
Foreign currency translation adjustments		8,000
Unrealized gains on securities		11,500
Unrealized holding gains arising during period	13,000	
Less: reclassification adjustment for gains included in net income	(1,500)	
Minimum pension liability adjustment		(2,500)
Other comprehensive income		17,000
Comprehensive income		80,250

We will not delve into the details of the different items of the other comprehensive income. The interested reader is encouraged to consult SFAS 130.

Real-life example

Table 6.12 illustrates (in a simplified manner) the two-statement approach of reporting comprehensive income. Aracruz is a Brazilian producer of bleached eucalyptus pulp, supplying about 20% of the world market for this product. This company follows the US GAAP.

Table 6.12 Aracruz

Consolidated statement of income (1999)
in millions of US dollars

Operating revenues	541
Operating costs	−407
Operating income	134
Financial income	101
Financial expenses	−128
Financial income	−27
Income before income taxes	107
Income taxes	−17
Net income	90

Consolidated statement of comprehensive income (1999) (adapted)
in millions of US dollars

Net income	90
Net unrealized gain*	12
Comprehensive income	102

* on available-for-sale securities

Government assistance: grants and subsidies

Government grants, also called subsidies, subventions, or premiums are relatively common in many countries. IAS 20 (IASC 1994) uses the term "government assistance" to show that the aid given takes many forms varying both in the nature of the assistance given and in the conditions which are usually attached to it. This assistance creates a serious revenue recognition problem, which can affect the interpretation of financial statements by users. Is government assistance a revenue (or a compensation of costs, which is equivalent to a revenue), or a source of financing?

There are several categories of government assistance, and each category may require a different answer to this question. They are:

- grants related to assets
- grants related to income
- forgivable loans (i.e., loans that will not need to be reimbursed if certain conditions are met).

Let us analyze in turn the specificity of each type of assistance.

Grants related to assets

Grants related to assets are government grants whose purpose is to specifically encourage qualified enterprises to purchase, construct or otherwise acquire long-term assets. These grants are mostly a targeted aid to investment in sectors or geographical areas selected for economic development. These grants, often called "investment grants", can be used to finance greenfield operations as well as part of the cost of additions or modifications to existing fixed assets.

Figure 6.6 illustrates the several possible ways to account for such government assistance. Figure 6.6 shows that the preferred treatment consists in recognizing the grant as revenue in systematic and rational sections that allow matching of the government assistance with the related costs (in practice the depreciation expenses) over the relevant periods. The full recognition of the whole investment grant in the first year would only be acceptable if no basis existed for allocating it to periods other than the one in which it was received.

Alternative solutions, however, exist without violating the intent of IAS 20. For example, under French GAAP, an investment grant appears not on the income statement but on the balance sheet as a separate item within shareholders' equity (in the unconsolidated financial statements) or as a non-current liability (in the consolidated financial statements). The amount so recorded is "amortized" following the method prescribed by IASC, i.e., a systematic and rational allocation to revenues. The separate item is then equivalent to the "deferred income" account prescribed by IASC as shown in Figure 6.6.

Theoretical example

Kunzen SA acquires an asset in exchange for a cash payment of 200 CU. This asset will be depreciated over five years on a straight-line basis. Because Kunzen is located in a special economic zone, it qualifies for government

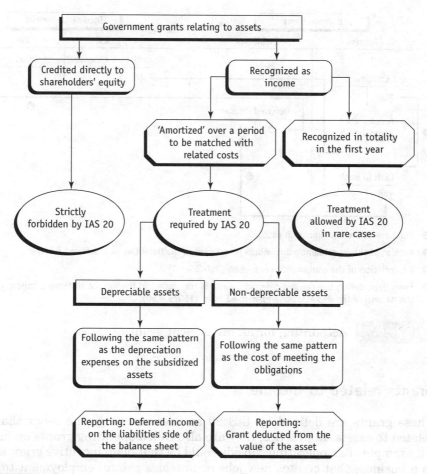

Figure 6.6   Accounting and reporting for investment grant in IAS 20

assistance related to this asset for an amount of 150 CU. Figure 6.7 illustrates the accounting for the grant in year 1.

Real-life example

Bayer, the German-based international chemicals and healthcare group, states in the notes to its annual report 1999 that, in accordance with IAS 20, grants and subsidies that serve to promote investment are treated as deferred income. The amounts – which are mainly from government sources – are gradually reversed during the useful lives of the respective assets and recognized in income. Deferred income as of 31 December 1999 includes €125 million in investment grants (in 1998, it amounted to €115 million); the amount reversed and recognized in 1999 was €16 million.

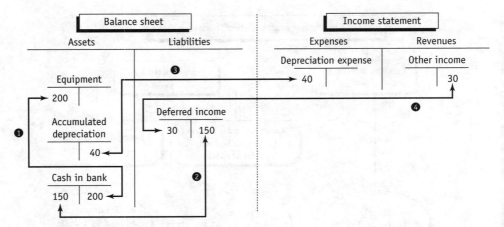

① Purchase of the equipment on cash

② Receipt of the investment grant, which is recorded in the liabilities as a deferred income

③ Depreciation of the equipment over 5 years (200/5 = 40)

④ Every year, during 5 years, the deferred income is transferred to the income statement, following the pattern of the depreciation of the fixed asset (150/5 = 30)

Figure 6.7　Accounting for an investment grant

Grants related to income

These grants are defined by IAS 20 as government grants other than those related to assets. In practice, they are also called operating grants or subsidies. An example of an operating subsidy could be that of an incentive grant awarded to a business that creates new jobs or provides gainful employment to certain categories of unemployed persons. Grants related to income are included in the income statement when they are received, as an income (in the category "other income") or as a deduction of the related expense.

Forgivable loans and repayable grants

These loans are defined as loans for which the lender accepts to waive repayment under certain prescribed conditions such as, for example, the effective creation within a specified time span of a given number of jobs. If the conditions are not met, the grant is, in principle, repayable. Other grants are repayable in case of success, such as for example a grant to help in research and development or a grant to help develop a new market. These grants are recorded in the balance sheet (on the liabilities side) until the condition has been met or it is established the conditions will not be met. It is recorded under the special caption "conditional advances received from the state" that lists the grant immediately next to shareholders' equity. At the end of the life of the grant, if the conditions are not met the grant is repayable and will be handled exactly as would a normal loan. If, on the contrary the conditions are met, an operating revenue or an exceptional revenue will be recorded.

KEY POINTS

- The issue of revenue recognition deals with when and how much revenue to recognize.
- Criteria for recognition vary according to the type of transaction: sales of goods, services or use of enterprise assets yielding interest, royalties, or dividends.
- Revenue from the sale of goods should be recognized when several conditions have been satisfied, and mainly when the enterprise has transferred to the buyer the significant risks and rewards of ownership of the goods.
- When the outcome of a transaction involving the rendering of services spanning several accounting periods (such as in long-term contracts) can be estimated reliably, revenue and costs associated with the transaction should be recognized on the balance sheet date as a function of the stage or percentage of completion of the transaction.
- There may be some divergence between tax regulation and accounting rules. When these differences relate to the timing of the recognition, they are called "temporary differences".
- Deferred tax assets or liabilities are created when the income tax expense is based on the pre-tax income (defined according to accounting rules) and not on the taxable income (based on the tax rules).
- The "percentage of completion method", which consists in recording costs and revenue associated with the contracts as the work proceeds, is the preferred method for the recognition of profit in long-term contracts.
- Accounting standards stipulate that for an income statement to be useful in terms of evaluation of performance and permitting extrapolations, it must present separately and distinctly what pertains to "normal" and recurrent business activities and what pertains to actions, decisions, and events that are occasional and unusual.
- The comprehensive income includes revenues and expenses that are usually excluded from net income (e.g., unrealized gains and losses on short-term investments). This concept aims at showing the global performance of the company.
- Government assistance (grants, subsidies, subventions or premiums) raise revenue recognition issues.

REVIEW

Review 6.1 Schultz Accountancy Firm (1)

Topic: Revenue recognition
Type: Group exercise
Related part of the chapter: Core Issues

Mr. Schultz, the managing partner of an accounting firm, is concerned by some of his clients who adopted specific rules in terms of revenue recognition. He provides the following list of some of the rules he has found in the notes to his customers' financial statements:

A An advertising agency records as revenue the full commission as soon as the advertisement campaign has been fully prepared.

B Atrium Auditorium Inc. (AA Inc.) sells subscription packages to several series of concerts to be held between October 20X1 and September 20X2. Most concerts will take place in the fall and the spring and a sprinkling of events will take place during the summer. Customers are expected to pay cash for their subscription. AA Inc.'s reporting year ends on 31 December. In its income statement for period 20X1, AA Inc. records as revenue 3/12 (3 months) of the amounts received as subscription from paying customers. The remaining 9/12 of the cash intake will be recognized in 20X2.

C Boticcelli Markets is specialized in home delivery of groceries, fruit, and produce. It expects cash on delivery. It recognizes revenue at the time of payment.

D The Olympic Sports Club is a membership-only club. The yearly admission fee allows the member to enter the premises. Members have the possibility of paying the membership fee in installments for a small surcharge. All services within the club are billed to the members at about 20% below the open enrolment market prices of competing clubs. Membership fees are recognized in the income statement in equal instalments over the duration of the membership (generally one year, although discounts are granted to members who pay upfront for longer periods).

Required

Evaluate whether the policies adopted by the different companies are acceptable or not. If you feel they are not, which policy should have been adopted?

Solution

a) Media commissions are recognized when the related advertisement or commercial appears before the public. The accounting treatment followed by this company is not correct.

b) Revenue from artistic performances, banquets, and other special events is recognized when the event takes place. When a subscription to a number of events is sold, the fee is allocated to each event on a basis which reflects the extent to which services are performed at each event.

c) Revenue is recognized when delivery is made and cash is received by the seller or its agent. The accounting treatment is correct.

d) Revenue recognition depends on the uncertainty of the collection of the membership fee. The fee is recognized as revenue when no significant uncertainty about collection exists. In the present case, since the fee permits only membership (and must be paid before the members gain access to other services that will be paid separately), the club should not defer the recognition on a straight-line basis and recognize it when it is paid, not by allocation over the months of the membership.

Review 6.2 Schall Company

Topic: Deferred taxation
Type: Individual exercise
Related part of the chapter: Core Issues

Schall Company realized in 20X1 a fiscal pre-tax income of 100 CU. This income includes taking into account a one off royalty fee expense for 10 CU (which was paid upfront in year 20X1). The royalty fee is for the use by Schall Co. of a new technology for 2 years. Accordingly, Schall Co.'s accountant chose to recognize, for reporting purposes, half the fee in year 20X1, and the second half in year 20X2. However, tax regulations require an immediate deduction in tax accounts. The income tax rate is 40%.

The following table summarizes the data:

Pre-tax income before recording the royalty fee	110
Royalty fee expense recorded for tax purposes	10
Pre-tax income after recording the fee	100
Royalty fee expense to be split over 2 years	10
Amortization of the fee expense over 2 years	5
Income tax rate	40%

Required

1 Compute the deferred taxation, assuming that the pre-tax income before recording the royalty fee expense is the same in 20X2 as in 20X1.

2 Record the deferred taxation in 20X1 and 20X2.

Solution

The impact on income tax calculations is as follows:

Financial statements	Year 1	Year 2
Pre-tax income before recording an expense	110	110
Expense recorded	–10	0
Pre-tax income after recording the expense	100	110
Expense split over 2 years	10	0
Depreciation of the expense split over 2 years	–5	–5
Pre-tax financial income	105	105
Income tax expense	–40	–44
Net income	65	61

Income tax return	Year 1	Year 2
Pre-tax income before recording an expense	110	110
Deduction of expense	–10	0
Taxable income	100	110
Income tax expense	40	44

In countries that authorize or require deferred taxation, the left-hand side of the table is not allowed because it mixes pre-tax income (coming from accounting for reporting calculations) and income tax which is the result of a fiscal calculation.

The following table illustrates what needs to be done if the use of deferred taxes is required.

Accounting for deferred income taxes

Tax expense based on financial reporting	Year 1	Year 2
Pre-tax income	105	105
Income tax expense (40% of pre-tax income)	42	42
Net income	63	63

Tax expense based on tax return	Year 1	Year 2
Pre-tax income	105	105
Income tax expense (40% of taxable income)	40	44
Net income	65	61

Recording

Year 1

IS (E+)		Income tax expense		42	
	BS (L+)		Income tax payable		40
	BS (L+)		Deferred tax liability		2

Year 2

IS (E+)		Income tax expense		42	
BS(L–)		Deferred tax liability		2	
	BS (L+)		Income tax payable		44

ASSIGNMENTS

Assignment 6.1 Schultz Accountancy Firm (2)

Topic: Revenue recognition
Type: Group exercise
Related part of the chapter: Core Issues

Mr. Schultz, the managing partner of an accounting firm, is concerned by some specific rules of revenue recognition adopted by some of his clients. The following list contains some of the rules he found in their notes to financial statements:

A DPS Business School Inc. invoices its students at the beginning of each quarter for the quarterly tuition fees. DPSBS Inc. recognizes revenue only when tuition is actually paid by the students (or whomever, on their behalf). The first quarter 20X2 tuition invoices were mailed on 1 December 20X1 and all the tuition fee payments have been received in full by 15 December 20X1. No adjusting entry has been recorded.

B The *Commercial Times* is a newspaper which receives payment for subscriptions. *Commercial Times* has a circulation of 750,000 copies and sells over three-quarters of these by subscription. Readers subscribe at any time during the year and there seems to be no clear seasonality in new subscriptions or cancellations. The *Commercial Times'* accountant is in the habit of recognizing as revenue for year 1 half of the cash received for subscriptions in that year and consequently to recognize in year 2 as revenue from subscription half the subscription payments of year 1 plus half the subscriptions payment for year 2.

C A bridge club invoices a membership fee to its members who receive in return the magazine *Bridge Forever* and are entitled to special prices on other magazines. The club, in order to simplify its recording of the fees, spreads the fees on a straight-line basis over the period of membership.

D A seller (shipper) sells goods to a buyer (recipient) who undertakes to sell the goods on behalf of the seller (consignment sales). The shipper recognizes the revenue at the time of delivery to the buyer.

Required

Evaluate whether the policies adopted by the different companies are acceptable or not. In the latter case, which policy should have been adopted?

Assignment 6.2 Nielsen Company

Topic: Deferred taxation
Type: Individual/group exercise
Related part of the chapter: Core Issues

During year 1, the Nielsen Company reported sales for 2,400 (thousands of CU) and total expenses for 1,800. It has no pre-existing deferred tax liability or tax asset. The following information is provided in relation to year 1:

1 Marketable securities held by Nielsen Co. have a market value at the end of the year which exceeds their book value by an amount of 8 CU. This potential gain is taxable as pertaining to year 1, but will be reported to shareholders only at the time of the sale.

2 The company accrued interest due on a bank loan for 16 CU. This interest (included in the expenses mentioned) will be tax deductible only when paid (which will be the case in year 2).

3 Nielsen Co. uses an accelerated method of depreciation for certain assets. The depreciation allowance for year 1 for tax purposes exceeds that reported to shareholders by 250 CU.

4 During year 1 a fine for an accidental pollution occurrence was paid for a total amount of 10 CU.

5 Part of the liquidity of Nielsen Co. is invested in tax-free municipal bonds. During year 1 these yielded a return of 40 CU.

6 Warranty costs are provisioned at the level of 1.5% of sales. The corresponding amount has been included in the expenses mentioned. Actual expenses incurred during year 1 for services and repairs included in the warranty contract amounted to 15 CU.

Assume the tax rate is 40%.

Required

1 Compute the income before income tax for shareholder reporting.

2 Analyze each information with regard to taxation in terms of permanent and timing differences.

3 Compute the income tax payable to the tax authorities and income tax expense for shareholder reporting.

4 Record the income tax expense for year 1.

Assignment 6.3 Repsol YPF*

Topic: Extraordinary/exceptional items
Type: Individual/group exercise
Related part of the chapter: Advanced Issues

Repsol YPF, a Spanish oil and gas company, publishes the following information (*source*: annual report 1999). The detail of the extraordinary revenues and expenses included in the accompanying consolidated statements of income for 1999, 1998, and 1997 follows.

Millions of euros	Revenues/(expenses)		
	1999	1998	1997
Extraordinary expenses			
Labor force restructuring	−59	−41	−40
Losses on fixed assets	−11	−3	−14
Variation in fixed asset provisions	−18	−41	−18
Changes in the discount rate for pension obligations	−10	−17	−5
Provision for commitments and contingent liabilities	−30	−34	−25
Provisions for estimated losses	−16	−38	−1
Other extraordinary expenses (1)	−160	−9	−26
	−304	−183	−129
Extraordinary income			
Gains on fixed asset disposals (2)	90	48	45
Gains on disposal of shareholdings	22	23	14
Subsidies and other deferred revenues transferred to income	23	8	6
Revenues from reversal of provisions for contingencies and expenses	18	32	36
Other extraordinary revenues	64	18	49
	217	129	150
	−87	−54	21

(1) Including in 1999 expenses of €128 million incurred in the acquisition of YPF
(2) The main revenues in 1999 relate to the sale of CLH's registered office, Repsol Butano's land in Hospitalet and the disposal of the holdings in Gas Natural México and Musini

Required

1 Compare the expenses and income with the definitions of extraordinary items given in the "Advanced Issues" section of this chapter.
2 What do you think of the terminology used by the Repsol group?
3 Explain the item "Subsidies and other deferred revenues transferred to income".

References

AICPA (1973) Accounting Principles Board Opinion No. 30, Reporting the Results of Operations – Reporting the Effects of Disposal of a Segment of a Business, and Extraordinary, Unusual and Infrequently Occurring Events and Transactions, New York.

FASB (1997) Statement of Financial Accounting Standards No. 130, Reporting Comprehensive Income, Norwalk, CT.

IASC (revised 1993a) International Accounting Standard No. 8, Net Profit or Loss for the Period, Fundamental Errors and Changes in Accounting Policies, London.

IASC (revised 1993b) International Accounting Standard No. 11, Construction Contracts, London.

IASC (revised 1993c) International Accounting Standard No. 18, Revenue, London.

IASC (reformatted 1994) International Accounting Standard No. 20, Accounting for Government Grants and Disclosure of Government Assistance, London.

IASC (revised 1996) International Accounting Standard No. 12, Income Taxes, London.

IASC (1998) International Accounting Standard No. 35, Discontinuing Operations, London.

Skousen F., Stice J., and Stice E.K. (2001) *Intermediate Accounting*, South-Western College Publishing, Cincinatti, OH.

Further readings

Artsbert, K. (1996) The link between commercial accounting and tax accounting in Sweden. *European Accounting Review*, 5 (Supplement), 795–814.

Ballas, A.A. (1999) Valuation implications of exceptional and extraordinary items. *British Accounting Review*, 31(3), 281–95.

Christiansen, M. (1996) The relationship between accounting and taxation in Denmark. *European Accounting Review*, 5 (Supplement), 815–33.

Eberhartinger, E.L.E. (1999) The impact of tax rules on financial reporting in Germany, France, and the UK. *International Journal of Accounting*, 34(1), 93–119.

Eilifsen, A. (1996) The relationship between accounting and taxation in Norway. *European Accounting Review*, 5 (Supplement), 835–44.

Forker, J., and Greenwood, M. (1995) European harmonization and the true and fair view: The case of long-term contracts in the UK. *European Accounting Review*, 4(1), 1–31.

Frydlender, A., and Pham, D. (1996) Relationships between accounting and taxation in France. *European Accounting Review*, 5 (Supplement), 845–57.

Holeckova, J. (1996) Relationship between accounting and taxation in the Czech Republic. *European Accounting Review*, 5 (Supplement), 859–69.

Hoogendoorn, M.N. (1996) Accounting and taxation in Europe – A comparative overview. *European Accounting Review*, 5 (Supplement), 783–94.

Hoogendoorn, M.N. (1996) Accounting and taxation in the Netherlands. *European Accounting Review*, 5 (Supplement), 871–82.

Jaruga, A., Walinska, E., and Baniewicz, A. (1996) The relationship between accounting and taxation in Poland. *European Accounting Review*, 5 (Supplement), 883–97.

Järvenpää, M. (1996) The relationship between taxation and financial accounting in Finland. *European Accounting Review*, 5 (Supplement), 899–914.

Jorissen, A., and Maes, L. (1996) The principle of fiscal neutrality: The cornerstone of the relationship between financial reporting and taxation in Belgium. *European Accounting Review*, 5 (Supplement), 915–31.

Lamb, M. (1996) The relationship between accounting and taxation: The United Kingdom. *European Accounting Review*, 5 (Supplement), 933–49.

Pfaff, D., and Schröer, T. (1996) The relationship between financial and tax accounting in Germany – The authoritativeness and reverse authoritativeness principle. *European Accounting Review*, 5 (Supplement), 963–79.

Pierce, A. (1996) The relationship between accounting and taxation in the Republic of Ireland. *European Accounting Review*, 5 (Supplement), 951–62.

Rocchi, F. (1996) Accounting and taxation in Italy. *European Accounting Review*, 5 (Supplement), 981–9.

Additional material on the website

Go to http://www.thomsonlearning.co.uk/accountingandfinance/stolowylebas for further information, journal entries and extra assignments for each chapter.

The following appendices to this chapter are available on the dedicated website:

Appendix 6.1: Illustration of the two methods for reporting of long-term contracts

Appendix 6.2: Recognition of a net deferred tax asset

Notes

1 The link between depreciation and cash flow is developed in Chapter 7, Advanced Issues.

2 The reader can refer to Skousen et al. (2001).

3 The practice of leasing cars is a good example of difficulties in evaluating risks. The vehicle lease value is based on some hypothesis of the resale value of the vehicle at the end of the contract. If the future used car market for a new vehicle is hard to anticipate, it is easy to under- or over-evaluate that resale value of the vehicle to be returned. Many North American automotive companies experienced serious difficulties on this topic in the last years of the 20th century.

Tangible fixed assets

The asset side of the balance sheet comprises both current and long-term or fixed assets. Current assets are those that are created or used in the operating cycle of the firm. They turn over rather rapidly, and, in the case of a well-managed firm, their turnover cycle is much shorter than the accounting period. Fixed assets are those that reflect the facilities and "capacity" provided by the firm for the operating cycle to take place. These assets create economic benefits over several periods, and represent significant investments that must be put in place before any activity can take place.

Among fixed assets, tangible assets represent a significant portion of total assets and the depreciation expense can be a large expense item, thus affecting the income calculation greatly. Table 7.1 illustrates the diversity of the proportion tangible assets represent in balance sheets of a non-scientific sample of industries and countries. The importance of tangible assets in financial statements is defined through two ratios: (net) tangible assets/total assets, and depreciation expense/net sales. All data are excerpted from 1999 annual reports. The currency is the one used in the annual report.

Companies are classified in decreasing order of percentage of tangible assets over total assets. The table shows that this ratio is heavily influenced by the sector of activity, services companies appearing at the bottom. The ratio varies from 71.3 to 8.1%.

After a short presentation of the various categories of fixed assets, this chapter will mainly deal with reporting and accounting issues (valuation and income effects) regarding tangible fixed assets.

Tangible distinguishes assets from intangible (see Chapter 8) or financial (see Chapter 13). A tangible asset is one that has a physical reality or substance

Major topics

Definitions

Cost of acquisition

Depreciation

Disposal

Financial aspects

Table 7.1 Weight of tangible assets

Company (country – activity)	Currency	Tangible assets (net amount)	Total assets (net amount)	% of total assets	Depreciation expense	Sales	% of sales
Irish Continental (Ireland – shipping, transport)	€m	284.1	398.3	71.3%	17.7	249.4	7.1%
Stora-Enso (Finland – paper production)	€m	10,717.6	16,034.0	66.8%	821.0	10,635.7	7.7%
Repsol (Spain – oil and gas)	€m	25,925	42,050	61.7%	1,666	25,633	6.5%
Club Méditerranée (France – leisure)	FRFm	6,071	10,029	60.5%	431	9,690	4.4%
Gaylord Container (USA – brown paper packaging products [production and distribution])	$m	558.9	1,018.0	54.9%	49.2	870.6	5.7%
Brau-Union (Austria – brewery group)	€m	402,495	772,153	52.1%	62,942	730,086	8.6%
Elkem (Norway – metals and materials [production])	NOKm	4,582	9,671	47.4%	457	9,583	4.8%
Interbrew (Belgium – brewery group)	€m	2,495.5	6,252.5	39.9%	291.9	4,346.4	6.7%
Pirelli (Italy – tires, cables and systems)	€000	2,424,771	7,821,335	31.0%	311,122	6,482,335	4.8%
Philips (Netherlands – consumer products)	€m	7,332	29,496	24.9%	1,510	31,459	4.8%
Honda Motor Co. (Japan – car and motocycles)	Yenm	1,121,040	4,898,428	22.9%	172,139	6,098,840	2.8%
Barmag (Germany – spinning and textile machines)	DM000	107,727	488,971	22.0%	23,908	662,112	3.6%
Roche (Switzerland – pharmaceuticals, chemicals)	CHFm	14,240	70,431	20.2%	1,246	27,567	4.5%
Securitas (Sweden – security systems)	SEKm	3,079.9	20,775.0	14.8%	725.0	25,646.3	2.8%
Taylor Nelson Sofres (UK – market information)	£m	42.9	289.9	14.8%	12.3	362.7	3.4%
ISS (Denmark – support services)	DKKm	1,105.1	13,673	8.1%	351.3	19,802.4	1.8%

such as a building or a piece of equipment, while an intangible asset does not have a physical substance but represents an idea (for example, the capitalized costs incurred in developing a product or a technology) or a right (for example, the price paid for a license to use a technology developed by someone else).

Fixed assets are, by nature, the most illiquid assets on the balance sheet. In countries where the accounting tradition is more "patrimonial" they will be shown at the top of the list of assets, while in countries where the accounting culture favors operations or liquidity, the tangible fixed assets will be listed at the bottom of the list.

CORE ISSUES

Categories of fixed assets

Fixed assets can be divided into three categories: tangible, intangible (see Chapter 8) and financial (see Chapter 13).

The first two categories are sometimes confused since their difference is not one of purpose or lifecycle but only one of physical substance. Table 7.2 presents the common and distinguishing characteristics of the three categories of asset.

Table 7.2 Tangible, intangible, and financial assets compared

Tangible assets	Intangible assets	Financial assets
Used in the course of the operations of the business (production, sale, or distribution of goods and services) and not acquired for the purpose of resale		
Long term (long lived) in nature and usually subject to depreciation		Long term (long lived) in nature
Possess physical substance	Lack physical substance	

Since all three categories of fixed assets are long lived, a distinguishing feature is also the way their cost is allocated (distributed) over time. Table 7.3 highlights how each category's and sub-category's cost of consumption of the capacity of the asset is recorded for reporting income to shareholders. Systematic allocation reflects an ongoing process of consumption (in the course of business and in a way reflecting as much as possible the pace of activity), while an unsystematic allocation reflects the recognition of some form of random, unpredictable, or catastrophic event that modifies the value of the asset rather than reflecting the consumption of the economic benefit provided by the fixed asset.

Table 7.3 Fixed assets and cost allocation

Asset classification	Examples	Systematic cost allocation	Unsystematic cost allocation
Tangible assets	Buildings, equipment, furniture	Depreciation	Impairment
	Land	No systematic cost allocation	Impairment
	Natural resources (oil and gas reserves, mineral deposits – e.g., mines and quarries)	Depletion	Impairment
Intangible assets	Patents, copyrights, trademarks, franchises, leaseholds, software, goodwill	Amortization	Impairment
Financial fixed assets	Investments	No systematic cost allocation	Impairment

Accounting issues relating to tangible assets

Figure 7.1 summarizes the various accounting issues that arise when reporting truly and fairly on tangible fixed assets. (The diagram also indicates in which part of this chapter each issue will be dealt with.)

The acquisition of a tangible fixed asset raises many other issues which will not be developed in this book such as the valuation of an asset acquired (1) by a lump sum purchase, (2) with deferred payments, (3) through the issuance of securities, (4) by donation, or (5) in exchange of other assets[1].

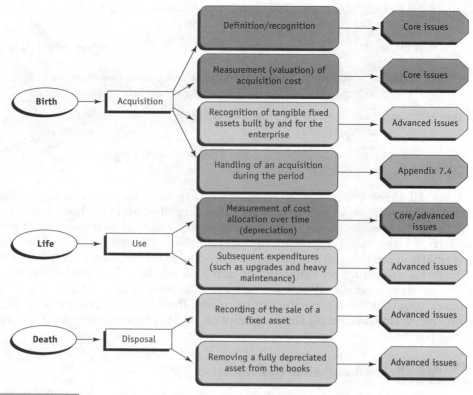

Figure 7.1 Accounting issues in reporting tangible assets

Definition of tangible fixed assets

General definition

Tangible fixed assets are also called "tangible assets", "property, plant and equipment" (PPE), "plant assets", "operational assets", or "fixed assets". IAS 16 (IASC 1998a) defines (§ 6) as "tangible assets [those] that:

(a) are held by an enterprise for use in the production or supply of goods or services, for rental to others, or for administrative purposes; and

(b) are expected to be used during more than one period."

In the remainder of this chapter, we will use the term "tangible assets" as synonymous for "property, plant and equipment" and all the other equivalent terms. Tangible assets include:

- land, freeholds, and leaseholds
- building structures (stores, factories, warehouses, offices)
- equipment (machinery, furniture and fixtures, tools)
- vehicles
- furniture and fittings

- payments on account (payments made by a company towards the acquisition of as yet undelivered tangible assets)
- tangible assets during their construction (cost of purchasing, constructing and installing tangible assets ahead of their productive use).

From the preceding definition, it would appear that the identification of a tangible asset should pose no problem. However, asset valuation and revenue recognition require that a clear distinction be made between fixed assets and inventories, on the one hand, and fixed assets and expenses, on the other.

Difference between tangible assets and inventories

The principal criterion used for making the distinction between tangible assets and inventories is the nature of the company's activity, which determines the purpose for which the asset is held – own use or resale. Thus, any category of tangible asset may be a fixed asset in one company and an inventory in another. The distinction is, of course, important because it affects the timing of income recognition. Tangible assets are subject to an annual depreciation expense over their normal useful life, while inventories are not. Interesting definitional issues can arise, for example, in the treatment of livestock. What kind of asset is an ox?

- A dray ox is a tangible asset.
- An ox reared for meat is inventory.
- A stud ox may be either a tangible asset or an inventory!

However, items that are carried in inventory are not all for resale. It is normal for businesses to have inventories of supplies, consumables, and maintenance parts. For example, for the latter, withdrawals from inventory will normally be expensed as repair and maintenance costs. However, when the unit cost of a spare part is significant, it may be accounted for as a fixed asset. For example, an airplane jet engine in working order kept in inventory to be used during maintenance operations or for a replacement would be treated as a tangible asset, and as such could be subject to an annual depreciation expense even before being brought into operational use.

Difference between assets and expenses (expenditures)

"An asset is a resource controlled by the enterprise as a result of past events and from which future economic benefits are expected to flow to the enterprise" (IASC 1989: § 49 and IASC 1998c: § 7). Some expenses or expenditures are incurred in the course of bringing an asset "online" or in upgrading it and as such change the potential for future economic benefits of the asset. It would, therefore, seem logical to consider such expenditure as an increase in the value of the asset in the books. However, it could also be considered to be a normal consumption of resources in the course of doing business and as such recognized as an expense of the period. All local GAAP specify their rules for distinguishing between capital, revenue expenditure, and expenses. Table 7.4 summarizes the most common practices.

Table 7.4 Assets and expenses

Type of expenditure	Definition	Accounting	Depreciation
Capital expenditure	Expenses incurred for the purpose of generating future economic benefits	Recorded as assets	Yes
Revenue expenditure	Expenses caused by the short-term usage – or maintenance – of the revenue-generating potential of an asset (examples: minor spare parts, oil and cooling fluids, maintenance expenses, minor repairs expenses)	Charged as expense as incurred	No
Expense	Ordinary expenses not subsequent to acquisition and not related to a specific asset	Charged as expense as incurred	No

How is the distinction made in practice? The solution generally depends on the impact of the expenditure. One generally distinguishes between capital and other expenditures.

Capital expenditures

Capital expenditures should meet at least one of the following criteria:

1 The quantity of services from the asset will be increased through a longer useful life.

2 The quantity of services from the asset will be increased with more units of output.

3 The quality of the services received from using the asset will be increased.

An expense or expenditure that meets at least one of the these three conditions is considered a capital expenditure.

Other expenditures

The choice of treating one specific expenditure as either a tangible asset or an expense is often made solely on grounds of materiality. Many countries' GAAP and tax regulations have established minimum threshold amounts (arbitrary, thus not necessarily coherent between the two sources of regulation) to facilitate the distinction between expense and asset. Thus acquired resources of small unitary value that may benefit future periods (such as software packages, small tools, furniture, and office equipment) may be fully expensed in the year of acquisition and not ever be listed as a fixed asset at all. For example, French tax law states that any industrial or office equipment with an invoiced price below 2,500 FF (or €381) can be expensed but must be treated as an asset if above that threshold. Thresholds are often relative to the size of the firm (however defined). For example, in the USA, practice acknowledges the following thresholds: $100 (for a "small" company) and $10,000 (for a "large" company).

As regulatory texts or practice allow companies to expense capital and revenue expenditures of an amount below a certain limit, most enterprises have generally opted for immediately expensing all those below that threshold. Doing so has two advantages:

- It will reduce taxable profits in the year of acquisition by an amount much greater than would have an allowance for depreciation expense.
- There will be no fiscal obligation to maintain, for these items, the detailed records of acquisition cost and accumulated depreciation that are usually mandated by tax regulations.

Cost of acquisition

Definition

Acquisition "cost is the amount of cash or cash equivalents paid or the fair value of the other consideration given to acquire an asset at the time of its acquisition or construction" (IAS 16: § 6). In general, the cost of acquisition is the cash or cash equivalents paid to obtain the asset and to bring it to the location and condition necessary for its intended use.

More precisely, IAS 16 (§ 15) states: "The cost of an item of property, plant and equipment comprises its purchase price, including import duties and non-refundable purchase taxes, and any directly attributable costs of bringing the asset to working condition for its intended use; any trade discounts and rebates are deducted in arriving at the purchase price. Examples of directly attributable costs are: (a) the cost of site preparation; (b) initial delivery and handling costs; (c) installation costs; (d) professional fees such as for architects and engineers; and (e) the estimated future cost of dismantling and removing the asset and restoring the site, to the extent that it is recognized as a provision under IAS 37, Provisions, Contingent Liabilities and Contingent Assets."

Recording of the acquisition

Let us take the example of a piece of equipment with a cost of acquisition, which can be broken down as follows (in currency units):

Purchase price	40
Import duties	3
Transportation	5
Professional fees	2
Total	50

The acquisition cost is therefore 50 CU. Figure 7.2 describes the recording procedure when the asset is acquired.

Examples of components of the acquisition cost

Appendix 7.1 lists some examples of components of the acquisition costs of tangible assets as reported in notes to financial statements.

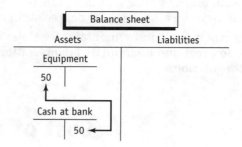

Figure 7.2 Recording of the acquisition

Depreciation

IAS 16 (§ 6) defines depreciation as "the systematic allocation of the depreciable [cost] of an asset over its useful life". In other words, depreciation is the process of allocating the cost of a long-term asset in a rational and systematic manner over its useful life in order to achieve a matching of expenses and revenues. The yearly depreciation allowance ("depreciation expense"), is therefore a normal component of the expense side of the income statement. The net book value (acquisition cost minus accumulated depreciation) of each and all fixed assets will diminish irreversibly, reflecting the diminution of productive potential through the effect of the passage of time, use, and any other reason. When the obsolescence of the potential for future benefits is unpredictable (unsystematic reduction in value due to unexpected or catastrophic events), the loss of value of an asset is not recognized through depreciation but will lead to a write-down (see the concept of "impairment" in "Advanced issues").

In the definition of depreciation, two concepts are important:

- *Rational manner*: The depreciation expense is related to the benefits expected to arise from the asset.

- *Systematic manner*: The computation of the depreciation expense is based on a formula which was decided at the time of acquisition or before, and cannot be modified during the life of the asset. This characteristic was introduced to prevent any possibility of income smoothing that might have happened if the amount of the depreciation allowance had been left to the whim of the management or of the accountant.

In order to establish the systematic and rational schedule of depreciation of a tangible asset, several parameters need to be documented:

- residual value of the asset
- depreciable amount
- useful life duration
- choice of a depreciation method.

They will lead to:

- a depreciation schedule
- a book value which is periodically updated.

Each of these points will be covered in succession. The last section of the Core Issues will introduce the procedures for recording depreciation. Some unusual methods of depreciation as well as impairment, the impact of depreciation on financial statements and the problem of partial years will be dealt with in the "Advanced issues" section of the chapter. "Depletion" (depreciation recorded for mineral deposits) is a specific topic especially relevant for countries with important exhaustible natural resources. It is not, however, covered in detail in this book[2].

Residual value

IAS 16 (§ 6) defines "residual value" as "the net amount which the enterprise expects to obtain for an asset at the end of its useful life after deducting the expected costs of disposal". The costs of disposal could include costs relating to dismantling, removing and selling the asset, as well as the costs of decontamination of the site or facility

The actual depreciable cost of an asset can only be the actual cost incurred to create the future benefits. The residual value is not depreciated because the company will recover it. If an asset, at the end of its useful economic life, still has a residual value (through for example scrap, resale or reuse), the depreciable asset value should conceptually be the cost of acquisition minus the residual value.

The residual value (also called salvage value, terminal value, end-of-life salvage value or scrap value) is often difficult to estimate. As a consequence, it is often neglected in the computation of the depreciation expense, i.e., assumed to be zero. Another possibility, often found in practice, is to adopt a discretionary standard percentage of the acquisition cost to determine the residual value, or to assume by convention the residual value is one currency unit (practice, for example, in Argentina, Austria, Germany, and Switzerland).

Depreciable amount

IAS 16 (§ 6) defines the "depreciable amount" as the "cost of an asset, or other amount substituted for cost in the financial statements, less its residual value":

Depreciable amount = Acquisition cost − Estimated residual value

If the residual value is negative, as could be the case with a polluting asset, the depreciable amount will be greater than the cost of acquisition. However, generally speaking, the depreciable amount is equal to or slightly smaller than the cost of acquisition.

It is in the interest of the firm to select as high a depreciable amount as possible as the depreciation expense generally reduces taxable profit and thus creates a higher cash flow[3] potentially retained in the firm.

Useful life (service life – economic life)

IAS 16 (§ 6) defines the "useful life" as "either:

(a) the period of time over which an asset is expected to be used by the enterprise; or

(b) the number of production [output] or similar units expected to be obtained from the asset by the enterprise."

> Useful life = Time period over which an asset is depreciated
>
> or
>
> Maximum expected number of units of output before the asset is declared unproductive

Theoretically, management has free choice of the method and duration of depreciation. However, this freedom applies only to innovative fixed assets used for the first time in a particular sector of economic activity. In all other cases, there is sufficient acquired experience for normal useful lives to be rationally established. The estimation of the duration of the useful life of a type of asset can vary from country to country but this is due more often to companies adopting depreciation rates consistent with that allowed for taxation purposes and these allowances vary between countries. Table 7.5 presents the most commonly accepted useful lives for a selection of classes of tangible assets.

Table 7.5 Common useful lives

Tangible assets	Useful life (years)	Corresponding rate (%)
Commercial buildings	20 to 50	5 to 2
Industrial buildings	20	5
Equipment	8 to 10	12.5 to 10
Industrial equipment (tooling)	5 to 10	20 to 10
Transportation (trucks, vans, cars)	4 to 5	25 to 20
Furniture	10	10
Computers	3	33
Office equipment	5 to 10	20 to 10
Fixtures and fittings	10 to 20	10 to 5

Long-haul truck tires are generally not depreciated *prorata temporis* but on the basis of mileage covered. For a tractor trailer, the expected mileage for a set of tires varies from country to country, but is generally in the range of 60,000 to 80,000 kilometers (37,290 to 49,720 miles).

In practice, as it is often difficult to forecast the real useful life of a fixed asset, the selected useful life may prove, *ex post* (i.e., after complete use of the asset), to be shorter than the real life of the asset. The principle of prudence (combined with the desire to create as much cash flow as early as possible) may explain the fact that many businesses deliberately choose shorter useful lives than they really expect to experience. The choice of a useful life may have a great impact on net income and on cash flows.

> For example, Willamette Industries, a forest products company, announced in 1999 that it would change its accounting estimates relating to depreciation. The estimated service lives for much of the company's machinery and equipment would be extended by approximately five years. The company estimated that this change would increase net income in 1999 by approximately $57m, thus creating a potential tax liability, which would reduce the disposable cash flow[4].

Choice of a depreciation method

Several methods have been developed. The choice of the appropriate method should theoretically be made so as to best reflect the pattern of decline in the asset's service potential and should therefore be specific to each class of tangible asset.

Classification of methods

Table 7.6 presents a classification of the main depreciation methods in two families: time-based and activity level-based methods.

Table 7.6 Main depreciation methods

Time-based depreciation methods	Depreciation methods based on activity level (or use)
1 Straight line	3 Productive output
2 Accelerated (reducing charge) 2.1 Sum of the years' digits (sum of digits) 2.2 Declining (reducing) balance	4 Service quantity
Depreciation expense will be determined regardless of the level of activity during the period	*Determination of a constant depreciation expense per unit of activity*

The methods most commonly used are the straight-line method and the declining balance method. They will be presented in this section of this chapter. The three other methods will be developed in the advanced issues section. All these methods will be described with the help of the example of an equipment purchased by the Purcell Company. This example is based on the following data (in thousands of CU):

Basic data

Acquisition cost	6,000
Residual value	1,000
Depreciable amount	5,000
Estimated useful life (in years)	5

Straight-line method

This method is appropriately used if the decline in service potential relates primarily to the passage of time rather than to the level of activity, and if it can be assumed the asset will be equally productive each year.

Principles

The asset is depreciated evenly over its useful life. In other words, the company allocates an equal amount of depreciation expense to each year of the asset's estimated useful life. Periodic depreciation expense is computed as follows:

$$D = \text{Depreciation expense} = (\text{Acquisition cost} - \text{Residual value})/\text{Number of years of useful life}$$

$$= \text{Depreciable amount}/\text{Estimated useful life}$$
$$= \text{Depreciable amount} \times \text{Depreciation rate}$$
$$(\text{with Depreciation rate} = 1/\text{Number of years of useful life of the asset})$$

The straight-line method is the most frequently used method because of its simplicity of application.

Illustration: Purcell Company

Table 7.7 shows an example of depreciation using the straight-line method. Depreciation rate = 1/5 years = a depreciation rate of 20%.

Table 7.7 Depreciation schedule – Straight-line method

End of year	Depreciable amount	Depreciation rate	Depreciation of the year	Balance: Accumulated depreciation	Year-end book value
Date of acquisition					6,000
Year 1	5,000	20%	1,000	1,000	5,000
Year 2	5,000	20%	1,000	2,000	4,000
Year 3	5,000	20%	1,000	3,000	3,000
Year 4	5,000	20%	1,000	4,000	2,000
Year 5	5,000	20%	1,000	5,000	1,000

Depreciable amount = 6,000 (acquisition cost) – 1,000 (residual value) = 5,000

Yearly depreciation expense = 5,000 (depreciable amount) × 20% (depreciation rate) = 1,000

Year-end book value (year 1) = 6,000 (year-end book value of the preceding year) – 1,000 (depreciation of the year)

Declining balance method

The objective of any **accelerated** (or **reducing charge**) method is to recognize greater amounts of depreciation in the early years of an asset's life and smaller amounts in the later years. The logic behind using an accelerated method of depreciation is twofold. First, it is a way of recognizing that the loss of resale value that is incurred in the first period of use (for example, the market value of a car is, according to published sales records in many countries, reduced by up to 15 to 20% in the first few months after acquisition – the market offers a premium for a pristine car). Second, it is also a way of shielding more income from taxation, thus leaving more cash in the firm in the early years to be used, hopefully, for the development of the firm.

However, depreciation methods are supposed, in keeping with the matching principle, to be first and foremost ways to allocate the cost of the asset to the periods during which the economic benefits are derived from the use of the asset.

Accelerated depreciation may be conceptually sound if the declining pattern of expense recognition is consistent with the actual contribution the asset makes to the revenue-generating process. Accelerated depreciation methods are conceptually attractive when an asset is believed to provide superior performance (i.e., operate with greater efficiency or provide more benefits) in the early years of its life, or if repairs and maintenance costs will burden the last years of the useful life more than the earlier years and the manager wishes to even out their cost of operating that asset.

Of the several variations of accelerated depreciation, the most widely used are the declining balance method (multiply a declining base by a constant rate) and the sum of the years' digits method (multiply a constant base by a declining rate).

Determination of a multiple in the declining balance method

The percentage applied to the base is defined as some multiple of the straight-line rate. The selection of the multiple is highly variable from country to country. In some countries, the choice of a multiple is totally open, subject to some unspecified criterion of reasonableness. In the USA, where the choice is essentially open, the most common application of this method is the double-declining balance, in which the accelerated percentage is twice the straight-line rate. By way of contrast, in some countries, such as France, the tax authorities have defined, for each class of assets, a standardized multiple.

Most accelerated methods have to switch, at some point in time, to a straight-line method, so as to arrive at a book value equal to the residual value at the end of the useful life. In order to avoid this switching, a method, mainly used in the UK, called "fixed percentage of book value method" or "fixed percentage of declining balance method" has been devised that selects a rate that depreciates the asset exactly down to the residual value. The formula for this method is shown in Table 7.8 along with some illustration of practice in other countries.

Table 7.8 Examples of multiples

Country	Determination of the multiple (or rate of depreciation) Where N = asset's useful life, expressed in years
France	M (multiple) = 1.25 if N = 3 or 4 years M= 1.75 if N = 5 or 6 years M = 2.25 if N > 6 years
Germany	Limitation of application of the accelerated rate to 30% of the depreciable amount
UK	Rate of depreciation = $1 - \sqrt[N]{\text{Residual value/Cost of acquisition}}$ If the residual value is 0, assume a residual value of 1
US	M = 2 (common practice). 1.5 is also used

Application to the declining book value

This fixed percentage is applied to the net book value of the asset, giving a depreciation figure that declines throughout the life of the asset.

Declining balance (DB) depreciation expense = (DB rate) × (Net book value)

or

DB depreciation expense = (DB rate) × (Depreciable cost minus accumulated depreciation)

Table 7.9 provides an illustration of the method.

How to end the depreciation process

If applied consistently, the mathematics of the method are such that the book value would never be equal to the residual value. If the method were applied without adjustments, not only would the asset never be fully depreciated but also its book value would eventually end up below the residual value. It is, therefore, important to decide beforehand how to terminate the depreciation to end up exactly at the level of the residual value.

In this context, several possibilities exist. They consist of either:

- Defining the depreciation expense as the difference between the preceding book value and the residual value in the year in which the accelerated depreciation expense would bring the book value to be lower than the residual value (illustrated in Table 7.9).
- Switching to a straight-line method (over the remaining useful life) at the point where the straight-line rate (calculated over the remaining useful life) exceeds the declining balance rate selected, or when the straight-line depreciation expense, which would have been computed at the acquisition date, exceeds the declining balance depreciation expense (illustrated in Table 7.10).
- Switching to straight-line (over the remaining useful life) at the midpoint of the life of the asset (illustrated in Table 7.11).

The "fixed percentage of book value method" used mainly in UK for computing the depreciation rate (see Table 7.8) avoids the entire problem of how to reach the residual value.

In choosing a method, the most important thing is to be rational and systematic. These conditions are met if the method for handling the end of depreciation is selected at the time of acquisition and applied to all assets of one homogeneous category.

Tables 7.9, 7.10 and 7.11 illustrate the three possibilities as applied to the Purcell Company. If we choose a multiple equal to 2, we have: DDB rate = straight-line rate × 2 = 20% × 2 = 40%.

Table 7.9	Simulation 1: Double-declining balance with switch as soon as DDB would lead to book value lower than residual value

End of year	Depreciable basis	Depreciation expense of the year	Balance: Accumulated depreciation	Year-end book value
Date of acquisition				6,000
Year 1	6,000	2,400	2,400	3,600
Year 2	3,600	1,440	3,840	2,160
Year 3	2,160	864	4,704	1,296
Year 4	1,296	296	5,000	1,000
Year 5	0	0	5,000	1,000

Depreciable amount = 6,000 (acquisition cost)
Depreciation expense of year 1 = 6,000 (depreciable amount) × 40% (DDB rate) = 2,400
Depreciation expense of year 2 = 3,600 (ending book value of the preceding year) × DDB rate = 1,440
In year 4, the DDB depreciation expense would bring the book value to be lower than the residual value [(1,296 – (1,296 × 40%)] = [1,296 – 518 = 778 < 1,000]. The depreciation expense is then set as the difference between the preceding book value and the residual value: 1,296 – 1,000 = 296
No depreciation in year 5

Table 7.10 Simulation 2: Double-declining balance with reversal to straight line when rate of SL over remaining life exceeds that of DDB

End of year	Depreciable basis	Depreciation expense of the year	Balance: Accumulated depreciation	Year-end book value
Date of acquisition				6,000
Year 1	6,000	2,400	2,400	3,600
Year 2	3,600	1,440	3,840	2,160
Year 3	2,160	864	4,704	1,296
Year 4	1,296	148	4,852	1,148
Year 5	1,296	148	5,000	1,000

In year 4, because the DDB approach would lead to a lower residual value than agreed upon (see notes to Table 7.9), reversal to straight line over the remaining useful life (2 years ® 50%) [note that we could also have said the switch was due to the straight-line rate over the remaining useful life, i.e., 50% exceeding the DDB rate i.e., 40%]. If we switch to straight line for the remaining two years the depreciation expense is 148 = [1,296 (the depreciable basis) – 1,000 (residual value)]/2

To illustrate this method, Barmag, a German company, explains in the notes to financial statements (annual report 1999) that "the declining balance method of calculating depreciation is replaced by the straight-line method in a year when the transition results in a higher depreciation than would be the case if the declining balance method were retained."

Table 7.11 Simulation 3: Declining balance with switch to straight line in mid-life

End of year	Depreciable basis	Depreciation expense of the year	Balance: Accumulated depreciation	Year-end book value
Date of acquisition				6,000
Year 1	6,000	2,400	2,400	3,600
Year 2	3,600	1,440	3,840	2,160
Year 3	1,160	387	4,227	1,773
Year 4	1,160	387	4,614	1,386
Year 5	1,160	386	5,000	1,000

Switch to straight line at the midpoint of the life of the asset (2.5 years is conventionally translated as 3rd year)
Depreciable amount at the time of the switch to straight line = 2,160 (book value at the end of year 2) – 1,000 (residual value) = 1,160
Depreciation allowance for years 3, 4 and 5 = 1,160 (the depreciable basis)/3 = 387 (or 386, due to rounding)

Depreciation schedule

The depreciation schedule is the list of depreciation amounts for each year of an asset's useful life. The elaboration of a depreciation schedule is based on the choice of depreciation method as illustrated in Tables 7.7, 7.9, 7.10, and 7.11.

Book value (or carrying amount)

The **book value** is the difference between the asset's cost and the balance of its accumulated depreciation. After the book value has reached the residual value (even equal to zero), the asset might not be taken out of service if it is still reliable and useful. It will be reported (carried) in the balance sheet for a book value of zero so that the asset remains identified.

Recording the depreciation expense

Principle

In countries where the income statement is organized by nature of expenses, depreciation is recorded the following way:

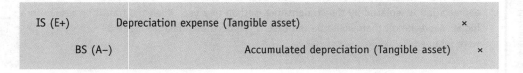

| IS (E+) | Depreciation expense (Tangible asset) | | × | |
| BS (A–) | | Accumulated depreciation (Tangible asset) | | × |

The credit entry to record the period's depreciation expense is to a "contra-asset" account usually called "accumulated depreciation".

In countries where the income statement is presented by function (see this concept in Chapter 3), the depreciation expense on a manufacturing asset is included in the cost of the goods manufactured at the stage of the manufacturing process when that asset is used. The depreciation expense is recorded as an increase (debit) of the "work in progress" account of that stage. The depreciation expense will flow to the cost of goods sold account after having transited through the various levels of inventories. The depreciation expense ends up, therefore, being potentially distributed over the cost of goods sold and the various inventories (if there has been an increase of the inventory levels). For non-manufacturing equipment (such as a computer used in the accounting department), the depreciation expense is a period cost that does not flow through inventory accounts, and the accounting entries are similar to the ones described for countries using a by nature income statement structure.

Illustration: Purcell Company

Figure 7.3 illustrates the accounting entries for the recording of depreciation (year 1 only) for the straight-line method.

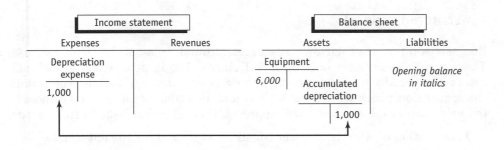

Figure 7.3 Recording depreciation expense

ADVANCED ISSUES

Definition and recognition of tangible assets

Particular issues relating to reporting land and buildings

Because they cannot be depreciated, land assets must always be reported separately from buildings, which are constructed on them. Even if a purchase contract provides only one global acquisition cost for a property comprising land and buildings, the firm acquiring the property has to obtain the necessary information to split the sum between two separate accounts. Such a correction is necessary not only to provide correct information on the assets (the market value of land and construction do not evolve in parallel), but also because buildings and constructions are depreciable assets.

Buildings shown in the tangible asset category on the balance sheet include only those that are held as long-term investments, thus excluding short-term or speculative holdings. This means that, in principle, all industrial, commercial and administrative buildings should be subject to an annual depreciation expense throughout their expected useful life.

During a very inflationary period, depreciation of buildings might not be coherent with truthful reporting because the residual value of the asset might increase to the point of exceeding the acquisition cost or the book value. Since the depreciable base is the difference between the cost of acquisition and the residual value, there might not be anything to depreciate in such a context. Such a situation is very rare in developed economies but was not rare in the 1980s in countries with high inflation rates such as Brazil or Argentina, and would require, in any case, full disclosure in a note to the financial statements.

Assets constructed by and for the enterprise (internally constructed assets)

Businesses often use their own resources to build an asset for their own use. These can be machinery, buildings, or fixtures. The issue of valuation of such assets is especially problematic since there is no "at arm's length" relation in the acquisition which would remove any and all ambiguity and arbitrariness in the valuation of the asset. We will approach this valuation issue in three steps:

1 Definition of what is an asset constructed by and for the enterprise.

2 Valuation of such asset (cost measurement).

3 Recording of such asset in the accounting system.

Definition – Principle

In certain circumstances companies construct or build their own tangible assets instead of acquiring them from other companies. This practice happens frequently in certain industry sectors such as construction, automotive, railroad, utilities (building a power plant or a water treatment facility or laying the network of pipes for gas distribution), etc. For instance, when Bouygues Company, a French-based global construction and civil engineering firm, built their showcase headquarters near Paris, they did it with their own human and physical resources. It would not have made sense to ask a competitor to develop such a building that is meant to showcase all the best facets of Bouygues' *savoir-faire*. Similarly, a machine tool manufacturer might develop its own machines to make the machine tools it sells or an automotive manufacturer might make the dies for its body shop or an airplane manufacturer might create a dedicated lift to hoist the tail reactor (for power and air conditioning) in place. The situation of an asset built by and for the firm is extremely common.

Valuation

Tangible assets, which are created or developed internally, must be valued at their historical cost. The cost of an object is generally broken down into several components, which can be traced to the object with varying degrees of accuracy:

- Cost of raw materials and components.
- Cost of the labor that was directly involved in the creation of the object (whether it is in the research and development phase or the manufacturing and testing phase).
- Overhead costs (or indirect) costs that include supplies, energy and fluids, supervisory labor, and all the costs of the facilities and support functions that permitted the creation of the object.
- Financial costs, which can be very significant when the asset is extremely costly and the construction process spans a long period, as is the case, for example, in the building of a power plant or the construction of a large office building.

Overhead

While there are generally few problems arising from the tracing of direct materials and components or direct labor cost to the object, allocation of overhead is a difficult issue (see Appendix 7.2).

Financing costs: interest cost (or borrowing cost)

While the asset is being constructed, resources are consumed but no revenue is generated. The revenue will be generated when the asset will be operational and for the duration of its useful life. The firm must, therefore, finance the cost of the resources consumed, either out of its own funds (possibly losing an opportunity to earn revenue) or by borrowing funds to cover the need. There is, therefore, little doubt that there is a causal link between the construction and the financial cost, but it is not so clear how much of it should be attached to the cost of the asset.

IAS 23 (IASC 1993) states that borrowing costs (interest and other costs incurred by an enterprise in connection with the borrowing of funds) should be recognized as an expense in the period in which they are incurred (§ 7). However, the interest costs can, under certain circumstances, be included in the cost of the construction (IAS 23: § 11). This possibility is referred to as the "capitalization" of interest costs. Directly attributable interest costs are capitalized as part of the cost of the asset when it is probable that they will result in future economic benefits to the enterprise and the costs can be measured reliably.

Table 7.12 shows that the capitalization of interest costs is generally accepted but that some exceptions exist.

Table 7.12 Capitalization of interest cost

Countries	Capitalization permitted	Capitalization prohibited	Countries	Capitalization permitted	Capitalization prohibited
Australia	x		Japan		x
Belgium	x		Luxembourg	x	
Brazil		x	Netherlands	x	
Canada	x		Norway	x	
Denmark	x		Spain	x	
Finland	x		Sweden	x	
France	x		Switzerland	x	
Germany	x		United Kingdom	x	
Ireland	x		USA	x	
Italy	x				

An example of capitalization of interest costs is provided in Appendix 7.3. Capitalized interest may represent a very large share of the asset cost and, thus, a big stake in the determination of income.

Real-life example

> For example, BAA (the British Airport Authority, the owner and operator of most British airports) changed their policy of capitalization in 1997. They had been capitalizing interest on Heathrow Airport's Terminal 5 since 1990. However, in 1997, they decided that it was no longer appropriate to do so until they had received proper planning commission authorization and government approval for the project. At the end of 1996, accumulated expenditure on Terminal 5 was £178 million, of which 28% (£49m) was capitalized interest. Financial statements for the year ending 31 March 1998 showed no interest capitalized and all interest previously accumulated were written off[5].

Recording of the transactions

Example

Let's take the example of a piece of machinery constructed by the Purcell Company for its own use. The production cost includes the following cost items (all are assumed to be paid for in cash, for simplicity sake):

- Materials and components: 30 CU.
- Labor (personnel expense): 55 CU.
- Overhead (various expenses): 15 CU.

The new machine will be depreciated over 5 years.

One way of recording the capitalization of the costs incurred in the construction is presented in Figure 7.4.

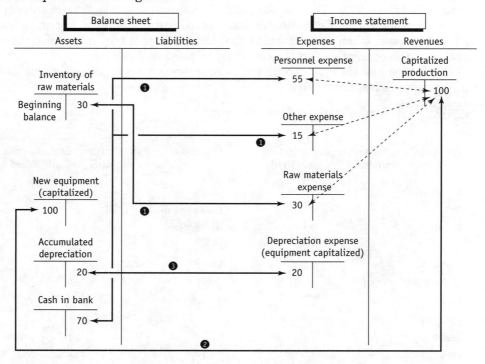

Figure 7.4 Accounting for tangible assets constructed by and for Purcell Co.

Across countries, several solutions are possible at the time of capitalization:

- to debit the income statement of the costs or expenses incurred for the capitalized asset (step 1) and credit a revenue account (production capitalized) (step 2) (this is the solution followed in Figure 7.4)
- to open a "project account" in which all the expenses pertaining to the new asset being developed are transferred, thus creating directly the value of the asset without having to go through the income statement. This solution is very simple but does not give the same visibility for shareholders to see what their business is really doing with its resources. This solution is not illustrated here
- depreciation of the new equipment over 5 years (100/5 = 20) is step 3.

After capitalization, the impact of the new machine on income for the first year is limited to the depreciation expense, i.e., 100/5= 20. If the machine built in-house had not been considered to be an asset and capitalized, the impact on the first year income would have been the full 100 monetary units or the full cost of the asset.

Depreciation: additional methods

This section will illustrate the three methods of depreciation mentioned but not covered in the Core Issues of this chapter. They are:

- sum of the years' digits method
- depreciation methods based on activity level (2 cases):
  - units-of-output method
  - service-quantity method.

We will use the same data as used previously of an acquisition by Purcell Company of a piece of equipment for 6,000 CU. Table 7.13 summarizes the data (in thousands of CU, unless otherwise specified).

Table 7.13 Basic data

Cost	6,000		
Residual value	1,000		
Depreciable amount	5,000		
Estimated useful life	**5 years**		
Expected units of output over the life of the asset	**25,000 units**	Expected number of machine hours over the life of the asset	**50,000 hours**
Year 1	8,000	Year 1	12,000
Year 2	7,000	Year 2	12,000
Year 3	6,000	Year 3	12,000
Year 4	3,000	Year 4	8,000
Year 5	1,000	Year 5	6,000

Sum of the years' digits method (sum of the digits method)

This method belongs to the category of accelerated (reducing charge) methods of depreciation.

Principle

This method calculates the annual depreciation expense by multiplying the depreciable amount by a fraction decreasing each year. The fraction is defined by the number of years remaining to depreciate (numerator) and the sum of the digits representing the number of years in the useful life (denominator). This method never has to reverse to straight line:

$$\text{Depreciation expense for 1 year} = \frac{\text{Number of remaining years of life}}{\text{Sum of digits}} \times \text{Depreciable amount}$$

For assets with relatively long lives, the following shortcut helps to calculate the sum of digits:

Sum of digits $= N(N+1)/2$ (where N is the number of years of the asset's useful life)

The sum of the years' digit method is rarely allowed by tax authorities and its use in reporting to shareholders is declining. For example, since the US Internal Revenue Service disallowed for tax calculations the sum of the years' digits method in 1980, the method's popularity has declined regularly in reporting to shareholders to become quite rare to date.

Illustration: Purcell Company

The useful life of the asset is 5 years. Thus the sum of the years' digits is $5 + 4 + 3 + 2 + 1 = 15$.

Table 7.14 Depreciation schedule – Sum of the years' digits

End of year	Depreciable basis	Applicable fraction	Annual depreciation expense	Balance: Accumulated depreciation	Year-end book value
					6,000
Year 1	5,000	5/15	1,667	1,667	4,333
Year 2	5,000	4/15	1,333	3,000	3,000
Year 3	5,000	3/15	1,000	4,000	2,000
Year 4	5,000	2/15	667	4,667	1,333
Year 5	5,000	1/15	333	5,000	1,000

Depreciation methods based on activity level

The use of such methods, matching the depreciation schedule with the "consumption" of the potential of economic benefits the asset can provide is appropriate only if the asset's output is discretely and distinctly measurable and if the useful life of the asset is better expressed in terms of maximum number of units of output than in terms of time periods.

Productive output method (units of output method)

Principle

The depreciation schedule matches the timing of the output of the asset expressed in units of products or services such as miles driven, units shipped, or tons produced. A depreciation cost per unit of output is calculated by dividing the depreciable amount by the total potential expected of that asset. This depreciation per unit is then applied to the actual output for the period to determine the depreciation expense.

The amount of depreciation expense cannot be determined in advance for any given period, because it is dependent on the level of output during the period.

$$\text{Depreciation expense} = \frac{\text{Depreciable amount}}{\text{Life expressed in units of output}} \times \text{Units of output for period} =$$

$$\text{Depreciation cost per unit} \times \text{Units of output for the period}$$

This method is easy to apply when the required information is readily available as, for example, for a bottling machine whose quantity of output would automatically be recorded.

One of the advantages of this method is that it allows the enterprise to record the depreciation expense in proportion to the intensity of use of the asset. It is clear that a machine that produces 48,000 containers of yogurt per hour during one 8-hour shift 5 days a week will not wear out as quickly as it would if it were used 20 hours a day for 6½ days a week (5 shifts).

However, the determination of the rated lifetime output is not completely objective: the difficulty of choosing the useful economic life is compounded with that of defining the output per period (generally estimated by the manufacturer or production engineers). For example, the yogurt-packaging machine just mentioned was rated by the manufacturer at 36,000 containers an hour but the dairy maintenance and production engineers were able to increase the rated output to 48,000 containers per hour after only three months of operation. Which is the appropriate figure in determining the denominator number: 36 or 48,000?

Another major source of ambiguity of the number of units constituting the life expected total number of units comes from the fact that there is no guarantee that the market will absorb the whole output potential over the expected useful life. If the cumulated market demand does not materialize and does not match the expected output, the asset may be completely obsolete much before it is fully depreciated. The method requires that the accountant use as the denominator only the total cumulated output that will reasonably be absorbed by the market.

The productivity of many plant assets, such as buildings and fixtures, however, cannot be measured in terms of a unit of output. For such classes of assets, this method of depreciation is inappropriate.

Table 7.15 offers an illustration of this method for the Purcell Company.

Table 7.15 Depreciation schedule – Productive output method

End of year	Annual output in units	Depreciation cost per unit	Annual depreciation expense	Balance: Accumulated depreciation	Year-end book value
					6,000
Year 1	8,000	0.20	1,600	1,600	4,400
Year 2	7,000	0.20	1,400	3,000	3,000
Year 3	6,000	0.20	1,200	4,200	1,800
Year 4	3,000	0.20	600	4,800	1,200
Year 5	1,000	0.20	200	5,000	1,000

The depreciable amount is 5,000 CU

The expected normal number of units of output the asset can create and which are expected to be sold has been estimated at 25,000 units

The estimated depreciation cost per unit of output is therefore 0.20 CU (5,000/25,000 = 0.20)

Depreciation of year 1 = 8,000 (units produced and sold) × 0.20 (depreciation cost per unit)

Service quantity method

Principle

While the mechanics of applying the service quantity (or unit depreciation) method are similar to those of the productive output method, the concepts underlying the methods are somewhat different. Under the service quantity method, the contribution to operation is stated in terms of productive output factors rather than physical sellable output of the production process. This method is commonly employed in air or ground transportation businesses. Aircraft are depreciated on the basis of flying hours (but the landing gear should logically be depreciated on the basis of the number of landings), locomotives or trucks are depreciated on the basis of kilometers (or miles) driven. The same issue arises as was found in the case of the productive output method, namely the definition of the accumulated number of units of service the equipment can handle. A truck may be rated for half a million miles for use over "normal roads under normal driving conditions" but the actual mileage that will be obtained from the same truck may vary greatly with the load factor and road conditions as well as with the driving style and intensity of use. For example, the mileage wear and tear cannot be equivalent between a truck driven over dirt roads in the Sahel and one driven over modern freeways in the Netherlands or over mountain roads in Switzerland or Austria. The issue of being able to actually "sell" the potential of units of service may also be an issue for the validity of this method of depreciation.

$$Depreciation\ expense = \frac{Depreciable\ amount}{Total\ quantity\ of\ productive\ service} \times Productive\ service\ for\ period =$$
$$Depreciation\ cost\ per\ unit\ of\ services \times Units\ of\ service\ for\ the\ period$$

The unit depreciation methods are not widely used, probably for two major reasons:

● These methods produce a schedule of depreciation for the first years of the asset that are often not very different from those that would be obtained through the use of the straight-line depreciation method;

● As mentioned in the text, the ambiguity on the figures can be rather large and the data-collection costs might prove to be expensive.

Table 7.16 provides an illustration.

Table 7.16 Depreciation schedule – Service quantity method

End of year	Life-time number of units of service	Depreciation cost per unit of service	Annual depreciation expense	Balance: Accumulated depreciation	Year-end book value
					6,000
Year 1	12,000	0.10	1,200	1,200	4,800
Year 2	12,000	0.10	1,200	2,400	3,600
Year 3	12,000	0.10	1,200	3,600	2,400
Year 4	8,000	0.10	800	4,400	1,600
Year 5	6,000	0.10	600	5,000	1,000

Depreciable amount: 5,000 CU

Estimated life time number of units of service: 50,000 units of service

Estimated cost per unit of service = 0.10 (5,000/50,000)

Depreciation expense for year 1 = 1,200 = 12,000 (number of units of service) × 0.10 (depreciation cost per unit of service)

Summary of the income statement impact of the different methods

Illustration: Purcell Company

Table 7.17 summarizes the depreciation expense and the book value of the same asset under the five main depreciation methods described in this chapter.

Table 7.17 Summary of the different methods

Year	Straight line		Sum of years' digits		Double-declining balance (simulation 1)		Productive output		Service quantity	
	Depr. expense	Book value	Depr. expense	Book value	Depr. expense	Book value	Depr. expense	Book value	Depr. expense	Book value
At acquisition		6,000		6,000		6,000		6,000		6,000
Year 1	1,000	5,000	1,667	4,333	2,400	3,600	1,600	4,400	1,200	4,800
Year 2	1,000	4,000	1,333	3,000	1,440	2,160	1,400	3,000	1,200	3,600
Year 3	1,000	3,000	1,000	2,000	864	1,296	1,200	1,800	1,200	2,400
Year 4	1,000	2,000	667	1,333	296	1,000	600	1,200	800	1,600
Year 5	1,000	1,000	333	1,000	0	1,000	200	1,000	600	1,000

Figure 7.5 shows evolution of the annual depreciation expense over time under each of the alternative depreciation methods and Figure 7.6 shows the resulting net book value at each year-end.

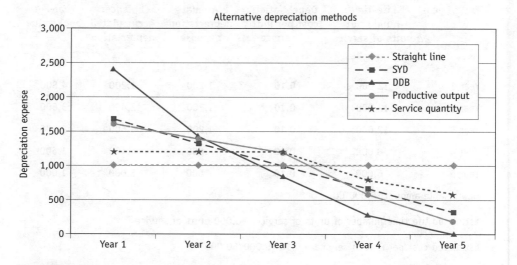

Figure 7.5 Annual depreciation expense

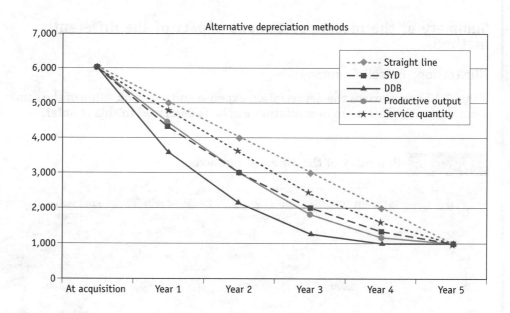

Figure 7.6 Book value

In practice, tangible assets are rarely purchased or sold on the first day of the accounting period. The treatment which arises for a purchase or sale during the year is dealt with in Appendix 7.4.

Impairment

Principle

IAS 16 (§ 6) defines an "impairment loss" as "the amount by which the carrying amount of an asset exceeds its recoverable amount". "To determine whether an item of property, plant and equipment is impaired, an enterprise applies IAS 36 [IASC 1998b]. That Standard explains how an enterprise reviews the carrying amount of its assets, how it determines the recoverable amount of an asset and when it recognizes or reverses an impairment loss" (§ 53).

Practically, if the fair market value of a tangible asset is less than its book value, such asset should be written down and a loss recognized ("lower of cost or market" is a consequence of the prudence principle) as an "impairment loss" expense or "loss from write-down" expense or "provision expense". If and when the impairment is no longer required, a reversal could and should be recorded as a negative expense or though a revenue account: "write-back on impairment" or "reversal of provisions" (it is, however, rarely done in practice).

Practice and regulation regarding impairment have varied over time and between countries in the world. Apart from IAS 36 (IASC 1998b), rules for impairment exist now in many countries, such as the USA (SFAS 121, Accounting for the Impairment of Long-Lived Assets and for Long-Lived Assets to Be Disposed Of) and the UK (FRS 11, Impairment of Fixed Assets and Goodwill).

The topic of impairment may become increasingly relevant, with the change of rules relating to impairment of intangibles (see Chapters 8 and, especially, 13). In practice, tests for impairment are very difficult to implement.

Real-life examples

Barlow

(Barloworld, since October 2000) (South Africa – South African GAAP – Source: Annual report 1999 – Heavy equipment, material handling equipment, motors, cement, and lime)

Note 31 to the financial statements for the year ended 30 September 1999

Change in accounting policy.

The accounting policy in respect of impairment of assets has been adopted to comply with International Accounting Standards. The standard prescribes that the recoverable amount of an asset should be estimated whenever there is an indication that an asset may be impaired. An impairment loss in respect of a cement mill, laser optics plant and a paper mill has been recognized and an amount of R85 million has been provided for in the current year through exceptional items.

This note is also a good illustration of reporting on an accounting change (see "Advanced Issues" in Chapter 6).

Lenzing

(Austria – US GAAP – Source: Annual report 1999 – Man-made cellulose fibers)

Note 8 to the financial statements for the year ended 31 December 1999

During 1999 and 1998 the management of Lenzing USA Corporation determined that, as a result of continuing losses and the depressed state of the American fiber industry, the Company's manufacturing facility and substantially all production equipment were impaired. As a result of the impairment of the carrying value of these assets, the Group recorded an impairment charge of €1,396,500 and €2,390,300 to write-down the assets to the estimated fair market value for 1999 and 1998, respectively. The impairment loss is recorded under the caption "cost of goods sold" in the income statement. The fair value of equipment was determined by using an independent appraisal.

Depreciation of land

Normally, land is accounted for at its acquisition cost and is not subject to any depreciation, since it theoretically neither gets consumed through use nor wears out, or becomes obsolescent. However, where land has been purchased as a natural resource for a productive activity – such as a quarry, a mine, oil field, or natural gas well – the acquisition cost relates not to the land surface but to the volume of riches which are hidden beneath it. In such cases, depreciation will be calculated on a unit consumption basis (proportional to the output extracted compared to the estimated life capacity of the deposit) since exploitation of the resource reduces the potential of future exploitation. This depreciation is recognized under the specific name of "**depletion**".

Another situation in which the land acquisition costs will be subject to value adjustment at the end of a financial year is when its current market value has fallen below the cost of acquisition. The required value adjustment will be recognized as an impairment.

Example: Britten Corp. purchased a well-located piece of suburban farm land for 850,000 CU (much higher than the price of farm land but much lower than the price of urban land) in the anticipation that it could be developed as a shopping center. However, three years later the company learns formally from its lawyer that, despite her efforts to obtain that the zoning regulations be changed, there will be no possibility of obtaining a building permit. As a consequence the market value of the land is not more than 85,000 CU (farm land price). In this case the company should take an impairment loss expense (exceptional depreciation expense) of 765,000 CU by debit to the income statement of the year.

Costs subsequent to acquisition

Costs incurred after the acquisition of an asset, such as additions, improvements, or replacements, are added to the asset's depreciable cost if they provide future service potential, extend the useful life of the asset, or increase either the quantity or quality of service rendered by the asset. Otherwise, they are expensed immediately.

IAS 16 (§ 23) indicates: "Subsequent expenditure relating to an item of property, plant and equipment that has already been recognized should be added to the carrying amount of the asset when it is probable that future economic benefits, in excess of the originally assessed standard of performance of the existing asset, will flow to the enterprise. All other subsequent expenditure should be recognized as an expense in the period in which it is incurred."

The International Standard (§ 24) gives some examples of improvements that result in increased future economic benefits:

● Modification of an asset to extend its useful life, including an increase in its capacity.
● Upgrading machine parts to achieve a substantial improvement in the quality of output.
● Adoption of new production processes enabling a substantial reduction in previously assessed operating costs.

An expenditure on repairs or maintenance of a tangible asset is made only to maintain or restore the stream of future economic benefits. As such, it is usually recognized as an expense when incurred. For example, the cost of servicing or overhauling plant and equipment is usually an expense since it restores, rather than increases, the originally assessed standard of performance (IAS 16: § 25).

The developments (in Core Issues) relating to the difference between an asset and an expense can be applied to the concept of "subsequent expenditure", especially in the case of small expenditures.

Disposal of long-term assets

Tangible assets are disposed of for many different reasons and in a variety of ways: sale, abandonment, and loss (flood, fire, natural disaster).

We will mainly deal with the sale of tangible assets, knowing that the other two categories of disposal can be assimilated to a sale without the entry recognizing the proceeds of the sale (see later).

Recording of the sale of an asset

When long-term assets are sold before their useful lives are completed, the difference between the book value and the disposition proceeds (**sales proceeds** or **selling price**) is treated as a gain or a loss.

Some countries (e.g., the USA) record the net impact from the sale in a single line (gain or loss, depending on the nature of this difference). Other countries record separately in the income statement the selling price as a revenue and the book value as an expense (e.g., France) or open an asset disposal account, the balance of which is transferred to the income statement account (e.g., the UK). Of course, the reported impact on net income is the same, whichever method is chosen. Depreciation must be recorded for the period of time between the date of the last depreciation entry and the date of sale. An illustration of the recording of a sale of fixed asset is given in Appendix 7.5 and the treatment of the removal of a fully depreciated tangible asset from the book is provided in Appendix 7.6.

Classification in the income statement

Gains and losses from the sale of long-term assets need to be reported to shareholders. The choice of where in the income statement to report these items (exceptional, extraordinary, or ordinary income) differs from country to country. In the USA, gains and losses from asset sales do not satisfy criteria for the extraordinary item treatment (see Chapter 6). They are included in the income statement "above the line", i.e., they are considered part of the normal business of the firm. In continental Europe, the book value of fixed assets sold and the sales price are classified as an exceptional item. In the UK, profits and losses on disposals (sales) of fixed assets must be disclosed after the operating profit as an exceptional item.

Financial aspects of tangible assets

Depreciation and cash flow

Depreciation expense is a non-cash expense. This means that the depreciation expense has no direct impact on the cash balance but an indirect one arising from the income tax effect of expenses. This will be illustrated through the example of the Purcell Company summarized in Table 7.18.

Assume that the company realized sales (all for cash) for 200 CU and operating expenses (all cash) for 120. In addition Purcell Co. also incurred a depreciation expense. If they use straight-line method, the depreciation expense for the first year amounts to 20 CU, while if they use the double-declining balance depreciation method, the first year depreciation expense amounts to 40 CU. In both cases we assume the income tax rate to be 40%. Table 7.18 presents the income statement and the operating cash flow (extracted from the cash flow statement – see Chapters 3 and 14).

Table 7.18 illustrates some important points:

- The choice of method of depreciation impacts both income before tax and after tax.
- Cash flow from operating activities is not influenced by depreciation expense because its calculation does not include the depreciation expense.
- However, income tax does influence the net cash flow.
- The higher the depreciation expense the larger the net after tax cash flow. This is due to the different income tax shield provided by each method. (In reality, this is the case only where tax regulation allows it.)

Table 7.18 Depreciation and cash flow

	Straight-line depreciation	Double-declining balance depreciation
Income statement		
Sales	200	200
Operating expenses	(120)	(120)
Depreciation expense	(20)	(40)
Income before income tax	60	40
Income tax expense (40%)	(24)	(16)
Net income after tax	36	24
Cash flow statement		
Cash received from customers	200	200
Cash paid for operating expenses	(120)	(120)
Cash flow before tax from operating activities	**80**	**80**
Cash paid for income tax	(24)	(16)
Cash flow after tax provided from operating activities	56	64
Alternative presentation of the cash flow statement		
Net income after tax	36	24
Plus Depreciation expense	20	40
Equals Cash flow (after tax) from operating activities	56	64
Plus Cash paid on income tax	24	16
Equals Cash flow from operating activities (before tax)	**80**	**80**

Reporting movements in tangible assets

Principle

In most countries, as well as under IAS 16 (IASC 1998a: § 60) or EU 4th Directive (EU 1978), the notes to financial statements must include two separate statements, one reporting the movements in the gross value of tangible assets and the other with the changes in accumulated depreciation (with the exception of the USA and Canada where both are merged). These statements are based on the principles listed in Table 7.19.

Table 7.19 Movements in tangible assets

Beginning value	+	Increases	–	Decreases	=	Ending value
Gross value	+	Acquisitions	–	Disposals	=	Gross value
Beginning accumulated depreciation	+	Depreciation expense	–	Cancellation of depreciation of fixed assets sold or disposed of	=	Ending accumulated depreciation

Barlo Company

an Irish buildings materials company publishes in its annual report 2000 the following statement relating to its parent company

€000	Freehold land and buildings	Motor vehicles	Fixtures and fittings	Total
Cost				
At 31 March 1999	485	147	448	1,080
Additions during year	0	15	246	261
Disposals during year	(485)	(23)	(416)	(924)
At 31 March 2000	0	139	278	417
Accumulated depreciation				
At 31 March 1999	48	59	195	302
Charge for the year	8	22	47	77
Disposals during year	(56)	(19)	(181)	(256)
At 31 March 2000	0	62	61	123
Net book amounts				
At 31 March 1999	437	88	253	778
At 31 March 2000	0	77	217	294

- Contrary to usual practice, which we have followed in the previous illustrations, the movements are presented in line and the assets in columns.
- The book value is computed as the difference between the gross value and the accumulated depreciation at year-end.

Financial statement analysis

Several ratios may be computed to help the user of financial information gain a better understanding of the financial position of the business regarding its ability to use its tangible fixed assets.

Capital intensity ratios

There are two key ratios:

Rate of return on tangible asset = Net income/Net tangible assets
Tangible asset turnover = Net sales/Average tangible assets (book value)

They answer the questions "how much profit does the business create" or "how much sales are generated per CU invested in tangible assets". These ratios are essential for extrapolating the consequences of an investment strategy. Their value is clearly influenced by the depreciation method chosen.

Average age and life of tangible assets

Shareholders (potential or actual) and financial analysts need to evaluate the risk of obsolescence of the assets of the firm. Failing to have exact, engineering-based knowledge of the average age or life of the assets, a quick estimate can be found by exploiting the fact that financial statements report both the gross value of the assets and their accumulated depreciation.

> Average age = Accumulated depreciation at year-end/Depreciation expense for the year
> Average life = Gross value of depreciable assets at year-end/Depreciation expense for the year

These two ratios suffer several limits since the depreciation allowance (and thus the timing of the accumulated depreciation) varies with the method of depreciation selected:

- They provide reasonably good information only in the case of straight-line depreciation method.
- They assume the cost of acquisition of equivalent assets over time is stable.
- They are influenced by acquisitions and disposals during the year.

A further problem with the meaningfulness of these ratios derives from the fact managers could manipulate tangible assets valuation and depreciation expense in order to increase (or decrease) net income. The three major sources of manipulation are:

- increase (or decrease) an asset's useful life
- change depreciation method (from straight-line to declining balance or the opposite, for example)
- decide to capitalize (or not) elements of the acquisition cost (such as financial expenses) or upgrade of the asset (by decomposing the upgrade in slices that all fit under the threshold.

The notes to financial statements, in particular the first part devoted to accounting policies, are very helpful for the user of financial statements. Managers must use them to reveal the accounting choices they have made during the year and thus allow the analyst or any reader to recast the figures in the light that suits them.

The impact of the choice of a depreciation method on the financial statements is dealt with in Appendix 7.7.

KEY POINTS

- Tangible fixed assets (property, plant and equipment (PPE), "plant assets", "operational assets" or "fixed assets") create economic benefits over several periods and represent significant investments that must be put in place before any economic activity can take place.
- Fixed assets are, by nature, the most illiquid assets on the balance sheet. In countries where the accounting tradition is more "patrimonial" they will appear at the top of the list of assets while in countries where the accounting culture favors liquidity, the tangible fixed assets will be listed at the bottom of the list.

- Fixed assets can be divided into three categories: (1) tangible assets; (2) intangible assets (see Chapter 8); and (3) financial fixed assets (see Chapter 13).
- The various accounting issues that arise when dealing with tangible fixed assets are related to their acquisition (definition, recognition, measurement), use (depreciation) and disposal (sale or removal).
- Depreciation is "the systematic allocation of the depreciable cost of an asset over its useful life".
- Several depreciation methods have been developed. The choice of the appropriate method should theoretically be made so as to best reflect the pattern of decline in the asset's service potential and should therefore be specific to each class of tangible asset.
- Two categories of methods are available: (1) time-based depreciation methods (straight-line, declining balance, and sum of the years' digits); and (2) methods based on activity level (productive output and service quantity).
- Depreciation expense is a non-cash expense. This means that the depreciation expense has no direct impact on the cash balance. There may be a relation between depreciation and cash, where choice of method is allowed for tax purposes.

REVIEW

Review 7.1 Gibbons

Topic: Determining the cost of acquisition
Type: Individual exercise
Related part of the chapter: Core Issues

Gibbons Co., a coffee shop company, purchases a new coffee machine. The list price for the machine is 1,500 CU. However, the manufacturer is running a special offer, and Gibbons Co. obtains the machine for a price which is 20% lower than the list price. Freight expenses for the delivery of the machine are 150 CU, and installation and testing expenses amount to 100 CU. During installation, uninsured damages are incurred resulting in repair expenses of 200 CU.

Required

1 Compute the acquisition cost of the machine.
2 Record the acquisition in the format of your choice ("ledger-financial statements", ledger, journal, financial statements).

Solution

1 *Computation of the acquisition cost*

Retail price		1,500
Discount	20%	–300
Net invoice cost		1,200
Freight expenses		150
Installation expenses		100
Total acquisition cost		1,450

The repair expenses are not considered a component of the machine's acquisition cost because those expenses are not necessary to obtain the machine.

2 Accounting entries

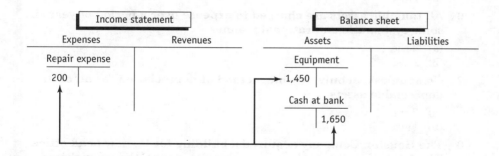

ASSIGNMENTS

Assignment 7.1

Multiple-choice questions
Type: Individual exercise
Related part of the chapter: Core Issues

Select the right answer.

1 The most appropriate method of depreciation of land is

(a) The straight-line method
(b) The declining balance method
(c) Either method
(d) None of these

2 Depreciation will directly generate

(a) An increase in cash
(b) An increase in liabilities
(c) A decrease in liabilities
(d) A decrease in assets
(e) A decrease in cash

3 At the end of the useful life of a tangible asset originally purchased for 100 CU and fully depreciated over 5 years, the gross value is

(a) 0
(b) 100
(c) 20
(d) None of these

4 Which of the following items would not be considered a tangible asset?

1. Land
2. Trademark
3. Building
4. Oil well
5. Software
(a) 1, 3, and 4
(b) 2 and 4
(c) 2 and 5

(d) 2, 3, 4, and 5

(e) 3 and 5

5 **Examples of tangible assets include land, buildings and equipment**

(a) True

(b) False

6 **All tangible assets are charged to expense over a period of years in some systematic and rational manner**

(a) True

(b) False

7 **Companies can only use one method of depreciation for all of its depreciable assets**

(a) True

(b) False

8 **The Houston Company acquired a building for its new head office. The following cash outlays were associated with the acquisition:**

Amount paid for the building	300,000
Legal fees	30,000
Property title search	3,000
Realtor's commissions	10,000

How should the Houston Company record the acquisition? Allocate the total cash outlays between the book value of the asset (to be depreciated) and expenses recognized in the current year

	Building	Expenses
(a)	300,000	43,000
(b)	330,000	13,000
(c)	333,000	10,000
(d)	343,000	0
(e)	310,000	33,000

9 **When using the double declining balance method, the depreciation rate is multiplied by the**

(a) Purchase cost of the asset

(b) Fair value of the asset at beginning of the period

(c) Depreciable amount

(d) Net book value at beginning of each year

(e) None of these

10 **The share of a natural resource deposit's cost of acquisition that is expensed each year is called**

(a) Depreciation

(b) Amortization

(c) Depletion

(d) Exhaustion

(e) None of these

Assignment 7.2

Discussion questions
Type: Group exercise
Related part of the chapter: Core/Advanced Issues

1 Give some arguments in favor of at least four different methods of depreciation.

2 Does depreciation provide or consume cash?

3 Give some arguments in favor of each method of reporting the sale of tangible assets.

4 Does the acquisition of a tangible asset influence net income?

Assignment 7.3

Topic: Reporting in different sectors of activity
Type: Group exercise
Related part of the chapter: Core Issues

On the internet, or in the library, find the annual reports of four companies from different sectors of activity in a given country or in different countries.

Required

1 How are tangible assets presented in the balance sheet? What decisions on the basis of this information can investors or shareholders take? What decisions would be difficult to take on the basis of just this information?

2 Are there any notes relating to tangible assets? How do they enlarge the decision analysis possibilities offered to shareholders and investors?

3 What are the accounting treatments applied to these assets?

4 What are the estimated useful lives of the major categories of assets?

5 What is the weight of tangible assets in percentage of total assets? What strategic implications do you derive from this ratio?

6 What is the weight of depreciation expense in percentage of income?

Assignment 7.4

Topic: Reporting in the same sector of activity
Type: Group exercise
Related part of the chapter: Core Issues

On the internet, or in the library, find the annual reports of three companies essentially in identical or similar industries in a given country or in different countries.

Required

Use questions from Assignment 7.3.

Assignment 7.5

Topic: Choice of depreciation methods
Type: Group exercise
Related part of the chapter: Core/Advanced Issues

Choose a country you know well, either because you come from this country or have worked there.

Required

Identify the depreciation methods which are mostly commonly used in practice. You can base your presentation on official statistics (if they exist) or on a sample of annual reports you will survey.

Assignment 7.6 Tippett

Topic: Popular depreciation methods
Type: Individual exercise
Related part of the chapter: Core/Advanced Issues

Tippett Company acquired new machine tools for 10 million CU. Their aggregate predicted useful lives is 4 years and predicted residual value is 1 million CU.

Depreciation expense of this class of asset can be computed through one of five methods:

- straight line
- double-declining balance
- sum of the years' digits
- units of output basis
- service hours basis.

Units of output and service hours for each year and in total are listed in the following table.

	Annual	Total
Units of output		15,000
. Year 1	7,000	
. Year 2	4,000	
. Year 3	2,000	
. Year 4	2,000	
Service hours		36,000
. Year 1	12,000	
. Year 2	9,000	
. Year 3	8,000	
. Year 4	7,000	

Required

Prepare a depreciation schedule comparing the five depreciation methods, assuming that the acquisition date was 1 January, Year 1.

Assignment 7.7 Britten Inc.

Topic: Determining the cost of acquisition – recording the acquisition and the depreciation
Type: Individual exercise
Related part of the chapter: Core/Advanced Issues

Britten Inc. is a large European civil engineering and construction enterprise. They have just finished building, for their own use, a large hangar which will serve as both a warehouse for their inventory of raw construction materials and as a garage for idle equipment between assignments. Construction began on 14 July 20X1 and was completed on 1 October of the same year. Resources consumed by the construction projects were:

- raw materials which were already in inventory for an amount of 10,000 CU
- labor costs amounting to 20,000 CU.

This type of light construction is generally depreciated over 10 years and Britten Inc. chose to use the double-declining balance method. The residual value of the building will be essentially zero. The hangar will be fully depreciated by:

- Either switching to the straight-line method when the double-declining rate on the balance becomes smaller than the straight-line rate over the remaining years.
- Or switching to straight-line method at the mid-point of useful life of the hangar.

The closing date is 31 December.

Required

1 Record the cost of the hangar (depreciable amount).
2 Prepare the depreciation schedule under both possibilities for switching to straight-line, assuming that the hangar is fully depreciated at the end of year 20X10.

3 Record the depreciation allowance pertaining to the hangar in the income statement of Britten Inc. for the year ended 31 December, Year 20X1.

Assignment 7.8 Saint-Gobain*

Topic: Reporting for movements of tangible assets
Type: Individual/group exercise
Related part of the chapter: Core Issues

Founded in France in 1665 as a manufacturer of flat glass, Saint-Gobain has undergone a major transformation of its operations. The group is now operating in three core sectors (glass, high-performance materials, and housing supplies), and operates in over 75 countries around the world.

Note 5 – Fixed assets – in the consolidated financial statements states the following (*source*: annual report 1999 – French GAAP):

In millions of €	31 December 1998	Changes in composition of the group	Additions	Disposals	Transfers	Translation adjustments	Depreciation charge	31 December 1999
Gross value								
Land	777	123	36	−10	6	38	–	970
Buildings	3,532	623	138	−49	74	124	–	4,442
Machinery and equipment	10,623	2,172	727	−551	406	496	–	13,873
Construction in progress	681	−75	811	−8	−486	47	–	970
Total gross value	15,613	2,843	1,712	−618	0	705	0	20,255
Depreciation								
Land	−46	−10	–	2	0	0	−7	−61
Buildings	−1,626	−273	–	28	1	−33	−184	−2,087
Machinery and equipment	−6,946	−1,061	–	382	−1	−185	−1,037	−8,848
Construction in progress	−41	0	–	0	0	0	0	−41
Total depreciation	−8,659	−1,344	0	412	0	−218	−1,228	−11,037

In the 31 December 1999 consolidated balance sheet, the following figures (in millions of €) appeared:

Assets	Note	1999	1998
(...)			
Property, plant, and equipment	5	20,255	15,613
Less: Accumulated depreciation		−11,037	−8,659
		9,218	6,954

Required

1 Explain the meaning of each column of the table in Note 5. NB. Although the topic of business combinations (see Chapter 13) has not been developed yet, we can deduct that the column "Changes in composition of the group" represents the impact of acquisitions and sales of companies and the column "Translation adjustments" is related to the translation of financial statements labeled in foreign currencies.

2 Reconcile the balance sheet figures and the statement of Note 5.

3 Explain the figure −75 under the heading "Construction in progress" in the column "Changes in composition of the group".

4 Explain what might the figure −46 represent under the heading "Depreciation" for "Land".

5 Explain and provide an illustration of what happens in the column "Transfers" (gross value).

6 Explain why, in the column "Disposals" (depreciation), the signs are positive.

7 Determine the book value of fixed assets sold during the year.

References

EU (European Union) (1978) 4th Directive on the annual accounts of certain types of companies no. 78/660/EEC. *Official Journal of the European Communities*, 14 August.

IASC (1989) Framework for the Preparation and Presentation of Financial Statements, London.

IASC (revised 1993) International Accounting Standard No. 23, Borrowing Costs, London.

IASC (revised 1998a) International Accounting Standard No. 16, Property, Plant and Equipment, London.

IASC (1998b) International Accounting Standard No. 36, Impairment of Assets, London.

IASC (1998c) International Accounting Standard No. 38, Intangible Assets, London.

Skousen F., Stice J., and Stice E.K. (2001) *Intermediate Accounting*, South-Western College Publishing, Cincinnati, OH.

Further readings

Burlaud, A. Messina, M., and Walton, P. (1996) Depreciation: concepts and practices in France and the UK. *European Accounting Review*, 5(2), 299–316.

Collins, L. (1994) Revaluation of assets in France: the interaction between professional practice, theory and political necessity. *European Accounting Review*, 3(1), 122–31.

Additional material on the website

Go to http://www.thomsonlearning.co.uk/accountingandfinance/stolowylebas for further information, journal entries and extra assignments for each chapter.

The following appendices to this chapter are available on the dedicated website:

Appendix 7.1: Examples of components of the acquisition cost

Appendix 7.2: Overhead

Appendix 7.3: Calculation of capitalized interest costs

Appendix 7.4: Depreciation for partial years (fractional year problems)

Appendix 7.5: Accounting for a sale of fixed asset: Illustration: Purcell Company

Appendix 7.6: Removing a fully depreciated tangible asset from the book

Appendix 7.7: Impact of the choice of a depreciation method on the financial statements

Notes

1   The reader can refer to Skousen *et al.* (2001) to find an explanation referring to US GAAP.

2   The interested reader can consult Skousen *et al.* (2001).

3   The concept of non-cash item and the mechanism relating the depreciation expense to the cash flow are developed in Chapter 14.

4   Based on *PR Newswire*, 11 March 1999.

5   Based on *Financial Times*, 25 April 1997 and 2 February 1998.

Intangible assets

As defined in Chapter 7, intangible assets are long-lived (long-term) assets that lack physical substance and whose acquisition and continued possession represent rights to future economic benefits. Intangible assets comprise patents, franchises, licenses, trademarks, brands, copyrights, etc., and capitalized R&D if certain conditions are met.

The valuation and reporting of intangibles has been controversial and a source of debate for many years because it is very difficult to objectively define and value future economic benefits. How can one establish an "objective" value for a brand, especially if the brand was developed by the firm itself and not purchased from someone else in an at "arm's length" transaction? Unlike with physical assets where the value is linked to ownership, it is the "quality" of the usage made of the intangible by a management team that creates the stream of future economic benefits. For example, when a pharmaceutical laboratory with a cosmetics division acquired a well-known perfume brand, their intention was to use the well-known brand as a locomotive for the rest of the division and develop the stream of future economic benefits of both the newly acquired firm but also, by ricochet and osmosis, of the other pre-existing products and brands in the portfolio of the division. However, the culture of that pharmaceutical laboratory was so different from that of a cosmetics and perfume business that it drowned the image of the acquired brand and was unable to capitalize on its acquisition. It ended up choosing to sell the whole cosmetics division a couple of years later at a loss. The buyer, in turn, with a culture more coherent with the potential of the brand was able to reap significant profit from the acquisition. Same intangible asset, different values.

Major topics

Definitions

Recognition

Changes in value

Research and development

Computer software

Financial statement analysis

Accountants and financial analysts have long been so cautious about intangible assets that they used to expense their cost of acquisition (or development) in the period incurred or, if recorded as assets, considered them as "virtual" assets and excluded them from their analyses of financial statements.

However, today's economy relies heavily on intangibles (see Table 8.1) and these assets have to be reported well if the financial statements are to give the shareholders a true and fair view of the business. Both accountants and financial analysts are therefore reconsidering their position. Brands or rights to patents may in some cases represent the major source of value creation by a business (for example, in retail, cosmetics or luxury products, biotechnology, or software development).

Intangible assets raise three major questions listed in Figure 8.1. Each will be dealt with in turn in the Core Issues part of the chapter.

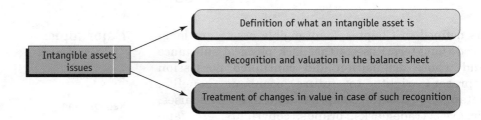

Figure 8.1 Intangible assets issues

Among the various intangibles, research and development costs and computer software deserve a special attention and will be covered in the Advanced Issues part.

CORE ISSUES

At the end of the 20th century many businesses reported some intangible assets in their year-end 1999 balance sheet as exemplified in Table 8.1.

Table 8.1   Weight of intangible assets

Company (country – activity)	Currency	Types of intangibles	Intangible assets (net)	Total assets (net amount)	% of total assets
ISS (Denmark – support services)	DKKm	Goodwill	7,553.3		55.2%
		Leasehold improvements	48.5		0.4%
		Intangible assets	7,601.8	13,672.9	55.6%
Racing Champions (USA – racing car replicas)	$000	Excess purchase price over net assets acquired, net	131,357	276,281	47.5%
Securitas (Sweden – security: guard services and alarm systems)	SEKm	Goodwill	7,178.4		34.6%
		Intangible rights	201.4		1.0%
		Other intangible assets	74.3		0.4%
		Intangible assets	7,454.1	20,775.0	35.9%

Table 8.1 Weight of intangible assets (continued)

Company (country – activity)	Currency	Types of intangibles	Intangible assets (net)	Total assets (net amount)	% of total assets
EMI (UK – music)	£m	Music copyrights	521.0		24.1%
		Goodwill	26.7		1.2%
		Total	547.7	2,164	25.3%
Interbrew (Belgium – brewery group)	€m	Intangible assets	49.4		0.8%
		Goodwill	1,368.0		21.9%
		Total	1,417.4	6,252.5	22.7%
Roche (Switzerland – pharmaceuticals, chemicals)	CHFm	Goodwill	5,389		7.7%
		Patents, licenses, trademarks, other	10,283		14.6%
		Intangible assets	15,672	70,431	22.3%
Saint-Gobain (France – glass)	€m	Goodwill	4,981		17.8%
		Other intangible assets	1,155		4.1%
		Intangible assets	6,136	27,916	22.0%
Repsol (Spain – oil and gas)	€m	Start-up expenses	172		0.4%
		Intangible assets	862		2.0%
		Goodwill	4,150		9.9%
		Total	5,184	42,050	12.3%
Club Méditerranée (France – leisure)	FRFm	Goodwill	659		6.6%
		Other	479		4.8%
		Intangible assets	1,138	10,029	11.3%
Philips (Netherlands – electronics)	€m	Intangible assets	2,822	29,496	9.6%
EVN (Austria – electricity, gas, heating)	ATS000	Goodwill	220,814		0.8%
		Other intangible assets	751,054		2.6%
		Intangible assets	971,868	29,240,624	3.3%
Pirelli (Italy – tires, cables and systems)	€000	Formation costs	6,331		0.1%
		Patents and design patent rights	7,473		0.1%
		Concessions, licenses, trademarks, similar rights	3,729		0.0%
		Goodwill	11,531		0.1%
		Consolidation difference	70,473		0.9%
		Intangible assets in progress and payments on account	3,367		0.0%
		Other intangible assets	68,777		0.9%
		Intangible assets	171,681	7,821,335	2.2%

Definition of intangibles

The definition of intangibles has evolved over the last few years trying to provide a better understanding of the concept, achieve reliable measurement of intangible investments and promote understanding and communication between researchers, management, users of financial information, and policy makers. Intangible assets are usually considered to have no physical substance and to be linked to legal rights (trademarks, patents, copyrights).

Definitions

All countries' GAAP refer to the idea of intangible assets. However, each may have its specific definition of the concept. Local GAAP's definitions of intangibles can be organized around two main types of approaches: conceptual and list based (see Figure 8.2).

In the conceptual approach, attributes, properties, and concepts are specified that, when used in a proper algorithm, allow one to classify any item appropriately as intangible assets or expense. This approach sometimes fails to provide a complete set of criteria and supplements these with a non-exhaustive list of illustrative cases, letting accountants, regulators and the courts classify new situation by similarity with listed cases.

In the list-based approach, the local GAAP provides a discrete "laundry list" of well-identified cases for which the creation of an intangible asset is appropriate and, by default, classifies any unlisted cost as one to be expensed in the year incurred. The list is eventually enriched by regulators on an ad hoc basis when the need arises.

The conceptual approaches can be divided into three sub-categories:

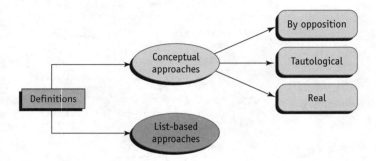

Figure 8.2   How intangible assets are defined

- definitions by opposition (for example, "fixed assets other than tangible or financial")
- tautological definitions (for example, "an intangible asset is characterized by a lack of physical substance"; "in order to be included in the balance sheet category entitled "Intangible Fixed Assets", an asset must be intangible", etc.)
- real definitions that make a genuine effort to determine what an intangible asset is.

Within the conceptual approach, a definition could include several "sub-approaches" at the same time. For example, UK (ASB 1997: § 2) defines as intangible assets those that are "non-financial assets that do not have physical substance but are identifiable and are controlled by the entity through custody or legal rights". This definition is broken down in its components in Figure 8.3.

Appendix 8.1 lists the position of several countries in their use of the opposition, tautological, real definitions, and of list-based approach.

No definition ever rests solely on the "tautological" approach. In fact, most definitions begin with a tautological statement (e.g., an intangible asset is intangible or lacks physical substance) and go on to define such assets either by opposition, and/or by providing criteria of what an intangible asset actually is. Table 8.2 provides examples of definitions.

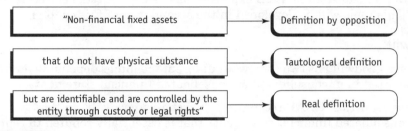

"Non-financial fixed assets	→	Definition by opposition
that do not have physical substance	→	Tautological definition
but are identifiable and are controlled by the entity through custody or legal rights"	→	Real definition

Figure 8.3 Definition of intangible assets in the UK

Table 8.2 Examples of definitions

"Real"	IASC	An intangible asset is "an identifiable non-monetary asset without physical substance held for use in the production or supply of goods or services, for rental to others, or for administrative purposes. An asset is a resource controlled by an enterprise as a result of past events; and from which future economic benefits are expected to flow to the enterprise" (IASC 1998b: § 7)
"Real"	UK, Ireland	"Non-financial fixed assets that do not have physical substance but are identifiable and are controlled by the entity through custody or legal rights" (ASB 1997: § 2)
"By opposition"	Austria, France, Germany	Fixed assets other than tangible or financial
"Tautological"	Switzerland	"Intangible assets are non-monetary without physical substance" (ARR No. 9, Intangible Assets)
"Tautological"	Canada	"An intangible asset is an asset, other than a financial asset, that lacks physical substance" (new Section 3062 of the CICA Handbook)
"List based"	Belgium	1 R&D expenditures 2 Licenses, patents, know-how, trademarks, franchises, and similar rights 3 Goodwill 4 Advance payments on intangible assets (Royal Decree, 8 October 1976)
"List based"	Italy	Separate line items in the balance sheet for: 1 Start-up and expansion costs 2 Research, development, and advertising costs 3 Rights for industrial patents and rights for the exploitation of intellectual properties 4 Concessions, licenses, trademarks, and similar rights 5 Goodwill 6 Intangible fixed assets in progress and payments on account 7 Others

Main categories of intangibles

Intangible assets are usually divided in three categories: research and development (R&D), goodwill, and other intangible assets.

Research and development

In certain circumstances, R&D expenses may be capitalized, i.e., recorded as an asset. This topic will be developed in the second part of this chapter.

Goodwill

The term goodwill has two somewhat different meanings depending on whether it is reported in unconsolidated or consolidated financial statements:

- Some countries' GAAP recognize a "purchased goodwill" in the unconsolidated financial statements that is essentially reputed to represent the value of the acquired customer base of the enterprise. Although this goodwill is reported in unconsolidated financial statements, it is also frequently reported in consolidated financial statements.

- In the consolidated financial statements, goodwill represents any excess of the cost of the acquisition over the acquirer's interest in the fair value of the identifiable assets and liabilities acquired as of the date of the exchange transaction. The calculation of this goodwill in the consolidated financial statements is presented in Chapter 13.

In the consolidated financial statements, many companies make the distinction between these two categories of goodwill and report two different figures. The first one is often referred to as "goodwill" or "purchased goodwill" while the latter is often called "consolidation goodwill". For example, Interbrew, the Belgian brewery group, discloses within intangible assets (€49.4m – see Table 8.1) a goodwill for €8.3m and, in a separate caption, a goodwill (on consolidation) for €1,368m.

Other intangible assets

Patent

A patent is a document granted by a government or an official authority bestowing on the inventor of a product or manufacturing process the exclusive right to use or sell the invention or rights to it. The duration of the protection offered by a patent varies between countries (17 years in the USA, 20 in France, etc.). A patent cannot be renewed, but obtaining a new patent on modifications and improvements to the original invention may extend its effective life.

Trademark

A trademark (or trade name or brand or brand name) is a distinctive identification (symbol, logo, design, word, slogan, emblem, etc.) of a manufactured product or of a service that distinguishes it from similar products or services provided by third parties. Legal protection for trademarks is usually granted by registration with a specialized office. This registration is effective for an initial duration which varies from country to country (20 years in the USA, 10 years in France, and so on) and which can be renewed periodically for the same period under specified conditions.

Copyright

A copyright provides the holder with exclusive rights to the publication, production, and sale of the rights for an intellectual creation be it a musical, artistic, literary, or dramatic work (and often, by extension, software). Usually, the protection is granted during the life of the author plus 50 years.

Franchises

A franchise is a contractual agreement that allows, for a fee and within a limited geographical territory, the holder (franchisee), with or without direct support from the franchisor, to sell certain products or services, to use certain trademarks, or to do other specific things identified in the franchise agreement without loss of ownership over these by the franchisor.

Licensing agreements

A licensing agreement allows a company to use properties or rights owned by other entities. It applies specifically to patents and trademarks.

Organization (or set-up) costs

Organization costs (incorporation or set-up costs) are the costs incurred during the process of establishing or incorporating a business. They include incorporation fees, legal fees (e.g., for the writing of by-laws or articles of incorporation), underwriting fees, accounting fees, and promotional fees. Some countries allow these costs to be recorded as intangible assets. In this case they must be amortized over a fairly short period (up to 5 years) generally using a straight-line approach.

Example: Albeniz NA was created on 1 January 20X1. Organization costs total 200 CU. The manager decides to amortize these costs over four years. Figure 8.4 describes the accounting entries.

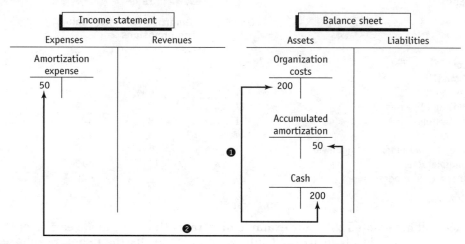

❶ Payment of organization costs
❷ Amortization: 200/4 years = 50

Figure 8.4 Accounting for organization costs

Computer software costs

Under certain circumstances, computer software can be considered as an "intangible asset". (See more on this point in "Advanced Issues".)

Deferred charges (deferred assets)

Deferred charges are sometimes considered to be intangible assets. They are conceptually identical to prepaid or deferred expenses but they have longer term economic benefits and must therefore be recognized over several periods to be coherent with the matching principle. Examples of such deferred charges are debt issuance costs or fixed assets acquisition costs (when they are not included in the cost of the asset). This category is often used as a catch-all by accountant for items hard to classify anywhere else. Deferred charges, therefore, deserve significant attention on the part of any user of financial information to understand what is actually covered in this category.

Transfer fees

In the UK, for instance, incorporated football clubs are allowed, although not required, to reflect the value of their players on their balance sheets and to amortize them over the length of their contracts. Until recently, these clubs could only charge transfer fees against profits in the year they occurred.

Real-life examples

Club Méditerranée
(France – French GAAP – Source: Annual report 1999 – Leisure)

This company provides for an interesting detail of its intangible assets.
Note 2.2 to the consolidated financial statements

FRF millions	31 Oct. 1999		
	Cost	Amortization and provisions	Net value
Start-up costs	19	7	12
Aquarius brand	150	150	0
Jet Tours brand	150	0	150
Other brands and licenses	17	8	9
Reservation system	351	228	123
Other software	144	38	106
Leasehold rights and purchased goodwill	53	7	46
Other intangible assets	29	16	13
Intangible assets in progress	20		20
	933	454	479

The reader will have noted that this example illustrates the point made earlier of the existence of two kinds of goodwill. Club Méditerranée distinguishes purchased goodwill (which is included in the note) from consolidation goodwill (which is mentioned in Table 8.1 and does not appear in note 2.2 which only deals with intangible assets other than consolidation goodwill).

EVN (Energie vernünftig nutzen)
(Austria – IAS GAAP – Source: Annual report 1998/99 – Energy – gas – heating)

Notes to financial statements

Other intangible assets [see Table 8.1] include electricity procurement rights, transportation rights on natural gas pipelines, and other rights, in particular software licenses.

Saint-Gobain

(France – French GAAP – Source: Annual report 1999 – Glass industry)

Note 1 to the consolidated financial statements

Other intangible assets [see Table 8.1] are represented by purchased goodwill, trademarks, patent, computer software and debt issuance costs.

Here again, purchased goodwill is distinguished from consolidation goodwill (which was mentioned in Table 8.1). The inclusion of debt issuance costs should be noticed.

Volvo Group

(Sweden – Swedish GAAP – Source: Annual report 1999 – Car industry)

Intangible assets (31 December 1999)(net amounts)	In millions of Swedish kroner (SEK)
Goodwill	6,929
Entrance fees, aircraft engine programs	1,293
Other intangible assets	1,727
Total	9,949

The second item in the list of intangible assets is relatively rare and is directly connected to the industrial activity of Volvo Group.

Interbrew

(Belgium – Belgian GAAP – Source: Annual report 1999 – Brewery group)

Note 3 to the consolidated financial statements

Intangible assets [see Table 8.1] include mainly supply rights and computer software. Since 1999 this caption also includes the consideration paid to acquire the internet domain Beer.com. All subsequent redesign and development costs were expensed as incurred.

Pirelli

(Italy – Italian GAAP – Source: Annual report 1999 – Tires, cables and systems)

The detail of intangible assets is given directly in the balance sheet (see Table 8.1). The notes provide for information on the nature of the items, which require such an explanation:

- Formation costs: capital increase costs of consolidated companies.
- Goodwill: amount paid for this purpose by the group companies for the acquisition of companies or other corporate transactions. [purchased goodwill.]
- Consolidation difference. [consolidation goodwill.]
- Other intangible assets: applied software acquisition costs, leasehold improvements, image awareness costs benefiting future periods, loan acquisition costs.

Repsol YPF

(Spain – Spanish GAAP – Source: Annual report 1999 – Oil and gas)

According to notes 2 and 4 to the consolidated financial statements, intangible assets include:

● Goodwill [purchased – the consolidation goodwill is reported separately – see Table 8.1].
● Transfer, easement and usage rights:
  – Costs relating to contracts for purchase of service station management rights and of usage and surface rights related to these assets.
  – Exclusive rights to use gas pipelines.
● Other intangible assets: costs relating to computer software, intellectual property, and administrative concessions.

Telecom Italia

(Italy – Italian GAAP – Source: Annual report 1999 – Telecommunications)

Parent company Intangible assets (31 December 1999) (net amounts)	In millions of Italian lire
Industrial patents, and intellectual property rights	1,192,288
Permits, licenses, trademarks, and similar rights	112,598
Goodwill	3,800
Work in progress and advances	740,383
Other	209,545
Total	2,258,614

Notes to the financial statements provide for the following additional information:

● Permits, licenses, trademarks, and similar rights refer mainly to the rights for the use of satellites.
● Goodwill: This item refers to the residual amount of goodwill paid by the company in connection with the acquisition of the Video On Line business segment from Exol.
● Work in progress and advances: They mainly represent the capitalization of costs incurred for software development projects currently in progress associated with network applications and administrative programming.
● The item Other consists primarily of:
  – Leasehold improvements: costs incurred to adapt leased properties to the company's operating needs.
  – Rights of transmission guarantee the extension of the transmission capacity of the company over a foreign territory.
  – "Great Jubilee 2000" includes the costs incurred to obtain the exclusive TLC provider rights for "Great Jubilee 2000".

Recognition of intangible assets

Different accounting principles favor or oppose recognition of intangible assets.

> **Matching principle**: The recognition of intangible assets allows their amortization over the period during which economic benefits are derived.
>
> **Prudence principle**: Since economic benefits derived from intangible assets are uncertain, the cost should be expensed in the period when incurred.

The recognition of intangible assets is the result of an informativeness trade-off between relevance and reliability or conservatism and prudence (see Høegh-Krohn and Knivsflå, 2000). Accounting standards in local GAAP generally provide recognition criteria for each of the three categories of intangible assets: research and development costs (R), goodwill (G), and other intangible assets (O).

Figure 8.5 illustrates the possibilities of recognizing (R) or not recognizing (NR) intangible assets.

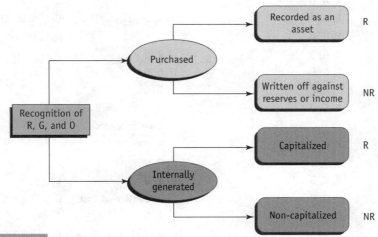

Figure 8.5 Recognition of intangible assets

Recognition policies are not the same for purchased and for internally generated intangible assets. Table 8.3 shows the distinction of recognition criteria for R&D costs, goodwill, and other intangible assets. Some local GAAP standards leave the choice of capitalization or expensing optional. Therefore Table 8.3 shows, when appropriate, the same item in both columns to reflect optionality.

Writing off goodwill against reserves in business combinations, which was exceptional, is no longer supported by the IASC, and is therefore more rarely recommended in national GAAPs. Denmark, Germany, the Netherlands, and Switzerland are the only remaining European countries allowing goodwill to be written off against reserves. The United Kingdom, a proponent for many years of goodwill write-off, has reversed its position and standard FRS 10 (adopted in 1997 by the ASB) disallows this possibility.

Appendix 8.2 illustrates another possible classification of intangibles on the basis of recognition criteria. Once recognized in the balance sheet, the crucial matter of reporting changes in the value of intangibles needs to be addressed.

Table 8.3 Intangibles recognized

Countries and organizations	Purchased intangibles		Internally generated intangibles	
	Recorded as an asset	Written-off against reserves or income	Capitalized	Non-capitalized
IASC (IAS 38)	R, G, O		D, O	R, G
European Union	R, G, O	R (research), G	R, O	G
Australia	R, G, O		R, O	G
Austria	R, G, O			R, G, O
Belgium	R, G, O		R, O	G
Canada	R, G, O		D	R, G
Denmark	R, G, O	G	D	R, G, O
Finland	R, G, O		R, O	G
France	R, G, O		R, O (software)	G, O (brands)
Germany	R, G, O	G		R, G, O
Greece	R, G, O	G	R, O	G
Ireland	R, G, O		D, O	R, G
Italy	R, G, O		D, O	R, G
Japan	R, G, O		O, D (classified as deferred assets)	R, G
Luxembourg	R, G, O		R, O	G
Netherlands	R, G, O	G	R, O	G
Norway	R, G, O		R, O	G
Portugal	R, G, O		R, O (start-up costs)	G
Spain	R, G, O		R, O	G
Sweden	R, G, O		R, O	G
Switzerland	R, G, O	G	D, O	R, G
UK	R, G, O		D, O	R, G
USA	R, G, O		O (namely software)	R, G

R = R&D costs; D = Only development costs (some countries and organizations make the difference between research and development costs); G = Goodwill; O = Other intangible assets

Reporting of changes in intangible assets value

As seen in Chapter 7, the process of allocation of the cost of an intangible asset over its useful life is called amortization instead of depreciation.

Different possibilities of changes in intangible assets value

Four possibilities for reporting changes in value of intangible assets exist and are summarized in Figure 8.6. Either the asset cost is amortized, its cost remains unchanged over time (no amortization), or a decrease in value is recognized through impairment. A revaluation based on the fair value of the intangible asset is allowed by some countries' GAAPs and represents the fourth possibility of recording a change in value of intangible assets.

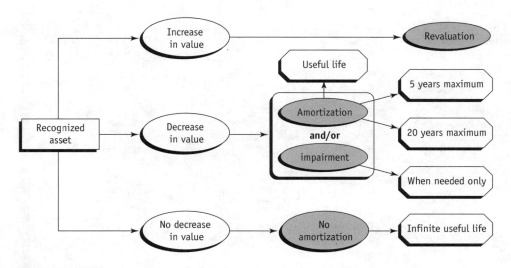

Figure 8.6 Treatment of changes in value

Duration and practices of amortization, when the method is allowed, vary between countries, rendering international comparisons often difficult without considerable rework. Some local GAAPs simply indicate that amortization must be recorded over the useful life of the asset without any further specification; others require amortization over the useful life up to an upper limit (5 or 20 years)[1] (see Table 8.4).

The large majority of countries require some form of amortization of intangible assets once they have been capitalized. Table 8.4 shows that the most common rule is to amortize the assets over their expected useful life, often subject to a legal maximum duration. In the USA, the Statement of Financial Accounting Standard No. 142, Goodwill and Other Intangible assets, adopted in June 2001, abolished amortization over 40 years and replaced it by an impairment test. The same modification has been adopted in Canada. The new regulation should be implemented in the majority of cases in 2002.

The impairment approach, in addition to amortization, put forward by the IASC (IAS 36 and 38) has been adopted by some countries such as the Netherlands for goodwill only, and Canada, Ireland, the UK, and the USA for goodwill and other intangibles. The conditions leading to an acknowledgment of an impairment of the asset may vary. For example, IAS 36 (IASC 1998a) requires that the recoverable amount of an asset be compared to the book value (carrying amount). In addition, IAS 38 (IASC 1998b) prescribes an impairment test when the amortization period exceeds 20 years. Despite the restrictive image given by Table 8.4, countries that have not "officially" adopted a rule on

Table 8.4 Treatment of decrease and increase in value (capitalized intangibles)[2]

Countries and organizations	Decrease in value[3]				No decrease in value	Increase in value
	Amortization			Impairment	No amortization	Revaluation
	Useful life	Max. 5 years	Max. 20 years		Unlimited useful life	
IASC	D, G, O		D, G, O	D, G, O		0[4]
European Union	R, G, O	R, G			0	
Australia	R, 0		G		0	0
Austria	0, G					
Belgium	R, G, O	R, G			R, G, O	
Canada	D			G, 0		
Denmark	D, G, O	D, G, O				
Finland		R, G	R, G, 0[5]			
France	0	R, G[6]			G, brands	
Germany	G, 0					
Greece	0	R, G, O				
Ireland	D, G, O			G, 0	G, 0	0[7]
Italy		D, G, 0[8]				
Japan	0	D, G	G[9]			
Luxembourg	R, G, 0[10]	R, G				
Netherlands	0	R, G[11]		G		
Norway	R, G, O	R, G				
Portugal	G, 0	R, G				
Spain	0	R	G[12]			
Sweden	R, G, O	R, G, O	G[13]			
Switzerland	R, G, O			R, G, O		
UK	D, G, O			G, 0	G, 0	0[14]
USA				G, 0		

R = R&D costs; D = Only development costs; G = Goodwill; 0 = Other intangible assets. If for a given country or organization, both the "useful life" column and a maximum duration column are marked, this means that the country or organization concerned amortizes the intangible asset over its useful life, subject to an upper limit which may be exceeded if relevant justification is disclosed in the notes

impairment generally have some form of an equivalent concept. It may take a different form (e.g., additional write-off) and it may not be specific to intangibles, but there is often a lower of cost and market rule for intangible assets. It is also important to remember that amortization and impairment are not exclusive concepts. Contrariwise, impairment can be added to amortization if the latter does not keep pace with the evolution of the fair market value of the asset.

In addition to the IASC, only Ireland, the UK, and Australia's GAAP specifically allow the revaluation of intangible assets.

Club Méditerranée

(France – French GAAP – Source: Annual report 1999 – Leisure)

Note 1.3.1 to the financial statements

Amortization is charged by the straight-line method over the following estimated useful lives:

- Computerized reservation system software: 12 years.
- Travel management module: 6 years.
- Financial information system: 6 years.
- Other purchased software: 5 years.
- Other intangible assets: 3 to 10 years.

Brands are not amortized but provisions are made for any impairment in value.

The different intangible assets are presented above. For example, with regard to impairment of brands, the Aquarius brand (worth 150 FRFm) was written down in full in fiscal 1997 following the decision to rebrand the Aquarius villages.

Saint-Gobain

(France – French GAAP – Source: Annual report 1999 – Glass industry)

We read in note 1 to the consolidated financial statements that trademarks other than retail are amortized on a straight-line basis over a period not exceeding 40 years. Retail trademarks are not amortized. Patents are amortized over their useful estimated lives not exceeding 20 years.

Debt issuance costs incurred in connection with issuance of debt securities or other long-term borrowings are capitalized as an asset and amortized over the term of the debt.

Repsol YPF

(Spain – Spanish GAAP – Source: Annual report 1999 – Oil and gas)

According to notes 2 and 4 to the consolidated financial statements, the following periods are adopted:

Purchased goodwill	10 years, the average years of useful life of the facilities
Contracts for purchase of service management rights	Related contract terms (from 15 to 25 years)
Exclusive rights to use gas pipelines	Term of the related right (currently 25 years)
Computer software and intellectual property	From 4 to 10 years
Administrative concessions	Concession term

BT (British Telecommunications)

(UK – UK GAAP – Source: Annual report 1999 – Telecommunications)

Note VI to the consolidated financial statements

License fees paid to governments, which permit telecommunication activities to be operated for defined periods, are amortized from the later of the start of the license period or launch of service to the end of the license period on a straight-line basis.

Telecom Italia

(Italy – Italian GAAP – Source: Annual report 1999 – Telecommunications)

Extracts from the notes to the parent company financial statements

- Industrial patents and intellectual property rights are amortized – over their estimated period of benefit – on a 5-year basis (industrial patents) or on a 3-year basis (software), starting from the year of their initial use.
- Permits, licenses, trademarks, and similar rights are amortized on the straight-line method on the basis of the useful life of the satellites.
- Goodwill is amortized in 5 years starting from the year in which the cost was incurred.
- Others:
  - Leasehold improvements: amortization calculated on the basis of the remaining duration of the lease contracts.
  - Rights of transmission: amortization over the period of the contracts entered with the foreign operators who own the installation to which the rights refer.
  - Exclusive rights to the "Great Jubilee 2000": amortization up to the expiration of the right (30 June 2001).

EVN (Energie vernünftig nutzen)

(Austria – IAS GAAP – Source: Annual report 1998/99 – Energy, gas, heating)

According to different notes to the financial statements, the electricity procurement rights at third-party power stations were subject to extraordinary depreciation resulting from the very significant pressure on electricity prices due to the deregulation of the electricity market. This depreciation was computed in accordance with IAS 36 (IASC 1998a). Its amount (990,396 thousands of ATS) represents 8% of sales revenues and should be related to the net income of 342,665 thousands of ATS.

Accounting for research and development

Definition

IAS 38 (IASC 1998b: § 7) states that:

(a) Research is "original and planned investigation undertaken with the prospect of gaining new scientific or technical knowledge and understanding". Examples of research activities are:

- activities aimed at obtaining new knowledge
- the search for, evaluation and final selection of, applications of research findings or other knowledge
- the search for alternatives for materials, devices, products, processes, systems, or services
- the formulation, design, evaluation, and final selection of possible alternatives for new or improved materials, devices, products, processes, systems, or services.

(b) Development is "the application of research findings or other knowledge to a plan or design for the production of new or substantially improved materials, devices, products, processes, systems or services prior to the commencement of commercial production or use". Examples of development activities include:

- the design, construction, and testing of pre-production or pre-use prototypes and models
- the design of tools, jigs, molds and dies involving new technology
- the design, construction, and operation of a pilot plant that is not of a scale economically feasible for commercial production
- the design, construction, and testing of a chosen alternative for new or improved materials, devices, products, processes, systems, or services.

Some countries distinguish fundamental and applied research within the category of research and development and recommend differentiated reporting:

- Pure research is experimental or theoretical work undertaken primarily to acquire new scientific or technical knowledge for its own sake rather than directed towards any specific aim or application.
- Applied research is original or critical investigation undertaken in order to gain new scientific or technical knowledge and directed towards a specific practical aim or objective.

Accounting for R&D

The default position, because of the prudence principle, is to expense research and development costs when incurred. However, under certain circumstances and if specified criteria are met, some development (and applied research – when the distinction is made) costs may be capitalized and recorded as an intangible asset.

Conditions for capitalization

Table 8.5 summarizes the seven necessary criteria stated in the IASC standards that must be met if capitalization is to be preferred over expensing. Each country standard for capitalization can be defined, as shown in Table 8.6, as a specific mix of the seven IASC conditions.

Table 8.5 Conditions of R&D capitalization

(1) Identifiability	• The projects concerned are clearly identifiable • A detailed description has been made of the product and process • The R&D work and the expenditures accrued on the work shall be well defined and the R&D work should have a fixed application
(2) Evaluation	• Their respective costs are distinctly evaluated in order to be allocated over time • Costs to be allocated are determinable • Ability to measure the expenditure attributable to the intangible asset during its development
(3) Technical feasibility	• Proof exists of technical feasibility of the product or process • The technical feasibility of the product or process has been established • The technical feasibility of completing the intangible asset so that it will be available for use or sale
(4) Commercial success	• Each project has a serious chance of commercial success at the date of closing of financial statements • The new product or process will be introduced in the market • There is a clear market potential or other beneficial use • The enterprise should demonstrate the existence of a market for the output of the intangible asset • Ability to use or sell the intangible asset
(5) Future economic benefits	• It will generate future economic benefits over several years
(6) Financial feasibility	• The development process can be completed (i.e., is financially feasible) • There must be resources both for the completion of the R&D work and for the marketing of the product or process if it is intended for sale • Adequate resources exist, or are expected to be available, to complete the project
(7) Intention to complete	• Intention to complete the intangible asset and use or sell it

Table 8.6 Examples of countries and conditions

Country/organization	Conditions
Canada	(1) (2) (3) (4) (6)
Denmark	(1) (5)
France	(1) (2) (4)
Ireland/UK	(1) (2) (3) (4) (5) (6)
Netherlands	(1) (2) (3) (4) (6)
Sweden	(1) (3) (4) (5) (6)
Switzerland	(1) (2) (5) (6)
IASC	(1) (2) (3) (4) (5) (6) (7)

Arguments for capitalization of R&D

Many users of financial statements (financial analysts and banks being among the most vocal) see capitalization of R&D as a grave violation of the prudence principle (see Chapter 5). Any position on the subject is therefore controversial. Arguments for and against are traded by both sides, arguing matching versus prudence.

Arguments in favor

R&D expenses, in case of a favorable outcome, should be related to future periods when the benefits will accrue (matching principle). Therefore, R&D expenses should be accrued (capitalized) and not expensed immediately.

Arguments against

Future economic benefits potentially derived from R&D are not sufficiently objectively defined or certain to flow to the enterprise at the time the expense is incurred to justify capitalization. The principle of prudence militates therefore in favor of expensing R&D costs as incurred.

The impact of capitalization

Let us take an example. Albeniz NA has incurred a development cost for a total amount of 150 CU (80 for labor expenses and 70 of depreciation expense for equipment and facilities used in carrying the development project). The manager of Albeniz NA has decided to capitalize the expenditure and to amortize it over the next 5 years as she feels the economic benefits will be derived for that period. Figure 8.7 illustrates the accounting entries required to record the first year of the project.

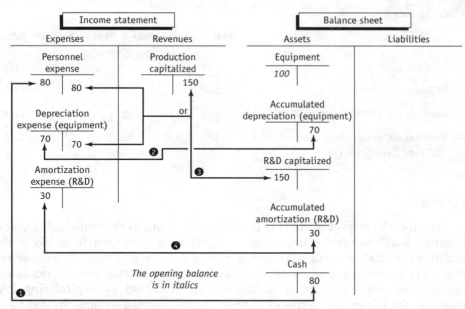

Entries ❶ and ❷ record the cost of the development project. If the conditions for capitalization are met, the total cost of the project is transferred to the asset side of the balance sheet (❸)
Two solutions are available in order to carry out this transfer:
- cancel (through a credit entry) the original expense accounts (labour expense and depreciation expense)
- create (through a credit entry) a revenue account (production capitalized)
 Each country GAAP recommends either one, and on a large sample of countries neither seems to show dominance
❹ Amortization is calculated on the basis of a useful life of 5 years (150/5 = 30)

Figure 8.7 Accounting for R&D

The impact of capitalization on the bottom line can be broken down as shown in Table 8.7.

Table 8.7   Simulation: Impact of capitalization

		Simulation 1 R&D expensed	Simulation 2 R&D capitalized
Net income before R&D		500	500
R&D expenses	Personnel expense	−80	−80
	Depreciation expense	−70	−70
Net income after R&D expenses		350	350
Capitalization of R&D		0	150
Net income after R&D capitalized		350	500
Amortization of R&D capitalized		0	−30
Net income		350	470
Differential net income due to treatment of R&D		+ 120	

The impact on net income of the choice of method for handling R&D over the amortization period shown in Table 8.8.

Table 8.8   Impact on net income over the period

	Year 1	Year 2	Year 3	Year 4	Year 5	Total
R&D expensed (1)	−150					−150
R&D capitalized (2)	+150					+150
Amortization of R&D capitalized (3)	−30	−30	−30	−30	−30	−150
Total impact of capitalization (versus R&D expensed) (2) + (3)	+120	−30	−30	−30	−30	0

Comments

In practice, the impact of R&D is more complex than in this simple illustration because R&D is rarely limited to a one-time project and it is likely that additional R&D costs will be incurred in year 2 and capitalized (to be coherent) and thus amortized, and so on. A business whose bottom line is not exactly prosperous may be tempted to improve its situation by capitalizing R&D expenses for the sole objective of improving the reported income. In this case it might find itself in a vicious circle: the annual amount of cumulated R&D amortization expense (on past projects) might become so large that the capitalization of the year's R&D expense might be needed for the sole purpose of offsetting the amortization of the previous year's R&D costs. In such a situation, the only sane issue is to stop capitalizing altogether, even if it leads to reporting significant losses in the first years after the decision.

Reporting R&D activity

R&D costs are an essential investment in the growth, profitability, and ability to remain a going concern. It should therefore be essential to report their amount as accurately and truthfully as possible, in all parts, financial and non-financial of the annual statements.

Income statement by function

The income statement presentation by function (Chapter 3) is the only one in which R&D expenses can be reported as such. The following examples show that three possibilities are used by companies:

- "R&D expenses" reported as a separate function, item or line
- R&D is not identified as such but is included in another function, such as selling, general and administrative expenses (e.g., Saint Gobain)
- R&D is not reported as such but since it is expensed as incurred, it becomes a part of the cost of goods sold (e.g., Sandvik).

Real-life examples

Taylor Nelson Sofres

(UK – UK GAAP – Source: Annual report 1999 – Market information)

Development expenditure relating to certain specific projects intended for commercial use is capitalized and amortized over the period expected to benefit (5 years or remaining life if shorter). The capitalized net amount is unknown because it is included in a global "development expenditure and other" for £7.1m. However, the finance director's review provides the amount of capitalized development expenditure for 1999: £1.5m.

Sandvik

(Sweden – Swedish GAAP – Source: Annual report 1999 – Engineering)

Note 5. Research, development and quality assurance

SEKm	1999	1998
Costs for research and development	1,114	1,070
Costs for quality assurance	479	498
Total	1,593	1,568

All research, development and quality assurance costs are expensed as incurred. These costs are included in the cost of goods sold.

Bayer

(Germany – German/IAS GAAP – Source: Annual report 1999 – Pharmaceuticals, chemicals)

Note 2 to the consolidated financial statements

According to IAS 9 (research and development costs) [this standard has been superseded by IAS 38], research costs cannot be capitalized; development costs can only be capitalized if specific conditions are fulfilled. (…) As in previous years, these conditions are not satisfied.

Saint-Gobain

(France – French GAAP – Source: Annual report 1999 – Glass industry)

R&D costs are expensed as incurred and recorded in selling, general, and administrative expenses.

Accounting for computer software

Accounting rules

Reporting computer software costs has long been a debated issue but today's practice is stabilized along the lines described in Figure 8.8.

As can be expected, the most delicate issue is deciding on the accounting treatment of internally developed software for use by the developing firm itself. The costs that can be capitalized in this case vary between countries (see an illustration in Appendix 8.3).

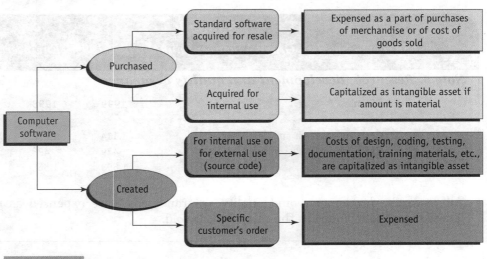

Figure 8.8 Accounting for computer software

Reporting computer software costs

Table 8.9 provides some examples of notes relating to computer software issues (excerpted from year 1999 annual reports).

Table 8.9 Examples of reporting for computer software

Company	Type of software and comments	Period of amortization
Bayer (Germany – German/IAS GAAP)	Purchased software	4
Bull (France – French/US GAAP)	Intangible assets (see Table 8.1) mainly include capitalized development costs for software products with identified markets which have reached a stage in their development at which there are no longer any major technical or commercial risks Capitalized development costs are amortized on a straight-line basis from the moment of capitalization over the estimated useful life of the product	3
Club Méditerranée (France – French GAAP)	Other purchased software The significant increase in other software between 1998 and 1999 corresponds to investments in the new accounting system and purchasing software, and transfers from intangible assets in progress of software development costs for the new accounting system	5
Philips (Netherlands – Dutch GAAP)	Beginning in 1999, computer software developed by Philips or purchased from third parties for the company's own use is capitalized and written off over its useful life	3
Saint-Gobain (France – French GAAP)	Purchased software	3 to 5

Financial statement analysis

Many financial analysts feel too many would-be-intangible assets are often omitted from the balance sheet due to "excessive" prudence on the part of accountants. As the economy is moving gradually into a knowledge-based, technology-intensive world, intangibles become ever more important in the competitive strategy of a firm. Investments in information technology, research and development, human resources, and advertising have become essential in order to strengthen the firm's competitive position and ensure its future viability (see Cañibano *et al*. 2000). Because some intangibles are not reflected in the balance sheet, a loss of relevance of accounting information has been highlighted by many studies and one evidence of this phenomenon is the gap existing between the book value and the market value of companies (Hope and Hope 1998; Lev and Zarowin 1999).

Among intangibles, R&D has received special attention on the part of financial analysts as it helps describe the effort of the firm to be innovative and build its future competence. Numerous academic studies (Lev and Sougiannis 1996, for example) have documented the positive relationship between a company's R&D investment and its market value both in the USA and in the UK.

Several ratios are often used in such evaluation, which we will explore further in turn. They are:

- R&D/sales, often called "R&D intensity".
- R&D/number of employees: R&D per employee.
- Annual growth rate of R&D [(R&D expenses year 2 – R&D expenses year 1)/R&D year 1].

R&D intensity

Table 8.10 provides some examples of R&D intensity based on 1999 annual reports.

Table 8.10 R&D intensity

Companies	Currency	R&D expenses	Sales	R&D/sales
Baltimore Technologies (UK – security for e-commerce)	£000	7,243	23,272	31.1%
Roche (Switzerland – pharmaceuticals, chemicals)	CHFm	3,782	27,567	13.7%
Bull (France – IT group)	€m	186	1,740	10.7%
Bayer (Germany – chemicals, healthcare)	€m	2,141	27,320	7.8%
Procter & Gamble (USA)	$m	1,726	38,125	4.5%
Sandvik (Sweden – tools and engineering)	SEKm	1,114	39,300	2.8%
Saint-Gobain (France – glass and building materials)	€m	342	22,952	1.5%

Table 8.10 confirms that the R&D intensity is clearly a function of the line of business of the firm. In industries with short product-life cycle (Baltimore Tech or Bull) or gigantic relative steps in innovation (Roche or Bayer), the need to invest in R&D is much greater than it is in industries where products and processes have a long lifecycle and innovation is incremental (Sandvik or Saint Gobain, for example). The average R&D intensity for a sample of 300 international firms (R&D Scoreboard) reported by the UK Department of Trade and Industry (DTI) is 4.9% for 1999 with very large standard deviations both between and within countries (see further developments on this topic in Appendix 8.4).

Link between R&D and growth

Several surveys showed that R&D intensity is linked to subsequent sales growth. For instance, Morbey (1988) demonstrated that companies sustaining R&D investment over 4% of sales were particularly likely to achieve higher long-term growth. The R&D Scoreboard reaches the same conclusion with a limit of 2% for R&D intensity.

Link between R&D and market value

The success of the NASDAQ a few years ago has drawn attention to the market value of technology-based companies. Numerous academic studies (Lev and Sougiannis 1996) have showed the relationship between a company's R&D

investment and its market value both in the USA and in the UK. It is therefore quite important, in a spirit of true and fair view, to inform the shareholders of the R&D expenditures of their company.

KEY POINTS

- Intangible assets are long-lived (long-term) assets that lack physical substance and whose acquisition and continued possession represent rights to future economic benefits.
- Intangible assets comprise patents, franchises, licenses, trademarks, brands, copyrights, etc., and may include R&D costs if these are capitalized.
- It is very difficult to be objective in the valuation of intangible assets as their value may be a function of the firm's ability to use them.
- Intangible assets raise three major questions: (1) what is an intangible asset? (2) recognition/valuation?, and (3) how to treat a change in value?
- When purchased, intangibles are valued without any ambiguity; the valuation of internally generated intangibles is a highly debated issue among accountants and analysts.
- The choice of capitalization versus expensing is the result of a trade-off between the matching and the prudence principles.
- Intangible assets may be amortized and/or impaired over an appropriate horizon regulated by local GAAP.
- Research and development costs are usually expensed when incurred. However, under certain circumstances, some development expenses may be capitalized and recorded as an intangible asset if specified "capitalization criteria" are met.
- R&D intensity, R&D per employee, and R&D growth rate are ratios that help analysts and investors monitor the policies of a management team regarding its investment in the future.

REVIEW

Review 8.1 Turina

Topic: Various intangibles
Type: Individual exercise
Related part of the chapter: Advanced Issues

The following information is given by the head accountant of the Turina Company.

1 The Turina Company acquired a franchise on 1 July 20X3 by paying an initial franchise fee of 160,000 CU. The franchise term is 8 years.

2 The Turina Company incurred advertising expenses amounting to 300,000 CU related to various products. According to the marketing department, these expenses could generate revenues for approximately 4 years.

3 During 20X3, Turina incurred legal fees of 40,000 CU in connection with the unsuccessful defense of a patent. The patent had been acquired at the beginning of 20X2 for 150,000 CU and was being amortized over a 5-year period. As a result of the unsuccessful litigation, the patent was considered to be worthless at the end of year 20X3.

Required

Analyze each piece of information and show its impact on financial statements (or record the journal entries).

Solution

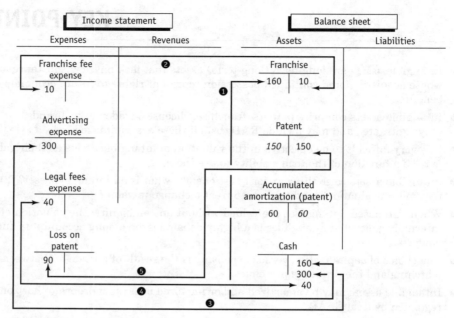

- ❶ Recording of the franchise as an intangible asset
- ❷ Franchise fee expense: 160 x 1/8 x 6 months
- ❸ The advertising expense is not considered an intangible asset
- ❹ The legal fees are recorded
- ❺ The patent and accumulated amortization accounts are canceled and a loss is recorded

Review 8.2 De Falla

Topic: Accounting for R&D
Type: Individual exercise
Related part of the chapter: Advanced Issues

During 20X1, the De Falla Company incurred the following costs in relation to its R&D activities (all figures in 000 of CU):

- Wages and salaries: 100.
- Supplies used from inventory: 20.
- Depreciation on building where R&D activities take place: 30.
- Depreciation on equipment specifically devoted to R&D: 50.
- Allocation of general and administrative expenses: 60.

Required

Assuming that the income statement is presented by function, show the impact of R&D on the financial statements.

Solution

Income statement		Balance sheet	
Expenses	Revenues	Assets	Liabilities

R&D expense
→ 260

Accumulated depreciation (building)
30 ←

Accumulated depreciation (equipment)
50 ←

Inventory
20 ←

Cash
100 ←
60 ←

All these expenses can be included in R&D expense. We assumed that wages and salaries, as well as general and administrative expenses, are paid in cash. "Payable" accounts could have been used instead of "cash".

ASSIGNMENTS

Assignment 8.1

Multiple-choice questions
Type: Individual exercise
Related part of the chapter: Core Issues

Select the right answer.

1   An example of an item that is not an intangible asset is

   (a) Patent
   (b) Goodwill
   (c) Computer
   (d) Computer software
   (e) Trademark

2   An example of a trademark which is capitalized is

   (a) The logo of a business school designed and created by the school
   (b) The Orangina trademark acquired by Pernod Ricard within the purchase of the whole Orangina company
   (c) The name "Oneworld", a group of airlines including American Airlines, British Airways, and Cathay Pacific
   (d) None of these

3 Albeniz company bought a patent for 100 (000 of CU) on 2 January 20X5. The legal life of the patent is 17 years. Albeniz estimated that the economic life of the patent is 5 years. What amount should be recognized for the year ended 31 December 20X5?

(a) Depreciation expense for 20
(b) Amortization expense for 5.88
(c) Depletion expense for 20
(d) Amortization expense for 20
(e) Depreciation expense for 5.88
(f) None of these

4 All recorded intangible assets are amortized

(a) True
(b) False

5 Albeniz company spent internally 500 (000 of CU) throughout 20X1 in promoting a not well-known trademark. This trademark is supposed to have an indefinite life. The company applies IAS GAAP in its financial statements. It should be

(a) Capitalized and amortized over 40 years
(b) Capitalized and not amortized
(c) Not capitalized and expensed in 20X1
(d) Capitalized and amortized over 20 years
(e) None of these

6 Same question as (5) but Albeniz applies US GAAP

(a) Capitalized and amortized over 40 years
(b) Capitalized and not amortized
(c) Not capitalized and expensed in 20X1
(d) Capitalized and amortized over 20 years
(e) None of these

7 Same question as (5) but Albeniz purchased the trademark and applies US GAAP

(a) Capitalized and amortized over 40 years
(b) Capitalized and not amortized
(c) Not capitalized and expensed in 20X1
(d) Capitalized and amortized over 20 years
(e) None of these

8 Training costs are

(a) Capitalized and amortized over 40 years
(b) Capitalized and not amortized
(c) Not capitalized and expensed
(d) Capitalized and amortized over 20 years
(e) None of these

9 Deferred assets are equivalent to

(a) Prepaid revenues
(b) Prepaid expenses
(c) Deferred tax assets
(d) Deferred revenues
(e) None of these

10 In IAS 38 of IASC (Intangible Assets), the limit of 20 years for amortization is a strict limit

(a) True
(b) False

Assignment 8.2

Discussion questions
Type: Group exercise
Related part of the chapter: Core/Advanced Issues

Required

1 Accounting for intangible assets. Discuss the choice between relevance versus reliability.

2 Goodwill. Discuss the choice between the different possible treatments (no amortization, amortization, impairment, immediate write-off).

3 Research and development costs. Discuss the choice between capitalization versus expensing.

Assignment 8.3

Topic: Reporting in different countries
Type: Group exercise
Related part of the chapter: Core/Advanced Issues

On the internet, or in the library, find the recent annual reports of four companies from different countries.

Required

1 How are intangible assets presented in the balance sheet? What decisions on the basis of this information can investors or shareholders take? What decisions would be difficult to take on the basis of just this information?

2 Are there any notes relating to intangible assets? How do they enlarge the decision analysis possibilities offered to shareholders and investors?

3 What are the accounting treatments applied to these assets?

Assignment 8.4

Topic: Searching for specific intangibles
Type: Group exercise
Related part of the chapter: Core Issues

Required

On the Web, or in the library, find recent illustrations or examples of industry specific intangible assets in the annual reports of four companies from different sectors of activity in a given country or in different countries (for example electricity procurement rights in the energy sector).

Assignment 8.5

Topic: R&D intensity
Type: Group exercise
Related part of the chapter: Advanced Issues

On the Web, or in the library, find the recent annual reports of 4 companies from sectors of activity in a given country or in different countries for which you anticipate R&D expenses may be quite important.

Required

Compare and contrast the firms in your sample.

1 Look for the data relating to R&D expenses and sales.
2 Compute the ratio R&D/sales.
3 Look for the data relating to the workforce.
4 Compute the ratio R&D/number of employees.

Assignment 8.6 CeWe Color*

Topic: Accounting for changes in intangibles
Type: Individual exercise
Related part of the chapter: Advanced Issues

CeWe Color is a German group operating in the development of films and color prints business. From the notes to the consolidated financial statements (annual report 1999), we extracted the following information (in thousands of €):

	Industrial property rights and similar rights	Goodwill
Change in consolidated group (depreciation)	6	326
Additions	800	0
Balance on 31.12.1999	4,083	20,528
Exchange rate adjustment	−3	−127
Depreciation	563	2,080
Disposals	142	0
Change in consolidated group	17	3,404
Amount carried forward 1.1.1999	3,411	17,251
Exchange rate adjustment (depreciation)	−2	0
Disposals (depreciation)	137	0
Balance on 31.12.1999 (depreciation)	3,036	6,905
Book value 31.12.1999	1,047	13,623
Amount carried forward 1.1.1999 (depreciation)	2,606	4,499

Required

1 From the information given, which is not presented in the right order, prepare a statement showing the movements in intangible assets, using the format presented in Chapter 7 for tangible assets.
2 Show which figures could be used as check figures in this exercise.

Assignment 8.7 Granados Company

Topic: Accounting for research and development
Type: Individual exercise
Related part of the chapter: Advanced Issues

Granados Company's accounting policies call for the expensing of R&D expenditures in the year incurred. The following table presents the amount of expenditures from Year 1 to Year 5.

Year 1	Year 2	Year 3	Year 4	Year 5
200	150	150	100	50

The managers of the company are considering modifying their accounting policies and capitalize R&D with an amortization over 5 years.

Required

1 Compute the impact of capitalization on net income for each year of the period.
2 Compute from which year the amount of amortization of past R&D will be at least equal to R&D expensed during the year.
3 What would you suggest to the managers of the company, with regard to possible modifications in accounting policies?

Assignment 8.8 Easynet*

Topic: Reporting for intangible assets
Type: Individual exercise
Related part of the chapter: Advanced Issues

Easynet, the British internet provider, reports in its financial statements for the year ended 31 December 1999 the following statement.

Tangible fixed assets

Depreciation on tangible fixed assets is provided on cost in equal annual installments over the estimated useful lives of the assets. The rates of depreciation used are as follows:

Leasehold improvements	Over the period of the lease
(...)	
Computer equipment	
– hardware	50% per annum
– software	33% per annum
(...)	

Required

Explain why this information is included in the "Tangible fixed assets" part of the notes?

References

ASB (1997) Financial Reporting Standard No. 10, Goodwill and Intangible Assets, London.

Cañibano, L., M. García-Ayuso, P., and Sánchez, M. (2000) Accounting for intangibles: A literature review. *Journal of Accounting Literature*, 19, 102–30.

FASB (2001) Statement of Financial Accounting Standards No. 142, Goodwill and Other Intangible Assets, Norwalk, CT.

Høegh-Krohn, N.E.J., and Knivsflå, K.H. (2000) Accounting for intangible assets in Scandinavia, the UK, the US, and by the IASC: Challenges and a Solution. *International Journal of Accounting*, 35 (2), 243–65.

Hope, T., and Hope, J. (1998) *Managing in the Third Wave*, Harvard Business Press, Cambridge, MA.

IASC (1998a) International Accounting Standard No. 36, Impairment of Assets, London.

IASC (1998b) International Accounting Standard No. 38, Intangible Assets, London.

Lev, B., and Sougiannis, T. (1996) The capitalization, amortization and value relevance of R&D. *Journal of Accounting and Economics*, 21, 107–38.

Lev, B., and Zarowin, P. (1999) The boundaries of financial reporting and how to extend them. *Journal of Accounting Research*, 37(2) (Autumn), 353–85.

Morbey G.K. (1988) R&D: Its relationship to company performance. *The Journal of Product Innovation Management*, 5(3), 191–201.

Further readings

Nixon, B. (1997) The accounting treatment of research and development expenditure: Views of UK company accountants. *European Accounting Review*, 6(2), 265–77.

Power, M. (1992) The politics of brand accounting in the United Kingdom. *European Accounting Review*, 1(1), 39–68.

Stolowy, H., Haller, A., and Klockhaus, V. (2001) Accounting for brands in France and Germany compared with IAS 38 (intangible assets) – An illustration of the difficulty of international harmonization. *International Journal of Accounting*, 36(2), 147–67.

Stolowy, H., and Jeny-Cazavan, A. (2001) International accounting disharmony: The case of intangibles. *Accounting, Auditing and Accountability Journal*, 14(4), 477–96.

Additional material on the website

Go to http://www.thomsonlearning.co.uk/accountingandfinance/stolowylebas for further information, journal entries and extra assigments for each chapter.

The following appendices to this chapter are available on the dedicated website:

Appendix 8.1: Definition of intangibles in accounting standards
Appendix 8.2: Another classification of intangibles
Appendix 8.3: Accounting for computer software
Appendix 8.4: R&D intensity

Notes

1 Forty years in the USA and Canada, before the regulation was modified in 2001.

2 When rules allow several alternatives or specify exceptions, the most frequently used practice is the one reported here.

3 We call this category by simplification "decrease in value" knowing that the amortization is not, strictly speaking, a decrease in value, but a cost allocation.

4 Reference to an active market.

5 Five years is the main rule.

6 Goodwill on consolidation can be amortized over longer than 5 years (no specified rule).

7 Only in rare cases ("readily ascertainable market value").

8 For goodwill, it is possible to increase this period "slightly" provided that this increased length does not exceed the period of use of the asset.

9 Consolidation goodwill (consolidation adjustment account).

10 Plus incorporation costs.

11 Goodwill on consolidation can be amortized over longer than 5 years.

12 Twenty years (new law dated 16 November 1998, effective 1 January 1999). No amortization rules mentioned for patents and trademarks.

13 Five years is the main rule.

14 Only in rare cases ("readily ascertainable market value").

Inventories

Inventories are a critical asset in the operating cycle of many organizations. An inventory helps in the application of the matching principle. An inventory is akin to a storage tank that can release its content (the costs) when certain triggering events take place. For example, as long as a product has not been sold, all costs attached to it are withheld from the income statement. They are temporarily stored in an inventory which is an asset, i.e., a potential source of future economic benefits.

Even if, in a world of just in time, the role of inventories is decreasing as a management tool for adjusting the needs of cost minimization and production smoothing to the randomness or seasonality of demand, inventories still create significant issues in reporting to shareholders: (a) inventories represent an immobilization of funds (required to finance the inventory), and (b) the choice of how to attach costs to objects held in inventory before their sale affects profit. It is therefore important to examine how inventories are recorded and reported[1].

The three major issues relating to accounting for inventories valuation are shown in Figure 9.1. They are: periodicity of recording, costing of inflows and outflows, and valuation adjustments.

Major topics

Classification

Recording systems

Costing inventory movements

Cash flow

Decline in value

Income statement format

Disclosures

Financial statement analysis

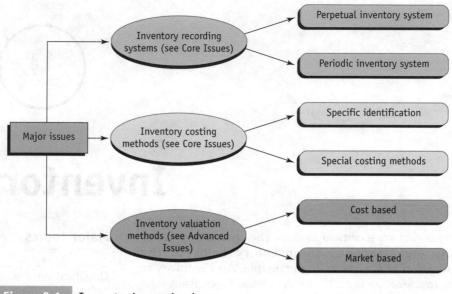

Figure 9.1 Inventories major issues

CORE ISSUES

Classification of inventories

Definition

According to IAS 2 (IASC 1993: § 4), "inventories are assets:

(a) held for sale in the ordinary course of business;

(b) in the process of production for such sale; or

(c) in the form of materials or supplies to be consumed in the production process or in the rendering of services."

Different types of inventory

Figure 9.2 illustrates the six basic types of inventories found on a balance sheet, each reflecting a different degree of saleability of the items it contains.

In Figure 9.2, the four inventory types shown in tinted boxes are the closest to the customer. They represent potential sales and it is only a question of time until these inventories can be turned into receivables or cash. By way of contrast the bottom two types of inventories represent items that are not potentially sellable in the condition in which they are held. They require either integration in the products themselves (raw materials and supplies) or being

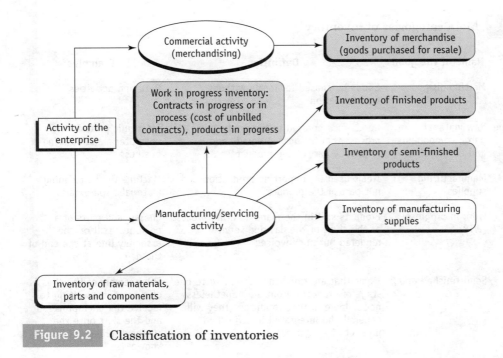

Figure 9.2 Classification of inventories

used in the production process or in the equipment that contributes to production (supplies).

Many businesses, as mentioned in Chapter 6, report in a single line their work in progress and their contracts in progress even though they are not of the same nature. Work in progress measures the value of the resources attached to items that are still left in the process of production on the closing date. Normally work in progress should be pretty small, equating at most less than half a day of production.

Contract(s) in progress (see Chapter 6) can legitimately represent large amounts since that item on the balance sheet measures the amount of resources consumed in realizing all or part of a (long-term) contract but for which no invoicing has been issued to the customer. If invoicing takes place, for example, every four months up to the cost of four months of production may be listed under contract in progress. As soon as an invoice is issued, all corresponding resources (application of the matching principle and subject to long-term contract rules) are carried, as cost of goods sold, to the income statement.

Although the terms "in progress" (UK usage) and "in process" (North American usage) are clearly interchangeable as already mentioned, we will use the first one (which is adopted by IASC). The reader will take solace in the fact that most of the time the initials WIP are used to refer to either of these items.

Table 9.1 presents and illustrates the various categories of inventory.

Weight of inventories in the balance sheet

Inventories sometimes represent a large portion of assets and therefore their correct valuation is essential for reporting shareholders' equity. The larger the proportion of total assets is represented by inventories, the more important it is to correctly estimate the physical inventory and its value.

Table 9.1 Main categories of inventory[2]

Activity	Name of the goods	Definition	Examples
Commercial activity	Merchandise	Goods purchased for resale without transformation	Retailing activities
Manufacturing activity	Raw materials, parts, components and consumables	Goods incorporated in the production process that become integrally and physically part of the product	Electronic parts in the computer manufacturing business
	Manufacturing supplies	Items used in supporting production and not part of the product	Machine fluids, cleaning materials, spare parts
	Work in progress (WIP)	Products still in the manufacturing process at the close of the day and services rendered but not invoiced	Chassis and parts of a computer still on the assembly line at the end of the day
	Semi-finished goods	Items that are finished with regard to one stage of production but are nonetheless not sellable in that condition. They will generally be integrated in a finished product at a later date	Subassembly of the chassis of a computer waiting to receive the microprocessor and the skirt once the customer order will be known
	Finished goods	Completed products ready for sale	Computers ready to be shipped
Service activity	Work in progress	Accumulated costs incurred in fulfilling a contract and not yet billed	Consultancy, law office, engineering firm

Real-life examples

Siemens

(Germany – German GAAP – Source: Annual report 1999 – Energy, industry components, automotive systems, information and communication products)

Excerpts from the notes to the consolidated balance sheet

Inventories (millions of DM)	30 Sep. 1999
Materials and supplies	3,020
Work in process	6,217
Finished products and merchandise	6,217
Cost of unbilled contracts	17,095
Advances to suppliers	1,716
Total inventories	34,265

Reasonable allowances of 3,509 millions of DM were provided for the net realizable values associated with long-term contracts and for inventory risks due to slow-moving items and technical obsolescence.

Comments

- The amounts in the notes are net of allowances for provisions (see Chapter 5 and Advanced Issues of this chapter).

- Finished products and merchandise are reported as a single item thus not allowing the shareholders to understand how much merchandise (for resale without transformation) is detained by Siemens.

- The very large amount listed under "work in process" possibly reflects a choice made by Siemens to pool together work in progress, work in process and semi-finished products. That choice is not unreasonable since a large part of Siemens' activity is in heavy equipment and long-term contracts and therefore much of the semi-finished products are probably part of a product that will take more than the interim reporting period to complete.

Sony Corporation

(Japan – Japanese/US GAAP – Source: Annual report 2000 –
Electronics, videogames, music, pictures)

Excerpts from the notes to the consolidated balance sheet

Inventories (millions of Yen)	31 March 2000
Current inventories	
● Finished products	461,675
● Work in process	106,749
● Raw materials, purchased components and supplies	165,866
● Film released	113,333
● Film in process	11,551
Sub-total current inventories	859,174
Non-current inventories	
● Film released	137,920
● Film in process	88,467
Sub-total current inventories	226,387
Total inventories	1,085,561

Comments

Sony is a very complex organization dealing both in manufacturing and selling diversified electronic equipment and in creating and selling cultural material (music and films). It has, therefore, distinguished current from non-current inventories (a rather unusual situation but quite legitimate in the entertainment field). The first ones are used in the course of the operating cycle (i.e., within less than 12 months after acquisition or creation). This includes both manufactured goods and entertainment products whose release is expected within the next 12 months. The non-current inventories represent film rights, which are held for use over a period of time extending beyond one year. Technically one might have been tempted to consider non-current inventories as long-lived (fixed) assets since they represent a right to future stream of economic benefits. However, such assets (films already released for which Sony holds future TV and video rights as well as films under development whose release date is not within 12 months, i.e., work in progress) do not qualify as tangible fixed assets since they have been acquired (or created) for the sole purpose of being sold as such.

For example, when Charbonnages de France (the now defunct French coal monopoly) was holding inventories of about one year's supply of coal in the early 1960s (and coal was still a major source of fuel in France), it was rumored that an error of estimation of less than 1% of the physical inventory of coal could either entirely wipe out the losses of the firm or double them. When one knows how difficult it is to estimate the physical quantity of coal in a coal storage bin (and even harder when we are talking about tens of millions of tons), one realizes that errors of more than 1% either way were very likely.

Each industry (and probably to some extent each firm's strategy) has its own appropriate level of inventory and there is a lot of diversity between industries (as can be seen in Table 9.2) but the interesting exercise is to compare firms in the same industry. However, the lower level of inventory is not always (but most of the time it probably is) synonymous with better management unless the services offered by the firm are completely comparable (a rare occurrence). In Table 9.2 Sony and Philips are not directly comparable because of the weight of the entertainment products in Sony's inventories, which Philips no longer has. However from the note on Sony's balance sheet (seen earlier) we know that the manufacturing inventories of Sony can be estimated at 734,290 million yen thus giving an industrial inventory as a percentage of total assets (netted of film assets) of 10.8% which compares favorably to Philips' 15%. This is, of course, a first pass at an analysis but it is the way financial reporting becomes useful.

Table 9.2 Weight of inventories

Company (country – activity)	Balance sheet date	Currency (in millions)	Inventory	Total assets	Inventories/ total assets
Siemens (Germany – energy, industry components, automotive systems, communication products)	30 Sep. 1999	DM	34,265	120,273	28.5%
Courtaulds (United Kingdom – textiles)	31 Dec. 1998	UK £	167	634	26.3%
Moulinex (France – small domestic appliances)	31 Mar. 1999	FF	1,518	5,821	26.1%
Kerry (Ireland – consumer foods, agribusiness)	31 Dec. 1998	Ir £	193	1,049	18.4%
Bosch (Germany – automotive equipment, consumer goods, communication technology, capital goods)	31 Dec. 1999	DM	6,525	40,743	16.0%
Sony (Japan – electronics, game, music, pictures)	31 Mar. 2000	Yen	1,085,561	6,807,197	15.9%
Volvo (Sweden – cars, trucks, buses, construction equipment, aero, marine and industrial engines)	31 Dec. 1998	SEK	32,128	204,426	15.7%
Unilever (Netherlands – foods business, home and personal care)	31 Dec. 1998	Dutch guilders	10,461	67,186	15.6%
Philips (Netherlands – technological consumer products, components, semiconductors)	31 Dec. 1998	Dutch guilders	9,419	62,041	15.2%
Pirelli (Italy – cables and systems, tires)	31 Dec. 1999	Euros	1,136	7,821	14.5%
L'Oreal (France – beauty and cosmetic products, toiletries and pharmaceuticals)	31 Dec. 1999	FF	6,427	69,830	9.2%
Norsk Hydro (Norway – oil and energy, light metals, agribusiness)	31 Dec. 1999	NOK	16,327	176,807	9.2%
Tractebel (Belgium – electricity and gas, communications)	31 Dec. 1998	BEF	85,058	973,146	8.7%
Compaq (USA – computers)	31 Dec. 1998	US $	2,005	23,051	8.7%
Telefónica (Spain – telecommunication, media)	31 Dec. 1998	Pesetas	49,172	8,246,124	0.6%

Not surprisingly a service industry like the telephone industry in which Telefónica operates shows little inventory compared to other assets (probably parts for repair of telephone exchanges and network).

Inventory recording systems

Chapter 2 introduced the two methods most commonly used to report inventory movements (whether they pertain to purchases of goods or raw materials or to addition of goods manufactured in-house): purchases recorded in the balance sheet and transferred to the income statement or, conversely, purchases recorded in the income statement and transferred to the balance sheet. In practice, there are two methods for recording inventory movements: perpetual and periodic inventory systems. We will now study these two practices in details as they impact differently on the profit and on the ending balance sheet structure. We will also examine the possibility that items carried in inventory are either so large, so valuable and/or so specific that they cannot be considered fungible (a basic assumption of both perpetual and periodic inventories) and are therefore kept in inventory under the so-called "specific identification method".

Perpetual (or permanent) inventory system

Under a perpetual inventory system, a continuous record of changes in inventory (entries as well as withdrawals) is maintained in the inventory account. Practically, all movements flow through an inventory account (in the general ledger). Purchases are recorded as increases of the inventory assets in the balance sheet and all withdrawals and consumption are reduction of the inventory asset.

The inventory account is presented in the following way:

Perpetual inventory account

Debit	Credit
• Beginning inventory	• Withdrawals from inventory (cost of goods sold or cost of goods consumed in the next segment of the "manufacturing" process)
• Purchases (cost of goods purchased) or additions to the inventory (cost of goods manufactured)	• Balance: Ending inventory (by deduction)

This system provides a continuous record of the balances in both the "inventory account" and the "cost of goods sold account".

Let us illustrate the mechanism with an example. The relevant complete data for the Borodine Company are:

Inventory of goods for resale (merchandise) at beginning of year	200
Purchases of goods for resale (merchandise) during year	900
Sales of goods for resale (merchandise)	1,200
Cost of goods sold (valued at their purchase price)	800
Inventory of goods for resale (merchandise) at end of year	300

In a perpetual inventory system, the fundamental inventory equation is used to calculate the ending inventory as follows:

Beginning inventory	+	Purchases or additions	–	Withdrawals	=	Ending inventory (the unknown)
200	+	900	–	800	=	X

$$X = 200 + 900 - 800 = 300$$

This system has two main characteristics:

1 All additions to inventory through manufacturing or purchase are debited to the inventory account.

2 All withdrawals for sale or further manufacturing are credited to the inventory account and are eventually charged to the income statement as cost of goods sold.

Dedicated accounting software will help any company record purchases, additions, and withdrawals nearly instantaneously at an acceptable cost if a proper system of control is introduced. However, creating a closed storeroom with rigorous controls counting all movements (in and out) can be a complex and expensive procedure, even if bar coding has often simplified recording. Many small companies do not have the administrative and technical capacity and resources to record all movements in and out of inventory. These companies, in particular, take advantage of the simplification allowed under the periodic inventory system.

Periodic inventory system

This method is minimalist. It simply follows the general requirement that at least once every period (commonly the year) a business physically counts – and attests to – what is really in inventory and what assets and liabilities really exist (opportunity to record impairment or provisions when needed). The periodic inventory system relies on the required periodic (annual) physical counting to establish the quantities in the ending inventory so that they can be valued.

This system has two main characteristics:

1 All beginning inventories and additions to inventory (through manufacturing or purchase) are, in a first step, presumed consumed and debited directly to the income statement.

2 In a second step, the presumed consumption cost is adjusted at the end of the period (adjusting entry) by deducting the independently measured ending inventory(ies).

The cornerstone of the periodic inventory method is therefore the physical inventory figures (always assumed to be measured on the balance sheet date[3]). The balance shown on an inventory account in the ledger is only changed when a new physical inventory is taken.

The inventory account is presented in the following way:

Periodic inventory account

Debit	Credit
● Beginning inventory	● Ending inventory (measured at year end)
● Purchases or additions (accumulated on an as-you-go basis)	● Cost of goods sold or cost of goods consumed (by deduction)

The fundamental inventory equation is expressed as follows (continuing the Borodine Company example):

Beginning inventory	+	Purchases or or additions	–	Consumption (cost of goods sold or transferred downstream) (the unknown)	=	Ending inventory
200	+	900	–	X	=	300

or, more accurately:

Beginning inventory	+	Purchases or additions	–	Ending inventory (independently measured)	=	Cost of goods sold or cost of goods transferred (deducted) (accumulated)
200	+	900	–	300	=	X

$$X = 200 + 900 - 300 = 800.$$

Comparison of recording

As the example shows, profit and inventory values are the same under either method, as long as the basic data do not show any inflation or deflation. The preference of most businesses for the perpetual inventory (subject to cost-benefit criteria) comes from the superior managerial information and internal control it provides. (A more detailed comparison of advantages and limits of both methods is presented in Appendices 9.1 and 9.2.)

Figure 9.3 illustrates side by side the impact of the perpetual and periodic inventory methods on the financial statements of Borodine Company.

Comments

● The ending inventory value, 300 CU, is the same under either method. It is calculated as follows:

– Perpetual inventory: Beginning inventory (i.e., 200) + Purchases or additions (i.e., 900) – Withdrawals (cost of goods sold or consumption) (i.e., 800) = 300.

– Periodic inventory: The ending inventory is declared to be 300 after an end of the period physical inventory count.

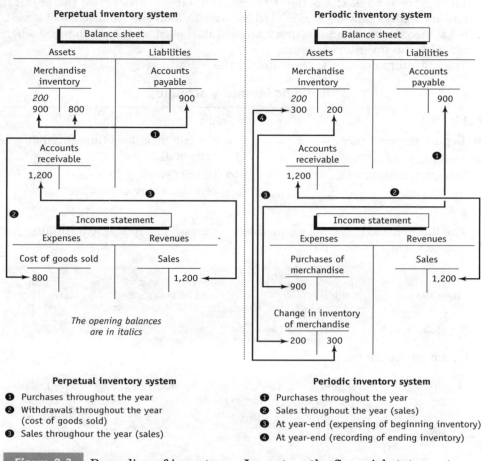

Perpetual inventory system

① Purchases throughout the year
② Withdrawals throughout the year
(cost of goods sold)
③ Sales throughour the year (sales)

Periodic inventory system

① Purchases throughout the year
② Sales throughout the year (sales)
③ At year-end (expensing of beginning inventory)
④ At year-end (recording of ending inventory)

Figure 9.3 Recording of inventory – Impact on the financial statements

- Both methods provide the same cost of goods sold (or cost of goods consumed) which is calculated as follows:
  - Perpetual inventory: directly by summing the withdrawal or requisition slips that recorded the movements.
  - Periodic inventory: by deduction: Purchases (i.e., 900) + Change in inventory (i.e., 200 – 300).
- The periodic inventory system is the by default minimum recommendation of the 4th European Union Directive for a retail business or for raw material and components in a manufacturing firm:

Purchases of goods for resale or used in manufacturing	900	This is considered an expense
Adjusted by the change in inventory of goods for resale or for use in production	–100	Here the sign is negative because the inventory actually increased thus it is equivalent to a reduction of the expense
Withdrawals (cost of goods consumed or cost of goods sold)	= 800	The expense recognized either as cost of goods sold or as a cost consumed in the manufacturing process

Presentation of inventories in the income statement by nature

Figure 9.4 illustrates how inventories are reported in an income statement presented by nature, in companies from countries such as Italy, Spain, and France.

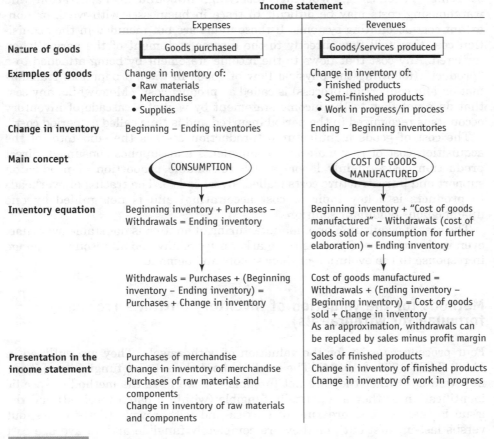

Income statement

	Expenses	Revenues
Nature of goods	Goods purchased	Goods/services produced
Examples of goods	Change in inventory of: • Raw materials • Merchandise • Supplies	Change in inventory of: • Finished products • Semi-finished products • Work in progress/in process
Change in inventory	Beginning – Ending inventories	Ending – Beginning inventories
Main concept	CONSUMPTION	COST OF GOODS MANUFACTURED
Inventory equation	Beginning inventory + Purchases – Withdrawals = Ending inventory	Beginning inventory + "Cost of goods manufactured" – Withdrawals (cost of goods sold or consumption for further elaboration) = Ending inventory
	Withdrawals = Purchases + (Beginning inventory – Ending inventory) = Purchases + Change in inventory	Cost of goods manufactured = Withdrawals + (Ending inventory – Beginning inventory) = Cost of goods sold + Change in inventory As an approximation, withdrawals can be replaced by sales minus profit margin
Presentation in the income statement	Purchases of merchandise Change in inventory of merchandise Purchases of raw materials and components Change in inventory of raw materials and components	Sales of finished products Change in inventory of finished products Change in inventory of work in progress

Figure 9.4 Inventories in the income statement by nature

Inventory valuation and reported income

The basic issue

The value of the cost of goods sold (which by definition is linked to the value of the ending inventory in the balance sheet) directly impacts on the gross margin, and, consequently, on net income. As a consequence, inventory valuation and costing methods have a great impact on net income.

IAS 2 (IASC 1993: § 7) states that "the cost of inventories should comprise all costs of purchase, costs of conversion and other costs incurred in bringing the inventories to their present condition and location" (i.e., historical cost of acquisition). IAS 2, like most accounting standards, defines the value of the inventory as the critical element (i.e., taking a balance sheet view of the firm) while to a manager whose responsibility is to allocate resources in order to manage a product and customer portfolios, it is the value of the cost of goods sold which is the most important element (and inventory valuation is residual information).

Some components of the acquisition cost such as supplier qualification, sourcing, purchasing, ordering, receiving, in-bound transportation and warehousing costs may be difficult to trace in businesses with weak or non-extant cost-accounting systems. If these items are not included in the acquisition cost they will flow directly to the income statement of the period when incurred. Any cost that flows to the income statement by being attached to a "product" (following the physical flow of goods in their production, transformation and conversion process) is called a "product cost". Meanwhile, any cost that does not flow to the income statement by way of a cascade of inventory accounts is recognized in the period incurred and is thus called a "period cost".

The cost of goods manufactured (production cost) is the sum total of the acquisition cost of raw materials, components and supplies consumed, direct production costs (mainly labor) and a reasonable proportion of production support and infrastructure costs (called "overheads"). The tracing of overheads to products is a key topic in cost accounting[4] and is not guided by one unambiguous dominant solution.

The cost of acquisition or of manufacturing of an item is not stable over time, even in the course of a year as the market price of any and all resources change in response to the evolution of their supply and demand.

Methods for the valuation of inventory outflows (costing formulae for withdrawals)

Four procedures exist for the valuation of withdrawals. They are outlined in IAS 2 (IASC 1993: § 19–24). The issue is about the relative fungibility of items in inventory. Either they are not fungible and we have the method of specific identification or they are partially fungible (within a batch received) and the issue is that of time ordering of entries and withdrawals (first-in, first-out versus last-in, first-out), or they are completely fungible and an average cost will be used.

Specific identification method

Items that are not ordinarily interchangeable or fungible (such as jewels, diamonds, paintings, etc.) and goods that were produced for a specifically identified project or customer will keep their specific cost when carried in inventory. This means that their cost upon withdrawal is absolutely identical to the one they had when entering in inventory (cost of acquisition or cost of goods manufactured). This method is known as the "specific identification method". When this method is used the concept of periodic or perpetual inventory system does not make much sense since the item will be entered or withdrawn only once during the accounting period. This method is simple but extremely costly to implement when the individual value of the items involved is moderate or small. It is also a method that could be used deliberately to affect (manipulate) the bottom line by carefully selecting those items that are sold and those that remain in inventories. Usually, this method is reserved for high-priced items or items that must not be considered to be fungible for legal reasons, such as cars, heavy equipment, farm equipment, works of art, furs, jewelry.

Methods used for fungible and semi-fungible items

When items are fungible to some degree, it is not simple (quasi-impossible?) to trace the cost of acquisition of a given item. The specific identification method is unworkable if large quantities of items flow through an inventory account, as it would be impractical to maintain individualized inventory records for each item. Specific identification would be impossible and unnecessary for generic microprocessors, nails or cans of beer, difficult for a hand-finished motor vehicle, necessary for a classical antique piece of furniture, essential for an item produced to a contractual customer specification. In other words, it is rarely feasible to trace the cost of a specific item in inventory.

As a consequence, businesses recognize the partial or total fungibility of products and make assumptions about the timing sequence according to which inventory items leave an inventory account to either become part of goods consumed in a further step of transformation (manufacturing) or become part of the cost of goods sold. There are two sets of hypotheses.

Either products are totally fungible or they are fungible only within a batch defined by a date of acquisition.

When products are considered partially or totally fungible, three possibilities for time ordering withdrawals exist[5], each reflecting a specific assumed pattern of goods flow:

1. Goods withdrawn are valued batch by batch in the order they entered inventory (first-in, first-out, or FIFO).

2. Goods withdrawn are valued batch by batch in the reverse order from the one they followed when entering inventory (last-in, first-out, or LIFO).

3. Goods withdrawn (considered totally fungible) are valued at the average cost of available goods (weighted average cost method, or WAC).

Both the FIFO and LIFO approaches require that a record of each acquisition be kept by date and that the withdrawals be valued by adding complete (or parts of) batches. The WAC is simpler and potentially less costly to operate. It consists in using a continuously updated weighted average for the unit cost of any item in inventory.

In periods of inflation the price (and thus the cost of acquisition) of resources does go up. FIFO or WAC methods do not give a true view of the financial condition of the business. Especially, they may lead to an overestimation of the real value created. If goods purchased three months ago for 100 CU, are sold for 150, the apparent profit margin is 50. But if the replacement of these units (required if the business is to remain a going concern) requires that 120 CU be spent, the "real" profit is only 30 CU. The LIFO[6] method is more reactive to the evolution (up or down) of the market price of resources and is often preferred to FIFO or WAC in the context of managerial decisions. However, the historical costing and prudence principles would tend to favor FIFO or WAC for reporting purposes.

LIFO is permitted as a valid basis for the valuation of withdrawal flows both by the European Union and by the International Accounting Standards Committee for consolidated accounts (reporting purpose) but not allowed under most European countries' local GAAP for unconsolidated accounts. The three main reasons for not using LIFO are:

- **Reporting**: Inflation is very limited today in developed economies and there is often simultaneously inflation and deflation on different products or resources thus the reporting benefit might not be significant.
- **Taxation**: With even a small inflation, the LIFO-based taxable income would be less than it would be under FIFO or WAC and, if there is a reversal of inflation, LIFO might create larger swings in taxable income levels than would WAC or FIFO. In fact, the use of LIFO is forbidden for tax purposes in many countries.
- **Accounting**: LIFO in periods of heavy inflation may lead to a negative valuation of an inventory that is physically and concretely real, thus giving less credibility to the balance sheet.

IAS 2 reflects a compromise between relevance and prudence:

- On the one hand, it states that inventories other than those valued under specific identification, should be valued by using either FIFO or WAC approaches (§ 21).
- On the other hand, it states (§ 23), that the last-in, first-out (LIFO) method is authorized as an alternative treatment.

Figure 9.5 summarizes the different costing methods.

The Glinka Company example summarized in Tables 9.3 and 9.4 illustrates the effect on income and the balance sheet of using FIFO, LIFO or WAC. In this illustration, we assume, without loss of generality, no beginning inventory. Glinka's relevant data for the period under scrutiny were the following:

- 1st purchase: 10 units are purchased and are recorded for an acquisition cost of 10 CU per unit.
- 2nd purchase: 10 units are purchased and are recorded for an acquisition cost of 12 CU per unit.
- 15 units are sold at the end of the period for a unit selling price of 18 CU per unit.

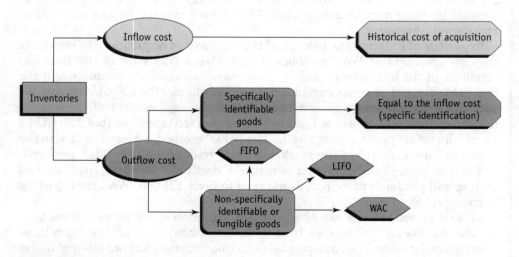

Figure 9.5 Costing inventories

Table 9.3 Cost of consumption and value of remaining inventory

FIFO	Transactions (in and out)			Ending inventory		
	Quantity	Cost per unit	Total cost	Quantity	Cost per unit	Total cost
Purchase 1	10	10	100	10	10	100
Purchase 2	10	12	120	20	10 units at 10	100
					10 units at 12	120
COGS	−10	10	−100			
	−5	12	−60	5	12	60
LIFO	Quantity	Cost per unit	Total cost	Quantity	Cost per unit	Total cost
Purchase 1	10	10	100	10	10	100
Purchase 2	10	12	120	20	10 units at 12	120
					10 units at 10	100
COGS	−10	12	−120			
	−5	10	−50	5	10	50
WAC	Quantity	Cost per unit	Total cost	Quantity	Cost per unit	Total cost
Purchase 1	10	10	100	10	10	100
Purchase 2	10	12	120	20	20 units at 11	220
COGS	−15	11	−165	5	11	55

Table 9.4 Impact on income statement

	FIFO	LIFO	WAC
Sales	270	270	270
Cost of goods sold (direct computation)	160	170	165
Alternatively the COGS can be obtained by applying the full equation			
Purchases	*220*	*220*	*220*
Plus beginning inventory	*0*	*0*	*0*
Equals cost of goods available for sale	*220*	*220*	*220*
Minus ending inventory	*−60*	*−50*	*−55*
Equals cost of goods sold	*160*	*170*	*165*
Gross margin (before tax)	110	100	105
− income tax (assuming a 40% rate)	−44	−40	−42
Gross margin (after tax)	66	60	63
Control			
Cost of goods sold + Ending inventory	220	220	220
Purchases + Beginning inventory	220	220	220

In this example, the sum of "cost of goods sold plus ending inventory" is equal to the sum of "purchases plus beginning inventory" as a consequence of the fundamental inventory equation which can be reformulated:

$$\text{Beginning inventory} + \text{Purchases} - \text{Cost of goods sold} = \text{Ending inventory} \rightarrow$$
$$\text{Beginning inventory} + \text{Purchases} = \text{Cost of goods sold} + \text{Ending inventory}$$

The example confirms that, in an inflationary world, LIFO gives the highest cost of goods sold of the three methods and thus the lowest value for ending inventory and the lowest reported income. The situation would be the exact opposite if Glinka had operated in a deflationary world. The effect of LIFO is that, after a period of years in an inflationary world, the balance sheet might no longer present a true and fair view of the company's real assets. However, over the same years the LIFO method has provided management with a true and fair measure of the COGS and thus allowed them to appropriately manage both products and customers to create more value for the shareholders. The debate between the various methods is thus a question of whether one prefers to have a "correct" income statement or a "correct" balance sheet.

Table 9.5 summarizes the impact on income and ending inventory of the three methods in the context of rising or falling costs of acquisition.

Table 9.5   Impact on net income and ending inventory

Context:		Impact on net income	Impact on ending inventory
Rising costs	FIFO →	higher income reported	FIFO → higher ending inventory reported
	WAC →	medium income reported	WAC → medium ending inventory reported
	LIFO →	lower income reported	LIFO → lower ending inventory reported
Falling costs	FIFO →	lower income reported	FIFO → lower ending inventory reported
	WAC →	medium income reported	WAC → medium ending inventory reported
	LIFO →	higher income reported	LIFO → higher ending inventory reported

All three methods are generally acceptable for financial reporting to shareholders (with the exceptions listed in Table 9.6), but, in practice, FIFO and WAC are the most commonly used methods.

Table 9.6   Accounting standards position regarding inventory valuation methods

Country and organization	First-in, first-out (FIFO)	Weighted average cost (WAC)	Last-in, first-out (LIFO)
IASC	Allowed	Allowed	Allowed
European Union	Allowed	Allowed	Allowed
Australia	Allowed	Allowed	Not allowed
Austria	Allowed	Allowed	Allowed[7]
Belgium	Allowed	Allowed	Allowed
Canada	Allowed	Allowed	Allowed[8]

continued opposite

INTERNATIONAL AND COMPARATIVE ACCOUNTING

Country and organization	First-in, first-out (FIFO)	Weighted average cost (WAC)	Last-in, first-out (LIFO)
Denmark	Allowed	Allowed	Not allowed
Finland	Allowed	Allowed	Not allowed
France	Allowed	Allowed	Not allowed[9]
Germany	Allowed	Allowed	Allowed
Greece	Allowed	Allowed	Allowed
Ireland	Allowed	Allowed	Not allowed[10]
Italy	Allowed	Allowed	Allowed
Japan	Allowed	Allowed	Allowed
Luxembourg	Allowed	Allowed	Allowed
Netherlands	Allowed	Allowed	Allowed
Norway	Allowed	Allowed	Not allowed
Portugal	Allowed	Allowed	Allowed
Spain	Allowed	Allowed	Allowed
Sweden	Allowed	Allowed	Not allowed
Switzerland	Allowed	Allowed	Not allowed
UK	Allowed	Allowed	Not allowed[11]
USA	Allowed	Allowed	Allowed

ADVANCED ISSUES

Effect of an inventory misstatement

Inventory misstatements may have an impact on net income (see Appendix 9.4).

Inventories and cash flow

The choice of inventory valuation methods has no impact on cash flow before tax. However, it has an impact on the tax expense that will accrue (because of the difference in gross margin). It will thus change the cash flow after tax. The effect of the choice of cost flow method on cash flows is illustrated in Table 9.7 using the data from the Glinka Company example (see earlier) assuming that sales and purchases are both paid cash.

Table 9.7 Impact on cash flow

	FIFO	LIFO	WAC
Cash inflow from sales	270	270	270
Minus Cash outflows for purchases	−220	−220	−220
Equals Cash flow before tax	50	50	50
Minus Income tax (40% rate) (see Table 9.4)	−44	−40	−42
Equals Cash flow after tax	6	10	8

Table 9.7 illustrates that in an inflationary resources market with stable market prices for units sold, it is the use of LIFO that generates the highest cash flow after tax because it provides the lowest net income (Table 9.4).

Decline in value (end-of-year adjustments)

Decline in replacement prices, physical deterioration or obsolescence are some of the reasons why the inventory at the end of the year may be worth less than its value shown in the books (assuming all physical discrepancies have been accounted for already). The rule of "lower of cost or market"[12] requires that a business realigns the books when it finds itself in a situation in which the book value of inventory is greater than its market value (expressed either in terms of disposal or liquidation cost or in terms of sale price that the business hopes to obtain from customers for the goods in inventory). If the "market value" is lower than the recorded cost, the inventory is written down to current market value. The unrealized loss must be recognized in the income statement.

Let us illustrate this point with an example. Glazunov Company purchased 1,000 stuffed wombats at a unit cost of acquisition of 20 CU. There has been a huge shipment from South East Asia of inexpensive stuffed wombats to all retailers competing with Glazunov Company. The wholesale market unit price of these stuffed wombats has dropped to 15 CU for the products that had been purchased for 20 CU. Glazunov GmbH still holds 100 units in inventory at the end of the accounting period. A provision for loss of value of inventory must be recorded. It amounts to (20 − 15) × 100 = 500 CU. Figure 9.6 illustrates the year-end adjusting entries.

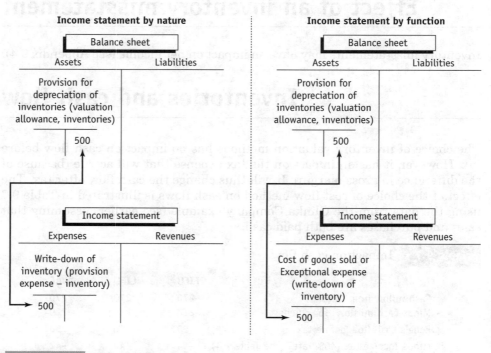

Figure 9.6   End-of-year adjustments

The "inventory" account is credited in the form of a contra-asset account so as to not lose the information. If the market value recovers by year-end, the write-down (provision) should be reversed either by reversing the expense itself or creating an income or a revenue:

BS (A+)	Provision for depreciation of inventories (Valuation allowance, inventories)		500
IS (E–)		Write-down of inventory (provision expense – inventory) or Cost of goods sold	500
or		**or**	
IS (R+)		Reversal of provision	

Income statement by nature and income statement by function

Expenses in the income statement can be classified either by nature or by function. In Chapter 3 we illustrated how to go from one presentation to the other for Brahms company, a retailer. We can now illustrate the passage from one presentation to the other for a manufacturing company. Our illustration will be about the Moussorgski Company. The relevant data are provided in Table 9.8 (in thousands of CU).

Table 9.8 Data

Beginning inventory of raw materials	20	Depreciation expenses	
		. Production equipment	19
Purchases of raw materials	40	. Sales equipment	5
Sales revenue (finished products)	100	. Administrative equipment	3
Raw materials consumed in manufacturing	50	Rent expenses	
		. Production	3
Ending inventory of raw materials	10	. Administration	1
Personnel expenses		Beginning inventory of work in process	2
. Direct labor	20		
. Supervisory labor	6	Units completed during the period	88
. Sales personnel	4	Ending inventory of work in process	12
. Accounting and administration personnel	3		
Cost of units sold during the period	80	Beginning inventory of finished products	3
		Ending inventory of finished products	11

Table 9.9 shows side by side the calculation of the operating income by nature and by function. The operating income is mechanically exactly the same under both approaches. The difference in presentation offers different possible interpretation and uses of the information contained in the income statement.

| Table 9.9 | Income statement by nature and by function |

Income statement by nature		Income statement by function	
Sales revenue from finished products	100	Sales revenue from finished products	100
+ Change in inventory of finished products (a)	8	− Cost of goods sold (f)	−80
+ Change in inventory of work in process (a)	10	= Gross margin	20
− Purchases of raw materials	−40	− Selling expenses (g)	−9
− Change in inventory of raw materials (b)	−10	− Administrative expenses (h)	−7
− Rent expenses (c)	−4	= Operating income	4
− Personnel expenses (d)	−33	Cost of goods sold (f)	
− Depreciation expense (e)	−27	+ Raw materials consumed	50
= Operating income	4	+ Direct labor	20
		+ Supervisory labor	6
(a) Ending minus beginning		+ Depreciation (production equipment)	19
(b) Beginning minus ending		+ Rent expense (production overhead)	3
(c) 3 + 1		= Cost of goods manufactured	98
(d) 20 + 6 + 4 + 3		− Change in inventory of finished products (a)	−8
(e) 19 + 5 + 3		− Change in inventory of work in process (a)	−10
		= Cost of goods sold (f)	80
		Selling expenses (g)	
		+ Personnel expenses (sales person)	4
		+ Depreciation (sales equipment)	5
		= Selling expenses (g)	9
		Administrative expenses (h)	
		+ Personnel expenses (administration)	3
		+ Depreciation (administration)	3
		+ Rent expense (administration)	1
		= Administrative expenses (h)	7

Disclosure of inventory valuation policies

Principles

Although disclosure practices in the notes to financial statements may vary between countries, the following minimum information should be given according to IAS 2 (§ 34):

- Accounting policies adopted in measuring inventories, including the cost formula used.
- Total carrying amount of inventories and carrying amount for each class of inventories appropriate for the enterprise.
- Carrying amount of inventories carried at net realizable value.
- Amount of any reversal of any write-down that is recognized as income in the period.
- Circumstances or events that led to the reversal of a write-down of inventories.
- Carrying amount of inventories pledged as security for liabilities.

Barmag

(Germany – German GAAP – Source: Annual report 1999 – Man-made fiber industry)

The first part of the income statement is presented as follows:

Consolidated income statement Thousands of DM	1999	1998
Sales	662,112	1,120,226
Increase/decrease in inventories of work in progress	–50,319	16,836
Own work capitalized	414	1,122
Total performance	612,207	1,138,184
Other operating income	69,851	53,160
Cost of materials	–264,915	–516,331

Note 2 to the consolidated balance sheet provides the following information:

	1999 DM 000	1998 DM 000
Raw materials and supplies	51,885	51,309
Work in progress	93,578	143,897
Advances to suppliers	1,784	2,852
	147,247	198,058
Advances received on orders	–52,786	–92,266
	94,461	105,792

Inventories have been valued at acquisition or manufacturing cost in compliance with the lower of cost or market principle. The manufacturing cost includes material costs and wage expenses, directly attributable costs as well as manufacturing and material overheads, including balance sheet write-offs. Interest payments on borrowings are not capitalized.

Provision has been made for risks due to limited usefulness of materials, e.g., for technological reasons, by way of appropriate value adjustments. Where the net realizable value is below cost or where there are special risks of loss on sales, the appropriate write-downs have been made.

Advance payments on orders have been applied in full to inventories.

Several comments can be made:

- The fact that the change in work in progress is shown both in the income statement (a reduction of 50,319,000 DM) and in the notes may appear to be redundant. But since the balance sheet figures are net amounts (i.e., after provision or valuation allowance) and the income statement figures are gross amounts (i.e., before provision), the notes act as a form of double-checking for the shareholder wanting to explore the accounts in details.
- Advances to suppliers are included in inventories.
- Advances received on orders are subtracted here from inventories. Usually, this item is reported as a liability. We could say the presentation adopted by Barmag appears to be in violation of the non-offsetting principle.
- The notes allow the calculation of the change in inventories of raw materials and supplies which could not be obtained from the income statement because Barmag reports the cost of goods sold and therefore these variations are hidden in the COGS.

- The reason why Barmag specifically mentions that "interest payments on borrowings are not capitalized" is due to the fact that interest expenses could (can) be capitalized and added to the inventory value exactly as it is done for tangible assets as shown in Chapter 7. Barmag chose not to use this possibility and dutifully reports on their accounting choice to the shareholders.

Sauer Inc.

(USA – US GAAP – Source: Annual report 1999 – Design, manufacture, and sale of highly engineered hydraulic systems and components for off-highway mobile equipment)

In the notes to consolidated financial statements for the year 1999, we find the following information:

Inventories are valued at the lower of cost or market, using various cost methods, and include the cost of material, labor, and factory overhead. The percentage of year-end inventory using WAC, LIFO, and FIFO was 59%, 34% and 7%, respectively, for 1999 and 61%, 33% and 6%, respectively for 1998.

The fact the note gives the opportunity to the reader of the financial statement to recast the income statement according to any of the three basic inventory valuation methods is rather unusual. It helps identify better the earnings potential of the firm in helping one understand what comes from past events (FIFO) and what comes from current competitive edge (LIFO) which is a good indicator of future earnings potential.

Financial statement analysis pertaining to inventories

Principles

The financial analyst's main concern is with the coherence of the level of inventory with the business's environment and strategy which define the desirable length of the operating cycle. Two metrics are commonly used in this respect:

- *Inventory turnover*: This metric is defined as the number of times the inventory "turns" during the accounting period. The shorter the operating cycle, the higher the turnover. This ratio is obtained by dividing the cost of goods sold by the average value of the relevant inventory (beginning inventory plus ending inventory divided by 2). For a given industry, the higher the turnover ratio, the more likely the management of the physical flows is efficient. With the development of just in time relations between suppliers and customers, ratios of 26 (equivalent to an inventory sufficient to meet the needs of 2 weeks of average demand or consumption) or even 52 (one week) are no longer unusual in the automotive industry or the assembly of washing machines.

● *Average days of inventory available*: This metric is the inverse of the turnover ratio. It expresses the inventory in terms of number of days of activity that can be "supplied" without having to purchase any new products or materials. It is obtained as the "number of activity days in the year divided by the turnover ratio".

The choice of presentation of the income statement (by nature or by function) facilitates or hinders the calculation of these ratios. In an income statement by nature, extensive information is available describing the inventories for each type of good (finished, intermediate, raw materials or merchandise) (see Table 9.10).

Table 9.10 Formulae for the calculation of the inventory turnover in the income statement by nature

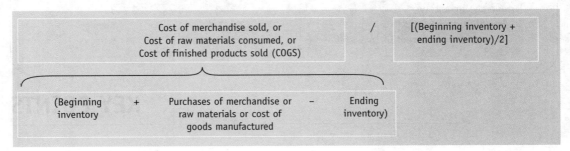

In an income statement presented by function, the cost of goods sold does not distinguish between merchandise, raw materials and finished products. A general inventory turnover is then calculated by dividing the cost of goods sold (obtained from the income statement) by the average inventory (obtained from the balance sheet).

Toray Industries

Japanese manufacturer of synthetic fibers and textiles.

Table 9.11, based on figures found in the 1999 annual report, shows the computation of inventory turnover and average days of inventory available.

Table 9.11 Inventory ratios

		Millions of yen 1999	1998
Balance sheet			
Finished goods and work in process		179,631	167,360
Raw materials and supplies		39,440	34,058
		219,071	201,418
Income statement			
Cost of goods sold	(1)	755,900	
Average inventory	(2)	212,243	
Inventory turnover	(3)=(1)/(2)	3.6 times	
Average days of inventory available	(4)=1/(3)*365	101.5 days	

KEY POINTS

- Inventories are essential assets (potential source of future economic benefits) (1) held for sale in the ordinary course of business; (2) in the process of production for such sale; or (3) in the form of materials or supplies to be consumed in the production process or in the rendering of services.

- As long as a product has not been sold, all costs attached to it are withheld from the income statement and essentially stored in an inventory account.

- The three major issues relating to accounting for inventories are: (1) inventory recording systems, (2) inventory costing methods, and (3) inventory valuation methods.

- The main categories of inventories are: (1) merchandise (commercial activity), and (2) raw materials, manufacturing supplies, work in progress and process, semi-finished goods and finished goods (manufacturing activity).

- Inventories sometimes represent a large portion of assets and therefore their correct valuation is essential for reporting accurately and fairly the value of the shareholders' equity.

- The fundamental inventory equation is withdrawals are equal to purchases or additions plus beginning inventory minus ending inventory.

- A perpetual inventory system is a continuous record of changes in inventory (additions as well as withdrawals).

- The periodic inventory system relies on the required periodic (annual) physical counting to establish and value the quantities in the ending inventory.

- Inventory valuation and costing methods have a great impact on net income.

- There are four methods for costing items withdrawn from inventory: "specific identification method", FIFO (first-in, first-out), LIFO (last-in, first-out) and WAC (weighted average cost).

- Financial analysts are mainly concerned with the coherence of the level of inventory with a business's environment and strategy. Their measures are (1) inventory turnover (number of times the inventory "turns" during the accounting period), and (2) average days of inventory available (inverse of the turnover ratio).

REVIEW

Review 9.1 Baltimore Technologies*

Topic: Reporting for inventory
Type: Group exercise
Related part of the chapter: Core/Advanced Issues

Baltimore Technologies is a UK provider of security products and services to enable companies develop trusted, secure systems for e-business, the internet and mobile commerce. The 1999 annual report shows inventories to be as follows.

	31 December 1999 £000	31 December 1998 £000
Current assets		
Stocks (inventories)	870	776

The notes to the consolidated financial statements contain the following information.

Inventories	31 December 1999 £000	31 December 1998 £000
Raw materials and consumables	380	307
Work in progress	214	278
Finished goods for sale	276	191
Balance at end of period	870	776
Provision for stock obsolescence		
Balance at beginning of year	179	151
Profit and loss account charge	5	28
Amounts utilized and other movements	−39	0
Balance at end of period	145	179

Required

1 What does the item "Profit and loss account charge" represent?
2 What does the item "Amounts utilized and other movements" represent?
3 Is the amount reported in the balance sheet a gross or a net amount?
4 What should you do to restate the balance sheet figure to obtain the other amount (gross or net)?

Solution

1 What does the item "Profit and loss account charge" represent?

It represents the provision expense (valuation allowance) for depreciation of inventories.

2 What does the item "Amounts utilized and other movements" represent?

It represents the reversal of provisions when the allowance is no longer necessary, for instance because inventories have been consumed or sold.

3 Is the amount reported in the balance sheet a gross or a net amount?

The amount reported can only be a net amount since the provision is shown separately in the notes (see the text of the problem and also it can be inferred from the fact that the provision can be reversed as shown in question 2). As a matter of fact, if the amount reported had been gross, the net amount would have been equal to 870 – 145 = 725.

4 What should you do to restate the balance sheet figure to obtain the other amount (gross or net)?

As the amount in the balance sheet is net, we could obtain the gross amount by adding the ending balance of the provision. For instance, in 1999, the gross amount would be: 870 + 145 = 1,015.

We should note that it is impossible to find the gross amount per category of inventory (raw materials, work in progress and finished goods).

Assignments

Assignment 9.1

Multiple-choice questions
Type: Individual exercise
Related part of the chapter: Core/Advanced Issues

1 **Raw materials and merchandise are included in**

(a) Expenses
(b) Fixed assets
(c) Cash
(d) Current assets
(e) None of these

2 **Ending inventory is reported in the liabilities side of the balance sheet**

(a) True
(b) False

3 **In the income statement by nature, change in inventory of finished products is reported**

(a) In the revenue, under the sales of finished products
(b) In the expenses, under the purchases of raw materials
(c) Both solutions are possible
(d) None of these

4 In the income statement by nature, change in inventory of merchandise is reported

(a) In the revenues, under the sales of merchandise
(b) In the expenses, under the purchases of merchandise
(c) Both solutions are possible
(d) None of these

5 In the balance sheet, the item "inventories" may be subject to

(a) Depreciation
(b) Amortization
(c) Depletion
(d) Provision
(e) None of these

6 The following inventory costing method provides a value for *ending inventory* which approximates most closely the current cost

(a) FIFO
(b) LIFO
(c) Neither of these

7 The following inventory costing method provides a value for *cost of goods sold* which approximates most closely the current cost

(a) FIFO
(b) LIFO
(c) Neither of these

8 Beginning inventory on 1 January 20X1 was overstated by 1,000 CU and the ending inventory was overstated by 400 CU. As a consequence, the cost of goods sold for 20X1 was

(a) Overstated by 1,000
(b) Understated by 1,000
(c) Overstated by 400
(d) Understated by 400
(e) Overstated by 1,400
(f) Understated by 1,400
(g) Overstated by 600
(h) Understated by 600
(i) None of these

9 In periods of steadily decreasing prices, the following method will give the highest ending inventory value (assuming purchases exceed withdrawals)

(a) FIFO
(b) LIFO
(c) Weighted average cost (WAC)

10 The average day's inventory available is defined as:
(Cost of goods sold/Average inventory) × 365

(a) True
(b) False

Assignment 9.2

Discussion questions
Type: Group exercise
Related part of the chapter: Core/Advanced Issues

Required

1   Give at least three arguments in favor of each of the three basic methods of inventory valuation (FIFO, LIFO and weighted average cost).

2   Provide at least three arguments in favor of perpetual and three for periodic inventory accounting methods.

Assignment 9.3 Taylor Nelson Sofres* and Irish Continental*

Topic: Nature of inventory
Type: Group exercise
Related part of the chapter: Core Issues

Taylor Nelson Sofres is a UK group specialized in market information, providing continuous and custom research and analysis. It is active in managing consumer panels and measuring television audience.

Irish Continental Group is a shipping, transport, and leisure group (Irish Ferries) principally engaged in the transport of passengers and cars, freight, and containers.

Both companies have in common the fact that their inventories are very low, particularly in relation to total assets as shown in the following table where figures have been extracted from the 1999 annual reports of each company.

Taylon Nelson Sofres	1999	1998
	£m	£m
Stocks [a]	32.6	30.7
Total assets	289.9	212.2
Inventories/total assets	11.2%	14.5%

Irish Continental Group	1999	1998
	€m	€m
Stocks [a]	0.6	0.4
Total assets	402.6	316.3
Inventories/total assets	0.15%	0.13%
(a) i.e. inventories		

Required

Provide a list of possible items that could be included under the item "inventories" (stocks) for each of these companies.

Assignment 9.4 Stravinsky

Topic: FIFO, LIFO and WAC
Type: Individual exercise
Related part of the chapter: Advanced Issues

Stravinsky Company, a retailer selling a single product, opened shop on 3 April. The first month's transactions were as follows:

April 02   Purchase of 220 units @ 22 CU each.

April 08   Purchase of 180 units @ 18 CU each.

April 17   Sale of 240 units @ 25 CU each.

Required

Using successively each of the three costing methods (FIFO, LIFO and WAC), prepare a table allowing you to compare the impact of the three methods on:

1   the ending inventory
2   the net income, assuming a 40% income tax rate
3   the cash flow.

Assignment 9.5 Stada*

Topic: Reporting for inventory
Type: Individual/group exercise
Related part of the chapter: Core Issues

Stada is a German group involved in the health and pharmaceutical sector. From the financial statements (annual report 1999), which are prepared in accordance with German GAAP, we extracted the following information relating to inventory.

Consolidated profit and loss statement for the period 1 January–31 December 1999	
	1999 DM 000s
Sales revenue	692,878
Increase in finished goods and work in progress	34,964
Other operating income	11,541
Cost of materials	
a) Cost of raw materials, consumables and supplies and of purchased materials	363,563
b) Cost of purchased services	6,239

Consolidated balance sheet as of 31 December 1999		
	1999 DM 000s	**1998** DM 000s
Inventories		
Raw materials and supplies	20,706	26,247
Work in progress	11,510	7,193
Finished goods and goods for resale	108,831	78,184
	141,047	111,624

Required

1 Identify the links between the figures of the balance sheet and the figures of the income statement.

2 Explain why some figures of the income statement cannot be double-checked.

Assignment 9.6 Tchaïkovsky

Topic: Income statement by nature and by function
Type: Individual exercise
Related part of the chapter: Advanced Issues

Tchaïkovsky Company has a manufacturing activity. Information relating to 20X1 is as follows (in 000 of CU).

Beginning inventory of raw materials	18	Rent expenses	
Purchases of raw materials	60	. Production	4
Sales of finished products	150	. Administration	5
Raw materials consumed	55	Beginning inventory of work in progress	10
Ending inventory of raw materials	23	Units completed during the period	105
Personnel expenses		Ending inventory of work in progress	5
. Direct labor	16	Beginning inventory of finished products	3
. Supervisory labor	5	Cost of units sold during the period	107
. Sales personnel	3	Ending inventory of finished products	1
. Accounting and administration	4		
Depreciation expenses			
. Production equipment	20		
. Sales equipment	6		
. Administrative equipment	4		

Required

Prepare an income statement by nature and an income statement by function. (Check figure (operating income) is 21.)

Assignment 9.7 Uno Restaurant* and others

Topic: Comparative inventory turnover
Type: Individual/group exercise
Related part of the chapter: Advanced Issues

The following information concerns eight US companies operating solely or mainly restaurants.

Uno Restaurant Corporation

Uno Restaurant Corporation runs 98 company-owned and 47 franchised Pizzeria Uno-Chicago Bar & Grill restaurants, 13 franchised Pizzeria Uno-Restaurant & Bar, and one Mexican restaurant. The company also operates a consumer products division which supplies American Airlines, movie theaters, hotel restaurants, and supermarkets with Pizzeria Uno brand products. Extracted from the consolidated balance sheet and income statement (annual report 1999) the following data are provided.

Thousands of US dollars	3 October 1999	27 September 1998
Inventory (balance sheet)	2,436	2,296
Cost of foods and beverage (income statement)	54,683	

A note to the financial statements indicates that inventory consists of "Food, beverages and supplies". The closing dates shown in the table are explained by the fact that the company's fiscal year ends on the close of business on the Sunday closest to 30 September in each year. The fiscal year consists of 52 weeks. Approximately every 6 or 7 years, a 53rd week is added. This practice is very frequent in the restaurant business (see below, with the exception of Meritage Hospitality Group).

Frisch's Restaurants

Frisch's Restaurants, Inc. operates and licenses family restaurants, most of which offer "drive-through" service, which use the trade name Frisch's Big Boy. Additionally, the company operates one Golden Corral grill buffet restaurant and two hotels with restaurants. Trademarks over which the company has rights include "Frisch's", "Big Boy", "Quality Hotel", "Clarion Hotel" and "Golden Corral". Lodging represents 7.2% of total sales revenue. From the consolidated balance sheet and income statement (annual report 1999), the following data were extracted.

US dollars	30 May 1999	31 May 1998
Inventories (balance sheet)	3,732,458	3,638,740
Cost of sales – Food and paper (income statement)	48,674,392	

A note to the financial statements indicates that inventory consists principally of food items. The closing date is the Sunday nearest to the last day of May.

Morton's Restaurant Group

Morton's Restaurant Group, Inc. operates 50 Morton's of Chicago steakhouse restaurants and 8 "Bertolini's" trattorias. From the consolidated balance sheet and income statement (annual report 1999), we extracted the following data.

Thousands of US dollars	2 January 2000	3 January 1999
Inventories (balance sheet)	7,134	6,400
Food and beverage (income statement)	69,873	

A note to the financial statements indicates that inventory consists principally of food, beverages, and supplies. The closing date is the Sunday nearest to the last day of December.

Dave & Buster's

Dave & Buster's owns and operates restaurant/entertainment complexes. Each Dave & Buster's offers food and beverage items, combined with an array of entertainment attractions such as pocket billiards, shuffleboard, state-of-the-art flight simulators, virtual reality, and traditional carnival-style amusements and games of skill. Whereas food and beverage represent one-half (49.1%) of sales revenues, amusement and other revenues represent the other half (50.9%). From the consolidated balance sheet and income statement (annual report 1999), the following data were extracted.

Thousands of US dollars	30 January 2000	31 January 1999
Inventories (balance sheet)	16,243	10,811
Cost of revenues (income statement)	45,720	

A note to the financial statements indicates that inventory consists principally of food, beverage, merchandise, and supplies. The closing date is the Sunday after the Saturday closest to 31 January.

Meritage Hospitality Group

Meritage Hospitality Group operates 30 "Wendy's Old Fashioned Hamburgers" restaurants. Besides traditional stand-alone Wendy's restaurants, the company runs non-traditional Wendy's restaurants which combine a full-service Wendy's restaurant with a convenience store and gas station facility. From the consolidated balance sheet and income statement (annual report 1999), we extracted the following data.

US dollars	30 November 1999	30 November 1998
Inventories (balance sheet)	207,563	165,156
Cost of food and beverages (income statement)	8,556,960	

A note to the financial statements indicates that inventory consists principally of restaurant food items, beverages, and paper supplies. The closing date is 30 November.

Benihana

Benihana Inc. operates 53 Japanese tepanyaki-style and sushi restaurants and franchises 13 others under the name Benihana of Tokyo. From the consolidated balance sheet and income statement (annual report 2000), the following data were extracted.

Thousands of US dollars	26 March 2000	28 March 1999
Inventories (balance sheet)	3,613	3,106
Cost of food and beverage sales (income statement)	36,588	

A note to the financial statements indicates that inventory consists principally of restaurant operating supplies, and food and beverages.

Rare Hospitality International

Rare Hospitality International, Inc. is a multi-concept restaurant company operating the following restaurants: LongHorn Steakhouse (118), Bugaboo Creek (18), The Capital Grille (11), and other specialty concepts (2). From the consolidated balance sheet and income statement (annual report 1999), the following data were extracted.

Thousands of US dollars	26 December 1999	27 December 1998
Inventories (balance sheet)	10,213	9,609
Cost of restaurant sales (income statement)	137,416	

A note to the financial statements indicates that inventory consists principally of food and beverages.

Diedrich Coffee

Diedrich Coffee, Inc. operates coffeehouses and sells light food items and whole-bean coffee through its coffeehouses. The company also operates a wholesale and a mail order business which sells whole-coffee beans and related supplies and equipment. From the consolidated balance sheet and income statement (annual report 1999), the following data were extracted.

US dollars	27 January 1999	28 January 1999
Inventories (balance sheet)	1,375,119	1,279,436
Cost of sales and occupancy costs (income statement)	9,263,286	

Note to financial statements indicates that inventory consists principally of unroasted coffee beans, roasted coffee beans (whole and ground), accessory and specialty items, other food, beverages, and supplies. The company's fiscal year ends on the Wednesday closest to 31 January.

Required

1 Compute the inventory turnover for each company.
2 Compute the average days' inventory available for each company.
3 Compare and contrast the figures obtained.

References

Drury, C. (2000) *Management and Cost Accounting*, Thomson Learning, London.
IASC (revised 1993) International Accounting Standard No. 2, Inventories, London.

Further readings

Ahmed, M.N., and Scapens, R.W. (2000) Cost allocation in Britain: Towards an institutional analysis. *European Accounting Review*, 9(2), 159–204.
Jennings, R., Simko P.J., and Thompson II, R.B. (1996) Does LIFO inventory accounting improve the income statement at the expense of the balance sheet? *Journal of Accounting Research*, 34(1), 85–119.
Knapp, M.C., and Knapp, C.A. (2000) Perry Drug Stores, Inc.: Accounting and control issues for inventory in a retail environment. *Issues in Accounting Education*, 15(2), 237–55.
Pfaff, D. (1994) On the allocation of overhead costs. *European Accounting Review*, 3(1), 49–70.

Additional material on the website

Go to http://www.thomsonlearning.co.uk/accountingandfinance/stolowylebas for further information, journal entries and extra assignments for each chapter.

The following appendices to this chapter are available on the dedicated website:

Appendix 9.1: Comparison of advantages and limits of perpetual and periodic inventory systems
Appendix 9.2: Differences between physical and accounting inventory count
Appendix 9.3: Other LIFO considerations
Appendix 9.4: Effect of an inventory misstatement

Notes

1 The reader wishing to explore the topics of inventory management or "costing" of inventory inflows is encouraged to consult books respectively on production management and managerial accounting. See, for example, Drury (2000).

2 Inventories related to long-term contracts have been developed in Chapter 6, Appendix 6.1.

3 Even if the physical inventory is not taken on the very date of closure of the books, the modification of said inventory between the two dates requires only minor adjustments which can be handled by keeping track, exceptionally, of each movement between inventory and closing dates.

4 See Drury (2000), for example.

5 In a physical inventory management system the first-in, first-out approach is the only one to make sense so as to avoid the build-up of obsolete inventories.

6 Some other LIFO considerations are shown in Appendix 9.3.

7 LIFO may not be used for tax purposes.

8 LIFO is not prevalent since it is not acceptable for tax purposes.

9 In consolidated financial statement, LIFO is accepted.

10 LIFO is not acceptable in the Republic of Ireland for tax purposes and is not commonly used.

11 LIFO is not acceptable in the UK for tax purposes and is not commonly used.

12 According to IAS 2 (§ 6), "Inventories should be measured at the lower of cost and net realizable value." Net realizable value is defined as the "estimated selling price in the ordinary course of business less the estimated costs of completion and the estimated costs necessary to make the sale" (IAS 2: § 4), i.e., "market value".

Current assets other than inventories

Current assets, excluding inventories, comprise essentially three types of accounts: receivables, current investments (marketable securities or short-term investments), and cash and cash equivalents. The valuation of receivables on the asset side of the balance sheet is strictly linked to the choice of revenue recognition rules (Chapter 6). These current assets are essential in the operating cycle of the firm and their valuation affect the way a user estimates how a firm would fare in a business downturn and evaluates the possible consequences on both income statement (provision expenses) and balance sheet of possible strategic actions.

Major topics

Accounts receivable

Current investments

Cash and cash equivalents

Notes receivable

Financial statement analysis

Value added tax

CORE ISSUES

In this first section, we will review sequentially the three main types of accounts: receivables, marketable securities, and cash.

Accounts receivable or "receivables"

Accounts receivable (A/R) often represent a sizeable component of the asset side of a balance sheet, as shown in Table 10.1, listing companies in decreasing percentage of accounts receivable in their 1999 annual financial statements. The percentage represented by receivables is, of course, much higher for a service activity (few fixed assets) than in a business involved in a heavy industry (large fixed assets components).

Table 10.1 Weight of accounts receivable (A/R)

Company	Currency	Account name	Receivables (rounded)	Total assets	A/R/total assets
Bull (France – IT group)	€ (millions)	Trade receivables	804	2,483	32.4%
ISS (Denmark – support services)	DKK (millions)	Trade accounts receivable	3,511	13,673	25.7%
Pernod Ricard (France – beverages)	€ (millions)	Current receivables	1,147	5,529	20.7%
Philips (Netherlands – electronics)	€ (millions)	Accounts receivable (net)	5,326	29,496	18.1%
Sulzer (Switzerland – medical equipment)	CHF (millions)	Trade accounts receivable	1,188	6,741	17.6%
Racing Champions (USA – manufacturing and sales of collectibles)	$US (thousands)	Accounts receivable	44,717	276,281	16.2%
Barmag (Germany – man-made fiber industry)	DM (thousands)	Receivables for goods and services provided	78,879	488,971	16.1%
Sony (Japan – consumer electronics and music)	Yen (millions)	Notes and accounts receivable, trade (net)	1,013,583	6,299,053	16.1%
Iberia (Spain – air transport)	Pesetas (mil.)	Accounts receivable	103,269	686,864	15.0%
Elkem (Norway – metals and materials)	NOK (millions)	Receivables from customers (net)	1,417	9,671	14.7%
BBAG (Austria – brewery)	€ (thousands)	Accounts receivable	101,288	904,178	11.2%
Stora-Enso (Finland – paper production)	€ (millions)	Accounts receivable	1,733	16,034	10.8%
Mayflower (UK – bus and coaches)	UK £ (millions)	Trade debtors	60	609	9.9%
Fiat (Italy – car manufacturing)	€ (millions)	Trade receivables	6,509	79,873	8.1%

This table, like equivalent tables in previous chapters, is provided for the sole purpose of illustrating the diversity of situations. It is interesting to note the variety of terms used in annual accounts to describe a similar reality.

Several accounting issues affect the reporting of receivables:

- non-offsetting principle
- subsidiary ledgers

- collectibility of the claim ("bad debts", "doubtful accounts")
- reporting
- handling of value added tax (VAT) (covered in Appendix 10.2).

Application of the non-offsetting principle to accounts receivable

Accounts receivable are the result of credit sales, whether they relate to individuals, retailers, wholesalers or manufacturers. In principle, accounts receivable should show a debit balance, since the account is debited when the sale (credit to the income statement) is recorded and balanced by a credit entry when the amount receivable is actually settled by the customer (debit cash). However, accounts receivable can show a credit balance in the case of payment by anticipation (down payment, for example) or error on the part of the customer (for example a payment in excess of the amount owed, or a duplicated payment).

When an account receivable shows a credit balance, it must be shown on the liability side of the balance sheet. Such an account represents a debt towards the customer. The "no offsetting principle" states that debit balances and credit balances in accounts receivable cannot under any circumstances be compensated. This rule applies even for subsidiary accounts concerning one given client as long as they do not correspond to the same transaction.

Subsidiary ledgers

In previous chapters we have recorded credit sales by debiting a generic "accounts receivable". For accounting to be useful to managers, such a generic account is not a sound basis for monitoring transactions with customers. Although reports to outside users of accounting information contain only one (or very few) line(s) for accounts receivable, internally the firm will use one account (or subsidiary ledger) per customer.

Most accounting software programs code accounts on an alphanumeric basis (see Chapter 4). At the end of the accounting period, individual subsidiary ledger accounts are centralized (accumulated) and transferred to the controlling "accounts receivable" in the general ledger.

Collectibility of receivables

The development of credit sales or sales on account is a legitimate way for reaching new customers and growing sales. The existence of receivables leads to the necessity of evaluating, at the end of each accounting period, the probability that the account will effectively be collected. This evaluation is based on both commercial information (customer satisfaction, returns, complaints, etc.) and external information pertaining to the economic or financial situation of the debtor. Figure 10.1 highlights the four categories of accounts receivable such an analysis will lead to.

Doubtful ❷ or disputed ❸ accounts, which are partly or totally uncollectible, are referred to as "bad" or "doubtful" debts[1]. The value of these accounts will have to be written down (provision expense – or valuation allowance – in the

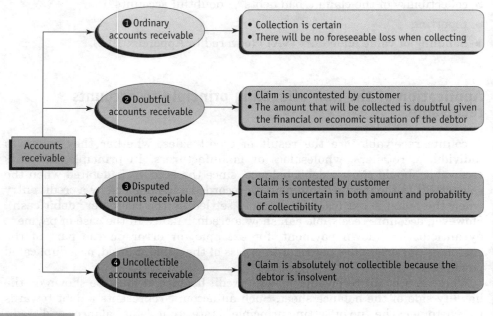

Figure 10.1 Different categories of claim

income statement). Uncollectible accounts ❹, must be written off (bad debt expense in the income statement). Sometimes, both written-down and written-off amounts are called "bad debt expense".

The write-down or write-off procedures are highlighted in Figure 10.2 and described subsequently.

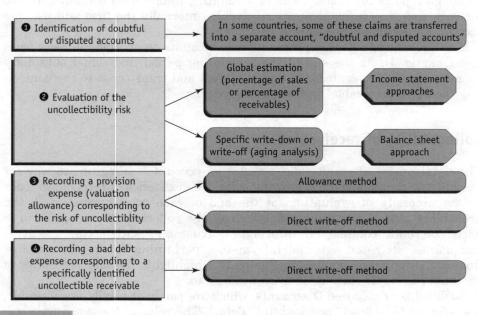

Figure 10.2 Doubtful accounts receivable

❶ Identification of doubtful or disputed accounts

The balances of each individual customer account are individually reviewed and structured by due date in an aged balance[2]. Any transaction whose age is considered to fall outside the customary credit terms for this type of clientele is potentially a doubtful or a disputed account. Further research about the cause of the lateness will establish whether the account should be considered doubtful or disputed. The range of credit terms shown in Table 10.2 illustrates, in increasing order, the range of average credit terms observed in several European countries.

Table 10.2 Average credit terms in some European countries in 2000[3]

Country	Number of days	Country	Number of days
Finland	29	Ireland	51
Sweden	32	France	58
Germany	34	Belgium	61
Denmark	34	Spain	74
Austria	37	Italy	87
Netherlands	46	Portugal	91
United Kingdom	49	Greece	94

The more a receivable exceeds the "normal" credit terms, the higher the likelihood of its uncollectibility.

❷ Evaluation of the risk of uncollectibility

Global estimation (percentage of sales or percentage of receivables)

The uncollectibility risk can be estimated globally using statistical elements as long as these are specific to the firm. The most commonly used methods consist in applying a selected percentage to either total sales or total receivables. This method is however less and less used in practice since the generalization of efficient accounting software permits the specific write-down (provision expense) or write-off (bad debt expense) of individualized transactions.

Specific write-down or write-off (aging analysis)

The aging analysis permits a transaction by transaction decision. The situation of each individual customer (or transaction) determined to be problematic is further documented through questions like the following:

● Has the customer challenged the validity of the receivable?

● Is the customer up to date in its payments according to the specifically agreed schedule pertaining to this transaction?

● Has there been any correspondence or other piece of data indicating that the customer had financial difficulties?

● Have any letters from the company been returned undelivered from the customer's address?

An overdue claim might often prove to be collectible if the conditions for its lateness are detected and handled appropriately. It is also critical to use the information about the uncollectibility of a claim to help prevent the occurrence of future uncollectible receivables.

❸ Recording a provision expense corresponding to the risk of uncollectibility

"When an uncertainty arises about the collectibility of an amount already included in revenue, the uncollectible amount, or the amount in respect of which recovery has ceased to be probable, is recognized as an expense, rather than as an adjustment of the amount of revenue originally recognized" (IAS 18, IASC 1993: § 22).

Generally, the uncollectibility risk is evaluated and an "allowance for uncollectibles" is recorded as a provision. This method is therefore known as the "allowance method". This procedure allows conformity with the matching principle, since the allowance will be expensed and matched with the sales which have generated the accounts receivable.

Brückner GmbH will provide an illustration of this procedure. Brückner has a claim of 100 CU over its customer Anton Corp. At the end of year 20X1, Anton Corp. experiences financial difficulties. The potential loss is estimated to reduce the collectible claim to 60 (a loss of 40% of the receivable). At the end of period 20X2, the estimation of the non-collectible part of the claim has grown to 70. During 20X3, Anton Corp. is liquidated and the receiver settles the claim in full with a payment of 10. These events are illustrated in Figures 10.3 through 10.5.

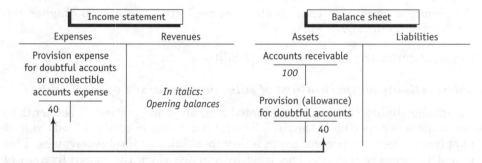

Figure 10.3 Doubtful accounts – Year 20X1

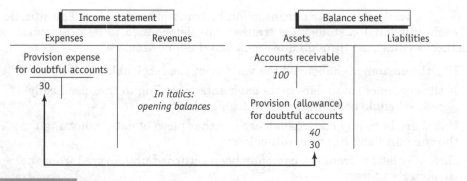

Figure 10.4 Doubtful accounts – Year 20X2

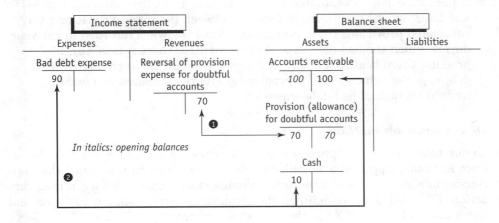

Figure 10.5 Doubtful accounts – Year 20X3

Brückner records an expense of 40 corresponding to its estimation of the uncollectibility risk. At this stage, the "accounts receivable" is not credited. A contra-asset account is used: "provision" (or "allowance") for "bad debts" (or "for doubtful accounts"). It is, of course, theoretically possible to credit directly the individual customer account.

In 20X2, the risk is now estimated to be 70. The allowance must be raised to recognize the further devaluation of the claim. An additional allowance amounting to 70 – 40 = 30 (40 was the estimation of the risk at the end of 20X1) should be recorded. The accumulated provision (recorded on the balance sheet) is now raised to 70.

When the client finally settles the account (even if it is not for the full amount remaining due and not yet provisioned), one must:

- cancel the cumulated provisions pertaining to this account or this receivable by recognizing the equivalent amount as revenue (or as a negative expense)
- record a bad debt expense corresponding to the difference between the original claim (here it is 100) which is settled and the amount actually collected (here it is 10).

Impact on income of each of the year's entries

Year 20X1	Provision expense	−40		
Year 20X2	Provision expense	−30		−90
Year 20X3	Reversal of provision expense	+ 70	−20	
	Bad debt expense	−90		

Comments

- The mechanism of allowance (provision) has the effect of distributing the net charge (here 90) over the years it takes to clear the receivable.
- The net impact is always equal to the "bad debt".

- If the risk is poorly evaluated (as was the case here, first evaluated at 40 and later revised at 70), the difference between the total expense and the cumulated provisions (here it amounts to 20) is always recorded in the year during which the bad debt expense is recognized (here it is 20X3). In practice, there is almost always a difference between the estimated bad debt expense (which led to provisioning) and the accounts receivable written off (actual bad debt expense).

Direct write-off method

Under this method, no provision (or allowance) is created when the risk of uncollectibility appears. The policy is, on the contrary, to wait until the non-recoverable amount is clearly and unambiguously known before taking any action. When all facts are definite, the accounting entry is similar to the second entry taken above in 20X3 in the Brückner example.

Not all countries allow this method since it shows receivables at their nominal value when in fact a risk of uncollectibility is actually known. The only situation where this approach might not create a misrepresentation of the financial situation of the firm is when the sales revenue and the percentage of uncollectible receivables is essentially constant or stable. Such a situation is obviously quite rare.

❹ Recording a bad debt expense corresponding to a specifically identified uncollectible receivable

When a specific receivable becomes definitely uncollectible, an expense is recorded. If a provision (allowance) had been created for this specific receivable, this provision has to be cancelled as was done in the Brückner GmbH example.

A concluding remark to this section is that the valuation of the uncollectibility risk constitutes one of the tools managers use to manage their earnings (see "accounts manipulation" in Chapter 15).

Reporting accounts receivable

In the balance sheet

Businesses follow one of four methods for reporting accounts receivable in their balance sheet. Each is now illustrated using the data from year 20X2 of the Brückner GmbH example:

Method 1 (detailed vertically and using a contra asset account)

Accounts receivable (gross)	100
Less provision for doubtful accounts	−70
Accounts receivable (net)	30

Method 2 (synthetic with detail in the balance sheet)

Accounts receivable (net of provision for doubtful accounts: 70)	30

Method 3 (synthetic with detail in a note to the balance sheet)

Accounts receivable (net) (see note X)	30

Notes to the financial statements:

Note X – Accounts receivable

The accumulated amount of provision for doubtful accounts is equal to 70.

Method 4 (detailed horizontally)

	Gross value	Amortization and provisions	Net value
Accounts receivable	100	70	30

Whichever method is used, the most important is, for the user of financial information, to get access to the gross amount of receivables, which is used to compute ratios (see developments on financial statement analysis later).

Real-life example

Ericsson
(Sweden – Swedish GAAP – Source: Annual report 1999 – Telecommunication)

Notes to the consolidated financial statements

11 Accounts receivable – trade SEK m	1999	1998
Notes and accounts receivable	63,380	53,775
Receivables from associated companies	204	125
	63,584	53,900

The allowance for doubtful accounts amounting to SEK 2,550 m (2,308) which has reduced the amounts shown above, includes amounts for estimated losses based on commercial risk evaluations. The allowance does not include provisions for potential losses of a political nature.

Reporting movements in provision for doubtful accounts

In Chapter 7 we evoked the changes in valuation of fixed assets concerning the evolution of the gross value of fixed assets and also of accumulated depreciation. It is possible to create a similar table to report the changes in the provision account. For example, Philips, the Dutch electricity and electronic applications group, publishes such a table in its 1999 annual report:

The changes in the allowances for doubtful accounts are as follows:	1999	1998	1997
Balance as of 1 January	186	155	114
Additions charged to income	198	179	122
Deductions from allowances*	–13	–60	–59
Other movements**	–93	–88	–22
Balance as of 31 December	278	186	155

*Write-offs for which allowances were provided
**Including the effect of translation differences and consolidation changes

The figures in the table come from a variety of events or components:

- Additions charged to income: they are provision expenses for the year (i.e., provisions on new receivables plus additional provisions on receivables for which the risk of uncollectibility is considered to have increased).

- Deductions from allowances: cancellation of provisions taken in previous years because the uncollectibility risk is perceived to have decreased on some of the receivables or cancellation of provisions because the receivable has been settled. This cancellation can be recorded as either a reduction in expenses or a revenue (reversal of provision).

- Other movements: they are movements linked to the consolidation of subsidiaries, such as:
  - translation differences on the conversion of financial statements of subsidiaries labeled in a currency other than the one of the parent company (see Chapter 13)
  - changes in the scope of consolidation resulting from acquisition or sale of subsidiaries (see Chapter 13).

Current investments

Definitions

"Current investments" are defined in IAS 25 (IASC 1994) as "investments that are by their nature readily realizable and are intended to be held for not more than one year" (§ 4). IAS 39 (IASC 1998: § 10), which supersedes IAS 25 and is applicable to the preparation of financial statements covering financial years beginning on or after 1 January 2001, introduces four different categories of financial assets composing current investments: "financial asset held for trading", "held-to-maturity investments", "loans and receivables originated by the enterprise", and "available for sale financial assets". We provide in Appendix 10.1 developments on this classification.

We will limit here current investments to "marketable securities" and "held-to-maturity investments", i.e., shares and bonds of other companies or loans to other companies that can be sold readily and which are held by the firm as a cash substitute with the intention of protecting the purchasing power of a liquid asset and possibly earning a return on the capital invested.

The valuation of current investments is critical as their value is constantly changing, thus creating potential (unrealized) gains or losses. The way these losses or gains are recognized, if at all, and handled in the reporting process may affect both the risk evaluation and the measurement of the value created by the business.

According to both IAS 39 and IAS 25 (§ 19), current investments "should be carried in the balance sheet at either market value; or the lower of cost or market value". A market valuation leads to recording potential gains or losses while the lower of cost or market rule leads to only recognize potential losses. The prudence principle would call for lower of cost or market (it seems prudent to consider that losses are rarely reversible while profits often are, alas, reversible). Conversely, the fair market value offers the best description of the reality of the financial situation of the firm. When "current investments are carried at the lower of cost or market value, the carrying amount can be determined either on an aggregate portfolio basis, in total or by category of investment, or on an individual current investment instrument basis" (IAS 25, § 19).

The option created by IAS 25 and maintained under IAS 39 of recognizing potential gains is an open door for using such valuation for "fine-tuning" financial results of a period (see "accounts manipulation" in Chapter 15). Fortunately, the consistency principle forces businesses to keep the same accounting method for several years thus reducing the risk of abuses of this option.

Accounting for current investments

The IASC allows the application of the lower of cost or market rule to either each discrete stock or investment (individual basis) or to the portfolio of investments as a whole (aggregate portfolio basis). The choice leads, of course, generally to different results as shown in Table 10.3.

Let us illustrate. Mozart Company holds in current investment equity securities of two other businesses (Alpha Company and Beta Company). Let us examine the key operations that can affect this current investment using the lower of cost or market rule.

Table 10.3 Data of Mozart Company's current investment example

Date of purchase	Security	Quantity	Unit cost	Total cost	Market value at year-end	Total market value	Period-end adjustment (individual basis)	Period-end adjustment (aggregate portfolio basis)
25/10/20X1	Shares Alpha Company	10	150	1,500	160	1,600		
23/11/20X1	Shares Beta Company	20	100	2,000	90	1,800	−200	
Total		30		3,500		3,400	−200	−100

Let us pursue the example using the individual basis method. Since only potential losses are recorded and the Alpha Company investment appreciated, it requires no adjusting entry. Only the investment in Beta Company will require adjusting entries since its value declined (see Figure 10.6).

On 20 April 20X2 10 shares of Beta Company are sold at a unit price of 95. Since they had been purchased for 100 each, there is a total loss of 50 on the sale. The appropriate entries are illustrated in Figure 10.7.

Some countries merge the two entries by recording in the income statement the difference between the reversal of the provision and the loss on the sale. In our example, a 150 CU revenue would have been recorded (200 − 50 = 150).

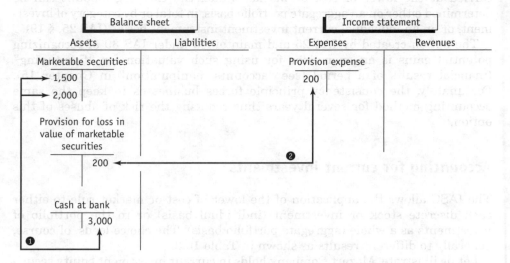

① Purchase of marketable securities
② At year-end, accounting for a potential loss (computed on an individual basis). The loss is only potential as long as the securities have not been sold. The terminology for unrealized losses or potential losses is not settled and several alternative terms can be found in financial statements.

Figure 10.6 Accounting for current investments – Year 20X1

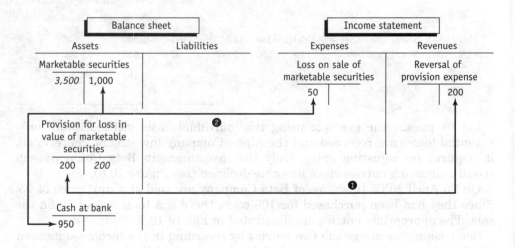

① The provision (allowance) is cancelled (reversed)
② The sale is recorded without taking the provision into account.
The loss is: 1,000 – 950 = (10 x 100) – (10 x 95) = 50

Figure 10.7 Accounting for current investments – Year 20X2

Reporting current investments

Current investments are found in annual statements to be reported in four different ways. If we use the Mozart company data for year 20X1, the current investments can be reported in one of the 4 following formats:

Format 1 (detailed vertically and using a contra asset account)

Current investments (gross -- at cost)	3,500
Minus provision for potential loss	−200
Current investments (net)	3,300

Format 2 (synthetic with detail in the balance sheet)

Current investments (net of provision for potential loss: 200)   3,300

Format 3 (synthetic with detail in a note to the balance sheet)

Current investments (net) (see note X)   3,300

Notes to the financial statements:

Note X – Current investments:

The accumulated amount of provision for potential losses is equal to 200.

Format 4 (detailed horizontally)

	Gross value	Amortization and provisions	Net value
Current investments	3,500	200	3,300

Real-life examples

Toray Industries
*(Japan – Japanese GAAP – Source: Annual Report 1999 –
Manufacturer of synthetic fibers and textiles)*

Consolidated balance sheet – 31 March 1999 and 1998 (in millions of yen)

	1999	1998
(...)		
Current assets		
Marketable securities (Note 4)	32,427	23,833
(...)		

Notes to the financial statements

1 Significant accounting policies

Marketable securities
Marketable securities in current assets (...) are generally carried at the lower of moving average cost or market.
(...)

4 Marketable securities
On 31 March 1999 and 1998 the marketable securities in current assets consisted of the following:

	1999	1998
Marketable equity securities	4,134	4,898
Marketable debt securities investments	20,671	—
Securities purchased under agreements with resale (Bond GENSAKI)	3,977	12,372
Other marketable securities	3,645	6,563
	32,427	**23,833**
Market value of marketable equity securities	11,498	14,769

Pernod Ricard

(France – French GAAP – Source: Annual Report 1999 – Beverages)

Consolidated balance sheet (€ million)

	Gross value	Amortization and provisions	31/12/1999 Net value	31/12/1998 Net value	31/12/1997 Net value
Marketable securities (see note 1.8)	154.0	3.9	150.1	120.9	112.7

Notes to the financial statements

Note 1.8 Marketable securities

Marketable securities are recorded on the balance sheet at their original value. When the market value of these securities at the close of the fiscal period is less than their original value, a depreciation reserve is set up.

Cash and cash equivalents

Definitions

IAS 7 (IASC 1992) states that "cash comprises cash on hand" (coins and currency available) and "demand deposits" (deposits in bank accounts that are available on demand). "Cash equivalents are short-term, highly liquid investments that are readily convertible to known amounts of cash and which are subject to an insignificant risk of changes in value" (§6). If the concept of "cash" is easily understandable, that of "cash equivalents" is more fuzzy. This is why IAS 7 specifies that cash equivalents are held for the purpose of meeting short-term cash commitments rather than for investment or other purposes. An investment normally qualifies as a cash equivalent only when it has a short maturity of, say, 3 months or less from the date of acquisition.

The weight of cash and cash equivalents in a balance sheet can vary greatly between companies (see Table 10.4). Unlike what we said before about other balance sheet items, there appears to be no link between the nature of the industrial sector the firm is involved in and its level of cash and cash equivalents. The level of cash and cash equivalent plus current investments is, in fact, considered to be the cash reserve a firm chooses to build in order to be able to strike rapidly in case opportunities appear. For example Microsoft's "cash plus cash equivalent plus current investments" during the year 2000 was in the area of US$23.5 billion. It is a strategic reservoir of resources coherent with a strategy of major acquisitions in a very turbulent world in which an exchange of shares may no longer be considered as attractive as it may have been in the previous year(s).

The topic of cash and cash equivalents is developed in greater detail in Chapter 14.

Table 10.4 Weight of cash and cash equivalents (C&CE)

Company (1999 annual reports)	Currency	Name of the account	Cash and cash equivalents	Total assets	C&CE/ total assets
Barmag (Germany – man-made fiber industry)	DM (th)	Cash	178,462	488,971	36.5%
Sulzer (Switzerland – medical equipment)	CHF (m)	Cash	1,144	6,741	17.0%
Elkem (Norway – metals and materials)	NOK (m)	Cash and bank deposits	1,106	9,671	11.4%
Sony (Japan – music)	Yen (m)	Cash and cash equivalents, time deposits	616,514	6,299,053	9.8%
Mayflower (UK – bus and coach)	UK £ (m)	Cash at bank and in hand	58.8	609.3	9.7%
Philips (Netherlands – electronics)	€ (m)	Cash and cash equivalents	2,331	29,496	7.9%
Bull (France – IT group)	€ (m)	Cash	154	2,483	6.2%
Pernod Ricard (France – beverages)	€ (m)	Cash	277	5,529	5.0%
BBAG (Austria – brewery)	€ (th)	Cash and deposits with credit institutions	45,097	904,178	5.0%
Racing Champions (USA – racing cars replicas)	US (th)	Cash and cash equivalents	12,265	276,282	4.4%
ISS (Denmark – support services)	DKK (m)	Liquid funds	515	13,673	3.8%
Stora-Enso (Finland – paper production)	€ (m)	Cash and cash equivalents	439.4	16,034.0	2.7%
Fiat (Italy – car manufacturer)	€ (m)	Cash	1,906	79,873	2.4%
Iberia (Spain – airline)	Pesetas (m)	Cash	2,396	686,864	0.3%

Real-life example of cash and cash equivalents

Philips
(Netherlands – Dutch GAAP – Source: Annual report 1999 – Consumer electronics)

Consolidated balance sheet as of 31 December (in € millions)

			1999	1998
	(...) Current assets			
11	Cash and cash equivalents		2,331	6,553
	(...)			

Note to the financial statements

Note 11: Cash and cash equivalents

Cash and cash equivalents includes time deposits with banks totaling €17 million (1998: €20 million) that are not freely available for withdrawal.

Notes receivable and sales returns deserve special attention, as well as the impact of value added taxes on the valuation of receivables (Appendix 10.2) and bank reconciliation (Appendix 10.3).

Notes receivable

Principle

Credit sales sometimes are settled through specific monetary instruments called "notes" or "commercial paper". These instruments are either a "draft" or "bill of exchange" when issued by the seller or a "promissory note" when issued by the purchaser. Such instruments are an extensively used practice mainly in southern Europe in countries such as Spain, Italy, France, and Greece. It is also found in other countries such as Japan, Finland, and the UK. Commercial paper or notes are defined as follows:

- A draft (or bill of exchange) is a written order by a first party (the drawer, i.e., the seller) instructing a second party (the drawee, i.e., the buyer) to pay a third party (the payee or beneficiary, who may be the drawer himself) a specified amount at a specified date (maturity) without conditions. It is common practice to have the draft prepared by the seller and sent to the buyer along with the invoice as a suggested preferred method of payment. The buyer then returns the signed ("accepted") draft to the seller, thus creating the contract by their signature.

- A promissory note is a written document in which a person or business (generally known as the "maker") promises to pay a given amount to a third party (individual or business), referred to as the "beneficiary", on a specified date (maturity date). The maker is the customer and the beneficiary is the supplier.

Since the accounting treatment is the same for a draft, a bill of exchange or a promissory note, we will refer to this class of financial instruments by using the generic term of "notes receivable" on the supplier side and "notes payable" on the buyer side (the latter is covered in Chapter 13).

Notes payable offer three advantages to the seller over the traditional credit sale in which an invoice leads the recording of a receivable:

- A note is a contract since it has been "accepted" by the buyer. It offers a higher level of guarantee of payment to the seller than a simple combination "order, delivery, acknowledgement of receipt plus invoice".

- A note is a regular financial instrument. A note can be endorsed over to a third party (not limited to financial institutions).

- A note is a negotiable credit instrument. The seller can sell a note (commercial paper) to a financial institution before its maturity date. The financial institution charges a fee for its services (generally proportional to the face value of the note plus a fixed administrative fee). The act of selling a note to a financial institution is referred to as "discounting" it.

The lifecycle process of a draft or bill of exchange is illustrated in Appendix 10.4 for a payment on the maturity date and in Figure 10.8 for a sale (discounting) of the note before that date.

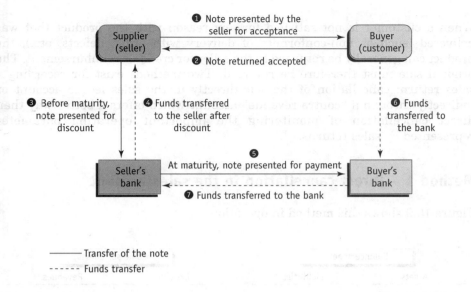

- Any holder of a note (even after an endorsement) can sell it whenever they feel the need
- In case of a discounting, in phase ❹ the holder of the note does not receive the full face amount of the note. The bank keeps a discounting fee which represents (1) the interest for the period separating the date of discounting and the maturity date, (2) an administrative fee, and eventually (3) a risk premium
- Discounting a note can be done in two ways that involve different risk levels:
  - *without recourse*: the note is sold with complete transfer to the buyer of the note of the default risk of the drawer
  - *with recourse*: i.e., a conditional sale. If the drawer defaults on the maturity date, the discounting financial institution will demand full reimbursement of the note plus fees from the seller of the note who discounted it in the first place

Figure 10.8 Note receivable discounted (sold) before maturity (draft emitted by the seller and accepted by the buyer)

Recording of notes receivable

The recording of notes receivable is developed in Appendix 10.5. The amount of discounted notes that have been removed from the assets but which still carry a recourse should be reported in the footnotes to financial statements, in the "commitments" or the "accounts receivable" sections. For example, Philips NV's annual report for the year 1999 discloses the following information in the section "receivables": "Discounted drafts of €22 million (1998: €29 million) have been deducted." It means that the accounts receivable represented by notes (or drafts) to that amount have been taken out of the assets at the time of discounting but still could represent a latent liability.

The amount of discounted notes is a necessary information to compute the average days of sale in a financial statement analysis.

When a customer is not satisfied for any reason with the product that was delivered (such as non-conformity of delivery with order, defects, etc.), the product can generally be returned to the seller for credit or reimbursement. The original sale must therefore be reversed. Two methods exist for recording a sales return: cancellation of the sale directly in the sales ledger account or indirectly through a "contra-revenue" account which offers a better way than direct cancellation of monitoring the important operating parameter represented by sales returns.

Method 1 – Direct cancellation in the sales account

Figure 10.9 shows this method in operation.

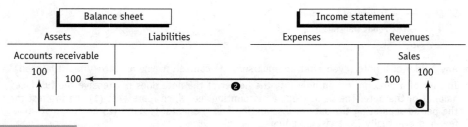

Figure 10.9 Recording of a sales return with direct cancellation

Method 2 – Use of a sales return account (contra account)

Figure 10.10 shows how this method works.

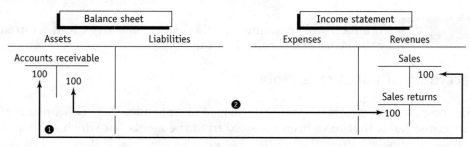

Figure 10.10 Recording of a sales return with use of a contra account

The sales returns account (a rarely reported, essentially internal account) creates a measure used by management to monitor the evolution of sales returns so as to better be able to research and manage their causes. Gross sales (before discounts and other price adjustments) are most of the time reported net of returns in the income statement.

When goods have been returned, they must be entered in inventory before resale or destruction. Accounting entries here depend on whether the firm is using a periodic or perpetual inventory[4].

If the firm uses a periodic inventory system, no specific entry is required at the time of the return since the returned goods will automatically be counted in the year-end physical inventory unless they have, by then, already been resold or destroyed.

If the firm uses a perpetual inventory system, and the goods are still in a sellable condition, the goods must be re-entered in the inventory account so as to adjust the cost of goods sold by the appropriate amount, otherwise they are simply ignored.

Financial statement analysis

Managers as well as many users are interested in monitoring the operating and cash cycles of a business. The credit policy of a firm has an impact on sales revenue (credit terms can be a key attribute in the customer's decision to buy), on the level of receivables and length of the cash collection cycle. Two ratios, actually linked, are commonly used to monitor the effects of a credit policy. They are the "average days of sales" and the "receivables turnover". They are defined as follows:

Average days of sales (in receivables) (or **Average collection period**) =
(Average net accounts receivable/Net sales) × 365 days

This ratio provides the average duration of credit terms offered to customer:

Receivables turnover = Net sales/Average net accounts receivable

This second ratio, which is proportional to the inverse of the previous one, measures the number of times receivables turned over during the year.

Observations about these ratios:
- The accounts receivable are generally averaged between beginning and end of year in an attempt to minimize seasonal variations. External analysts generally only have, in the worst case, annual and, in the best case, quarterly data to build the averages, thus not freeing themselves completely of seasonal variations within the period. An internal manager probably uses rolling averages over 12 months based on monthly balances for a better vision of the impact of the interaction of the credit policy and the state of the economy and the behavior of customers.
- Some analysts suggest that only credit sales be used in the calculation in order to not introduce a favorable bias due to cash sales. Although theoretically more accurate than the averaging of total sales versus total receivables, this approach is difficult to implement as the breakdown between cash and credit sales is rarely reported in annual statements.
- Notes receivable that have been discounted to a bank and have been removed from accounts receivable should be added to the book receivables in order to get as accurate a picture of the real situation as possible. In fact, the possibility for the seller to sell their notes to a financial institution is an encouragement to feel free to extend credit without having to bear the requisite increase in working capital it would involve.

- When sales are eligible for VAT the accounts receivable balance includes VAT. Therefore, in order to use coherent figures in the calculation of ratios one must verify that numerator and denominator are expressed coherently either VAT-included or VAT-excluded. However, such coherence is not always easy to achieve as, for example, export sales are generally not submitted to VAT in the country of origin and domestic sales are exposed to different VAT rates in different countries. Current practice calls for ignoring VAT and accept that the figures do not give the true value of the ratio but that it is not a dramatic error in that the general trend of evolution is still the same as long as no major changes in the mix of sales (cash versus credit as well as domestic versus export) take place.

Real-life example

Ericsson

The Swedish telephone equipment manufacturer shows an excellent example of the difficulty of evaluating the average days of sales when a large proportion of sales are export sales or sales not realized by the parent's country operations. In its 1999 annual report they report their average days of sales at approximately 100 days:

		Millions of SEK
Net sales	1999	215,403
Net sales in Sweden	1999	7,551
Accounts receivable – trade	1999	63,584
Accounts receivable – trade	1998	53,900
Accounts receivable – trade	Average	58,742
Average days' sales (58,742/215,403) × 365		99.5
Receivables turnover (215,403/58,742)		3.7

In this example, we have chosen to not extract the VAT which is included in the receivables because the proportion of total sales originating from domestic operations is very small. The credit term appears to be intrinsically long but, as we will see in Chapter 15, no ratio can ever be interpreted on its face value but only by comparing its value to equivalent ratios pertaining to other comparable firms in the same line of business.

KEY POINTS

- Current assets, excluding inventories, comprise receivables, marketable securities (or short-term investments), and cash.
- The percentage of total assets represented by receivables is generally related to the business activity in which the company is involved: higher for a service activity, lower in a heavy industry, because of the relative importance of fixed assets.

- The probability that an account receivable will effectively be collected must be evaluated at the end of each accounting period. Doubtful or disputed accounts, which are partly or totally uncollectible, are referred to as "bad" or "doubtful" debts, or "doubtful accounts". Their value has to be written down by recognizing a provision expense.
- Uncollectible accounts must be written off by recognizing a bad debt expense.
- "Current investments" are semi-liquid assets that are readily realizable and are intended to be held for not more than one year.
- Current investments should be carried in the balance sheet at either market value or the lower of cost or market value.
- Cash comprises "cash in hand" (coins and currency available) and "demand deposits" (deposits in bank accounts that are available on demand).
- Cash equivalents are short-term, highly liquid investments that are readily convertible to known amounts of cash and which are subject to an insignificant risk of changes in value.
- The two main indicators relevant with regard to accounts receivable are (1) the average days of sales, and (2) the receivables turnover.

REVIEW

Review 10.1 Berg

Topic: Accounting for provision on receivables
Type: Individual exercise
Related part of the chapter: Core Issues

At the end of their accounting period, on 31 December 20X3, Berg Enterprises have reviewed their receivables and found two doubtful accounts.

Customer	A/R balance	Comments	Probable loss
Alban	200	Filed for protection from creditors	25%
Adam	300	Ditto	40%

As of 31 December 20X4, these doubtful accounts are as follows.

Customer	A/R balance	Comments	Probable loss
Alban	200	Filed for protection from creditors	70%
Adam	300	Paid 50 in total settlement of account	250

Required

1 Prepare the doubtful accounts provisions at the end of 20X3.
2 Prepare the appropriate entries at the end of 20X3.
3 Prepare the doubtful accounts provisions at the end of 20X4.
4 Prepare the appropriate entries at the end of 20X4.

Solution

1 Doubtful accounts provisions at the end of 20X3

Customer	A/R balance	Probable loss	Provision
Alban	200	25%	200 × 25% = 50
Adam	300	40%	300 × 40% = 120
Total	500		170

2 Entries at the end of 20X3

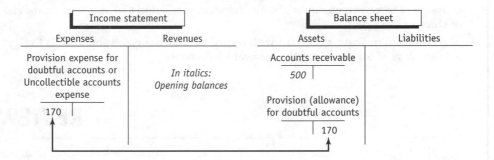

3 Doubtful accounts provisions at the end of 20X4

Customer	Accounts receivable	Probable loss	Provision
Alban	200	70%	200 × 70% = 140 − 50 (provision year 20X3) = 90
Adam	300	—	Payment of 50. Reversal of provision (120)

4 Entries at the end of 20X4

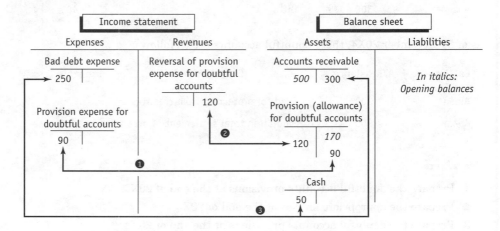

ASSIGNMENTS

Assignment 10.1

Multiple-choice questions
Type: Individual exercise
Related part of the chapter: Core/Advanced Issues

Select the right answer (only one possible answer, unless otherwise stated).

1 **Doubtful debts represent**
   (a) Liabilities which are challenged by one of the parties
   (b) Receivables which might not be collected
   (c) All of these
   (d) None of these

2 **Accounts receivable is equivalent to (several answers possible)**
   (a) Trade creditors
   (b) Trade debtors
   (c) Trade accounts payable
   (d) Trade accounts receivable
   (e) All of these
   (f) Note of these

3 **A bank overdraft should be**
   (a) Included in the financial fixed assets
   (b) Reported as a current asset
   (c) Reported as a current liability
   (d) Netted against positive cash balances at other banks
   (e) None of these

4 **The direct write-off method is consistent with the matching accounting principle while the allowance method is not**
   (a) True
   (b) False

5 **Accounts receivable are generally valued at the**
   (a) Amounts invoiced to customers
   (b) Net realizable value
   (c) Present value of future cash flows
   (d) None of these

6 **Given the following information, determine the accounts receivable turnover (two possible answers)**

Beginning accounts receivable 20
Ending accounts receivable 40
Beginning cash 50
Ending cash 60
Cash sales 40
Credit sales 300
Net income 35

   (a) 15   (g) 1
   (b) 7.5   (h) 2
   (c) 10   (i) 2.5
   (d) 17   (j) 3
   (e) 8.5   (k) None of these
   (f) 11.33

7 An accounts receivable with a 100% probability of being collected is a cash equivalent

(a) True
(b) False

8 When a note receivable is discounted

(a) The note is removed from the assets
(b) The note is maintained in the assets and a liability is recorded
(c) The note is removed from the assets or maintained in the assets with a liability recorded, depending on the national GAAP
(d) None of these

9 When a provision (allowance) is no longer necessary

(a) An expense account is decreased (credited)
(b) A revenue account is increased (credited)
(c) Both solutions are possible, it depends on the country
(d) None of these

10 In a monthly bank reconciliation, the statement begins with

(a) The cash balance per books at the end of the month
(b) The cash balance per books at the beginning of the month
(c) The cash balance on the bank statement at the beginning of the month
(d) The cash balance on the bank statement at the end of the month
(e) None of these

Assignment 10.2 Mahler

Topic: Estimating provision for doubtful accounts
Type: Individual exercise
Related part of the chapter: Core Issues

Mahler Company provides the following information relating to sales, accounts receivable and the provision for doubtful accounts for year 20X2 (000 CU omitted).

Sales for 20X2	3,000
Sales returns on credit sales	100
Accounts receivable balance on 1 January 20X2	400
Provision for doubtful accounts balance on 1 January 20X2	40
Cash collected on accounts receivable during 20X2	1,000
Accounts written off as bad debt expenses during 20X2	30

Required

1 Record the write-off of uncollectible doubtful accounts during 20X2.

2 Prepare the adjusting entry required on 31 December 20X2 to record the provision on doubtful accounts for each of the following *independent* assumptions:

(a) The provision for doubtful accounts is based on the ending balance of accounts receivable. Eighty percent of the sales for 20X2 were credit sales. The accountant of Mahler Company, Mr. Gustav, estimates, from past experience, that 10% of the 31 December 20X2 accounts receivable will prove to be doubtful.

(b) The provision for doubtful accounts is based on net credit sales. The accountant estimated that 80% of the sales are credit sales, and that 5% of the net credit sales will prove to be doubtful.

(c) The provision for doubtful expense is based on aging of accounts receivable. The following aging schedule has been prepared by the accountant.

Days outstanding	Amount	Probability of collection
0–30 days	900	95%
31–60 days	500	90%
61–90 days	250	80%
More than 90 days	20	70%

Assignment 10.3 Barmag AG*

Topic: Reporting for receivables
Type: Group exercise
Related part of the chapter: Core Issues

Barmag AG is a German company offering the man-made fiber industry a complete range of products for the manufacture and the processing of man-made fibers. The consolidated balance sheet (*source*: annual report 1999), shows the following elements relating to receivables.

Consolidated balance sheets (excerpts)		
DM (000)	31.12.1999	31.12.1998
Assets		
Receivables for goods and services provided	78,879	27,614
Other accounts receivable and other assets	22,059	82,012

Notes to the consolidated financial statements.

(3) Receivables and other assets

	Due date within 1 year DM (000)	in over 1 year DM (000)	1999 Total DM (000)	1998 Total DM (000)
Receivables for goods and services provided	75,957	2,922	78,879	27,614
Receivables from affiliated companies	9,083	—	9,083	68,911
Other assets	9,891	3,085	12,976	13,101
	94,931	6,007	100,938	109,626

With regard to receivables and other assets, all discernible one-off risks are taken into account by individual value adjustments. Provision is made for general risks in receivables for goods and services provided in the form of a flat-rate adjustment

Receivables from affiliated companies include DM 686,000 in short-term loans to AGIV within the framework of the group's central financial management

Required

1 Relate the balance sheet items shown to the information contained in the notes.

2 What plausible conclusion can be drawn about the format of presentation of the balance sheet from the existence of the two columns "within one year" and "in over one year"?

3 In your best judgement, are the amounts reported in the notes gross or net? Explain your position and eventually its possible implications.

4 Which method do you feel was used to calculate the provision for doubtful accounts?

5 What are affiliated companies and is it normal that receivables pertaining to trade with these companies still appear on a consolidated balance sheet (see Chapter 13)?

Assignment 10.4 Atos*

Topic: Financial statement analysis of receivables
Type: Group exercise
Related part of the chapter: Advanced Issues

Atos is a French group operating as an information technology services provider. Atos was formed in January 1997 through the merger of Axime and Sligos. The consolidated balance sheet and notes to financial statements (*source*: annual report 1999) include the following data.

€ millions	On 30 Sept. 1999	On 30 Sept. 1998	On 30 Sept. 1997
Balance sheet			
Accounts and notes receivable, trade (net)	363.3	368.3	344.4
Income statement			
Revenues (restated to include VAT)	1,277.8	1,148.1	818.7
Notes to financial statements			
13. Accounts receivable			
Gross value	368.5	374.3	350.8
Provisions	–5.2	–6.0	–6.4
20. Other liabilities			
Payments on account received on orders	52.0	52.6	42.2
23. Other financial commitments			
Discounted bills	1.8	0	0.3
Other information			
Deferred income and amounts due to clients (including VAT)	41.7	73.0	–60.4

Required

1 In order to compute the average days of sales, you must restate the "accounts receivable" integrating the data provided.

2 Compute the average days of sales (also called the number of days' revenue outstanding). Note: Because of the merger which took place at the end of the first quarter of 1997, the data for that year pertain only to the last 9 months of the fiscal year.

3 Comment on these figures.

Assignment 10.5 Holmen*

Topic: Reporting for receivables
Type: Group exercise
Related part of the chapter: Advanced Issues

Holmen (formerly MoDo) is a Swedish company operating in the paper industry. In the notes to the 1999 consolidated financial statements (*source*: annual report 1999), the company disclosed the following data with regard to operating receivables.

	Group		Parent company	
	1999	1998	1999	1998
Accounts receivable	2,051	3,586	1,761	2,066
Receivables from group companies	—	—	159	280
Receivables from associate companies	272	45	265	45
Prepaid costs and accrued income	130	323	86	240
Tax receivable	6	44	—	—
Other receivables	507	616	216	343
	2,966	4,614	2,487	2,974

In the income statement, the net turnover (net sales) amounts to the following.

	1999	1998
Net turnover	20,508	22,676

Required

1 Explain why the "receivables from group companies" do not appear in the "group" financial statements.

2 Which of the 6 lines describing operating receivables is generally presented separately in financial statements' assets?

3 Compute the average days of sales (in receivables) for 1999 and 1998. Comment on these figures.

References

FASB (1993) Statement of Financial Accounting Standard No. 115, Accounting for Certain Investments in Debt and Equity Securities, Stamford, CT.

IASC (revised 1992) International Accounting Standard No. 7, Cash Flow Statements, London.

IASC (revised 1993) International Accounting Standard No. 18, Revenue, London.

IASC (reformatted 1994) International Accounting Standard No. 25, Accounting for Investments, London.

IASC (1998) International Accounting Standard No. 39, Financial Instruments: Recognition and Measurement, London.

Lymer, A., and Hancock, D. (2000) *Taxation: Policy & Practice*, 7th edn, Thomson Learning, London.

Nexia International (1994) *VAT in Europe*, Tolley Publishing, Croydon.

Additional material on the website

Go to http://www.thomsonlearning.co.uk/accountingandfinance/stolowylebas for further information, journal entries and extra assignments for each chapter.

The following appendices to this chapter are available on the dedicated website:
Appendix 10.1: Current investments in IAS 39
Appendix 10.2: Value added tax
Appendix 10.3: Bank reconciliation
Appendix 10.4: Note receivable paid at maturity
Appendix 10.5: Recording of notes receivable

Notes

1 The term debt is still often used in practice. A more accurate (but rarely used) term ought to be "bad" or "doubtful receivables". Some countries use the term "doubtful accounts" or "uncollectible accounts".

2 Aging accounts receivable is the process of classifying individual receivable transactions by the time elapsed since the claim came into existence. Most accounting software programs provide an automatic partitioning of the accounts receivable by age class, i.e., due date or overdue delay (30 days, 31 to 60 days, etc.).

3 Source: MOCI (France) 1462, 5 October 2000, p. 48.

4 See Chapter 9.

Shareholders' equity

As shown in Figure 1.3 (in Chapter 1), in order to create value or wealth for its creators, a business, must finance upfront the acquisition of its initial means of production. The two main sources of seed financial resources of a firm are (1) capital provided by the entrepreneur or by investors in exchange for a claim on the future returns of the business venture, and (2) borrowed funds, generally provided by external financial institutions. Additional financial resources will be generated on an ongoing basis through operations but if these are not sufficient to support growth, further calls on external sources of financing might be required.

Capital can be provided in the form of cash contributions, contribution of tangible or intangible assets, of intellectual property, or even of labor (in lieu of remuneration). Capital, unlike borrowed financial resources, has no specified reimbursement date to the provider(s) and generally no return is guaranteed.

The term used to refer to investors (providers of capital) is a function of the legal form of the business organization. In a corporation they are shareholders, in a partnership they are partners or associates. A sole proprietor is the investor in a business she or he owns entirely. Whatever the legal organizational format, the separation of private and business rights and responsibilities is essential.

Capital is an investment at risk that implies the investor's participation (even if sometimes only nominal or virtual) in managerial decision making. Investors are therefore liable for the consequences of the actions of "their" business. That liability may be limited to their contribution to the capital of the firm, for example in "limited liability corporations", while it may be unlimited, for example in an unincorporated sole entrepreneurship.

Major topics

Forms of business organization

Share capital

Profit appropriation

Non-cash capital contributions

Reduction of capital

Treasury shares

Stock options plan

Share dividend

Comprehensive income

Financial statement analysis

Since capital often represents the upper limit of the potential liability assumed by investors, its nominal or face value must be communicated to all persons dealing (or potentially dealing) with the business. It cannot be modified without public notice and without conforming to the rules defined in the business's by-laws or their equivalent.

Understanding what capital and shareholders' equity are and how they are recorded and reported is crucial in the definition of standardized key investment return metrics (such as earnings per share, cash flow per share, share yield, dilution, share (stock) options, etc.) that are used by financial market investors to inform their investment decisions.

This chapter is devoted to business owners' equity: definitions and processes through which equity and capital can be increased (whether it be through operations or through additional capital contributions) or modified (for example through the payment of dividends or the, hopefully rare, resorption of accumulated losses).

CORE ISSUES

The term equity is a universal concept referring to the value of a property beyond the total amount owed on its mortgages, liens, etc. In the case of a business, it is a synonym of net worth. The IASC Framework (1989) defines equity as "the residual interest [of the investors] in the assets of the enterprise after deducting all its liabilities" (§ 49).

Because businesses that are incorporated represent a much larger part of the global gross wealth creation (measured, for example, by the gross national products) than do the unincorporated firms, the most important form of equity or net worth, from an economic point of view, is that of "shareholders' equity". For simplicity sake, we will use in this text the term shareholders' equity to refer to any investor's residual claim on the worth of the company regardless of the organizational form retained in the by-laws by the founders of the firm. The alternative forms of organization are evoked briefly first as they are important for understanding the extent of the responsibility assumed by the investors in each case.

The two principal components of shareholders' equity will then be reviewed: (share) capital and retained (accumulated) earnings (or reserves). The mechanism of their modification will subsequently be examined: decrease or increase of capital as well as payment of dividends are some of the most common events that impact on the shareholders' equity.

Forms of business organization

Three generic and alternative legal forms of organization specify the roles and responsibilities of the capital providers: (1) sole proprietorship; (2) partnership; and (3) limited company. Each country's legal system defines precisely the rules applying to each generic form. It would be beyond the scope of this book to explore the more detailed specific elements of any country.

A business represents a legal or economic entity that is separate from the individual or corporate capital provider(s). Any business must report on its economic activity by issuing periodic financial statements, even if only for tax purposes. If incorporated as a legal entity, a business can possess wealth, own property, make decisions, contract debts, pay money in its own right, go to court, or be taken to court, etc.

It is essential that the accounting and the reporting systems completely separate economic transactions that concern the business exclusively, from those that concern its individuals or corporate capital providers. Capital providers are distanced and separated from the firm in which they invested. This separation suffers one exception pertaining to risk sharing (assumption of liability for the firm's actions) as mentioned before: some legal organizational forms limit responsibility while others do not.

Sole proprietorship

In a sole proprietorship, the single capital provider holds claim to 100% of the future wealth creation of the business and bears all the risks of the venture. This legal form is not well adapted to the needs of large businesses. Creating a sole proprietorship generally is simple. This simplicity and the corollary low organizational costs may explain its common usage in the creation of small enterprises.

Partnership

A partnership is a business with two or more owners. In many countries, a partnership is not incorporated and each of the associates or partners is fully responsible for all the consequences of the actions of the business. Some countries do not specifically offer the partnership form as such, but generally offer other forms approximating the partnership format such as the "unlimited liability company", also called "incorporated partnership". Examples of such national variations on the theme are: *Société en nom collectif* (SNC) in Belgium and France, *Interessentskab* (I/S) in Denmark, *Offene Handelsgesellschaft* (OHG) in Germany, *Omorrythmos Etairia* (OE) in Greece, Unlimited company in Ireland and the UK, *Società in nome collettivo* (SNC) in Italy, *Vennootschap Onder Firma* (VOF) in the Netherlands, *Sociedad regular colectiva* (SRC) in Spain, and *Sociedade em nome colectivo* in Portugal.

This form of organization is best suited for a limited number of associates or partners. Each country's legislation specifies the minimum number of partners and sometimes an upper limit to that number. Both lower and, occasionally, upper limits vary greatly between countries. This form of legal organization is flexible enough to allow a significant expansion of the business activities. New partners (i.e., additional capital providers) can often be added on with minimal formality. The organizational costs of setting up a partnership are greater than those incurred in setting up a sole proprietorship but the procedures are nonetheless not very complex or burdensome.

Limited liability company

The limited liability company, also called corporation in North America, is the most common form of organization for larger businesses. The liability assumed by the investors does not extend beyond their investment. The capital is partitioned in small homogeneous and tradable increments called shares. Each share represents both a contribution to the capital and a claim on future profits. Investors are called shareholders. They may generally trade their share independently of the enterprise.

Most countries require a minimum level of capital funds be provided by investors as this type of organization is meant to grow and expand, and their level of responsibility of potential liability with them. Since capital measures the maximum level of liability an incorporated enterprise assumes, its trading partners (suppliers, customers, banks, etc.) generally require that the capital be brought to a level coherent with the size of the business activities.

Limited liability companies generally raise capital in the open market. They have an obligation of reporting to their shareholders. An auditor generally is required to certify that the financial statements have been prepared in accordance with the rules and requirements of the country and also that they represent fairly the financial situation of the business. Corporations are generally highly regulated and the incorporation process is often complex, leading to significant organizational costs.

Many countries distinguish two types of limited liability companies:

- *Private limited companies*: They generally have a fairly low minimum level of capital and at least two share capital providers, although there are exceptions such as in Belgium (SPRLU), France (EURL), Germany (Einmann GmbH), and Portugal (EIRL) where a single capital provider (individual or corporate entity) may incorporate her, his or its business as a private limited company. Country specific business legislation generally specifies a maximum number of capital providers. For example, it is 50 shareholders in France, Ireland, Spain, and the UK. Because the number of shareholders is often small, the shares are not traded on a financial market and their sale may even require approval (as is the case for partnerships) by a majority of the remaining shareholders. These shares are thus not very liquid and often represent a cumbersome investment instrument for the capital provider.

- *Public limited companies*: A minimum number of capital providers is required, but no maximum is ever specified. The minimum number of shareholders varies greatly between countries (2 in Belgium, Greece, Italy, the Netherlands and the UK, 3 in Denmark and Spain, 5 in Germany and Portugal, 7 in France and Ireland, etc.) Each country's legislation also specifies a minimum amount of capital and such minimum is generally higher for the public limited companies than it is for the private limited companies. Most of the time, shares of public limited companies can be traded freely on open financial markets. When such a market exists, these shares are liquid and offer a preferred medium of investment for capital providers who can go in and out of an investment with a low transaction cost. A side benefit of such liquidity is that it generally provides a lower cost of capital than the one incurred by businesses where the capital is not as liquid.

Figure 11.1 summarizes the principal characteristics of the various forms of legal organization.

Although shareholders' equity is defined by the IASC as a residual, its framework states that it "may be sub-classified in the balance sheet [i.e., for reporting purposes]. For example, in a corporate [i.e., incorporated] enterprise, funds contributed by shareholders, retained earnings, reserves representing appropriations of retained earnings and reserves representing capital maintenance adjustments may be shown separately. Such classifications

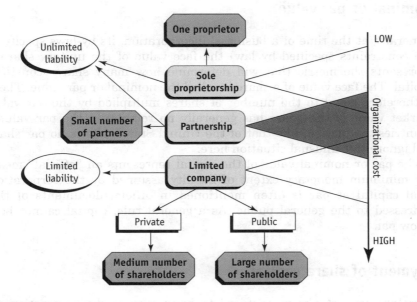

Figure 11.1 Forms of business organization

can be relevant to the decision-making needs of the users of financial statements when they indicate legal or other restrictions on the ability of the enterprise to distribute or otherwise apply its equity. They may also reflect the fact that parties with ownership interests in an enterprise have differing rights in relation to the receipt of dividends or the repayment of capital" (IASC, 1989: § 65). The following sections will explore these sub-categories of shareholder's equity.

Share capital

Definition

Shares or stock certificates represent the capital. They are evidence of the contribution of the shareholder to the formation of the capital. Shares are attributed to investors proportionately to the value of the resource they provided. A share is a certificate of property. It can generally be sold, bought or transferred by the shareholder without the consent of the corporation. Each shareholder has the right to:

- influence management decision making by participating in and voting in general assembly meetings
- receive dividends and a proportionate share of any eventual liquidations surplus
- first pass at acquiring additional shares (proportionately to the current holding) in the case of a new issue of shares.

Nominal or par value

Generally, at the time of a business' incorporation, its by-laws specify (within the constraints specified by law) the face value of the unitary share, which represents the metric that will determine how many shares constitute the capital. The face value of a share is called the nominal or par value. The capital is therefore equal to the number of shares multiplied by the par value. The market value of the share has generally no relation to the par value. Some countries' regulation, like that of the United States, allows no par shares. We will ignore this unusual situation here.

The par or nominal value of the capital represents an "official" measure of the minimum monetary extent of liability assumed by the corporation. The total capital at par is often mentioned in official documents of the firm addressed to the general public. As a general rule, capital cannot be issued below par.

Payment of share capital

Investors are not always required to hand over to the corporation the full amount of their investment as represented by the number of shares they receive. This is due to the fact a newly created business often does not need to have all the capital available right at the beginning and would not be able to provide the shareholders a return that would be competitive. Corporations can therefore offer their shareholders the possibility to subscribe to (or buy on credit) their shares by delivering their funds or resources to the corporation over a period specified by the board of directors but generally not to exceed five years. This subscription process is useful to shareholders as it gives them time to accumulate the funds or resources they will use to pay for the shares they have purchased upon issuance. The 2nd European Directive states that at least only one-quarter of the capital needs be handed over to the corporation upon incorporation and initial issuance of shares.

The vocabulary reflects the complexity of this situation:

Authorized capital is the maximum amount of capital (at par) the charter state the corporation can issue when needed. It is the maximum number of shares authorized multiplied by the par value.

Subscribed or issued capital is that part of the capital authorized that the shareholders have agreed to purchase and pay when called to do so. Some countries require that subscribed capital be equal to authorized capital. The fact that there are authorized shares in excess of subscribed shares however gives great flexibility to the management of the business in issuing new shares as they see fit as is for example the case when the compensation package of executives or senior personnel includes stock options or share options. For example British Telecom's 2000 annual report in the notes to consolidated financial statements (note 24) states that: "Of the authorized but un-issued share capital at 31 March 2000, 232 million ordinary shares were reserved to meet options granted under the employee share-option schemes."

Called-up capital is the fraction of the subscribed capital that the corporation's board decided to collect from the investors (the amount of the par or only a portion of the par).

Paid-in capital or **contributed capital** is the part of the capital that has been actually contributed by the shareholders and is available to the corporation.

Uncalled capital (or capital receivable) is the part of the subscribed capital that has either not been called up or remains unpaid. It will represent a declining balance as the investors actually deliver on their promise to fund the company.

Outstanding capital (outstanding shares times the par value) is subscribed capital (at par) minus the par value of any share that has been bought back by the corporation (treasury shares).

To sum up:

> Outstanding shares < Issued shares < Authorized shares
> and
> Capital subscribed = Paid-in capital + Uncalled capital

Different categories of shares

Shares are negotiable instruments that grant certain rights to their owner. However, a corporation may find an interest in giving different rights to different categories of shareholders in order, for example, to make the capital subscription more attractive to certain types of investors or more attractive at certain times such as when the ongoing nature of the business is not fully assured. Shares carrying special rights are called "preferred shares" or "preference shares". They form a category distinct from "ordinary shares".

Preferred versus ordinary shares

The special rights of preferred shares, that make them more attractive to purchase when issued than ordinary shares can take many forms which can be combined:

- pecuniary advantage such as fully or partially guaranteed dividend, larger dividend than common shares, priority dividend, cumulative dividends,[1] etc.
- different voting rights in the general assembly (often double but occasionally no voting right at all) than those held by the ordinary shares.

The basic idea behind preferred shares is that they allow raising of capital without necessarily creating a proportional dilution or without creating a shift in stewardship away from the original shareholders (case of no voting shares), or, on the contrary, shifting control towards a certain class of shareholders (case of multiple voting rights).

Preferred shares generally represent a trade-off between return and control: either higher dividends but reduced voting rights, or higher voting rights but lower returns. The common or ordinary shareholders are the residual owners of the corporation after the preferred shareholders have received their dues. Shares carrying the same rights are organized in homogeneous classes.

Redeemable or convertible preference shares

When the special rights attached to preferred shares are only temporary, these shares may be redeemable or convertible. In this first case, the preferred shares can be retired or redeemed at the initiative of the corporation at a price that was

Barloworld

Barloworld (formerly Barlow), a South African group with manufacturing interests in capital equipment, materials handling, motor, cement, and lime, has created preference shares as indicated in Note 14 to its financial statements (annual report 2000 – the currency is the rand):

		2000 R'm	1999 R'm
Authorized share capital			
500,000	6 percent cumulative preference shares of R2 each	1	1
300,000,000	ordinary shares of 5 cents each	15	15
		16	16
Issued share capital			
375,000	6 percent cumulative preference shares of R2 each	1	1
214,309,448	ordinary shares of 5 cents each (1999: 214,309,448)	11	11
		12	12

These figures have been rounded by the company

mentioned in the preference share contract (and which is often conditional on the market performance of common shares). Depending on the terms of the contract, redeemed preferred shares could either be exchanged for cash or converted into a predetermined number of common shares or bonds. In the second case, convertible shares can be converted, within a certain time range and at the initiative of the bearer, into bonds or ordinary shares.

Shares with amended voting rights

The voting power of a common shareholder is strictly proportional to the number of common shares she or he holds. Preferred shares may hold voting rights that deviate from the normal "one share one vote". Preferred shares with special voting rights are often used in new share issuance when the original shareholders are willing to incur a dilution of earnings but not of their power to direct the affairs of the firm. They are also used as defensive or offensive tactics in acquisitions, mergers or takeover bids.

For example, Quebecor Inc., a Canadian company operating in the fields of communications, printing and forest products, reports the existence of multiple voting rights shares in a footnote to capital stock in its 1998 annual report:

a) Authorized capital stock
An unlimited number of Class A Multiple Voting shares with voting rights of ten votes per share (herein referred to as "A shares"), convertible at any time into Class B Subordinate Voting Shares on a one-for-one share basis.

An unlimited number of Class B Subordinate Voting Shares (herein referred to as "B shares"), convertible into A shares on a one-for-one basis only if a takeover bid regarding A shares is made to holders of A shares without being made concurrently and under the same terms to holders of B shares.

Holders of B shares are entitled to elect 25% of the Board of Directors of Quebecor Inc. Holders of A Shares may elect the other members of the Board of Directors.

Other illustrations:

- Volvo Group (Swedish car and truck manufacturer): "The share capital of the Parent Company is divided into two series of shares: A and B. Both series carry the same rights, except that each Series A share carries the right to one vote and each Series B share carries the right to one tenth of a vote" (Note 21 to the 1999 consolidated financial statements).
- Ericsson (Swedish telephone equipment manufacturer): Class B shares are entitled to one thousandth of one vote per share (Annual report 1999, note 14 to consolidated financial statements).

Share premium

The par value of a share is only a way of defining the number of shares in the legal capital and thus the relative power of decision of each shareholder. A share is valued by the market as the net present value of the estimated future cash flows (or dividends plus liquidation value) of the business venture. Most shares are issued above their par.

The share premium is the difference between the issue price and the par value. It records a contribution from the "new" shareholders in excess of the legal share capital. The share premium is also called "additional paid-in capital" or "capital in excess of par" or, in the USA, "capital surplus". It is reported as a part of the shareholders' equity.

Accounting for share capital

Accounting for capital issuance follows the same rules whether it is when the capital is first issued or when further capital is raised through a flotation of new shares. It is illustrated here through the entries required to record the issuance of capital by Gershwin Corporation. This business entity was incorporated at the beginning of year 20X0. Its authorized capital is 100,000 ordinary shares with a par of 1 CU. The initial issue was for 10,000 ordinary shares sold at par. This issue was entirely subscribed (paid in) for a total cash inflow of 10,000 CU. During year 20X1, 90,000 additional shares were floated at the price of 1.2 CU per share. The terms of the flotation are that the acquirers of the new shares must contribute immediately 50% of the par (the rest to be contributed when called) and 100% of the share premium. This flotation creates a share premium for a total of 18,000 CU [90,000 shares × (1.2 CU – 1 CU at par)]. Of the par value of the 90,000 shares (i.e., 90,000 CU), only 45,000 CU will be contributed while another 45,000 will remain uncalled for the time being. The total cash raised is therefore 63,000 CU.

Figure 11.2 illustrates the accounting mechanism required for recording both transactions (000 CU).

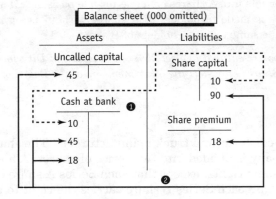

① Recording of the capital issued at the time of the incorporation of the company
② Issuance of additional shares for cash

Figure 11.2 Accounting for issuance of share capital

The capital is increased by the par value of the 90,000 shares issued even though one-half has not yet been contributed and remains uncalled. However, in some countries (e.g., the United States), the uncalled portion of capital (subscriptions receivable) is not shown as an asset as done here but as a reduction of share capital, i.e., a contra-liability account. However, the end result is the same and the different treatments, giving full disclosure, provide a true and fair view of the financial situation of the firm. When the uncalled capital will be called and the shareholders will pay in the rest of their contribution, the only additional entry required will be to balance cash against either the uncalled capital (receivable) or the contra-liability of uncalled capital.

Reporting share capital

International standard

IAS 1 (IASC 1997) stipulates rather detailed rules for the reporting of share capital in financial statements. Article 74 states that "an enterprise should disclose the following, either on the balance sheet or in the notes:

(a) For each class of share capital
  - The number of shares authorized;
  - The number of shares issued and fully paid, and issued but not fully paid;
  - Par value per share, or that the shares have no par value;
  - A reconciliation of the number of shares outstanding at the beginning and at the end of the year;
  - The rights, preferences and restrictions attaching to that class including restrictions on the distribution of dividends and the repayment of capital;

- Shares in the enterprise held by the enterprise itself or by subsidiaries or associates of the enterprise; and
- Shares reserved for issuance under options and sales contracts, including the terms and amounts;

(b) A description of the nature and purpose of each reserve within owner's equity;

(c) The amount of dividends that were proposed or declared after the balance sheet date but before the financial statements were authorized for issue;

(d) The amount of any cumulative preference dividends not recognized.

An enterprise without share capital, such as a partnership, [still has equity and] should disclose information equivalent to that required above, showing movements during the period in each category of equity interest and the rights, preferences and restrictions attaching to each category of equity interest."

Real-life example

Procter & Gamble
(a US-based multinational corporation) reports several types of shares
(source: annual report 1999)

Consolidated balance sheet

Amounts and quantities in millions except per share amounts	30 June 1999	1998
Shareholders' equity		
Convertible Class A preferred stock, stated value $1 per share (600 authorized)	$1,781	$1,821
Non-Voting Class B preferred stock, stated value $1 per share (200 shares authorized; none issued)	—	—
Common stock, stated value $1 per share (5,000 shares authorized; shares outstanding: 1999 – 1,319.8 and 1998 – 1,337.4)	1,320	1,337
Additional paid-in capital (...)	1,337	907

Profit appropriation

As mentioned in Chapter 2, all earnings generated by a business are theoretically available for appropriation and distribution to shareholders. However, although the right of ownership by shareholder over all after-tax earnings is not challenged, yearly earnings are partitioned in two categories: some will be "retained" in the business as retained earnings (i.e., a voluntary reinvestment), also called reserves, and some will effectively be distributed as dividends.

Dividends

A dividend is a distribution of the earnings of the business to its shareholders. Dividends are allocated proportionately to the rights attached to the shares held by the shareholders on a date of record.[2] The management team of the business generally proposes the dividend payout ratio for approval by the general assembly of shareholders once the financial statements have been approved. Shareholders have the final say (through the general assembly) in what to do with the earnings. Dividends are paid to the shareholders following a schedule which varies with the traditions of each country: monthly or quarterly and mostly by anticipation in the United States or annually and *ex post* in most European countries.

Reserve accounts

According to the IASC Framework (IASC 1989: § 66): "The creation of reserves is sometimes required by statute or other law in order to give the enterprise and its creditors an added measure of protection from the effects of losses. Other reserves may be established if national tax law grants exemptions from, or reductions in, taxation liabilities when transfers to such reserves are made. The existence and size of these legal, statutory and tax reserves is information that can be relevant to the decision-making needs of users. Transfers to such reserves are appropriations of retained earnings rather than expenses."

Reserve accounts must be funded before dividends can be paid out. It means that the earnings available to the shareholders for distribution or voluntary reinvestment is equal to:

> Annual earnings minus sum of the allocations to reserve accounts
> = Earnings available for distributing or retaining

The main categories of reserves are the following: legal reserve, statutory reserve, regulated reserve, revaluation reserve, reserve for own shares, optional (or voluntary) reserves, profit/loss brought forward and reserve for conversion of accounts to euros. These different categories are presented in Appendix 11.1.

Reporting retained earnings

A balance sheet may be presented "before" or "after appropriation". The term "appropriation" here refers to the decision taken by the shareholders or directors to distribute dividends and/or to transfer the income to retained earnings (also called reserves).[3] In the "after appropriation" method, the earnings of the year are not reported explicitly in the balance sheet; only additions to the retained earnings will be reported. The earnings of the period are added to the "retained earnings". The formula defining retained earnings at any point in time is presented in Table 11.1.

Table 11.1 Retained earnings

	Retained earnings (up to end of previous period)
plus	Net income (after tax) of the year
minus	Dividends declared
=	Retained earnings (at year-end)

Table 11.1 is a bare bone template for the "statement of retained earnings" that is required in the USA, in Canada, and generally in the annual statements of financial position of any business reporting under the US GAAP (most firms quoted on the New York Stock Exchange) or under a local GAAP which is based on the US GAAP. That statement explains how the retained earnings of the previous year are transformed, in a recurring fashion, into the retained earnings of the current year.

Most of the time the term "retained earnings" is a part of "shareholders' equity". However, an analyst of the financial position of the firm must beware of the fact that the term retained earnings may cover different realities depending on the country whose laws and practices are followed (see more on this topic in Appendix 11.2).

Reporting and accounting for shareholders' equity

Simple example of reporting of reserves and retained earnings

Gershwin Corporation's income and dividend payment for years 1 and 2 are as follows (000 CU):

	Year 1	Year 2
Profit	50	70
Dividends	0	30

Table 11.2 illustrates the presentation of shareholders' equity according to each of the two methods commonly used by corporations.

Table 11.2 Presentation of shareholders' equity in the balance sheet

	Year 1	Year 2
Method 1 (after appropriation)		
Share capital	100	100
Share premium	18	18
Retained earnings	50	90 *
Shareholders' equity	168	208
Dividends payable (liabilities)	0	30
Total shareholders' equity and liabilities	168	238
Method 2 (before appropriation)		
Share capital	100	100
Share premium	18	18
Reserves	0	50
Net income	50	70
Shareholders' equity (before dividends)	168	238

*[50 (beginning balance) + 70 (income of the period) − 30 (dividends payable)]

The choice of method has no impact on the actual total shareholders' equity plus liabilities.

When method 1 is used, there is a "dividends payable" only as long as the dividends have not actually been paid out at balance sheet date. If they had already been paid out by the date the financial statements are approved, in our example the 30 CU of the paid-out dividend would already have reduced the cash account and would not need to be reported as a liability

Accounting for profit appropriation

Figure 11.3 illustrates the impact of profit appropriation for year 2 on the balance sheet of Gershwin Corporation. Since the accounting entries for methods 1 and 2 are essentially the same (but the timing is different), we chose to only illustrate method 2, i.e., reporting before appropriation, which appears to be the most frequently used method in Europe.

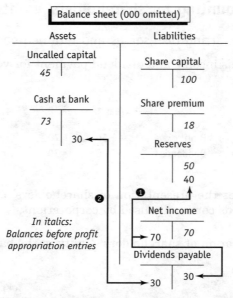

❶ Cancellation of net income, and transfer to reserves and to dividends payable. Dividends have been declared but not paid
❷ Payment of dividends

Figure 11.3 Accounting for profit appropriation

Method 1 – Balance sheet after appropriation

Ispat International NV

NV (Netherlands – US GAAP – Source: Annual report 1999 – Steel company)

Consolidated balance sheet – 31 December, millions of US dollars

	1998	1999
Shareholders' equity		
Common shares	4	4
Additional paid-in capital	480	480
Retained earnings	253	320
Cumulative other comprehensive income	64	50
Total shareholders' equity	801	854

- The topic "Cumulative other comprehensive income" was introduced in Chapter 6 and is further developed in the Advanced Issues section of this chapter.
- The evolution of retained earnings between 1998 and 1999 is explained in the statement of changes in shareholders' equity, which contains the following information:

Balance on 31 December 1998	253
Net income [from the income statement]	85
Dividends on common shares	(18)
Balance on 31 December 1999	320

Dividends have been paid during the year but they only are reported in the cash flow statement (financing activities). (For refresher and further developments on the cash flow statement, see Chapters 3 and 14.)

Barlo Group Plc

(Ireland – Irish/UK GAAP – Source: Annual report 2000 – Light building materials with operations in sheet plastics and radiators)

Consolidated balance sheet – as of 31 March – in thousands of €

	2000	1999
Capital and reserves		
Called-up share capital	21,270	21,615
Share premium account	8,531	8,531
Other reserves	16,978	16,504
Profit and loss account	59,743	39,601
Shareholders' funds – equity	106,522	86,251

Consolidated profit and loss account – year ended 31 March – in thousands of €

	2000	1999
(...)		
Profit for the financial year attributable to shareholders	21,469	15,998
Dividend on equity shares – paid	(1,531)	(3,238)
Dividend on equity shares – proposed	(2,713)	—
Retained profit for the year	17,225	12,760
Balance [of retained earnings] at the beginning of the year	39,601	27,388
Currency translation adjustment	3,355	(547)
Acquisition of own shares	(438)	—
Balance [of retained earnings] at the end of the year	59,743	39,601

These elements of the financial statements are reported after profit appropriation since the dividends are deducted already.

- The dividends paid in 2000 are interim dividends while the ones for 1999 is the net of all dividends paid pertaining to the earnings of that year.
- The issues pertaining to "acquisition of own shares" are covered in the "Advanced Issues" section of this chapter.
- The coherence of the 1999 and 2000 "profit and loss account" is explained in the lower part of the profit and loss account shown in the following table. For the sake of clarity, the order of the items has been modified to facilitate understanding.

Consolidated profit and loss account – year ended 31 March – in thousands of €

		2000	1999
	Balance [of retained earnings] at the beginning of the year	39,601	27,388
+	Profit for the financial year attributable to shareholders	21,469	15,998
–	Dividend on equity shares – paid	(1,531)	(3,238)
–	Dividend on equity shares – proposed	(2,713)	—
+	Currency translation adjustment	3,355	(547)
–	Acquisition of own shares	(438)	—
=	Balance [of retained earnings] at the end of the year	59,743	39,601

Method 2 – Balance sheet before appropriation

Ericsson
(Sweden – Swedish GAAP – Source: Annual report 1999 – Communication industry)

Consolidated balance sheet – 31 December SEK millions

	1999	1998
Stockholders' equity		
Capital stock	4,893	4,878
Reserves not available for distribution	32,618	28,053
Restricted equity	37,511	32,931
Retained earnings	19,535	17,140
Net income [from the income statement]	12,130	13,041
Non-restricted equity	31,665	30,181
	69,176	63,112

- Ericsson's annual report indicates clearly restricted and unrestricted equity. (This distinction is developed in Appendix 11.3.)
- The "retained earnings" only represent accumulated earnings in unrestricted reserves.

Repsol YPF
(Spain – Spanish GAAP – Source: Annual report 1999 – Oil and gas)

Consolidated balance sheet – 31 December – in millions of €

	1999	1998
Shareholders' equity		
Capital stock	1,188	902
Paid-in surplus	6,064	687
Other reserves in parent company:		
Restatement reserves	3	3
Other reserves	1,388	1,312
Reserves in consolidated companies	2,813	2,396
Translation differences	249	41
Net income for the year [same as in income statement]	1,011	875
Interim dividend paid during the year	(190)	(173)
Total shareholders' equity	12,526	6,043

- The topic "translation differences" is covered in Chapter 13.
- This excerpt of a balance sheet is a good illustration of a rather detailed description of shareholder's equity.
- An interesting detail in this statement can be found in the fact that the interim dividends are shown and deducted, as is to be expected, from shareholders' equity.

This part of the chapter will address special situations that deviate from the general principles presented in Core Issues. Issues that are covered in this section are:

- New shares may be the result of non-cash contributions.
- Share issuance costs need to be recorded and reported appropriately.
- Shareholders' equity is affected by the possibility most corporations have to purchase their own shares and cancel them. This is used when there exist no investment alternatives to increase the return on equity for the shareholders (by reducing the denominator, while productive investment opportunities would have increased the numerator).
- The comprehensive income (discussed in Chapter 6) may appear in the shareholders' equity.
- The statement of changes in shareholders' equity is an important document.

Accounting issuance of shares for non-cash capital contributions

Not all shares are issued against cash. There are three basic situations that may lead to the issuance of shares in return for something other than cash:

1 Shares can be issued in return for a capital contribution in kind.
2 New shares may be issued as the result of a "capitalization" of reserves.
3 New shares may be the result of the conversion by a creditor of their claim into shares.

Issuance of shares for capital contributions in kind

Shareholders may contribute assets other than cash. For example, intangible assets such as patents, specific knowledge, uncompensated work, provision of access to a market, or tangible assets such as fixed assets, inventories or receivables (all net of attached liabilities) are often important capital contributions, especially in the early phases of the life of a corporation. Shares issued for capital contributions in kind are also frequent in the case of business combinations such as acquisitions or mergers (see Chapter 13). The contributed value is theoretically the "fair value" of the net assets but such a value is often difficult to estimate since their value may be a function of their coherence with the strategy of the buyer.

The mechanism of recording is similar to that of a cash capital contribution, with the only difference that the debit is to an asset account different from cash.

To illustrate the mechanism of recording a contribution in kind, let us go back to the Gershwin Corporation. In year 3, new shareholders contribute a patent valued at 15,000 CU. In exchange for the property transfer of the patent, these new shareholders receive 10,000 ordinary shares with a par of 1 CU. A 5,000 CU share premium therefore needs to be recorded. Figure 11.4 describes the mechanism.

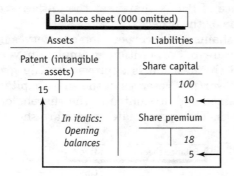

Figure 11.4 Accounting for a share issuance in kind

Issuance of new shares due to capitalization of reserves

To incorporate reserves into the share capital is called capitalization. When the balance of the accumulated undistributed earnings becomes very large in proportion to the share capital, it may be a good idea to incorporate all or part of the reserves into the capital. It is so because (1) it may improve the liquidity of the shares if new shares are issued; and (2) it increases the protection of creditors to a higher level of responsibility assumed by the shareholders.

After the incorporation of reserves in the share capital (restructuring and consolidation of the shareholders' equity), the total book value of the shareholders' equity is unchanged but the number or par value of shares has been modified. Such an operation is called by different names: "stock split"[4] mainly in North America (where an increase of the par value would be extremely unusual), and "bonus issue" or "capitalization of reserves" elsewhere (depending on whether or not new shares are issued).

Unless the corporation chooses to reflect this action by increasing the par value of the share, the procedure will lead to the issuance of new shares that will generally be given to the current shareholders. It leads to a "bonus issue" and the shareholders of record on the date of the issue receive the new shares in proportion to their previous holdings.

Most reserves that are unambiguously the property of the shareholders (essentially all reserves) can be incorporated into share capital. Although each country may have its own specific rules regarding the incorporation of reserves, the eligible reserves are generally composed of (see the definition of each reserve in Appendix 11.1):

- legal reserve (after its capitalization, this reserve must be reconstituted)
- statutory reserves
- regulated reserves
- optional (voluntary) reserves
- revaluation reserves

- profit brought forward
- net income of the year
- share premium.

While some countries allow both an increase of the par value of the existing shares and the issuance of bonus shares, at the initiative of the corporation, others forbid either one or the other.

To illustrate the mechanism of incorporation of reserves in the share capital, let us revisit the Gershwin Corporation example. In year 4, the board of directors decides (and the decision is approved by the general assembly) to incorporate 30,000 CU worth of reserves in the share capital. Some 30,000 new shares of par 1 are created and attributed to the shareholders proportionately to their current holdings. The appropriate entries are shown in Figure 11.5.

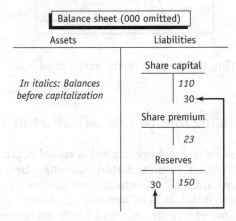

Figure 11.5 Share issuance by capitalization of reserves

Such an entry involves a mere transfer from reserves to capital. The history of the 150 CU beginning balance of the reserves account is the sum of the undistributed earnings up to and including those of year 3.

Issuance of shares resulting from an increase in capital due to a conversion of liabilities

Creditors of the corporation (suppliers or bankers) may accept to receive shares of capital as a counterpart for canceling their claim. In this case the shares they receive are new shares, thus creating an increase of the share capital.

Any combination of the following three reasons may explain the decision of the creditors to surrender a fixed claim in exchange for a conditional claim:

- The debtor corporation is experiencing serious cash difficulties and/or the total interest charge is not compatible with the current possibilities of the business. In order to avoid bankruptcy of their debtor, the creditors may find the conversion of loans or payables a less risky operation than the significant loss that the failure of their client might entail. In many cases the creditors use this opportunity to effectively take control of the board of directors to reorient the business activities in a way that provides for what they feel might be a more secure future for their investment.

- The corporation had issued convertible debt. The choice of issuing convertible debt is generally the result of a bad image of the corporation on the share market. It allows lenders to reduce the risks they are taking: they receive a fixed remuneration if things go not so well, and a dividend remuneration – which may be greater than the fixed return – if things go well. This way the lender can take the time to see how the business is evolving before deciding to become a shareholder.
- The lender is, for example, the parent company of the borrower and such an operation belongs to the long-term strategy of the parent. It may, for example, be an opportunity for the parent to increase its control over the subsidiary, or even to create a possibility for a de facto transfer of the debt to an outside party when shares are easier to sell than debt.

The increase in capital is recorded by a simple accounting entry in which debt is eliminated and "share capital at par" is increased and "capital surplus" or "share premium" is incremented for the balance.

Accounting for share issuance costs

Incorporating a corporation or increasing its capital are operations that cause the incurrence of significant costs. These costs include legal costs, auditors' fees, bankers' commissions, etc. These costs can be handled in three different ways at the initiative of the firm. They can be:

- considered to be a period cost and recognized in the corresponding income statement
- capitalized as an intangible asset and amortized (in general over a maximum of 5 years)
- written off against the total accumulated share premium.

The last possibility, when it is authorized by the laws and regulations of the country, offers the advantage of not impacting on income, thus not biasing the time series of earnings.

Capital reduction

A corporation may be led to reducing its capital for essentially either of two reasons:

- taking into account the reality created by accumulated losses (see Appendix 11.5)
- cancellation of shares to acknowledge the reduction in the total liability assumed by the population of shareholders because, for example, the business has repurchased its own shares.

The second case is so important that we will devote the following section to the issues such a practice raises. As a reduction of share capital reduces the maximum liability assumed, company laws in most countries strictly regulate reductions of share capital to protect creditors.

Treasury shares (or own shares or treasury stock)

Treasury shares occur when the corporation acquires its own shares.

Why repurchase one's own shares?

Corporations generally do not normally acquire or hold their own shares. However, in most countries such a practice is perfectly legal. Corporations are allowed to purchase their own shares (i.e., create treasury stock, in North American terminology) under certain circumstances. The following situations offer a far from exhaustive list of such conditions:

- A corporation can repurchase its shares so as to reduce its capital by canceling the repurchased shares. This is generally done with the intent of boosting the earnings per share ratio when no better alternative exists to develop the numerator of that ratio.
- Shares can be repurchased and given to employees in the context of a profit-sharing plan or in their exercising the stock options they have received. Such a policy would be coherent only if (a) the remaining shareholders do not want to see any dilution take place due to the distribution, or (b) all the authorized shares have already been issued and it would be difficult to increase the number of authorized shares.
- A listed corporation may repurchase its own shares with the intent of smoothing the market value of its shares in a turbulent environment.
- A listed corporation may wish to repurchase its own shares as a preventive measure if it fears a potential takeover. If fewer shares are on the open market, it may be harder for the "predator" to obtain a majority of the voting rights.
- In some countries, the by-laws may require that the sale of a block of shares by a shareholder be made conditional on the approval of the new shareholder by the remaining previous shareholders. In such a situation, the corporation may act as a broker and thus allow the shareholder wanting to sell to find an acceptable candidate.

Among these five possible situations, the first one does not strictly lead to the creation of "own shares" or "treasury stock" since the shares are rapidly cancelled and taken off the books.

Purchase of treasury shares to reduce the share capital

As we have seen, the main reason for such action, called retirement of shares, is generally a way of boosting the earnings per share or to stabilize the market price of the share. However it may be used in other circumstances. Retirement of shares may take place, for example, in a small corporation, when one of the shareholders wants to leave the group of shareholders for whatever reason. For example, let us assume that the shareholders of Gershwin Corporation have a falling-out. One of the shareholders, Mr. George, owns 20% of the shares and wants out. The remaining shareholders wish neither to buy George's shares nor to welcome an outside buyer of his shares.

The total share capital amounts 140,000 (at par). Mr. George's claim on the par capital amounts to 28,000 CU but the equity book value of Mr. George's shares is 20% of (140 + 23 + 120), i.e., 56.6 thousand CU. The remaining shareholders and Mr. George have agreed to value the shares at only 56,000 CU. The simplest solution is to have the corporation repurchase Mr. George's shares and cancel them. As shown in Figure 11.6, this transaction is carried out in two steps. The difference between the market value of the shares in the transaction and their par value will be taken out of the reserves and share premium accounts (the former for 20% of the reserves and the latter only for the balance). In this simplified example, we assume that the share premium and the reserves are unrestricted (see Appendix 11.3).

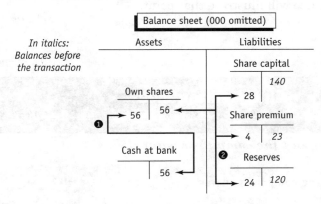

Figure 11.6 Accounting for retirement of shares to reduce share capital

❶ Purchase of the corporation's own shares for the amount accepted by the seller and the remaining shareholders. In North america the "own shares" tend to be reported as a negative entry in the shareholders' equity while we used here the approach that is most common in Europe and which recognizes the shares on the asset side

❷ Reduction of the capital by canceling these shares and all the rights pertaining to them:

- Generally, phase 2 (entry ❷) happens at the same time as phase 1

- In some countries, both entries are merged into only one and the account "own shares" is not used

- In some European countries, the law requires that despite canceling shares, the total amount of the restricted reserves/capital remain unmodified. In such a case a special reserve (reserve for own shares) must be created for the amount of the capital and share premium that were reduced. Here such a reserve would amount to (20% of 140 = 28) + (56 – 20% 3 120 – 20% 3 140 = 4) = 32 CU. The following entry would be recorded:

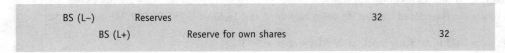

| BS (L–) | Reserves | | 32 | |
| | BS (L+) | Reserve for own shares | | 32 |

Purchase of treasury shares held by the corporation

When own shares are purchased and held for some time for whatever purpose (regulating the market of the share, anti-takeover bid strategy, employees' profit-sharing plan, etc.), the accounting transaction recording the purchase is identical to that of phase 1 in the preceding paragraphs. When the shares are eventually sold (or handed over to employees under a profit sharing plan), the entry is simply reversed as long as the amounts are the same. However the amounts are rarely identical. When the resale value is different from the purchase value, the difference is recorded, varying between countries, either:

- in the income statement, as an income or a loss
- in the shareholders' equity, as an increase or decrease of the share premium (this is notably the case in North America).

Reporting for treasury shares

There are many ways to report the ownership of one's own shares. Some examples of practice will illustrate that point.

Real-life examples

Club Meditérranée
(France – French GAAP – Source: Annual report 1999 – Leisure)

General information about the company's capital

Authorization to trade in the company's shares

The Annual Shareholders' Meeting of 25 March 1999 renewed the authorization given to the Executive Board to trade in the Company's shares on the stock market, as provided under Articles 217-2 to 217-5 of the French Companies Act of 24 July 1966. Under the terms of this authorization, which is valid until the Annual Shareholders' Meeting to be called to approve the accounts for the year ended 31 October 1999, the number of shares purchased may not exceed 10% of capital stock, the purchase price per share may not exceed €106.71 (FRF 700) and the sale price per share may not be less than €45.73 (FRF 300). This minimum sale price also applies to shares acquired prior to the renewal of the authorization.

The authorization may be used to purchase shares on the open market, in order to stabilize the share price or for allocation on exercise of stock options granted with the aim of promoting employee share ownership. Alternatively, the shares may be exchanged for stock in other companies, in order to minimize the cost of external growth transactions or generally enhance the transaction terms. Shares not used for any of the above purposes may be resold on the open market, depending on market opportunities.

The Company used this authorization in the year ended 31 October 1999 to purchase 25,109 shares and to sell 29,312 shares. The related transaction costs amounted to €14,514.64 (FRF 95,209.79) excluding tax.

No shares were held in treasury stock as of 31 October 1999 (...).

This footnote is interesting in that it explains what happened during the period and what were the safeguards placed by the executive board on these treasury stock transactions.

Toray Industries

(Japan – Japanese GAAP – Source: Annual report 1999 – Manufacturer of synthetic fibers and textiles)

Consolidated balance sheet – 31 March 1999 and 1998

Liabilities and stockholders' equity	Millions of yen	
	1999	1998
(…)		
Stockholders' equity		
Common stock	96,937	96,937
Additional paid-in capital	85,792	85,792
Consolidation surplus	308,770	310,638
	491,499	493,367
Treasury stock, at cost	(2)	(1)
Total stockholders' equity	491,497	493,366

The own shares (treasury stock) are shown as a reduction of stockholders' equity, as is common in a North American balance sheet.

Interbrew

(Belgium – Belgian GAAP – Source: Annual report 1999 – Brewery)

Consolidated balance sheet

ASSETS	31.12.1999	31.12.1998
	Millions of €	Millions of €
(…)		
CURRENT ASSETS AND LONG-TERM RECEIVABLES		
(…)		
Term deposits and marketable securities		
Own shares Note 7	34.7	3.3
(…)		

Notes to the financial statements

Note 7
During the year, the group bought back some own shares and options for a total value of 31.4 million euro. At the end of the year, the group held through an affiliate 2,126,600 own shares representing 1.3% of the shares outstanding.

The own shares detained on the closing date are shown as part of the group assets.

Stock options plan ("share options plan")

A stock option plan is a motivational device in which the corporation grants employees the right to acquire a specified personalized number of shares of the corporation at a predetermined invariant price and for a specified time window. These options are generally granted only after a given number of months or years of employment (the vesting period) and if the performance of either or both the employee and the business have met prespecified levels. The implementation of such a plan is at the discretion of the management of the firm.

Employees exercise their option to buy only when the current market price is sufficiently high for the difference between the exercise price and the current market price to cover the transaction costs (often the employee must borrow funds to exercise her/his options[5]) and leave an appreciable surplus.

If the shares sold to the employees are new shares, the entries are the same as the ones seen in Figure 11.2. However, if no authorized shares remain unissued, the firm will need to have acquired the shares on the market and sell them to the employees at the option price which could be lower (or higher) than the market price paid. The entry will be identical to that seen in the earlier section when the purchase and the sale prices are different, i.e., the difference between these two prices (positive or negative) is recorded either in the income statement or directly in shareholders' equity.

Share dividend and dividend in kind

Normally, dividends are paid out in cash. However, they could also be paid out by giving assets to the shareholders (dividend in kind). For example, the corporation may distribute third-party securities held in portfolio or may hand over some real property. Such an approach, although perfectly conceivable, encounters significant legal issues about property rights and is, therefore, very rarely used.

More frequently corporations issue dividends by giving their own shares to their shareholders without requiring any additional contribution on their part (share dividend or stock dividend). This method is interesting to an organization because it allows the "payment" of dividends without placing any strain on the cash situation of the firm. This is an especially attractive approach for often cash-strapped new ventures or fast growing businesses.

By-laws often allow the shareholders to elect, individually or collectively (in the general assembly) whether they prefer their dividend to be paid-out in cash or in the form of additional shares.

In the calculation of the number of shares to be given as dividends, there are several valuation options and the actual choice varies from country to country. The possibilities are:

● par value
● fair value
● par value or fair value, at the discretion of the management team
● par value or fair value depending on the size of the dividend distribution. (In the United States the choice is essentially based on the size of the distribution relative to shareholder's equity. If it is a "small stock distribution" fair value is to be used; if it is a large stock distribution, par value is to be used.)

When it distributes its dividends in the form of shares, the corporation has to record a capital increase and a share premium (capital surplus).

The accounting recording of the payment of a share dividend is illustrated below. MacDowell Corporation has a capital composed of 100 shares with a par value of 1 CU plus 900 in retained earnings. For period 20X1, the annual general meeting has decided to vote a dividend of 100 CU in total and to give the choice to the individual shareholders between a payment in cash or as a share dividend. Shareholders holding a total of 10 shares prefer payment in cash while the others, holding a total of 90 shares, prefer to receive a share dividend.

The average market quote over the 6 weeks prior to the distribution was 15 CU per share. Figure 11.7 illustrates the recording of these share dividends.

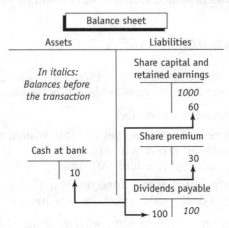

Figure 11.7 Accounting for share dividends

- The dividends owed to those shareholders who prefer a share dividend amounts to 90 CU. The fair value of that dividend is equivalent to 60 shares at fair market value (90 CU/1.5 CU per share = 60 shares).
- A share dividend is essentially similar to a share issuance by capitalization of reserves.

The practice may be different in North America (see Appendix 11.6).

Comprehensive income

In "Advanced Issues" in Chapter 6, comprehensive income was defined. It was also stated that the comprehensive income could be detailed either directly in the income statement or in the shareholders' equity. According to SFAS 130 (FASB 1997: § 26): "The total of "other comprehensive income" for a period shall be transferred to a component of equity that is displayed separately from retained earnings and additional paid-in capital in a balance sheet at the end of the accounting period. A descriptive title such as "accumulated other comprehensive income" could be used for that component of equity." It is also important to highlight the non-distributive nature of the "other comprehensive income".

An illustration of reporting for comprehensive income is developed in Appendix 11.7.

Changes in shareholders' equity

Given the complexity of the shareholders' equity account and the many changes that can affect its composition during the year, International Accounting Standard IAS 1 (IASC 1997) and the GAAP of many countries require (or suggest) that a table be provided that explains changes in shareholders' equity.

The prescriptive content of IAS 1

IAS 1 (IASC 1997: § 86) states that an enterprise should present, as a separate component of its financial statements, a statement showing:

(a) the net profit or loss for the period

(b) each item of income and expense, gain or loss which, as required by other standards, is recognized directly in equity, and the total of these items (such as revaluation surpluses and certain foreign exchange differences)

(c) the cumulative effect of changes in accounting policy and the correction of fundamental errors dealt with under the benchmark treatments in IAS 8.

In addition, an enterprise should present, either within this statement or in the notes:

(a) capital transactions with owners and distributions to owners

(b) the balance of accumulated profit or loss at the beginning of the period and at the balance sheet date, and the movements for the period

(c) a reconciliation between the carrying amount of each class of equity capital, share premium and each reserve at the beginning and the end of the period, separately disclosing each movement.

Presentation of the changes in equity

The requirements of IAS 1 or of the local national regulations may be met in a number of ways. The approach adopted in many jurisdictions follows a columnar format that reconciles the opening and closing balances of each element within shareholders' equity. An alternative is to present a separate component of the financial statements called "statement of changes in shareholders' equity" or "statement of changes in equity".

Columnar format

IAS 1

IAS 1 provides an example of a statement, which presents those changes in equity that represent gains and losses (see Table 11.3).

Table 11.3 XYZ Group – Statement of recognized gains and losses for the year ended 31 December 20X2

thousands of CU	20X2	20X1
Surplus/(deficit) on revaluation of properties	(x)	x
Surplus/(deficit) on revaluation of investments	x	(x)
Exchange differences on translation of the financial statements of foreign entities	(x)	(x)
Net gains not recognized in the income statement	x	x
Net profit for the period	x	x
Total recognized gains and losses	x	x
Effect of changes in accounting policy		(x)

Real-life examples

EMI Group

(UK — UK GAAP – Source: Annual report 2000 – Music company)

This firm provides the reconciliation in a slightly modified columnar format. The reconciliation table begins with the opening balance of shareholders' funds and ends by the closing balance of shareholders' funds.

Reconciliation of movements in shareholders' funds (for the year ended 31 March 2000)

	2000		1999	
	£m	£m	£m	£m
Opening shareholders' funds:				
As reported		(794.0)		(652.6)
Prior-year adjustments				(126.2)
Opening shareholders' funds (restated)		(794.0)		(778.8)
Profit for the financial year	158.4		122.6	
Dividends (equity)	(125.1)		(125.6)	
Other recognized gains (losses)	29.3		(9.3)	
Goodwill adjustments	0.2		(5.2)	
Shares issued	3.6		2.3	
Net increase (decrease) in shareholders' funds for the year		66.4		(15.2)
Closing shareholders' funds		(727.6)		(794.0)

The figures that appear as "other recognized gains (losses)" are, in fact, extracted from the statement of total recognized gains and losses.

Barlo Group Plc

(Ireland – Irish/UK GAAP – Source: Annual report 2000 – Light building materials with operations in sheet plastics and radiators)

Notes to the financial statements

The detail of the shareholders' equity was introduced earlier in this chapter. The total shareholders' equity was reported as follows:

Consolidated balance sheet – as of 31 March – (€000)		
	2000	1999
Shareholders' funds – equity	106,522	86,251

The notes to financial statements provide the following explanation of the change in equity:

Note 25 Reconciliation of movements in shareholders' funds (€000)			
		2000	1999
Total recognized gains and losses		24,953	15,404
Capital introduced:	At par		112
	Share premium		328
Dividends:	Paid	−1,531	−3,238
	Proposed	−2,713	
Acquisition of own shares		−438	
Net increase in shareholders' funds		20,271	12,606
Opening in shareholders' funds equity		86,251	73,645
Closing shareholders' funds – equity		106,522	86,251

This table can only be fully understood and related to both the balance sheet and the income statement when one adds another table, the "statement of total recognized gains and losses" (€000), which reads as follows.

	2000	1999
Profit for the financial year attributable to group shareholders	21,469	15,998
Currency translation difference on revaluation reserves	129	−47
Currency translation on net investment in foreign subsidiaries	3,355	−547
Total recognized gains and losses for the year	24,953	15,404

The first line of this last statement was already mentioned in the profit and loss account (see earlier in "Core Issues"). The total recognized gains and losses for the year is the starting point of the statement of changes in equity.

Statement format

IAS 1

IAS 1 provides in its appendix an illustration of a statement of change in equity. We consider it to be an illustration of best practice. Table 11.4 is a simplified abstract of that example.

Table 11.4 XYZ Group – Statement of changes in equity for the year ended 31 December 20X1

	Share capital	Share premium	Revaluation reserve	Translation reserve	Accumulated profit	Total
Balance on 31 December 20X0	x	x	x	(x)	x	x
Changes in accounting policy					(x)	(x)
Restated balance	x	x	x	(x)	x	x
Surplus on revaluation of properties			x			x
Deficit on revaluation of investments			(x)			(x)
Currency translation differences				(x)		(x)
Net gains and losses not recognized in the income statement			x	(x)		x
Net profit for the period					x	x
Dividends					(x)	(x)
Issue of share capital	x	x				x
Balance on 31 December 20X1	x	x	x	(x)	x	x

Financial statement analysis

Impact on financial structure

Table 11.5 summarizes the different possible key types of capital increase. It also reports their impact on the structure of the balance sheet. In order to facilitate the understanding of the right-most column, the following definitions may prove useful (the concepts are fully defined in Chapter 15):

- Working capital = Equity + Long-term liabilities – Fixed assets (or current assets including cash – current liabilities)
- Working capital need = Current assets (excluding cash) – Current liabilities (excluding bank overdrafts) = Inventories + Receivables – Payables (simplified definition)
- Cash = Cash at bank and in hand – Bank overdrafts.

Holmen (formerly MoDo)

(Sweden – Swedish GAAP – Source: Annual report 1999 – Newsprint and magazine paper as well as paperboard)

Notes to the financial statements (parent company)

Note 15 Equity (million SKr)

	Share capital	Restricted equity		Non-restricted equity		Total
		Revaluation reserve	Other restricted equity	Profit brought forward	Profit for the year	
Opening balance 1 January 1999	4,443	100	1,998	4,754	1,745	13,040
Transfer of profit of the year 1998				1,745	−1,745	0
Dividend paid						0
Ordinary				−889		−889
Extra				−3,110		−3,110
Profit for the year					4,675	4,675
Closing balance 31 December 1999	4,443	100	1,998*	2,500	4,675	13,716

* Other restricted equity consists of statutory reserves SKr 1,952 million and share premium reserve SKr 46 million

- The item "profit brought forward" represents accumulated optional reserves.
- That table explains the variation between the opening and closing shareholders' equity in the balance sheet.

SKr million	1999	1998
Equity		
Restricted equity		
Share capital	4,443	4,443
Revaluation reserve	100	100
Statutory reserve	1,952	1,952
Share premium reserve	46	46
Non-restricted equity		
Profit brought forward	2,500	4,754
Profit for the year	4,675	1,745
	13,716	13,040

Ratios

The share yield (earnings per share divided by market value of the share – see the definition of the earnings per share in Chapter 15) is a key ratio for analysts and investors alike in deciding whether to move their investment or not. However, many other ratios help analysts evaluate shareholders' equity.

Return on equity

The most common one is undoubtedly the return on equity (ROE). The formula is as follows:

Net income/Average equity

Table 11.5 Different types of capital increase

Types of increase	Objectives	Procedure	Impact on the balance sheet	Impact on the financial structure
In cash	To obtain additional long-term financial resources without term limits in order to buttress the development potential of the firm	Issuance of new shares either at a price greater than the par value (thus creation of a "share premium" for the difference) or increase in the par value of the existing shares	Increase of current asset, and increase of the capital account on the liability side	Increase in working capital Increase in cash
Capitalization of reserves	Reconcile the level of legal capital with the actual value of the assets and/or strengthen the capital as a gesture of responsibility towards the firm's trading partners	Distribution of shares or increase of the par value	Reduction of the reserves on the liability side Increase of capital on the liability side	Financial structure unchanged
In kind	Reinforce the growth potential of the firm by adding new tangible and intangible assets that will enhance the firm's future development	New shares are valued close to their fair market value	Increase on the asset side (the contributed asset) and possibly increase on the liability side if the contribution is not net of debt Increase of capital	If the contribution is a fixed asset, the financial structure is not modified If the contribution is a current asset: ● increase in working capital ● increase in working capital need If the contribution includes a financial (i.e., LT) debt the financial structure is unchanged If the contribution includes operating (i.e., ST) or non-operating debts: ● increase in working capital ● increase in working capital need
Conversion of liabilities	Reimburse debt without impacting on cash: the creditor abandons its claim in exchange for shares	New shares are valued close to their fair market value	Decrease in liabilities Increase of shareholders' equity (capital)	If the cancelled debt was long-term debt, the financial structure is unchanged If the cancelled debt was short term (operating or non-operating): ● increase in working capital ● increase in working capital need If the conversion is one of short-term bank credit such as overdraft: ● increase in working capital ● increase in cash
Share dividend	Reinforce the capital structure without strapping either the firm or the shareholders for cash	New shares are valued close to their fair market value	Reduction of the debt (dividends payable) Increase of capital	Increase in working capital Increase in working capital need

Managers use this ratio to compare investments opportunities, hopefully from the point of view of the shareholders. A variant, called "return on common equity" is sometimes used when only the point of view of the common shareholders needs to be taken into account:

(Net income minus preferred dividends)/Average common equity

Economic value added

This metric, designed by and proprietary to the financial consulting firm Stern Stewart, and developed in Chapter 15, addresses the concept of return on equity from a slightly different point of view by restating both the income (to reflect the long-term dynamics of the firm) and the equity to show the real investment (beyond the book value of equity) of the shareholders in the firm.

Equity ratio

This ratio measures the contribution of the shareholders in providing the resources required by the firm's operations.

Shareholders' equity/Total shareholders' equity and liabilities (or total assets)

Debt/equity ratio

This ratio describes the financial leverage the shareholders have obtained. This ratio has many different definitions as will be shown in the following examples.

Long-term debts/Shareholders' equity

Market to book ratio

Shareholders' equity defines the book value of the company. However, the amount at which equity is shown on the balance sheet is dependent on the valuation of assets and liabilities. Since (a) assets and liabilities are recorded in accounting systems at their historical cost and (b) the market value of a firm (and thus of its shares) is largely a function of its intangible assets (expertise, legitimacy, knowledge base, customer loyalty, employee loyalty, etc.), the market value of a firm is generally much greater than the book value of its equity. Even the resale value of the assets in the context of a liquidation often exceeds their book value by a large amount.

The "market to book" ratio measures the under valuation represented by the book value of equity. The higher the ratio, the higher the intangible assets are likely to be (since they are not recorded in the balance sheet – see Chapter 8). The formula is very simple:

Market price per share/Book value per share

This ratio represents the amount investors appear to be willing to pay for each CU of a firm's net assets.

Real-life examples

Table 11.6 compares three ratios as published by three industrial companies in the same country so as to minimize discrepancies that might be due to differing GAAPs (all data are from the companies' own 1999 annual reports). Even in the same country, here Sweden, discrepancies exist because technologies (thus assets required), markets, financing and reporting strategies are different. This diversity implies that when ratios are being used to compare companies around the world, great care must be taken to ensure comparability.

Table 11.6 Examples of ratios based on equity

Company	Name of the ratio	Computation	1999	1998
Holmen (newsprint and magazine paper)	Return on equity (in %)	Profit/loss for the year, expressed as a percentage of the average equity	10.6	14.4
Rottneros (production of pulp)	Return on equity after full tax (in %)	Profit after tax in relation to average equity	7	10
Sandvik (engineering)	Return on shareholders' equity (in %)	Consolidated net profit for the year as a percentage of average shareholders' equity during the year	12.4	11.9
Holmen	Equity ratio (in %)	Equity plus minority interests expressed as a percentage of the balance sheet total	54.4	60.4
Rottneros	Equity/assets ratio (in %)	Equity in relation to balance sheet total	62	81
Sandvik	Equity ratio (in %)	Shareholders' equity and minority interests in relation to total assets	52	47
Holmen	Debt/equity ratio (in times)	Net financial liabilities (financial liabilities and interest-bearing provisions less financial receivables, short-term placements and cash and bank) divided by the sum of equity and minority interests	0.13	0.17
Rottneros	Debt/equity ratio (in times)	Current and long-term liabilities, plus deferred tax liability, in relation to equity	0.5	0.2
Sandvik	Debt/equity ratio (in times)	Interest-bearing current and long-term debts (including pension liability) divided by the total of shareholders' equity and minority interests	0.4	0.5

KEY POINTS

- The two main sources of seed long-term financial resources of a firm are (1) the entrepreneur or investors, and (2) the providers of borrowed funds.
- The wealth contributed by the entrepreneur or by investors as capital to a business can be in the form of cash contributions, contribution of tangible or intangible assets, of intellectual property or even of labor, etc.

- Investors bring in capital to the business venture in return for a claim on a portion of the wealth potentially created by the enterprise over the years following the investment.

- Equity is "the residual interest [of the investors] in the assets of the enterprise after deducting all its liabilities".

- The two principal components of shareholders' equity are (share) capital, and retained earnings (or reserves).

- Shares or stock certificates represent the capital of incorporated firms. They are evidence of the contribution of the shareholder to the formation of capital.

- The face value of a share is called the nominal or par value. The capital is, therefore, equal to the number of shares multiplied by the par value.

- "Ordinary" (or common) shares are distinct from "preferred" shares. The latter carry rights different from those of common shares.

- The share premium is the difference between the issue price and the par value.

- The profit of a period can be either distributed to the shareholders in the form of dividends or kept in the organization either as a voluntary re-investment by the shareholders as retained earnings (reserve) or as a legally required reserve for a purpose specified by the law.

- The statement of changes in shareholders' equity is an important document that details how the current year's decisions (beyond operating decisions) have affected shareholder's equity.

- Several important ratios are related to shareholders' equity: return on equity, equity ratio, debt/equity ratio and market to book ratio.

REVIEW

Review 11.1 Copland Company

Topic: Share issuance in cash
Type: Individual exercise
Related part of the chapter: Core Issues

Copland has a capital of 300,000 CU, divided into 3,000 shares each with a par of 100 CU. It issues 1,000 new shares (par 100) for a price of 170 each. The legislation of the country in which Copland operates requires that the full share premium (here 70 CU per share) be paid up at the time of the new shares subscription but only requires that a minimum of 25% of the par value be paid up. The share issuance costs pertaining to this issuance (legal fees, auditors fees, printing costs, financial commissions and sundry fees) are recognized as an intangible asset and will be amortized over 5 years. All providers, whose bills are summed up under issuance costs for an amount of 5,000 CU, have been paid cash by check.

Required

1 Prepare the accounting entries necessary to record this capital increase.
2 Prepare a comparison of the relevant excerpts of the balance sheet before and after the issuance of new shares.

Solution

(In the following answers all 000 are omitted.)

1 Accounting entries

❶	BS (A+)	Cash at bank (100/4 + 70) × 1,000		95
	BS (A+)	Uncalled capital 100 × 3/4 × 1,000		75
	BS (L+)		Share capital	100
	BS (L+)		Share premium	70
❷	BS (A+)	Share issuance costs		5
	BS (A−)		Cash at bank	5
❸	IS (E+)	Amortization expense		1
	BS (A−)		Amortization of share issuance costs	1

2 Balance sheet excerpts

Balance sheet excerpt before new share issuance

Assets		Shareholders' equity and liabilities	
(...)		*Shareholders' equity*	
		Share capital (incl. 300 paid)	300
		(...)	

Balance sheet excerpt after new share issuance

Assets		Shareholders' equity and liabilities	
Uncalled capital	75	*Shareholders' equity*	
Intangible assets		Share capital (incl. 325 paid)	
(Share issuance costs)	5	(300 + 100)	400
Minus accumulated amortization	−1	Share premium	70
Intangible assets (share issuance costs) – net	4		
(...)		(...)	
Cash at bank (95 − 5)	90		

Review 11.2 Menotti Company

Topic: Profit appropriation
Type: Individual exercise
Related part of the chapter: Core Issues

As of 1 January 20X1, Menotti's capital comprised 4,000 shares of 100 CU par. These shares are divided in two classes: 1,000 class-A shares and 3,000 class-B shares. Class-A shares enjoy a 5% of par preference dividend over and above the ordinary dividends.

Before appropriation of the annual earnings, the books show the following year-end data (in CU).

Legal reserve	39,000
Regulated reserves	8,000
Losses brought forward	−5,000
Net income after tax	40,000

Tax regulations require that the regulated reserve be incremented by 2,000 CU. The by-laws contain the following stipulations:

- Each year the legal reserve must be incremented by an amount of 5% of the net income for the year net of any loss carry-forward (if the net is positive) as long as the legal reserve is less than 10% of the par capital.
- Class-A shares must receive a preference dividend of 5% of their par value.
- All A and B shares are equally entitled to the payment of ordinary dividends.

The board of directors proposes that (a) an optional reserve be created for an amount of 10,000 CU and (b) that an ordinary dividend of 4 CU per share be paid out. The general meeting approves these propositions.

The balance of income after appropriation will be carried forward.

Required

1 Prepare a table detailing the profit appropriation calculations (including the per share dividend for each class of shares).
2 Prepare the appropriation accounting entries.
3 Prepare a table detailing the shareholders' equity and liabilities before and after appropriation.

Solution

1 Prepare a table detailing the profit appropriation calculations (including the per share dividend for each class of shares)

Net income				40,000
Losses brought forward				−5,000
Subtotal				35,000
Legal reserve	Basis		35,000	
	Rate		5%	
	Amount		1,750	
	Share capital		400,000	
	Rate		10%	
	Required legal reserve ceiling		40,000	
	Current legal reserve		39,000	
	Contribution required		1,000	−1,000
Distributable profit				34,000
Regulated reserve				−2,000
Optional reserve				−10,000
Preference dividend (Class A shares)	Number of shares		1,000	
	Par value		100	
	Rate		5%	
	Amount		5,000	−5,000
Ordinary dividends (Class-A and B shares)	Number of shares		4,000	
	Amount per share		4	
	Amount		16,000	−16,000
Profit brought forward to retained earnings				1,000

Notes:

- Since the legal reserve only requires an increment of 1,000 CU to reach the level of 10% of the capital at par, the amount appropriated to that purpose is limited (and will be nil for the next period).
- All shares are entitled to receiving the ordinary dividend.
- The dividends per share are as follows:
  - preference shares (class-A): 5 (preference dividend) + 4 (ordinary dividend) = 9 CU
  - ordinary shares (class-B): 4 CU (ordinary dividend).

2 Prepare the appropriation accounting entries

BS (L–)	Net income		40,000
BS (L+)		Loss brought forward	5,000
BS (L+)		Legal reserve	1,000
BS (L+)		Regulated reserve	2,000
BS (L+)		Optional reserve	10,000
BS (L+)		Dividends payable	21,000
BS (L+)		Profit brought forward	1,000

3 Prepare a table detailing the shareholders' equity and liabilities before and after appropriation

	Before appropriation	After appropriation
Shareholders' equity		
Share capital	400,000	400,000
Reserves		
Legal reserve	39,000	40,000
Regulated reserve	8,000	10,000
Optional reserve		10,000
Profit/loss brought forward	–5,000	1,000
Net income	40,000	0
Total shareholders' equity	482,000	461,000
Liabilities (dividends payable)		21,000
Total shareholders' equity and liabilities	482,000	482,000

ASSIGNMENTS

Assignment 11.1

Multiple-choice questions
Type: Individual exercise
Related part of the chapter: Core Issues

Select the right answer (only one possible answer, unless otherwise stated).

1 The sale by a shareholder of shares of a company to another shareholder should be recorded by the company
   (a) True
   (b) False

2 A company received cash subscriptions for 5,000 shares of 20 CU nominal (par) value at 100 CU per share. A down-payment of 50% of the issuance price is required. The remainder of the purchase price is to be paid the following year. At the time that the share is subscribed, share capital should be credited for
   (a) 500,000
   (b) 250,000
   (c) 100,000
   (d) 50,000
   (e) 400,000
   (f) 200,000
   (g) None of these

3 Dividends cannot be distributed if net income is not greater than zero
   (a) True
   (b) False

4 The difference between the price paid for a company's common share and the par value of each share can be called (several possible answers)
   (a) Capital surplus
   (b) Share premium
   (c) Additional paid-in capital
   (d) Paid-in capital
   (e) Additional contributed capital
   (f) Ordinary share capital
   (g) Capital in excess of par value
   (h) Premium fund
   (i) All of these
   (j) None of these

5 A company's board has authorized 20,000 shares and 10,000 shares were issued and are outstanding. In April 20X2, the company declared a 2.00 CU per share ordinary dividend. Which of the following journal entries would be necessary at the time of the declaration?

   (a) Net income (or retained earnings)   20,000
         Cash   20,000
   (b) Net income (or retained earnings)   40,000
         Dividend payable   40,000
   (c) Net income (or retained earnings)   40,000
         Cash   40,000
   (d) Net income (or retained earnings)   20,000
         Dividend payable   20,000
   (e) Dividend payable   40,000
         Net income (or retained earnings)   40,000
   (f) Dividend payable   20,000
         Net income (or retained earnings)   20,000

   (g) None of these

6 A company has the following shareholders' equity section:

Ordinary shares: par = 2 CU; 250,000 shares authorized; 100,000 shares issued and outstanding	200,000
Share premium	30,000
Reserves	50,000
Net income	20,000
Shareholders' equity	300,000

The market price per share is 15 CU. What is the book value per share?

(a) 2
(b) 1.2
(c) 3
(d) 0.8
(e) 15
(f) 2.3
(g) 0.92
(h) None of these

7 In all types of limited liability companies, it is possible to defer the payment of one part of the subscribed capital

(a) True
(b) False

8 The number of authorized shares is greater than the amount of issued shares which is greater that the amount of outstanding shares

(a) True
(b) False

9 A share may grant a voting right greater than one but never lower than one

(a) True
(b) False

10 The main objective of the legal reserve is to protect the shareholders of the company

(a) True
(b) False

Assignment 11.2 Ives Company

Topic: Impact on shareholders' equity
Type: Individual exercise
Related part of the chapter: Core/Advanced Issues

Transactions related to Ives Company's shareholders' equity (far left column) are listed in the following table. For each line you are provided with three choices of impact of the transaction on the total of shareholders' equity: increase, decrease or no impact.

Required

Indicate by a checkmark the impact of each transaction.

	Impact on shareholders' equity		
	Increase	Decrease	No impact
Core Issues			
Issuance of ordinary shares in cash at par value			
Issuance of preference shares in cash at par value			
Declaration of the year's cash dividend			
Payment of a cash dividend			
Issuance of ordinary shares in cash at a price greater than par value			
Issuance of preference shares in cash at a price greater than nominal value			
Conversion of preference shares to ordinary shares			
Advanced Issues			
Issuance of share dividends			
Issuance of ordinary shares at par (nominal) value by capitalization of reserves (retained earnings)			
Issuance of ordinary shares by conversion of bonds for a price greater than nominal value			
Issuance of shares in kind for a price greater than nominal value			
Repurchase and retirement of shares by the company			
Purchase of treasury shares (own shares)			

Assignment 11.3 Bernstein Company

Topic: Share issuance in cash
Type: Individual exercise
Related part of the chapter: Core Issues

Bernstein Co. is a limited liability company. The annual general meeting, held on 6 May 20X1, voted to issue an additional 2,500 shares (each with a par of 550 CU). The public offering price is set at 700 CU. The capital will be called for the full amount of the legal minimum. Bank X received the subscriptions from 7 to 30 May. On 30 May, the bank issued a certificate stating that the sale was complete and all funds had been collected.

Required

Prepare the appropriate entries in either one of the following formats:

● journal entries
● T-accounts entries
● balance sheet entries,

   under both of the following hypotheses:

   1 The legal minimum that must be called is half the issuance price.
   2 The legal minimum that must be called is half the par value and the entire share premium.

Assignment 11.4 Gilbert Company

Topic: Profit appropriation
Type: Individual exercise
Related part of the chapter: Core Issues

Gilbert Company was created in early 20X1. Its original capital was 2,500 shares with a par value of 100 CU. The composition of the capital as of 31 December 20X9, is described in article 7 of the amended by-laws (see exhibit).

At the end of 20X9 the shareholders' equity account before appropriation stands as shown in the table.

Share capital	3,780,000
Share premium	7,560,000
Legal reserve	370,000
Optional reserve	2,000,000
Profit/loss brought forward	−100,000
Net income for 20X9	1,000,000
Total	14,610,000

The board of directors has approved a motion in which in addition to the appropriation of the earnings from 20X9, there will be a second dividend which will be paid to shares of all classes. This second dividend will be the maximum legally possible without, however, exceeding 10 CU per share. The remaining balance, if there is any, will be transferred to the optional reserve account.

The prime rate mentioned in the by-laws and applicable to the year 20X9 is 6% per annum.

The amount of the legal reserve may be limited to 10% of the share capital.

Required

1 Prepare a suggested appropriation of the 20X9 net income.

2 Prepare the appropriate accounting entries that your suggested appropriation requires.

3 Prepare a table describing the shareholders' equity after appropriation.

Exhibit

Article 7 – **Share capital**

The capital of Gilbert is 3,780,000 (three million seven hundred eighty thousand) CU.

The capital is composed of 37,800 (thirty seven thousand eight hundred) fully subscribed shares, each with a par of 100 (one hundred) CU.

The shares are partitioned in two classes:

- 27,000 A Shares, numbered 1 to 27,000, and
- 10,800 B Shares numbered 27,001 to 37,800.

The B shares are preference shares with a preference dividend for the fiscal years 20X9 to 20X15 inclusive. This preference dividend will be calculated as a fixed remuneration on the basis of the prime rate minus 1% for fiscal year 20X9, prime rate plus 2% for fiscal year 20X10, and prime rate plus 5% for years 20X11 to 20X15.

The fixed remuneration rate will be applied to the full subscription price (including the capital surplus), i.e., 800 CU per share of 100 CU. All holders of B shares will receive this dividend. The dividend will be payable in keeping with the conditions defined by law.

(...)

Assignment 11.5 Graphit Kropfmühl AG*

Topic: Reporting for profit appropriation
Type: Group exercise
Related part of the chapter: Core Issues

Graphit Kropfmühl AG is a German raw material refiner (graphite and silicon) for high-tech applications (chemical, electronics and aluminum-processing industry). The following data concerning the parent company Graphit Kropfmühl AG were excerpted from the 1999 annual report.

Balance sheet (excerpts) (000 DM)		
	31 Dec 1999	31 Dec 1998
Equity		
Subscribed capital	14,400	14,400
Capital reserve	13,389	13,389
Revenue reserves		
1 Statutory reserve	1,200	1,200
2 Other revenue reserves	7,042	5,800
	8,242	7,000
Balance sheet profit	4,320	4,351
	40,351	39,140

Income statement (excerpts) (000 DM)		
	1999	1998
Year's net income	5,531	6,832
Profit brought forward from the previous year	31	19
Allocation to other revenue reserves	1,242	2,500
Balance sheet profit	4,320	4,351

Required

1 Explain the computation of the balance sheet profit in the income statement.

2 What does this balance sheet profit represent? Is the balance sheet presented before or after profit appropriation?

3 Explain the change in the "Other revenue reserves".

4 From the data excerpted from the balance sheet and income statement provided, find the amount of the dividends distributed in 1999 with regard to 1998.

5 The annual report indicates that the dividends distributed in 1999 relating to the 1998 profit amounted to 1.5 DM per share. It also states that the share capital includes 2,880,000 shares. Double-check the amount of dividends paid in 1999 as found in question 4.

Assignment 11.6 Easynet*

Topic: Statement of changes in equity
Type: Individual/group exercise
Related part of the chapter: Advanced Issues

The 1999 financial statements for Easynet, a British internet provider, contain the following information on "shareholders' equity" for the year ended 31 December 1999.

Parent company balance sheet (excerpts)		
	1999	*1998*
	£000	*£000*
Capital and reserves		
Called-up share capital	992	820
Share premium account	10,409	5,951
Profit and loss account	−35	−247
Shareholder's funds	11,366	6,524

Profit for financial year 1999 is equal to £212,000. During 1999, Easynet issued 4,301,295 new shares of 4 pence par each (1 pence equals 1% of a pound). Of these new shares: 4,022,845 came from outright sales and 278,450 came from exercise of share options. The total issuance amount received was £4,892,000 (£4,734,000 from sales and £158,000 from exercise of share options). The expenses incurred in the sale of new shares amounted to £262,000. These were offset against the share premium account.

Required

Prepare the statement of changes in shareholders' equity for the year 1999.

Assignment 11.7 Munksjö*

Topic: Ratios based on equity
Type: Individual/group exercise
Related part of the chapter: Advanced Issues

Munksjö is a Swedish company that operates in four business areas: paper, packaging, pulp, and hygiene. Its consolidated balance sheet shows the following "shareholders' equity and liabilities" information (*source*: annual report 1999).

Consolidated balance sheet (excerpts)		
Millions of Swedish kroners	31 Dec. 1999	31 Dec. 1998
SHAREHOLDERS' EQUITY AND LIABILITIES		
SHAREHOLDERS' EQUITY		
Restricted equity		
Share capital	216.7	216.7
Restricted reserves	777.2	707.6
Total restricted equity	993.9	924.3
Non-restricted equity		
Non-restricted reserves	922.2	872.0
Net earning for the year	157.9	245.4
Total non-restricted equity	1,080.1	1,117.4
TOTAL SHAREHOLDERS' EQUITY	**2,074.0**	**2,041.7**
Minority interest	1.0	0.8
PROVISIONS		
Interest-bearing provisions	179.3	180.4
Non-interest-bearing provisions	298.6	227.5
TOTAL PROVISIONS	**477.9**	**407.9**
LIABILITIES		
Long-term interest-bearing liabilities		
Convertible loan	73.7	71.6
Other long-term liabilities	1,048.4	696.0
	1,122.1	767.6
Short-term non-interest-bearing liabilities		
Operating liabilities	847.2	713.8
Tax liability	42.5	115.1
	889.7	828.9
Short-term interest-bearing liabilities		
Short-term portion of long-term debt	0.0	131.9
Other current liabilities	429.7	0.0
	429.7	131.9
TOTAL LIABILITIES	**2,441.5**	**1,728.4**
TOTAL SHAREHOLDERS' EQUITY AND LIABILITIES	**4,994.4**	**4,178.8**

From the assets, we extracted the following items:

Millions of Swedish kroners	31 Dec. 1999	31 Dec. 1998
Financial assets	22.0	17.8
Short-term investments	0.0	10.8
Cash and bank balances	23.0	23.7

In addition, the annual report mentions that the amount of shareholders' equity on 31 December 1997 was equal to 1,930 million Swedish kroners.

Required

Compute the following three ratios based on equity, as defined by the company in its annual report:

1 *Return on equity*: Net earnings for the year as a percentage of average reported shareholders' equity.

2 *Equity ratio*: Shareholders' equity in relation to the balance sheet total.

3 *Debt ratio*: Net debt in relation to shareholders' equity at the end of the period. Net debt is defined as interest-bearing liabilities less liquid funds and long-term investments at the end of the period.

Comment on these ratios.

References

FASB (1997) Statement of Financial Accounting Standards No. 130, Reporting Comprehensive Income, Norwalk, CT.

IASC (1989) Framework for the Preparation and Presentation of Financial Statements, London.

IASC (1997) International Accounting Standard No.1, Presentation of Financial Statements, London.

Further readings

Dhaliwal, D., Subramanyam, K R., and Trezevant, R. (1999) Is comprehensive income superior to net income as a measure of firm performance? *Journal of Accounting & Economics*, 26(1–3), January, 43–67.

Additional material on the website

Go to http://www.thomsonlearning.co.uk/accountingandfinance/stolowylebas for further information, journal entries and extra assignments for each chapter.

The following appendices to this chapter are available on the dedicated website:

Appendix 11.1: Different categories of reserves
Appendix 11.2: Differences in the meaning of retained earnings
Appendix 11.3: Unrestricted and restricted reserves
Appendix 11.4: Share (stock) split
Appendix 11.5: Reduction of the share capital due to accumulated loss
Appendix 11.6: Share dividend in North America
Appendix 11.7: Reporting for comprehensive income

Notes

1 A *cumulative* dividend means that if there are not enough earnings to pay out the guaranteed dividend during one period, the dividends in arrears (i.e., that were not paid) will be carried over to the next period and paid in priority before any other dividend can be paid out.

2 The date of record is a cut-off. Investors who acquired shares beyond this date do not receive dividends emanating from earnings relating to the period(s) during which they were not actually shareholders.

3 This topic was introduced in Chapter 2.

4 The concept of "stock split" (or "share split") is developed in Appendix 11.4.

5 Borrowing the funds, exercising the option, reselling all or enough shares to reimburse the loan in full may all be done in a 24- to 48-hour window.

Liabilities and provisions

Liabilities are one of the three major components of the balance sheet. They represent, beside shareholders' equity, the other source of funding for any business (through either direct contribution of cash or postponement of cash outlays). A liability is the result of a business's past transactions that recognizes an obligation to transfer in the future and for the benefit of "liability holders" (for example, lenders), some of the business' resources such as assets – and particularly cash payments – or provide services.

The liability funds providers can be persons or organizations whose main activity is to do so (such as bond holders – private or institutional – or financial institutions such as banks or insurance firms) or business "partners" such as customers (who prepaid for services, as would be the case, for example, of a subscription to a magazine), suppliers (accounts payable), tax or para-fiscal authorities (such as a social security authority, for example), or even salaried employees (who get paid – or receive a bonus – after they provided the work and thus are owed their salary or bonus until payday and thus provide some cash float to the business). As was the case for assets, the problems of definition (what constitutes a liability), recognition (when to recognize the obligation), valuation (what is the amount of the obligation) and classification in reporting apply to liabilities.

The principles of liabilities reporting as well as the handling of provisions and equivalent will be addressed in "Core Issues", while a certain number of special issues including those created by bonds and "quasi-liabilities" like leases will be dealt with in "Advanced Issues".

Major topics

Definitions

Long-term liabilities

Current liabilities

Reporting liabilities

Provisions

Contingent liabilities

Bonds

Leased assets

Environmental liability

Employee benefits

A liability reflects an obligation to pay or deliver in the future. However, the definitions of what an obligation is and how definitive it is or to how much it amounts are difficult points the IASC has attempted to clarify. Liabilities or obligations are generally divided between current and non-current. The weight of these obligations in the financing of a business as well as the mix of current and non-current varies from business to business and between industrial or service sectors.

Definitions

International Accounting Standard 37 (IASC 1998a: § 10) defines a liability as a "present obligation of the enterprise arising from past events, the settlement of which is expected to result in an outflow from the enterprise of resources embodying economic benefits". In this definition, several concepts are important; each will be reviewed in turn.

Present obligation

The IASC Framework (IASC 1989: § 60) specifies that an "essential character-istic of a liability is that the enterprise has a present obligation". The concept of obligation is then defined as: "A duty or responsibility to act or perform in a certain way. Obligations may be legally enforceable as a consequence of a binding contract or statutory requirement. This is normally the case, for example, with amounts payable for goods and services received. Obligations also arise, however, from normal business practice, custom and a desire to maintain good business relations or act in an equitable manner. If, for example, an enterprise decides as a matter of policy to rectify faults in its products even when these become apparent after the warranty period has expired, the amounts that are expected to be expensed in respect to goods already sold are liabilities."

Past events

"Liabilities result from past transactions or other past events. Thus, for example, the acquisition of goods and the use of services give rise to trade payables (unless paid for in advance or on delivery) and the receipt of a bank loan results in an obligation to repay the loan. An enterprise may also recognize future rebates based on [accumulated] annual purchases by customers as liabil-ities; in this case, the sale of the goods in the past is the transaction that gives rise to the liability" (IASC 1989: § 63).

Settlement of the obligation

"The settlement of a present obligation usually involves the enterprise giving up resources embodying economic benefits in order to satisfy the claim of the other party." This settlement "may occur in a number of ways, for example, by: (a) Payment of cash; (b) Transfer of other assets; (c) Provision of services; (d) Replacement of that obligation with another obligation; or (e) Conversion of the obligation to equity [see Chapter 11]. An obligation may also be extinguished by other means, such as a creditor waiving or forfeiting its rights" (IASC 1989: § 62).

The current/non-current distinction

Principles

We have seen in Chapter 3 that IAS 1 (IASC 1997a) left businesses relatively free to choose their format for reporting liabilities as separate classifications on the balance sheet. Alternative acceptable classifications to the current/non-current classification include order of maturity (short term versus long term) and distinguishing interest-bearing liabilities from non-interest-bearing ones (and possibly ranking by order of maturity within each category). Reporting of liability is aimed at informing investors, partners and analysts. Any classification is a choice reflecting an emphasis on a given focus. For example, the distinction current/non-current (❶ in Figure 12.1) emphasizes the operating cycle, while the short term/long term (❷ in Figure 12.1) refers to a preoccupation with solvency.

IAS 1 (IASC 1997a) specifies (§ 60) that "a liability should be classified as a current liability when it:

(a) is expected to be settled in the normal course of the enterprise's operating cycle; or

(b) is due to be settled within twelve months of the balance sheet date.

All other liabilities should be classified as non-current liabilities."

Figure 12.1 summarizes the two classifications of liabilities.

The expressions "short term" and "current" are often used interchangeably because they both refer to a period of 12 months or less. The distinction between "current/non-current" and "short/long term" is therefore fuzzy.

The concept of "operating cycle" was introduced in Chapter 3. "Some current liabilities, such as trade payables and accruals for employee and other operating costs, form part of the working capital used in the normal operating cycle of the business. Such operating items are classified as current liabilities even if they are due to be settled after more than twelve months from the balance sheet date" (IASC 1997a: § 61). However, other liabilities classified as current (such as dividends payable, income taxes and other non-trade payables) do not belong to the operating cycle in a strict and narrow sense. They are, however, considered current because they are due to be settled within 12 months of the balance sheet date.

When the current/non-current classification is adopted, the IASC prescribes that an enterprise should "disclose for each (…) liability item that combined amounts expected to be (…) settled both before and after twelve months of the

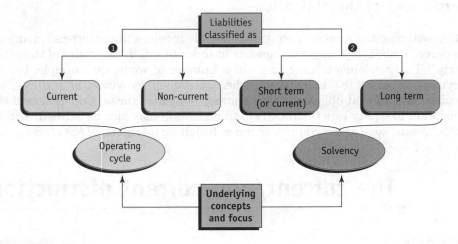

Figure 12.1 Classification of liabilities

balance sheet date, the amount expected to be (...) settled after more than twelve months". This disclosure should be carried out in a note to the financial statements or in a footnote to the balance sheet.

Real-life examples

Sandvik

(Sweden – Swedish GAAP – Source: Annual report 1999 – Engineering)

Consolidated balance sheet (excerpts)

Amounts in SEK M	1999	1998
SHAREHOLDERS' EQUITY AND LIABILITIES		
Shareholders' equity	20,109	18,621
Minority interests	888	872
Provisions	5,972	6,348
Interest-bearing liabilities		
Bond loans	—	194
Loans from financial institutions	4,587	7,335
Convertible debenture loan	1,024	—
Other long-term liabilities	483	220
	6,094	7,749
Non-interest-bearing liabilities		
Advance payments from customers	307	286
Trade payables	2,117	2,323
Bills payable	199	288
Due to associated companies	53	50
Income tax liabilities	426	560
Other liabilities	1,191	1,408
Accrued expenses and deferred income	2,840	3,101
	7,133	8,016
Total shareholders' equity and liabilities	40,196	41,606

This excerpt of Sandvik balance sheets illustrates a presentation of liabilities first according to their interest-bearing and non-interest-bearing nature and second, within each category by range of maturity date (information provided in the notes).

Sony Corporation

(Japan – Japanese/US GAAP – Source: Annual report 2000 – Electronics, games, music, motion pictures)

Excerpts from the consolidated balance sheet

	Millions of yen	
	1999	2000
LIABILITIES AND STOCKHOLDERS' EQUITY		
Current liabilities		
Short-term borrowings	40,877	56,426
Current portion of long-term debt	87,825	158,509
Notes and accounts payable, trade	722,690	811,031
Accounts payable, other and accrued expenses	670,631	681,458
Accrued income and other taxes	107,031	87,520
Other	313,491	365,398
Total current liabilities	1,942,545	2,160,342
Long-term liabilities		
Long-term debt	1,037,460	813,828
Accrued pension and severance costs	129,115	129,604
Deferred income taxes	120,822	184,020
Future insurance policy benefits and other	913,937	1,124,873
Other	195,382	177,059
Total long-term liabilities	2,396,716	2,429,384

This excerpt of the balance sheet of this company illustrates the classification of liabilities in a decreasing order of maturity.

Relative weight of liabilities in the balance sheet

Between businesses, countries, and even between firms in the same economic sector, liabilities (and provisions) represent different weights in the balance sheet. Such diversity is illustrated in Table 12.1 based on the 1999 annual reports of a not statistically significant sample of companies.

Table 12.1 Weight of liabilities

Company (country – activity)	Currency	Types of liability	Liabilities	Total equity and liabilities (=assets)	% of total equity and liabilities
Morton's Restaurant (USA – restaurants)	$000	Current liabilities	34,468		30.1%
		Obligations to financial institutions and capital leases	60,970		53.3%
		Other liabilities	6,855		6.0%
		Total liabilities	102,293	114,361	**89.4%**
Ispat International (Netherlands – steel)	$m	Current liabilities	1,440		24.1%
		Long-term debt	2,184		36.6%
		Deferred tax liabilities	130		2.2%
		Deferred employee benefits	1,227		20.6%
		Other long-term obligations	131		2.2%
		Total liabilities	5,112	5,966	**85.7%**
Renault (France – automotive industry)	€m	Deferred tax liabilities	223		0.5%
		Pensions and other post-retirement benefit obligations	1,252		2.7%
		Other provisions for risks and liabilities	2,645		5.7%
		Interest-bearing borrowings	20,344		43.8%
		Trade and other payables	7,402		15.9%
		Other liabilities and deferred income	5,741		12.4%
		Total	37,607	46,422	**81.0%**
Statoil group (Norway – oil and gas)	NOKm	Provisions for liabilities and charges	32,540		19.4%
		Long-term debt	46,030		27.4%
		Current liabilities	47,957		28.5%
		Total liabilities	126,527	168,137	**75.3%**
Iberia (Spain – airline)	Ptas m	Deferred revenues	3,759		0.5%
		Provisions for contingencies and expenses	159,701		23.3%
		Long-term debt	112,668		16.4%
		Current liabilities	240,973		35.1%
		Total	517,101	686,864	**75.3%**
Sony (Japan – music) (2000)	Y m	Current liabilities	2,160,342		31.7%
		Long-term liabilities	2,429,384		35.7%
		Total	4,589,726	6,807,197	**67.4%**
Easynet (UK – internet provider)	£000	Creditors (amounts falling due within one year)	15,457		42.8%
		Creditors (amounts falling due after more than one year)	6,236		17.3%
		Total	21,693	36,109	**60.1%**
Elkem (Norway – metals and materials production)	NOK m	Provisions	417		4.3%
		Interest-bearing long-term debt	1,652		17.1%
		Current liabilities	2,272		23.5%
		Total	4,341	9,671	**44.9%**
Fielmann (Germany – eye glasses)	DM000	Accruals	63,440		10.3%
		Liabilities	145,028		23.5%
		Deferred income	78		0.01%
		Total	208,546	616,079	**33.9%**
Mountain Province Mining (Canada – mining)	C$000	Current liabilities	145		0.4%
		Total liabilities	145	37,172	**0.4%**

Long-term liabilities

Figure 12.2 illustrates the fact that businesses have both long-term and short-term financial needs that cut across the operating/non-operating cycles.

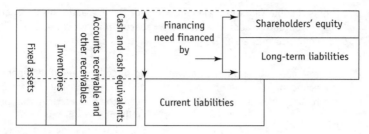

Figure 12.2 Financing need

A business's financing needs come essentially from a combination of three factors:

- **Growth**: In order to grow, a business must invest in both long-term fixed assets (tangible or intangible) and in operating assets.
- **The operating cycle**: Inventories, receivables and payables will generally grow with the expansion of the business's activity unless the speed of the operating cycle can be increased in a lower proportion as the expansion (which is a highly improbable occurrence). Because the need for operating assets is recurrent, a large part of the growth in these items must be financed through long-term (semi-permanent) funds.
- **Temporary imbalances in the equilibrium** between the various components of the operating cycle (for example due to a strong seasonality factor). Although such imbalances are generally short lived and self-correcting, they tend to reoccur on a regular basis and often require long-term funding as a way of avoiding the transaction costs that would be incurred in the activities required to securing appropriate funding each time the problem occurs.

The financing need (Figure 12.2) is equal to (Fixed assets + Current assets – Current liabilities). It is satisfied (or covered) by two sources of long-term finance:

- shareholders' equity (see Chapter 11)
- long-term liabilities (developed later).

The relative interest of funding through shareholders' equity or long-term liabilities is an issue constantly debated in all businesses. The leverage effect it creates is generally a major topic in corporate finance or financial statement analysis textbooks[1]. Table 12.2 summarizes some of the key issues looked at when choosing whether to go the equity or the liability route.

Long-term liabilities are generally divided between two categories:

- **Bank borrowings**: A lump sum liability, generally from a single source.
- **Bonds**: In this case, the debt is broken up in small (generally equal) increments represented by certificates. The holder of a debt certificate

	Liabilities	Shareholders' equity
Repayment term	Repayment of principal is required	No repayment required
Flexibility	Highly flexible (duration, amount, ease of obtaining additional funds, possibility to refinance, etc.)	Not flexible and high transaction costs. Decision is not reversible
Cost of funds	Interest must be paid regardless of the economic outcome of the use of the funds. Rates are market based	No directly required remuneration Dividends paid only if there is enough net income or accumulated previously undistributed income Part of the remuneration may come from a market appreciation of the shares
Deductibility of the cost of funds	Interest expense is generally tax deductible	Dividends are generally not tax deductible
Rights of the funds providers	Debt holders generally have no influence or control over the decisions or the management of the firm New debt holders affect previous debt holders only because the interest expense of the new liability may overburden the earnings and increase the likelihood of bankruptcy	Shareholders generally have influence and control over decisions and management Additional shareholders may cause a dilution of the power of current shareholders
Use of funds	Funds and projects may be linked explicitly (for example, through specific securing or guarantee agreements such as mortgages)	Funds cannot be targeted to a specific project

(bond) can trade it on a financial market. Each certificate has a face (or par) value and coupon rate (interest rate) that jointly specify the periodic interest paid to the bond bearer.

The specificities of accounting for bonds will be dealt with in the "Advanced Issues" section of this chapter.

Bank borrowings can take on many different forms depending on whether or not they are secured. For example, a mortgage liability is a debt secured by real property.

Accounting for current liabilities

Current liabilities are liabilities that relate to the operating cycle. They include accounts payable, notes payable, employee benefits payable, income taxes payable, sales or value added taxes payable, and the current portion of long-term liabilities.

Accounts payable

An **"account payable"** (or **"trade payable"**) represents the obligation of a business to a creditor (generally a supplier) usually arising from the purchase of goods and services on credit. Most businesses around the world show their accounts payable (the sum of all individual accounts payable) as a separate line item under current liabilities on their balance sheet.

Figure 12.3 illustrates the accounts payable mechanism. Larsson Company, a video equipment manufacturer, acquires electronic components, on credit, from Gynt AB. The components will be kept in inventory for a few days before being consumed in the manufacturing process. The purchase of these components amounts to 100 CU. It will be settled in two installments: a first payment of 90 after 30 days and the balance after 45 days. Figure 12.3 illustrates both the acquisition ❶ and the first payment ❷.

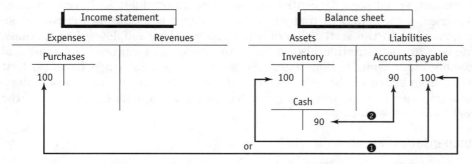

The transaction recorded as ❶ happens on the date of the purchase. It either involves recognizing the transaction as a purchase (i.e., in traditional financial accounting that assumes all purchases are presumed consumed and the cost of materials consumed is obtained by deducting the net increase/decrease in inventory between 2 physical inventories) or incrementing the inventory if the cost of part of merchandise consumed is calculated by accumulating the requisitions for withdrawals from inventory (see Chapters 2 and 9).

Entry ❷, recorded on the date of the first settlement, accounts for the first payment.

Figure 12.3 Accounts payable

Notes payable

Chapter 10 introduced "notes receivable" (bills of exchange and promissory notes) in the accounts of the buyer. Notes payable are the equivalent items in the seller's books. Figures 10.8 and 10.2A (Chapter 10) are applicable without complexity (mirror image) to notes payable.

When notes are payable within the next 12 months, they are shown as current liabilities. Otherwise, they are recorded as long-term liabilities (if a presentation by maturity term is adopted). An illustration of the recording of notes payable is given in Appendix 12.1.

Short-term employee benefits

Employers pay salaries or wages to their employees in exchange for their "labor". Salaries are paid on a periodic basis (every two weeks or every month) as a fixed installment of an agreed upon total amount defined as the remuneration for the person making her or his services available to the employer for an agreed upon annual number of hours, regardless of the level of occupation the employer will be able to provide. Wages refer to the payment (daily, weekly, biweekly or monthly) of an amount defined by an agreed hourly rate or piecework applied to the actual number of units of labor provided during the period for which the wages are calculated. In accounting terms, wages and salaries are handled in the same way and are recorded as "compensation expense".

Employers often withhold part of their employee's compensation to pay the worker's share of the contributions due for such things as health insurance premiums, social security contributions, labor union dues, and even, in some countries, income tax. In that case, the employer is assuming the role of an intermediary in the settlement of otherwise personal employees' obligations. The cost of compensation also includes the employer's share of the same and possibly other contributions (such as payroll taxes and fringe benefits) that derive from either the benefits package of their workforce or (and) legal obligations imposed by regulatory agencies. These expenses increase the cost of the workforce to the employer.

Compensation expense

Figure 12.4 is an illustration of the recording of the compensation expense for Larsson Company. The total monthly payroll amounts to 300 CU. This amount corresponds to a net payment to the workers of 235 CU, a total of employee withholdings of 20 CU for contribution to the social security program and a withholding of 45 CU which will be paid to the fiscal authorities in the name of the employees in settlement of personal income taxes.

The amounts withheld are not an additional employer cost. The compensation cost is 300 CU.

Payroll taxes and fringe benefits

Payroll taxes and **fringe benefits** are employee-related costs that are paid by the employer in addition to the compensation package (wages or salaries). They are sometimes called "**social expenses**" or "**social charges**".

Payroll taxes are amounts paid to the government for items such as the employer's portion of social security, unemployment taxes (federal and state taxes as the case may be), and workers' compensation taxes. Fringe benefits include the employer's share of employees' pension contributions, life and health insurance premiums, and vacation pay.

The Larsson Company, in its country of operation, is required (a) to pay an employer's social security contribution equal to 12% of the gross salary, and (b) to contribute to the workforce's retirement account paying an employer's contribution amounting to 20% of gross salaries. The following entry would be recorded:

IS (E+)		Employee benefit expense (social expenses)	96	
	BS (L+)	Pension liability payable		60
	BS (L+)	Employer social security payable		36

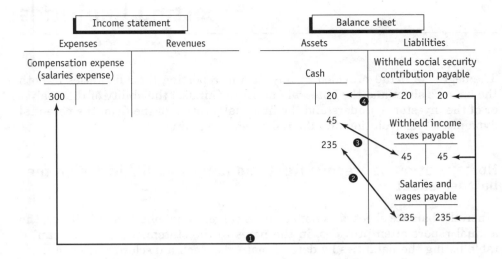

① Compensation expense. The net amount due to the employees is recorded in the "salaries payable" account but the expense that will eventually be recognized in the income statement is the compensation expense

②, **③** and **④** Payment (separately) of each liability on the appropriate date when it is due

Figure 12.4 Accounting for compensation expense

Income taxes payable

The recording of income taxes has been presented in Chapter 6.

Sales tax and value added tax (VAT) collected

Value added tax (VAT) collected has been introduced and developed in Chapter 10 (Appendix 10.2). Sales tax collected would follow a mechanism similar to that of VAT. When sellers (whether retailers or business to business enterprises) collect sales taxes, they are agents of the state or local government. Appendix 12.2 illustrates the sales tax payable accounting entries.

Current portion of long-term debt

When a company has decided to separately show long-term and short-term debts in their reporting of liabilities, the part of long-term debts due within a year should be reclassified as part of current liabilities. The following entry would be recorded when preparing financial statements:

BS(L–)	Long-term liability		x
	BS (L+)	Current portion of long-term liability	x

The degree of detail provided by any firm in reporting their liabilities in both the balance sheet and the notes will assist (or hinder) the ability of the analyst or of the investor to understand the financial position of the firm, the potential dynamics of its evolution and the risks they are taking.

No separation between current and long-term liabilities on the balance sheet

When the balance sheet does not separate current and long-term liabilities, the annual report often provides, in the notes to the statement, a fairly detailed table listing the liabilities by date of maturity. Such a disclosure is even more essential when the balance sheet does not structure the liabilities by relative maturity dates. For example, Continental, a global German-based manufacturer of tires, systems, and modules for the automotive industry, discloses the following figures in its financial statements (*source*: annual report 1999):

Excerpts from the consolidated balance sheet		
Shareholders' equity and liabilities	As of 31/12/1999 In millions of €	As of 31/12/1998 In millions of €
(...) Other liabilities (...)	1,505.8	1,267.1
Total	7,403.8	6,765.7

Excerpts from the notes to the consolidated financial statements						
(23) Other liabilities						
In millions of €		31 December 1999			31 December 1998	
	Total	Thereof < 1 year	Thereof > 5 years	Total	Thereof < 1 year	Thereof > 5 years
Trade accounts payable	752.4	752.4	—	649.3	648.8	—
Payables to affiliated companies	4.7	4.2	—	5.1	5.1	—
Payables to companies in which a participation is held	16.3	16.3	—	16.3	16.3	—
Miscellaneous liabilities	732.4	626.8	13.4	596.4	566.3	13.4
	1,505.8	1,399.7	13.4	1,267.1	1,236.5	13.4

The details of the liabilities maturity ranges are provided in note 23. The liabilities with a maturity date between 1 and 5 years are not explicitly indicated and can only be obtained by deduction.

Current and long-term liabilities reported separately on the balance sheet

The most common situation is to report liabilities separately by showing the current liabilities distinctly from the long-term liabilities with the "long-term" concept meaning more than one year. A typical example is provided by the Elkem annual report.

Elkem

(Norway – Norwegian GAAP – Source: Annual report 1999 – Metals and materials production)

This company discloses in its balance sheet the following categories of liabilities, in decreasing order of maturity date:

- provisions
- interest-bearing long-term debt
- interest-bearing short-term debt
- other short-term liabilities.

Notes 24 and 25, for example, provide even more information about the last two categories:

Note 24 Interest-bearing short-term debt

NOKm	1999	1998	1997
Bank overdrafts	48	131	64
Short-term loans	20	479	101
Current portion of long-term debt	9	299	79
	77	909	244

Note 25 Other short-term liabilities

NOK m	1999	1998	1997
Payable to suppliers	911	962	1,112
Value added taxes, vacation pay and employee taxes payable	210	244	199
Dividends	315	296	296
Taxes payable	296	177	200
Other short-term liabilities	463	573	506
	2,195	2,252	2,313

Liabilities, provisions, and contingent liabilities

Quasi-liabilities often render "liabilities" reporting complex. Liabilities are the materialization of a future obligation. However, the reality and immediacy of that obligation may be subject to debate. Quasi-liabilities are obligations for which either the triggering event may not come from a transaction with a third party, or the timing of the obligation may not be clear, or the amount may not well defined, or any combination of the three. Liabilities (in the strict sense) must be distinguished from:

- provisions
- accrued liabilities
- contingent liabilities.

Figure 12.5 illustrates the characteristics of each and summarizes the differences on the basis of the certainty of three distinguishing characteristics of the obligation they represent: principle creating the obligation, timing, and valuation or amount of the obligation.

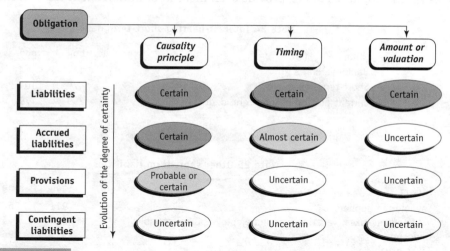

Figure 12.5 Liabilities and related concepts

Provision versus liability

A provision is an obligation that could eventually be reversed because some degree of estimation is involved in its amount and timing (Figure 12.5). It represents a real although potential obligation, the amount of which cannot be easily determined with precision at the time. A liability, however, is generally irreversible and can only be settled according to the terms of the contract or event that created it.

Principle and definition

The IASC Framework (IASC 1989: § 64) explains that: "Some liabilities can be measured only by using a substantial degree of estimation. Some enterprises

INTERNATIONAL AND COMPARATIVE ACCOUNTING

describe these liabilities as provisions. In some countries, such provisions are not regarded as liabilities because the concept of a liability is defined narrowly so as to include only amounts that can be established without the need to make estimates." The IASC definition of a liability favors the broader approach. Thus, according to the IASC, "when a provision involves a real and present obligation and satisfies the rest of the definition, it is a liability even if the amount has to be estimated." Examples include provisions for payments to be made under existing warranties provided to customers and provisions to cover pension obligations.

For IASC (1998a: § 10), a provision is "a liability of uncertain timing or amount". A provision should therefore be recognized "when:

(a) an enterprise has a present obligation (legal or constructive) as a result of a past event;

(b) it is probable that an outflow of resources embodying economic benefits will be required to settle the obligation; and

(c) a reliable estimate can be made of the amount of the obligation.

If these conditions are not met, no provision should be recognized" (§ 14).

The debate about what does or does not constitute a provision is extremely important to understand and particularly in studying a company's reported performance.

The notion of "time value of money" is developed in Appendix 12.3.

The **provision for restructuring** is quite frequently found in annual reports. IAS 37 (IASC 1998a, §70) states that such a provision is created when any or all of the following events or circumstances occur that create an obligation to incur future costs:

- sale or termination of a line of business
- closure of business locations in a country or region or relocation of business activities from one country or region to another
- changes in management structure, for example, eliminating a layer of management
- fundamental reorganizations that have a material effect on the nature and focus of the enterprise's operations.

The restructuring provision amount should be calculated so as to reflect estimates of "only the direct expenditures arising from the restructuring, which are those that are both (a) necessarily entailed by the restructuring; and (b) not associated with the ongoing activities of the enterprise" (IAS 37, 1998a: § 80).

Because estimates of future costs are often difficult to establish objectively, many managers have long used "provisions for restructuring" as a privileged tool of earnings management or income smoothing. An overestimation of the amount of the provision (for example, decided by a new management team) offers the possibility of improving future earnings when the actual expense reveals itself to be lower than anticipated (i.e., provisioned) since the excess provision will be reversed and added to the income of the period.

Movements in the provision accounts are generally reported in the notes to the financial statements. Since the appropriate reporting is similar to that of accounts receivable variations as described in Chapter 10, this topic will not be developed further.

ISS-International Service System

(Denmark – Danish GAAP – Source: Annual report 1999 – Support services)

The consolidated balance sheet and notes include the following elements:

In DKK m	1999	1998	Other provisions	1999	1998
Pensions and similar obligations	194.2	138.9	Restructuring	15.5	43.9
Deferred tax	136.2	133.6	Labor cases	45.4	16.8
Other provisions	530.6	245.5	Self-insurance	12.8	12.9
Total provisions	861.0	518.0	Integration cost	318.4	84.5
			Other provisions	138.5	87.4
				530.6	245.5

The "pensions and similar obligations" also called "provision for pensions" or "pension liability" will be developed in the advanced issues section of this chapter. "Deferred taxes" were introduced in Chapter 6. The details of "Other provisions" is given in one of the notes to the consolidated financial statements:

As the effect of time value of money is not material, the provisions are not discounted.

Restructuring: The restructuring provision relates to the restructuring of the group, which was announced in December 1998.

Labor cases: The provision relates to labor cases in Brazil, France, and Spain.

Self-insurance: In the UK, ISS carries an insurance provision excess on employers' and public liabilities. ISS UK is self-insured up to £300,000 for employers' liability and £150,000 for public liability.

Integration costs: The provision includes primarily provisions to cover costs arising as a direct consequence of acquisitions.

Other provisions: In 1999 the provisions comprise, e.g., provisions for legal costs and provisions relating to disposal of companies in previous years.

Provision versus accrued liabilities

Accrued liabilities are the results of both the accrual process and the time lag between an event and its complete resolution in the course of the cycle of operations.

Principle and definition

IAS 37 states (IASC 1998a: § 11) that: "Provisions can be distinguished from other liabilities such as trade payables and accruals because there is uncertainty about the timing or amount of the future expenditure required in settlement. By contrast:

(a) trade payables are liabilities to pay for goods or services that have been received or supplied and have been invoiced or formally agreed with the supplier; and

(b) accruals are liabilities to pay for goods or services that have been received or supplied but have not been paid, invoiced or formally agreed with the supplier, including amounts due to employees (for example, amounts relating to accrued vacation pay). Although it is sometimes necessary to estimate the amount or timing of accruals, the uncertainty is generally much less than for provisions.

Accruals are often reported as part of trade and other payables, whereas provisions are reported separately."

Accrued liabilities are usually recorded as part of the end-of-period entries (Chapter 5). Many annual reports do not distinguish clearly between "liabilities" and "accrued liabilities" and merge them under only one category in the balance sheet. However, it is clear that such a distinction could considerably help the analyst or the investor in understanding the effect of the operating cycle on the liquidity and solvency of the firm. Notes often provide much needed details.

Real-life example

Sulzer

(Switzerland – IAS GAAP – Source: Annual report 1999 – Medical equipment)

Notes to the consolidated financial statements

Note 28 Other current and accrued liabilities		
In millions of Swiss francs (CHF)	1999	1998
Other current liabilities		
Notes payable	12	12
Employee benefit plans	26	15
Social security institutions	21	33
Taxes	58	44
Commissions payable	19	23
Other liabilities	147	97
Total other current liabilities	**283**	**224**
Accrued liabilities		
Interest	13	23
Vacation and overtime claims	67	68
Salaries, wages and bonus	89	80
Contract-related costs	190	209
Other accrued liabilities	113	105
Total accrued liabilities	**472**	**485**
Total other current and accrued liabilities	**755**	**709**

While only the "Total other current and accrued liabilities" is reported on the balance sheet, Sulzer Company discloses the details of this category of liabilities, separating the current and the accrued liabilities.

Contingent liabilities

Contingent liabilities, as shown in Figure 12.5, are the liabilities for which there is uncertainty simultaneously on causing principle, timing and amount. Contingent liabilities, as their name implies, are obligations that are contingent (conditional) on events that are not entirely under the control of the firm.

IAS 37 (IASC 1998a: § 10) defines a contingent liability as:

(a) "a possible obligation that arises from past events and whose existence will be confirmed only by the occurrence or non-occurrence of one or more uncertain future events not wholly within the control of the enterprise; or

(b) a present obligation that arises from past events but is not recognized because:

    (i) it is not probable that an outflow of resources embodying economic benefits will be required to settle the obligation; or

    (ii) the amount of the obligation cannot be measured with sufficient reliability."

Provisions versus contingent liabilities

Discussion

The borderline between provisions and contingent liabilities is not always clear cut. IAS 37 (§12) explains that, "in a general sense, all provisions are contingent because they are uncertain in timing or amount". In this context, IAS 37 explains in its paragraph 13 the distinction "between provisions and contingent liabilities:

(a) provisions are recognized as liabilities (assuming that a reliable estimate can be made) because they are present obligations and it is probable that an outflow of resources embodying economic benefits will be required to settle the obligations; and

(b) contingent liabilities are not recognized as liabilities because they are either:

    (i) possible obligations, as it has yet to be confirmed whether the enterprise has a present obligation that could lead to an outflow of resources embodying economic benefits; or

    (ii) present obligations that do not meet the recognition criteria in this Standard (because either it is not probable that an outflow of resources embodying economic benefits will be required to settle the obligation, or a sufficiently reliably estimate of the amount of the obligation cannot be made)."

An illustration of the difficulty of distinguishing between accrued liabilities, provisions and contingent liabilities will be given in the Advanced Issues section of this chapter using an environmental liability as an example. IAS 37 does not address the recognition issue of obligations derived from "commitments" (such as loan repayment guarantees given by a solid parent for the benefit of helping a fledgling subsidiary secure a lower cost of financing). These commitments actually and conceptually represent an obligation that meets the same criteria as a contingent liability. In fact, most businesses report commitments in the same footnote to the financial statements in which they give the details pertaining to their "contingent liabilities".

Litigation liabilities

The provisions created in anticipation of the possible worst outcome of litigation cases are often mentioned as contingent liabilities. Since litigation takes a significant amount of time to settle, creating such a provision as close as possible in time to the triggering event is coherent with the matching principle. Litigation provisions are often mentioned as part of the contingent liabilities as exemplified by the following excerpt from the Honda Motor Company annual statement.

Real-life examples

Honda Motor Co.

(Japan – US GAAP – Source: Annual report 2000 – Manufacturer of automobiles, motorcycles, and other motorized durable equipment)

Notes to consolidated financial statements

(18) Commitments and contingent liabilities

(...) Honda is subject to potential liability under various lawsuits and claims. Such lawsuits and claims include product liability and personal injury lawsuits, lawsuits from dealers alleging impropriety in allocation of products and other claims. Although the aggregate ultimate liability under these lawsuits and claims at 31 March 2000 was not determinable, on the basis of legal advice received, management is of the opinion that such liability would not have a significant adverse effect on the consolidated financial statements.

In some cases the information provided is much more precise as can be seen in the annual report of Strora Enso.

Stora Enso

(Finland – IAS GAAP – Source: Annual report 1999 – Production of paper)

Note to the consolidated financial statements

Note 26 Commitments and contingent liabilities

Contingencies

Stora Enso is a party to certain legal proceedings that have arisen in the normal course of business. Stora Enso received a statement of objection from the European Commission relating to newsprint producers' operations during the period 1989–1995. Stora Enso has given its reply within the stipulated time schedule denying all allegations. Should the company be found to have participated in a prohibited pricing behavior, it would be subjected to a substantial fine. Management is currently not in a position to assess the final outcome of the investigation. No provision has been made in the accounts in relation to the matter. Except for the administrative proceeding just described, there is no reason to believe that any single ongoing or expected legal or arbitration proceeding will have any material effect on Stora Enso's results of operations.

Reporting precise information about a litigation or lawsuit places the business in a conundrum: if detailed information is published such as a quantified estimate of the possible out of court settlement or court verdict or award, such reporting might be construed by the opposing party as an acknowledgment of responsibility. By the same token, if there is not enough information about the case and the risks involved, users of financial information might consider themselves maligned (and, in turn, sue the business!).

Contingent liability derived from discounted notes or bills of exchange

Principles

The discount mechanism for bills of exchange and notes (see Chapter 10) creates a contingent liability often mentioned in the footnote pertaining to the notes payable. The mention of such a liability is critical in the calculation of the average days' sales ratio that must take into account the notes discounted in the denominator since the final responsibility is still borne by the company in case the discounted note is not paid in the end.

Real-life examples

<table>
<tr><td>

Mitsubishi Electric

(Japan – US GAAP – Source: Annual report 2000 – Electrical equipment)

Notes to consolidated financial statements

(15) Commitments and contingent liabilities

(…) It is common practice in Japan for companies, in the ordinary course of business, to receive promissory notes in settlement of trade accounts receivable and to subsequently discount such notes at banks. At 31 March 2000, the companies were contingently liable on trade notes discounted in the amount of ¥3,373 million ($31,821 thousand). Notes discounted are accounted for as sales. The aggregate amounts of proceeds from notes discounted for the years ended 31 March 2000, 1999 and 1998 are not available; however, based on its financial policy, the company believes that the balance of such contingent liabilities should not have significantly fluctuated during the year ended 31 March 2000.

There is no established or normalized terminology for reporting discounted notes. For example, CeWe Color, a German company, reports the amounts of discounted notes-related contingent liabilities as amounts "arising from the issue and assignment of bills of exchange".

</td></tr>
</table>

Other contingent liabilities

A variety of other contingent liabilities are found in annual reports. Toray Industries, for example, reported both a contingent liability as loan guarantor and one to cover its product warranty obligations.

Toray Industries

(Japan – Japanese GAAP – Source: Annual report 1999 – Manufacturer of synthetic fibers and textiles)

Notes to consolidated financial statements

11. Contingent liabilities

At 31 March 1999, contingent liabilities were as follows:

	Millions of yen	Thousands of US dollars
Notes discounted	6,155	50,868
As guarantors of loans to:		
Affiliates	11,458	94,694
Others	9,126	75,422
	20,584	170,116
Obligations of guarantee	102	843

The obligation of guarantee (or warranty) might also have been reported as a provision or not reported at first and only later reported as a contingent liability when warranty issues would have materialized.

ADVANCED ISSUES

Among financial liabilities, several offer specific accounting challenges. Bonds, financial leases, environmental liabilities as well as pension liabilities are examples of specific liabilities that require specific solution for quality reporting. In this part of the chapter we will also cover the importance of liabilities in financial statement analysis.

Bonds

Definition

In order to attract interest-bearing funds from investors, a company may issue bonds. A bond is a certificate allowing the division of a debt between a large number of investors (bondholders) each of whom can contribute only a small amount of the debt (the face value, or the selling price if sold at a discount or with a premium). If the face value of a bond is small, it makes this lending instrument accessible to a large public. In the aggregate the bond issue may represent a very large amount of borrowed funds to cover all or part of the company's financing needs. The larger the bond issue, the larger the number of bonds that can be sold individually or in blocks.

The bond or certificate shows the evidence of the claim held by the bondholder. The claim is based on a lending agreement between the provider of funds who purchases the bond (bondholder or investor) and the business (the borrower and the issuer of the bond). Each bond has a par or face value and a coupon rate (interest rate). Bond issuance offers businesses an alternative to bank loans. Instead of dealing with a single (or a limited pool of) financial institution(s), the bond-issuing company goes to the open financial markets to collect funds from a variety of sources (institutional as well as private) who value the liquidity offered by the bond.

A company that issues bonds assumes two obligations:

1 To pay investors a specified amount of cash on an agreed upon maturity date (when the bond will be redeemed) – which may be either a specified and unmodifiable date or a date which can be established later at the initiative of the borrower, generally after a period during which early retirement of the bond is not allowed. The amount that will be given to the bondholder on the date of redemption is called principal, par value, face value, or maturity value.

2 To pay investors a cash interest at periodic intervals on specified dates (generally before the maturity date) at a rate of interest defined on the date of issuance (fixed rate or conditional rates linked, for example, to the evolution of the prime rate or to the market price of some commodity).

Bonds are most of the time traded on financial markets, thus providing the lender with the possibility of making their investment liquid if needed. There are at least two basic types of bonds:

- **Term bonds** in one bond issue mature all on the same date. All the bonds are repaid *in fine*, i.e., at the end of the maturity period. For example, 500 term bonds of 1,000 CU each with a maturity date of 5 years from the date of issuance represent a total maturity value of 500,000 CU that will be paid on the fifth anniversary of the issuance.

- **Serial bonds** mature in predetermined installments (but the specific bonds called in a given installment are often drawn through a lottery). For example, 500 serial bonds of 1,000 CU face value each would in this case, for example, mature at the rate of 100,000 CU per year over a 5-year period.

Zero bonds (or Zeroes) are bonds that do not pay interest during their life and for which the face value or maturity value is the result of the compounding of the specified interest rate over the maturity period of the bond. Such bonds sell for an amount that is, of course, much reduced compared to the maturity value and offer a tax advantage to the holder as no taxable interest is earned by the lender during the entire life of the bond until it matures.

Interest, discount, and premium

Bonds are generally issued with a fixed or variable stated interest rate. The main concepts related to bonds issue will be illustrated through the example of Berwald Company. The data for this illustration are given in Table 12.3.

In this example, the bond is a term bond. It will be repaid *in fine*, at the end of year 20X5. The selling price of a bond should be equal to the present value of the future cash flows the lender will receive, i.e., all the interest payments (during the lending period) and the reimbursement of the principal (at the end). (Time value of money and present value are developed in Appendix 12.3.) In this computation, the interest rate (also called discount rate) used is the market rate of interest at the issue date for like instruments with similar risk.

Table 12.3 Berwald Company – Basic data

Date of issuance	1 January 20X1
Term	5 years
Face value (1)	500,000
Stated interest rate (2)	8%
Annual interest expense (1) × (2)	40,000
Payment of interest	Annually, 31 December
Maturity date	31 December 20X5

Table 12.5 shows the value of the bond issue described in Table 12.3 for market interest rates of 8%, 6%, and 10%.

Table 12.4 summarizes the current cash flows (in CU), while Table 12.5 illustrates the present value of those cash flows.

Table 12.4 Cash flows linked to the bond

	1 Jan. 20X1	31 Dec. 20X1	31 Dec. 20X2	31 Dec. 20X3	31 Dec. 20X4	31 Dec. 20X5
Interest payment		40,000	40,000	40,000	40,000	40,000
Principal						500,000
Total	Value of bonds = Net present value of future payments	40,000	40,000	40,000	40,000	540,000

Table 12.5 Present value of the cash flows from Table 12.4

Market rate 1 Jan. 20X1	Basis	Number of years		8%	6%	10%
Present value of principal	500,000	5	(1)	340,292	373,629	310,461
Present value of interest payments	40,000/year	5	(2)	159,708	168,495	151,631
Selling price			(3)=(1)+(2)	500,000	542,124	462,092
Stated value of principal			(4)	500,000	500,000	500,000
Premium/(discount)			(5)=(3)–(4)	0	42,124	(37,908)
Effective yield on the selling price				8%	6%	10%

(1) Present value = $\dfrac{1}{(1 + \text{assumed discount rate})^5}$. See Appendix 12.3 and Table 12.1A

(2) Present value of an ordinary annuity (see Appendix 12.3 and Table 12.3A)

In this table no issuance cost is assumed. Such cost would of course have to be covered by the funds received and the issuer of the bonds would receive less than the amount stated as the selling price in Table 12.5.

Case 1: Interest assumed in discounting is 8% or the same as in the bond issue. When the rate that investors can earn on investments of similar risk is 8%, that is the stated rate, the bonds will sell at par (face) value and yield 8%.

Case 2: assumed discount rate of 6%. When the market rate of interest is 6%, investors will bid up the price of the bonds to 542,124 because the stated rate of 8% is more favorable than the current (opportunity) market rate. In this case, the effective yield will correspond to the market rate of 6% and the bonds will sell at a premium of 42,124 CU (i.e., above face value).

Case 3: assumed discount rate is 10%. When the market rate of interest is 10%, the price of the bonds will be only 462,092 because the stated rate of 8% is less favorable than the current (opportunity) market rate. In this case, the effective yield will correspond to the market rate of 10% and the bonds will sell at a discount of 37,908 CU (i.e., below face value) to attract investors.

The difference between what was received at the date of issue and what must be paid at maturity is a premium (if the market rate is lower than the stated rate) or a discount (if the market rate is higher than the stated rate).

Accounting for bonds

The mechanism is illustrated in Figures 12.6, 12.7 and 12.3A.

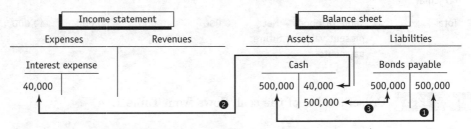

❶ On 1 January 20X1. At issuance: receipt of the principal
❷ On 31 December 20X1 (and on 31 December for each of the 4 following years): payment of the interest due
❸ At maturity (31 December 20X5): repayment of the principal

Figure 12.6 Accounting for bonds issued at par

Amortization

A premium represents a reduction of future interest expense. The premium needs to be amortized to follow the matching principle. Two methods of amortization are possible:

- effective interest method
- straight-line method.

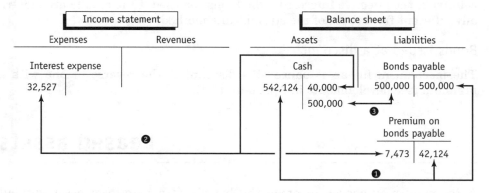

- ❶ On 1 January 20X1. At issuance: receipt of the principal. It is also possible to record the bonds in one account, including the premium
- ❷ On 31 December 20X1 (and on 31 December for each of the 4 following years): payment of the interest and amortization of the premium (see Table 12.6). (In this context, the term "amortization" has not the same meaning as for the amortization of intangible assets – see Chapter 8)
- ❸ At maturity (31 December 20X5): repayment of the principal

Figure 12.7 Accounting for bonds issued at a premium

Effective interest method

The periodic interest expense is determined by multiplying the book value at the beginning of each period by the effective interest rate at the time the bonds are issued. The premium amortization for each (interest) period is the difference between the interest calculated at the stated rate (8%) and the interest calculated at the effective rate (6%). Table 12.6 presents an illustration of such a calculation.

Table 12.6 Schedule of interest and book value – Effective interest method, premium case

Year ending	Interest expense	Cash (interest paid)	Premium amortization (decrease in book value)	Book value of bonds
	(1)=(4) previous line × 6%	(2)	(3)=(1)-(2)	(4)
				542,124
31 Dec. 20X1	32,527	40,000	-7,473	534,651
31 Dec. 20X2	32,079	40,000	-7,921	526,730
31 Dec. 20X3	31,604	40,000	-8,396	518,334
31 Dec. 20X4	31,100	40,000	-8,900	509,434
31 Dec. 20X5	30,566	40,000	-9,434	500,000
Total	157,876	200,000	-42,124	

Straight-line method

Interest expense is a constant amount each year equal to cash interest minus the annual premium amortization (premium/5). The interest patterns under the effective interest method conform more closely to economic reality. In most countries, the effective interest method must be used if the results are materially different from those of the straight-line method.

Bonds issued at a discount

The mechanism for an issuance at a discount is the reverse of one with a premium (see developments in Appendix 12.4).

Leased assets

A company may choose to enjoy the benefit of a long-term asset without necessarily wanting to own it. In this case, the user (lessee) will enter into a leasing contract with the supplier or a specialized enterprise (the lessor).

In a leasing contract, title to the asset does not change hands. An analyst or an investor would want to know what lease agreement the business has entered into both because the access to the assets involved is source of value creation and because the lease contract creates an obligation to pay a rent for the equipment, property or building. Leases are therefore an important element of the financial situation of a firm at any point in time and must be reported to the users of financial information.

IAS 17 (IASC 1997b: § 3) defines a "lease" as "an agreement whereby the lessor conveys to the lessee in return for a payment or series of payments the right to use an asset for an agreed period of time". This standard further distinguishes between:

- finance leases which are "leases that transfer substantially all the risks and rewards incident to ownership of an asset. Title may or may not eventually be transferred", and
- operating leases which are "leases other than a finance lease" (IASC 1997b: § 3).

In this definition,

- risks include the possibilities of losses from idle capacity or technological obsolescence and of variations in return due to changing economic conditions
- rewards may be represented by the expectation of profitable operation over the asset's economic life and of gain from appreciation in value or realization of a residual value.

Concretely, a finance lease is essentially equivalent to the acquisition of a fixed asset with debt financing.

Accounting treatment of leased assets

The distinction between the concepts of "finance" and "operating" leases plays a major role in the way leased assets will be reported. Figure 12.8 illustrates the issues at hand.

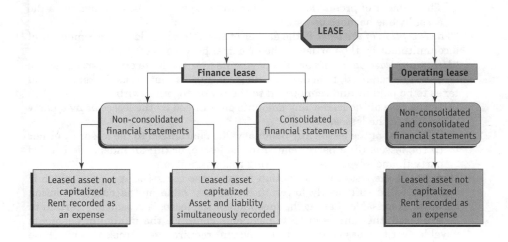

Figure 12.8 Accounting treatment of leased assets

We will only examine here the accounting issues from the point of view of the lessee. Leases in the financial statements of lessors will not be developed and the reader interested in this topic can consult IAS 17 (§§ 28–48).

Finance and operating leases

IAS 17 (IASC 1997b, § 8) states that a lease is either a "finance lease or an operating lease depend[ing] on the substance of the transaction rather than the form of the contract. Examples of situations that would normally lead to a lease being classified as a finance lease are:

(a) the lease transfers ownership of the asset to the lessee by the end of the lease term;

(b) the lessee has the option to purchase the asset at a price which is expected to be sufficiently lower than the fair value at the date the option becomes exercisable such that, at the inception of the lease, it is reasonably certain that the option will be exercised;

(c) the lease term is for the major part of the economic life of the asset even if title is not transferred;

(d) at the inception of the lease the present value of the minimum lease payments amounts to at least substantially all of the fair value of the leased asset; and

(e) the leased assets are of a specialized nature such that only the lessee can use them without major modifications being made."

In these situations, several terms are defined in the IASC standard (§ 3):

> "*Fair value* is the amount for which an asset could be exchanged or a liability settled, between knowledgeable, willing parties in an at arm's length transaction."
>
> "*Economic life* is either:
>
> (a) The period over which an asset is expected to be economically usable by one or more users; or

(b) The number of production or similar units expected to be obtained from the asset by one or more users."

"The *inception of the lease* is the earlier of the date of the lease agreement or of a commitment by the parties to the principal provisions of the lease."

"*Minimum lease payments* are the payments over the lease term that the lessee is, or can be required, to make excluding contingent rent, costs for services and taxes to be paid by and reimbursed to the lessor, together with:

(a) In the case of the lessee, any amounts guaranteed by the lessee or by a party related to the lessee; or

(b) In the case of the lessor, any residual value guaranteed to the lessor by either (i) the lessee, (ii) a party related to the lessee, or (iii) an independent third party financially capable of meeting this guarantee.

However, if the lessee has an option to purchase the asset at a price which is expected to be sufficiently lower than the fair value at the date the option becomes exercisable that, at the inception of the lease, is reasonably certain to be exercised, the minimum lease payments comprise the minimum payments payable over the lease term and the payment required to exercise this purchase option."

"The *lease term* is the non-cancelable period for which the lessee has contracted to lease the asset together with any further terms for which the lessee has the option to continue to lease the asset, with or without further payment, which option at the inception of the lease it is reasonably certain that the lessee will exercise."

When a contract meets even only one of the criteria laid out by the IASC, it should be considered as a finance lease. The IASC criteria are different from the criteria laid out by SFAS 13 (FASB 1976) under US GAAP. The key differences between financial and operational leases pertain mainly to two criteria which are: "*the major part* of the economic life of the asset" criterion and the "present value of the minimum [accumulated] lease payments amounts to *at least substantially all of the fair value* of the leased asset."

The IASC favors a professional appreciation of the situation over specifying precise conditions. Any precise list of conditions can always be bypassed or played with "at the limit" in order to avoid reporting a useful piece of information to investors and analysts.

In the United States, SFAS 13 lists the four conditions that create a finance lease (meeting only one of these conditions is enough, however):

1 The lease transfers ownership of the asset to the lessee by the end of the lease term.

2 The lease contains a bargain purchase option.

3 The non-cancelable lease term is 75% or more of the estimated economic life of the leased asset.

4 The present value of the minimum lease payments equals or exceeds 90% of the fair value of the leased asset.

Under condition (3), "the major part" (IAS 17) is replaced by 75% (SFAS 13) and under condition (4), "substantially" (IAS 17) is replaced by 90% (SFAS 13).

Capitalization of finance-leased assets

IAS 17 recommends that finance leases be recognized as assets (the use of the leased object is to create future economic benefits) and liabilities (representing future lease payments) on the balance sheet. Such recording of finance leases is often known as the "capitalization" of the leased asset. As shown in Figure 12.8, capitalization is generally adopted in the consolidated financial statements. However, in the non-consolidated financial statements, some countries' GAAP do not follow the IAS recommendation and do not recognize leased assets at all (France and Italy, for example). In fact, legally the property belongs to the owner throughout the duration of the lease and for that reason EU countries with accounting systems based on commercial law do not capitalize leases and treat the rental payments as expenses in the income statement. The 4th Directive does not formulate a recommendation on the capitalization of leases. Some European countries, for example UK and Netherlands, prefer to respect the accounting principle of "substance over form" and include the assets held under a finance lease agreement in their balance sheet, following, implicitly or explicitly, the prescription of IAS 17.

If a company decides to capitalize leased assets, it can follow the IAS 17 prescriptions (§ 12): "The amount used for capitalization is equal at the inception of the lease to the fair value of the leased property or, if lower, at the present value of the minimum lease payments. In calculating the present value of the minimum lease payments the discount factor is the interest rate implicit in the lease, if this is practicable to determine; if not, the lessee's incremental [marginal] borrowing rate should be used." This "incremental borrowing rate" is "the rate of interest the lessee would have to pay on a similar lease or, if that is not determinable, the rate that, at the inception of the lease, the lessee would incur to borrow over a similar term, and with a similar security, the funds necessary to purchase the asset" (IASC 1997b: § 3).

If leased assets are capitalized, lease payments are apportioned between the finance expense and the reduction of the outstanding liability. Simultaneously, the asset is depreciated consistently with the depreciable assets that are owned by the company. "If there is no reasonable certainty that the lessee will obtain ownership by the end of the lease term, the asset should be fully depreciated over the shorter of the lease term or its useful life" (IAS 17: § 19). Otherwise, the period of expected use is the useful life of the asset.

In practice, "the sum of the depreciation expense for the asset and the finance expense for the period is rarely the same as the lease payments payable for the period" (IAS 17: § 21). Therefore, it is inappropriate to simply recognize the lease payments as an expense in the income statement. It is necessary to restate the lease payment (see Lindblad Company example that follows.)

Example of accounting for leased assets

The Lindblad Company leases equipment (worth 600 CU at fair market value) under a finance lease. The contract is for a 5-year period. The annual lease payment amounts to 150 CU. The purchase option at the end of the lease has been established at 10 CU. Such equipment would usually, if owned outright, be depreciated over an 8-year period.

The interest rate implicit in the lease may be determined by applying the method described below (and see additional information in Appendix 12.3).

Value of the equipment	600 CU
Total payments (5 × 150 + 10)	760 CU

The value of the asset is provided by the following formula:

$$\text{Value of the leased equipment} = \text{Lease payment} \times \sum_{t=1}^{5} \frac{1}{(1+i)^t} + \frac{\text{Purchase option}}{(1+i)^5}$$

$$= 150 \times \sum_{t=1}^{5} \frac{1}{(1+i)^t} + \frac{10}{(1+i)^5}$$

In this formula, the factor $\sum_{t=1}^{5} \frac{1}{(1+i)^t}$ can be replaced by the following formula $\frac{1-(1+i)^{-n}}{i}$ where n represents the duration of the contract.

Since the purchase value of the asset is known, one can solve the above equation for i. The interest rate i may be obtained from a statistics table (such as the one provided in the Appendix 12.3) or by using some advanced handheld calculators, spreadsheet or statistics software. Our example yields an implied rate of interest $i = 8.357\%$. In the case where the implicit rate is impossible to determine mathematically, the lessee's incremental borrowing rate may be used. Table 12.7 shows the schedule of financial amortization of the debt.

Table 12.7 Repayment schedule of the debt

Year	Beginning lease liability	Interest expense	Repayment of liability	Lease payment	Ending lease liability
	(1)	(2)=(1)×8.357%	(3)=(4)−(2)	(4)	(5)=(1)−(3)
Year 1	600.00	50.14	99.86	150.00	500.14
Year 2	500.14	41.80	108.20	150.00	391.94
Year 3	391.94	32.76	117.24	150.00	274.70
Year 4	274.70	22.96	127.04	150.00	147.66
Year 5	147.66	12.34	137.66	150.00	10.00
Purchase	10.00		10.00	10.00	0.00
Total		160.00	600.00	760.00	

The depreciation of the equipment will follow the depreciation schedule shown in Table 12.8, given that the useful life is 8 years, which makes a depreciation rate of 12.5% (1/8) if straight-line were used.

Table 12.8 Depreciation schedule of the leased equipment

Year	Depreciable basis	Depreciation expense	Book value
Year 1	600.00	75.00	525.00
Year 2	525.00	75.00	450.00
Year 3	450.00	75.00	375.00
Year 4	375.00	75.00	300.00
Year 5	300.00	75.00	225.00
Year 6	225.00	75.00	150.00
Year 7	150.00	75.00	75.00
Year 8	75.00	75.00	0.00

Figure 12.9 illustrates the accounting of the leased asset in year 1 as both an asset and a liability, using the information from both Tables 12.7 and 12.8.

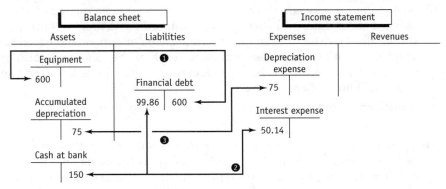

❶ The leased equipment is recorded as both an asset and a liability (for the same amount)

❷ The leased payment (150) is split between interest expense and repayment of the financial debt (figures are derived from Table 12.7)

❸ The leased asset is depreciated over 8 years (figures are derived from Table 12.8)

Figure 12.9 Capitalization of leased equipment

Because the time schedule of the expense paid (lease payment of 150) differs from that of the reported expense (Depreciation expense + Interest expense = 75 + 50.14 = 125.14, for example in year 1), a deferred taxation situation arises (see Chapters 6 and 13).

Operating leases

According to IAS 17 (§ 25): "Lease payments under an operating lease should be recognized as an expense in the income statement on a straight-line basis over the lease term unless another systematic basis is representative of the time pattern of the user's benefit."

Sales and leaseback transactions

Sales and leaseback transactions are developed in Appendix 12.5.

Reporting lease agreements to the users of financial information

Since leases are a very important way through which a business acquires control over assets (alternative to outright acquisition), it is very important to agree on how the commitment created by the lease is reported.

The IASC position

IAS 17 (§ 23) states that lessees should disclose the following elements regarding their finance leases:

(a) "for each class of asset, the net carrying amount at the balance sheet date;

(b) reconciliation between the total of minimum lease payments at the balance sheet date, and their present value. In addition, an enterprise should disclose the total of minimum lease payments at the balance sheet date, and their present value, for each of the following periods: (i) not later than one year; (ii) later than one year and not later than five years; (iii) later than five years.

(c) contingent rents recognized in income for the period;

(d) (…)

(e) a general description of the lessee's significant leasing arrangements including, but not limited to, the following: (i) the basis on which contingent rent payments are determined; (ii) the existence and terms of renewal or purchase options (…), and (iii) restrictions imposed by lease arrangements, such as those concerning dividends, additional debt, and further leasing."

Real-life examples

Benihana
(USA – US GAAP – Source: Annual report 2000 – Japanese restaurants: tepanyaki-style and sushi)

Excerpts from the notes to consolidated financial statements

Note 8: Lease obligations

The company generally operates its restaurants in leased premises. The typical restaurant premises lease is for a term of between 15 to 25 years with renewal options ranging from 5 to 25 years. The leases generally provide for the payment of property taxes, utilities, and various other use and occupancy costs. Rentals under certain leases are based on a percentage of sales in excess of a certain minimum level. Certain leases provide for (built-in) increases based upon changes in the consumer price index. The company is also obligated under various leases for restaurant equipment and for office space and equipment.

Minimum payments under lease commitments are summarized as follows for capital and operating leases. The imputed interest rates used in the calculations for capital leases vary from 9.75% to 12% and are equivalent to the rates which would have been incurred to borrow, over a similar term, the amounts necessary to purchase the leased assets.

The amounts of operating and capital lease obligations are as follows (in thousands):

Fiscal year ending:	Operating leases	Capital leases
2001	4,741	893
2002	4,868	893
2003	4,788	784
2004	4,750	458
2005	4,632	289
Thereafter	33,219	27
Total minimum lease payments	56,998	3,344
Less amount representing interest		642
Total obligations under capital leases		2,702
Less current maturities		629
Long-term obligations under capitalized leases at 26 March 2000		2,073

This example also illustrates the required disclosure for operating leases.

Environmental liability

More and more businesses are aware that their business activity may create environmental risks. They not only explicitly manage such risk but also want to report the potential liabilities this creates (both as a signaling move to customers and other stakeholders, and for the sake of completeness of reporting to shareholders, analysts, and investors). This "environmental liability" is presented in Appendix 12.6.

Employee benefits and pension accounting

Employee benefits give rise to complex future obligations. International Accounting Standard 19 (IASC 1998b) deals with this topic. Its paragraph 4 distinguishes short-term employee benefits (while being employed) and post-employment benefits. It defines these as:

(a) *"short-term employee benefits* include monetary benefits such as wages, salaries and Social Security contributions, paid annual leave and paid sick leave, profit sharing and bonuses (if payable within twelve months of the end of the period) and non-monetary benefits (such as health and medical care program contributions, housing, company cars and free or subsidized goods or services) for current employees.

(b) *post-employment benefits* such as pensions, other retirement benefits, post-employment life insurance and post-employment health and medical care."

Figure 12.10 summarizes, in a simplified way, the accounting issues arising from the handling of employee benefits.

Let us now examine the various components of Figure 12.10.

Short-term employee benefits

Accounting for short-term employee benefits, as seen earlier, is generally straightforward because no actuarial assumption is required to evaluate the obligation and its cost. A business should recognize the undiscounted amount of short-term employee benefits expected to be paid in exchange of the service rendered by employees:

- as an expense for the amount paid whenever payment takes place
- as a liability (accrued expense) for the amount accrued and still due (the expense of the period minus any amount already paid).

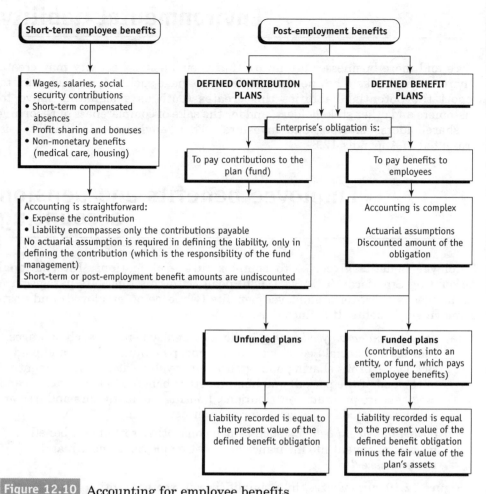

Figure 12.10 Accounting for employee benefits

Post-employment benefits

As explained in IAS 19 (IASC 1998b: § 24), "post-employment benefits include, for example:

(a) retirement benefits such as pensions; and

(b) other post-employment benefits, such as post-employment life insurance [or payment of premiums to a life insurance plan] and post-employment medical care [or contribution to a health and medical care plan for the retirees and their beneficiaries].

Arrangements whereby an enterprise provides post-employment benefits are [referred to as] post-employment benefit plans."

Accounting for post-employment benefits will depend on a very important distinction made regarding the nature of the benefit plan: defined contribution plans or defined benefit plans. Reporting the obligations created vary greatly between the two types of plans.

Defined contribution plans

Under this type of plan, the retirement benefit obligation of the firm to its employees is entirely turned over to a third party. The employer pays a premium or contribution to a capital fund managed by a third party that will provide the service contractually agreed with the employee(s) (capital or annuity). The business needs not recognize any obligation, provision or liability. Accounting for the contribution expenses to a defined contribution plan is absolutely identical to that of short-term employee benefits.

Defined contribution plans are quite common in Europe where many state-run, -controlled or -appointed agencies have been created specifically to be the third party relieving the employer from any post-employment benefit obligation management beyond the payment of the contributions and pay out the pension benefits to the employee when she/he has retired.

Defined benefit plans

In defined benefit plans, the enterprise itself assumes the obligation to provide in the future the agreed benefits to current and former employees. This obligation needs to be measured (quantified), managed and reported in the balance sheet. However, "accounting for defined benefit plans is complex because actuarial assumptions are required to measure the obligation and expense and there is a possibility of actuarial gains and losses. Moreover, the obligations are measured on a discounted basis because they may be settled many years after the employees render the related service" (IASC 1998b: § 48).

Defined benefit plans are the most common types of plans in North America as primary retirement benefit plans and in Europe for optional secondary or supplementary retirement benefit plans.

In addition to providing retirement pay until the former employee or his beneficiaries decease, many businesses have chosen or negotiated the payment of a retirement bonus (at the time of retirement) that is most of the time proportional to the length of employment in the firm. Since the calculation method of the bonus is public knowledge and cannot be modified without negotiation, such bonuses are considered to be defined benefits and should be recognized as an expense (and funded) throughout the period of employment since they are part of the compensation package for services rendered.

An enterprise has a choice of alternatives in handling defined benefit plans:

- *The plan may be unfunded.* In this case the business bears the sole responsibility of the obligation and pays the agreed upon benefits to the employees, either on a pay-as-you-go basis (no savings, the expense is covered as incurred – a very risky proposition either when headcount is reduced or when there is an economic downturn affecting the profitability and liquidity of the firm), or by saving privately to cover the obligation and managing the fund inside the firm itself. Unfunded plans tend to be unusual for both these reasons. In addition, unfunded pension plans tend to create ethical issues: when the savings created by the enterprise have increased in value (due to a bull market, for example) the value of the fund may vastly exceed the needed funds and the enterprise may be tempted to recapture the contributions it appears to have paid in excess of the need. Such situations have not been uncommon in the past. They have potentially dramatic consequences when the market turns bearish.

- *The plan may be funded*, either partly or completely. In this case the enterprise pays a contribution premium to an entity (or fund) that is legally and completely separate and independent from the reporting business. The contribution premiums will be managed by the fund so as to allow the payment of the agreed benefits. This type of plan is the most common. The contribution premium expenses are equivalent to a "forced" saving plan for the firm. Insurance companies have made it a specialty of managing this type of fund as they have the actuarial expertise in establishing the level of the contributions that will guarantee the ability to honor the contractual obligation of the fund to the employer and the employees.

In a simplified way, the amount recognized as a defined benefit liability in the balance sheet will be the net total of the following amounts:

- net present value of the defined benefit obligation as of the balance sheet date
- minus the fair value on the balance sheet date of the plan's assets (if the plan is funded).

In practice, the calculations required for the quantification of defined benefits obligations are rather complex. They require the use of the services of actuaries. Such a topic is generally well covered in an intermediate accounting course[2].

Financial statement analysis

The choices made regarding how to value, record and report the business's future obligations to a variety of constituencies impact on the understanding of and the ability to decode the firm's situation through its financial statements. Choices made about liability reporting affect also the asset side (through the capitalization of leases) and the value of various ratios.

Capitalized leased assets

Even if the firm does not capitalize its leases (the frontier between finance and operational leases is fuzzy at times), analysts generally restate the published financial information and treat any ambiguous lease as a finance lease to create the financial statement that would have been obtained if the asset had been acquired and 100% financed by debt. In the restated income statement, the interest portion of the lease payment is classified as "interest expense" and the depreciation expense of the lease payment is a part of the depreciation expense. Both the balance sheet and the income statement are affected by the handling of leases and thus many ratios are also affected.

Ratios

Although ratios will be covered extensively as part of Chapter 15, Table 12.9 lists some of the key ratios pertaining to liabilities. These ratios are especially important in evaluating both the risk and the return on investment a business can offer to investors. All these ratios can be affected greatly by the choices made in handling the recognition of liabilities. Provisions (which, as mentioned, can sometimes be used for income smoothing) are generally included in liabilities for the computation of debt ratios. Some analysts exploit the notes to the financial statements to eventually restate the provisioned amounts and the

Table 12.9 Debt ratios

Name of the ratio	Computation	Interpretation or meaning
Debt ratio or debt to total assets ratio	Total debt/total assets	Firm's long-term debt-paying ability
Debt to equity ratio	Debt[3]/Shareholders' equity or Debt/(Shareholders' equity + Debt)	The lower this ratio, the better the company's position
Long-term debt to equity ratio	Long-term debt/Shareholders' equity or Long-term debt/(Shareholders' equity + Debt)	Firm's degree of financial leverage
Interest coverage ratio	Operating income (before interest expense and income taxes)/Interest expense	Number of times that a firm's interest expense is covered by operation earnings. Rule of thumb: minimum of 5

income statement or simulate the range of values the ratios could take if the provisions were either accepted at face value or restated under specified hypotheses.

These ratios are critical for a potential lender or investor who may need to evaluate the risk attached to a transaction with another firm. One critical element of the dynamics of the risk evaluation is that the larger the shareholders' equity is, the lower are the liabilities to third parties and thus the less risky the business appears to be to a lender (and conversely). The first three ratios in Table 12.9 relate to that aspect of the evaluation of the firm's risk. They reflect the weight of third-party liabilities in the long-term financial resources of the firm. The fourth ratio in Table 12.9 (interest coverage) reflects the likely capability of the firm to face its interest obligation. This ratio is often considered to be a good proxy for the ability of the firm to cover its short-term or current liabilities or obligations.

The generic definitions of the ratios presented in Table 12.9 are subject to many variations and adaptations to serve the specific needs of the analyst. Amendments can be made to either or both of the numerator or the denominator. For example, some practitioners restrict long-term liabilities in their ratio calculations to long-term interest-bearing liabilities.

Minority interests in consolidated statements (percentage of a subsidiary's shareholders' equity held by shareholders different from the parent company) add a little complexity to the calculation of the key liability-based ratios. Chapter 13 deals with these issues. A key question is to decide whether minority interests are part of liabilities or part of shareholders' equity. Both choices are possible in reporting the financial position of the firm.

KEY POINTS

● Liabilities are obligations to pay cash or to provide goods and services to third parties in the future. They represent a major source of financing in any business.

- Liabilities are classified as current versus non-current (operating cycle emphasis) or short-term (current) versus long-term (emphasis on solvency).
- Weight represented by liabilities in the balance sheet as well as liabilities reporting practices are extremely variable across countries, business sectors, and firms.
- Liabilities should be distinguished from related but different concepts: (1) accrued liability; (2) provision; and (3) contingent liability on the basis of their varying degrees of certainty in (1) the principle causing the obligation, (2) its timing, and (3) its amount.
- The value of bonds depends on the market rate at the time of the issuance. Bonds may be issued with a premium (sold above par) or with a discount (sold below par).
- Leasing is a very convenient and flexible medium for obtaining the right to use a fixed asset. Operating leases and finance leases respond to different business needs, follow different business models and need to be handled differently in the accounting and the reporting systems. A finance lease is equivalent to the acquisition of an asset completely financed by a loan. Most countries require that financial leases be reported in the balance sheet as both a fixed asset and a financial liability.
- Costs relating to short-term employee benefits and defined contribution plans for post-employment benefits are expenses as incurred.
- Defined benefits plans for post-employment benefits open complex issues of valuation and accounting. They mainly require provisioning (or recognizing the (ever) increasing pension liability) during the period of employment of the eligible workforce.

REVIEW

Review 12.1 Stenborg

Topic: Repayment of a bank loan
Type: Individual exercise
Related part of the chapter: Core Issues

The Stenborg Company has subscribed a bank loan on 30 June 20X1, with the following terms and conditions:
- Amount: 100,000 CU.
- Annual interest: 10%.
- Reimbursement by ordinary annuities starting on 30 June 20X2 (annual payment).
- Number of years of the loan: 5 years.
- Closing date used by Stenborg in its books: 31 December.

Required

1 Compute the amount of the constant annuity (interest expense plus part of the principal) following the effective interest rate method.
2 Present the repayment schedule of the debt.
3 Show the accounting entries:
- on the date of subscription
- on closing date
- on the first repayment date.

Solution

1 Compute the amount of the constant annuity following the effective interest rate method

The constant annuity allowing for the repayment of a debt is given by the following formula:

$$\text{Annual cash flow} = \text{Amount of the debt} \times \frac{i}{1 - (1 + i)^{-n}}$$

where i is the interest rate and n the number of years.

$$\text{Annual cash flow} = 100{,}000 \times \frac{0.10}{1 - (1.10)^{-5}} = 100{,}000 \times \frac{10\%}{0.379078677}$$

$$= 100{,}000 \times 0.263797481 = 26{,}380 \text{ CU (rounded)}$$

2 Present the repayment schedule of the debt

			Repayment schedule		
Years	Beginning balance (1)=(5) previous	Interest expense (2)=(1)× 10%	Repayment (3)=(4)–(2)	Annuity (4)	Ending balance (5)=(1)–(4)
30/6/20X1	100,000	10,000	16,380	26,380	83,620
30/6/20X2	83,620	8,362	18,018	26,380	65,602
30/6/20X3	65,602	6,560	19,820	26,380	45,784
30/6/20X4	45,784	4,578	21,802	26,380	23,982
30/6/20X5	23,982	2,398	23,982	26,380	0
		31,898	100,000		

3 Show the accounting entries: on the date of subscription, on closing date, and on the first repayment date.

Year 20X1

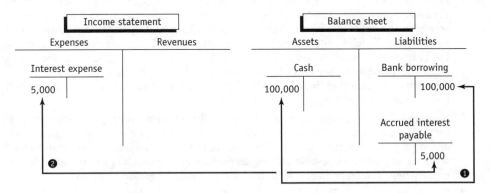

❶ On 30 June 20X1, subscription of the debt. Receipt of the principal

❷ On the closing date (31 December 20X1), accrual of the interest relating to 20X1 (10,000 × 6 months from July to December = 5,000)

Year 20X2

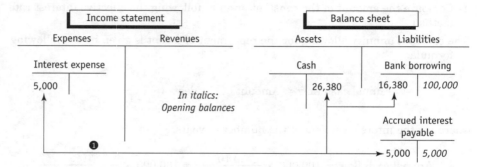

● At the first maturity date (30 June 20X1), repayment of the principal according to the schedule
(16,380 CU), cancellation of the accrued interest payable (5,000 currency units) and
recording of the second part of the interest (10,000 currency units x 6 months from January to June)

Review 12.2 Haeffner PLC (1)

Topic: Provisions and contingent liabilities
Type: Group exercise
Related part of the chapter: Core Issues

Haeffner PLC is an accounting firm. Some of its clients face the following situations. For
each, it is assumed that a reliable estimate can be made of any outflows expected:

1 Acme Manufacturing Enterprises (AME) provide a warranty on their products at
   the time of sale. Under the terms of the warranty contract, AME undertakes to
   make good, by repair or replacement, any manufacturing defect that becomes
   apparent within three years from the date of sale. Based on past experience, it is
   probable that there will be some claims under the warranties.

2 Stone Oil Industries (SOI) have been a medium-size oil producer and refiner for
   the past 50 years. They operate in many parts of the world. On occasions, SOI
   units have incurred spills of crude or refined products that have contaminated
   land and water. It is SOI's management philosophy that clean-up should be
   organized only when the firm is required to do so under the laws of the country
   in which the spill took place. One country in which SOI operates has until now
   not had any legislation requiring cleaning up, and SOI has been contaminating
   land and water in that country for several years without taking any corrective
   action. On 31 December 20X1 it becomes virtually certain that a draft law
   mandating retroactive clean-up of land and waterways already contaminated will
   be enacted shortly after the year-end.

3 Sudstrom is a large upscale retail store established in most major consumer
   market areas. It has built its reputation on selection and quality of its products
   and on a well-advertised policy of refunding purchases to dissatisfied customers
   without asking any question as long as Sudstrom carries the product, even in
   cases where the store may not be under any legal obligation to do so.

4 On 18 December 20X1 the board of Zygafuss Agglomerated Enterprises (ZAE)
   decided to close down one of its industrial divisions. By closing date (31
   December) the decision had not yet been communicated to any of those affected
   (not even to the Works Council), and no other steps had been taken to implement
   the decision.

5 During 20X1 Mutter GmbH had provided a loan guarantee for the benefit of
   Tochter SA, a trading partner (in which Mutter does not hold any share interest)
   opening the market for Mutter products in Transmoldavia. Tochter's financial

condition at that time is considered to be sound and economic prospects bright. Bankers have, however, requested a loan guarantee because of the short history of Tochter in this market and the possible instability of the Transmoldavian market. During 20X2 the market in Transmoldavia experiences a serious economic downturn and Tochter's financial condition deteriorates. On 30 June 20X2 Tochter SA actually files for protection from its creditors.

Required

Analyze each of these 5 situations and make a recommendation for each as to the necessity of recording or not an appropriate provision.

Solution[4]

Situations	Past obligating event ...	... resulting in a present obligation	Outflow of resources embodying economic benefits in settlement	Conclusion
1 Warranties	Sale of the product with a warranty	Legal obligation	Probable for the warranties as a whole	Recognize provision for the best estimate of the costs of the warranty for products sold before the balance sheet date
2 Contaminated land – legislation virtually certain to be enacted	Contamination of the land	Virtual certainty of legislation requiring cleaning up	Probable	Recognize provision for the best estimate of the costs of the clean-up
3 Refunds policy	Sale of the product	Constructive obligation because the conduct of the store has created a valid expectation on the part of its customers	Probable, based on the proportion of the goods returned for refund	Recognize provision for the best estimate of the costs of refunds
4 Closure of a division – no implementation before closing date	No obligating event	No obligation	—	No provision need be recognized
5 Single guarantee At 31 December 20X1	Giving of the guarantee	Legal obligation	No outflow probable	No provision recognized but disclosure of the guarantee as a contingent liability unless the probability of any outflow is regarded as remote
At 31 December 20X2	Giving of the guarantee	Legal obligation	Probable	Provision recognized for the best estimate of the obligation

Assignment 12.1

Multiple-choice questions
Type: Individual exercise
Related part of the chapter: Core Issues

Select the right answer (one possible answer, unless otherwise stated).

1 Provisions for risks and liabilities are recorded

(a) In the expenses
(b) In the revenues
(c) In the shareholders' equity and liabilities
(d) As a contra-asset
(e) None of these

2 An example of financial liabilities is

(a) Income tax payable
(b) Unearned revenues
(c) Bank borrowings
(d) Salaries payable
(e) None of these

3 An example of a current liability is

(a) Bank borrowing (long-term portion)
(b) Unearned revenues
(c) Share capital
(d) Retained earnings
(e) None of these

4 An example of an item that is not a current liability is

(a) Accrued expenses
(b) Prepaid expenses
(c) Salaries payable
(d) Accounts payable
(e) Unearned revenues
(f) None of these

5 Warranty costs are recognized as an expense

(a) At the time the products covered by the warranty are sold
(b) At the time the costs are really incurred
(c) None of these

6 When the balance sheet is presented by nature, the current portion of a long-term liability is still included in the financial liability section of the balance sheet

(a) True
(b) False

7 Notes payable represent bills of exchange or promissory notes

(a) True
(b) False

8 The net salary (after deduction of withholdings) is recorded as such an expense

(a) True
(b) False

9 A contingent liability is recorded

    (a) As part of the assets

    (b) As part of the shareholders' equity and liabilities

    (c) As part of the revenues

    (d) As part of the expenses

    (e) None of these

10 A provision for restructuring can be recorded as soon as a company has decided to close a business entity

    (a) True

    (b) False

Assignment 12.2

Topic: Reporting for liabilities in different sectors of activity
Type: Group exercise
Related part of the chapter: Core Issues

On the internet, or in the library, find the annual reports of four companies from different sectors of activity in a given country or in different countries.

Required

1 How are liabilities presented in the balance sheet? What decisions on the basis of this information can investors or shareholders take? What decisions would be difficult to take on the basis of just this information?

2 Are there any notes relating to liabilities? How do they enlarge the decision analysis possibilities offered to shareholders and investors?

3 What are the accounting treatments applied to these liabilities?

4 What is the weight of liabilities as a percentage of total shareholders' equity and liabilities? What strategic implications do you derive from this ratio?

Assignment 12.3

Topic: Reporting for liabilities in the same sector of activity
Type: Group exercise
Related part of the chapter: Core Issues

On the internet, or in the library, find the annual reports of four companies essentially in identical or similar industries in a given country or in different countries.

Required

Use questions from Assignment 12.2.

Assignment 12.4 Club Méditerranée*

Topic: Bonds, bank loans and debts
Type: Group exercise
Related part of the chapter: Core Issues

Club Méditerranée, the French leisure company, reports the following information relating to its financial liabilities (*source*: annual report 1999, financial year ended 31 October 1999).

Consolidated balance sheet (excerpts)			
FRFm	Notes	1999	1998
Liabilities and shareholders' equity			
(...)			
Bonds	2.14	1,888	1,912
Bank loans and debts	2.14	1,355	1,478
(...)			

2.14 Bonds, bank loans and debts		
FRFm	1999	1998
Convertible bonds	1,045	1,066
Bonds with equity warrants	843	843
Other (1)	0	3
Total bonds	**1,888**	**1,912**
Bank loans and debts		
Short-term bank loans and overdrafts	242	274
Current maturities of long-term debt	140	240
Long-term debt	973	964
Total bank loans and debts	**1,355**	**1,478**
TOTAL	**3,243**	**3,390**

(1) Club Med Inc. bonds redeemed during the year

Required

1 What do "convertible bonds" represent?
2 What do "bonds with equity warrants" represent?
3 What do "bonds redeemed during the year" represent?
4 What is the difference between "Current maturities of long-term debt" and "Short-term loans"?
5 Are "short-term bank loans" and "overdrafts" equivalent?

Assignment 12.5 Haeffner PLC (2)

Topic: Provisions and contingent liabilities
Type: Group exercise
Related part of the chapter: Core Issues

Haeffner PLC is an accounting firm. Some of its clients face the following situations. For each, it is assumed that a reliable estimate can be made of any outflows expected:

1 Stone Oil Industries (SOI) have been a medium-size oil producer and refiner for the past 50 years. They operate in many parts of the world. In Outer Boulimia (which is a country without any environmental legislation) an unfortunate accident during the capping of a gusher has caused significant contamination of a nearby stream and of the soil around the well. SOI has a widely published new environmental policy in which it mandates that effective clean-up of any and all

contaminations SOI causes directly or indirectly be undertaken immediately. SOI has a record of honoring this published policy.

2 On 9 December 20X1 the board of Shankar Inc. decided to close down its defense division, effective 1 June 20X2. On 20 December 20X1 a detailed plan for closing down the division was agreed by the board. The plan was further discussed and amended during a scheduled meeting of the Works Council on 21 December. In the following week, letters were sent to customers warning them to seek an alternative source of supply and redundancy notices were sent to the staff of the division who would not be offered other positions in the company. The accounting closing date of Shankar Inc. is 31 December.

3 The government introduces a number of changes in legislation, which will generate the need for Acme Amalgamated Enterprises to retrain its security and quality control staff. At closing date, no retraining of staff has taken place.

4 Five people were severely injured in an industrial accident in which machinery and equipment sold by Lang Sein Enterprise was involved. The injured parties' lawyers have started legal proceedings against Lang Sein Enterprise, seeking damages. Lang Sein disputes its liability. As of the date of approval for publication of the financial statements for the year ending 31 December 20X1, Lang Sein's lawyers are of the opinion that the evidence will probably show that the enterprise will not be found liable. However, one year later, due to new developments in the case, the Lang Sein lawyers believe that it is probable the enterprise will be found at least partially liable.

Required

Analyze each situation and conclude about the necessity to record a provision or not.

Assignment 12.6 Stora Enso*, Repsol YPF*, Barlow*, Cobham* and Thomson-CSF*

Topic: Reporting movements in provisions
Type: Group exercise
Related part of the chapter: Core Issues

You are provided with excerpts from notes to consolidated financial statements of five companies reporting movements in provisions.

Stora Enso (Finland – IAS GAAP – *Source*: Annual report 1999 – Production of paper)

Other provisions			
€m	Restructuring	Pension	Other
Carrying value on 31 Dec. 1998	151	570	105
Translation difference	3	26	9
Increase	5		19
Decrease	−96	−21	−9
Carrying value on 31 Dec. 1998	63	575	124

Repsol YPF (Spain – Spanish GAAP – *Source*: Annual report 1999 – Oil and gas)

€m	Pension costs	Provisions for labor force restructuring	Tanker repairs	Dismantling of fields	Commitments and contingent liabilities	Reversion reserves	Other provisions	Total
Balance as of 31 December 1998	196	54	7	36	176	31	173	673
Period provisions charged to income	14	22	3	8	30	5	40	122
Allowance released with a credit to income	(1)	—	(1)	—	(6)	—	(12)	(20)
Amount used	(51)	(7)	(2)	(1)	(2)	—	(38)	(101)
Effects of inclusion of YPF	36	—	—	111	—	—	281	428
Translation differences	4	1	—	5	—	—	12	22
Reclassifications and variations in scope of consolidation	(23)	(12)	—	(3)	18	—	(5)	(25)
Balance as of 31 December 1999	175	58	7	156	216	36	451	1,099

The "Other provisions" caption includes mainly technical reserves for insurance, provisions for environmental contingencies, provisions for litigation in progress, and other provisions for future contingencies

Barlow (now Barloworld) (South Africa – South African GAAP – *Source*: Annual report 1999 – Heavy equipment, material handling equipment, motors, cement, and lime)

Movement of provisions

Millions of SA rands	Total 1999	Retirement benefits	Discontinued operations	Warranty provisions	Insurance claims	Other
Balance at beginning of year	901.0	274	379	63	41	144
Amounts added	279.0	46	83	18	12	120
Amounts used	(476.0)	(41)	(301)	(12)	(11)	(111)
Amounts reversed unused	(24.0)	(2)	(4)	(5)		(13)
Arising on acquisitions	3.0			3		
Exchange adjustments	(13.0)	(13)		(1)		1
Other	(2.0)					(2)
Balances at end of year	668.0	264	157	66	42	139

Cobham (United Kingdom – UK GAAP – *Source*: Annual report 1999 – Equipment, systems and components for aerospace and defense industries)

Provisions for liabilities and charges

£m	Deferred taxation	Acquisitions	Other	Total
At 1 January 1999	11.1	1.3	1.9	14.3
Provisions created	3.3	—	0.8	4.1
Provisions realized	—	—	(0.4)	(0.4)
Provisions acquired on acquisition	0.2	—	—	0.2
Expenditure charged against provisions	—	(1.0)	(2.0)	(3.0)
At 31 December 1999	14.6	0.3	0.3	15.2

Acquisition provisions of £0.3m relate to a legal claim. Other provisions include amounts of £0.2m relating to legal claims and £0.1m relating to a retirement indemnity. The legal claims are expected to be resolved in the near future and the retirement indemnity has been calculated on the basis of an actuarial assessment

Thomson-CSF (France – French GAAP – *Source*: Annual report 1999 – Electronics)

	Accrued contract costs and other				
€m	Balance at beginning of period	Changes in reporting entity – Exchange rates and other	Charges to costs and expenses	Deductions	Balance at end of period
31 December 1999					
Estimated losses on long-term contracts	281.7	18.3	38.2	(120.0)	218.2
Accrued costs on completed contracts	38.0	(19.4)	7.4	(6.9)	19.1
Accrued penalties claims	79.4	15.1	33.7	(33.5)	94.7
Litigation	107.6	9.0	29.9	(42.1)	104.4
Guarantees	174.2	15.1	41.4	(65.1)	165.6
Restructuring reserves	373.8	64.2	55.5	(163.6)	329.9
Other	200.0	(7.8)	84.7	(87.5)	189.4
Total	1,254.7	94.5	290.8	(518.7)	1,121.3

For the five studied companies, all the figures mentioned in the caption "total" or "balance at end of period" have been recorded in the balance sheet.

Required

1 What is (are) the main formal difference(s) you can notice in the presentation of the tables between the first four companies and the fifth one?

2 Identify and comment on the differences in the terminology used to name each table.

3 Explain each component of the movements for the five studied companies.

4 Explain the nature of each provision.

5 What difference(s) do you notice in the way these companies record reductions in provisions?

Assignment 12.7 Nilsson Company

Topic: Leasing
Type: Group exercise
Related part of the chapter: Advanced Issues

Nilsson Company closes its books on 31 December each year. During the past year they have taken a 3-year lease on a computer web server to support the development of their e-business activities. The terms and conditions of the lease agreement are provided as Appendix 1. The lease contract itself is summarized in Appendix 2.

Required

1 Explain how this contract should be recorded in Nilsson's books if the company does not capitalize the lease.

2 Calculate the implicit interest rate in this lease contract. Prepare the schedule of amortization of a loan that would have the same principal, the same semi-annual reimbursements and the same residual value. Break down each semi-annual reimbursement between interest expense and principal reimbursement.

3 Illustrate the accounting entries (T-accounts or journal entries) required if the lease were capitalized.

4 Prepare the relevant information that should be placed in the notes to the financial statements if the leased equipment were not capitalized.

Note: In the case of an outright acquisition of the web server, Nilsson would have depreciated it on a straight-line basis over 5 years.

Appendix 1: Everylease PLC

26 December 20X0

Customer: Nilsson Company

Object: File number no. 982 (Nilsson)

Characteristics of the equipment provided by Everylease PLC to Nilsson Company:

- Price of the web server (in CU)   1,500
- Date of availability   1 January 20X1
- Purchase residual value of the web server at the end of the contract (in CU)   10

Schedule of payments and terms of the contract (all payments are due at the end of the relevant period): There will be six semi-annual rent payments of 280 CU each on the following dates: 30 June 20X1, 31 December 20X1, 30 June 20X2, 31 December 20X2, 30 June 20X3, 31 December 20X3.

Appendix 2: Lease contract

The following lease agreement is between,

On one hand, Everylease, Public Limited Company, with a Capital of 2,000,000 CU; Headquarters address: 15, Lost Rents Avenue, London, UK, hereafter called "the lessor" and

Nilsson Company, on the other hand, hereafter called "the lessee". The parties agree to the following:

1 Order and commitment to lease

The lessor has ordered from:

Micro Server Incorporated (hereafter called "supplier"), the equipment selected directly by the lessee from the supplier. Equipment consists of the following: Microcomputer Server Hexium V, 1,200 Mhz purchased at a price of 1,500 CU.

- The lessee has committed to take delivery of the equipment as ordered.
- The actual price in the lease will reflect the prices practised by the supplier and the lessee acknowledges knowing what this price is going to be or accept what it will be.
- Delivery of the equipment will take place in accordance to the terms and conditions enumerated in Article 1 of the General Conditions of Lease Contracts and on the date agreed to by both supplier and lessee.

2 Lease date and duration

- The lease agreement is for an irrevocable 36-month period and will be effective as of the signing of the contract pursuant to the terms and conditions of Article 1 of the General Conditions of Lease Contracts.
- Residual value: The residual value at the end of the irrevocable lease period pursuant to Articles 5, 9 and 10 of the General Conditions of Lease Contracts granting the lessee an option to buy is set at 0.67% of the actual price of the equipment.
- If the purchase option is exercised by the lessee, the residual value will be paid by lessee to lessor on 31 December 20X3.

3 Schedule and amount of the rent

- The first semi-annual rent payment is due at the end of the semester during which the delivery took place as attested by the invoice of the supplier and the signed delivery notice; a copy of each shall be forwarded to lessor.
- The lease payments will be in 6 semi-annual payments of equal amount.

Signed   *Signed*
The lessor   The lessee

Assignment 12.8 Easynet*

Topic: Reporting for leasing
Type: Individual exercise
Related part of the chapter: Advanced Issues

Easynet, the British internet provider, reports in its financial statements for the year ended 31 December 1999 the following simplified balance sheet (*source*: annual report 1999).

Simplified balance sheet		
	1999 £000	1998 £000
Fixed assets	26,242	4,945
Current assets	9,867	4,758
Creditors (amounts falling due within one year)	(15,457)	(8,268)
Net current liabilities	(5,590)	(3,510)
Total assets less current liabilities	20,652	1,435
Creditors (amounts falling due after more than one year)	(6,236)	(824)
Minority interests	0	408
Total net assets	14,416	1,019
Shareholders' funds	14,416	1,019

In the notes to the accounts, the detail of creditors is provided.

Creditors (amounts falling due within one year)	1999 £000	1998 £000
Bank loans and overdrafts	0	60
Obligations under finance leases	2,292	891
Trade creditors	5,919	3,149
Other creditors	242	256
Taxation and social security	1,563	757
Corporation tax	503	0
Accruals and deferred income	4,938	3,155
	15,457	8,268

Creditors (amounts falling due after more than one year)	1999 £000	1998 £000
Obligations under finance leases	6,236	824
Obligations under finance leases are due as follows:		
Within 1–2 years	1,715	682
Within 2–5 years	4,521	142
	6,236	824

The group has a bank facility of £4,000,000 net of group credit balances against which each United Kingdom group member has given the bank a fixed and floating charge over its assets.

The notes also reports special information on leases.

Assets held under finance leases and hire purchase contracts are capitalized at their fair value on the inception of the leases and depreciated over their estimated useful lives. The finance charges are allocated over the period of the lease in proportion to the capital amount outstanding.

Rentals under operating leases are charged to the profit and loss account as they accrue. Minimum lease payments under finance leases as at 31 December 1999 were as follows:

	1999 £000	1998 £000
Payable within one year	2,528	1,083
Payable in two years	6,344	892
Minimum lease payments	8,872	1,975
Less: amount representing interest	(344)	(260)
Net present value of minimum lease payments	8,528	1,715

Required

1 Reconcile the figures reported for creditors in the notes and the figures given in the balance sheet.

2 Identify in the notes the figures relating to finance leases.

3 Reconcile the detail of creditors and the special information given on finance leases.

4 In the notes, what information relating to interest implicit in lease payments is not given?

5 In the table providing future lease payments, what information could have been added at the bottom of the table?

Assignment 12.9 Ispat international*

Topic: Debt ratios
Type: Group exercise
Related part of the chapter: Advanced Issues

Ispat International N.V. is a Dutch company operating in the steel industry as a global producer. The balance sheet and income statement for the years 1998 and 1999 (*source*: annual report 1999), prepared in accordance with US GAAP, is provided as follows.

Consolidated balance sheets

Millions of US dollars	31 December 1998	1999
Assets		
Current assets	2,324	2,156
Property, plant, and equipment	3,179	3,333
Investment in affiliates	273	305
Deferred tax assets	39	58
Other assets	112	114
Total assets	5,927	5,966
Liabilities and shareholders' equity		
Current liabilities	1,334	1,440
Long-term debt	2,400	2,184
Deferred tax liabilities	87	130
Deferred employee benefits	1,213	1,227
Other long-term obligations	92	131
Total liabilities	5,126	5,112
Shareholders' equity	801	854
Total liabilities and shareholders' equity	5,927	5,966

Consolidated statements of income

Millions of US dollars	Year ended 31 December 1998	1999
Net sales	3,492	4,680
Costs and expenses:		
Cost of sales	2,871	4,052
Depreciation	91	164
Selling, general, and administrative	126	156
	3,088	4,372
Operating income	404	308
Other income (expense) – net		15
Financing costs:		
Interest (expense)	(178)	(209)
Interest income	46	25
Net gain (loss) from foreign exchange	16	(11)
	(116)	(195)
Income before taxes	288	128
Income tax expense	51	43
Net income	237	85

Required

1 For the years 1998 and 1999 compute the four "debt ratios" introduced in the "Advanced Issues" section of this chapter: debt ratio, debt to equity ratio, long-term debt to equity ratio, and interest coverage ratio.

2 Analyze these ratios.

References

FASB (1976) Statement of Financial Accounting Standard No. 13, Accounting for leases, Norwalk, CT.

IASC (1989) Framework for the Preparation and Presentation of Financial Statements, London.

IASC (1997a) International Accounting Standard No. 1, Presentation of Financial Statements, London.

IASC (1997b) International Accounting Standard No. 17, Leases, London.

IASC (1998a) International Accounting Standard No. 37, Provisions, Contingent Liabilities and Contingent Assets, London.

IASC (1998b) International Accounting Standard No. 19, Employee Benefits, London.

Palepu, K., Healy, P., and Bernard, V. (2000) *Business Analysis and Valuation – Using Financial Statement*, 2nd edn, South-Western College Publishing, Cincinnati, OH.

Skousen, F., Stice, J., and Stice, E.K. (2001) *Intermediate Accounting*, South-Western College Publishing, Cincinnati, OH.

Walton, P. (2000) *Financial Statement Analysis – An International Perspective*, Thomson Learning, London.

Further readings

Cravens, K.S., and Goad Oliver, E. (2000) The influence on culture on pension plans. *International Journal of Accounting*, 35(4), 521–37.

Garrod, N., and Sieringhaus, I. (1995) European Union accounting harmonization: The case of leased assets in the United Kingdom and Germany. *European Accounting Review*, 4(1), 155–64.

Moneva, J.M., and Llena, F. (2000) Environmental disclosures in the annual reports of large companies in Spain. *European Accounting Review*, 9(1), 7–29.

Additional material on the website

Go to http://www.thomsonlearning.co.uk/accountingandfinance/stolowylebas for further information, journal entries and extra assignments for each chapter.

The following appendices to this chapter are available on the dedicated website:

Appendix 12.1: Accounting for notes payable

Appendix 12.2: Accounting for sales tax

Appendix 12.3: Interest and time value of money

Appendix 12.4: Bonds issued at a discount

Appendix 12.5: Sales and leaseback transactions

Appendix 12.6: Environmental liability

Notes

1 See, for example, Walton (2000), or Palepu *et al*. (2000).

2 See for example Skousen *et al*. (2001).

3 "Debt" represents long-term and short-term interest-bearing liabilities.

4 These review answers are based on the appendix to IAS 37.

Financial fixed assets and business combinations

Enterprises create value for their owners by utilizing and transforming resources to satisfy solvent customer demand. This means extracting more resources from the customer in exchange for the services or products provided than it took to create these and make them available to the customer.

We have seen that financial statements, and especially the income statement and the cash flow statement, reflect the transformation process that is implemented through the operations of a firm. However, the process of value creation may require that the firm look (and be proactive) beyond the frontiers of the "legal entity" and start developing a network of relationships in order to secure a superior ability to deliver customer satisfaction in a sustainable way, and thus a higher return to its investors.

Beside strategic alliances that are beyond the scope of this text, the development of such a network organization can lead a business to engage in intercorporate investments. These are the focus of this chapter. We saw in Chapter 10 that when excess resources (cash or equivalent) are created through operations, investing in marketable securities is a way (at least in the short run) to create value for the shareholders (an alternative solution being a share repurchase and/or the issuance of large dividends). Such investments are passive (the investing firm has no right or possibility to influence the behavior of the enterprise whose marketable securities it purchased) and short lived in general, coherent with a position of "wait and see" until an active investment opportunity presents itself.

This chapter deals with active financial investment of the resources of the firm. We use the term active in

Major topics

Financial fixed assets

Business combinations

Consolidation methods

Deferred taxation

Foreign currency translations

Legal mergers

the sense that the investor (the firm) chooses to apply its resources to deliberately grow its value creation potential and do so with a long-term, strategic view requiring that the investing firm take an active role in the decisions of the firm in which they have invested.

Such active financial investment can take several forms. There are three generic models that can easily be combined to create a customized solution:

1 The simplest is probably to lend resources to another corporate entity (controlled or not) in order to foster their development so as to create a reliable supplier or a reliable customer.

2 The business can also enter into an active partnership with an existing firm or create another corporate entity (alone or in partnership) that would be more nimble and reactive or able to deal, more effectively than the investing firm, with a core competence or core market (by being "closer" to either the technology or the customers or both). In this category of investments we find close-knit or loose networks around a larger firm of specialized production or commercial businesses. The aerospace and automotive industries with their system of concentric first-, second- and third-tier suppliers are examples of such networks. The idea here is to partition the risk and increase speed of reactivity of the whole network to the needs and opportunities of both technology and markets while focussing each firm on its core competence and thus gaining in efficiency of use of resources. The issue here becomes one of degree of autonomy granted to or left in the third-party entity by the provider of capital. Two terms are generally used to recognize these differing degrees of autonomy (i.e., of integration in the value creation process of the investing firm): influence (having between 20 to 50% of the capital) and control (having more than 50% of the capital of the third-party entity.)

3 A third approach consists in acquiring a controlling interest in an existing entity, either to gain access to a technique or a market segment or to grow the size of the business to enjoy greater economies of scale and/or scope. Recent examples abound in the financial press of business entities creating closer links between their activities: AOL/Time Warner, Rhône-Poulenc/Hoechst, Pfizer/Warner-Lambert, DaimlerBenz/Chrysler, Exxon/Mobil or Total-Fina/Elf, etc.

Whichever strategic move a business chooses, there is creation of long-term (fixed) financial assets in the accounts of the investing firm or in the accounts of the entity resulting from the operation of integrating the two or more partners. Reporting to shareholders the financial situation and value creation potential of the sometimes complex, more or less close-knit network of firms thus created is the focus of this chapter.

If the organizing firm (or pivot of the network) were to only report its own activities without acknowledging the potential created by the preferred linkages its active financial investments have created, it would not give much information to the shareholders or potential investor. Its only visible assets might be loans granted or the shares acquired or funded. The nature of the business and its potential and correlated risks may not be apparent in the balance sheet.

Consolidated financial statements create a description of the financial position of an economic entity that is the agglomeration or conglomeration of diverse and, often, distinct legal entities connected by relations of intercorporate investments or lending relationships. A subsidiary is generally not liable for the liabilities of another. The issue of the degree of autonomy of the members and the definition of rules partitioning the wealth created by the networked entity will be central to this chapter.

The fact that complex, more or less loosely coupled "groups" are now often more the norm than are the "integrated" single legal entity firms has led countries such as the USA and Canada to even cease asking the pivot firm to report as a stand-alone entity as its balance sheet would generally be pretty meaningless for a potential investor.

We first look at the Core Issues pertaining to the establishment and interpretation of consolidated financial reports. The Advanced Issues explore more advanced and technical points created in the process of acquisition, merger or consolidation such as deferred taxation, currency translation of financial statements established in foreign currency (i.e., different from the currency used by the consolidating firm), and the reporting of advanced forms of combination of entities such as absorption or legal merger.

CORE ISSUES

Consolidated financial statements describe the financial position of an economic entity resulting from the existence of active intercorporate financial investments or fixed financial assets. The latter can take different forms.

Types of financial fixed assets

The three combinatorial strategies evoked in the introduction lead to the existence of five types of financial fixed assets:

- shares in subsidiaries
- shares in associated companies
- shares in other investments
- loans to subsidiaries, associated companies and other investments
- other loans.

Figure 13.1 illustrates the distinguishing criteria suggested by IAS 28 to separate an associated company (associate) from a subsidiary (IASC 1998b: § 3).

"Investment" is defined in IAS 25 (IASC 1994a: § 3): [It] "is an asset held by an enterprise for the accretion of wealth through distribution (such as interest, royalties, dividends and rentals), for capital appreciation or for other benefits to the investing enterprise such as those obtained through trading relationships." Additionally, IAS 25 states that "the cost of an investment includes acquisition charges such as brokerage [and other] fees, duties, and bank fees" (§ 15).

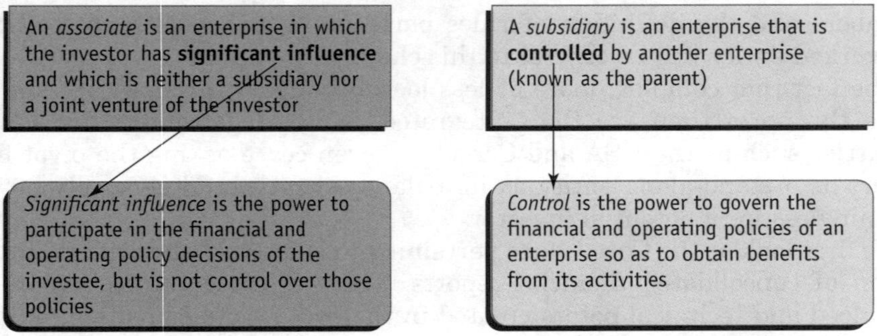

An *associate* is an enterprise in which the investor has **significant influence** and which is neither a subsidiary nor a joint venture of the investor

A *subsidiary* is an enterprise that is **controlled** by another enterprise (known as the parent)

Significant influence is the power to participate in the financial and operating policy decisions of the investee, but is not control over those policies

Control is the power to govern the financial and operating policies of an enterprise so as to obtain benefits from its activities

Figure 13.1 Definition of associate and subsidiary

Treatment of changes in value

By their very nature, financial fixed assets are not subject to regular annual depreciation. However, value adjustments should be made when the market value falls below the acquisition cost. In this case, an exceptional provision (or valuation allowance) expense will be recognized in the income statement to reduce the value to its market level. This entry could (conceptually) be partly or completely reversed in any subsequent year to the extent that the market value increases. This type of entry is essentially identical to the one shown in Chapter 10 with current investments. The reader may revisit the Mozart Company example (Chapter 10) to have an example of reversal of provision. Appendix 13.1 illustrates the mechanism of value adjustment to lower of cost or market.

Business combinations: principles and methods

Types of business combinations

A business combination is "the bringing together of separate enterprises into an economic entity as a result of one enterprise uniting with or obtaining control over the net assets and operations of another enterprise" (IASC 1998a: § 8). There is a variety of scenarios that can be followed in order to create a business combination. The following list is illustrative of some of the most commonly observed scenarios but is in no way exhaustive. Merger and acquisition specialists (financiers and lawyers alike) compete in creativity in designing approaches best tailored to each specific situation. Essentially all solutions are combinations of the generic scenarios described as follows:

● Company X obtains control over Company Y by acquiring enough shares of Y in exchange for cash or in exchange of shares of X (acquisition of stock) or a combination of the two. In this case, Company Y continues to exist as a separate legal entity but becomes a subsidiary of X. Its financial statements are integrated in the consolidated financial statements of X, which becomes the reporting entity.

- Company X acquires all the shares of Company Y. The latter is dissolved as a legal entity and all its assets and liabilities are merged in the accounts of Company X. This is a legal (or statutory) merger.

- Company X and Company Y decide jointly to combine all their activities to become the Z Company entity. Both Company X and Company Y are dissolved as legal entities and their assets and liabilities are entirely integrated in the accounts of the Z entity. This is a statutory consolidation.

- Company X and Company Y decide jointly to combine all their activities but, unlike in the previous case, neither of the combining companies is dissolved. The shareholders of each company exchange their shares against those of a newly formed Holding Company H (formation of a holding company). Holding company H becomes the sole shareholder of both Company X and Company Y. These in turn become subsidiaries of H and their activities, assets and liabilities are consolidated in the accounts of the Holding Company.

- Company X acquires directly all the assets of Company Y, without acquiring its shares (acquisition of assets). Company Y is essentially liquidated as it currently exists and the cash received in exchange for its assets is used to settle its liabilities and company Y either returns the surplus cash to its shareholders before dissolving itself or becomes a totally different business by investing the available funds in a new venture.

Figure 13.2 illustrates the two generic methods (purchase and uniting of interests) used to account for business combinations. Since within the purchase approach three further possibilities exist, there are four generic ways to record business combinations.

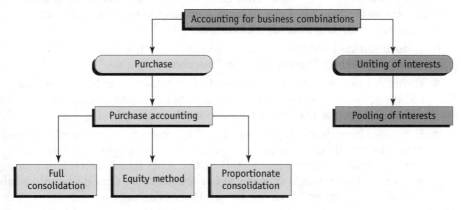

Figure 13.2 Accounting for business combination

Most of the time in a business combination (except in the case of merger between equals), one of the combining enterprises obtains control over the other combining enterprise. The former is known as the acquirer and the latter as the acquired. However, "in exceptional circumstances, it may not be possible to identify an acquirer. (…) The shareholders of the combining enterprises join in a substantially equal arrangement to share control over the whole, or effectively the whole, of their net assets and operations. (…) The shareholders of the combining enterprises share mutually in the risks and benefits of the combined entity" (IAS 22: § 13). Such a business combination is accounted for as a "uniting of interests" (also known as "pooling of interests"). This method, developed in Appendix 13.4, was forbidden in the USA in June 2001, and should be less and less used in the world.

Usefulness of consolidated financial statements

A corporation owning shares of another holds power over the second. The economic entity resulting from the combination of two or more enterprises linked by intercorporate investments of sufficient importance to warrant effective control of one over the other is called a "group". In most countries (with the notable exception of Germany) a group is generally not a legal entity as such and the parent company (pivot of the combination) and each controlled corporation are the only legal entities. If an investor or a shareholder wants or needs to shape her or his opinion about the financial position and the performance potential of this group, it is essential to develop group accounts, also called consolidated accounts or consolidated financial statements.

Group or consolidated accounts are needed because the accounts of the pivot company (parent or holding company) contain little useful information about the performance potential and the assets and obligations of the group. Some of the reasons for the lack of representativeness of the unconsolidated accounts of the parent are listed as follows. Each is a justification for developing consolidated statements:

1 *If the parent company is a "pure" holding company* (i.e., the case of a corporation whose sole purpose is to own – hold and manage – the shares of the members of the group and coordinate their activities without directly exercising any industrial, commercial or service activity itself). The income statement of the holding company is very "simple" and characterized by the following elements:

   - It does not include any of the "traditional" items such as "sales revenue", "cost of goods sold" or "purchases".
   - Revenues are essentially comprised of "management fees" (internal billing of "services" to each group member company) and "investment income" which is the sum of all dividends received.
   - Expenses include mainly administrative expenses (personnel expenses, depreciation of equipment) of an often very light coordination team. For example the direct headcount at the ABB Headquarters (a holding parent company based in Zürich) is reputed to be only 65 people while the whole group employs around 200,000 persons!

The balance sheet is also somewhat unusual:

   - It probably does not include any significant (or relevant for evaluating the financial position) amounts under accounts receivable, accounts payable, and inventories.
   - The value of tangible and intangible assets is often low.
   - However, the amount of financial investments is proportionately very high, representing the cost of acquisition of the shares of group companies owned by the parent company.

2 *If the parent company is a "mixed" holding company* (i.e., a corporation which both exercises an economic activity of its own and, in addition, administers a group of companies), the unconsolidated financial statements of the parent may have a more informative content since they reflect at least the stand-alone economic activity of the parent as well as the financial result of the holding activity. Despite their somewhat greater relevance than those of a pure holding company, the unconsolidated financial statements of the parent still are very far from giving a true and fair view of the performance potential of the group and of its risks, assets and obligations: importance of financial investments, importance of investment income and management fees hide the reality of the relationships of the group with its markets.

Given each and all of these weaknesses and insufficiencies of unconsolidated statements, it is judicious to prepare financial statements that reflect the economic activity of a group. As stated in IAS 27 (IASC 1994b: § 6): "Consolidated financial statements are the financial statements of a group presented as those of a single enterprise."

Nature of relations between the parent company and group entities

The nature of the relation(s) existing between the parent company and the different group entities is a determinant of the way the financial statements of each of the individual group entities will be taken into account in the consolidation process to create the group financial statements.

Table 13.1 lists the definitions suggested by the IASC of the three types of group companies that result from a classification and a qualification of the subsidiarity relationship that exists between a parent and another corporation. Any corporation for which its relation to the "parent" does not fall in one of the three types shown in Table 13.1, will not be considered to be a group company and thus will not be consolidated.

Table 13.1 Relations between a "parent" and another company

	Type of relation		Type of group company
Control	"Power to govern the financial and operating policies of an enterprise so as to obtain benefits from its activities" (IAS 27: § 6)	Subsidiary	"Enterprise that is controlled by another enterprise (known as the parent)" (IAS 27: § 6)
Significant influence	"Power to participate in the financial and operating policy decisions of the investee" (but it has no control over those policies) (IAS 28: § 3)	Associate	"Enterprise in which the investor has significant influence and which is neither a subsidiary nor a joint venture of the investor" (IAS 28: § 3)
Joint control	"Contractually agreed sharing of control [between two or more legal entities] over a [third] economic activity" (IAS 31: § 2)	Joint venture	"Contractual arrangement whereby two or more parties undertake an economic activity which is subject to joint control" (IAS 31: § 2)

Let us now expand on the types of relations provided in Table 13.1.

Control

According to IAS 27 (§ 12): "Control is presumed to exist when the parent owns directly, or indirectly through subsidiaries, more than one half of the voting power of an enterprise (…). Control also exists even when the parent owns one half or less of the voting power of an enterprise when there is:

(a) Power over more than one half of the voting rights by virtue of an agreement with other investors;

(b) Power to govern the financial and operating policies of the enterprise under a statute or an agreement;

(c) Power to appoint or remove the majority of the members of the board of directors or equivalent governing body; or

(d) Power to cast the majority of votes at meetings of the board of directors or equivalent governing body."

"Control" may exist even though less than a majority of the capital is held by the parent since voting rights alone define control (as seen in Chapter 11, multiple voting rights or no voting rights may be attached to shares). What matters is the actual ability to exercise control. The concepts, vocabulary and procedure put forward in IAS 27 are more or less identical to those of the 7th European Directive of 1983 which covers consolidated accounts.

Significant influence

According to IAS 28 (IASC 1998b: § 4): "If an investor holds, directly or indirectly through subsidiaries, 20% or more of the voting power of the investee, it is presumed that the investor does have significant influence, unless it can be demonstrated that this is not the case. Conversely, if the investor holds, directly or indirectly (…) less than 20% of the voting power of the investee, it is presumed that the investor does not have significant influence, unless such influence can be clearly demonstrated." The standard adds: "A substantial or majority ownership by another investor does not necessarily preclude an investor from having significant influence."

In practice: "The existence of significant influence by an investor is usually evidenced in one or more of the following ways:

(a) Representation on the board of directors or equivalent governing body of the investee;

(b) Participation in policy-making processes;

(c) Material transactions between the investor and the investee;

(d) Interchange of managerial personnel; or

(e) Provision of essential technical information" (IAS 27: § 5).

Joint control

Joint ventures take on many different forms and structures and are described in IAS 31 (IASC 1998c). All joint ventures result from a contractual arrangement between two or more economic entities in which joint control is established.

Percentage of control and percentage of interest

The percentage of control and the percentage of interest affect the way the accounts will be consolidated and how the value created will be shared:

- **Percentage of control** (also called percentage of stake, of vote, or of voting rights) is the term used to reflect the degree of dependency in which a parent company holds its subsidiaries or associates. The higher the percentage, the higher the dependency of the group company. This percentage measures the proportion of total voting rights held by the parent in its related company. This percentage will be used to determine whether full consolidation, equity method, or proportionate consolidation is used in establishing the consolidated financial statements.

- **Percentage of interest** (also called percentage of ownership) represents the claim held by the parent company over the shareholders' equity (including net income) of its subsidiaries or associates. This percentage is used in the process of consolidation of accounts and calculations to define majority and minority interests.

Figure 13.3 Percentages of control may differ from percentages of interest

The percentage of control held by a parent may be different from the percentage of interest it holds in a given subsidiary or associate. This is the case, for example, when there is a cascade of dependency links. Figure 13.3 illustrates a situation in which a parent company P is linked to corporation C2 both directly and indirectly by way of another corporation C1 in which the parent holds a non-controlling interest.

The *percentage of control* of the parent P over C2 is equal to only 42% and not to 82% (42% + 40%) because P does not have control over C1 (30% only) thus the "possible influence" branch that goes through C1 gives zero control to P over C2. With 42% control by the parent and without any additional element qualifying the relationship between P and C2, we can only say that there is significant influence.

The *percentage of interest* of P in C2 however is equal to 54% [42% + (30 % × 40%), i.e., (42% + 12%)]. Even with a percentage of interest equal to 54% (which is higher than 50%), there is nonetheless not more than significant influence as the insufficient percentage of control (42%, which is lower than 50%) dominates.

Note that the percentage of control equals the percentage of interest in case of a direct link (30% between P and C1, 40% between C1 and C2 and 42% between P and C2).

Consolidation methods

Table 13.1 introduced the three main types of relationships and to each corresponds a method of consolidation as shown in Figure 13.4.

Each method is now analyzed from a conceptual viewpoint and its mechanism illustrated both in a schematic diagram and through a quantified example.

Full consolidation per IAS 27

Figure 13.5 shows the operation of full consolidaton.

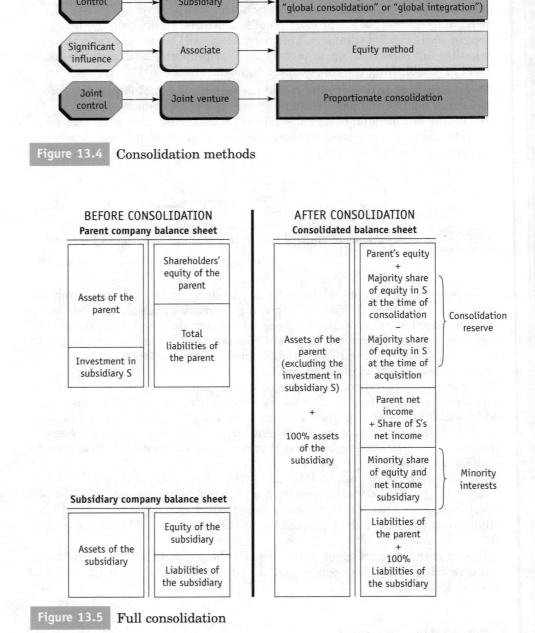

Figure 13.4 Consolidation methods

Figure 13.5 Full consolidation

The founding principle of full consolidation is that all assets and liabilities of the subsidiary are added to those of the parent (excluding, of course, the investment the parent holds in the subsidiary, which is eliminated in the process). Technically, if the percentage of interest of the parent is not 100%, part of the assets and liabilities of the subsidiary belong to "minority shareholders" and will be identified as such in the consolidated statements – see Simulation 2).

In order to illustrate the schematics of Figure 13.5, let us look at a quantified example. At the end of 20X1 Lentz Company acquires 100% of the Meder Company which continues to exist and becomes its subsidiary. The price paid in cash (320 CU) is equal to the shareholders' equity (book value of the subsidiary). It corresponds to 100% of the subsidiary's shareholders' equity (share capital, reserves, and undistributed net income).

Acquisition of company Meder (S)

Table 13.2 shows the unconsolidated balance sheet of Lentz Company before and after acquisition. The only modification between the two stems from the investment in Meder and the corresponding decrease in cash. It is important to remember that the balance sheet of Lentz Company after the acquisition is not the consolidated balance sheet.

| Table 13.2 | Balance sheet at acquisition |

Balance sheets as at 31 December 20X1	Lentz before acquisition	Meder (stand-alone)	Lentz after acquisition
Assets			
Investment in Meder	0		320
Other assets (incl. cash)	2,000	500	1,680
Total	2,000	500	2,000
Equity and liabilities			
Share capital	600	200	600
Reserves	460	100	460
Net income	30	20*	30
Liabilities	910	180	910
Total	2,000	500	2,000

*The net income will not be distributed

Simulation 1: Consolidation – 100% of interest

Lentz Company is headquartered in a country where consolidation is compulsory only if the group size exceeds a certain threshold. At the time of acquisition, Lentz Co. does not meet the threshold level. Two years later, because of the growth of Lentz Co.'s business, preparing consolidated financial statements is now required. The unconsolidated financial statements of both companies at the end of 20X3 are shown in Table 13.3.

Table 13.4 presents the consolidated balance sheet.

When applying the full consolidation mechanism, as stated in IAS 27 (IASC 1994b: § 15): "The financial statements of the parent and its subsidiaries are combined on a line-by-line basis by adding together like items of assets, liabilities, equity, income and expenses." However, this combined balance sheet does not provide a "true and fair view" of the group because it includes the investment in Meder as an asset and in the equity the corresponding share of equity of the subsidiary, which belongs to the parent company. In other words, the combined balance sheet shows an investment of the group in itself. This investment must be eliminated along with the corresponding share of equity of the

Table 13.3 Financial statements as at 31 December 20X3

Balance sheets as at 31 December 20X3	Lentz	Meder
Assets		
Investment in Meder	320	0
Other assets (incl. cash)	1,880	600
Total	2,200	600
Equity and liabilities		
Share capital	600	200
Reserves	500	300
Net income	50	40
Liabilities	1,050	60
Total	2,200	600

Income statement – Year 20X3	Lentz	Meder
Sales	1,000	400
Expenses	950	360
Net income	50	40

Table 13.4 Consolidated balance sheet

	Lentz (stand-alone)	Meder (stand-alone)	Combined	Elimination entries and adjustments	Consolidated balance sheet
	(1)	(2)	(3)=(1)+(2)	(4)	(5)=(3)+(4)
Assets					
Investment in Meder	320	0	320	(a) –320	0
Other assets (incl. cash)	1,880	600	2,480		2,480
Total	2,200	600	2,800	–320	2,480
Equity and liabilities					
Share capital	600	200	800	(a) –200	600
Reserves	500	300	800	(a) –300	500
Consolidation reserve				(a) 180	180
Net income	50	40	90		90
Liabilities	1,050	60	1,110		1,110
Total	2,200	600	2,800	–320	2,480

carrying amount of the parent's investment in each subsidiary and the parent's portion of equity of each subsidiary are eliminated".

This elimination is carried out as operation (a) in the Lentz example. Consequently, the consolidated equity represents only the share capital and reserves of the parent company (plus the undistributed net income of both parent and subsidiary companies).

Figure 13.5 shows a "consolidation reserve". This reserve is the difference between (i) the share of the subsidiary equity held by the consolidating parent (majority share of subsidiary's equity) excluding undistributed net income at the time of consolidation, and (ii) the share of the subsidiary equity held by the consolidating parent including undistributed net income at the time of acquisition. In our example, the reserve amounts to:

$$(200 + 300) \times 100\% - (200 + 100 + 20) \times 100\% = 180$$

An alternative description of the full consolidation process is to say that the investment in the subsidiary is mathematically and mechanically replaced by the book assets and liabilities of the subsidiary.

Intra-group balances and intra-group transactions (i.e., transactions between the parent and the subsidiary or between subsidiaries) resulting in unrealized profits should be eliminated in full. For example, if Lentz Company had held accounts receivable in the amount of 50 CU on Meder Company – which means the latter has recorded accounts payable to Lentz for the same amount – both balances would have been eliminated when calculating the consolidated assets and liabilities since these balances are of equal amount and opposite sign.

Table 13.5 illustrates the resulting consolidated income statement which can be used to report the profit generation potential of the combined businesses.

Table 13.5 Consolidated income statement

	Lentz (stand-alone)	Meder (stand-alone)	Combined	Elimination entries and adjustments	Consolidated income statement
Sales	1,000	400	1,400		1,400
Expenses	950	360	1,310		1,310
Net income	50	40	90		90

As Table 13.5 shows, the preparation of the consolidated income statement requires no adjusting or eliminating entry. The consolidated income statement is thus the result of combining mechanically the parent and subsidiary income statements with, of course, the elimination of any intra-group transactions. Such elimination is mathematically automatic since the sales revenue recognized in one of the income statement is part of the costs incurred in the other's income statement. However, even though the intra-group transactions do not affect the income of the consolidated entity, it is critical to explicitly cancel out all intra-group transactions to avoid the risk of biasing operating ratios involving sales revenue and cost of sales separately (by artificially inflating the balances).

Simulation 2: Consolidation – 90% interest – Minority interest

Let us now assume that Lentz Company does not acquire a 100% interest in Meder Company but only 90% of its shares. The purchase price is established at 90% of the shareholders' equity of the acquired firm (share capital, reserves and undistributed net income of Meder Company), which means the purchase price is (200 + 100 + 20) × 90% = 288 CU, which we will still assume, for the sake of simplicity, will be paid out of cash holdings.

As mentioned earlier, the parent company integrates 100% of the assets and liabilities of the subsidiary in its consolidated accounts because it holds effective economic control over the decisions of the subsidiary company. However, 10% of the Meder shareholders ("minority shareholders") still hold a (proportional) claim to the assets, liabilities and past and future profits of Meder Company. The consolidated statements specifically recognize the existence of these claims as "minority interests" or "third-party interests".

Minority interests are defined in IAS 27 (§ 6) as: "That part of the net results of operations and of net assets of a subsidiary attributable to interests which are not owned directly or indirectly through subsidiaries, by the parent." Table 13.6 illustrates the calculation and reporting of minority interests in the consolidated balance sheet at the end of 20X3.

Table 13.6 Consolidated balance sheet with minority interests

	Lentz (stand-alone)	Meder (stand-alone)	Combined	Elimination entries and adjustments	Consolidated balance sheet
	(1)	(2)	(3)=(1)+(2)	(4)	(5)=(3)+(4)
Assets					
Investment in Meder	288	0	288	(a) −288	0
Other assets (incl. cash)	1,912	600	2,512		2,512
Total	2,200*	600	2,800	−288	2,512
Equity and liabilities					
Share capital	600	200	800	(a) −180	
				(b) −20	600
Reserves	500	300	800	(a) −270	
				(b) −30	500
Consolidation reserve				(a) 162	162
Net income	50	40	90	(b) −4	86
Minority interest				(b) 54	54
Liabilities	1,050	60	1,110		1,110
Total	2,200	600	2,800	−288	2,512

*For the sake of simplicity, we assume that the balance sheet total of Lentz here is again equal to 2,200. The amount of other assets is then determined by difference between the total and the price of the investment in Meder

In this example, two elimination entries are required. Entry (a) in Table 13.6 serves to eliminate the investment of Lentz in Meder (for the same reasons as in Simulation 1). The purchase price of 288 CU corresponds to 180 CU (90% of share capital of Meder, i.e., 0.9 × 200) plus 90 CU (90% of the accumulated reserves of Meder, i.e., 0.9 × 100) plus 18 CU (90% of the undistributed net income of Meder). The 270 figure corresponds to the elimination of 90% or reserves of Meder. A consolidation reserve appears for 162 ([200 + 300] × 90%) − [200 + 100 + 20] × 90%).

Entry (b) establishes the claim of the minority shareholders regarding both shareholders' equity and income. The minority rights over the equity of Meder is 54 CU which is the sum of 20 CU (10% of share capital of 200) plus a 10% claim on the accumulated reserves of 300. The minority interest also represents a claim of 10% over the undistributed income of the period (10% of 40 CU). The minority interests represent therefore a total amount of 20 + 30 + 4 = 54 CU.

As in the previous simulation, assets and liabilities are added to create their consolidated balances, the consolidated share capital and reserves represent share capital and reserves of the parent company, and the minority interest line item in the balance sheet acts as a mechanism to offset the "over-incorporation" of assets and liabilities and help calculate the net claim held by the combined entity over the assets and liabilities it effectively controls.

Table 13.7 presents the mechanism of establishing the consolidated income statement when there are minority interests. The net income attributable to the group differs from the net income of the combined operation by the amount of the claim held by minority interests over income. This claim is established by the third component of the (b) entry mentioned earlier.

Table 13.7 Consolidated income statement

	Lentz (stand-alone)	Meder (stand-alone)	Combined	Elimination entries and adjustments	Consolidated income statement
Sales	1,000	400	1,400		1,400
Expenses	950	360	1,310		1,310
Net income	50	40	90		90
Minority interest (10 %) in subsidiary's net income				−4	−4
Net	50	40	90	−4	
Net income of consolidated entity					86

Principles guiding reporting for minority interests

Reporting of minority interests is described in IAS 27 (§ 15) in the following terms:

- "Minority interests in the net assets [assets minus liabilities] of consolidated subsidiaries are identified and presented in the consolidated balance sheet separately from liabilities and the parent shareholder's equity."

- "Minority interests in the net income of consolidated subsidiaries for the reporting period are identified and adjusted against the income of the group in order to arrive at the net income attributable to the owners of the parent."

If we consider this IASC definition, minority interests appear to be some kind of hybrid between shareholders' equity and liabilities. Choosing in which of the two categories to incorporate minority interests will affect the ratios and financial analysis that will be carried out on the consolidated financial statements.

The way minority interests are reported (either as a liability to a third party, or as a part of shareholder's equity, or even ignored altogether) stems from the perceived purpose of consolidated financial statements held by each company in its reporting to shareholders and investors. Three types of beliefs (property, parent, and entity) lead to four reporting positions (three pure positions and a hybrid).

- *Property concept*: Its foundation is that consolidated financial statements are meant to describe what shareholders have invested in the company. In this case what is of foremost interest is the description of their shareholders' ownership in the subsidiary company.

- *Parent company concept*: Its conceptual foundation is that the consolidated statements must focus mainly on informing the shareholders of the parent company because they are the ones who control the managerial decisions and orientations. In this case, minority shareholders are considered residual and are treated as third parties.

- *Entity concept*: Its foundation is that the consolidated financial statements are established mainly for internal decision-making purposes. Consolidated financial statements should therefore give a fair view of what the consolidated entity actually controls, i.e., assets, shareholders' equity and liabilities of the whole group, without making any reference to the specificity of the legal claim of some special class of shareholders (minority or majority).

- *Parent company extension concept*: This fourth case is a hybrid in that the minority shareholders are considered as a special and distinct class of shareholders and not dealt with as if they had been a third party.

Each set of beliefs regarding the foundations of consolidated financial statements leads to a specific way of reporting minority interests. These are outlined in Table 13.8.

Reporting for minority interests (real-life example)

Stora-Enso
(Finland – IAS GAAP – Source: Annual report 1999 – Production of paper)

The following tables illustrate an application of IAS 27. Only selected and aggregated relevant data are provided here.

Consolidated balance sheet

€ mill.	31 Dec. 1999	31 Dec. 1998
Shareholders' equity	5,953.2	5,266.3
Minority interests	202.0	278.8
Long-term liabilities	6,184.1	6,537.0
Current liabilities	3,694.7	3,331.0
Total shareholders' equity and liabilities	16,034.0	15,413.1

Consolidated income statement

€ mill.	1999	1998
(...)		
Profit after taxes	757.0	191.2
Minority interests [share of profit]	–4.5	–0.2
Profit for the period [share of the group]	752.5	191.0

Table 13.8	Minority interests and theories of consolidation

Theory	Reporting of minority interests
Property concept	No minority interests are reported (theory implies proportionate consolidation)
Parent company concept	Minority interests are part of liabilities of consolidated entity
Entity concept	Minority interests are included as a part of shareholders' equity
Parent company extension concept	Minority interests are reported between shareholders' equity and liabilities

Simulation 3: Consolidation with 100% of interest but purchase price of controlling interest has a different value from that of book value of assets being purchased

Let us here enrich the Lentz company example to be closer to everyday life. Most of the time the acquired entity's book value of net equity is lower than the amount paid by the acquiring firm (otherwise the acquiree's shareholders would have little incentive to enter into a cession agreement). In this example, Lentz Company still acquires 100% of the outstanding shares of Meder Company. However where the purchase price was previously 320 CU (equal to the book value of equity), Lentz must now, in this version of the example, pay 420 CU in cash on 31 December 20X1 to acquire Meder company. As seen before, at the time of acquisition, the book value of the shareholders' equity (including net income) of company Meder was 320. There is therefore a premium of 100 CU paid by Lentz Co. which amounts to the difference between the price paid (420 CU) and the book value of equity of the subsidiary (320 CU).

The premium finds its roots in two sources as shown in Figure 13.6. Part of the premium originates from a difference between fair and book values of identifiable assets and liabilities (valuation difference) and the other part reflects the excess value embedded in the purchase price over and above the fair market value of the identifiable assets and liabilities. This difference is called the "difference arising on first consolidation". The term "first consolidation" refers to the fact the difference is computed and analyzed the first time the consolidation statements are prepared, whenever such action takes place (and the difference will not change ever after).

The part of the difference that is not explained by valuation differences is the "goodwill" (as seen in Chapter 8). Goodwill is defined in IAS 22 (IASC 1998a: 41) in the following terms: "Any excess of the cost of the acquisition over the acquirer's interest in the fair value of the identifiable assets and liabilities acquired as at the date of the exchange transaction should be described as goodwill and recognized as an asset." IAS 22 adds: "Goodwill arising on acquisition represents a payment made by the acquirer in anticipation of future economic benefits. The future economic benefits may result from synergy between the identifiable assets acquired or from assets which, individually, do not qualify for recognition in the financial statements but for which the acquirer is prepared to make a payment in the acquisition" (§ 42).

For the sake of our example, let us assume that the fair market value of Meder's identifiable assets and liabilities (tangible or intangible) amounts to 390 CU. The global gross difference (100 CU) between cost of acquisition and

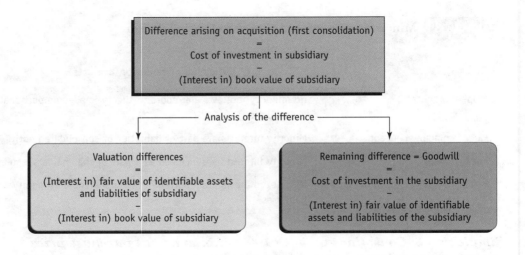

Figure 13.6 Analysis of the difference arising on first consolidation

Table 13.9 Analysis of the difference arising on first consolidation

Purchase price	420	(1)
Book value of shareholders' equity (excluding net income) of subsidiary at the time of acquisition	320	(2)
Interest in book value of shareholders' equity (excluding net income) of subsidiary at the time of acquisition	320	(3)=(2)*100%
Difference arising on first consolidation	100	(4)=(1)−(3)
Fair value of identifiable assets and liabilities of subsidiary	390	(5)
Interest in fair value of identifiable assets and liabilities of subsidiary	390	(6)=(5)*100%
Valuation difference	70	(7)=(6)−(3)
Goodwill	30	(8)=(4)−(7)

book value of what was acquired and which is computed at the time of acquisition is analyzed as shown in Figure 13.6. This difference arising on first consolidation is analyzed in Table 13.9.

Table 13.10 presents the consolidated balance sheet that results from the acquisition of Meder Company by Lentz Company for 420 CU.

If we refer to the consolidated balance sheet (see Table 13.10), transaction (a) is similar to the one described in Simulation 1 (elimination of investment in Meder). Let us emphasize here that the elimination entry concerns only the book value of equity of Meder (320). In a second step (transaction (b)), the difference arising on first consolidation (100) is broken up and distributed between "other assets" for an amount of 70 CU and "goodwill" for an amount of 30 CU.

We will not cover in this text the complexity introduced by the coexistence of goodwill and minority interests. The reader wishing to explore this situation is encouraged to consult advanced textbooks[1].

Table 13.10 Consolidated balance sheet

	Lentz (stand-alone)	Meder (stand-alone)	Combined	Elimination entries and adjustments		Consolidated balance sheet
	(1)	(2)	(3)=(1)+(2)		(4)	(5)=(3)+(4)
Assets						
Investment in Meder	420	0	420	(a)	–320	
				(b)	–100	0
Goodwill				(b)	30	30
Other assets (incl. cash)	1,780	600	2,380	(b)	70	2,450
Total	2,200	600	2,800		–320	2,480
Equity and liabilities						
Share capital	600	200	800	(a)	–200	600
Reserves	500	300	800	(a)	–300	500
Consolidation reserve				(a)	180	180
Net income	50	40	90			90
Liabilities	1,050	60	1,110			1,110
Total	2,200	600	2,800		–320	2,480

Treatment of goodwill after recording

The treatment of goodwill has been presented in detail in Chapter 8. It suffices here to recall that pursuant to the prescriptions of IAS 22 (§ 44): "Goodwill should be amortized (like any asset) on a systematic basis over its useful life. The amortization period should reflect the best estimate of the period during which future economic benefits are expected to flow to the enterprise. There is a rebuttable presumption that the useful life of goodwill will not exceed twenty years from initial recognition." We must also recall that, in the USA, the Statement of Financial Accounting Standard No. 142, Goodwill and Other Intangible Assets (FASB 2001b), adopted in June 2001, abolished amortization over 40 years and replaced it by an impairment test. The same modification has been adopted in Canada. The new regulation should be implemented in the majority of cases in 2002.

In the case of the Lentz company all calculations have ignored amortization of any goodwill since the acquisition took place on 31 December and the consolidated accounts were established on the same date.

Reporting goodwill amortization

Table 13.11 offers some examples of the diversity of the period of amortization of goodwill chosen by a random sample of firms in a diversity of industries.

Equity method

Principles

The equity method consists in re-evaluating, in the accounts of the parent company, the investment in the associate (or affiliated) company over which the

Table 13.11 Examples of amortization of goodwill (1999 annual reports)

Company (country – GAAP)	Activity	Method	Number of years
Baltimore Technologies (UK – UK GAAP)	Security services for e-commerce	Straight line	5
Bayer (Germany – German/IAS GAAP)	Chemicals and healthcare	Straight line	15
BT (UK – UK GAAP)	Telecommunications	Straight line	20
Bull (France – French/US GAAP)	IT group	Straight line	20
Club Méditerranée (France – French GAAP)	Leisure	Not mentioned	20
EMI (UK – UK GAAP)	Music	Straight line	20
Interbrew (Belgium – Belgian GAAP)	Brewery group	Not mentioned	40
ISS (Denmark – Danish GAAP)	Support services	Straight line	20
Philips (Netherlands – Dutch GAAP)	Consumer products (electronics)	Straight line	20
Pirelli (Italy – Italian GAAP)	Tires, cables and systems	Not mentioned	10 to 20
Racing Champions (USA – US GAAP)	Racing replicas	Straight line	40
Repsol YPF (Spain – Spanish GAAP)	Oil and gas	Straight line	20
Roche (Switzerland – IAS GAAP)	Pharmaceuticals, chemicals	Not mentioned	20
Saint Gobain (France – French GAAP)	Glass	Straight line	40
Sandvik (Sweden – Swedish GAAP)	Engineering	Straight line	5 to 20
Securitas (Sweden – Swedish GAAP)	Guard services and alarm systems	Straight line	5 to 20

Bayer – Goodwill, including that resulting from capital consolidation, is capitalized in accordance with IAS 22 and amortized on a straight-line basis over its estimated useful life, which currently is a maximum period of 15 years. The value of goodwill is reassessed regularly and any impairment is written down if considered irreversible in the foreseeable future

Sandvik – While amortized goodwill is normally on a straight-line basis over 5 to 10 years, amortization periods up to 20 years may be decided in cases of important strategic acquisition. Amortization is reported as a part of selling expenses

Securitas – The duration of goodwill amortization depends on the type of company acquired:

● 5 years in the case of acquisition of companies where customer contracts, systems or specially trained personnel constitute the greatest asset

● 10 years in the case of acquisition of well-established companies, with independent and well-known trademarks

● 20 years in the case of companies that also constitute strategic acquisitions, with respect to either products or markets

parent company exerts a significant influence. This method, therefore, excludes any idea of cumulating assets and liabilities. This method is not, in the strict sense, a consolidation since there is no "integration" of the financial statements of the associate. IAS 28 (IASC 1998b: § 3) defines the equity method as: "A method of accounting whereby the investment is initially recorded at cost and adjusted thereafter for the post acquisition change in the investor's share of the net assets of the investee. The income statement reflects the investor's share of the results of the operations of the investee." The asset value of the intercorporate investment will therefore be called "at equity" since it will reflect the share of the shareholders' equity controlled by the "parent".

Figure 13.7 illustrates schematically the application of the basic principles in the equity method.

In Figure 13.7, the term "consolidated" as applied to the balance sheet of the combined businesses is placed between quotation marks to emphasize the fact that it is not a true consolidation but more a revaluation.

Going back to the Lentz Company example, let us now assume that Lentz acquires only 30% of the outstanding shares of Meder company. The "consolidated" balance sheet, i.e., valued at equity, is shown in Table 13.12.

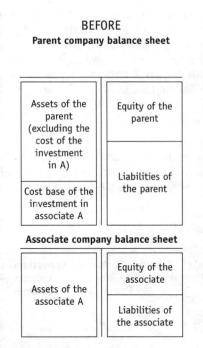

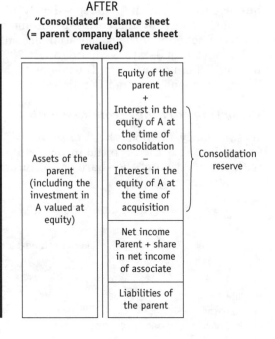

BEFORE
Parent company balance sheet

Assets of the parent (excluding the cost of the investment in A)	Equity of the parent
	Liabilities of the parent
Cost base of the investment in associate A	

Associate company balance sheet

| Assets of the associate A | Equity of the associate |
| | Liabilities of the associate |

AFTER
"Consolidated" balance sheet
(= parent company balance sheet revalued)

Assets of the parent (including the investment in A valued at equity)	Equity of the parent + Interest in the equity of A at the time of consolidation − Interest in the equity of A at the time of acquisition	} Consolidation reserve
	Net income Parent + share in net income of associate	
	Liabilities of the parent	

Figure 13.7 Equity method

Table 13.12 Consolidated balance sheet with equity method

	Lentz after acquisition	Lentz after acquisition and equity adjustment
Assets		
Investment in Meder	96	162*
Other assets (incl. cash)	2,104	2,104
Total	2,200	2,266
Equity and liabilities		
Share capital	600	600
Reserves	500	500
Consolidation reserve		54
Net income	50	50
Net income resulting from equity		12
Liabilities	1,050	1,050
Total	2,200	2,266

*Valued at equity

Investment in the associate has been paid 96 CU [(200 + 100 + 20) × 30%]. The consolidation reserve is the difference between the interest in the equity of the associate (excluding net income) at the time of consolidation and the interest in the equity of the associate (including net income) at the time of acquisition. Here, given our hypotheses, this reserve is 54 [(200 + 300) × 30% − (200 + 100 + 20) × 30%]. After the acquisition is completed and the two businesses begin to cooperate or coordinate their actions, the value of the equity of the associate has begun to fluctuate independently of the cost of the acquisition by the "parent" (hopefully increasing if the move was strategically justified and the expected benefits of the cooperation actually accrue to the combination).

The fact that Lentz company owns 30% of Meder Company leads to Lentz having a claim over 30% of the income of Meder or 12 CU (40 CU × 30% = 12). The investment in Meder is now valued 162 [(200 + 300 + 40) × 30%].

Reporting earnings from associates

In the equity method, the "consolidated" income statement is equivalent, as shown in Table 13.13, to the income statement of the parent company (Lentz) with the addition of the share of net income of the associate Meder pertaining to Lentz' interest.

Table 13.13 Income statement (equity method)

	Lentz (stand-alone)	Adjustment due to the equity interest in Meder	Consolidated income statement
Sales	1,000		1,000
Expenses	950		950
Net income resulting from equity		12	12
Net income	50	12	62

Proportionate consolidation

Under this method there is a simple line-by-line addition of parts (proportion) of the financial statements of the parent company (called the "venturer") and of the corporate entities whose shares are owned by the parent in the context of a joint control. Such a corporate entity is generally referred to as a joint venture or JV.

IAS 31 (IASC 1998c: § 2) defines proportionate consolidation as: "A method of accounting and reporting whereby a venturer's share of each of the assets, liabilities, income and expenses of a jointly controlled entity is combined on a line-by-line basis with similar items in the venturer's financial statements or reported as separate line items in the venturer's financial statements."

Figure 13.8 illustrates the mechanism of this method.

As shown in Figure 13.8, proportionate consolidation is a true consolidation method in that the investment in the joint venture is eliminated at the same time as the share of parent company in the equity of the joint venture is. There is, however, a major difference between proportionate consolidation and full consolidation: the assets and liabilities of the joint venture are integrated only proportionately to the interest held by the venturer in JV.

Let us now assume Lentz Company shares joint control over Meder Company with Marcus SA which is an equal partner. Lentz company acquired its 50% control over the joint venture by paying 160 CU. The price of the investment, at the time of acquisition, equals 50% of the shareholders' equity: 160 = [(200 + 100 + 20) × 50%]. The consolidated balance sheet that results is illustrated in Table 13.14.

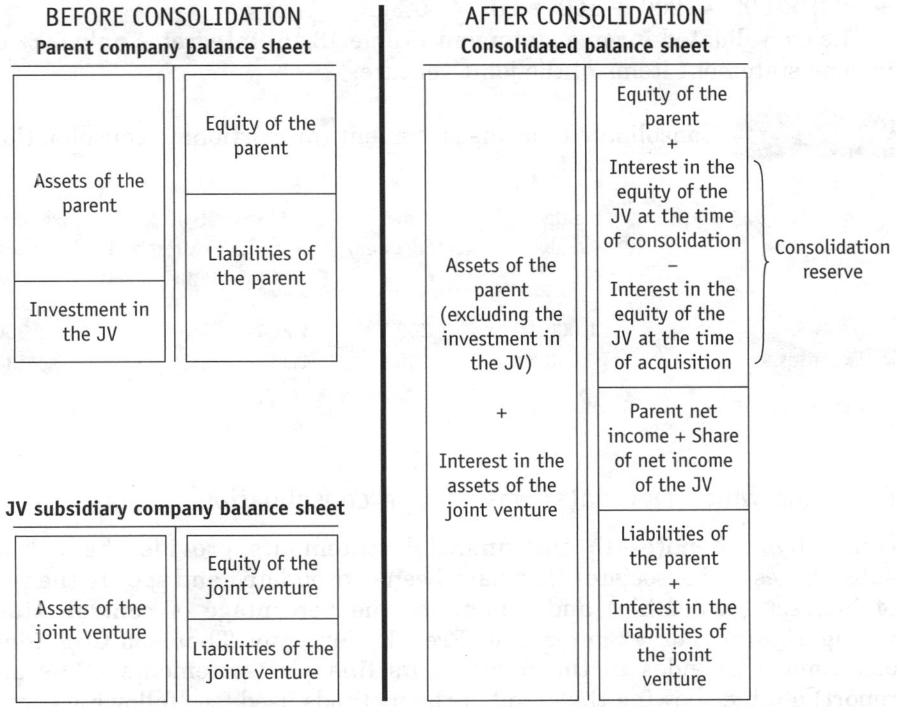

BEFORE CONSOLIDATION
Parent company balance sheet

| Assets of the parent | Equity of the parent |
| Investment in the JV | Liabilities of the parent |

JV subsidiary company balance sheet

| Assets of the joint venture | Equity of the joint venture |
| | Liabilities of the joint venture |

AFTER CONSOLIDATION
Consolidated balance sheet

Assets of the parent (excluding the investment in the JV) + Interest in the assets of the joint venture	Equity of the parent + Interest in the equity of the JV at the time of consolidation − Interest in the equity of the JV at the time of acquisition	Consolidation reserve
	Parent net income + Share of net income of the JV	
	Liabilities of the parent + Interest in the liabilities of the joint venture	

Figure 13.8 Proportionate consolidation

Table 13.14 Consolidated balance sheet (proportionate consolidation)

	Lentz (stand-alone)	Meder (Lentz's interest in Meder's assets and liabilities)	Combined	Elimination entries and adjustments	Consolidated balance sheet
	(1)	(2)	(3)=(1)+(2)	(4)	(5)=(3)+(4)
Assets					
Investment in Meder	160		160	(a) −160	0
Other assets (incl. cash)	2,040	300	2,340		2,340
Total	2,200	300	2,500	−160	2,340
Equity and liabilities					
Share capital	600	100	700	(a) −100	600
Reserves	500	150	650	(a) −150	500
Consolidation reserve				(a) 90	90
Net income	50	20	70		70
Liabilities	1,050	30	1,080		1,080
Total	2,200	300	2,500	−160	2,340

For the sake of simplicity, we assume that the balance sheet total of Lentz is once again equal to 2,200. The amount of other assets is then determined by difference between the total and the price of the investment in Meder

The consolidation reserve is computed as in the two previous methods: [(200 + 300) × 50% − (200 + 100 + 20) × 50%].

The consolidated income statement (Table 13.15) integrates only 50% of the income statement items of the joint venture.

Table 13.15 Consolidated income statement (proportionate consolidation)

	Lentz (stand-alone)	Meder (stand-alone)	Combined	Elimination entries and adjustments	Consolidated income statement
Sales	1,000	200	1,200		1,200
Expenses	950	180	1,130		1,130
Net income	50	20	70		70

Reporting which method(s) was used in consolidation

Generally, the notes to the financial statements provide the list of all subsidiaries and associates that have been consolidated and specify the percent of interest (ownership) and sometimes the percentage of control (stake or voting rights). For example, the French Company Thomson-CSF (defense electronics) provides in the notes to its financial statements (1999 annual report) a table showing the detail of the methods used (see following excerpts):

	31/12/1999		31/12/1998	
Number of companies	**French**	**Foreign**	**French**	**Foreign**
● Consolidated	90	65	90	55
● Accounted for under the equity method	2	6	3	6
● Accounted for by proportionate consolidation	13	23	10	16
Subtotal	**105**	**94**	**103**	**77**
Total	**199**		**180**	

ADVANCED ISSUES

The consolidation process follows a rigorous methodology which is covered in the first section. Then we address two especially sticky points in the consolidation process: deferred taxation arising from consolidation entries (due among other reasons to timing differences as seen in Chapter 6) and translation of financial statements established in a currency different from the one used by the reporting entity (the parent company). We go on to cover the reporting issues resulting from a "legal merger" in which the two or more combining entities literally disappear into a third entity.

Consolidation process

The consolidation process is a complex and rigorous sequential process that requires good organization. Preliminary steps include:

- Creating detailed record of all companies that could be included in the scope of consolidation so that all relevant information be located in the same database or file.

- Setting up a consolidation guide, continuously updated and describing the various steps in the consolidation activities, the procedures to be followed and an allocation of responsibilities, etc.

- Issuance of a group accounting guide setting down the principles, rules and methods of valuation the group companies involved in the consolidation perimeter or scope must follow to facilitate the consolidation work. The accounting guide will also specify the types of adjustments needed when required local practice or principles are not coherent with the group's principles and methods.

- Preparation of the "consolidation package", i.e., the work documents, files and tables that each group company must prepare following strict rules to prepare the consolidation calculations.

The consolidation process follows four standard steps:

Step 1: Identify the companies to be consolidated

Decide for each company in which the parent holds an investment whether they should be included in the scope of consolidation. Based on the finding as to control and interest, decide on the method of consolidation that will be retained for each company.

Step 2: Pre-consolidation

This step is generally carried out locally as it consists essentially of restatements of the local statements to align them with the accounting policies of the parent:

- Individual financial statements of all companies included in the scope of consolidation are restated so they present their financial position in an homogeneous way and follow the prescriptions of the group accounting guide.

- If the need exists, the restated financial statements must be converted to the currency used by the parent.

Step 3: Consolidation entries and operations

- Preparation of a comprehensive balance of all restated accounts.

- Elimination of intra-group operations and entries (between subsidiaries or between a subsidiary and the parent). The consolidation process retains only the operations and results arising from transactions with (third) parties external to the consolidation scope. Transactions that generate trivial or immaterial amounts are generally ignored as the potential benefit in improved reporting that would be obtained rarely balances the cost of their elimination activity.

- Elimination of the intra-group investments (in group companies) and partition of equities and net income of each consolidated company between the group and minority interests if the need arises.

Step 4: Preparation of the consolidated financial statements

The trial balance of consolidated accounts (as they stand after step 3) serves to prepare consolidated balance sheet, consolidated income statement and consolidated notes to financial statements, and sometimes both consolidated cash flow statement and statement of changes in consolidated shareholders' equity.

The elimination of intra-group transactions (step 3) represents a very important part of the consolidation process and the key elimination entries are generally reported in the notes as can be seen in the few examples of notes that follow.

Real-life examples

Repsol YPF

(Spain – Spanish GAAP – Source: Annual report 1999 – Oil and gas)

Notes to the consolidated financial statements – financial year ended 31 December 1999

Transactions between consolidated companies

All material accounts, transactions and profits between the companies consolidated by the global integration method and the income derived from transactions with associated companies were eliminated in consolidation. In the case of the companies consolidated by the proportional integration method, the receivables, payables, revenues, expenses and results of operations with other group companies were eliminated in proportion to Repsol's percentage of these companies.

Fielmann

(Germany – German GAAP – Source: Annual report 1999 – Optician, glasses)

Notes to consolidated accounts as at 31 December 1999

Intra-group profits on fixed assets have not been eliminated as they were negligible.

Deferred taxation on consolidation

The consolidation operations bring together companies that may not follow the same tax calendar as the parent, or whose financial statements are established in accordance with tax or reporting rules that differ from those selected in the group accounting guide or that apply to the parent. Chapter 6 showed that these differences create deferred taxation issues. Appendix 13.2 develops the specificity of deferred taxation arising on consolidation.

Foreign currency translations

Once the individual non-consolidated financial statements have been restated and harmonized in keeping with the prescriptions of the group accounting guide, and before they can be aggregated, it is essential to express all accounts in the same currency. The unique currency or "reporting currency" used in establishing the consolidated accounts is generally the parent's. Foreign exchange rates therefore affect the translation of financial statements, established originally in foreign currencies, for all entities that are included in the parameter of either a full or proportionate consolidation or the application of the equity method. The treatment of foreign currency translations is further developed in Appendix 13.3.

Legal mergers

A "legal merger" between two companies may take two different forms. Either:

- The assets and liabilities of one company (the merged company) are transferred to the other company (the merging company) and the former (merged) company is dissolved.

- Or the assets and liabilities of both companies are transferred to a new company and both original companies are dissolved.

The major accounting issues pertaining to a legal merger are:

- determination of the value of each business
- determination of the rate of exchange of shares
- determination of the number of shares to issue
- determination of the merger premium
- accounting entries for recording for the merger so as to be able to produce a relevant new balance sheet.

Let us illustrate and discuss these points around an example.

Hol Company merges with Van Rennes Company. Table 13.16 presents the balance sheet of each of the firms before the merger (in thousands of the same CU).

Table 13.16 Balance sheets of merging and merged companies

Assets (000 omitted)	Hol	Van Rennes	Equity and liabilities (000 omitted)	Hol	Van Rennes
Assets	1,500	500	Capital	400	200
			Reserves	800	50
			Liabilities	300	250
Total	1,500	500	Total	1,500	500
Number of shares included in the capital				4,000	2,000
Par value				100	100

The facts of the merger are as follows:

- Hol merges with Van Rennes, which is dissolved (essentially and to all intents and purposes, Hol purchases Van Rennes: the purchase method is applied).
- All book values do not reflect the economic (fair) values of the different Van Rennes balance sheet items, as indicated in the following table:

Van Rennes assets (excerpts)	Book value	Fair value
Assets	500	520
Non-identifiable difference	0	30

Determination of the value of both companies

Table 13.17 shows the determination of the value of each company.

Table 13.17 Value of companies (000 omitted, except for shares and per share data)

		Hol	Van Rennes
Capital	(1)	400	200
Reserves	(2)	800	50
Shareholders' equity	(3)=(1)+(2)	1,200	250
Number of shares	(4)	4,000	2,000
Book value	(5)=(3)/(4)*1,000	300	125
Potential gain on assets	(6)		20
Goodwill	(6)		30
Net assets	(7)=(3)+(6)	1,200	300
Fair value per share	(8)=(7)/(4)*1,000	300	150

Determination of the rate of exchange of shares

The ratio of the per share value is:

$$\frac{\text{Value of a share of Van Rennes}}{\text{Value of a share of Hol}} = 150/300 = 1/2$$

The rate of exchange is then equal to 1 share Hol for 2 shares Van Rennes. We can check that one share Hol has the same value as 2 shares Van Rennes: $300 \times 1 = 150 \times 2$.

Determination of the number of shares to issue in the merger

The merging company Hol should issue: 2,000 (number of shares in Van Rennes) $\times$ 1/2 = 1,000 new shares of Hol to be awarded to the former shareholders of Van Rennes so the latter will retain the same value as they gave up in agreeing to the merger.

Determination of the merger premium

The capital increase is equal to 100 (par value) × 1,000 = 100,000. The difference between net assets of Van Rennes (300) and the capital increase is the merger premium (see Table 13.18).

Table 13.18 Determination of the merger premium

	Computations	Share capital Hol	Merger premium
Capital Hol		400	
Net assets of Van Rennes	300		
Share capital increase	−100	100	
Merger premium	200		200
Total		500	200

Accounting for the merger

Table 13.19 illustrates the balance sheet after the merger.

Table 13.19 Balance sheet after merger

	Hol	Merger entries		B/S after merger
Assets	1,500	520	(a)	2,020
Goodwill		30	(a)	30
Total	1,500	550		2,050

	Hol	Merger entries		B/S after merger
Capital	400	100	(b)	500
Merger premium		200	(b)	200
Reserves	800			800
Liabilities	300	250	(a)	550
Total	1,500	550		2,050

a Integration of the net assets of the merged company at fair value (520 + 30 − 250 = 300)
b Increase of the capital of the merging company (100 + merger premium of 200)

The resulting balance sheet calls for several observations that affect the decision-making usefulness of the merged financial statements:

- The reported assets of the merged entity end up being valued by mixing assets at book value (from Hol) and assets at fair value (from Van Rennes).
- The reserves are only those of Hol Company.
- The merger premium is the difference between the net value of the assets contributed to the merger and the nominal (or par value) of the shares of capital issued by Hol.

In this example, we took the position that the balance sheet of the merged business was combined at fair value, which could be done because of the simplicity of the data. It was assumed possible to know the fair market value of every asset or asset class. In the real world it would be extremely difficult and cumbersome to identify the fair market value of each line item asset, or even of classes of assets. It is however, especially if the merged company is quoted on a financial market, possible to estimate the fair market value of the aggregate represented by the merged company. In practice, many mergers use the fair market value only in the calculation of the exchange of shares and merge the accounts at book value, thus using the merger premium to balance the entry. If it had been the case here, the merger premium would have been reduced (from 200 to 150). The interested reader could refer to Fischer *et al*. (1999) for further developments.

Appendix 13.4 presents the "pooling of interests" method and compares it to the "purchase method".

KEY POINTS

- Consolidated financial statements create a description of the financial position of an economic entity which is the agglomeration or conglomeration of diverse and often distinct legal entities connected by relations of intercorporate investments, control or lending relationships.

- Financial assets include mainly: (1) shares in subsidiaries, (2) shares in associated companies, (3) shares in other investments, (4) loans to subsidiaries, associated companies and other investments, and (5) other loans.

- A *subsidiary* is an enterprise that is controlled by another enterprise (known as the parent) and an *associate* is an enterprise in which the investor has significant influence.

- When market value of a financial asset falls below its acquisition cost, an exceptional provision (or valuation allowance) expense is recognized in the income statement to reduce the value to market.

- A business combination is the bringing together of separate enterprises into the economic entity as a result of one enterprise uniting with or obtaining control over the net assets and operations of another enterprise.

- Accounting for business combinations is based on two exclusive generic hypotheses: purchase and uniting of interests. The latter is now forbidden in the USA.

- Usefulness of consolidated financial statements partly arise from the lack of representativeness of the unconsolidated accounts of the parent (holding) company.

- The nature of subordination and control relationship linking group companies to the parent drives the choice of the consolidation method.

- There are three main types of relationships (control, significant influence and joint control) and to each corresponds a method of consolidation (full consolidation, equity method and proportionate consolidation).

- In full consolidation, if the percentage of control is below 100, minority interests are reported. They represent that part of the net results of operations and of net assets of a subsidiary attributable to interests which are not owned directly or indirectly through subsidiaries by the parent.

- If the purchase price of a subsidiary exceeds the interest in the book value of the acquired company, the difference arises from both valuation differences on identifiable assets and liabilities of the subsidiary and "goodwill".

- The consolidation process follows a rigorous methodology.

- Consolidation often gives rise to deferred taxation.
- The financial statements of all group companies should be expressed in the same currency. Financial statements of companies prepared in a currency which is different from the reporting one should be translated into the reporting currency.
- A legal merger raises accounting issues regarding value of each business, rate of exchange of shares, number of shares to issue, merger premium, etc.

REVIEW

Review 13.1 Mater & Filia

Topic: Consolidated balance sheet (three methods)
Type: Individual/group exercise
Related part of the chapter: Core Issues

The balance sheet of the Mater & Filia companies, as of 31 December 20X1, are given in the following (Mater Co. is the parent company, and Filia Co. is the subsidiary company).

Balance sheet as of 31 December 20X1 (in thousands of CU)		
	Mater	Filia
Assets		
Fixed assets (net)	1,500	550
Investment in Filia Company (1)	160	—
Inventories	930	510
Other current assets	1,210	740
Total Assets	3,800	1,800
Equity and liabilities		
Capital	500	200
Retained earnings	780	600
Net income (2)	220	150
Debts	2,300	850
Total liabilities	3,800	1,800

(1) Mater acquired 80% of the capital of Filia when this latter was incorporated
(2) Net income will not be distributed

Required

Prepare the consolidated balance sheet by each of the following methods:

- full consolidation
- proportionate consolidation
- equity method.

Solution

1 Full consolidation

	Mater	Filia	Combined statements	Elimination entries and adjustments		Consolidated balance sheet
				Elimination of investment	Minority interests	
Fixed assets (net)	1,500	550	2,050			2,050
Investment in Filia Company	160	—	160	−160		0
Inventories	930	510	1,440			1,440
Other current assets	1,210	740	1,950			1,950
Total assets	**3,800**	**1,800**	**5,600**	**−160**	**0**	**5,440**
Group interests						
Share capital	500	200	700	−160	−40	500
Reserves	780	600	1,380	−480	−120	780
Consolidation reserve				480		480
Net income	220	150	370		−30	340
Minority interests						
Share capital of F					40	40
Reserves of F					120	120
Net income of F					30	30
Liabilities	2,300	850	3,150			3,150
Total equity and liabilities	**3,800**	**1,800**	**5,600**	**−160**	**0**	**5,440**

In the elimination of investment, the investment is canceled and the share of reserves of Filia belonging to the parent company, Mater, is transferred to the consolidation reserve. The minority interests are shown by transferring the share of minority shareholders over the share capital, reserves, and net income of the subsidiary Filia.

2 Proportional consolidation and equity method

In reality, the three methods could not be used in the same situation with the same percentage of interest (here, 80%). This review has the pedagogical objective to show the difference between the three methods, which explains why the three methods are applied to the same companies, as shown now.

Consolidated balance sheet as at 31 December 20X1 (000 CU)			
Comparison of the three methods			
	Full consolidation	Proportional consolidation	Equity method
Fixed assets (net)	2,050	1,940	1,500
Investment in Filia Company	0	0	0
Investment valued at equity	—	—	760
Inventories	1,440	1,338	930
Other current assets	1,950	1,802	1,210
Total assets	**5,440**	**5,080**	**4,400**
Group interests (shareholders' equity)			
Share capital	500	500	500
Reserves	780	780	780
Reserve from consolidation	480	480	480
Net income	340	340	340
Minority interests			
Share capital of Filia	40	0	0
Reserves of Filia	120	0	0
Net income of Filia	30	0	0
Liabilities	3,150	2,980	2,300
Total equity and liabilities	**5,440**	**5,080**	**4,400**

In the proportionate consolidation, all assets and liabilities are the result of the combination of the Mater Company items + 80% of Filia items. For instance, for fixed assets, $1,500 + 550 \times 80\% = 1,500 + 440 = 1,940$. However, the group interests (shareholders' equity) are the same as with full consolidation.

In the equity method, there is no integration. Consequently, the assets (with the exception of investment) and liabilities are taken from the parent (Mater) balance sheet. The share capital and reserves are also those of the parent company. However, the investment in Filia (160 originally) is revalued. The current value is: Shareholders' equity of Filia (including net income) × percentage of interest = $(200 + 600 + 150) \times 80\% = 760$. The difference between this value and the acquisition price $(760 - 160 = 600)$ is split between the consolidation reserve (480 which represents the share of the reserves of Filia which did not exist at the time of acquisition: $600 \times 80\%$) and net income (120 which represent the share of the net income of Filia: $150 \times 80\%$).

ASSIGNMENTS

Assignment 13.1

Multiple-choice questions
Type: Individual exercise
Related part of the chapter: Core Issues

Select the right answer (one possible answer, unless otherwise stated).

1 **The percentage of interest**
   (a) Is used to define the dependency link
   (b) Is used to decide about the inclusion of a company in the consolidation scope
   (c) Reflects the interests that are controlled directly and indirectly
   (d) None of these

2 **In the situation described in the diagram, the percentage of control (stake, voting rights, vote) is**

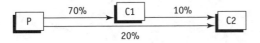

   (a) 10%
   (b) 20%
   (c) 30%
   (d) 27%
   (e) None of these

3 **In the diagram in question 2, the percentage of interest (ownership) is**
   (a) 10%
   (b) 20%
   (c) 30%
   (d) 27%
   (e) None of these

4   Minority interests can be reported (several possible answers)

(a)   As a part of shareholders' equity
(b)   As a part of long-term liabilities
(c)   As a part of current liabilities
(d)   Between shareholders' equity and long-term liabilities
(e)   As a negative liability within financial fixed assets
(f)   None of these
(g)   All of these

5   Associate and affiliate are often considered as synonymous

(a)   True
(b)   False

6   The only possibility to hold control of a company is to own more than 50% of the voting rights of this entity

(a)   True
(b)   False

7   Minority interests are reported when which method is used?

(a)   Full consolidation
(b)   Equity method
(c)   Proportionate consolidation
(d)   None of these

8   Goodwill is the difference between the purchase price (cost of investment) of shares and the book value of these shares

(a)   True
(b)   False

9   The study of annual reports shows that goodwill is generally amortized over 20 or 40 years

(a)   True
(b)   False

10   The equity method should be used when the percentage of control is more than 30% and less than 50%

(a)   True
(b)   False

Assignment 13.2 Mutter & Tochter

Topic: Preparation of a consolidated balance sheet
Type: Individual/group exercise
Related part of the chapter: Core Issues

The balance sheet of the Mutter & Tochter companies, as of 31 December 20X1, are given in the following (Mutter Co. is the parent and Tochter Co. is the subsidiary).

Balance sheet at 31 December 20X1 (000 CU)				
	Mutter		**Tochter**	
Fixed assets (net)	22,000		16,000	
Investment in Tochter Company	10,000	(1)	—	
Inventories	34,000		10,000	
Other current assets	25,700	(2)	9,200	
Total assets	91,700		35,200	
Capital	40,000		15,000	
Reserves	14,000		6,000	
Net income	7,000		4,000	
Debts	30,700		10,200	(3)
Total equity and liabilities	91,700		35,200	

(1) When Mutter acquired 60% of the capital of Tochter, the shareholders' equity (capital, retained earnings and net income) of the subsidiary was valued at 16,000

(2) Includes a loan to Tochter   1,000

(3) Includes a debt to Mutter   1,000

Required

Prepare the consolidated balance sheet by each of the following methods:

- full consolidation
- proportionate consolidation
- equity method.

Assignment 13.3 Saint-Gobain*

Topic: Presentation of the consolidated income statement
Type: Group exercise
Related part of the chapter: Core Issues

Founded in France in 1665 as a manufacturer of flat glass, Saint-Gobain has undergone a major transformation of its operations. The group is now operating in three core sectors: glass, high-performance materials, and construction materials.

Excerpts from the consolidated income statement (*source*: annual report 1999 – French GAAP) show the following figures.

Consolidated statements of income			
In millions of €	**1999**	**1998**	**1997**
(...)			
Gross margin	6,851	4,573	4,118
(...)			
Operating income	2,314	1,776	1,593
(...)			
Income before profit on sale of non-current assets and taxes	1,821	1,393	1,220
(...)			
Net operating income from consolidated companies before amortization of goodwill	1,503	1,198	1,011
Amortization of goodwill	−142	−102	−91
Net operating income from consolidated companies	1,361	1,096	920
Share in net results of equity investees	28	86	50
Net income before minority interests	1,389	1,182	970
Minority interest in consolidated companies	−163	−85	−112
Net income	1,226	1,097	858

Required

1 What is the meaning of the item "Amortization of goodwill"? What questions does it raise for an analyst or an investor?

2 What is the meaning of the line item "Share in net results of equity investees"?

3 What is the meaning of the line item "Minority interest in consolidated companies"?

4 What is the real meaning of the item "Net income"? How useful is this item for an analyst or an investor?

Assignment 13.4 Honda*, Miba*, and Ares-Serono*

Topic: Reporting for minority interests
Type: Group exercise
Related part of the chapter: Core Issues

The following are excerpts of the equity and liabilities section of the balance sheet (with notes when applicable) of three companies.

Honda Motor Co. (Japan – US GAAP – *Source*: Annual report 2000 – Manufacturer of automotive vehicles, motorcycles, and light farming equipment)

Yen (millions) – 31 March 1999 and 2000	1999	2000
Liabilities and stockholders' equity		
Current liabilities	2,265,196	2,202,311
Long-term debt	673,084	574,566
Other liabilities (see note 8)	332,112	191,178
Total liabilities	3,270,392	2,968,055
Stockholders' equity	1,763,855	1,930,373
	5,034,247	4,898,428

Notes to consolidated financial statements		
Note (8) Other liabilities		
Yen (millions) – 31 March 1999 and 2000	1999	2000
(…)		
Minority interest	25,186	30,278
(…)		

Miba (Austria – Austrian GAAP – *Source*: Annual report 1998/99 – Supplier to the motor and automotive industry)

Consolidated balance sheet (extracts)		
Austrian shillings (thousands)	**As of 31.1.1999**	**As of 31.1.1998**
Equity		
Capital stock	130,000	130,000
Capital reserves	248,904	248,604
Revenue reserves	458,409	393,105
Minority stockholders' interest	882	2,008
Net profit	37,283	29,439
	875,478	803,156

Ares-Serono (Switzerland – IAS GAAP – *Source*: Annual report 1999 – Biotechnology)

Consolidated balance sheet (extracts)		
US$ (000)	**1999**	**1998**
Liabilities		
Current liabilities	507,364	476,626
Long-term liabilities	256,575	297,594
Total liabilities	763,939	774,220
Minority interests	574	621
Shareholders' equity	836,188	771,060
Total liabilities, minority interests, and shareholders' equity	1,600,701	1,545,901

Required

1 Compare and contrast the way minority interests are reported in the three companies.

2 Suggest a coherent set of arguments that support the solution that has been adopted by each firm. How robust is your set of arguments? In other words, what hypotheses could be challenged that might change the outcome in terms of reporting the minority interests?

Assignment 13.5 LVMH* and others

Topic: Accounting policy for goodwill and intangibles
Type: Group case study
Related part of the chapter: Core Issues

Excerpts from annual reports of six very different companies are provided in the following exhibit. They are:

- LVMH
- Cap Gemini Sogeti
- Allied-Lyons
- Rank Hovis McDougall (RHM)
- Seita
- Seb

Required

Analyzing the data provided in the exhibit below, identify the accounting policies followed by each company relating to:

- the analysis of the difference arising on first consolidation
- the treatment of goodwill and other intangibles.

Comments:

- The annual reports provided relate to different time periods (some of the reports are quite old). The choice here is deliberate as the years selected correspond to periods during which each firm made a significant accounting policy choice. The historical perspective also illustrates the diversity of practices that IAS 38 attempts to limit.

- Some of the excerpted paragraphs may refer to other sections of the annual report that are not provided here. If the information is not provided, it is because we felt it was not relevant. However all elements pertaining to goodwill and intangible assets that were in the annual report have been provided.

- Except where specifically mentioned, all data are extracted from the official English-language version of the annual report established by the firm itself and released to the public. Texts have not been edited for content or style.

- The reader is encouraged to refresh her or his knowledge by revisiting Chapter 8 in connection with this assignment.

Exhibit

LVMH (France – IAS/French GAAP – *Source*: Annual report 1990 – Luxury products)

Consolidated balance sheet (excerpts)			
Assets (in millions of French francs)	Notes	31 December 1990	31 December 1989
Investments and other assets			
Cost in excess of net assets of acquired businesses (minus amortization of 288; 1989: 1,880)	9	4,222	2,178
Brands and other intangible assets (less amortization of 108; 1989: 333)	10	1,781	1,622

Notes to the consolidated financial statements (excerpts)

1. ACCOUNTING POLICIES

1.1 General

The consolidated financial statements are prepared in compliance with the French law of 3 January 1985 and in accordance with IAS (International Accounting Standards).

1.4 Brands and other intangible assets

Brands very often represent the most significant component of costs in excess of tangible net assets acquired in connection with the company's investments and acquisitions. Only brands which are very well known and established, individually identifiable and for which it is possible to verify their utility are assigned values in the company's financial statements. Brands are stated at cost, valued by reference to their contribution to the earnings of the related activity acquired.

Prior to 1990, the company's policy was to amortize costs assigned to brands on a straight-line basis over their estimated useful lives, limited to 40 years (the maximum period accepted under US GAAP). The majority of French and European companies do not amortize costs assigned to legally protected brands. As such, beginning 1 January 1990, LVMH changed its policy to conform with this practice. Provision for depreciation will be recorded only in those instances where a permanent impairment of value, using the same criteria established at the date of acquisition, arises. The impact of this change in accounting principle is discussed further in Note 2 to these financial statements.

Other intangible assets are stated at cost and are amortized on a straight-line basis over their estimated useful lives, not exceeding 40 years.

1.5 Cost in excess of net assets of acquired businesses

Cost in excess of net assets of acquired businesses represent the difference between the purchase price of acquired businesses, net of specific amount assigned to assets and liabilities, and the fair value of the group's share of their underlying net assets at the date of acquisition. Amortization is computed using the straight-line method over periods not exceeding 40 years. The amortization charge is included under the heading "Administrative expenses" where related to consolidated companies and under the heading "Equity in net income (losses) of associated companies" where related to equity accounting for companies.

1.9 Research and development costs

Research and development costs are expensed in the year they are incurred.

2 IMPACT OF CHANGE IN ACCOUNTING PRINCIPLE RELATING TO THE AMORTIZATION OF COSTS ASSIGNED TO BRANDS

In an effort to conform to accepted practices used by the majority of other French and European companies, LVMH changed its policy with respect to the amortization of costs assigned to brands beginning in 1990. The impact of the company's decision to discontinue amortization of such costs is detailed as follows.

In millions of French francs, except per share amounts	1990	1989 (restated)	1989
Income from operations	5,672	5,711	5,671
Income before income taxes	5,039	4,996	4,956
Equity in net income of associated companies	792	517	428
Net income	3,375	3,061	2,932
Earnings per share	254.69	239.47	229.41
Fully diluted earnings per share	248.57	227.19	217.76

Brand amortization for the year ended 31 December 1989 is summarized as follows, in million of French francs:

Relating to income from operations	40
Relating to equity in net income of associated companies taxes	89
Net income	129

3 INCREASE IN INVESTMENT IN GUINNESS PLC

During June 1990, LVMH increased its investment in the outstanding share capital of Guinness PLC from 12.09% to 23.46%. The cost of this additional investment totaled 8,174 millions of FF. The cost of this additional investment exceeded LVMH's proportionate share of Guinness' net assets by 5,067 M of FF. On this excess, 2,918 M of FF was allocated to the leading brands of the Guinness Group (beers: Guinness, Harp, Smithwicks..., whiskies: Johnnie Walker, Bells, Dewars...; gins and vodkas: Gordon's, Tanqueray). The remaining cost in excess of LVMH's share of net assets acquired, net of specific amounts assigned to other assets and liabilities totaled 2,094 M of FF, and is being amortized on a straight-line basis and over 40 years.

9 COST IN EXCESS OF NET ASSETS OF ACQUIRED BUSINESSES

In millions of French francs	1990		1989	
	Gross	Amortization	Gross	Amortization
Guinness Group (note 3)	2,094	26	—	—
Veuve Clicquot Group	1,912	191	1,912	143
Other	504	71	465	56
	4,510	288	2,377	199

10 BRANDS AND OTHER INTANGIBLE ASSETS

In millions of French francs	1990		1989	
	Gross	Accumulated Amortization	Gross	Accumulated Amortization
Brands	1,648	12	1,792	279
Patented and proprietary products	19	15	17	13
Leasehold rights	112	35	98	25
Other	110	46	48	16
	1,889	108	1,955	333

Following a change in the Company's accounting principles, beginning 1 January 1990, LVMH no longer systematically amortizes costs assigned to brands. Unamortized costs remaining at 31 December 1989 have been reflected at their net values in the 1 January 1990 opening balance sheet. A provision for depreciation has been recorded in those instances where an impairment of value relating to specific brands has been identified.

CAP GEMINI SOGETI (France – IAS/French GAAP – *Source*: Annual report 1994 – Software and information technology)

Consolidated balance sheet as of 31 December 1993 and 1994 (excerpts)		
Assets (in thousands of French francs)	**1993**	**1994**
Non-current assets		
Intangible assets (note III)	7,183,569	6,881,245

Notes to the 1994 consolidated financial statements (excerpts)

I ACCOUNTING POLICIES

The consolidated financial statements have been prepared in accordance with current statements of accounting practices issued by the International Accounting Standards Committee (IASC) and with the French law on consolidated accounts.

4 Market share

When the acquisition of companies allows the group to obtain a significant share of a specific market, the excess of purchase cost over the fair value of assets acquired is allocated to the market share acquired.

Such market share is valued at the date of acquisition in relation to objective economic data with reference to activity and profitability indicators.

In view of its nature, acquired market share is not amortized. However, at each accounting date it is revalued in accordance with the same criteria used as of the date of acquisition and a provision is set up if there is a diminution in value.

5 Goodwill

Goodwill, consisting of the excess of cost over the group's equity in the fair value of the underlying net assets at the date of acquisition of companies consolidated or accounted for by the equity method, after allocation of purchase cost to identified tangible or intangible assets such as market share, is amortized on a straight-line basis over a maximum period of 40 years.

III INTANGIBLE ASSETS

As of 31 December (in thousands of French francs)	1993	1994
Market share	3,805,957	3,726,419
Goodwill	3,782,583	3,690,854
Software and user rights	225,615	134,370
Gross	7,814,155	7,551,643
Accumulated amortization	(630,856)	(670,398)
Intangible assets, net	7,183,299	6,881,245

1 Market share

As of 31 December (in thousands of French francs)	1993	1994
Hoskyns	2,224,606	2,127,020
Cap Volmac	1,178,434	1,192,790
Cap Programator	402,917	406,609
Total	3,805,957	3,726,419

Market share is valued according to the method described in note I.4 and represents part of the excess of purchase cost over the fair value of the net assets of Hoskyns, Programator and Volmac as of the date of acquisition. The changes in market share value are due to fluctuations in exchange rates (note XXV).

2 Goodwill

As of 31 December (in thousands of French francs)	1993	1994
Fully consolidated subsidiaries	2,937,611	2,896,296
Proportionally consolidated subsidiaries	716,772	31,644
Investments accounted for by the equity method	128,200	762,914
Gross	3,782,583	3,690,854
Accumulated amortization	(519,937)	(591,493)
Goodwill, net	3,262,646	3,099,361

Goodwill is almost completely amortized over a period of 40 years.

The change in the gross value of goodwill on full consolidated subsidiaries is primarily attributable to fluctuations in the exchange rates used to translate goodwill on foreign subsidiaries. Translation adjustments had a negative impact of FF 43,027 thousand as of 31 December 1994 and FF 9,686 thousand as of 31 December 1993.

Changes in the gross value of goodwill on proportionally consolidated subsidiaries and investments accounted for by the equity method arise from the mergers carried out in Germany (note II.2).

ALLIED-LYONS (UK – UK GAAP – *Source*: Annual report 1994 – Brewery)

In the balance sheet, no indication of intangible assets.

Group reconciliation of movements in shareholders' equity 52 weeks ended 3 March 1994		
	1994 £m	1993 £m
(...)		
Goodwill written back on disposals	21	6
Goodwill and intangibles written off	(196)	(156)
(...)		

RANK HOVIS MCDOUGALL (UK – UK GAAP – *Source*: Annual report 1988 – Flour miller)

Consolidated balance sheets at 3 September 1988 (pounds in millions) (excerpts)			
	Notes	1988	1987
Fixed assets			
Intangible assets	12	678.0	0

Accounting policies

Basis of accounting and consolidation. The accounts have been prepared under the historical cost convention (...) and in compliance with the provisions of the Companies Act.

Intangible assets. Until the end of the current financial year intangible assets (including brands) have been written off to reserves. With effect from 3 September 1988, brands, both acquired and created within the group, are included at their "current cost". Such cost, which will not be subject to amortization, will be reviewed each year. The accounting treatment of additions to goodwill is considered, as previously, on an individual basis and elimination against reserves has been selected as appropriate for the current year. The prior year figures, including reserves, have not been restated because of the impracticality of establishing a meaningful cost of all brands previously acquired; the group results of the previous year are unaffected. An amount has been transferred from revaluation reserve in respect of the estimated cost of brands acquired in the last six years.

12 Intangible assets (in £ millions)

	The group 1988	The company 1988
Brands		
At 5 September 1987	—	
Valuation at 3 September 1988	678.0	
At 3 September 1988	678.0	

The group has valued its brands at their "current use value to the group" at 3 September 1988 in conjunction with Interbrand Group Plc branding consultants.

The basis of valuation ignores any possible alternative use of a brand, any possible extension to the range of products currently marketed under a brand, any element of hope value and any possible increase of value of a brand due to either a special investment or a financial transaction (e.g., licensing, which would leave the group with a different interest from the one being valued).

SEB (France – US/French GAAP – *Source*: Annual report 1993 – Small domestic appliances)

Consolidated balance sheets (excerpts) (as of 31 December in thousands of French francs)			
Assets	Notes	1993	1992
Fixed assets			
Intangible assets	6	533,003	552,945

Notes to the consolidated financial statements (excerpts)
(all figures in thousands of French francs, as of 31 December)

Note 1 – Accounting principles

The consolidated financial statements, prepared in accordance with the French Consolidation Act, are in conformity with the accounting principles generally accepted in the United States of America.

1.3 Accounting principles and valuation methods

a) Intangible assets

Trademarks, licenses, patents, and lease rights are booked at acquisition cost and are amortized on a straight-line basis over the shorter of the duration of legal protection or the period of use, with a maximum of 40 years for the trademarks and of 20 years for licenses, patents, and lease rights.

The goodwill is the excess of the cost of the acquired enterprise over the sum of the amounts assigned at acquisition to identifiable assets, less liabilities assumed. It is amortized on a straight-line basis over the estimated useful life, with a maximum of 40 years.

Note 6 – Intangible assets

	1993	1992
Rowenta trademark	251,265	252,122
Other trademarks and licenses	69,946	67,706
Goodwill	370,642	370,174
Other intangible assets	249	157
	692,102	**690,159**
Amortization	(159,099)	(137,214)
	533,003	**552,945**

The Rowenta trademark is amortized over 40 years, and goodwill is amortized over 33 years. This amortization expense is not tax deductible.

SEITA (France – French GAAP – *Source*: Annual report 1993 – Tobacco products)

Consolidated balance sheets at 31 December (excerpts) (in millions of French francs; all amounts are net of amortization or depreciation)		
Assets	**1993**	**1992**
Goodwill	48.0	77.7
Intangible assets	85.3	41.0

These figures are taken from the French version of the annual report. In the English version, they are grouped under one line "Intangible assets".

Notes to the consolidated financial statements (excerpts)

SUMMARY OF SIGNIFICANT ACCOUNTING POLICIES

The consolidated financial statements have been prepared in accordance with French generally accepted accounting principles.

Intangible fixed assets …

Research and development expenses are charged against income as incurred.

Depreciation is charged by the straight-line method over the following estimated useful lives:

Intangible assets: 3 to 5 years

Goodwill is generally amortized over periods not exceeding 20 years.

Goodwill

	in millions French francs		
	Gross	Amortization	Net
At 1 January 1993	118.2	(40.5)	77.7
Movement for the year	—	(29.7)	(29.7)
At 31 December 1993	118.2	(70.2)	48.0

This goodwill is being amortized over 10 years. Goodwill arising on the acquisition of Coralma was written down by an additional FF 20 million in 1993, to take account of the potential decline in the group's earnings following the devaluation of the CFA franc.

Brands acquired by the MKI group have been assimilated to goodwill and amortized. Due to the evolution of sales, the remaining amortization period has been shortened from 9 to 5 years in MKF and from 9 to 7 years in MKS [data taken from the French version of the annual report, as they were not inserted in the English version].

Assignment 13.6 Bosmans and Badings

Topic: Legal merger
Type: Individual/group exercise
Related part of the chapter: Advanced Issues

Bosmans Company merges with the Badings Company which will be dissolved after the merger. The balance sheet of each company is provided here (in 000 of CU).

Balance sheets of the merging companies		
Assets	Bosmans	Badings
Fixed assets	700	500
Inventories	600	400
Receivables and cash	150	200
Total	1,450	1,100
Equity and liabilities	Bosmans	Badings
Capital	400	600
Reserves	500	280
Liabilities	550	220
Total	1,450	1,100
Number of shares	4,000	6,000
Par value	100	100

You are informed that, for some assets of Badings Company, the fair value is different from the book value, as indicated in the following table.

Assets (excerpts)	Book value	Fair value
Fixed assets	500	560
Inventories	400	390
Receivables and cash	200	170

Required

1 Prepare, step by step, the balance sheet of Bosmans after its merger with (absorption of) Badings under the following two sets of hypotheses:
- The net assets of Badings are integrated at fair value.
- The net assets of Badings are integrated at book value.

2 Discuss the pros and cons of each method, using the data of the Bosmans–Badings merger.

References

Alexander, D., and Britton, A. (2001) *Financial Reporting*, 6th edn, Thomson Learning, London.

Bine, P., and Péricard, A. (2000) Vers la suppression du "pooling of interests" aux Etats-Unis. *Les Echos*, 29 February, 71.

EU (European Union) (1978) 4th Directive on the annual accounts of certain types of companies no. 78/660/EEC. *Official Journal of the European Communities*, 14 August.

EU (European Union) (1983) 7th Directive on consolidated accounts of companies no. 83/349/EEC. *Official Journal of the European Communities*, 18 July.

FASB (1981) Statement of Financial Accounting Standard No. 52, Foreign Currency Translation, Norwalk, CT.

FASB (2001a) Statement of Financial Accounting Standards No. 141, Business Combinations, Norwalk, CT.

FASB (2001b) Statement of Financial Accounting Standards No. 142, Goodwill and Other Intangible Assets, Norwalk, CT.

Fischer, P.M., Taylor, W.J., and Cheng, R.H. (1999) *Advanced Accounting*, 7th edn, South-Western College Publishing, Cincinnati, OH.

IASC (revised 1993) International Accounting Standard No. 21, The Effects of Changes in Foreign Exchange Rates, London.

IASC (reformatted 1994a) International Accounting Standard No. 25, Accounting for Investments, London.

IASC (reformatted 1994b) International Accounting Standard No. 27, Consolidated Financial Statements and Accounting for Investments in Subsidiaries, London.

IASC (revised 1998a) International Accounting Standard No. 22, Business Combinations, London.

IASC (revised 1998b) International Accounting Standard No. 28, Accounting for Investments in Associates, London.

IASC (revised 1998c) International Accounting Standard No. 31, Financial Reporting of Interests in Joint Ventures, London.

PricewaterhouseCoopers (PwC) (1999) *Student's Manual of Accounting*, ITBP, London.

Skousen, F., Stice, J., and Stice, E.K. (2001) *Intermediate Accounting*, South-Western College Publishing, Cincinatti, OH.

Further readings

Feige, P. (1997) How "uniform" is financial reporting in Germany? – The example of foreign currency translation. *European Accounting Review*, 6(1), 109–122.

Higson, C. (1998) Goodwill. *British Accounting Review*, 30(2), 141–58.

Johnson, L.T., and Petrone, K.R. (1998) Is goodwill an asset? *Accounting Horizons*, 12(3), September, 293–303.

Lamb, M. (1995) When is a group a group? Convergence of concepts of "group" in European Union corporation tax. *European Accounting Review*, 4(1), 33–78.

Mora, A. and Rees, W. (1998) The early adoption of consolidated accounting in Spain. *European Accounting Review*, 7(4), 675–96.

Additional material on the website

Go to http://www.thomsonlearning.co.uk/accountingandfinance/stolowylebas for further information, journal entries and extra assignments for each chapter.

The following appendices to this chapter are available on the dedicated website:

Appendix 13.1: Value adjustment to lower of cost or market
Appendix 13.2: Deferred taxation on consolidation
Appendix 13.3: Foreign currency translations
Appendix 13.4: Uniting of interests and the pooling of interests method

Note

1   See, for example, Alexander and Britton (2001) and PwC (1999).

Financial statement analysis

Cash flow statement

Neither balance sheet nor income statement provides a dynamic view of the evolution of the financial structure of a business, i.e., the changes in structure in general, and changes in the cash position in particular. Yet understanding such evolution over a period of time is of interest to both the company's management and external financial analysts. As IAS 7 puts it (IASC 1992: § 3): "Users of an enterprise's financial statements are interested in how the enterprise generates and uses cash and cash equivalents. This is the case regardless of the nature of the enterprise's activities and irrespective of whether cash can be viewed as the product of the enterprise, as may be the case with a financial institution. Enterprises need cash for essentially the same reasons, however different their principal revenue-producing activities might be. They need cash to conduct their operations, to pay their obligations, and to provide returns to their investors."

The cash flow statement or statement of cash flows was developed to meet these informational needs. A rudimentary cash flow statement was presented in Chapter 3, showing how it related to both balance sheet and income statement. In this chapter the Core Issues develop the model of cash flow statement adopted by the IASC and many countries. The Advanced Issues look at differences in classification of certain cash flows and at a model called the statement of changes in financial position, which is still used in several countries.

Major topics

Structure

Benefits

Content

Operating cash flow

Cash and cash equivalents

Preparation

Reporting

Other models

Financial statement analysis

According to IAS 7 (IASC 1992: § 1): "An enterprise should prepare a cash flow statement (...) as an integral part of its financial statements for each period for which financial statements are presented." In some countries (the USA and the UK, for instance) publishing a cash flow statement is compulsory, whereas in others (France and Italy, for instance), it is optional. In practice, most major listed companies include a cash flow statement in their annual report.

Structure of the cash flow statement

One of the objectives of a cash flow statement is, by definition, to provide information on the transactions which affect the cash position. The cash flow statement reports cash generated or provided and used during a given period. It classifies cash flows in three categories of activities: operating, investing, and financing, as shown in Table 14.1.

Table 14.1 Cash flow statement structure

Net cash provided by/used in **operating** activities	A
Net cash provided by/used in **investing** activities	B
Net cash provided by/used in **financing** activities	C
Net increase/(decrease) in **cash and cash equivalents**	D = A + B + C
Cash and cash equivalents at beginning of year	E
Cash and cash equivalents at end of year	F = D + E

This classification by activity, as mentioned in IAS 7 (IASC 1992: § 11): "Provides information that allows users to assess the impact of those activities on the financial position of the enterprise and the amount of its cash and cash equivalents. This information may also be used to evaluate the relationships among those activities."

Usefulness of the cash flow statement

"A cash flow statement, when used in conjunction with the rest of the financial statements, provides information that enables users to evaluate the changes in net assets of an enterprise, its financial structure (including its liquidity and solvency) and its ability to affect the amounts and timing of cash flows in order to adapt to changing circumstances and opportunities" (IAS 7: § 4). The cash flow statement is a useful statement in its own right, explaining the changes in cash, just as the income statement explains the components of net income.

The importance of cash

IAS 7 (IASC 1992: § 4) stresses the fact that "cash flow information is useful in assessing the ability of the enterprise to generate cash and cash equivalents and to finance investments". The cash position is a key indicator for management and financial analysis, both in the short-(assessing solvency) and the long-term (measuring financing requirements). The importance of the cash position, in both absolute and relative terms, and its sign (positive or negative) may reveal the company's situation: financially healthy, vulnerable, struggling, etc. Many researchers have demonstrated that cash is a valuable indicator in forecasting business difficulties and possible bankruptcy.

Cash is objective

Cash flow statements enhance the comparability of reported operating performance by different enterprises because they eliminate the effects of using different accounting treatments for the same transactions and events.

A valuable forecasting tool

The cash flow statement is well suited for both retrospective analysis and forecasting. It enables users to assess and compare the present value of future cash flows of different enterprises. It can also be used as part of a business plan and in the preparation of budgets.

Developments in international practice

There is currently a clear movement towards the adoption of a relatively uniform cash flow statement format, replacing a variety of previously used statements such as the funds flow statement, or statement of changes in financial position, which are discussed later in the chapter. Table 14.2 lists the countries which allow or have adopted the publication of a cash flow statement as part of the annual report (other possible models may coexist in any given country). Many companies in countries where the standards do not require a cash flow statement still publish one if they apply international accounting standards in their annual report or if they are quoted on a major stock exchange.

Table 14.2 Countries allowing or requiring a cash flow statement

Date of adoption	Date of revision	Country	Reference of the standard	Title of the document (translated in English)
1985	1998	Canada	Section 1540 of the CICA handbook	Cash flow statements
1987	*	USA	SFAS 95	Statement of cash flows
1987	1989	New Zealand	SSAP 10	Statement of cash flows
1988	—	South Africa	AC 118	Cash flow information
1988	1997	France	Recommendation 1.22 superseded by Opinion 30	Statement of cash flows
1991	1996	UK/Ireland	FRS 1	Cash flow statements
1992	—	IASC	IAS 7	Cash flow statements
1997	—	Australia	AASB 1026	Statement of cash flows
1999	—	Germany	GAS 2	Cash flow statements

*Standard affected by several subsequent standards

Clear partitioning of the cash flow statement between the various "activities" creating or consuming cash (operating, investing and financing) is vital. Each activity is defined by IAS 7 and we will follow that position. These definitions are used in international accounting practice and are coherent with the principal national standards regarding cash flow statements (SFAS 95 in the USA, FRS 1 in the UK, Opinion 30 in France, etc.).

The classification of certain operations is sometimes difficult. For example, deciding where financial expenses should be classified has been hotly debated as it impacts on the very philosophy of what a business does. In addition, a single transaction may include cash flows components that belong to two or more distinct categories. For example, the monthly or quarterly cash repayment of an installment loan generally includes both an interest component and a partial reimbursement of the capital or principal. The interest element is generally classified as an operating activity while the reimbursement of the principal is classified as a financing activity.

Operating activities

Cash flows from operating activities are primarily derived from the main or core revenue-producing activities of the enterprise. They generally result from the transactions and other events that enter into the determination of net profit or loss. The amount of cash flows from operating activities is a key indicator of the extent to which the operations of the enterprise have generated sufficient cash flows to keep it afloat. That implies the ability to maintain the operating capability of the enterprise, repay loans, pay dividends without recourse to external sources of financing and, possibly make new investments for the development of the firm.

Examples of cash flows from operating activities, as given in IAS 7 (§ 14) are provided in Table 14.3 and in Appendix 14.1. Some transactions, such as the sale of a fixed asset, may give rise to a gain or loss which is included in the determination of net profit or loss. However, the cash flows relating to such transactions will be included in cash flows from investing activities. A later section is dedicated to the methods and approaches to calculating operating cash flows.

Investing activities

The separate disclosure of cash flows arising from investing activities is important because these cash flows represent the extent to which expenditures have been made for resources intended to generate future income and cash flows (see examples of investing cash flow in Table 14.3 and Appendix 14.1).

Financing activities

The separate disclosure of cash flows arising from financing activities is important because it is useful in predicting claims on future cash flows by providers of capital to the enterprise. It also helps understand how much of the cash available in a business comes from influxes of "fresh capital" by shareholders or financial partners of the firm (see examples of financing cash flows in Table 14.3 and Appendix 14.1).

Calculating cash flows from operating activities

There are two ways of determining cash flows from operating activities: the *direct method* and the *indirect method*.

The *direct method* calculates the cash flows by grouping cash effects of transactions classes. In other words, it presents receipt and payment flows separately for each category of operating activities: selling, purchasing, securing employees labor, etc. In practice, there are two sub-categories of the direct method:

- a "semi-direct" method, where accounting flows (sales, purchases, labor costs, etc.) are adjusted for changes in inventories and operating or trade receivables and payables to give cash flows of the period, for instance, cash received from customers equals "sales" minus "changes in accounts receivable"
- a "true" direct method, where cash flows are entered directly into the cash flow statement from the accounting records of cash movements in the "cash at bank" account.

The *indirect method* calculates the net cash flow from operating activities by adjusting net profit or loss for the effects of:

- changes during the period in inventories and operating receivables and payables
- non-cash items such as depreciation, provisions, deferred taxes (see Chapter 6), unrealized foreign currency gains and losses, undistributed profits of associates, and minority interests (see Chapter 13)
- all other items for which the cash effects are investing or financing cash flows. For instance, the gain or loss from sale of fixed assets is adjusted because it will be included in the investing activities (see later).

Figure 14.1 summarizes these methods.

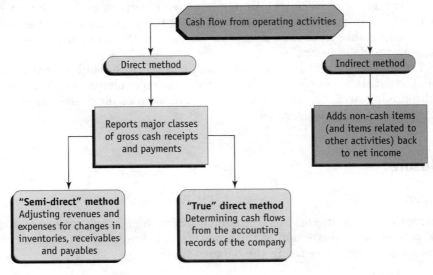

Figure 14.1 Reporting cash flows from operating activities

Most standards (IAS 7, SFAS 95 in the USA, FRS 1 in the UK, etc.) recommend the direct method while allowing the indirect method. Although the direct method provides information which may be useful in estimating future cash flows and which is not available under the indirect method, it is, however, difficult to implement and may also be seen by managers as too revealing of the actual operations of their firm. The "semi-direct" method is also relatively complex. Thus the vast majority of businesses – in fact almost all of them – report cash flows from operating activities using the indirect method, which is much simpler. Unfortunately, the information thus provided by the cash flow statement is also much less valuable as a result.

Cash and cash equivalents

Definitions

According to IAS 7 (IASC 1992: § 6): "Cash comprises cash on hand and demand deposits. Cash equivalents are short-term, highly liquid investments that are readily convertible to known amounts of cash and which are subject to an insignificant risk of changes in value." An investment normally qualifies as a cash equivalent only when it has a short maturity of, say, 3 months or less from the date of acquisition. Equity investments are excluded from cash equivalents unless they are, in substance, cash equivalents, for example in the case of preferred shares acquired within a short period of their maturity with a specified redemption date.

Bank borrowings are generally considered to be financing activities. However, the treatment of bank overdrafts is a matter of debate. For instance, in some countries, such as Germany, France, and the UK, bank overdrafts, which are repayable on demand, form an integral part of an enterprise's cash management approach. The inclusion of bank overdrafts in cash equivalents is not without its critics. The separation of short-term credits and other debts makes it impossible to explain the total change in debt and to measure the leverage on the debt accurately.

IAS 7 considers that in the circumstances just described, bank overdrafts are included as a negative component of cash and cash equivalents. A characteristic of such banking arrangements is that the bank balance often fluctuates from being positive to being overdrawn.

Disclosure

Principles

An enterprise should disclose the components of cash and cash equivalents and should present a reconciliation of the amounts in its cash flow statement with the equivalent items reported in the balance sheet.

The Vermont Teddy Bear Co., Inc.

(USA – US GAAP – Source: Annual report 1999 – Designer, manufacturer and direct marketer of teddy bears and related products)

Notes to the financial statements – 30 June, 1999

Cash and cash equivalents

All highly liquid investments with initial maturities of three months or less are considered cash equivalents. At 30 June 1999 and 1998, approximately $363,000 and $361,000 of the company's cash was restricted, respectively. The largest component of the restricted cash is $300,000 restricted by a debt service reserve, which was required as part of the company's loan agreement with the Vermont National Bank and was required to be maintained as part of the company's sale-leaseback transaction.

The first sentence of this note is standard and can be found in many annual reports. The remainder, however, is more interesting because it describes the company's specific circumstances. (Leaseback operations are discussed in Chapter 12.)

Stora Enso

(Finland – IAS GAAP – Source: Annual report 1999 – Production of paper)

Notes to the financial statements – 31 December 1999

Cash and cash equivalents

For the purpose of the cash flow statement, cash and cash equivalents comprise cash in hand, deposits held at call with banks, and investments in money market instruments, net of bank overdrafts. In the balance sheet, bank overdrafts are included in borrowings in current liabilities.

Interestingly, the company supplies a breakdown of "cash and cash equivalents" at the bottom of the cash flow statement:

Consolidated cash flow statement		
€ mill.	**1999**	**1998**
(...)		
Cash and cash equivalents at end of period	642.2	348.6
Cash and cash equivalents include:		
Bonds and shares	122.8	
Short term deposits	80.0	
Cash in hand and at banks	439.4	348.6
	642.2	348.6

Furthermore, the company states that bank overdrafts are treated as short-term debts (current liabilities).

Sulzer
(Switzerland – IAS GAAP – Source: Annual report 1999 – Medical equipment)

Corporate accounting principles

Cash

Cash comprises bills, postal giro and bank accounts, together with deposit balances. These include fixed deposits and money market paper with maturities of under 3 months.

Example of a cash flow statement

Table 14.3 summarizes the contents of each cash-related activity. As will be seen later in this chapter, the classification of certain items is subject to debate. Our table reflects current standard practice.

Table 14.3 Classification of cash flows

Activities	Cash inflows (receipts)	Cash outflows (payments)
Operating activities	Sale of goods and rendering of services to customers Royalties, fees, commissions and other revenue Interests on loans and investments	Purchase of goods and services Salaries and social expenses Taxes Interests on borrowings
Investing activities	Sale of fixed assets (intangible, tangible, financial – securities which are not cash equivalents) Receipt of repayment of loans and advances	Purchase of fixed assets (intangible, tangible, financial – securities which are not cash equivalents) Loans and advances made
Financing activities	Proceeds from issuing shares Proceeds from issuing debts	Repayment of shares Repayment of debts Payment of dividends

Table 14.4 presents an example of a generic cash flow statement template reflecting the most common practices. The third column in Table 14.4 is presented for pedagogical reasons only to show the source of information for each line.

Table 14.4 shows, for pedagogical purposes, both the direct and the indirect method for the cash flow from operating activities. Of course, in practice, only one of these methods is applied in any cash flow statement.

Table 14.4 Example of a cash flow statement

		Source of the information
Cash flow from operating activities (indirect method)		
Net income/loss	±	IS
Adjustments to reconcile net income/loss to net cash provided by/used in operating activities		
Depreciation and amortization (excluding changes in current assets – inventories and accounts receivable)	+	IS
Gain/loss on sale of fixed assets	±	IS
Changes in operating assets and liabilities		
Change in accounts receivable (net amount)	±	BS
Change in inventories (net amount)	±	BS
Change in prepaid expenses	±	BS
Change in accounts payable and accrued expenses	±	BS
Net cash provided by/used in operating activities = (A)	=	
Cash flow from operating activities (direct method)		
Cash received from customers	+	IS/BS
Cash paid to suppliers*	–	IS/BS
Cash paid to employees*	–	IS/BS
Cash dividend received	+	IS/BS
Other operating cash receipts	+	IS/BS
Other operating cash payments	–	IS/BS
Interest paid in cash	–	IS/BS
Income taxes paid in cash	–	IS/BS
Net cash provided by/used in operating activities = (A)	=	
Cash flows from investing activities		
Purchase of fixed assets	–	BS/AI
Proceeds from sale of fixed assets	+	IS/AI
Loans granted	–	BS/AI
Repayment of loans	+	BS/AI
Net cash provided by/used in investing activities = (B)	=	
Cash flows from financing activities		
Proceeds from issuance of long-term debt	+	BS/AI
Proceeds from issuance of shares	+	BS/AI
Dividends paid	–	BS/AI
Payment on long-term debt	–	BS/AI
Payment on reduction of share capital (repayment of shares)	–	BS/AI
Net cash provided by/used in financing activities = (C)	=	
Net increase in cash and cash equivalents = (A) + (B) + (C) = (D)	=	
Cash and cash equivalents at beginning of year = (E)		
Cash and cash equivalents at end of year = (F) = (E) + (D)		

IS: Income statement
BS: Balance sheet
AI: Additional information
*These 2 lines are often merged

Preparation of a cash flow statement

Tables 14.5 and 14.6, pertaining to the published statements of the Liszt Company, a retail and wholesale commercial business, provide the raw material for the construction of a cash flow statement.

Table 14.5 Liszt Company – Comparative balance sheets before appropriation – Years ended 31 December 20X2 and 20X1

000 CU	20X2	20X1	Changes (X2 – X1)
Assets			
Fixed assets			
Tangible assets			
Equipment	615	460	155
Accumulated depreciation	–116	–70	–46
Equipment (net)	499	390	109
Loans	115	174	–59
Total fixed assets	614	564	50
Current assets			
Inventory	144	100	44
Accounts receivable	44	63	–19
Cash	25	15	10
Prepaid expenses*	4	7	–3
Total current assets	217	185	32
Total assets	831	749	82
Shareholders' equity and liabilities			
Shareholders' equity			
Share capital	282	200	82
Share premium	198	115	83
Reserves	124	122	2
Net income	9	10	–1
Total shareholders' equity	613	447	166
Liabilities			
Long-term liabilities (bonds)	155	245	–90
Current liabilities			
Accounts payable	62	54	8
Income taxes payable	1	3	–2
Total current liabilities	63	57	6
Total liabilities	218	302	–84
Total shareholders' equity and liabilities	831	749	82

*Related to "Other operating expenses"

Table 14.6 Liszt company – Income statement – Year 20X2

000 CU	
Sales	800
Cost of goods sold	–570
Gross profit	230
Depreciation expense	–60
Other operating expenses	–162
Operating profit	8
Interest expense	–15
Investment income	18
Gain on sale of equipment	3
Profit before taxes	14
Income taxes	–5
Net profit	9

Additional events took place during the year that are relevant for the preparation of the cash flow statement for the year 20X2:

● Equipment was purchased for 175.

● Equipment with an original cost of 20 and accumulated depreciation of 14 was sold for 9.

● No new loan was either granted or obtained.

● 135 CU were raised from the issue of shares in cash (share capital of 66 plus share premium of 69).

● Bonds were converted into capital for 30 (share capital for 16 and share premium for 14).

● Bonds were repaid at face (nominal) value at maturity for 60.

● Dividends (relating to net income of 20X1) were paid in cash for 8.

Cash flows from operating activities

The direct method and the indirect method will be used successively.

Direct method

We use the "semi-direct" method described earlier, where income statement items are adjusted for changes in inventories and operating receivables and payables to give cash flows[1]. This, in effect, transforms a fund flow (a transaction), calculated on an accrual basis (income statement item), into a cash flow. This calculation can be systematized into the equation shown as Figure 14.2.

● One difficulty is the correct association of related income statement and balance sheet items for inventories, receivables and payables.

● Changes in balance sheet items have been calculated by a simplified method: Year 2 minus Year 1. However, assets and liabilities have different impacts, as shown in the following:

	Change (ending minus beginning)	Impact on cash
Assets	increase decrease	− +
Liabilities	increase decrease	+ −

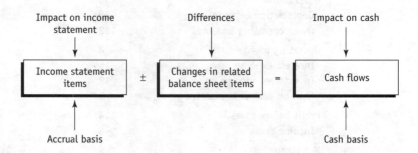

Figure 14.2 Determination of cash flows using the semi-direct method

The components of the generic equation of Figure 14.2 can thus be shown as follows:

$$\text{Income statement items} \left\{ \begin{array}{l} - \text{ Increase in related receivables} \\ + \text{ Decrease in related receivables} \\ + \text{ Increase in related liabilities} \\ - \text{ Decrease in related liabilities} \end{array} \right\} = \text{Cash flow}$$

The way this equation works is illustrated with the calculation of each component of the cash flow.

Cash received from customers

Income statement items	±	Change in related balance sheet items	=	Cash flows
Sales		Change in accounts receivable		Cash received from customers
800	+	19 (decrease)	=	819

- "Sales" are obtained from the income statement and flow through the "accounts receivable".
- The change in accounts receivable is taken from the "changes" column of the comparative balance sheet.
- The nature of the change in accounts receivable (positive or negative) is important. A negative figure in the comparative balance sheet indicates a decrease, and this has a positive impact on cash (it means that more customers paid off their trade debt than new customers added to the trade debt balance).
- The cash flow, in this example, exceeds sales by the amount of the change in accounts receivable.

- The receivable arising on the sale of a fixed asset (if there were one – which is not the case here) should be kept separate from "accounts receivable". If there were one it would be included as part of the investing activities.

Cash paid out in relation to cost of merchandise sold (cash paid to suppliers of goods for resale)

This is calculated in two steps. First of all, the amount of purchases is reconstructed by eliminating the effect of changes in inventory. As already seen in Chapter 9, the cost of merchandise sold can be computed as follows for a trading (retailer) company:

> Purchases + Changes in inventory (beginning – ending) = Cost of merchandise sold

Given that in Table 15.5 the balance sheet changes are calculated by deducting Year 1 figures from Year 2 figures (i.e., ending – beginning), this formula becomes:

> Purchases – Changes in inventory (ending – beginning) = Cost of merchandise sold

Purchases are consequently calculated as follows:

> Purchases = Changes in inventory (ending – beginning) + Cost of merchandise sold
>
> | Purchases | = | Change in inventory | + | Cost of merchandise sold |
> |---|---|---|---|---|
> | 614 | = | 44 | + | 570 |

The second step is now to calculate cash flow.

Income statement items	±	Change in related balance sheet items	=	Cash flows
Purchases		Change in accounts payable		Cash paid out for purchases
– 614	+	8 (increase)	=	– 606

Cash paid for other operating expenses (cash paid to suppliers of other operating expenses)

Income statement items	±	Change in related balance sheet items	=	Cash flows
Other operating expenses		Change in prepaid expenses		Cash paid out for other operating expenses
– 162	+	3 (decrease)	=	– 159

- If there had been any accrued liabilities, or salaries and social expenses payable in the balance sheet, then these items would have been included in the adjustment of other operating expenses.
- Depreciation expense (and amortization expense, which does not exist in this example) has no impact on cash. These expenses are not included in the direct method.

Cash paid for interest

In our example, there is no accrued interest payable on the balance sheet. The cash outflow is thus equal to the interest expense: –15. In general, cash paid for interest is equal to the interest expense adjusted for the change in accrued interest payable.

Cash received from investment income

Our example does not include any accrued interest receivable on the balance sheet. The cash inflow is thus equal to the investment income (dividends received): 18.

Cash paid for income taxes

This is calculated as was done for other expenses.

Income statement items	±	Change in related balance sheet items	=	Cash flows
Income taxes		Change in income taxes payable		Cash paid on income taxes
– 5	–	2 (decrease)	=	– 7

Gain on sale of equipment

The gain on sale of equipment is not included in the direct method.

Summary of adjustments

Table 14.7 shows balance sheet items (receivables and payables) related to income statement items.

Table 14.7   Income statement items and related balance sheet items

Income statement items	Related receivables (and inventory)	Related liabilities
Sales	Accounts receivable	Revenues recorded in advance (unearned revenues)
Cost of merchandise sold	Inventory	Accounts payable
Rent expense	Prepaid rent (expenses recorded in advance)	Rent payable Accrued rent payable
Salaries and social expenses	Prepaid salaries and social expenses (expenses recorded in advance)	Salaries and social expenses payable Accrued salaries and social expenses payable
Other operating expenses	Prepaid other operating expenses (expenses recorded in advance)	Other expenses payable Accrued other expenses payable
Taxes Income taxes	Prepaid taxes – prepaid income taxes (expenses recorded in advance)	(Income) taxes payable Accrued (income) taxes payable

Depreciation expense and amortization expense are not included in this table because they have no impact on cash. Income statement items may be related to both assets and liabilities at the same time.

Schedule of cash flows from operating activities (direct method)

Table 14.8 shows how cash flows from operating activities are calculated.

Table 14.8 Cash flows from operating activities (direct method)

Cash received from customers	819
Cash paid in relation to cost of merchandise sold	−606
Cash paid in relation to other operating expenses	−159
Cash paid on interest	−15
Cash received from investment income	18
Cash paid on income taxes	−7
Net cash provided by/used in operating activities	50

Indirect method

The indirect method, which consists in adjusting net income for non-cash items (such as depreciation expense) and changes in receivables and payables is illustrated in Figure 14.3.

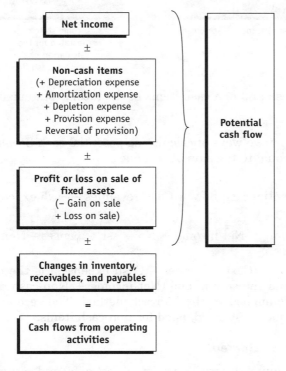

Figure 14.3 Indirect method

The following comments apply to Figure 14.3.

Non-cash items

The cash flow from operating activities cannot be obtained directly from the income statement, because the latter records revenues and expenses, not receipts and payments. Therefore, the first step is to determine a "potential cash flow". This is done by separating revenues and expenses in two categories:

first, those which, by nature, will eventually generate a real cash flow (they are called cash items or monetary items); second, those which do not generate a real cash flow (non-cash items or non monetary items). Cash items make up most of the income statement (sales, cost of merchandise sold, operating expenses, etc.). Non-cash items include depreciation expense, amortization expense, depletion expense, provision expense and reversal of provision. Figure 14.4 illustrates that the income statement can be converted easily into the needed format for the calculation of the potential cash flow.

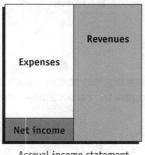
Accrual income statement

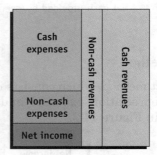
Income statement restated for the calculation of the potential cash flow

Figure 14.4 Cash and non-cash items in the income statement

There are, then, two ways of calculating potential cash flow since the sum of the expenses is equal to the sum of revenues:

Potential cash flow = Cash revenues – Cash expenses

OR

Potential cash flow = Net income + Non-cash expenses – Non-cash revenues

The first formula (Cash revenues – Cash expenses) is the one used in the direct method, and the second one (Net income + Non-cash expenses – Non-cash revenues) is applied in the indirect method. The second formula shows that the net income must be adjusted for non-cash items.

Gain on sale of equipment

In our example, equipment with an original cost of 20 and accumulated depreciation of 14 was sold for 9. A gain of 3 CU on the sale was computed in the following way:

Sales price		9
Original cost	20	
Accumulated depreciation	– 14	
Book value	6	– 6
Gain on sale		3

The sales price cash inflow is recorded as part of the investing activities ("proceeds from sale of equipment"). If the gain on the sale were included in the operating activities it would end up being recorded twice in the cash flow statement: once under operating activities, and once in investing activities (since it is part of the sales price of 9). The gain on the sale must, therefore, be eliminated from operating activities. In fact, many companies consider gains/losses on sales of fixed assets as a non-cash item and thus include them as such in the calculation of their potential cash flow.

Changes in inventory, receivables, and payables

As in the direct method, the "potential cash flow" determined by adjustment of net income for non-cash items, then corrected for gains or losses on sales of fixed assets, now has to be adjusted by the amount of changes in inventory, receivables and payables. These changes are exactly the same as those included in the direct method calculation, with the same positive or negative signs, except for inventory changes which follow a different logic. For the inventory, the same principle is applied as for receivables: an increase has a negative impact on cash and a decrease has a positive impact on cash.

Schedule of cash flows from operating activities (indirect method)

Table 14.9 shows how cash flows from operating activities are computed.

Table 14.9	Cash flow from operating activities (indirect method)		
Net income			9
Adjustments to reconcile net income/loss to net cash provided by/used in operating activities			
Depreciation expense		60	
Gain on sale of fixed assets		−3	
Changes in operating assets and liabilities			
Change in accounts receivable		19	
Change in inventories		−44	
Change in prepaid expenses		3	
Change in accounts payable		8	
Change in income taxes payable		−2	
Total adjustments		41	41
Net cash provided by/used in operating activities			50

Since the cash flows from operating activities must be the same under both methods (in our example this is indeed the case: 50), the indirect method can be used as a rapid verification of the detailed figures calculated through the direct method.

Cash flows from investing activities

The second cash flow to determine is the cash flow from investing activities. The relevant data for this activity are:

- Equipment was purchased for 175.
- Equipment with an original cost of 20 and accumulated depreciation of 14 was sold for 9.
- No new loans were granted.

For balance sheet items affected by investing activities, the following equation is key (the same equation applies to any balance sheet item). It allows the calculation of any one of the four items when the other three are known.

Beginning balance	+	Increases	–	Decreases	=	Ending balance
A	+	B	–	C	=	D

An application of this equation is illustrated as follows.

Purchase of equipment

Beginning balance	+	Increases	–	Decreases	=	Ending balance
Equipment (gross value)	+	Purchase at cost	–	Sale at original cost	=	Equipment (gross value)
460	+	175	–	20		615

Sale of equipment

As just stated, the sales price (9) must be included in the cash flow statement, since it represents the cash inflow (unless the sale was on credit, in which case the price should be adjusted by the changes in accounts receivable to give the net cash flow from that transaction).

The change in accumulated depreciation between the beginning and end of the year should be verified.

Beginning balance	+	Increases	–	Decreases	=	Ending balance
Accumulated depreciation	+	Depreciation expense	–	Accumulated depreciation of fixed assets sold	=	Accumulated depreciation
70	+	60	–	14	=	116

Repayment of loan

In our example, no new loan was granted but the ending balance of loans granted to third parties is lower that the beginning balance. We therefore know that some borrowers have repaid their loans. As an external user we can deduct the amounts that were reimbursed and are therefore cash inflows for Liszt Company. The equation yields the missing datum:

Beginning balance	+	Increases	–	Decreases	=	Ending balance
Loan	+	New loan granted	–	Repayment of loan	=	Loan
174	+	0	–	?	=	115

$174 + 0 - X = 115$ thus $X = 174 - 115 = 59$. Loans granted by Liszt Company were repaid by borrowers for a total amount of 59.

Schedule of cash flows from investing activities

Table 14.10 summarizes the cash flows from investing activities.

Table 14.10 Cash flows from investing activities

Purchase of equipment	-175
Proceeds from sale of equipment	9
Repayment of loan by borrowers	59
Net cash used in investing activities	-107

Cash flows from financing activities

The relevant information available is:

- 135 was raised from the issue of shares in cash (66 of share capital and 69 of share premium).
- Bonds were converted into capital for 30 (share capital of 16 plus share premium of 14).
- Bonds were repaid at face value at maturity for 60.
- Dividends (relating to net income of 20X1) were paid in cash for 8.

Issuance of share capital

The changes in share capital and share premium are due to both issuance of new shares and conversion of bonds:

Beginning balance	+	Increases	–	Decreases	=	Ending balance
Share capital	+	Issued	–	Repayment	=	Share capital
200	+	66 + 16 = 82	–	0	=	282
Share premium		Issued		Repayment		Share premium
115		69 + 14 = 83		0		198

These two transactions are separated in Table 14.11.

Table 14.11 Share issues

Share capital	Issue in cash	66
	Issue by conversion of debts	16 → 135
	Total	82
Share premium	Issue in cash	69
	Issue by conversion of debts	14 → 30
	Total	83

Only the issue of new shares in cash should be included in the cash flow statement. The debt-conversion issue is a non-cash financing activity and will be mentioned in a separate schedule as a footnote to the cash flow statement.

Beginning balance	+	Increases	–	Decreases	=	Ending balance
Bonds	+	New issue	–	Repayment or conversion	=	Bonds
245	+	0	–	90	=	155

The decrease just seen comprises the following components:

- Repayment: 60.
- Conversion into capital: 30.

Dividends

When the balance sheet is presented before profit appropriation, changes in reserves can be explained as follows:

Beginning balance	+	Increases	–	Decreases	=	Ending balance
Reserves	+	Net income of Year 1	–	Dividends paid in Year 2 in relation to Year 1 or capitalization to reserves	=	Reserves
122	+	10	–	8	=	124

We have no information here concerning any transfer of reserves to capital, and the changes in capital have already been explained. Consequently, the decrease in reserves can only be explained by dividends paid out.

Table 14.12 shows how cash flows from financing activities are computed.

Table 14.12 Cash flows from financing activities

Proceeds from issuance of shares	135
Payments on long-term debt	–60
Dividends paid	–8
Net cash provided by/used in financing activities	67

Cash flow statement

Since we have calculated its three components, the cash flow statement can now be established. For the sake of simplicity Table 14.13 uses the indirect method. The direct method would be obtained by replacing, in Table 14.13, the operating cash flow (indirect method) by Table 14.8 which summarized the cash flow from operating activities using the direct method.

The total cash flow (net increase in cash and cash equivalents) is equal to the sum of all three cash flows: 50 – 107 + 67 = 10. This figure corresponds to the changes in cash as reported in the balance sheet (25 – 15 = 10).

Reporting

Companies often report additional cash information such as:

- non-cash investing and financing transactions
- other cash flow information (interest and taxes paid)
- business acquisitions, net of cash acquired.

Examples of such disclosures follow, together with comments.

Table 14.13 Cash flow statement of Liszt Company – Year 2 (indirect method)

Cash flow from operating activities (indirect method)	
Net income	9
Adjustments to reconcile net income to net cash provided by in operating activities	
Depreciation expense	60
Gain on sale of fixed assets	–3
Changes in operating assets and liabilities	
Change in accounts receivable	19
Change in inventories	–44
Change in prepaid expenses	3
Change in accounts payable	8
Change in income taxes payable	–2
Total adjustments	41
Net cash provided by/used in operating activities	50
Cash flows from investing activities	
Purchase of equipment	–175
Proceeds from sale of equipment	9
Repayment of loan	59
Net cash used in investing activities	–107
Cash flows from financing activities	
Proceeds from issuance of shares	135
Payments on long-term debt	–60
Dividends paid	–8
Net cash provided by financing activities	67
Net increase in cash and cash equivalents	10
Cash and cash equivalents at beginning of year	15
Cash and cash equivalents at end of year	25
Schedule of non-cash investing and financing transactions	
Conversion of bonds into capital	30

Real-life examples

Mitsubishi Electric

(Japan – US GAAP – Source: Annual report 2000 – Electrical equipment)

Notes to consolidated financial statements (year ended 31 March 2000)

(18) Supplementary cash flow information

	2000	Yen (millions) 1999	1998
Cash paid during the year for:			
Interest	42,010	48,902	41,486
Income taxes	36,135	30,918	61,131
Non-cash financing activities:			
Convertible debt converted into common stock and capital surplus	13	—	26

The "cash paid" information is given because the company used the indirect method to compute the cash flows from operating activities. As a result, the statement does not show interest- and tax-related cash flows separately, and so the company provides these additional details. Non-cash financing activities, as mentioned before, are not included in the cash flow statement but disclosed separately.

Benihana Inc.

(USA – US GAAP – Source: Annual report 2000 – Japanese restaurants)

Consolidated statements of cash flows

In thousands of dollars	26 March 2000	28 March 1999	29 March 1998
(...)			
Investing activities			
Business acquisition, net of cash acquired	(8,445)		(19,138)
(...)			
Business acquisitions, net of cash acquired:			
Fair value of assets acquired, other than cash	2,830		8,888
Liabilities assumed	(157)		(2,577)
Purchase price in excess of the net assets acquired	5,772		12,827
	8,445		19,138

During fiscal year ended 28 March 1999, 300 shares of preferred stock were converted into 45,113 shares of Class A common stock.

The table provides details of the acquisition of a company, while the sentence underneath concerns a change in the nature of shares (see Chapter 11) that has no impact on cash.

ADVANCED ISSUES

Differences in classification

Most items fold neatly into one of three classes: operating, investing, and financing activities. "Operating activities" reflect, in most local GAAP standards, one common line of thinking namely that cash flows from operations must translate the cash effect of transactions and other events that enter into the determination of net income. Operating activities include operating activities in the strictest sense (manufacturing and selling for example), trade financing and cash management, and taxes and employee profit sharing. All affect cash flows.

Some items are difficult to classify clearly in one of the three classes. They include interest paid, dividends paid, interest received, dividends received, and taxes paid. As shown in Table 14.14, most countries give clear instructions favoring a particular solution for some items while leaving maneuvering room for others. Meanwhile the IASC leaves the choice to the reporting body.

Appendix 14.2 provides some developments on the contents of Table 14.14. The best reporting practice, regardless of the classification adopted is to provide as much specific information to allow users of financial statements to make any reclassifications they judge useful and to assess the effect of the company's policy. Appendix 14.3 presents the model adopted in the UK and Ireland.

Table 14.14 Differences in classification

	Interest paid	Interest received	Dividends paid	Dividends received	Taxes paid
IASC	OPE or FIN	OPE or INV	OPE or FIN	OPE or INV	OPE or INV or FIN
Australia	OPE or FIN	OPE	FIN	OPE	OPE or INV or FIN
Canada	OPE or FIN	OPE or INV	OPE or FIN	OPE or INV	OPE or INV or FIN
France	OPE or FIN	OPE or INV	FIN	OPE or INV	OPE or INV
Germany	OPE (FIN)	OPE (INV)	FIN	OPE (INV)	OPE (INV/FIN)
New Zealand	FIN	INV	FIN	INV	OPE
South Africa	OPE	OPE	OPE	OPE	OPE
UK/Ireland	RETURNS	RETURNS	EQUITY DIVIDENDS PAID	RETURNS	TAXATION
USA	OPE	OPE	FIN	OPE	OPE

OPE = Operating activities
INV = Investing activities
FIN = Financing activities
RETURNS = Returns on investments and servicing of finance (the UK/Irish statement has four classes)
Brackets indicate that this classification may be used in exceptional circumstances

Non-cash investing and financing transactions

Some transactions affecting the capital and asset structure of an enterprise do not have any direct impact on current cash flows. They are, however, part of the investing and financing activities. Examples of such transactions are:

- The acquisition of assets either by assuming directly related liabilities or by means of a finance lease (see Chapter 12).
- The acquisition of an enterprise exclusively by means of an equity issue.
- The conversion of debt to equity (see Chapter 11).
- The issuance of shares by capitalization of reserves (see Chapter 11).

Under IAS 7 (§ 43), and accordingly under most national standards, investing and financing transactions that do not require the use of cash or cash equivalents should be excluded from a cash flow statement. Such transactions should be disclosed elsewhere in the financial statements in a way that provides all the relevant information about these transactions (see examples earlier in this chapter).

Funds flow statement or statement of changes in financial position

Certain countries, and certain companies, are in the habit of publishing a funds flow statement (or statement of changes in financial position), built around a breakdown of the change in working capital (defined as the difference between equity and long-term debts and fixed assets, or the difference between current assets and current liabilities). Some developments on this statement are presented in Appendix 14.4.

Different titles and different models

Cash flow statements are known by a wide variety of names:

- financing statement (*cuadro de financiación* in Spain)
- capital flows statement (*Kapitalflussrechnung* in Germany and Switzerland)
- *statement of cash flows* in the USA
- *funds flow statement*
- *statement of sources and applications of funds*
- *statement of changes in financial position*.

Appendix 14.5 presents some developments on the different titles.

Analysis of the cash flow statement

There are several possible ways in which users of financial statements can analyze a cash flow statement.

Algebraic sign of cash flows

Generally, the operating cash flow is expected to be positive[2]. In fact, many financial analysts believe it must be positive: in other words, the core activity of the company should generate a positive cash flow. A negative operating cash flow is a serious indicator of potential weakness or of a need to generate rapid growth to reach the more stable situation created by a positive cash flow from operation.

The investing cash flow is almost always negative, as the company invests more in new assets than it receives on sales of its underused or obsolete fixed assets.

The financing cash flow can be positive or negative depending on the circumstances.

Available cash flow and free cash flow

The *"available cash flow"* is the difference between the cash flow from operating activities (assumed positive) and the cash flow from investing (assumed to be negative). Table 14.15 illustrates how the available cash flow is linked to the change in cash position.

If the "available cash flow" is positive, the financing cash flow can be negative. For example, it allows the firm to engage in a policy of repayment of its long-term debt or distribution of dividends. If, however, the available cash flow is negative, the business will have to compensate this situation by creating a positive financing cash flow, which is achieved, for example by issuing new shares or by contracting new debt. The anticipated evolution of the available cash flow is, therefore, a very important tool for understanding the likely future financing policy of a business.

Some companies also report their variation of the available cash flow: operating cash flow minus purchases of fixed assets plus proceeds from sales of fixed assets. This "excess" cash flow represents the amount available for acquisitions of companies and for the financing activities. The possible strategic moves of a firm can be guided by the existence of such truly available cash flow.

The so called *"free cash flow"*, preferred by some analysts, is a variation on the available cash flow. It is the available cash flow minus the dividends paid. Its reconciliation with the change in cash position is illustrated in Table 14.15.

The free cash flow is seen by many as more useful than the available cash flow because, since the payment of a dividend is a requirement for keeping the support of shareholders, it represents the only amount of cash truly unencumbered for a possible reimbursement of debt or for investment.

Both the free cash flow and the available cash flow assume that the investing activity is supposed to be financed first by cash from operations and that the financing strategy is the consequence of any insufficiency in cash from operations. Such a hypothesis is pretty robust in a reasonably non-inflationary economy.

Going back to the Liszt company example (see Table 14.13), we can determine the available and free cash flows (see Table 14.15).

Table 14.15   Liszt Company – Available and free cash flows

Net cash provided by operating activities	50
Net cash used in investing activities	–107
Available cash flow	**–57**
Dividends paid	–8
Free cash flow	**–65**
Other financing cash flows	75
Net increase in cash and cash equivalents	10

Given that the available cash flow is negative, the free cash flow is not surprisingly negative. This means the operating cash flow is not sufficient to finance the investing strategy of the firm, and it must therefore obtain new sources of financing (capital issuance will be the answer in this example) to balance its cash flows.

Ratios

Several ratios are particularly appropriate for analyzing cash flow statements.

Cash flow as percentage of sales

By comparing the operating cash flow to net sales over several years, the "transformation of sales into cash" can be measured. For Liszt company, this ratio is $(50/800) = 6.25\%$ in the year examined. Knowing the evolution of this metric over time would give a better understanding of the prospects of the firm.

Cash flow yield

Operating cash flow/Net income

For Liszt, this ratio is equal to $(50/9) = 5.55$, which indicates a very good yield.

Cash liquidity ratios

Operating cash flow/Average current liabilities

This ratio indicates the company's ability to repay its current liabilities using its operating cash flows. For the Liszt company, the ratio is $50/[(63 + 57)/2] = 83.3\%$.

Operating cash flow/Average total liabilities

This ratio indicates the company's ability to repay its total liabilities using its operating cash flows. For the Liszt company, it is $50/[(218 + 302)/2] = 19.2\%$.

Structure of each cash flow

In order to examine the contents of each activity, it is possible to divide each cash flow by the total cash flow of the activity. For example, the proceeds from issuance of shares can be divided by the financing cash flows, over several years if required.

KEY POINTS

- Users of an enterprise's financial statements are interested in how the enterprise generates and uses cash and cash equivalents.
- The cash flow statement or statement of cash flows is the tool designed to help users understand better how a firm creates and uses cash.
- The cash flow statement is an integral part of a firm's financial statements. In some countries, it is compulsory to publish a cash flow statement, whereas in others, it is optional. In practice, most major listed companies include a cash flow statement in their annual report.

- The cash flow statement classifies cash flows of a period in three activities: operating, investing, and financing.

- Cash flows from operating activities are primarily derived from the principal revenue-producing activities of the enterprise. Therefore, they generally result from the transactions and other events that enter into the determination of net profit or loss.

- The cash flows arising from investing activities represent the expenditures which have been made for resources intended to generate future income and cash flows.

- The financing cash flows help predict claims on future cash flows by providers of capital to the enterprise. They are the net result of cash proceeds from issuing shares or debt, cash repayments of amounts borrowed and dividends paid.

- There are two ways of determining cash flows from operating activities: the detailed *direct method* (which discloses major classes of gross cash receipts and gross cash payments) and the aggregated *indirect method* (which discloses the net cash flow from operating activities by adjusting net profit or loss for the effects of several items including non-cash items and is thus easily created by an outside user).

- The available cash flow is defined as the difference between the cash generated by operations and the cash flow used to finance the investing activity of the firm.

- Several ratios capture the dynamics of the cash flow statement. They include the "cash flow as percentage of sales" and "cash flow yield" (Operating cash flow/Net income).

REVIEW

Review 14.1 Dvorak Company

Topic: Preparation of a cash flow statement
Type: Individual exercise
Related part of the chapter: Core Issues

The balance sheets and income statements of Dvorak Company for the years 20X1 and 20X2 are presented in the following.

Balance sheet		
ASSETS	*20X1*	*20X2*
Fixed assets (gross amount)	12,000	14,950
Minus accumulated depreciation	−3,700	−4,300
Fixed assets (net amount)	8,300	10,650
Inventories (gross amount)	2,300	2,000
Minus accumulated provision	0	0
Inventories (net amount)	2,300	2,000
Accounts receivable	1,650	2,300
Cash at bank	190	80
TOTAL ASSETS	*12,440*	*15,030*

continued overleaf

EQUITY AND LIABILITIES	20X1	20X2
Share capital	3,000	3,200
Reserves	3,600	3,800
Net income/loss	2,780	2,560
Shareholders' equity	9,380	9,560
Financial liabilities (1)	3,000	4,350
Accounts payable	60	870
Fixed assets accounts payable	0	250
TOTAL LIABILITIES	12,440	15,030
(1) Including bank overdrafts	200	950

Income statement

EXPENSES	20X1	20X2
Purchases of merchandise	3,000	3,700
Change in inventory of merchandise	150	300
Other purchases and external expenses	700	550
Taxes and similar expenses	600	70
Personnel expenses	4,900	4,310
Depreciation expenses	1,200	1,400
Provision expenses	0	0
Total operating expenses	10,550	10,330
Financial expenses	650	580
Exceptional expenses (1)	0	250
Income tax	1,390	1,280
Net income	2,780	2,560
TOTAL EXPENSES	15,370	15,000

REVENUES	20X1	20X2
Sales of merchandise	15,000	14,100
Other operating revenues	20	150
Total operating revenues	15,020	14,250
Financial revenues	350	300
Exceptional income (2)	0	450
Net loss	0	0
TOTAL REVENUES	15,370	15,000
(1) Book value of sold items	0	250
(2) Sales price of fixed assets	0	450

The following additional information was taken from the company's records.

Additional information				
	31/12/20X1	+	–	31/12/20X2
Fixed assets (gross amount)	12,000	4,000	1,050	14,950
Accumulated depreciation	3,700	1,400	800	4,300
Accumulated provision	0			0
Financial liabilities (excluding overdrafts)	2,800	1,000	400	3,400
	20X2			
Dividends paid	2,580			

Required

Prepare a cash flow statement for 20X2 using the direct or the indirect method.

Solution

We first present the solution with the indirect method.

Cash flow statement	
	20X2
Cash flows from operating activities (indirect method)	
Net income/loss	2,560
Adjustments to reconcile net income/loss to net cash provided by/used in operating activities	
Depreciation and provision expense (excluding provision movements on current assets)	1,400
Gain/loss on sale of fixed assets	−200
Potential cash flow	3,760
Change in operating assets and liabilities	
Change in inventories (net amounts)	300
Change in account receivable (net amounts)	−650
Change in accounts payable	810
Net cash provided by/used in operating activities (1)	4,220
Cash flows from investing activities	
Purchase of fixed assets	−4,000
Change in fixed assets payable	250
Cash paid on purchase of fixed assets	−3,750
Proceeds from sales of fixed assets	450
Net cash used in investing activities (2)	−3,300
Cash flows from financing activities	
Dividends paid	−2,580
Proceeds from issuance of share capital	200
Proceeds from issuance of financial liabilities	1,000
Repayment of financial liabilities	−400
Net cash provided by financing activities (3)	−1,780
Net increase/decrease in cash and cash equivalents (4)=(1)+(2)+(3)	−860
Cash and cash equivalents at beginning of year (5)	−10
Cash and cash equivalents at end of year (6)=(5)+(4)	−870
Cash and cash equivalents at end of year (balance sheet) (7)	−870
Control: (7)=(6)	

We now show the operating cash flow computed with the direct method.

Cash flows from operating activities (direct method)	
Sales of merchandise	14,100
Change in account receivable (net amounts)	−650
Cash received from customers	13,450
Purchases of merchandise	−3,700
Change in accounts payable	810
Cash paid to suppliers	−2,890
Other operating revenues	150
Financial revenues	300
Other purchases and external expenses	−550
Taxes and similar expenses	−70
Personnel expenses	−4,310
Financial expenses	−580
Income tax	−1,280
Net cash provided by/used in operating activities	4,220

In the cash flow statement, we assumed that the bank overdrafts formed an integral part of the cash management. As a consequence, they were excluded from the financing activities and included in the "cash and cash equivalents", as a negative cash. Another solution is possible: to include the change in bank overdrafts in the financing activities. In this case, the cash and cash equivalents will only comprise the "cash at bank". The following table discloses this second solution.

Cash flows from financing activities	
Dividends paid	−2,580
Proceeds from issuance of share capital	200
Proceeds from issuance of financial liabilities	1,000
Repayment of financial liabilities	−400
Change in bank overdrafts*	750
Net cash provided by financing activities (3)	−1,030
Net increase/decrease in cash and cash equivalents (4)=(1)+(2)+(3)	−110
Cash and cash equivalents at beginning of year (5)	190
Cash and cash equivalents at end of year (6)=(5)+(4)	80
Cash and cash equivalents at end of year (balance sheet) (7)	80
Control: (7)=(6)	
*Line which is different from the first solution	

Review 14.2 Mitsubishi Electric*

Topic: Understanding and analyzing a cash flow statement
Type: Group exercise
Related part of the chapter: Advanced Issues

Mitsubishi Electric Corporation is a multinational concern headquartered in Japan (Tokyo). It develops, manufactures and distributes a broad range of electrical equipment in fields as diverse as home appliances and space electronics.

The company's principal lines of business are: (1) information, telecommunications, and electronic systems and devices (41% of net sales in 2000), (2) heavy machinery (22%), (3) industrial products and automation equipment (16%), and (4) consumer and other products (21%).

The financial statements are reported in conformity to the US generally accepted accounting principles.

The following presents the cash flow statements of the group for the period 1998–2000 (*source*: annual report 2000).

Consolidated statements of cash flows, years ended 31 March			
Yen (millions)	2000	1999	1998
Cash flows from operating activities			
Net income (loss)	24,833	−44,548	−105,920
Adjustments to reconcile net income (loss) to net cash provided by operating activities:			
Depreciation	215,969	230,600	237,546
Deferred income taxes	−13,882	−87,768	3,906
Decrease (increase) in trade receivables	42,304	−54,133	−7,125
Decrease (increase) in inventories	2,444	99,622	−12,130
Decrease (increase) in prepaid expenses and other assets	1,707	31,876	−8,134
Increase (decrease) in trade payables	56,405	−50,879	3,122
Increase (decrease) in other liabilities	61,551	33,770	−72,603
Other, net	1,467	12,197	9,249
Net cash provided by operating activities	392,798	170,737	47,911
Cash flows from investing activities			
Capital expenditure	−190,289	−261,178	−326,116
Proceeds from sales of property, plant, and equipment	14,366	24,701	17,917
Purchase of short-term investments and investment securities	−65,407	−143,419	−85,952
Proceeds from sale of short-term investments and investment securities	69,379	222,274	67,982
Other, net	4,076	−555	6,395
Net cash used in investing activities	−167,875	−158,177	−319,774
Cash flows from financing activities			
Proceeds from long-term debt	79,846	283,357	346,426
Repayment of long-term debt	−100,762	−228,790	−78,885
Increase (decrease) in bank loans, net	−220,800	−110,032	24,687
Dividends paid	−11,809	0	−19,323
Net cash provided by (used in) financing activities	−253,525	−55,465	272,905
Effect of exchange rate changes on cash and cash equivalents	−13,052	−10,686	4,704
Net increase (decrease) in cash and cash equivalents	−41,654	−53,591	5,746
Cash and cash equivalents at beginning of year	367,983	421,574	415,828
Cash and cash equivalents at end of year	326,329	367,983	421,574

From the balance sheet and income statement, we have extracted the following information.

Yen (millions)	2000	1999	1998
Sales	3,774,230	3,794,063	3,801,344
Net earnings	24,833	−44,548	−105,920
Current liabilities	1,835,502	1,925,833	N/A
Total liabilities	3,274,077	3,613,996	N/A
N/A = not available			

Required

Step 1: Understanding

1 What is the method used to compute the operating cash flow?

2 Compute the potential cash flow.

3 Why does the statement report "decrease (increase)" for changes in trade receivables, inventories, and prepaid expenses and "increase (decrease)" for changes in trade payables and other liabilities?

4 Make comments on the way short-term investments are reported. What would have been the other possibility?

5 Bank loans can be considered as equivalent to "bank overdrafts". Comment on the way they are reported. What would have been the other possibility?

Step 2: Analyzing

6 Analyze the cash flow statements over the period.

Solution

1 What is the method used to compute the operating cash flow?

The method used to compute the operating cash flow is the indirect method, which starts from the net income and adjusts it by adding back non-cash expenses, subtracting non-cash revenues, and integrating the changes in inventories, receivables, and payables.

2 Compute the potential cash flow

The potential cash flow is the net income adjusted for non-cash items. In this example, the only non-cash items are the depreciation and the deferred income taxes.

Yen (millions)	2000	1999	1998
Net income (loss)	24,833	−44,548	−105,920
Depreciation	215,969	230,600	237,546
Deferred income taxes	−13,882	−87,768	3,906
Potential cash flow	226,920	98,284	135,532

3 Why does the statement report "decrease (increase)" for changes in trade receivables, inventories, and prepaid expenses and "increase (decrease)" for changes in trade payables and other liabilities?

The statement indicates the changes having a positive impact on cash with a + sign and the changes having a negative impact with a – sign (or brackets).

For the changes in inventories, trade receivables, and prepaid expenses (which are assets), an increase will generate less cash (minus sign) and a decrease means more cash (plus sign). Conversely, for the changes in trade payables and other liabilities, an increase is synonymous of more cash (plus sign) and a decrease leads to less cash (minus sign).

4 Comment on the way short-term investments are reported. What would have been the other possibility?

Short-term investments are reported under the investing activities. Alternatively they could have been considered as cash equivalents, that is "short-term, highly liquid investments that are readily convertible to known amounts of cash and which are subject to an insignificant risk of changes in value" [IAS 7 (§ 6)].

5 Bank loans can be considered as equivalent to "bank overdrafts". Make comments on the way they are reported. What would have been the other possibility?

Bank loans are loans granted by banks. In other words, they represent a debt (liability) for the company. They are reported under the financing activities. They could have been included as negative cash in "cash and cash equivalents".

6 Analyze the cash flow statements over the period.

Although the company showed a steady level of sales over the period, it has realized a significant increase in its net income. However, the change in cash and cash equivalents is negative and we will explain why.

The following table discloses the general structure of the cash flow statement.

Yen (millions)	2000	1999	1998
Net cash provided by operating activities (1)	392,798	170,737	47,911
Net cash used in investing activities (2)	−167,875	−158,177	−319,774
Available cash flow (3)=(1)+(2)	224,923	12,560	−271,863
Net cash provided by (used in) financing activities (4)	−253,525	−55,465	272,905
Effect of exchange rates (5)	−13,052	−10,686	4,704
Change in cash and cash equivalents (6)= (3)+(4)+(5)	−41,654	−53,591	5,746

The available cash flow becomes highly positive in 2000, which shows an improvement. The operating cash flow is in fact able to finance the investing cash flow (in 2000 and 1999), which was not the case in 1998. This available cash allows the company to have a negative financing cash flow. In other words, the company is able to repay its debts (see below).

Operating activities

The operating cash flow has increased significantly over the period for the following reasons:

● In 2000, the potential cash flow (see question 2) has risen.
● Positive impact of the changes in inventories, receivables and payables.

This improvement appears in the computation of the operating cash flow to sales ratio.

	2000	1999	1998
Operating cash flow to sales	10.4%	4.5%	1.3%

Investing activities

Cash used in investing activities has decreased almost by one-half, mainly through the reduction of capital expenditure. In 1999, the company sold short-term investments to generate cash.

Financing activities

Whereas the company required external financing in 1998, it was able to reduce its debt in 1999 and especially in 2000.

In conclusion, we could say that the company, although it showed a decrease in cash, improved its financial situation with regard to its cash flows by increasing the operating cash flow, reducing the investing cash flow, and repaying debts.

Review 14.3 Bartok Company

Topic: Comparative financial analysis – cash flow statement
Type: Group exercise
Related part of the chapter: Advanced Issues

You receive information extracted from the financial statements of three companies.

	Company 1	Company 2	Company 3
Increase in capital	800		700
Purchase of tangible fixed assets	900	900	1,400
Purchase of financial assets	700		400
Increase in long-term debts	100	1,500	1,100
Repayment of long-term debts		300	
Potential cash flow*	1,000	400	100
Dividends paid	200	600	

*Net income adjusted for non-cash items

Required

1 From the information, prepare the cash flow statements.

2 Comment on the resulting statements.

Solution

1 Cash flow statements

	Company 1	Company 2	Company 3
Cash flows from operating activities			
Potential cash flow	1,000	400	100
Net cash provided by operating activities	*1,000*	*400*	*100*
Cash flows from investing activities			
Purchase of tangible fixed assets	−900	−900	−1,400
Purchase of financial assets	−700	0	−400
Net cash used in investing activities	*−1,600*	*−900*	*−1,800*
Cash flows from financing activities			
Dividends paid	−200	−600	0
Proceeds from share issuance	800	0	700
New debt	100	1,500	1,100
Repayment of long-term debts	0	−300	0
Net cash provided by financing activities	*700*	*600*	*1,800*
Increase in cash and cash equivalents	100	100	100

2 Comments

As an introduction, it should be stressed that the proposed exercise is intentionally simplified, without any changes in inventory, receivables, or payables.

Stage 1

It may be useful to draw up the following table summarizing the information already received.

	Company 1	Company 2	Company 3
Net cash provided by operating activities (OCF)	1,000	400	100
Net cash used in investing activities (ICF)	−1,600	−900	−1,800
Available cash flow (ACF)	−600	−500	−1,700
Net cash provided by financing activities (FCF)	700	600	1,800
Change in cash	100	100	100

All three companies have the same change in cash, although their cash structures are very different.

Company 1

- It has the highest OCF of the 3 companies. This is a good sign.
- Its ICF is negative, as is almost always the case, since it represents investments.
- The ACF is negative, which means that the company will need financing to restore financial equilibrium. It does this through its FCF.

Company 2

- Its OCF is lower than for company 1. This is not as good, but not yet a real cause for concern.
- The ICF is negative and quite low compared to that of company 1. This is apparently logical, since company 2's investments are not as high.
- This is reflected in the ACF, which is almost identical to that of company 1.
- Once again, financing is necessary, hence the positive FCF.

Company 3

- The OCF is very low; this is an early warning of future difficulties.
- At the same time, the ICF is enormous, with the company making particularly large investments.
- The ACF is dramatically negative.
- The only solution is to use external financing, and this is reflected in the FCF.

Stage 2

After commenting on the main items in the cash flow statements, the contents of each function may be examined. For example, it might be interesting to point out that in its search for financing, company 3 uses loans but also, although to a lesser extent, calls on its shareholders.

ASSIGNMENTS

Assignment 14.1

Multiple-choice questions
Type: Individual exercise
Related part of the chapter: Core Issues

Select the right answer (one possible answer, unless otherwise stated).

1   **Which of the following cannot be the main objective of a cash flow statement?**
   (a) To provide relevant information on the cash receipts and cash payments of an enterprise during a given period
   (b) To explain changes in cash in the same way as the income statement explains the components that comprise the net income
   (c) To provide information on the operating, financing and investing activities of an entity and the effects of those activities on cash resources

(d) To explain the changes in working capital between opening and closing balance sheets

(e) To report on a standard basis the cash generation and cash absorption for a period

(f) To provide relevant information to users of the cash inflows and cash outflows of an entity during a reporting period

(g) To provide information on the historical changes in cash and cash equivalents

2 **Which of the following would not be integrated in the computation of the cash flow from operating activities?**

(a) Cash received from customers

(b) Cash paid to suppliers

(c) Proceeds from sale of fixed assets

(d) Depreciation and amortization

(e) Gain on sale of fixed assets

3 **Which of the following would not be included in investing activities? (more than one answer possible)**

(a) Repayment of a loan granted to a subsidiary

(b) Dividends paid

(c) Purchase cost of fixed assets

(d) Depreciation and amortization

(e) Gain on sale of fixed assets

4 **Which of the following would not be included in financing activities? (more than one answer possible)**

(a) Proceeds from issuance of shares

(b) Dividends received

(c) Repayment of debt

(d) Issuance of share capital by capitalization of reserves

(e) Dividends paid

5 **When using the indirect method to compute the operating cash flow, which of the following items will not be included?**

(a) Change in inventory

(b) Depreciation expense

(c) Gain on sale of fixed assets

(d) Cash paid to employees

(e) Net income

6 **When using the direct method to compute the operating cash flow, which of the following items will not be included?**

(a) Cash received from customers

(b) Depreciation expense

(c) Cash paid to suppliers

(d) Cash paid to employees

(e) Cash paid on other operating expenses

7 **Depending on the country, interest expenses are included in either operating activities or investing activities**

(a) True

(b) False

8 **Under IAS 7, bank overdrafts are included in either cash or financing activities**

(a) True

(b) False

9 **Dividends received are usually included in**

(a) Operating activities

(b) Investing activities

(c) Financing activities

10 Which of these stages are included in the indirect method? (more than one answer possible)

(a) Add any increase in inventory
(b) Subtract any increase in accounts receivable
(c) Add any loss on sale of fixed assets
(d) Subtract depreciation expense
(e) Subtract any increase in accounts payable

Assignment 14.2 Janacek Company (1)

Topic: Preparation of cash flow statement
Type: Individual/group exercise
Related part of the chapter: Core Issues

The Janacek Company has a commercial activity in the beauty cream business.

Required

1 With the help of the following balance sheet, income statement, and additional information, prepare a cash flow statement for the years 20X2 and 20X3 using the direct method.

2 Prepare a separate statement reconciling the net income and the net cash provided by/used in operating activities.

3 Comment on the cash flow statement.

Balance sheet (000 CU)			
ASSETS	***20X1***	***20X2***	***20X3***
Fixed assets (gross amount)	15,000	22,000	27,400
Less accumulated depreciation	−4,900	−5,500	−6,000
Fixed assets (net amount)	10,100	16,500	21,400
Inventories (gross amount)	3,200	4,500	5,700
Less accumulated provision	0	0	−100
Inventories (net amount)	3,200	4,500	5,600
Accounts receivable	2,020	3,500	5,300
Cash at bank	1,150	250	240
TOTAL ASSETS	*16,470*	*24,750*	*32,540*
EQUITY AND LIABILITIES	***20X1***	***20X2***	***20X3***
Share capital	3,000	5,000	7,500
Reserves	3,800	4,200	4,400
Net income/loss	1,728	474	246
Shareholders' equity	8,528	9,674	12,146
Financial liabilities (1)	3,900	8,500	11,500
Accounts payable	4,042	6,126	5,094
Accounts payable to suppliers of fixed assets	0	450	3,800
TOTAL EQUITY AND LIABILITIES	*16,470*	*24,750*	*32,540*
(1) Including bank overdrafts	100	1,000	2,000

Income statement (000 CU)			
EXPENSES	**20X1**	**20X2**	**20X3**
Purchases of merchandise	3,500	7,100	9,000
Change in inventory of merchandise	200	−1,300	−1,200
Other purchases and external expenses	750	1,000	1,530
Taxes and similar expenses	100	200	500
Personnel expenses	7,561	11,000	13,000
Depreciation expenses	800	1,000	1,500
Provision expenses	0	0	100
Total operating expenses	12,911	19,000	24,430
Financial expenses	717	1,149	1,931
Exceptional expenses (1)	145	600	100
Income tax	864	237	123
Net income	1,728	474	246
TOTAL EXPENSES	*16,365*	*21,460*	*26,830*
REVENUES	**20X1**	**20X2**	**20X3**
Sales of merchandise	16,000	20,900	25,500
Other operating revenues	310	220	710
Total operating revenues	16,310	21,120	26,210
Financial revenues	55	140	220
Exceptional income (2)	0	200	400
Net loss	0	0	0
TOTAL REVENUES	*16,365*	*21,460*	*26,830*
(1) Book value of items sold	0	600	100
(2) Sale price of fixed assets	0	200	400

It should be noted that this income statement is presented by nature.

Additional information

	31/12/20X1	+	−	31/12/20X2	+	−	31/12/20X3
Fixed assets (gross)	15,000	8,000	1,000	22,000	6,500	1,100	27,400
Accumulated depreciation	4,900	1,000	400	5,500	1,500	1,000	6,000
Accumulated provision	0			0	100		100
Financial liabilities (excluding overdrafts)	3,800	4,000	300	7,500	3,000	1,000	9,500

	20X2	20X3
Dividends paid	1,328	274

Assignment 14.3 Smetana Company

Topic: Preparation of cash flow statement
Type: Individual/group exercise
Related part of the chapter: Core Issues

Smetana Company is an industrial activity.

Required

1 With the help of the following income statement, balance sheet, statement of retained earnings, and additional information, prepare a cash flow statement for the year 20X2 using the direct method.

2 Prepare a separate statement reconciling the net income and the net cash provided by/used in operating activities.

3 Comment on the cash flow statement.

Smetana Company – Income statement (000 CU) – Year 20X2

Sales	1,000
Cost of goods sold	−600
Gross profit	400
Depreciation expense	−60
Other operating expenses	−150
Operating profit	190
Interest expense	−18
Investment income	16
Loss on sale of equipment	−5
Profit before taxes	183
Income taxes	−60
Net profit	123

Smetana Company – Comparative balance sheets (000 CU) – Years ended 31 December 20X2 and 20X1

	20X2	20X1	Changes (X2 − X1)
Assets			
Current assets			
Cash	65	20	45
Accounts receivable	55	80	−25
Prepaid expenses*	8	10	−2
Inventory	131	80	51
Total current assets	259	190	69
Fixed assets			
Loans	150	140	10
Tangible assets			
Equipment	700	600	100
Accumulated depreciation	−110	−80	−30
Equipment (net)	590	520	70
Total fixed assets	740	660	80
Total assets	999	850	149
Shareholders' equity and liabilities			
Liabilities			
Current liabilities			
Accounts payable	136	135	1
Income taxes payable	40	35	5
Total current liabilities	176	170	6
Long-term liabilities (bonds)	160	180	−20
Total liabilities	336	350	−14
Shareholders' equity			
Share capital	300	250	50
Share premium	150	120	30
Retained earnings	213	130	83
Total shareholders' equity	663	500	163
Total shareholders' equity and liabilities	999	850	149

*related to other operating expenses

Retained earnings (end of year 20X1)	130
Net income year 20X2	123
Dividends paid year 20X2	−40
Retained earnings (end of year 20X2)	213

The following additional information is also relevant for the preparation of the cash flow statement for the year 20X2:

- Equipment with an original cost of 50 and accumulated depreciation of 30 was sold for 15.
- A new loan was granted. No loan was repaid.
- 80 was raised from the issue of shares in cash (share capital of 50 plus share premium of 30).
- Bonds were repaid at face value at maturity for 70.

Assignment 14.4 Pernod Ricard*

Topic: Comments on the reported cash flow statement
Type: Group exercise
Related part of the chapter: Core/Advanced Issues

Pernod Ricard is a French group based in Paris and operating in the beverage business (wine and spirits, fruit, and soft drinks). Among its numerous brands are Pastis 51, Clan Campbell, Cognac Bisquit and Orangina.

In its 1999 annual report, the group reports the following consolidated cash flow statement (see opposite).

€ million	1999	1998
Net income	213.2	202.2
Minority interests	7.1	7.3
Interest in earnings of equity companies (net of dividends)	−0.5	6.6
Depreciation of fixed assets	86.3	78.7
Amortization of goodwill	20.9	14.2
Change in provisions and deferred taxes	14.2	0.6
Gains on disposals of fixed assets	−38.0	6.3
Cash flow	303.2	315.9
Change in working capital need	25.0	−119.1
Cash provided by operating activities	328.2	196.8
Acquisition of property, plant, and equipment (net of disposals)	−112.1	−119.2
Acquisition of financial assets (net of disposals)	−62.7	−29.1
Effect of change in scope of consolidation (a)	−53.1	−95.1
Net change in receivables and payables on assets	−25.2	1.2
Cash used in investment activities	−253.1	−242.2
Increase in capital	0.0	0.0
Dividends paid	−92.5	−82.9
Cash used in financing activities	−92.5	−82.9
Currency translation adjustment (b)	−63.5	24.6
Change in net debt	−80.9	−103.7
Net debt at the beginning of the year	−677.0	−573.3
Net debt at the end of the year	−757.9	−677.0

(a) Impact of acquisitions and sales of subsidiaries on the consolidated financial statements – see Chapter 13

(b) Impact of the translation of financial statements reported in foreign currencies – see Chapter 13

The following note accompanies the statement: the change in net debt consists of the change in loans, long-term debts, and cash. The net debt consists of the following.

	1/1/00	1/1/99	1/1/98
Loans and long-term debt	−1,185.0	−1,092.9	−1,022.3
Marketable securities	150.1	120.9	112.7
Cash	277.0	295.0	336.3
Opening net debt	−757.9	−677.0	−573.3

Required

1 Which method is used for computing the cash flow from operating activities?

2 What does the "cash flow" item in the operating activities represent?

3 What does the "change in working capital need" item in the operating activities represent?

4 How does the statement balance? Is this the traditional method of balancing a cash flow statement?

5 With the help of the note accompanying the cash flow statement, restate the final part of the statement in order to balance it with cash and cash equivalents. (Marketable securities are assumed to be a cash equivalent.)

Assignment 14.5 Procter & Gamble*

Topic: Analysis of a cash flow statement
Type: Group exercise
Related part of the chapter: Core/Advanced Issues

Procter & Gamble, the US group involved in various sectors, such as fabric and homecare (Ariel, Mr. Clean), feminine protection (Always), healthcare, food and beverages, beauty care (Head & Shoulders), and baby care (Pampers)[3], publishes the following consolidated statement of cash flows in its 1999 annual report.

Amounts in millions of US dollars	Years ended 30 June		
	1999	1998	1997
Cash and cash equivalents, beginning of year	1,549	2,350	2,074
Operating activities			
Net earnings	3,763	3,780	3,415
Depreciation and amortization	2,148	1,598	1,487
Deferred income taxes	−60	−101	−26
Change in accounts receivable	−207	42	8
Change in inventories	−96	−229	−71
Change in accounts payable, accrued, and other liabilities	792	−3	561
Change in other operating assets and liabilities	−926	−65	503
Other	130	−137	5
Total operating activities	5,544	4,885	5,882
Investing activities			
Capital expenditures	−2,828	−2,559	−2,129
Proceeds from asset sales	434	555	520
Acquisitions	−137	−3,269	−150
Change in investment securities	356	63	−309
Total investing activities	−2,175	−5,210	−2,068
Financing activities			
Dividends to shareholders	−1,626	−1,462	−1,329
Change in short-term debt	689	1,315	−160
Additions to long-term debt	986	1,970	224
Reductions of long-term debt	−334	−432	−724
Proceeds from stock options	212	158	134
Treasury purchases	−2,533	−1,929	−1,652
Total financing activities	−2,606	−380	−3,507
Effect of exchange rate changes on cash and cash equivalents	−18	−96	−31
Change in cash and cash equivalents	745	−801	276
Cash and cash equivalents, end of year	2,294	1,549	2,350

Required

1 What is unusual about this statement as regards its presentation of cash and cash equivalents at beginning and end of year?

2 Which method is used for computing the cash flow from operating activities?

3 Why are the operating cash flows higher than the net income each year?

4 With the help of the additional information provided in the following, prepare an analysis of the cash flow statement.

In millions of US dollars	1999	1998	1997
Sales	38,125	37,154	35,764
Net earnings	3,763	3,780	3,415
Current liabilities	10,761	9,250	7,798
Total liabilities	20,055	18,730	15,498

The information for 1997 is extracted from the 1998 annual report

References

ASB (1991, revised 1996) Financial Reporting Standard No. 1, Cash flow statements, London.

FASB (1987) Statement of Financial Accounting Standards No. 95, Statement of Cash Flows, Norwalk, CT.

IASC (revised 1992) International Accounting Standard No. 7, Cash Flow Statements, London.

Further readings

Boussard, D., and Colasse, B. (1992) Funds-flow statement and cash-flow accounting in France: evolution and significance. *European Accounting Review*, 1(2), 229–254.

Cheng, C.S.A., Liu, C.S., and Schaefer, T.F. (1997) The value-relevance of SFAS No. 95 cash flows from operations as assessed by security market effects. *Accounting Horizons*, 11(3) (September), 1–15.

Dhar, S. (1998) Cash flow reporting in India – A case study. *Indian Accounting Review*, 2(2) (December), 39–52.

Haller, A., and Jakoby, S. (1995) Funds flow reporting in Germany: A conceptual and empirical state of the art. *European Accounting Review*, 4(3), 515–34.

Kinnunen, J., and Koskela, M. (1999) Do cash flows reported by firms articulate with their income statements and balance sheets? Descriptive evidence from Finland. *European Accounting Review*, 8(4), 631–54.

McEnroe, J.E. (1996) An examination of attitudes involving cash flow accounting: Implications for the content of cash flow statements. *The International Journal of Accounting*, 31(2), 161–74.

Nissan, S., Kamata, N., and Otaka, R. (1995) Cash reporting in Japan. *The International Journal of Accounting*, 29, 168–80.

Nurnberg, H., and Largay III, J.A. (1996) More concerns over cash flow reporting under FASB statement No. 95. *Accounting Horizons*, 10(4) (December), 123–36.

Stolowy, H., and Walser-Prochazka, S. (1992) The American influence in accounting: Myth or reality? The statement of cash flows example. *The International Journal of Accounting*, Autumn, 185–221.

Wallace, R.S.O., Choudhury, M.S.I., and Pendlebury, M. (1997) Cash flow statements: An international comparison of regulatory positions. *The International Journal of Accounting*, 32(1), 1–22.

Wallace, R.S.O., Choudhury, M.S.I., and Adhikari, A. (1999) The comprehensiveness of cash flow reporting in the United Kingdom: Some characteristics and firm-specific determinants. *The International Journal of Accounting*, 34(3), 311–47.

Yap, C. (1997) Users' perceptions of the need for cash flow statements – Australian evidence. *European Accounting Review*, 6(4), 653–72.

Additional material on the website

Go to http://www.thomsonlearning.co.uk/accountingandfinance/stolowylebas for further information, journal entries and extra assignments for each chapter.

The following appendices to this chapter are available on the dedicated website:

Appendix 14.1: Contents of activities according to IAS 7
Appendix 14.2: Differences in classification
Appendix 14.3: The UK/Ireland model
Appendix 14.4: Funds flow statement or statement of changes in financial position
Appendix 14.5: Different titles and different models

Notes

1 The "true" direct method is not presented, since it requires access to internal company information, and this is not consistent with the users' perspective adopted in this book.

2 Known exceptions are start-up companies, and especially dot.com firms that require a large discretionary investment in operating facilities upfront and build their business slowly. When speaking of many dot.com firms before the year 2000 crash or of weakened airlines such as TWA in 2000, their negative cash flow from operating activities is referred to in the economic press as their "cash burn rate" (the $ millions required per month). Such firms require a constant influx of cash from either shareholders or financial institutions and the question of their survival revolves around their ability to turn a cash burn rate into a positive cash flow from operating activities.

3 The group possesses many other brands besides the brands quoted.

Financial statement analysis

Although in all previous chapters we already emphasized the decision-making support offered by financial reporting information, this chapter focusses in more details on the use of such information by decision makers. The data reported to shareholders and the financial community are not directly useable in decision making. They need to be analyzed and interpreted.

Financial statement analysis addresses the informational concerns of internal and external decision makers regarding future performance and risk. It builds on understanding past performance or achievements as well as present condition(s) and opportunities. It uses various techniques integrating accounting data and additional information, emphasizing comparative and relative analysis over time for one firm and between firms. Users are interested in understanding liquidity, solvency, leverage effects, and profitability of a firm as well as its asset management policy and ability to deliver a return to investors.

Although practical financial statement analysis may vary across countries, the main techniques used (and developed early in this chapter) include:

- Trend or horizontal analysis[1] (comparison over time of the evolution of a specific expense or revenue item or a particular asset or liability item).

- Common-size or vertical analysis (comparison of the evolution of the structure of the financial statements).

- Ratio analysis (evaluation of the relation between components of financial statements).

Major topics

Trend analysis

Common-size analysis

Ratio analysis

Sources of information

Return to investors

Value added

Segment reporting

Accounts manipulation

Scoring models

Additional specific instruments, such as earnings per share, and economic value added are presented later.

CORE ISSUES

Trend analysis

Definition and terminology

Since users are interested in gaining an understanding of the characteristics of the stream of future income of the firm, the analysis of the evolution over time of each or some constituents of its current and past income represent a fundamental element of reflection. A measurement of the changes over the past accounting period (or over a longer period of time) of a limited number of items, or, by way of contrast, of the whole set of financial statements (income statement, cash flow statement, and balance sheet) can help the analyst or the user of the analysis understand the dynamics of the income generation model. Such a comparison over time is known as "trend analysis".

This comparison is carried line item by line item (in absolute value and in percentage) against the like value in a base year (often the previous year).

If the percentage change approach is used, the base year item amount (sales revenue, cost, liability, asset, etc.) is used as an index with a base value of 100. Other periods are then measured against that index. For example: sales this year are 120% of last year's and COGS is 125% of last year's and commercial expenses are 150% of last year's.

Advantages and limitations

This method allows the examination of long trends (evolution over 10 years for example) but such long trends often are not always meaningful because the parameter of the enterprise may have changed greatly over time and the environmental and competitive conditions may have changed greatly also. For example there would be very little meaning to a trend analysis of Vivendi Universal: this company evolved in less than 10 years from Générale des Eaux (water distribution and environmental services) to become successively Vivendi (communication and environmental services) and is now Vivendi Universal (communication and entertainment). For trends to be meaningful, the business model must be stable over the period of comparison.

Example of trend analysis

Bernstein AG is a provider of computer services to medium and small enterprises. Its income statements for years 20X1 and 20X2 are compared in Table 15.1 (in millions of CU).

Table 15.1 Trend analysis

	20X2	20X1	Amount of change	% of change
Net sales	28,500	25,000	3,500	14%
Costs and expenses				
COGS (cost of goods sold)	14,700	12,000	2,700	23%
Selling, general, and administrative expenses	10,500	10,100	400	4%
Interest expense	745	570	175	31%
Interest income	−50	−90	40	−44%
Income before tax	2,605	2,420	185	8%
Income tax expense	1,042	847	195	23%
Net income	1,563	1,573	−10	−1%

This simple illustration shows that income and selling general and administrative (SG&A) expenses remained pretty stable. Some people may consider such stability positive. But the situation has, probably, deteriorated: (a) COGS grew faster than sales leading to a reduction of the gross margin; (b) interest expenses are higher; (c) interest income is lower; and consequently (d) profit declines despite a growing volume of sales. The fact that SG&A expenses remained pretty stable in a growing market can be seen as an indicator of a dangerous situation because it can be surmised that it is an indication the customer base is not developed or enlarged. We can assume that the management sacrificed SG&A to save (somewhat successfully in the short run) the income margin which was threatened by the runaway COGS. Of course, an optimistic view, always possible, would highlight the fact that it costs the firm less in 20X2 to create one CU of revenue and therefore there has been an increase in commercial productivity.

This example shows immediately the limits of trend analysis. What is important is not only the evolution of one line item over time but its relative evolution, or the evolution of its relative weight in the determination of income. What is important is the evolution of the structure of financial statements. It confirms that the causal relations creating the income for a year are changing from one year to the next.

That is the reason why common-size analysis of financial statements is generally used as a complement to trend analysis.

Common-size (or vertical) analysis

Common-size analysis is based on the preparation of common-sized financial statements, i.e., an income statement and a balance sheet presented in percentage of a base figure (indexed as 100). The base is generally net sales for the income statement and total assets or total liabilities for the balance sheet. This analysis provides an understanding of the relationships between items in the financial statements, or, preferably, series of financial statements by combining vertical and horizontal analyses with the trend analysis. The common-size financial statements are often referred to as "income statement structure or structural income statement" and "balance sheet structure or structural balance sheet".

The income statement structure for Bernstein AG is as shown in Table 15.2.

Table 15.2 Common-size analysis

	20X2	20X1
Net sales	100%	100%
Costs and expenses		
COGS (cost of goods sold)	52%	48%
Selling, general, and administrative expenses	37%	40%
Interest expense	3%	2%
Interest income	ns%	ns%
Income before tax	9%	10%
Income tax expense	4%	3%
Net income	5%	6%

ns = not significant

Table 15.2 confirms, for example, that the moderate (4%) increase in SG&A reveals a change in either strategy or cost control over the consumption of these resources. The drift in COGS is confirmed by the fact that it increases to 52% of sales from a previous 48%.

Neither trend analysis nor common-size analysis gives sufficient or final answers but they help (especially when carried out in parallel) raise questions that need to be explored by the decision maker in seeking further information to interpret the data provided. Some of these additional data are of non-accounting nature. For example, the same increase in COGS can be due either to Bernstein AG introducing a large number of different and totally new products in 20X2 (with some birthing difficulties in production and undoubtedly some large increase in the cost of complexity) or to a growth in sales due mainly to maturing products (which would indicate either a decrease in efficiency in production, or/and a saturation of the current productive capacity). Depending on the circumstances, the growth in COGS cannot be interpreted in the same way in terms of anticipating future performance.

The common-size analysis also permits the analyst to compare and contrast more easily the financial statements of two and more companies in the same industrial sector or risk class. It effectively reduces the problem of the size difference between companies. It helps the analyst formulate hypotheses about the most efficient business model between the firms compared and identify possible thresholds in economies of scale.

Finally, common-size financial statements can be used to compare a company's financial data with industry norms or averages. Figure 15.1 summarizes the use of common-size financial statements.

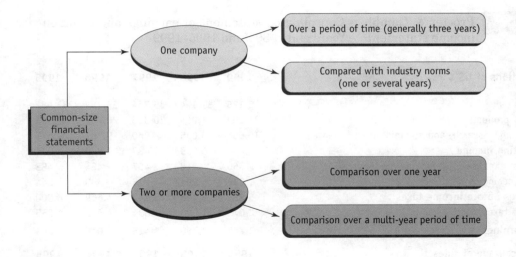

Figure 15.1 The use of common-size financial statements

Income statement

As mentioned before, the base line is the net sales figure. We examine separately the presentation of the income statement by function and by nature (see Chapter 3) since each structure reveals different aspects of performance.

Common-size income statement by function

Table 15.3 illustrates the common-size consolidated income statements by function of the US company Procter & Gamble. Each line item on the income statement is divided by the net sales of the corresponding year.

Common-size income statements are used to identify structural changes in a company's operating results.

Common-size income statement by nature

When the income statement is presented by nature it is important to restructure it to identify the key intermediate balances that help describe the value creation process such as commercial margin, value added and gross operating profit. The income statement, when all the intermediate balances have been clearly computed, becomes a "statement of intermediate balances". Figure 15.2 is an example of such a statement which reports the succession of levels in the formation of income for the period.

Essentially, such a statement dissects the income statement into meaningful blocks of data to help in the user's financial understanding and interpretation of the firm's economic activity. The intermediate balances may be presented in absolute monetary amounts, as percentages of variations from one period to another (trend analysis), or as percentages of some relevant basis. This restructured income statement can prove to be particularly useful to the user when a company has side by side a manufacturing activity (manufacture of goods or services for sale) and a dealership or brokerage activity (merchandise purchased for resale).

| Table 15.3 | Procter & Gamble – Consolidated statement of earnings and common-size income statements – Years ended 30 June 1995–1999 |

In millions of US $	1999	1998	1997	1996	1995
Net sales	38,125	37,154	35,764	35,284	33,482
Cost of products sold	21,206	21,064	20,316	20,762	19,561
Marketing, research, and administrative expenses	10,666	10,035	9,960	9,707	9,677
Operating income	6,253	6,055	5,488	4,815	4,244
Interest expense	650	548	457	484	488
Other income, net	235	201	218	338	244
Earnings before income taxes	5,838	5,708	5,249	4,669	4,000
Income taxes	2,075	1,928	1,834	1,623	1,355
Net earnings	3,763	3,780	3,415	3,046	2,645
In percentage of sales	1999	1998	1997	1996	1995
Net sales	100.0%	100.0%	100.0%	100.0%	100.0%
Cost of products sold	55.6%	56.7%	56.8%	58.8%	58.4%
Marketing, research, and administrative expenses	28.0%	27.0%	27.8%	27.5%	28.9%
Operating income	16.4%	16.3%	15.3%	13.6%	12.7%
Interest expense	1.7%	1.5%	1.3%	1.4%	1.5%
Other income, net	0.6%	0.5%	0.6%	1.0%	0.7%
Earnings before income taxes	15.3%	15.4%	14.7%	13.2%	11.9%
Income taxes	5.4%	5.2%	5.1%	4.6%	4.0%
Net earnings	9.9%	10.2%	9.5%	8.6%	7.9%

Source: Annual reports 1997 and 1999

Following is an analysis of the main sections of this "restructured" income statement.

Margin on sales

The commercial margin expresses the difference between sales of merchandise and cost of merchandise sold.

Current period "production"

The company's industrial output during the period is the total of sold production at sales price, plus increases in the finished goods and work in progress inventories at cost and the cost of self-produced fixed assets.

Value added

The term value added is a basic concept used in national income accounting, which refers to the amount contributed by a particular enterprise to the national wealth. It is the creation or increase in value, resulting from the enterprise's current professional activities, over and above that of goods and services provided by third parties and consumed by the firm. This concept is used in several countries, and especially in Australia, France, Germany, South Africa, and the United Kingdom. It is developed in Appendix 15.1

EBITDA or gross operating profit

The EBITDA (earnings from operations before interests, taxes, depreciation and amortization and provisions), or gross operating profit, measures the

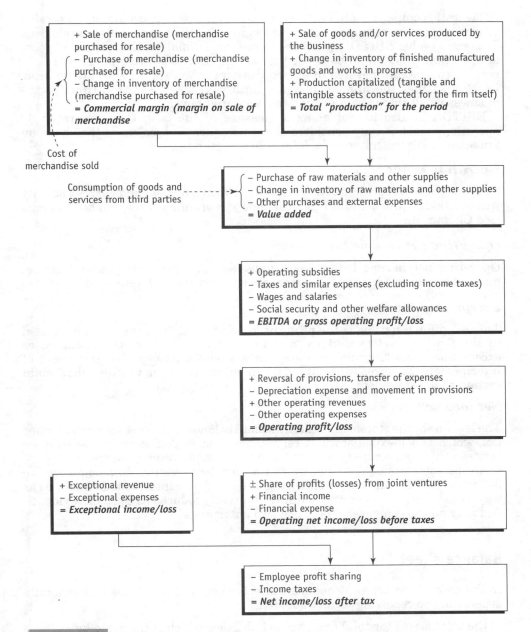

Figure 15.2
Structure of the income statement by intermediate balances of financial performance

wealth created by the enterprise from its operations, independently of its financial income and expenses, charges for depreciation and amortization, and other adjustments such as provisions for doubtful accounts. This indicator helps in evaluating the firm's management's short-term ability to create wealth since it is not affected by long-term strategic decisions regarding financing (capital structure) and capital investment policies. The ratio of EBITDA to sales (or accounting "production") is often considered to be a measure of the "business profitability" of the firm, allowing inter-enterprise comparisons.

The ratio comparing EBITDA to the value of the enterprise (net market value of equity), serves as a measure of the vulnerability of the firm to a takeover. This ratio (Value/EBITDA) provides, in fact, an estimate of the number of years of operations that would be needed for an acquirer to get to a payback, i.e., to recover the capital invested in an acquisition of the firm. The lower the ratio, i.e., the smaller the number of years until payback, the more attractive the business is, all things being equal, to a potential buyer.

EBITDA is also looked at as a measure of the cash flow generated by operations since it only considers those revenues and expenses that have an impact on cash (cash items, as defined in Chapter 14).

Operating profit

Operating profit represents the result of the firm's normal and current activity without taking into account financial and extraordinary (exceptional) elements (see Chapter 6).

Operating net income before taxes

Operating net income before taxes indicates economic and financial performance before consideration of extraordinary (exceptional) items and taxes.

Exceptional income

The exceptional income is the profit or loss from activities that are not related to the firm's usual operations, and are, therefore, out of the ordinary, or exceptional. This "income" is shown as a separate item on the statement of intermediate balances without addition or subtraction to any other main section of the statement.

Net income/loss

The last line of the statement of intermediate balances is the net income/loss after tax, which is self-explanatory. It serves, however, to double-check the equality between this restructured statement and the original income statement.

An income statement by nature can always be presented in a common-size format, even without the restructuring to identify the intermediate balances as we just did, but, of course, its usefulness is greatly reduced as the metrics identified may not be comparable between two enterprises.

Balance sheet

In the case of the balance sheet, the selected common-size basis will generally depend on the reporting format adopted:

● the total assets (or total equity plus liabilities, which is the same by definition) in the United States, in the majority of continental European countries, and in Japan

● the shareholders' equity (total shareholders' funds) in the UK and Ireland

● the shareholders' equity plus long-term debts in the Netherlands.

Traditional common-size balance sheet

The common-size balance sheet (in millions of US dollars) is illustrated in Table 15.4 through that of Procter & Gamble.

As is generally the case in a common-size presentation, the balance sheet reported in Table 15.4 is rather aggregated and several items such as shareholders' equity, property, plant and equipment, goodwill, and intangibles are more detailed in the published balance sheet.

Table 15.4 Procter & Gamble – Consolidated balance sheets and common-size balance sheets – Years 30 June 1996–1999

Assets	1999	1998	1997	1996	1999	1998	1997	1996
Current assets								
Cash and cash equivalents	2,294	1,549	2,350	2,074	7.1%	5.0%	8.5%	7.5%
Investment securities	506	857	760	446	1.6%	2.8%	2.8%	1.6%
Accounts receivable	2,940	2,781	2,738	2,841	9.2%	9.0%	9.9%	10.2%
Inventories	3,338	3,284	3,087	3,130	10.4%	10.6%	11.2%	11.3%
Deferred income taxes	621	595	661	598	1.9%	1.9%	2.4%	2.2%
Prepaid expenses and other current assets	1,659	1,511	1,190	1,718	5.2%	4.9%	4.3%	6.2%
Total current assets	11,358	10,577	10,786	10,807	35.4%	34.2%	39.2%	39.0%
Property, plant, and equipment (net)	12,626	12,180	11,376	11,118	39.3%	39.3%	41.3%	40.1%
Goodwill and other intangible assets (net)	6,822	7,011	3,949	4,281	21.2%	22.6%	14.3%	15.4%
Other non-current assets	1,307	1,198	1,433	1,524	4.1%	3.9%	5.2%	5.5%
Total assets	32,113	30,966	27,544	27,730	100.0%	100.0%	100.0%	100.0%
Liabilities and shareholders' equity	1999	1998	1997	1996	1999	1998	1997	1996
Current liabilities								
Accounts payable	2,300	2,051	2,203	2,236	7.2%	6.6%	8.0%	8.1%
Accrued and other liabilities	4,083	3,942	3,802	3,981	12.7%	12.7%	13.8%	14.4%
Taxes payable	1,228	976	944	492	3.8%	3.2%	3.4%	1.8%
Debt due within one year	3,150	2,281	849	1,116	9.8%	7.4%	3.1%	4.0%
Total current liabilities	10,761	9,250	7,798	7,825	33.5%	29.9%	28.3%	28.2%
Long-term debt	6,231	5,765	4,143	4,670	19.4%	18.6%	15.0%	16.8%
Deferred income taxes	362	428	559	638	1.1%	1.4%	2.0%	2.3%
Other non-current liabilities	2,701	3,287	2,998	2,875	8.4%	10.6%	10.9%	10.4%
Total liabilities	20,055	18,730	15,498	16,008	62.5%	60.5%	56.3%	57.7%
Shareholders' equity	12,058	12,236	12,046	11,722	37.5%	39.5%	43.7%	42.3%
Total liabilities and shareholders' equity	32,113	30,966	27,544	27,730	100.0%	100.0%	100.0%	100.0%

Source: Annual reports 1997 and 1999

Balance sheet structure

A company's simplified balance sheet can be structured by identifying two separate "time horizons" (current or short term; and non-current or long term), each corresponding to different types of decisions for both assets, on one hand, and shareholders' equity and liabilities on the other, as well as separating operating from financial activities. Table 15.5 illustrates such structure.

A firm's financial structure is sometimes analyzed through the use of the structurally simplified balance sheet just presented but the best way probably remains the preparation of a common-size simplified balance sheet.

Cash equation

Principles

One extension of the simplified balance sheet described already, beyond the common-size analysis, is that of net cash. The simplified balance sheet can be restructured in turn to identify some critical metrics which are very useful in both managing the firm and evaluating its income growth potential and risks (see Table 15.6).

Table 15.5 Balance sheet structure

Assets	Shareholders' equity and liabilities
● Fixed (non-current assets) (FA)	● Shareholders' equity and long-term (financial) liabilities (= Long-term capital) (LTC)
● Current assets (CA)	● Current liabilities (CL)
● Cash and cash equivalents (positive cash) (PC)	● Bank overdrafts (negative cash) (BO)
Total assets	Total shareholders' equity and liabilities

Table 15.6 Cash equation

(+)	Shareholders' equity and long-term (financial) debts (LTC)
(−)	Fixed (non-current) assets (FA)
(=)	**Working capital (WC)**
(+)	Current assets (except cash) (CA)
(−)	Current liabilities (CL)
(=)	**Working capital need (financing need arising from the operating cycle) (WCN)**
(+)	Positive cash and cash equivalents (PC)
(−)	Bank overdrafts (BO)
(=)	**Net cash (NC)**

Table 15.6 can be summarized as the cash equation:

Working capital – Working capital need = Net cash

Working capital can be calculated in two ways (as shown in Table 15.7):

(a) shareholders' equity *plus* long-term debts *minus* fixed assets, or

(b) current assets (inventories plus receivables) *plus* cash *minus* current liabilities and bank overdrafts.

Table 15.7 Link between balance sheet structure and cash equation

Assets	=	Shareholders' equity and liabilities
FA + CA + PC	=	LTC + CL + BO
(CA − CL) + (PC − BO)	=	(LTC − FA)
WCN + NC	=	WC
(PC − BO)	=	(LTC − FA) − (CA − CL)
NC	=	WC − WCN

Each approach, although it provides the very same figure in the end, communicates a different message.

The (a) approach gives an indication of the financial solidity of the enterprise and its state of health: it essentially identifies how much long-term capital is available to finance the operating cycle (see Figure 15.3).

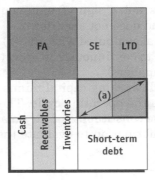

Figure 15.3   The (a) approach: WC(a) = SE + LTD – FA

The (b) approach (most commonly used approach in North America) shows the capacity of the company to face up to its short-term debts through its available cash, receivables and inventory accounts: it essentially shows the ability of the firm to survive if it were to lose all short-term financial support. Clearly if the operating cycle were to continue in the case of a credit crunch, it is best to still have some cash, some receivable and some inventories, a situation the working capital illustrates well (see Figure 15.4).

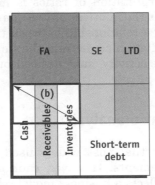

Figure 15.4   The (b) approach: WC(b) = Cash + Receivables + Inventories – Short-term debt

Although it is impossible to establish a normative value for working capital (it depends on the speed and variance in the speed of the operating cycle), it is a useful indicator especially when viewed dynamically over time and in comparison with other enterprises operating in the same or similar economic or geographic sector of activity.

Originally, analysts were only looking at working capital, ignoring the working capital need. Working capital was expected to always be positive and was considered to represent a measure of security and survival ability of the firm. The existence of distribution companies and the development of the new economy have made a negative working capital situation perfectly normal. For example when a retailer has an inventory that rotates 52 times a year, has customers that pay cash (and the cash is immediately reinvested), and obtains 45 days of effective credit from its suppliers, the working capital need is by construction negative. It is not a sign of imminent danger (inability to pay suppliers) as long as demand does not slow down.

A negative working capital computed with the (b) approach (it is a source of funds) encourages retailers to continuously to grow (and the growth is actually, de facto, financed by the suppliers).

The working capital need (working capital minus cash on hand) defines the financing need arising from the operating cycle. The cash equation establishes a critical liaison between the constituents of the balance sheet and allows users and analysts of financial information to evaluate the position of the firm with regard to its operating cycle.

Scenarios

On the basis of the cash equation just defined, six different types of financial structure are possible (see Figure 15.5).

As shown in Appendix 15.2, the working capital need can be expressed in sales days.

Ratio analysis

The computation and interpretation of ratios is more or less homogeneous between countries. A ratio is the quotient of two quantities, the numerator and the denominator, assuming a relationship between them. In financial analysis quantities used in the calculation come from the financial statements or from descriptors of the business's activity (such as headcount, volume of sales, share of market, etc.).

Conditions of use of ratio analysis

Ratio analysis is probably the most widely used analytical technique for interpreting financial statements. However, caution should be exercised in using such tools. A ratio reflects a business model relationship between two or more quantities. A causal interpretation of the variation over time of a ratio may weigh differently a variation of the numerator alone, of the denominator alone, or of both simultaneously.

It is also essential to verify the coherence of the quantities that are related: they may not correspond to the same parameter of analysis (possibly as the result of mergers, acquisition or divestment, etc.), may not result from similar accounting or classification rules (WAC to FIFO costing of inventory flows, for example – see Chapter 9), may not reflect the same operating assumptions (possibility of a divergence of news about the useful life of a tangible or intangible asset), etc.

When using comparative ratio analysis, it is important to remember that the causal relationship behind a certain value of a ratio may not apply similarly to two different enterprises (Ford Motor Company relies heavily on outsourcing of

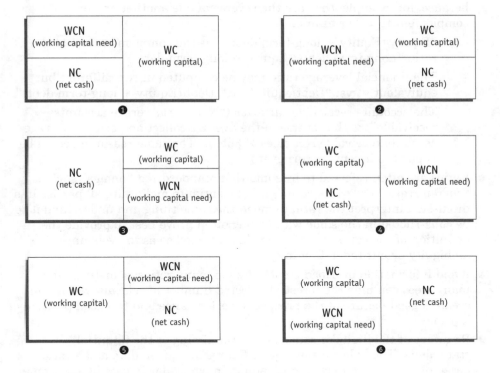

① Financial structure for a manufacturing company with positive net cash
② Financial structure for a manufacturing company with negative net cash
③ Financial structure for a distribution company for which the working capital need is a source of financing arising from the operating cycle
④ Financial structure for a distribution company for which the working capital need is a financing source arising from the operating cycle and working capital is negative indicating an excess of investment in fixed assets
⑤ Not a typical structure: the negative cash and the financing source arising from the operating cycle finance the investments
⑥ Not a typical structure: the negative cash finances the investments and the need arising from the operating cycle

Figure 15.5 Different types of financial structure

many key car components, while Volkswagen believes in producing a much higher proportion of its own components); or that practices between countries may be very different (supplier credit or the role of financial institutions, for example).

Essentially, it is important to remember that ratios should be used to raise questions. They rarely provide a direct interpretation. A ratio calculation is generally the first step in an investigative research to get to the root cause of the situation described by the financial statement.

Some suggestions follow for an appropriate use of ratios in financial analysis.

● Base the analysis on comparisons.

● Avoid information overload which would result from computing seemingly different ratios, which in reality have the same informational content because, for example, they are the reverse of one another or the complement to 1. For example,

- "Equity/(Equity + long-term debts)" is the complement to 1 of the ratio "Long-term debts/(Equity + long-term-debts)".
- The financial leverage ratio may be computed in two different but equivalent ways: "Debt/equity" or "(Debt/(Equity + long-term debt)".
- The accounts receivable turnover ("Net sales/Average accounts receivable") is the reverse of the average collection period ("Average accounts receivable/Net sales × 365"). (The same reasoning could be applied to inventory turnover.)

- Ratios are often referred to by somewhat standardized "names" such as "current ratio" or "quick ratio". It is essential to make sure all parties in a discussion interpret the ratio to mean the same thing and understand it to be constructed in the same way. It may often prove best to provide the definition of the ratio next to the value reported so as to avoid any ambiguity or misunderstanding.

- Avoid information overload created by too many ratios: sometimes too many trees can hide the forest. A selected number of relevant ratios will create a good picture of the prospects, performance and financial position of a firm.

- Be aware of the limits of ratios due to the timing of the financial statements. The balance sheet gives figures at a given date and a ratio based on this figure may be misleading, in particular in case of a seasonal or cyclical activity. One solution consists in averaging beginning and ending balance sheet figures.

- Be aware of the limits of the ratios due to the quality of financial statements.

- Be aware of the difficulty of interpreting negative ratios (because either the numerator or the denominator is negative – for instance, a negative net income). In general, the negative sign of the ratio is mentioned, but the absolute value is difficult to interpret and is often omitted altogether.

- Do no look for a standardized list of universally applicable ratios. Frustrating though it might be, such "ready-to-use" list cannot exist. There are hundreds of possible different ratios, due to the existence of numerous items in the financial statements and the almost unlimited possibility of combinations. The following ratios are some examples of the most frequently used and discussed ratios but they may not be appropriate for a given situation of a specific firm. Each firm is case specific and the analyst should first understand the business to be able to choose the relevant ratios (rather than doing the opposite, although sometimes a few fundamental ratios may help identify the key questions to understand the business).

- Ratios defined in a given country should only be applied to financial statements of another country with great caution. Ratio analysis is dependent on accounting principles followed, business practices and culture. For instance, some ratios describing liquidity and solvency imply a given presentation of the balance sheet (increasing liquidity or decreasing liquidity (see Chapter 3). In countries where the balance sheet is presented by "nature", the concepts of liquidity and solvency are more difficult to implement.

- Financial statement analysis is based on judgement calls and interpretation on the part of the analyst. Never overestimate the explanatory power of ratios. Always place ratio analysis within a more comprehensive analysis of the whole set of financial statements and of the business.

Comparisons of ratios

Figure 15.6 illustrates the fact there are three possible types of ratios, according to the basis of their comparisons:

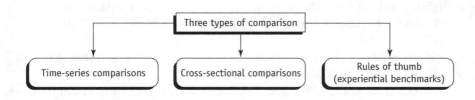

Figure 15.6 Ratio comparisons

1 **Time-series comparison** (or **longitudinal ratio analysis**): Ratios are computed yearly (or for several periods) over a given period of time. The ratios of one year are then compared to the historical ratios of the company. Although the period is not standardized, practice seems to imply that a 3-year period provides useful information.

Example:

	20X1	**20X2**	**20X3**
COGS to sales	55%	57%	54%

It appears that year 20X2 performance seems to have shown a deterioration in the gross margin and that year 20X3 has shown an improvement. Further inquiry is required to understand why this happened as no action comes directly from the data. Managers should not take solace in the fact that 20X3 clearly shows an improvement over 20X2, unless they have a clear understanding of the causality of the improvement so they can create the conditions for the continuation of the positive trend.

2 **Cross-sectional comparisons**: Ratios are compared to equivalent ratios of other companies, a competitor for instance, or against industry averages. One limit of such industry comparisons stems from the fact that the activities of compared companies rarely offer a consistent basis for comparison. Another issue is the difficulty in obtaining the relevant ratios for competitors or businesses in the same economic sector (this topic will be developed in the second part of this chapter).

Example:

	Firm A	**Firm B**	**Firm C**
Average days of inventory available	25	42	27

Firm B appears to be an outlier in this industry (a fast turnover of inventories is generally considered preferable). However if Firm B's strategy is different from that of A and C (for example A and C offer little variety at low prices, while B offers a great diversity of products and extracts a price premium for such a service to customers), it may very well be normal for B to have a slower turnover of inventory.

3 **Rules of thumb** (experiential benchmarks): Ratios are compared to selected references. These can be either competitive measures (compare to the "best in class" – with all the problems implied by the concept) or rules of thumb based on industry-wide "experience". For example one often speaks of the *rule of the three-thirds* for a "sound" equity and liability side of the balance sheet: this *rule* implies one-third for shareholders' equity, one-third for long-term debt and one-third for short-term debt.

Such reference for interpreting ratios can prove to be difficult to use effectively for the following reasons:

– If the ratio is based on industry statistics, all problems already raised about cross-sectional comparisons apply. For example, the *rule* that used to say that the working capital was supposed to be positive is continuously challenged (appropriately) in distribution and retail activities. Another rule of three-thirds applies to the restaurant business in which one often hears that in order to be "normally" profitable the price *ought to be* three times the cost of the raw materials; but even if this is often true, the same so-called *rule* probably cannot apply to institutional kitchens (rule of thumb is *twice*) or gastronomic restaurants (rule of thumb is *four to six times*).

– If the ratio is based on a "rule of thumb" built over the years without any reasoned basis, the results of the ratio analysis may be then subjected to doubt. For example, one often hears that a healthy firm is one that generates at least €150,000 revenue per person employed. However, this does not specify the degree of value addition provided by the firm or the intrinsic price of the raw materials (raw materials in a three-star restaurant probably are more expensive than they are in a neighborhood diner; rare metals dealers and software manufacturers have very different situations in terms of added value, etc.).

Some key ratios

Ratios are organized in four categories serving each some of the needs expressed by shareholders: (a) evaluation of short-term liquidity and solvency; (b) evaluation of long-term solvency and financial leverage; (c) evaluation of profitability and generation of profitability; and (d) measures of shareholders' return.

Table 15.8 lists some key ratios, and the reader is reminded to keep great caution in using such a list as the ratios suggested may not all be appropriate or the best suited for any given situation. This list is a "tool box" and the user must first identify the nature and issues of the business evaluated before selecting the appropriate tools from the box.

There are hundreds of possible different ratios, since the number of combinations of all the items on the financial statements plus the possibility of relating these to non-financial activity descriptors is limitless. As a consequence, ratios are frequently classified in subgroups which reflect a particular aspect of financial performance or position. Appendix 15.3 identifies some of the classifications suggested by different authors.

Table 15.8 Some key ratios

Name of the ratios	Computation	Comments
Short-term liquidity ratios (firm's ability to finance its day-to-day operations and to pay its liabilities as they fall due)		
Current ratio (or working capital ratio)	Current assets[2]/Current liabilities (creditors: amounts falling due within one year)[3]	Firm's ability to pay its current liabilities from its current assets Rule of thumb: 2:1 as an "ideal"
Quick ratio (or quick asset or acid test or liquidity)	(Cash + marketable securities + accounts receivable)/Current liabilities	Firm's ability to pay its current liabilities from its current assets excluding the sale of inventories
Cash ratio	(Cash + marketable securities)/Current liabilities	Firm's ability to pay its current liabilities from its cash and cash equivalents
Average collection period	[(Accounts receivable year 2 + Accounts receivable year 1)/2 × 365]/Sales	Average length of time to collect accounts receivable
Average payment period	[(Accounts payable year 2 + Accounts payable year 1)/2 × 365]/Purchases of goods and services	Average length of time to pay accounts payable
Inventory turnover	Cost of sales/[(Inventories year 2 + Inventories year 1)/2]	Number of times that a firm sells or turns over its inventory per year
Long-term solvency ratios (firm's ability to pay its long-term liabilities)		
Debt ratio	Total debt/Total assets	Firm's debt-paying ability The lower this ratio, the better the company's position Firm's degree of financial leverage
Debt to equity ratio	Debt[4]/Shareholders' equality or Debt/ Shareholders' equity + Debt)	
Debt to tangible net worth	Debt/Shareholders' eaity – intangible assets)	
Long-term debt to equity ratio	Long-term debt/Shareholders' equity or Long-term debt/Shareholders' equity + Debt)	Firm's long-term debt-paying ability The lower this ratio, the better the company's position Firm's degree of financial leverage
Interest coverage ratio (interest cover ratio)	Operating income (before interest expense and income taxes)/Interest expense	Number of times that a firm's interest expense is covered by operation earnings Rule of thumb: minimum of 5

continued overleaf

Table 15.8 Some key ratios (continued)

Name of the ratios	Computation	Comments
Profitability ratios (measure of the firm's performance)		
Return on shareholders' equity (ROE)	Net income/Average equity[5] (or income before interest and Tax/Average equity)	Return to shareholders
Return on investment (ROI) (return on capital employed or ROCE)	Net income/(Average long-term liabilities + equity = net income/capital employed or earnings before interest and tax (EBIT)/capital employed	Measure of the income earned on the invested capital
Gross profit rate (gross profit margin)	Gross profit/Sales	Percentage of each sales CU not absorbed by the cost of sales
Return on sales (net profit margin)	Net income/Sales	Percentage of each sales CU that contributes to net income
Asset turnover	Sales/[Assets year 2 + assets year 1)/2]	Firm's ability to generate sales relative to its investment in assets
Return on assets (ROA)	Net income/[Assets year 2 + assets year 1)/2]	Firm's ability to use its assets to create profits
Sales per employee	Sales/Number of employees	Measure of the sales productivity of the workforce
Market price and dividend ratios (capital markets' perception of the firm's share)		
Earnings per share	Net income/Average shares outstanding	Measure of share performance
Price/earnings ratio (P/E or PER)	Market price per share/Earnings per share	Amount that investors are willing to pay for each CU of a firm's earnings – market confidence in a company
Market to book ratio	Market price per share/Book value per share	Amount that investors are willing to pay for each CU of a firm's net assets
Dividend yield ratio	Cash dividends per share/Market price per share	Cash return on the investment in a company
Dividend payout ratio	Cash dividends per share/Earnings per share	Proportion of earnings paid out in the form of dividends

Additional remarks about ratios computation

1 Table 15.8 includes the "average payment period" (accounts payable/purchases × 365) but it cannot be easily calculated by an outside analyst since the value of purchases is not provided in an income statement by function. However, with companies presenting their income statement by nature, this ratio is often computed. It is also a ratio which is pretty systematically calculated in an internal financial analysis as it is a key element of the speed of the operating cash cycle.

2 When net income is used in ratios, it is sometimes replaced by the earnings before interest and taxation (EBIT) because doing so takes away the financing policy effect as well as the income tax effects, thus facilitating cross-sectional and longitudinal comparisons.

3 There is a link between several "return" ratios, as shown in Figure 15.7.

4 The earnings per share (EPS) ratio is critically important for financial markets as it is used as a common metric for most businesses. As we have seen repeatedly, the definition of "earnings" is quite complex and therefore many countries (essentially those with active financial markets) have felt the need to clarify the process of calculation of EPS by issuing accounting standards or reporting regulations so that the markets be able to operate efficiently with every one understanding data to mean the same thing. This topic will be further developed in Advanced Issues.

Additional remarks on ratios computation are presented in Appendix 15.4.

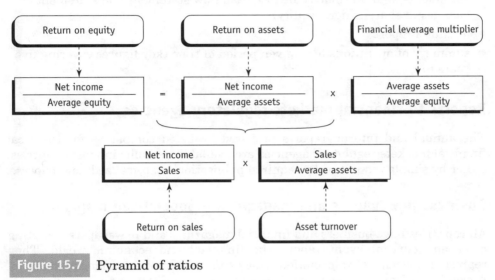

Figure 15.7 Pyramid of ratios

ADVANCED ISSUES

Sources of information about companies

Public sources of financial and operational information about companies are plentiful and all give a partial view of the whole and must be used conjointly as much as possible: annual statements reporting to shareholders, reports to financial markets regulatory agencies, business magazines and papers, databases and statistical publication by trade associations or consulting firms and legal filings (with tax authorities or courts depending on the regulatory environment).

Annual report to shareholders

When analyzing public companies, their annual report to shareholders is an important source of information. The content of annual reports is very similar throughout the world. They contain:

- chairman's letter to shareholders (highlights of the year and perspectives)
- management discussion and analysis (segmental analysis of the business with an analysis of the past and the identification of perspectives)
- financial statements (balance sheet, income statement, notes to financial statements, and, in some countries, cash flow statement and statement of changes in shareholders' equity)
- auditor's report
- summary of operations for a given period of time (key figures covering five years in general).

Reports to financial markets regulatory agencies

The annual and interim reports prepared by listed companies for the local financial markets regulatory agencies are available to public in most countries, either by simple request or by required publication in specialized newspapers.

Business newspapers and magazines – Specialized magazines

All countries have business and financial magazines and newspapers reporting news and current events about the financial and economic world. They represent a wealth of information which can be helpful for financial analysts. Appendix 15.5 provides some examples of such magazines and newspapers.

Databases and statistics publications

Appendix 15.6 lists several sources of government statistics or publications from private organizations.

Financial statements filed with tax or judicial authorities

In some countries (mainly European countries), there is an obligation for certain companies (in general limited companies) to file their financial statements with an administration. The Appendix 15.7 presents the obligation in several countries.

Measures of return to investors

The performance of an enterprise, both in terms of past results and in terms of creation of potential prospects is not all that the shareholders want to monitor. They want to see whether they earn enough to keep their money invested in this firm at that level of risk. Two families of indicators are used here: earnings per share and return on capital invested.

Earnings per share

Earnings per share (EPS) is one of the prime metrics used in financial markets. It is the ratio of net income after taxes (and after preferred dividends if there are any)[6] to average number of shares during the period for which the income has been calculated. As we have seen the calculation of earnings (income) for the numerator as well as the definition of the denominator (ordinary, preference, treasury shares) can be complex. Many countries have issued statements or standards aimed at clarifying earnings, denominator shares and earnings per share. Examples of such regulations are FRS 14 in the UK and SFAS 128 in the US. At the international level, IASC adopted IAS 33 in 1997.

A difficulty comes from the existence of share equivalents such as stock options and stock warrants, or convertible instruments such as bonds which can be turned into shares at any time the conditions specified when they were issued are met. The fully diluted earnings per share reveals the risk that the EPS be much lower than currently calculated if all those holding options or warrants or convertible instruments were to convert their rights effectively into shares.

For example, a high-tech firm with a capital of one million CU (100,000 shares with a 10 CU par) has issued stock options to lure and retain managerial and creative talent. Options amount to a potential of 200,000 shares. Let us assume that today the EPS is 2 CU per share (i.e., total earnings were $2 \times 100,000 = 200,000$ CU). If total earnings were to increase by 50% to 300,000 CU in the next year, and all options were exercised, the original shareholders would see the EPS fall to only 1 CU:

$$\frac{200,000 \times 1.5}{100,000 + 200,000} = 1$$

Each standard prescribes principles for the determination and presentation of earnings per share that improve comparisons of performance between enterprises in one period and between different periods for the same enterprise.

All regulations adopted apply to publicly traded companies and specifically to their consolidated financial statements. However these rules and recommendations are common sense and may usefully be applied to not publicly traded companies and to unconsolidated financial statements.

IAS 33 makes a distinction between basic and diluted earnings per share. Numerous companies compute adjusted earnings after the impact of both operating and non-operating exceptional items and amortization of goodwill in order to provide a better understanding of the underlying performance of the company on a normalized basis. By doing so, four earnings per share may be computed:

- basic EPS
- diluted EPS
- adjusted basic EPS
- adjusted diluted EPS.

Basic earnings per share

Basic earnings per share is defined as (IAS 33, IASC 1997a: § 10):

In this definition, the net profit is computed after deducting preference dividends. The weighted average number of ordinary shares outstanding during the period is computed according to one of the two methods shown in Table 15.9.

Table 15.9 Time-weighted average number of shares

		Shares issued (1)	Treasury shares (2)	Shares outstanding	
1 January 20X1	Balance at beginning of year	3,100	400	2,700	=(1)–(2)
30 April 20X1	Issue of new shares for cash	900	—	3,600	
1 November 20X1	Purchase of treasury shares for cash	—	600	3,000	
31 December 20X1	Balance at end of year	4,000	1,000	3,000	=(1)–(2)

		Balance (1)	Number of months (2)	Weighted balance (1)×(2)/12
Method 1	1 January 20X1–30 April 20X1	2,700	4	900
	1 May 20X1–1 November 20X1	3,600	6	1,800
	1 November 20X1–31 December 20X1	3,000	2	500
	Weighted average number of shares			3,200
Method 2	1 January 20X1–31 December 20X1	2,700	12	2,700
	30 April 20X1–31 December 20X1	900	8	600
	1 November 20X1–31 December 20X1	–600	2	–100
	Weighted average number of shares			3,200

The time-weighting factor is the number of days that the specific shares are outstanding as a proportion of the total number of days in the period. Moreover, as shown in Table 15.9, there are two different ways to compute the weighted average number of outstanding shares.

Diluted earnings per share

As indicated in IAS 33 (IASC 1997a: § 24), in order to calculate diluted earnings per share: "The net profit attributable to ordinary shareholders and the weighted average number of shares outstanding should be adjusted for the effects of all dilutive potential ordinary shares." We must recall that a potential ordinary-share is a financial instrument or other contract that may entitle its holder to ordinary shares.

The amount of net profit or loss should be adjusted (§ 26) for the following after-tax elements:

● "Any dividends on dilutive potential-ordinary-shares which have been deducted in arriving at the net profit attributable to ordinary shareholders (…);

● interest recognized in the period for the dilutive potential-ordinary-shares; and

● any other changes in income or expense that would result from the conversion of the dilutive potential-ordinary-shares."

In other words, the net profit or loss of the period is increased by the amount of dividends, interest and other income or expense that will be saved on the conversion of the dilutive potential ordinary shares into ordinary shares. Table 15.10 presents an example of computation of diluted earnings per share based on the conversion of bonds.

In order to compute diluted earnings per share, an enterprise should assume the full exercise of dilutive options and other dilutive ordinary shares of the enterprise. The assumed proceeds from these issues should be considered to have been received from the issue of shares at fair value. In practice, options and other share purchase arrangements are dilutive when they would result in the issue of ordinary shares for less than fair value. The amount of the dilution is fair value less the issue price.

Table 15.10 Computation of diluted earnings per share

Net income	(1)	5,000
Ordinary shares outstanding	(2)	2,500
Basic earnings per share	(3)=(1)/(2)	2
Number of convertible bonds	(4)	200
Conditions of conversion: 10 bonds for 4 shares	(5)	0.4
New shares issued from the conversion	(6)=(4)×(5)	80
Interest expense for the current year relating to the liability component of the convertible bond	(7)	50
Current and deferred tax relating to that interest expense	(8)	20
Adjusted net profit	(9)=(1)+(7)−(8)	5,030
Number of ordinary shares used to compute diluted earnings per share	(10)=(2)+(6)	2,580
Diluted earnings per share	(11)=(9)/(10)	1.95

Real-life examples

Irish Continental Group

(Ireland – UK/Irish Gaap – Source: Annual report 1999 – Shipping, transport and leisure group principally engaged in the transport of passengers and cars (Irish Ferries), freight and containers)

In Note 8 to financial statements, the group indicates that diluted earnings per share is computed in accordance with FRS 14 and is based on the weighted average shares in issue, including options exercisable as of the date of this report (31 October 1999). Table 15.11 presents the computation of the number of diluted weighted average shares and earnings per share (both basic and diluted).

Table 15.11 Irish Continental Group – Computation of earnings per share

		1999	1998
Total options in issue (millions)	(1)	2.12	1.9
Options not yet exercisable (millions)	(2)	−0.88	−0.86
Options exercisable (millions)	(3)=(1)+(2)	1.24	1.04
Average option price (€cents)	(4)	308	236
Average fair value of share price during the year (€cents)	(5)	1,136	1,330
Number of shares which would have been issued at fair value (millions)	(6)=−(3)×(4)/(5)	−0.34	−0.18
Dilutive options (millions)	(7)=(3)+(6)	0.90	0.86
Basic weighted average shares (millions)	(8)	26.23	26.02
Diluted weighted average shares (millions)	(9)=(7)+(8)	27.13	26.88
Profit attributable to shareholders of Irish Continental Group plc (€millions)	(10)	26.4	22.7
Basic earnings per share (€cents)	(11)=(10)/(8)×100	100.6	87.2
Diluted earnings per share (€cents)	(12)=(10)/(9)×100	97.3	84.4

Lines 10, 11 and 12 are taken from the profit and loss account (income statement). The number of shares which would have been issued at fair value (line 6) is computed by applying the ratio [average option price over average fair value] to the number of options exercisable

The EMI Group reports multiple versions of EPS. Table 15.12 is excerpted from the company's financial statements.

Table 15.12   EMI – Computation of earnings per share

	2000 £	1999 £
Earnings/basic EPS	158.4 m	122.6 m
Adjustments:		
Operating exceptional items	4.0 m	0.0 m
Non-operating exceptional items	−42.5 m	−3.7 m
Amortization of goodwill and music copyrights	34.6 m	27.3 m
Attributable taxation	−0.6 m	1.5 m
Minority interest (re: music copyright amortization)	−3.8 m	−3.7 m
Adjusted earnings/adjusted EPS	150.1 m	144.0 m
Basic earnings per ordinary share is calculated as follows:		
Earnings (1)	158.4 m	122.6 m
Weighted average number of ordinary shares in issue (2)	780.9 m	778.9 m
Earnings per ordinary share (1)/(2) × 100	20.3 p	15.7 p
Diluted earnings per ordinary share is calculated as follows:		
Earnings	158.4 m	122.6 m
Adjusted weighted average number of ordinary shares	781. m	779.4 m
Earnings per ordinary share	20.3 p	15.7 p
Adjusted basic earnings per ordinary share is calculated as follows:		
Adjusted earnings	150.1 m	144.0 m
Weighted average number of ordinary shares in issue	780.9 m	778.9 m
Adjusted earnings per ordinary share	19.2 p	18.5 p
Adjusted diluted earnings per ordinary share is calculated as follows:		
Adjusted earnings	150.1 m	144.0 m
Adjusted weighted average number of ordinary shares	781.8 m	779.4 m
Adjusted earnings per ordinary share	19.2 p	18.5 p

The number of ordinary shares has been adjusted for dilutive share options

Residual income and economic value added

Principles

The idea behind these methods is that the profit reported in the accounting statements only accounts for the cost of borrowed capital when in fact shareholders also have provided capital and expect a return (higher even than that of borrowed capital because shareholders assume much more risk). The original idea is that the "real" profit of the firm (called residual income) is the income after taking into account a fair (but nominal) remuneration for the shareholders.

If we assume the shareholders place a risk-factor of 10% on this firm and the risk-free rate is 5%, the shareholders implicitly expect a return of 15%. The residual income for a firm that earned an after-tax income of 1,000 CU and has a capital of 10,000 CU is $1,000 - (10,000 \times 0.15) = -500$ CU. The firm which showed an accounting profit is in fact not returning enough for the shareholders' expectations. Many businesses actually show a negative residual income.

The financial consulting firm Stern Stewart updated the old concept of residual income under the name of Economic Value Added® or EVA®. Their position is that many accounting elements used in the determination of income do not take a long-term vision and thus does not reflect the point of view of the shareholder (interested more in the future than in the past). In total they suggest some 150 adjustments to the income figure. One such adjustment is the consideration that R&D is really an investment and not an outright expense (see Chapter 8). Other consulting firms have coined their own proprietary approaches such as MVA (for market value added).

Example (assuming a shareholders' expectation of a 15% return)

Table 15.3 shows how the method works.

Table 15.13 Example of economic value added calculation

Income statement	
Sales revenue	5,000
Gross margin (after depreciation expense)	3,000
R&D expenses	500
Selling, administrative, and general expenses	1,000
EBIT	1,500
Financial expenses	200
Taxable income	1,300
Tax expense (assumes to be at 33%)	429
Net income after tax	871
Balance sheet	
Fixed assets (net)	1,500
Current assets	300
Current liabilities	200
Long-term liability	600
Shareholders' equity	1,000
Residual income calculation	
Profit after tax and before interest 871 + 200 (1–0.33) =	1,005
Cost of long term capital (1,000 +600) × 15%	240
Residual income	**765**
EVA calculation	
Profit after tax and before interest	1,005
Reintegration of R&D expenses (considered to be an investment)*	500
Adjusted income base	1,505
Long-term capital	1,600
Adjustment for R&D*	500
Adjusted long-term capital	2,100
Cost of capital (15%)	315
EVA (1,505 – 315)	**1,190**

*The R&D expense is considered as an investment. Consequently, the profit is increased and the shareholders' equity (included in the long-term capital) also increased by the same amount corresponding to the change in profit (see the capitalization of R&D in Chapter 8)

Source: Adapted from Lebas (1999)

All methods such as EVA® try to provide what they feel is a "better" answer to the question "Does a business really create value?" than traditional financial analysis. As usual no method provides a complete answer and each metric sheds light on a different aspect of financial performance, especially as it pertains to an estimation of the potential for future profits.

New methods appear continuously that try to compensate for the weaknesses or limitation of a previous method. For example, very few of the items examined in this chapter account for the fact that the cash flow generation ability of a firm is essential to its survival and growth. For example, in 2000 the Boston Consulting Group introduced a new metric which they call the Cash Value Added or CVA. This metric attempts to measure the value generated by a business by looking at the cash influx (after-tax income before interest plus depreciation) minus the cost of economic depreciation (i.e., the investment required to keep the production potential at the current level) minus the cost of long-term capital. Such a measure is clearly much more conducive to investing to grow the firm than many of the other synthetic metrics. A ratio of CVA to capital invested shows the cash flow return on investment. An aggressively investing firm that chooses the right sectors to invest will be rewarded with a good indicator while the management team that invests in the "wrong" sector will be shown to be poor performers by this metric.

Segment reporting

Segmenting the activity of a business means breaking it down into homogeneous subtotals or segments. Segmenting may be by markets, by customer profiles, by families of products or services, by families of technologies, by geographical areas, by type of currency exposure, etc. Reporting financial information by segment may help the financial statements users:

- better understand the enterprise's operating model and thus better interpret past performance as a leading indicator of future performance
- better assess the enterprise's risks and returns, opportunities and threats
- make more informed judgements about the enterprise as a whole.

Segments often yield differing profitability rates, offer different opportunities for growth, represent different future prospects and risks. Segment reporting is essential for both the management of the firm (for resource allocation especially) and for shareholders. The principles and practices of segment reporting are documented through SFAS 131 (FASB 1997) in the USA and IAS 14 (IASC 1997b) for the IASC. These standards requiring reporting of segment information apply mainly to publicly traded companies and especially to consolidated financial statements. However, the standards may in general be applied to not publicly traded companies and to non-consolidated financial statements.

Definitions

IAS 14, Segment Reporting (revised in 1997) defines a business segment (§ 9) as: "A distinguishable component of an enterprise that is engaged in providing an individual product or service or a group of related products or services and that is subject to risks and returns that are different from those of other business segments. Factors that should be considered in determining whether products and services are related include:

(a) the nature of the products or services;

(b) the nature of the production processes;

(c) the type or class of customer for the products or services;

(d) the methods used to distribute the products or provide the services;

(e) if applicable, the nature of the regulatory environment, for example, banking, insurance, or public utilities."

A geographical segment (IAS 14, IASC 1997b: § 9) is: "A distinguishable component of an enterprise that is engaged in providing products or services within a particular economic environment and that is subject to risks and returns that are different from those of components operating in other economic environments. Factors that should be considered in identifying geographical segments include:

(a) similarity of economic and political conditions;

(b) relationships between operations in different geographical areas;

(c) proximity of operations;

(d) special risks associated with operations in a particular area;

(e) exchange control regulations; and

(f) the underlying currency risks."

Disclosure

Each enterprise may choose to report both a primary and a secondary segment reporting format: for example, business segments as primary information and geographical segments as secondary information (or the opposite). The choice is based on the source and nature of the enterprise's perceived risks and returns.

Primary reporting format

The following information should be reported for the primary segment(s):

- segment revenue (with the split between revenue from sales to external customers and revenue from transactions with other segments)

- "income" of the segment (which open up the issue of whether it is income – which would mean the consolidation of these amounts gives the total income of the firm) or simply a margin (which leaves some costs unaccounted for)

- total carrying amount (book value) of segment assets

- segment liabilities

- total cost incurred to acquire segment tangible and intangible assets (capital expenditures)

- total depreciation and amortization of segment assets included in the segment "income"

- total amount of significant non-cash expenses (other than depreciation and amortization).

Toray Industries

(Japan – Japanese GAAP – Source: Annual report 1999 – Manufacturer of synthetic fibers and textiles)

The company operates principally in five industrial segments (see Table 15.14).

Table 15.14 Primary reporting by business segment, 1999

	million Yen							
	Fibers and textiles	Plastics and chemicals	Housing and engineering	Pharma-ceuticals and medical products	New products and other businesses	Total	Elimination and corporate	Consolidated total
Sales to outside customers	420,040	295,537	132,343	47,796	105,401	1,001,117	0	1,001,117
Intersegment sales	1,144	25,578	61,192	25	21,066	109,005	−109,005	0
Total sales	421,184	321,115	193,535	47,821	126,467	1,110,122	−109,005	1,001,117
Operating income	15,690	17,156	1,041	4,237	8,976	47,100	464	47,564
Assets	466,269	478,255	204,021	66,497	249,596	1,464,638	−27,278	1,437,360
Depreciation and amortization	26,763	30,756	2,957	2,887	15,626	78,989	−1,373	77,616
Capital expenditures	37,203	51,086	3,666	2,661	27,579	122,195	−1,227	120,968

Although the term "primary" is not used in the annual report, the information published refers obviously to the primary format.

The company operates in three major geographic segments (see Table 15.15).

Table 15.15 Secondary reporting by geographic segment, 1999

	million Yen					
	Japan	Asia	North America and Europe	Total	Elimination and corporate	Consoli-dated total
Sales to outside customers	759,745	110,455	130,917	1,001,117	0	1,001,117
Inter-segment sales	70,490	11,510	8,249	90,249	−90,249	0
Total sales	830,235	121,965	139,166	1,091,366	−90,249	1,001,117
Operating income	26,239	8,530	12,817	47,586	−22	47,564
Assets	1,051,582	176,754	180,647	1,408,983	27,374	1,436,357

Reconciliation of segment data with enterprise-wide data must be carried out, so that any unassigned asset, liability, cost or revenue is accounted for:

● segment revenues with the total revenue to external customers
● segment "income" with a comparable measure of enterprise profit or loss as well as with the net profit or loss
● segment assets with the enterprise's assets
● segment liabilities with the enterprise's liabilities.

Secondary reporting format

The following information should be reported for the secondary segment(s):

● segment revenue from external customers

- total carrying amount of segment assets
- total cost incurred to acquire segment tangible and intangible assets (capital expenditure).

In general, this information is not required if the amount relating to a given segment represents less than 10% of the corresponding enterprise total amount.

Accounts manipulation and quality of financial statements

Principles

A major part of financial statement analysis is based on figures including net income (the "bottom line") or another intermediate level of measurement of income (such as gross margin or total contribution). It is therefore important to evaluate the quality of such figures, in other words the "quality of earnings". This quality is influenced by three factors:

- accounting methods
- accounting estimates
- classification of exceptional (or extraordinary) items in the income statement.

These three factors, joined together, have given rise to a practice known broadly as "accounts manipulation" which encompasses earnings management, including income smoothing and "big bath" accounting, and creative accounting. Copeland (1968: 101) defined manipulation as some ability to increase or decrease reported net income at will. At the same time, he implicitly acknowledged that the notion of manipulation may result from at least three types of behavioral patterns: "income maximizers", "income minimizers", and "income smoothers". However, we believe that accounts manipulation has a broader meaning than what Copeland describes. It also includes income statement classificatory practices, presented by Barnea et al. (1975, 1976) and Ronen and Sadan (1975), and also those related to the balance sheet, which are far less well described in the literature (Black et al., 1998). Actually, these practices represent a more important phenomenon now than when Copeland published his seminal article. Such accounts manipulation practices are based on a common functional fixation view of share price determination which states that accounting numbers contribute to determining share prices. Financial markets are essentially efficient and generally would "see through" accounting manipulation engaged in by listed firms. However, unlisted firms are not subject to the scrutiny of market analysts and the functional fixation view of the world may well apply in their case. In any case accounting manipulations may affect both cash flow and risks perceived by analysts (through the impact of manipulations on ratios).

We distinguish different streams of accounts manipulation, based on the fundamental principle that the aim of providing financial information is the reduction of the cost at which capital is obtained for the firm's endeavors. This reduction is related to the perception of the firm's risk by investors. The risk is technically measured by the *beta*, which is based on the relative variance of earnings.[7] Moreover, there is a structural risk revealed by the equilibrium between debt and equity. As a consequence, the objectives of accounts manipulation are to alter both: the variance of earnings per share and the debt/equity ratio. Earnings per share can be modified in two ways: first, by adding or removing revenues or expenses (modification of net income) and second, by listing an item "before" or "after" the profit definition used to calculate the earnings per share (classificatory manipulations). Figure 15.8 presents our framework for classifying accounts manipulation.

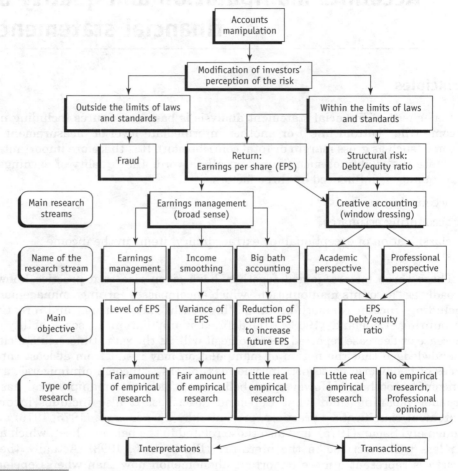

Figure 15.8 A framework for classifying accounts manipulation
Source: Co-authored with Gaétan Breton

Regarding the nature of practices, the literature has mainly discussed manipulations that are interpretations of standards, for instance, decisions on the level of accruals. But manipulation can also be premeditated, i.e., transactions can be designed in order to allow a desired accounting treatment. For instance, a leasing contract might be written in such a way that the leased equipment does not need to be capitalized (see Chapter 12).

The different streams of accounts manipulation

Earnings management

In this family of manipulation practices, management artificially manages earnings to achieve or meet some pre-established level of "expected" earnings (e.g., analyst forecasts, management's prior estimates or continuation of some earnings trend) (Fern *et al.*, 1994).

Income smoothing

Income smoothing has the clear objective of producing a steadily growing stream of profits. This form of manipulation can be, for example, the result of creating and canceling provisions (which means that at some point profit was enough to allow these provisions), or through the appropriate choice of the date of recognition of profit on long-term contracts, or through the ad hoc sale of inventories or long-lived assets which were undervalued (as was the case for example for a firm that sold TV rights to a large inventory of films it had obtained through an acquisition). Income smoothing is mainly a reduction of the variance of the profit.

Big bath accounting

Intuitively, big bath accounting is easy to understand. When a new CEO is appointed, she or he may wish to "clean up" the accounts to (a) start on a sound base that will allow a growing income figure to obtain more easily, or (b) so as to create provisions which will later be used to create some form of income smoothing. Such practices in reducing drastically earnings when the "new" administration takes over is believed to be reassuring to the shareholders and facilitating the creation of a future positive stream of revenues. As Moore (1973: 100) explained, new management has a tendency to be very pessimistic about the values of certain assets with the result that these values are often adjusted downward more than necessary. This type of behavior is colloquially known as "taking a bath".

Creative accounting

Creative accounting is an expression that has been developed by both practitioners and commentators (journalists) of the market activity. Creative accounting is using inappropriately accounting standards with the aim of misleading investors by presenting them with what they want to see, like a nice steadily increasing profit figure. Creative accounting has been studied by authors like Griffiths (1986, 1995) and Smith (1996), an investment analyst, who refers to "accounting sleight of hand". Mathews and Perera (1996: 260) include under the term such activity as "fiddling the books", "cosmetic reporting" and "window dressing the accounts". Griffiths (1986) starts, in his introduction, from the assumption that: "Every company in the country is fiddling its profits. Every set of accounts is based on books, which have been gently cooked or completely roasted." Creative accounting has been used with various meanings and brings some confusion into the field of accounts manipulation. It mainly includes earnings management (without any reference to income smoothing) and focusses a lot on classificatory manipulations (either related to income statement or to balance sheet).

Creative accounting practices

Numerous practices are available, and can be referred to as "manipulating variables". There follows a non-comprehensive list of such practices:

- Changes in accounting policies (this includes many possibilities and could be considered as a generic activity – see Chapter 6).
- R&D costs (capitalized or expensed? expenses deferred or anticipated? – see Chapter 8).
- Change from accelerated to straight-line depreciation (see Chapter 7).
- Capitalization (or not) of interest costs (see Chapter 7).
- Change in inventory valuation method (FIFO, WAC, LIFO – see Chapter 9).
- Accounting treatment of government grants (liability or revenue? – see Chapter 6).
- Long-term contracts (percentage of completion versus completed contract method – see Chapter 6).
- Treatment of unusual gains and losses (exceptional versus operating or extraordinary versus ordinary: classificatory manipulation; to anticipate or postpone: inter-temporal manipulation – see Chapter 6).
- Evaluation of provisions (inventories, doubtful accounts, long-term and marketable securities, loan loss, risks – see Chapters 9, 10 and 12).
- Capitalization of leases (see Chapter 12).
- Discretionary accounting decisions (expenses split over several years or deferred expenses, in countries allowing this practice – see Chapter 8).
- Purchase versus pooling decision (see Chapter 13).
- Pension costs (see Chapter 12).
- Analysis of the difference arising on first consolidation (see Chapter 13).

Conclusion on accounts manipulation

Some analysts believe that financial statements have no value because of these manipulations. We do not agree with such an idea. Financial statements are always useful, but the user must be aware of the limitations on their reliability. The notes to financial statements are a very good source of information which can be used to restate the financial statements and to perform a comparative analysis. Moreover, the consistency accounting principle (see Chapter 5) often works as a good limitation to manipulations. One should also never forget that most of the manipulations, principally those based on provisions, will have an opposite effect at the time of their reversal. This is also an efficient limitation.

Finally, the role of auditors is, among other things, to help verify that no manipulation practice took place during the period covered by the financial statements. We should also point out the responsibility of directors in conforming with standards and the increasing liability that rests with company directors for the content of the companies reports.

Scoring models

One main preoccupation of analysts is to identify the risk of a business failing. The scoring models (see Appendix 15.8) constitute one tool to help analysts to achieve this objective.

KEY POINTS

- Financial statement analysis analyzes and interprets the data reported to shareholders and the financial community to facilitate its usability in decision making.

- Financial statement analysis can be carried out by both managers and outsiders to the firm in order to assess a firm's past performance or achievements, present condition and future prospects.

- It uses various techniques integrating accounting data and additional information, emphasizing comparative and relative analysis over time for one firm and between firms.

- Understanding current and past performance of a business helps users of financial statements, and principally investors, derive the firm's business model and its correlated risks.

- Users are interested in understanding liquidity, solvency, leverage, and profitability of a firm as well as understand its asset management policies and the resulting return to investors.

- The main techniques of financial statements analysis include: (1) trend or horizontal analysis (comparison over time of the evolution of a specific expense or revenue item or a particular asset or liability item); (2) common-size or vertical analysis (comparison of the evolution of the structure of the financial statements); and (3) ratio analysis (evaluation of the relation between items in the financial statements).

- "Trend analysis" measures the changes over past accounting period(s) of a limited number of items or, on the contrary, of the whole financial statements (balance sheet, income statement, and cash flow statement). It reveals the dynamics of the income generation model.

- Common-size analysis is prepared by presenting each financial statement component in terms of its percentage of a selected base figure, generally indexed as 100, such as net sales for income statement items or total assets for balance sheet elements.

- The common-size analysis permits the analyst to compare and contrast more easily the financial statements of two and more companies in the same industrial sector or risk class.

- A company's simplified balance sheet can be structured by identifying two separate "time horizons" (current or short term; and non-current or long term), each corresponding to different types of decisions for both assets, on one hand, and shareholders' equity and liabilities on the other.

- One extension of this simplified balance sheet, beyond the common-size analysis, is the "cash equation" relating three major concepts: working capital, working capital need, and net cash.

- A ratio is the quotient of two quantities, the numerator and the denominator, showing the relationship between them.

- Ratio analysis must be used cautiously as the numerator and denominator must be coherent within the business model and correspond to the same time period.

- Three types of evaluation of the meaningfulness of ratios: (1) time-series comparisons; (2) cross-sectional comparisons; and (3) comparison against a competitive or rule of thumb-based benchmark.

- A financial analyst supplements the accounting data by additional information from a variety of sources. Earnings per share and return on capital invested help shareholders decide whether or not to keep their money invested in this firm. The economic value added measures the excess value generated by a business after its cost of long-term capital (which includes shareholders' expected remuneration).

- Segmenting the activity of a business means breaking down its business model in homogeneous sub-models or segments to help improve the predictability of future streams of economic benefits.
- The "quality of earnings" is influenced by (1) accounting methods changes; (2) accounting estimates, especially of required provisions; and (3) classification of exceptional (or extraordinary) items in the income statement.
- "Accounts manipulation" is the result of earnings management including income smoothing and "big bath" accounting, and creative accounting.
- Financial analysts strive to identify the risk of a business failing or bankruptcy. Scoring models establish, for each firm, a synthetic index or "score" which indicates whether a firm should be considered as healthy or in difficulty.

REVIEW

Review 15.1 Chugoku Electric Power Company*

Topic: Common-size income statements by nature
Type: Group case study
Related part of the chapter: Core Issues

Chugoku Electric Power Company, Inc., was established in 1951 as one of 10 electric power companies in Japan. It maintains its head office in the city of Hiroshima and supplies electricity to the Chugoku region through an integrated structure that encompasses all stages of power supply, from generation through to transmission and distribution. In fiscal year 1999, ended 31 March, it supplied 51.6 billion kWh of electricity.

The income statements of the parent company for the years 1997–1999 follow. Consolidated figures are very close to the non-consolidated ones because the parent is the heaviest actor in the group.

Non-consolidated statements of income

Millions of yen	1997	1998	1999
Operating revenues	1,001,835	1,029,045	1,000,160
Operating expenses			
Personnel	125,754	141,902	124,352
Fuel	122,883	110,225	109,559
Purchased power	142,315	151,304	134,414
Depreciation	163,999	189,218	204,265
Maintenance	124,891	114,548	100,250
Taxes other than income taxes	63,796	65,146	65,123
Purchased services	33,037	33,237	33,827
Other	90,895	88,695	94,514
	867,570	894,275	866,304
Operating income	134,265	134,770	133,856
Other expenses (income):			
Interest expense	94,571	88,531	83,496
Interest income	(804)	(864)	(851)
Other, net	(1,358)	(1,050)	3,119
	92,409	86,617	85,764
Income before special item and income taxes	41,856	48,153	48,092
Special item:			
Reversal of (provision for) reserve for drought*	0	(688)	688
Extraordinary loss:			
Loss on sale of securities	0	0	(1,507)
Income before income taxes	41,856	47,465	47,273
Provision for income taxes	19,192	20,310	19,187
Net income	22,664	27,155	28,086

*The company is required to set up a reserve for drought under the Electric Utility Industry Law to stabilize its income position for variations in water levels. In the year ended 31 March 1998 the company provided for such a reserve in accordance with legal requirements. A drought occurred during the year ended March 1999, and, accordingly, this reserve was added back to income to compensate for the higher cost of electricity produced

Source: Annual report 1999

Required

1 Prepare common-size statements on the basis of the income statement, as published by the company.
2 Restate the income statement and prepare common-size intermediate balances following the format of figure 15.2.
3 Comment on these different statements.

The item "Other, net" in "Other expenses (income)"can be assumed to refer to "financial expenses and income".

Solution

The reader must pay attention to the signs of other expenses (income): Positive sign for expenses and negative sign for income.

1 Prepare common-size statements on the basis of the income statement, as published by the company

Millions of yen	Common-size income statements		
	1997	1998	1999
Operating revenues	100.0%	100.0%	100.0%
Operating expenses	0.0%	0.0%	0.0%
Personnel	12.6%	13.8%	12.4%
Fuel	12.3%	10.7%	11.0%
Purchased power	14.2%	14.7%	13.4%
Depreciation	16.4%	18.4%	20.4%
Maintenance	12.5%	11.1%	10.0%
Taxes other than income taxes	6.4%	6.3%	6.5%
Purchased services	3.3%	3.2%	3.4%
Other	9.1%	8.6%	9.4%
	86.6%	86.9%	86.6%
Operating income	13.4%	13.1%	13.4%
Other expenses (income):			
Interest expense	9.4%	8.6%	8.3%
Interest income	−0.1%	−0.1%	−0.1%
Other, net	−0.1%	−0.1%	0.3%
	9.2%	8.4%	8.6%
Income before special item and income taxes	4.2%	4.7%	4.8%
Special item:			
Reversal of (provision for) reserve for drought	0.0%	−0.1%	0.1%
Extraordinary loss:			
Loss on sale of securities	0.0%	0.0%	−0.2%
Income before income taxes	4.2%	4.6%	4.7%
Provision for income taxes	1.9%	2.0%	1.9%
Net income	2.3%	2.6%	2.8%

The income statement is drawn by nature and vertically. This second characteristic is very important because only a vertical statement can show the intermediate financial performance balances (see Chapter 3).

2 Restate the income statement and prepare common-size intermediate balances following the format of figure 15.2.

Statement of intermediate balances

	In millions of yen			In percentage		
	1997	1998	1999	1997	1998	1999
Cperating revenues	1,001,835	1,029,045	1,000,160	100.0%	100.0%	100.0%
Total production for the period	1,001,835	1,029,045	1,000,160	100.0%	100.0%	100.0%
Fuel	122,883	110,225	109,559	12.3%	10.7%	11.0%
Purchased power	142,315	151,304	134,414	14.2%	14.7%	13.4%
Maintenance	124,891	114,548	100,250	12.5%	11.1%	10.0%
Purchased services	33,037	33,237	33,827	3.3%	3.2%	3.4%
Consumption from third parties	423,126	409,314	378,050	42.2%	39.8%	37.8%
Value added	578,709	619,731	622,110	57.8%	60.2%	62.2%
Taxes other that income taxes	63,796	65,146	65,123	6.4%	6.3%	6.5%
Personnel	125,754	141,902	124,352	12.6%	13.8%	12.4%
Gross operating profit	389,159	412,683	432,635	38.8%	40.1%	43.3%
Depreciation	163,999	189,218	204,265	16.4%	18.4%	20.4%
Other	90,895	88,695	94,514	9.1%	8.6%	9.4%
Operating profit	134,265	134,770	133,856	13.4%	13.1%	13.4%
Interest expense	94,571	88,531	83,496	9.4%	8.6%	8.3%
Interest income	−804	−864	−851	−0.1%	−0.1%	−0.1%
Other, net	−1,358	−1,050	3,119	−0.1%	−0.1%	0.3%
Operating net income before taxes	41,856	48,153	48,092	4.2%	4.7%	4.8%
Reversal of (provision for) reserve for drought	0	−688	688	0.0%	−0.1%	0.1%
Loss on sale of securities	0	0	−1,507	0.0%	0.0%	−0.2%
Exceptional result	0	−688	−819	0.0%	−0.1%	−0.1%
Provision for income taxes	19,192	20,310	19,187	1.9%	2.0%	1.9%
Net income/loss after tax	22,664	27,155	28,086	2.3%	2.6%	2.8%

3 Comment on these different statements

With regard to the different intermediate financial performance balances, many are the same as those in the non-restated income statement. The new information concerns mainly the upper part of the statement. A statement of financial performance intermediate balances is interesting and useful mainly because it offers an actionable decomposition of the operating profit:

- The added value rate increases over the period. It may be an indication of a modification in the production structure (such as more internal maintenance and less outsourcing), or an indication of a decrease in the unit value of raw materials (fuel oil).
- This increase (57.8 up to 62.2) is not carried directly to the income line. Income only increases by 0.5%. This is not a favorable signal, as it indicates that the management has not been able to find actions to keep the impact of the increase in added value rate.
- The increase is about the same for the gross operating profit.
- It is, therefore, at the level of the operating profit that the business was not able to keep the benefits of the increase of added value by what appears to be an increase of the depreciation expenses. We do not have enough information about fixed assets and investments during the period to know what the source of the increase was. Only an analysis of the full annual report could let us know whether there was an increase in investments or a change in the depreciation policy.

Review 15.2 Elkem*

Topic: Balance sheet structure
Type: Group case study
Related part of the chapter: Core Issues

Elkem, a Norwegian group based in Oslo, is one of the world's leading suppliers of metals and materials within its core areas. Its main products are silicon metal, aluminum, hydro-power, ferroalloys, carbon and micro-silicon. Elkem has production plants in Norway, Iceland, the USA, Canada, and Brazil. It is listed on the Oslo and Frankfurt Stock Exchanges.

The consolidated balance sheet for the period 1997–1999 follows.

Consolidated balance sheet			
NOK million	31.12.99	31.12.98	31.12.97
ASSETS			
Intangible fixed assets	77	83	13
Tangible fixed assets	4,582	4,833	3,786
Investment in associates	89	76	59
Investment in shares	240	147	73
Long-term receivables	403	404	820
Financial fixed assets	732	627	952
Fixed assets	5,391	5,543	4,751
Inventories	1,297	2,378	2,063
Current receivables	1,654	1,906	1,963
Market-based financial current assets	223	120	88
Cash and bank deposits	1,106	275	276
Current assets	4,280	4,679	4,390
TOTAL ASSETS	9,671	10,222	9,141
EQUITY AND LIABILITIES			
Share capital	986	986	986
Nominal value of own shares	−16	0	0
Other equity	4,102	3,654	3,370
Shareholders' equity	5,072	4,640	4,356
Minority interest	258	272	246
Shareholders' equity and minority interest	5,330	4,912	4,602
Pension liabilities	167	256	244
Deferred taxes	207	112	151
Other long-term liabilities	43	40	26
Provisions	417	408	421
Interest-bearing long-term debt	1,652	1,741	1,561
Interest-bearing short-term debt	77	909	244
Other short-term liabilities	2,195	2,252	2,313
Current liabilities	2,272	3,161	2,557
TOTAL EQUITY AND LIABILITIES	9,671	10,222	9,141

Source: Annual report 1999

Required

1 Prepare a simplified balance sheet with three sub-headings in the assets and three sub-headings in the equity and liabilities (see "Core Issues" in this chapter).

2 Compute working capital, working capital need, and net cash.

3 Comment on your findings.

Solution

1 Prepare a simplified balance sheet with three sub-headings in the assets and three sub-headings in the equity and liabilities

Simplified balance sheet						
	Amounts (NOK million)			Structure (%)		
	31.12.99	31.12.98	31.12.97	31.12.99	31.12.98	31.12.97
Fixed assets	5,391	5,543	4,751	55.7%	54.2%	52.0%
Current assets	3,174	4,404	4,114	32.8%	43.1%	45.0%
Cash	1,106	275	276	11.4%	2.7%	3.0%
Total assets	9,671	10,222	9,141	100.0%	100.0%	100.0%
Equity and long-term liabilities	7,399	7,061	6,584	76.5%	69.1%	72.0%
Current liabilities	2,272	3,161	2,557	23.5%	30.9%	28.0%
Bank overdrafts	0	0	0	0.0%	0.0%	0.0%
Total equity and liabilities	9,671	10,222	9,141	100.0%	100.0%	100.0%

- The market-based financial current assets have been included in current assets and not in cash, because a note to the financial statements indicates that it represents shares of other companies.
- Apparently, the company has no bank overdraft.

2 Compute working capital, working capital need and net cash

Financial structure			
NOK million	31.12.99	31.12.98	31.12.97
Equity and long-term liabilities	7,399	7,061	6,584
less Fixed assets	−5,391	−5,543	−4,751
Working capital	2,008	1,518	1,833
Current assets	3,174	4,404	4,114
less Current liabilities	−2,272	−3,161	−2,557
Working capital need	902	1,243	1,557
Cash	1,106	275	276
less Bank overdrafts	0	0	0
Net cash	1,106	275	276
Control: Working capital less Working capital need = Net cash			
Net cash	1,106	275	276
Synthesis	31.12.99	31.12.98	31.12.97
Working capital	2,008	1,518	1,833
Working capital need	902	1,243	1,557
Net cash	1,106	275	276

The following graph shows the variation of the three items over the three years (the order of the years has been reversed in order to make the graph more readable).

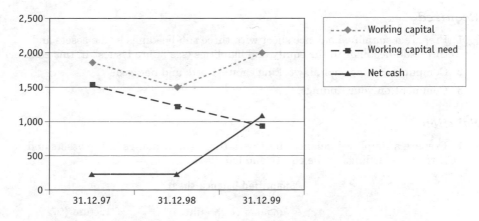

3 Comment on your findings

Over the three years, the financial structure of the business corresponds to scenario 1 described in "Core Issues" earlier in this chapter. The structure can be considered to be sound. In addition there was an increase in cash over the period. The graph shows that this increase in cash arises from both an increase in working capital and a reduction in the working capital need.

ASSIGNMENTS

Assignment 15.1 Janacek Company (2)

Topic: Preparation of a statement of intermediate balances and statement of financial structure
Type: Individual/group exercise
Related part of the chapter: Core Issues

The Janacek Company has a commercial activity in the sector of beauty creams.

Required

1 With the help of the balance sheet, income statement, and additional information (see assignment Janacek company (1), in Chapter 14), prepare a statement of intermediate balances for the years 20X1, 20X2, and 20X3.

2 Prepare a simplified balance sheet.

3 Prepare a statement showing the financial structure of the company.

4 Evaluate and comment on these statements.

Assignment 15.2 Procter & Gamble*

Topic: Common-size income statements
Type: Group case study
Related part of the chapter: Core Issues

The common-sized income statements of Procter & Gamble have been prepared for the years 1995–1999 (see Table 15.3).

Required

1 What financial performance intermediate balance does not appear in the income statement and would be useful to your analysis?

2 Comment on the common-size statements over the period.

Assignment 15.3 Barmag* (1)

Topic: Common-size income statements by nature
Type: Group case study
Related part of the chapter: Core Issues

Barmag AG is a German company offering the man-made fiber industry a complete range of products for the manufacture and the processing of man-made fibers. Its sales can be split between three activities (in 1999).

	DM 000	%
Spinning machines	353,522	53%
Textile machines	96,365	15%
Other (customer service, chemical pumps...)	212,225	32%
	662,112	100%

In 1999, a crisis developed in the industry. It was caused by significant surplus capacity on the part of the company's customers and resulting low market prices for end products. This situation led manufacturers to cut back their production and investments.

The consolidated income statements for the years 1997–99 are provided in the following.

Consolidated income statement			
Thousands of DM	1999	1998	1997
Sales	**662,112**	**1,120,226**	**1,013,653**
Increase/decrease in inventories of work in progress	−50,319	16,836	23,259
Own work capitalized	414	1,122	806
Total performance	**612,207**	**1,138,184**	**1,037,718**
Other operating income	69,851	53,160	60,006
Cost of materials	−264,915	−516,331	−503,163
Personnel expenses	−260,042	−344,082	−315,638
Depreciation of intangible and tangible assets	−25,830	−25,430	−23,762
Other operating expenses*	−111,564	−225,351	−209,365
Investment income	143	205	446
Net interest income/expense	3,227	5,920	4,376
Income/loss from ordinary operations	**23,077**	**86,275**	**50,618**
Other taxes	−1,500	−1,171	−1,249
Earnings before income tax	**21,577**	**85,104**	**49,369**
Taxes on income	−6,342	−10,079	1,032
Net income for the year	**15,235**	**75,025**	**50,401**
*Including additions to reserves (provision expense)	12,510	52,094	57,344

Source: Annual reports 1999 and 1998

According to the notes to the financial statements, the other operating income mainly includes "revenue" from reversal of provisions. The other operating expenses comprise essentially external costs (special sales costs, maintenance, legal and consultancy costs, travel, other outside services), and provision expense (see footnote).

Required

1 Prepare common-size statements on the basis of the income statement, as published by the company.

2 Restate the income statement and prepare common-size intermediate balances as explained in "Core Issues" earlier in this chapter.

3 Comment on the documents and information that arise out of questions 1 and 2.

Assignment 15.4 Club Méditerranée*

Topic: Balance sheet structure
Type: Group case study
Related part of the chapter: Core Issues

The French group Club Méditerranée is an active service provider in the field of leisure with, in particular, its famous "villages". The balance sheets for the period 1997–1999 follow (*source*: annual reports 1999 and 1997).

Consolidated balance sheet			
FRF million	**1999**	**1998**	**1997**
Assets			
Intangible assets	**1,138**	**625**	**657**
Goodwill	659	363	413
Other	479	262	244
Tangible assets	**6,071**	**5,172**	**5,184**
Land	898	840	859
Property and equipment	4,237	3,662	3,710
Other	936	670	615
Financial assets	**621**	**466**	**554**
Investments, loans, and advances	315	214	274
Deposits	227	186	207
Other	79	66	73
TOTAL FIXED ASSETS	**7,830**	**6,263**	**6,395**
Inventories	178	156	197
Trade receivables	342	249	227
Other receivables	683	428	543
Marketable securities	79	20	16
Bank and cash	595	1,606	672
TOTAL CURRENT ASSETS	**1,877**	**2,459**	**1,655**
Deferred taxes	10	7	8
Prepaid expenses and deferred charges	312	221	220
TOTAL ASSETS	**10,029**	**8,950**	**8,278**
LIABILITIES AND SHAREHOLDERS' EQUITY			
Common stock	385	375	344
Additional paid-in capital	2,845	2,709	2,329
Reserves	31	−400	993
Group net income (loss)	253	171	−1,294
SHAREHOLDERS' EQUITY	**3,514**	**2,855**	**2,372**
MINORITY INTEREST	**102**	**98**	**103**
PROVISIONS FOR CONTINGENCIES AND CHARGES	**937**	**1,235**	**1,540**
Bonds	1,888	1,912	1,083
Bank loans and debts*	1,355	1,478	1,670
Trade payables	662	374	407
Amounts received for future vacations	837	364	411
Other	606	594	651
TOTAL DEBT	**5,348**	**4,722**	**4,222**
Deferred taxes	6	5	6
Accrued expenses and deferred income	122	35	35
TOTAL LIABILITIES AND SHAREHOLDERS' EQUITY	**10,029**	**8,950**	**8,278**
*Including current maturity portion of long-term debt	140	240	270
*Including bank overdrafts	242	274	318

1 Prepare a simplified balance sheet with three sub-headings in the assets and three sub-headings in the equity and liabilities (see Table 15.5).

2 Compute the working capital, working capital need, and net cash.

3 Comment on the results and information created in questions 1 and 2.

Assignment 15.5 Nokia & Ericsson*

Topic: Comparative financial statement analysis
Type: Group case study
Related part of the chapter: Core Issues

Nokia and Ericsson are two well-known players in the field of telecommunications, in particular in the area of mobile phones.

Nokia comprises three business groups: Nokia Networks, Nokia Mobile Phones and Nokia Communications Products. At the end of 1999, Nokia had sales in over 130 countries, research and development in 14 countries, and a global network of distribution, sales, customer services, and other operational units. Headquartered in Finland, Nokia is listed on the New York, Helsinki, Stockholm, London, Frankfurt, and Paris Stock Exchanges and employs over 55,000 people:

- Nokia Network (29% of net sales in 1999) is a leading supplier of data, video, and voice network solutions.
- Nokia Mobile Phones (66% of sales) is the world's largest mobile phone manufacturer.
- Nokia Communications Products (5% of sales) comprises Nokia Multimedia Terminals, a pioneer in digital multimedia terminals for digital TV and interactive services via satellite, cable, or terrestrial networks.

Based in Sweden, Ericsson is a leading provider in the telecom world, with communication solutions that combine telecom and datacom technologies with freedom of mobility for the user. With more that 100,000 employees in 140 countries, the group operates in four major business segments:

- Network operators and service providers (mobile systems according to all mobile standards, third-generation 3G mobile systems, GPRS, mobile internet) (65% of net sales including inter-segment sales).
- Consumer products (mobile phones) (20% of sales).
- Enterprise solutions (8% of sales).
- Other operations (components, microwave systems) (7% of sales).

Balance sheets, income statements, cash flow statements, and key data for both groups for the years 1999, 1998, and 1997 follow (*sources*: Nokia and Ericsson annual reports 1999 and 1998). The Nokia financial statements are prepared in accordance with International Accounting Standards (IAS) whereas those of Ericsson comply with the recommendations of the Swedish Financial Accounting Standards Council.

Required

Prepare a complete comparative financial statement analysis of both groups. The two economic entities are competitors on several (but not all) business segments.

Appendix
Nokia – Consolidated profit and loss account

Financial year ended 31 December	1999 €m	1998 €m	1997* €m
Net sales	**19,772**	**13,326**	**8,849**
Cost of goods sold	−12,227	−8,299	−5,718
Research and development expenses	−1,755	−1,150	−767
Selling, general and administration expenses	−1,811	−1,368	−942
Amortization of goodwill	−71	−20	0
Operating profit	**3,908**	**2,489**	**1,422**
Share of results of associated companies	−5	6	9
Financial income and expenses	−58	−39	−23
Profit before tax and minority interests	**3,845**	**2,456**	**1,408**
Tax	−1,189	−737	−382
Minority interests	−79	−39	−17
Profit from continuing operations	**2,577**	**1,680**	**1,009**
Discontinued operations	0	0	44
Cumulative prior year net effect of change in accounting policies	0	70	0
Net profit	**2,577**	**1,750**	**1,053**

*With regard to Nokia, all the financial statements for 1997 have been converted from Finnish marks to euros

31 December	1999 €m	1998 €m	1997 €m
ASSETS			
Fixed assets and other non-current assets			
Intangible assets	838	484	347
Property, plant and equipment	2,031	1,331	1,050
Investment in associated companies	76	90	56
Investment in other companies	68	75	76
Deferred tax assets	257	196	0
Other assets	217	44	60
	3,487	**2,220**	**1,589**
Current assets			
Inventories	1,772	1,292	1,230
Receivables	4,861	3,631	2,141
Short-term investment	3,136	2,165	1,575
Bank and cash	1,023	726	485
	10,792	**7,814**	**5,431**
Total assets	**14,279**	**10,034**	**7,020**
SHAREHOLDERS' EQUITY AND LIABILITIES			
Shareholders' equity			
Share capital	279	255	252
Share issue premium	1,079	909	803
Treasury shares	−24	−110	−110
Translation differences	243	182	129
Retained earnings	5,801	3,873	2,546
	7,378	**5,109**	**3,620**
Minority interests	**122**	**63**	**33**
Long-term liabilities			
Long-term interest-bearing liabilities	269	257	226
Deferred tax liabilities	80	88	0
Other long-term liabilities	58	64	50
	407	**409**	**276**
Current liabilities			
Short-term borrowings	792	699	506
Current portion of long-term debt	1	61	48
Accounts payable	2,202	1,357	2,446
Accrued expenses	3,377	2,336	91
	6,372	**4,453**	**3,091**
Total shareholders' equity and liabilities	**14,279**	**10,034**	**7,020**

Nokia – Consolidated cash flow statement

Financial year ended 31 December	1999 €m	1998 €m	1997 €m
Cash flow from operating activities			
Operating profit	3,908	2,489	1,422
Adjustments, total	597	501	429
Operating profit before change in net working capital	4,505	2,990	1,851
Change in net working capital	−21	−451	148
Cash generated from operations	4,484	2,539	1,999
Interest received	189	134	118
Interest paid	−212	−210	−173
Other financial income and expenses	−113	−3	47
Income taxes paid	−1,246	−773	−275
Net cash from operating activities	**3,102**	**1,687**	**1,716**
Cash flow from investing activities			
Acquisition of group companies, net of acquired cash	−178	−76	−85
Treasury shares acquired	−25	0	−8
Investments in other shares	−37	−51	−160
Additions in capitalized R&D costs	−271	−182	−404
Capital expenditures	−1,302	−761	14
Proceeds from disposal of shares in group companies, net of disposed cash	27	85	1
Proceeds from sale of treasury shares	0	0	14
Proceeds from sale of other shares	121	16	38
Proceeds from sale of fixed assets	318	182	85
Dividends received	6	7	4
Net cash used in investing activities	**−1,341**	**−780**	**−500**
Cash flow from financing activities			
Share issue	152	108	12
Capital investment by minority shareholders	28	16	0
Proceeds from (+), payments of (−) long-term liabilities	−6	66	−173
Proceeds from (+), payments of (−) short-term borrowings	−126	275	−165
Proceeds from (+), payments of (−) long-term receivables	−171	−8	18
Proceeds from (+), payments of (−) short-term receivables	128	−146	42
Dividends paid	−597	−374	−178
Net cash used in financing activities	**−592**	**−63**	**−444**
Net increase in cash and cash equivalents	1,169	844	772
Cash and cash equivalents at beginning of period	2,990	2,047	1,288
Cash and cash equivalents at end of period	**4,159**	**2,891**	**2,060**

The difference (which should not exist) between the beginning cash balance of one year and the ending reported for previous year corresponds to foreign exchange adjustment

Nokia – Key figures

	1999	1998	1997
Key data			
Number of shares (in thousands, nominal value €0.24)			
K (common)	—	254,061	314,750
A (preferred)*	1,163,516	957,132	884,659
Total	1,163,516	1,211,193	1,199,409
Average number of shares excluding shares owned by the group during the year (in thousands)	1,148,440	1,138,341	1,133,128
(Nominal) dividend per share, €**	0.80	0.48	0.31
Share prices, € (Helsinki Exchanges)			
K share (year-end)	—	52.14	16.40
A share (year-end)***	180	52.14	16.31
Average personnel	51,177	41,091	35,490

*As of 9 April 1999 one class of shares only

**1999: proposed by the board of directors

***As of 9 April 1999 one class of shares only. Consequently, the figures concern total number of all the shares

Ericsson – Consolidated income statement

Years ended 31 December	1999 SEK m	1998 SEK m	1997 SEK m
Net sales	215,403	184,438	167,740
Cost of sales	−125,881	−105,251	−97,868
Gross margin	89,522	79,187	69,872
Research and development and other technical expenses	−33,123	−28,027	−24,242
Selling expenses	−31,205	−24,108	−20,464
Administrative expenses	−10,078	−8,922	−7,755
Other operating revenues	2,224	995	866
Share in earnings of associated companies	250	148	480
Operating margin	17,590	19,273	18,757
Financial income	2,273	2,228	2,413
Financial expenses	−2,971	−2,465	−2,365
Income after financial items	16,892	19,036	18,805
Minority interest in income before taxes	−506	−826	−1,587
Income before taxes	16,386	18,210	17,218
Taxes			
Income taxes for the year	−4,358	−5,409	−5,755
Minority interest in taxes	102	240	478
Net income	12,130	13,041	11,941

31 December	1999 SEK m	1998 SEK m	1997 SEK m
Assets			
Fixed assets			
Intangible assets	10,548	6,354	748
Tangible assets	24,719	22,516	19,225
Financial assets			
Equity in associated companies	2,712	2,777	2,643
Other investments	1,751	1,438	1,434
Long-term customer financing	6,657	5,937	2,000
Other long-term receivables	4,972	2,902	3,365
	51,359	**41,924**	**29,415**
Current assets			
Inventories	25,701	26,973	23,614
Receivables			
Accounts receivable – trade	63,584	53,900	46,151
Short-term customer financing	1,749	3,837	
Other receivables	31,227	22,589	19,133
Short-term cash investments	13,415	6,356	20,416
Cash and bank	15,593	11,877	8,711
	151,269	**125,532**	**118,025**
TOTAL ASSETS	**202,628**	**167,456**	**147,440**
STOCKHOLDERS' EQUITY, PROVISIONS AND LIABILITIES			
Stockholders' equity			
Capital stock	4,893	4,878	2,436
Reserves not available for distribution	32,618	28,053	29,172
Restricted equity	37,511	32,931	31,608
Retained earnings	19,535	17,140	9,075
Net income	12,130	13,041	11,941
Non-restricted equity	31,665	30,181	21,016
	69,176	**63,112**	**52,624**
Minority interest in equity of consolidated subsidiaries	**2,182**	**2,051**	**4,395**
Provisions	**22,552**	**22,284**	**21,095**
Long-term liabilities			
Notes and bond loans	17,486	4,470	2,476
Convertible debentures	5,453	6,241	6,034
Liabilities to financial institutions	1,448	1,898	2,209
Other long-term liabilities	567	459	510
	24,954	**13,068**	**11,229**
Current liabilities			
Current maturity portion of long-term debt	1,491	1,188	742
Current liabilities to financial institutions	10,519	5,427	4,242
Advances from customers	6,437	8,398	7,633
Accounts payable – trade	21,618	18,246	14,803
Income tax liabilities	2,397	1,957	4,100
Other current liabilities	41,302	31,725	26,577
	83,764	**66,941**	**58,097**
TOTAL STOCKHOLDERS' EQUITY, PROVISIONS AND LIABILITIES	**202,628**	**167,456**	**147,440**

Ericsson – Consolidated cash flow statement

Years ended 31 December	1999 SEK m	1998 SEK m	1997 SEK m
Operations			
Net income	12,130	13,041	11,941
Adjustments to reconcile net income to cash			
Minority interest in net income	404	586	1,109
Undistributed earnings of associated companies	18	−359	−90
Depreciation and amortization	7,382	6,081	5,756
Capital gains (−)/losses on sale of fixed assets	−1,399	−230	152
Taxes	−947	−2,301	619
Changes in operating net assets			
Inventories	714	−2,056	−3,396
Customer financing, short term and long term	722	−5,727	−347
Accounts receivable – trade and other operating assets	−19,562	−10,695	−15,828
Provisions and other operating liabilities	13,463	9,054	14,986
Cash flow from operating activities	**12,925**	**7,394**	**14,902**
Investments			
Investments in tangible assets	−9,085	−8,965	−7,237
Sales of tangible assets	625	632	642
Acquisitions/sales of other investments, net	−4,768	−8,865	−69
Net change in capital contributed by minority	134	35	21
Other	−2,270	−56	−513
Cash flow from investing activities	**−15,364**	**−17,219**	**−7,156**
Cash flow before financing activities	**−2,439**	**−9,825**	**7,746**
Financing			
Changes in current liabilities to financial institutions, net	3,854	955	96
Issue of convertible debentures	58	19	4,875
Proceeds from issuance of other long-term debt	15,163	3,366	2,571
Repayments of long-term debt	−1,515	−1,332	−2,672
Dividends paid	−4,010	−3,800	−2,805
Cash flow from financing activities	**13,550**	**−792**	**2,065**
Effect of change in rate changes on cash	−336	−277	256
Net change in cash	**10,775**	**−10,894**	**10,067**
Cash, beginning of period	18,233	29,127	19,060
Cash, end of period	**29,008**	**18,233**	**29,127**

Ericsson – Key figures

	1999	1998	1997
Key data			
Average number of shares outstanding (in thousands)	1,954,291	1,950,225	1,938,742
Cash dividends per share (SEK)*	2.00	2.00	1.75
Share prices, SEK, Stockholm Stock Exchange			
A at 30 December**	575.0	209.5	157.0
B at 30 December	548.0	193.0	149.0
Average number of employees	104,996	101,485	100,774

*As of 9 April 1999 one class of shares only
** A shares carry one vote. B shares carry one-thousandth of vote

In order to simplify the analysis, if it appears to be interesting to convert the financial statements of Ericsson from Swedish kroner to euros, a unique currency exchange rate will be used for the 3 years and all the items of the financial statements: €1 = 8.857 SEK.

Assignment 15.6 4 Kids Entertainment, Inc.*

Topic: Earnings per share
Type: Individual/group exercise
Related part of the chapter: Advanced Issues

4Kids Entertainment is a US company that receives revenues from a number of sources, principally licensing and media buying. It represents such well-known properties as Pokémon and Nintendo. The company's common stock is traded on the NASDAQ. The annual report 1999 (for the year ended 31 December) contains the following information: The company applies SFAS No. 128 which requires the computation and presentation of earnings per share (EPS) to include basic and diluted EPS. Basic EPS is computed based solely on the weighted average number of common shares outstanding during the period. Diluted EPS reflects all potential dilution of common stock.

The number of common shares is 10,741,082 and the number of stock options is 1,625,267. The income statement shows net income to be US $23,638,426.

Required

Prepare a statement showing the computation of basic and diluted earnings per share for the year 1999.

References

Altman, E.I. (1968) Financial ratios, discriminant analysis and the prediction of corporate bankruptcy. *The Journal of Finance*, (23) September, 589–609.

Altman, E.I., and McGough, T.P. (1974) Evaluation of a company as a going concern. *Journal of Accountancy*, December, 50–57.

Barnea, A., Ronen, J., and Sadan, S. (1975) The implementation of accounting objectives: An application to extraordinary items. *The Accounting Review*, January, 58–68.

Barnea, A., Ronen, J., and Sadan, S. (1976) Classificatory smoothing of income with extraordinary items. *The Accounting Review*, January, 110–22.

Black, E.L., Sellers, K.F., and Manly, T.S. (1998) Earnings management using asset sales: An international study of countries allowing noncurrent asset revaluation. *Journal of Business Finance and Accounting*, 25(9) and (10), November/December, 1287–317.

Blake, J., and Amat, O. (1996) *Interpreting Accounts*, International Thomson Business Press, London.

Copeland, R.M. (1968) Income smoothing. *Journal of Accounting Research, Empirical Research in Accounting, Selected Studies*, 6, Supplement, 101–16.

FASB (1997) Statement of Financial Accounting Standard No. 131, Disclosures about Segments of an Enterprise and Related Information, Norwalk, CT.

Fern, R.H., Brown, B., and Dickey, S.W. (1994) An empirical test of politically-motivated income smoothing in the oil refining industry. *Journal of Applied Business Research*, 10(1) Winter, 92.

Gibson, C.H. (2001) *Financial Reporting Analysis: Using Financial Accounting Information*, South-Western College Publishing, Cincinnati, OH.

Gray, R., Laughlin, R., and Bebbington, J. (1996) *Financial Accounting – Method and Meaning*, 2nd edn, International Thomson Business Press, London.

Gray, S.J., and Needles, B.E. (1999) *Financial Accounting: A Global Approach*, Houghton Mifflin Company, Boston, MS.

Griffiths, I. (1986) *Creative Accounting*, Irwin, London.

Griffiths, I. (1995) *New Creative Accounting*, Macmillan, London.

Horngren, C.T., Sundem, G.L., and Elliott, J.A. (1999) *Introduction to Financial Accounting*, Prentice Hall, 7th edn, Upper Saddle River, NJ.

IASC (1997a) International Accounting Standard No. 33, Earnings Per Share, London.

IASC (revised 1997b) International Accounting Standard No. 14, Segment Reporting, London.

Knapp, M.C. (1998) *Financial Accounting – A Focus on Decision Making*, 2nd edn, South-Western College Publishing, Cincinnati, OH.

Laidler, J., and Donaghy, P. (1998) *Understanding UK Annual Reports and Accounts*, International Thomson Business Press, London.

Lebas, M. (ed.) (1999) *Management Accounting Glossary*, ECM, Paris, and CIMA, London.

Mathews, M.R., and Perera, M.H.B. (1996) *Accounting Theory and Development*, Nelson–ITPC, Melbourne.

Moore, M.L. (1973) Management changes and discretionary accounting decisions. *Journal of Accounting Research,* (Spring), 100–7.

Ronen, J., and Sadan, S. (1975) Classificatory smoothing: Alternative income models. *Journal of Accounting Research* (Spring), 133–49.

Smith, T. (1996) *Accounting for Growth – Stripping the Camouflage from Company Accounts*, 2nd edn, Century Business, London.

Sutton, T. (2000) *Corporate Financial Accounting and Reporting*, Financial Times/Prentice Hall, London.

Walton, P. (2000) *Financial Statement Analysis – An International Perspective*, Thomson Learning, London.

Further readings

Alford, A., Jones, J., Leftwich, R., and Zmijewski, M. (1993) The relative informativeness of accounting disclosures in different countries. *Journal of Accounting Research*, 31 (Supplement), 183–223.

Arnold, J., Holder, W.W., and Mann, M.H. (1980) International reporting aspects of segment disclosure. *International Journal of Accounting, Education and Research*, 16 (Fall), 125–35.

Barth, E.M., and Clinch, G. (1996) International accounting differences and their relation to share prices: Evidence from UK, Australian, and Canadian firms. *Contemporary Accounting Research*, 13(1) (Spring), 135–70.

Cote, J.M., and Latham, C.K. (1999) The merchandising ratio: A comprehensive measure of working capital strategy. *Issues in Accounting Education*, 14(2), 255–67.

Deppe, L. (2000) Disclosing disaggregated information. *Journal of Accountancy*, 190(3), September, 47–52.

Emmanuel, C.R., and Gray, S.J. (1977) Segmental disclosures and the segment identification problem. *Accounting and Business Research*, Winter, 37–50.

Emmanuel, C., and Garrod, N. (1994) Segmental reporting in the UK. How does SSAP 25 stand up to international comparison? *European Accounting Review*, 3(3), 547–62.

Gray, S. (1999) A new era of segment reporting. *Accountancy*, 123(1268), April, 76–8.

Haller, A., and Park, P. (1994) Regulation and practice of segmental reporting in Germany. *European Accounting Review*, 3(3), 563–80.

Haller, A., and Stolowy, H. (1998) Value added in financial accounting: A comparative study of Germany and France. *Advances in International Accounting*, 11, 23–51.

Herrmann, D., and Thomas, W.B. (2000) An analysis of segment disclosures under SFAS No. 131 and SFAS No. 14. *Accounting Horizons*, 14(3), September, 287–302.

Lainez, J.A., and Callao, S. (2000) The effect of accounting diversity on international financial analysis: Empirical evidence. *International Journal of Accounting*, 35(1), 65–83.

Plenborg, T. (1998) A comparison of the information content of US and Danish earnings. *European Accounting Review*, 7(1), 41–63.

Sanders, J., Alexander, S., and Clark, S. (1999) New segment reporting: Is it working? *Strategic Finance*, 81(6), December, 35–8.

Springsteel, I. (1998) Sliced, diced, and still obscure: New rules on reporting business segment information set by the Financial Accounting Standards Board. *CFO: The Magazine for Senior Financial Executives*, February, 85.

Street, D.L., Nichols, N.B., and Gray, S.J. (2000) Segment disclosures under SFAS No. 131: Has business segment reporting improved? *Accounting Horizons*, 14(3), September, 259–85.

Additional material on the website

Go to http://www.thomsonlearning.co.uk/accountingandfinance/stolowylebas for further information, journal entries and extra assignments for each chapter.

The following appendices to this chapter are available on the dedicated website:

Appendix 15.1: Value added
Appendix 15.2: Working capital need in sales days
Appendix 15.3: Classifications of ratios
Appendix 15.4: Complementary remarks on ratios computation
Appendix 15.5: Business newspapers and magazines – specialized magazines
Appendix 15.6: Databases and statistics publications
Appendix 15.7: Filing of financial statements
Appendix 15.8: Scoring models

Notes

1 See, for example, Gibson (2001) or Gray and Needles (1999).

2 Current assets include cash.

3 Current liabilities include bank overdrafts.

4 "Debt" represents long-term and short-term interest-bearing liabilities.

5 Average equity = (Beginning shareholders' equity + Ending shareholders' equity)/2.

6 The relevance of extraordinary items in the determination of the income integrated in the EPS computation has been discussed and the practice differs a lot.

7 The *beta (β)* measures the risk of the company's shares. It relates the variance of earnings of a company with the average variance of earnings of the market.

index

[A indicates an appendix (on the website and CD Rom); S indicates a supplement (on the website for instructors); * indicates a real company]